BLACK AUTHORS

GARLAND REFERENCE LIBRARY
OF THE HUMANITIES
(VOL. 1260)

BLACK AUTHORS
A Selected
Annotated Bibliography

James Edward Newby

GARLAND PUBLISHING, INC. • NEW YORK & LONDON
1991

Library of Congress Cataloging-in-Publication Data

Newby, James Edward.
   Black authors : a selected annotated bibliography /
James Edward Newby.
      p.   cm. — (Garland reference library of the humanities; vol.
1260)
   Includes bibliographical references and indexes.
   ISBN 0–8240–3329–9 (alk. paper)
   1. United States—Imprints. 2. Afro-Americans—Bibliography.
3. Afro-American authors—Bibliography. 4. American literature—
Afro-American authors—Bibliography. I. Title. II. Series.
Z1215.N57   1991
015.73—dc20   90-13875
                                                               CIP

Printed on acid-free, 250-year-life paper
Manufactured in the United States of America

To Pat
And to the memory of my mother, father, and son.

CONTENTS

PREFACE   ix

ACKNOWLEDGMENTS   xiii

GUIDE TO SYMBOLS AND ABBREVIATIONS   xv

CHAPTER 1. AUTOBIOGRAPHIES AND BIOGRAPHIES   3

CHAPTER 2. BIBLIOGRAPHIES AND LIBRARY SCIENCE   55

CHAPTER 3. EDUCATION   •   71

CHAPTER 4. FINE ARTS, ENTERTAINMENT,
               AND SPORTS   187

CHAPTER 5. HISTORY   205

CHAPTER 6. JUVENILE LITERATURE   277

CHAPTER 7. LANGUAGE AND LITERATURE   355

CHAPTER 8. PHILOSOPHY, PSYCHOLOGY,
               AND RELIGION   467

CHAPTER 9. SCIENCE AND TECHNOLOGY   491

CHAPTER 10. SOCIAL SCIENCE   507

NOTES   601

SELECTED BIBLIOGRAPHY   603

AUTHOR INDEX   605

TITLE INDEX   635

PREFACE

The present work is the culmination of a research project I undertook nearly two decades ago. The major objective of the project was to compile a bibliography of books on education[1] and educational policy by black authors covering the period from the 1800s to the 1980s to (1) update existing knowledge of works by black authors; (2) meet the growing needs of instructional and research programs, particularly in Afro–American studies and fields related to teaching ethnic groups; (3) assist research scholars, administrators, teachers, students, and the public–at–large in identifying literature on education by black authors; and (4) ensure that the role and contributions of black authors to the intellectual development of this nation will not be "lost, strayed, or stolen."

To accomplish these objectives, I mailed a survey sheet with a cover letter to individuals, organizations, publishers, and four–year colleges and universities throughout the country to obtain the identity of black authors who had published one or more books in the field of education. In addition to these names, however, the results yielded names of authors whose books encompass a variety of disciplines.

From that research, I published a bibliography of books in the field of education and several bibliographies in other subject areas.[2] However, the works of the overwhelming majority of black authors were not included in the above publications because they were not in those particular subject areas. Those works—along with my previously published bibliographies, which constitute about 10 percent of this total work—are included in this bibliography.

The present work is an attempt to provide a selected bibliography of works written, coauthored, or edited *by* black Americans. A few African and Caribbean authors who are living and/or publishing in the United States are included. Two asterisks (**) by an author's name signify that the author or editor is *not* black; one asterisk (*) means that the author's ethnic identity was not verified.[3] Whenever there was an illustrator of one of these texts (which occurs primarily in the chapter on juvenile literature), a similar method of identification was used. The bibliography includes over 3,200 titles in all subject areas, fiction and nonfiction, spanning over 200 years of publication. The earliest work cited was published in 1773 and the most recent in 1990.

The bibliography is divided into ten chapters, based primarily on the Library of Congress classification system.[4] Each chapter is arranged alphabetically by author, but consecutive numbering of entries is continued throughout the book. No entry is listed more than once. Many books, however, could have been logically put in more than one chapter. When an author is responsible for more than one work, the entries are entered alphabetically by title. Entries are confined to book–length works, monographs, or separately published essays. Each entry contains author(s), title, place of publication, publisher, and copyright date. Nearly half the entries are annotated. An effort was made to avoid pronouncing judgment on the various works.

In compiling this bibliography, I consulted many sources, including publishers and their catalogues, periodicals, computer databases, bibliographies, and biographical dictionaries, such as Barbara Rollock, *Black Authors and Illustrators of Children's Books: A Biographical Dictionary* (New York: Garland Publishing, Inc., 1988); Dorothy Burnett Porter, *Working Bibliography on the Negro in the United States* (Ann Arbor, Mich.: Xerox, University Microfilms, 1969), among others. A few annotations in the bibliography, particularly in the Juvenile section, consist of a quotation taken from the summary statement in the book or in the Library of Congress record.

This bibliography is neither a complete record of books by black authors nor a complete listing of all black authors who have published a book. My attempt to maximize the number of different authors was sometimes done at the expense of my attempt to ensure the inclusion of all titles by a particular author. Undoubtedly many important works by black authors have been overlooked. However, I plan to update the bibliography and would appreciate any information that would enable me to rectify omissions or references in subsequent editions. Please address the information to me at Howard University, School of Education, 2400 Sixth Street, N.W., Washington, D.C., 20059. In the meantime, I hope this work serves as a viable research/teaching tool and a primary source for identifying some black authors who have contributed to the literary discourse in this country.

James E. Newby
Howard University

ACKNOWLEDGMENTS

Many persons and organizations, too numerous to mention by name, have contributed directly or indirectly to this work. Thanks go to Earle H. West who initially sparked my interest in bibliographical research; colleagues at Howard University who shared their knowledge of black authors; my former undergraduate and graduate assistants who provided invaluable help, especially Jo Anne Manswell who patiently spent many hours doing library and computer searches and recording data; publishers and individuals throughout the country who identified works by black authors.

I am indebted to several bookstores and their staff for their assistance in identifying black authors and for giving me the opportunity to scrutinize their books. In this respect, I want to thank Pam and the staff of Cheshire Cat Children's Book Store; Barbara Carney of African American Literature Service; and Edwin and Toni Brittenum of Triple "A" Literary Connection. For their cooperation and support, thanks also are extended to the staff of Howard University Technical Services Department, Moorland–Spingarn Research Center, Reference Department of Founders Library, and Howard University Press.

Appreciation goes to *The Journal of Religious Thought* for permission to use material from "Black Authors in Philosophy, Psychology, and Religion: An Annotated Bibliography of Selected Books," by James E. Newby. Copyright 1979, by James Edward Newby; *Journal of Black Studies* for permission to use material from "Language, Literature, and Communication: An Annotated Bibliography of Books By Black Authors," by James E. Newby. Copyright 1984, by James Edward Newby; *Black Books Bulletin* for permission to use material from "Black Authors: An Annotated Bibliography of Autobiographies and Biographies," by James Edward Newby. Copyright 1980, by James Edward Newby; and University Press of America for permission to use material from *Black Authors and Education: An Annotated Bibliography of Books*, by James Edward Newby. Copyright 1980, by James Edward Newby.

Finally, I would like to extend my gratitude to Pat—my wife—for her enduring support, patience, and inspiration.

GUIDE TO SYMBOLS
AND ABBREVIATIONS

*   Author's ethnic identity was not verified

**   Author is not black

N.p. No place of publication appears on the title page.

Black Authors

CHAPTER 1

AUTOBIOGRAPHIES AND BIOGRAPHIES

1. Abdul-Jabbar, Kareem, with Peter Knobler.** *Giant Steps: The Autobiography.* New York: Bantam Books, 1983.

   This book is a social history and an autobiography of a sports superstar. Written with the assistance of Peter Knobler, it traces the evolution of Lew Alcindor into Kareem Abdul-Jabbar, a devout Muslim and articulate advocate of black causes. The basketball superstar takes the reader behind-the-scenes in professional sports and speaks candidly about drugs, racism, and sex in the athletic ranks. He also explains the story behind the tragedy that made national headlines when several Muslims were found murdered in a Washington, D.C., house he owned. Includes sixteen pages of photographs.

2. Abdul-Jabbar, Kareem, with Mignon McCarthy.** *Kareem.* New York: Random House, 1990.

   Based on a diary of his final season in basketball, 1988–1989, this book is an intimate and detailed story of Kareem's farewell NBA season with the defending champion Los Angeles Lakers. It provides a rare window on the behind-the-scenes world of the Lakers, including astute portraits of Magic Johnson, James Worthy, Byron Scott, Michael Cooper, Pat Riley, and Jerry

West. It also gives a sketch of the music– and film–industry people at courtside, including Jack Nicholson.

In addition the athlete reflects on his boyhood in New York; the early inspiration of Bill Russell and Jackie Robinson, and, later, John Wooden at UCLA; his relationship with Wilt Chamberlain; his pro years in Milwaukee with Oscar Robertson; and his good times with the Lakers. The book includes photographs and Kareem's lifetime statistics.

3.   Abernathy, Ralph David. *And the Walls Came Tumbling Down: An Autobiography.* New York: Harper and Row, 1989.

In this autobiography, Rev. Ralph Abernathy includes an account of his early years in rural Alabama, his time in a segregated Army, his days as a student at Alabama State University and at Atlanta University, his role in the Montgomery bus boycott, and his work in the Southern Christian Leadership Conference. His story also provides the reader with a personal portrait of Dr. Martin Luther King, Jr., his best friend and fellow freedom fighter in the civil rights movement, including details of King's activities on the night before he died in Memphis. Includes photographs and an index.

4.   Ali, Muhammad, with Richard Durham. *The Greatest: My Own Story.* New York: Random House, 1975.

Written in the train–of–thought style, the book is an intimate story of the world heavyweight champion himself. The exhibitionism for which Ali was often criticized is minimal; instead there is an attempt to be open and honest and to discuss such personal things as prefight anxiety and fantasies. The autobiography covers Ali's boxing career from his first fight to his championship bout in Manila against Joe Frazier. While not in chronological order, the book includes important events in Ali's life, as well as his professional fight record.

5.   Angelou, Maya. *All God's Children Need Traveling Shoes.* New York: Random House, 1986.

6. ———. *Gather Together in My Name.* New York: Random House, 1974.

7. ———. *The Heart of a Woman.* 1st ed. New York: Random House, 1981.

This fourth volume of Angelou's autobiography finds her moving to New York and chronicles her involvement with black artists and writers and the civil rights movement.

8. ———. *I Know Why the Caged Bird Sings.* New York: Random House, 1969.

This autobiography, in which one black woman of talent comes alive, is a message not only to black people of talent, but to *all* black people, urging them to face their lives with dignity and courage.

9. ———. *Singin' and Swingin' and Gettin' Merry Like Christmas.* 1st ed. New York: Random House, 1976.

This third volume of Angelou's autobiography carries her into the adult world of marriage, show business, and foreign travel.

10. Armstrong, Louis. *Satchmo: My Life in New Orleans.* New York: Prentice–Hall, 1954. Reprint. New York: Da Capo Press, 1986.

With a new introduction by Dan Morgenstern, this 240–page memoir tells how Armstrong grew up in New Orleans. It recounts his early encounter with music before leaving home for Chicago at age twenty–two to join his idol Joe Oliver ("King Oliver") and his band. It describes his neighborhood—an environment with its share of hustlers, gamblers, and musicians—and his various jobs, including his stints on the riverboat and in the coal mine. Includes photographs.

11. Ashe, Arthur R., Jr., with Clifford G. Gewecke, Jr.* *Advantage Ashe.* New York: Coward–McCann, 1967.

12. Bailey, Pearl. *Between You and Me: Loving Reminiscences.* 1st ed. New York: Doubleday, 1989.

13. ———. *The Raw Pearl.* New York: Harcourt, Brace and World, 1968.

14. ———. *Talking to Myself.* New York: Harcourt Brace Jovanovich, 1971.

15. Baraka, Imamu Amiri. *The Autobiography of LeRoi Jones/Amiri Baraka.* New York: Freundlich Books, 1984.

   A chronicle of the first forty years of his life, this book describes how Jones/Baraka, black writer and political activist, comes into being from his middle–class roots in Newark. It relates how his journey through Howard University, the Air Force, Greenwich Village among the beatniks, incendiary Harlem, polemic Newark, and the caverns of his heart dictated his reactions to a racist society.

16. Basie, William (Count), with Albert Murray. *Good Morning Blues: The Autobiography of Count Basie.* 1st ed. New York: Random House, 1985.

   In this autobiographical account, as told to Albert Murray, Basie takes the reader behind the scenes of his journey from Red Bank, New Jersey, through his apprenticeship in New York City and his years in Kansas City, to the peaks of the musical world. He recounts his association with Billie Holiday, Lester Young, Jimmy Rushing, Jo Jones, and Joe Williams. There are also stories and recollections of his command performances, the triumphant tours of Japan and Europe, and the recordings of his autumnal years.

17. Bates, Daisy. *The Long Shadow of Little Rock, a Memoir.* New York: David McKay Co., 1962.

Little Rock, Arkansas, became a prominent symbol of the struggle for school integration and is paramount in black Americans' continuing quest for freedom. As Daisy Bates reveals her life experiences, she underscores a deep–seated hatred caused by the death of her mother at the hands of a white rapist. She tells how this experience placed her regard for mankind on a more philosophical plane. The love, compassion, and belief in brotherhood are the motivating forces in her perseverance throughout and her emergence as a leader in the pursuit for human quality.

18. Becket, Sidney. *Treat It Gentle: An Autobiography.* London: Cassell, 1960. Reprint. New York: Da Capo Press, 1978.

19. Bellegarde, Ida Rowland. *Black Heroes and Heroines.* Book 1, *Mary McLeod Bethune and James Weldon Johnson.* Pine Bluff, Ark.: Bell Enterprises, 1979.

Describes the life and accomplishments of Mary McLeod Bethune, the famed educator, and James Weldon Johnson, the noted poet and civil rights leader. Robert Russa Moton, Paul Laurence Dunbar, Phillis Wheatley, and Benjamin Banneker are the focus of books 2, 3, 4, and 5, respectively.

20. ———. *Black Heroes and Heroines.* Book 2, *Robert Russa Moton.* Pine Bluff, Ark.: Bell Enterprises, 1979.

21. ———. *Black Heroes and Heroines.* Book 3, *Paul Laurence Dunbar.* Pine Bluff, Ark.: Bell Enterprises, 1979.

22. Berry, Chuck. *Chuck Berry: The Autobiography.* New York: Simon and Schuster, 1987.

Chuck Berry talks about his St. Louis boyhood, reform school, the first hit single, touring, racism on the road, the prison stints, the comebacks, the romances, the stories behind the songs, and much more. The book includes a foreword by Bruce Springsteen,** photographs, a list of recording sessions, a discography/filmography, and an index.

23. Blockson, Charles, with Ron Fry.* *Black Genealogy.* Englewood
     Cliffs, N.J.: Prentice Hall, 1977.

24. Bontemps, Arna Wendell, ed. *Five Black Lives: The
     Autobiographies of Venture Smith, James Mars, William
     Grimes, G. W. Offley, and James L. Smith.* Middletown,
     Conn.: Wesleyan University Press, 1971.

     Presents ex–slave narratives written from 1729 to 1870 by
     fugitive slaves who settled in Connecticut. These autobiographies
     provide a unique and essential perspective on slavery. Some
     accounts are rare.

25. Brawley, Benjamin Griffith. *Negro Builders and Heroes.* 1937.
     Reprint. Chapel Hill: University of North Carolina Press,
     1965.

     This book is an introduction to black biography. Much of
     the work focuses on history and literature. The early chapters
     present such individuals as Crispus Attucks, Phillis Wheatley,
     Benjamin Banneker, John Chavis, Paul Cuffe, Frederick
     Douglass, Harriet Tubman, and Blanche Kelso Bruce, the first
     black to serve a full term in the U.S. Senate. The later chapters
     of the book deal with groups, as opposed to individuals. They
     describe leaders in science, education and religious work, blacks
     in sports, black women in American life, and inventions by
     blacks.

26. Bricktop, with James Haskins. *Bricktop.* New York: Atheneum
     Publishers, 1983.

     Bricktop—she was born Ada Beatrice Queen Victoria Louis
     Virginia Smith in 1894 and later adopted the name Bricktop and
     became the queen of nightclubs—and writer James Haskins tell
     the colorful, high–spirited story of prohibition Harlem, café
     society Paris, and movie–mad Rome. The book presents
     anecdotes about rich and powerful and famous figures such as
     Jack Johnson, Josephine Baker, Martin Luther King, Jr., Jelly

Roll Morton, Frank Sinatra, John Barrymore, Edward G. Robinson, and Paul Robeson.

27. Brooks, Gwendolyn. *Report from Part One: An Autobiography.* Detroit: Broadside Press, 1972.

28. Brown, Claude. *Manchild in the Promised Land.* New York: Macmillan Co., 1965.

    The autobiography of a young man who abandoned the crime and drugs of his Harlem youth to make a new life for himself. It recreates the Harlem streets of the 1940s and 1950s.

29. Browne, Rose Butler, and James W. English.* *Love My Children: An Autobiography.* 2d ed. Elgin, Ill.: David C. Cook Publishing Co., 1974.

    In this story of pride and hard work, Rose Butler Browne—one of seven children in a struggling, impoverished family—describes how she grew up in South Boston. She goes on to recount her successful quest for a doctorate at Harvard University in the 1930s.

30. Buckley, Gail Lumet. *The Hornes: An American Family.* New York: Alfred A. Knopf, 1986. Reprint. New York: New American Library, 1988.

    Gail Lumet Buckley, Lena Horne's daughter, tells the story of an American and an Afro–American family. In words and pictures—photographs and memorabilia culled from scrapbooks kept by family and friends—she traces eight generations of Hornes and their ancestors. Highlighted are the achievements, conflicts, and traditions of this family.

31. Burrell, Natelkka E., with Elizabeth S. McFadden.** *God's Beloved Rebel: An Autobiography.* Mountain View, Calif.: Pacific Press, 1982.

32. Callender, Red, and Elaine Cohen.* *Unfinished Dream: The Musical World of Red Callender.* Winston–Salem, N.C.: Salem House Publishers, 1986.

Unclouded by heroin, nightmare withdrawals, and pointless self–destruction, this book describes the life of bassist–composer Red Callender and the rich musical history of Los Angeles' Central Avenue. Callender and coauthor Elaine Cohen also provide behind–the–scenes portraits of Louis Armstrong, Billie Holiday, Duke Ellington, and other great jazz artists.

33. Callum, Agnes Kane. *Kane–Butler Genealogy: History of a Black Family.* N.p.: Author, 1979.

This book traces the Kane–Butler family from its origin in St. Mary's County, Maryland, in 1681 to many parts of the United States in 1978. Callum shows that many descendants of the Kane–Butler lineage still reside in St. Mary's County.

34. Campanella, Roy. *It's Good To Be Alive.* 1st ed. Boston: Little, Brown and Co., 1959.

Reveals the life and times of the celebrated Roy Campanella, who almost became the first black in the major leagues. Signed by the Dodgers in 1946, he won Most Valuable Player on three separate occasions—1951, 1953, and 1955. An automobile accident, which left him paralyzed and confined to a wheelchair, ended his playing career in 1958.

35. Carroll, Diahann, with Rose Firestone.* *Diahann: An Autobiography.* Boston: Little, Brown and Co., 1986.

This book presents a glimpse into the life of Diahann Carroll, a singer–actress who won a Tony Award for *No Strings*, an Oscar nomination as best actress for *Claudine*, an Emmy nomination for her television series "Julia," and superstar status for her role in "Dynasty." It covers her early life in Harlem, her singing debut as part of the Tiny Tots choir in Adam Clayton Powell's Abyssinian Baptist Church, her first marriage to and her daughter by the jazz impresario Monte Kay, her marriages to Freddie Glusman and Robert DeLeon, her relationships with men, including Sidney Poitier and David Frost. Includes photographs and an index.

36. Cazort, Jean E., and Constance Tibbs Hobson. *Born to Play: The Life and Career of Hazel Harrison.* Westport, Conn.: Greenwood Press, 1983.

Hazel Harrison (1883–1969) claims distinction as having been not only the most highly accomplished black concert pianist of her day, but also the first black American performing artist to have appeared as a soloist with the renowned Berlin Philharmonic Orchestra (1904). The authors trace Harrison's career from her formative years in La Porte, Indiana (1883–1911), through her years of study and concertizing in Germany (1911–1914), on to her years of maturity back in America, where she continued her work as a private teacher and performer (1914–1931), and finally, as an artist/teacher in academia (1931–1936 at Tuskegee Institute, 1936–1955 at Howard University, and 1958–1963 at Alabama State College).

37. Chamberlain, Wilt, and David Shaw.** *Wilt: Just Like Any Other 7-Foot Black Millionaire Who Lives Next Door.* New York: Macmillan Publishing Co., 1973. Reprint. New York: Warner Paperback Library, 1975.

Chamberlain stresses his successes with making money, "coping" with women, scoring points, and drawing large crowds. He gives the reader a guided tour of his life—from his early childhood successes to his status as an ace basketball player. Included are photographs of Chamberlain the boy, Chamberlain the youth, and Chamberlain the man. Photographs of his dream house and his dogs are also included.

38. Charles, Ray, with David Ritz.** *Brother Ray: Ray Charles' Own Story.* New York: Dial Press, 1978.

The autobiography of the famous musician showcases Charles's triumph over poverty and pain. The discography and notes are by David Ritz.

39. Chisholm, Shirley. *Unbought and Unbossed.* Boston: Houghton Mifflin Co., 1970.

40. Church, Annette Elaine, and Roberta Church. *The Robert R. Churches of Memphis: A Father and Son Who Achieved in Spite of Race.* Memphis, Tenn.: Authors, 1974.

This is the biography of Annette Elaine Church's father (Robert Reed Church, Sr., 1839–1912) and brother (Robert Reed Church, Jr., 1885–1952). Annette Church and Roberta Church—her niece—describe the life and times of the two men in a segregated society, and reveal how Robert, Sr., a self-made man, who was considered to be the South's first black millionaire, created a legacy.

41. Church, Roberta, and Ronald Anderson Walter. *Nineteenth Century Memphis Families of Color, 1850–1900.* 1st ed. Memphis, Tenn.: Authors, 1987.

Using materials from a variety of sources, particularly from the descendants of individuals included, this 150–page work provides biographical sketches of some of Memphis's notable black families and their achievements. The authors include photographs and an index.

42. Clark, Septima Poinsette. *Echo in My Soul.* New York: E. P. Dutton and Co., 1962.

This autobiography tells about Clark's career as a schoolteacher on John's Island in South America and her work with the Highlander Folk School in Tennessee. It concludes with her endeavors with the Southern Christian Leadership Conference in setting up citizenship schools.

43. Coan, Josephus Roosevelt. *Daniel Alexander Payne, Christian Educator.* Philadelphia: AME Book Concern, 1935.

44. Comer, James Pierpoint. *Beyond Black and White.* New York: Quadrangle Books, 1972.

    Comer recounts his experiences as a black man and as a psychiatrist to demonstrate the impact of racism on both blacks and whites in America. He contends that "Black and white conflict is a by–product of a more basic problem: the failure of this society to develop a social system that enables all people to meet their basic human needs at a reasonable level. Until this is done, we will not be able to move beyond black and white." Includes an introduction by Robert Coles, a foreword by Richard G. Hatcher, footnotes, a bibliography, and an index.

45. ————. *Maggie's American Dream: The Life and Times of a Black Family.* New York: New American Library, 1988.

    This book is Comer's "family biography in the context of the Afro–American experience." More specifically it is his autobiography and a window into his mother's life.

46. Cromwell, Adelaide M. *An Afro-Victorian Feminist: The Life and Times of Adelaide Smith Casely Hayford, 1868–1960.* Totowa, N.J.: F. Case, 1986.

47. Daniel, Sadie Iola. *Women Builders.* Washington, D.C.: Associated Publishers, 1931.

    This book is a collection of biographies of twelve outstanding women who made an invaluable contribution to the development of black youth in general and who opened the way for black women in particular. Their leadership role in the community and their moral and spiritual values are magnificently portrayed.

48. Davis, Allison. *Leadership, Love, and Aggression.* New York: Harcourt Brace Jovanovich, 1983.

This book focuses on four individuals—Frederick Douglass, W. E. B. DuBois, Richard Wright, and Martin Luther King, Jr.—and discusses the psychological factors that propelled them to leadership. These four men represent four different periods of American history and four different leadership styles. Three were political leaders while the fourth, Richard Wright, was a leader in literary arts.

49. Davis, Angela Yvonne. *Angela Davis: An Autobiography.* New York: Random House, 1974. Reprint. New York: International Publishers, 1988.

50. Davis, Arthur Paul. *A Black Diamond in the Queen's Tiara.* N.p. 1974.

   This rare piece of history is the biography of Pyrrus Concer, former slave. The book gives one insight into the early history of *Southhampton Magazine,* spring issue of 1912. It ends with an epilogue containing more biographical information on Pyrrus Concer and a finale in which gratitude is expressed to those who helped in the author's research. Included in the book is a picture of the "diamond," Pyrrus Concer, and other pictures of historical events.

51. ————. *Isaac Watts: His Life and Works.* New York: Dryden Press, 1943.

52. Davis, Marianna White, et al.* *South Carolina's Blacks and Native Americans: 1776–1976.* Columbia, S.C.: State Human Affairs Commission, 1976.

53. Davis, Miles, with Quincy Troupe. *Miles: The Autobiography.* New York: Simon and Schuster, 1989.

54. Douglass, Frederick. *The Life and Times of Frederick Douglass: From 1817–1882.* London: Christian Age Office, 1882. Reprint. Boston: DeWolfe Fiske and Co., 1892; New York: Pathway Press, 1941; New York: Macmillan Co., 1962.

According to the editor of the 1941 edition, "*The Life and Times* is the final form of an autobiography first published as a small Narrative in 1845, expanded in *My Bondage and My Freedom* in 1855, further extended in the first edition under the same title in 1881, and completed and revised in 1893. A reprint appeared in 1895. . . . This . . . is substantially a reproduction of the text of the last revised and complete work."

This is the renowned autobiography of the runaway slave who became Abraham Lincoln's adviser and the consul general to Haiti. Includes an introduction by Rayford W. Logan, a bibliography, and an index.

55. ————. *The Life and Writings of Frederick Douglass*. Edited by Philip Sheldon Foner.** New York: International Publishers, 1950, 1975.

56. ————. *My Bondage and My Freedom*. 1855. Reprint. New York: Arno Press, 1968; Salem, N.H.: Ayer Co., 1984.

In this autobiography—his second, originally published in 1855—Douglass not only tells of his life as a slave but also presents a vivid picture of his life as a free man and an active member of the abolitionist movement. Includes some of his most significant speeches and writings on the evils of slavery, and a foreword by Lerone Bennett, Jr.

57. ————. *Narrative of the Life of Frederick Douglass, An American Slave, Written by Himself.* Boston: Published at Anti–Slavery Office, 1845. Reprint. Garden City, N.Y.: Dolphin Books, 1963.

This autobiography, Douglass's first, details the life of one of this country's revered Afro–Americans. It tells how Douglass—who was born a slave in Talbot County on the Eastern Shore of Maryland—endured life as a slave, how he eventually escaped from slavery, how he was encouraged to address the antislavery convention in Nantucket, and how he became a leading abolitionist.

58. DuBois, Shirley Lola Graham. *DuBois: A Pictorial Biography.* 1st ed. Chicago: Johnson Publishing Co., 1978.

> The life of W. E. B. DuBois is recalled through these photographs. This volume shows him at every stage of his life from infancy to the days shortly before his death in Accra, Ghana. The foreword and the introduction are by David Graham DuBois and Lerone Bennett, Jr., respectively. Includes index.

59. ————. *His Day Is Marching On: A Memoir of W. E. B. DuBois.* Philadelphia: Lippincott, 1971. Reprint. New York: Third Press, 1974.

60. DuBois, Shirley Lola Graham, and George Dewey Lipscomb.* *Dr. George Washington Carver, Scientist.* New York: Julian Messner, 1944.

> This book is a biography of the black scientist whose childhood love for plants led him into a botanical and cultural career.

61. DuBois, W. E. B. *The Autobiography of W. E. B. DuBois: A Soliloquy on Viewing My Life from the Last Decade of Its First Century.* New York: International Publishers, 1968.

62. Dunbar–Nelson, Alice Moore. *Give Us Each Day: The Diary of Alice Dunbar–Nelson.* Edited with a critical introduction and notes by Gloria T. Hull. New York: W. W. Norton and Co., 1984.

> This rare diary by the widow of Paul Laurence Dunbar presents the life of an educated middle–class woman in the early twentieth century and her participation in black organizations and cultural life.

63. Dunham, Katherine, and J. Harbrace.* *A Touch of Innocence.* 1st ed. New York: Harcourt, Brace and Co., 1959. Reprint. Freeport, N.Y.: Books for Libraries Press, 1980.

Written in the third person, this nontraditional autobiography covers the first eighteen years of Katherine Dunham's life. It is her account of a girl (and her family) growing up during the years after World War I and the early years of the Great Depression. She reveals a domineering father, a vaguely remembered mother, an adored older brother, a devoted stepmother, and a girl who fought against her parents' rule and dreamed of becoming a choreographer.

64. Dunnigan, Alice Allison. *A Black Woman's Experience: From Schoolhouse to White House.* Philadelphia: Dorrance and Co., 1974.

This is the glowing autobiography of Alice Allison Dunningan, the first Afro-American woman to receive accreditation from the White House. There are three sections to this autobiography: "Those Years," "Exploring a Great New World," and "The Political Arena." The first two parts are drawn from memory, but the final section, which reports contemporary history, is from veritable sources. Numerous pictures of herself and family enhance the book.

65. Emecheta, Buchi. *Head Above Water.* London: Fontana Paperbacks, 1986.

66. Evers, Charles James. *Evers.* New York: World Publishing Co., 1971.

The autobiography of the mayor of Fayette, Mississippi, and also gubernatorial candidate. In addition to discussing his own life, Evers provides a glimpse into the life of his famed brother, Medgar Evers. Edited with an introduction by Grace Halsell.

67. Evers, Myrlie, with William Peters.* *For Us, the Living.* New York: Doubleday and Co., 1967.

The widow of civil rights leader Medgar Evers writes of their life and aspirations, of his beliefs and participation in the

Mississippi civil rights movement during the 1950s and early 1960s, and of his tragic assassination.

68. Farris, Christine King. *Martin Luther King, Jr.: His Life and Dream.* Lexington, Mass.: Ginn and Co., 1986.

One of a group of books, same title and author, designed for the three educational levels: elementary, elementary–intermediate, and intermediate. A teacher–annotated edition is associated with this publication. Includes a bibliography.

69. Ferguson, Ira Lunan. *I Dug Graves at Night to Attend College by Day: An Autobiography.* Brooklyn, N.Y.: Theodore Gaus' Sons, 1968.

70. Fields, Mamie Garvin, with Karen Fields. *Lemon Swamp and Other Places: A Carolina Memoir.* New York: Free Press, 1983.

71. Flipper, Henry Ossian. *Autobiography of Lieut. Henry Ossian Flipper, U.S.A., First Graduate of Color from U.S. Military Academy.* New York: Homer Lee and Co., 1878. Reprint. New York: Arno Press, 1969; Salem, N.H.: Ayer Co., 1986.

Originally published under the title *Colored Cadet at West Point*, this autobiography of the first Afro–American graduate of West Point deals with such things as a description of the institution (including its aristocracy, classes, privileges, and life) and comments about Smith, the only other Afro–American to have attended West Point then. Of special interest is the preface by Sara Dunlap Jackson, who provides a short biography of Flipper that includes his life as a slave, his army life and court–martial, his distinguished civilian life, and his death in 1940.

72. Fowler, Carolyn. *A Knot in the Thread: The Life and Work of Jacques Roumain.* Washington, D.C.: Howard University Press, 1980.

The author examines Jacques Roumain's brief thirty-seven years, during which he was a journalist, politician, revolutionary, diplomat, professor, ethnographer, and also the leading Haitian poet–novelist of his generation. Includes introduction, appendix, bibliography, and an index.

73. Franklin, John Hope. *George Washington Williams: A Biography.* Chicago: University of Chicago Press, 1985.

Franklin pays tribute to the pioneering, controversial black scholar—born in 1849 in Bedford Springs, Pennsylvania—who wrote the first history of black people in America, published in 1882. Using a wide range of sources, Franklin evokes the personality, strengths, and weaknesses of George Washington Williams, who dedicated his life to uplifting the race through journalism, the ministry, oratory, law, and politics. In the process, Franklin touches on major social, economic, intellectual, and political concerns of the black community during that time.

74. Franklin, John Hope, and August Meier,** eds. *Black Leaders of the Twentieth Century.* Urbana: University of Illinois Press, 1982.

75. Frazier, Walt, with Neil Offen.** *Walt Frazier: One Magic Season and a Basketball Life.* New York: Times Books, 1988.

Walt "Clyde" Frazier, a Hall of Famer, reflects on the New York Knickerbockers' legendary championship season of 1969–1970. He describes his development as an athlete and as a person—first as one of nine children growing up poor in Atlanta, then as a student at Southern Illinois University, a rookie with the Knicks, a celebrity, a faded star, and finally a businessman starting a new life. He offers insight into his defensive secrets and shares his views of the changes that have affected the nature of the game, players, coaches, and fans. He also offers revealing profiles of past and present stars. Includes four pages of individual and team statistics.

76.   Gaines, Ernest J. *The Autobiography of Miss Jane Pittman.* New York: Dial Press, 1971.

Beginning from the time of emancipation, Jane Pittman, former slave child, recounts her life story to writer Ernest Gaines. For young Jane and for many other freed slaves, freedom held the initial hope of opportunity, change, and relief from the burden of an evil system. But as life unfolds, this hope is almost shattered by the reality of life in the South. The story of Miss Jane Pittman is the story of perseverance and hope, and offers an intriguing insight into human nature. In spite of the odds against blacks after the Emancipation Proclamation, she succeeds in building for herself a life of ease and happiness. Her experiences in and after slavery provided her with immense maturity at an early age and a deep understanding and acceptance of the flaws and strengths of human nature. She nurtured many who later became influential advocates for the advancement of blacks. Gaines won the Best Writer of the Year Award for this book, which became a television award–winning piece.

77.   Gayle, Addison, Jr. *Oak and Ivy: A Biography of Paul Laurence Dunbar.* Garden City, N.Y.: Doubleday and Co., 1971.

This is an attempt to give the reader a glimpse into the life of Paul L. Dunbar the, "elevator boy," as well as Paul L. Dunbar, the poet. Gayle relates the story of a genius fallen victim to American racism. Dunbar's life is described as one of "quiet desperation" because "others dictated the route" his poetry and life were to take. Gayle says it is because of his frustrations, so visible in his poetry, that blacks readily identified with him. For students of Dunbar, the book includes a chronology and a listing of Dunbar's work.

78.   ————. *Richard Wright: Ordeal of a Native Son.* 1st ed. New York: Anchor Press/Doubleday and Co., 1980.

The fifth full–scale biography of the world–famous Richard Wright, this book was prompted specifically by Gayle's gaining access to "previously classified documents on American citizens by various government agencies" (e.g., the FBI, CIA). These documents "assume an overwhelming importance" in the last years of Richard Wright's life in exile. Includes a bibliography and an index.

79. ———. *Wayward Child: A Personal Odyssey.* Garden City, N.Y.: Anchor Press, 1977.

A moving chronicle of the life of a dynamic personality. The autobiography tells of Gayle's hardships and of his consequent rise above them. It includes a few interesting and appropriate excerpts from his diary. Note the short digression on Richard Nixon to be found toward the end of the book.

80. Gibson, Althea. *I Always Wanted To Be Somebody.* As told to Ed Fitzgerald.* Specially abridged by Stephen M. Joseph.* New York: Noble and Noble, 1970.

81. Gilliam, Dorothy Butler. *Paul Robeson, All-American.* Washington, D.C.: New Republic Book Co., 1976.

82. Giovanni, Nikki. *Gemini: An Extended Autobiographical Statement on My First Twenty-Five Years of Being a Black Poet.* Indianapolis: Bobbs-Merrill, 1971. Reprint. New York: Penguin Books, 1980.

83. Golden, Marita. *Migrations of the Heart.* 1st ed. Garden City, N.Y.: Doubleday and Co., 1983.

A personal odyssey by an Afro-American woman who returned to America after the breakup of her marriage to an African.

84. Gordy, Berry, Sr. *Movin' Up.* New York: Harper and Row, 1979.

With an introduction by Alex Haley, this autobiography of "Pop" Gordy, founder of Motown Records, was completed shortly before Gordy's death at age ninety.

85. Grant, Moses Alexander, with Janie Aiken Grant. *Looking Back: Reminiscences of a Black Family Heritage on Hilton Head Island.* Orangeburg, S.C.: Williams Associates, 1988.

   The author tells about the Grant and the Aiken families of Hilton Head Island—one of the Sea Islands off the coast of South Carolina. He describes five generations of his family tree. Includes photographs and a selected bibliography.

86. Green, Ely. *Ely: An Autobiography.* New York: Seabury Press, 1966.

   Ely Green, the son of a black servant and a white man, tells of his search for identity and of his life in a small Southern town at the turn of the century.

87. Greene, Lorenzo Johnson, and Arvarh E. Strickland, eds. *Working with Carter G. Woodson, the Father of Black History: A Diary, 1928–1930.* Baton Rouge: Louisiana State University Press, 1989.

88. Gregory, Dick, with Robert Lipsyte.* *Nigger: An Autobiography.* New York: E. P. Dutton, 1964. Reprint. New York: Washington Square Press, 1986.

   Dick Gregory uses wit and subtlety to tell his story of growing up poor in Chicago, his career as a comedian, and his evolution into an activist in civil rights. He gives a message to those concerned with human rights.

89. Gregory, James M. *Frederick Douglass: The Orator.* Springfield, Mass.: Willey Co., 1893.

   This is a study of the character, early life, fight for freedom, and important events in the life of Frederick Douglass. Direct quotations taken from an autobiography entitled *The Life and Times of Frederick Douglass* and extracts of speeches are included with obituary tributes delivered at his funeral. Historical illustrations of Douglass and other figures of importance are presented in the book.

90. Griffith, Helen. *Dauntless in Mississippi: The Life of Sarah A. Dickey, 1838-1904.* 2d ed. South Hadley, Mass.: Dinosaur Press, 1966. Reprint. Washington, D.C.: Zenger Publishing Co., 1978.

This is a biography of a northern white woman in the second half of the nineteenth century, a woman "dauntless" in the face of obstacles. The story is also one of the growth of friendly race relations in a town where she was almost ostracized.

91. Hall,* Donald, with Dock Ellis. *Dock Ellis in the Country of Baseball.* New York: Coward, McCann and Geoghegan, 1976. Reprint. New York: Simon and Schuster, 1989.

92. Hamilton, Virginia. *W. E. B. DuBois: A Biography.* New York: Thomas Y. Crowell Co., 1972.

Hamilton views DuBois as a father of change in the attitudes of black people toward themselves and their conditions in American society because he made them aware of the first reason for their discontent. Discussed in the book are the Niagara Movement and the N.A.A.C.P., two organizations founded by DuBois. The author also discusses DuBois's influence in the founding of *The Crisis* magazine and the back–to–Africa movement. While investigating the reasons for DuBois's influence, the author points out that despite all these involvements, DuBois was largely ignored for many years.

93. Hampton, Lionel, with James Haskins. *Hamp: An Autobiography.* New York: Warner Books, 1989.

94. Handy, William Christopher. *Father of the Blues: An Autobiography.* New York: Macmillian Co., 1941, 1955. Reprint, Edited by Arna Bontemps. New York: Da Capo Press, 1985.

95. Harris, Joseph Earl, ed. *Recollections of James Juma Mbotela.*
     Nairobi, Kenya: East African Publishing House, 1977.

     A synthesis of the paper written by Mbotela (in Swahili) and
     of data from personal interviews. It is a short account of the life
     of Mbotela, whose memories provide insight into the changes
     within one Kenyan community over several generations. The
     book combines autobiographical fragments written by Mbotela
     with oral testimonies elicited by Harris and a question–and–
     answer exchange between the two men.

96. Haskins, James. *About Michael Jackson.* Hillside, N.J.: Enslow
     Publishers, 1985.

97. ————. *Adam Clayton Powell: Portrait of a Marching Black.*
     New York: Dial Press, 1974.

     The goal of this book is to provide some insight into Adam
     Clayton Powell, the man. This biographical study traces Powell's
     life from early childhood up to and including his death. His
     escapades as an adolescent, his deep personal life as a family
     man, and his devout belief in both the Almighty Creator and the
     equality of his people are among the essential ingredients
     considered to have gone into the molding of his charismatic
     character. The book shows that Powell the man had much more
     impact than Powell the preacher–politician. Includes eighteen
     photographs.

98. ————. *Always Movin' On: A Biography of Langston Hughes.*
     New York: Franklin Watts, 1976.

99. ————. *Babe Ruth and Hank Aaron: The Home Run Kings.*
     New York: Lothrop, Lee and Shepard Co., 1974.

     The baseball successes of Babe Ruth and Hank Aaron are
     compared in this dual biography. The development of both these
     men to prominence is shown beginning with their early
     childhood. Their statistics and batting averages are compared,

together with their most famous games. There are photographs illustrating the text.

100. ————. *Bill Cosby: America's Most Famous Father.* New York: Walker and Co., 1988.

101. ————. *Bob McAdoo: Superstar.* New York: Lothrop, Lee and Shepard Co., 1978.

102. ————. *Corazon Aquino: Leader of the Philippines.* Hillside, N.J.: Enslow Publishers, 1988.

103. ————. *Diana Ross: Star Supreme.* New York: Viking Press, 1985.

104. ————. *Dr. J: A Biography of Julius Erving.* Garden City, N.Y.: Doubleday and Co., 1975.

Julius Erving is described as an ambitious young man who grew up on the outskirts of New York City with an immense desire to make something big out of life. The book traces Dr. J's development from early adolescence to prominence as a leading basketball player. Sixteen photographs illustrate the text.

105. ————. *Fighting Shirley Chisholm.* New York: Dial Press, 1975.

Haskins presents Chisholm as a fiery black woman who dared to enter the male–dominated arena of politics. Her early years are traced as far back as her life in Barbados. From there she entered the New York scene and began her rise to prominence as an assemblywoman, congresswoman, and even presidential candidate. Of particular interest is the appendix showing her impressive legislative record.

106. ————. *From Lew Alcindor to Kareem Abdul Jabbar.* 1973. Reprint. New York: Lothrop, Lee and Shepard Co., 1978.

107. ————. *George McGinnis: Basketball Superstar.* New York: Hastings House, 1978.

108. ————. *I'm Gonna Make You Love Me: The Story of Diana Ross.* New York: Dial Press, 1980.

109. ————. *Katherine Dunham.* New York: Coward, McCann and Geoghegan, 1982.

Relates the story of the famous choreographer who, wherever she has lived, has worked at bringing creative arts participation to the community.

110. ————. *Lena Horne.* New York: Coward, McCann, 1983.

111. ————. *The Life and Death of Martin Luther King, Jr.* New York: Lothrop, Lee and Shepard Co., 1977.

Dr. King is pictured here as a man who, during his lifetime, continually championed the cause of civil rights for his people. His life is examined from early childhood, with special note taken of his development into a proponent of the concept of nonviolence. This book also includes a re-examination of the circumstances surrounding his assassination. A few selected photographs are included.

112. ————. *Mabel Mercer: A Life.* New York: Atheneum Publishers, 1988.

A biography of the entertainer Mabel Mercer, who lived during the period from 1900 to 1984. Appendix A includes a partial list of songs by Mercer, and appendix B includes a discography.

113. ————. *Magic: A Biography of Earvin Johnson.* Hillside, N.J.: Enslow Publishers, 1982.

114. ————. *Pele: A Biography.* Garden City, N.Y.: Doubleday and Co., 1976.

This is the biography of the man who is considered by Haskins to be the world's premier soccer player. His life is traced from early childhood, when his love of the sport was nurtured. The text comprises many action–filled photographs that fully illustrate Pele's unequaled success. The first two chapters present the history of the sport and give a basic outline of the rules of the game. Soccer lovers may especially wish to note Pele's goal–scoring prowess, documented at the back of the text.

115. ———. *Pinckney Benton Stewart Pinchback.* New York: Macmillan Co., 1973.

Haskins identifies Pinchback, a former governor of Louisiana, as one of the most complex and flamboyant figures in American history. Haskins starts by cautioning that information about this mulatto is very questionable since most records were destroyed either by Pinchback himself or by others. He then says that he has had to draw together the few references available; the legends; and the physical, social, and political realities of various places at various times, and that he has had to resort to his inferences to give a coherent and living sense to Pinchback, the boy and the man.

116. ———. *Ralph Bunche: A Most Reluctant Hero.* New York: Hawthorn Books, 1974.

This book acquaints the uninitiated with Ralph Bunche. It points out the very fulfilled life of this black man, who played a significant role in opening the door to high–ranking positions to qualified blacks as well as in providing a positive image for young blacks. His life and times are traced from early childhood on, fully illustrating the hard work he undertook to attain success. The text includes many illustrative photographs of his rise to greatness as arbitrator for the United States and as peacemaker for the world.

117. ———. *Richard Pryor: A Man and His Madness.* New York: Beaufort Books, 1984.

118.   ———. *Shirley Temple Black: Actress to Ambassador.* New York: Viking Press, 1988.

119.   ———. *Sugar Ray Leonard.* New York: Lothrop, Lee and Shepard Co., 1982.

120.   ———. *Winnie Mandela: Life of Struggle.* New York: G. P. Putnam's Sons, 1988.

121.   Haskins, James, with Kathleen Benson.** *Lena: A Personal and Professional Biography of Lena Horne.* New York: Stein and Day, 1985.

This biography is a thorough account of Lena Horne's sometimes rocky road to fame. The reader is taken from her birth in Brooklyn in 1917 through a singing career that starts in the Cotton Club but suddenly has the songstress singing in the midst of whiteness; through Broadway appearances and a contract with MGM; through her external struggles with her husband and band director, Lennie Hayton; and finally to a Tony Award in 1981 for *Lena Horne: The Lady and Her Music.*

122.   ———. *Nat King Cole.* New York: Stein and Day, 1984.

123.   ———. *Scott Joplin: The Man Who Made Ragtime.* New York: Doubleday and Co., 1978. Reprint. New York: Stein and Day, 1980.

This book, winner of the ASCAP Deems Taylor Award for excellence in writing in the field of music, is the biography of the ragtime musician and creator of the opera *Treemonisha.*

124.   Haskins, James, and N. R. Mitgang.** *Mr. Bojangles: The Biography of Bill Robinson.* New York: William Morrow and Co., 1988.

125. Haskins, James, and J. M. Stifle.* *Donna Summer: An Unauthorized Biography.* 1st ed. Boston: Little, Brown and Co., 1983.

126. Haskins, James, with Kathleen Benson** and Ellen Inkelis.* *The Great American Crazies.* New York: Condor Press, 1977.

127. Haskins, Jim. *Queen of the Blues: The Story of Dinah Washington.* New York: William Morrow and Co., 1987.

128. Henderson, Thomas (Hollywood), and Peter Knobler.** *Out of Control: Confessions of an NFL Casualty.* New York: G. P. Putnam's Sons, 1987.

Henderson looks at the steamy side of professional football from the vantage point of its flashiest stars. A Dallas Cowboys defensive standout, Henderson ruined his million-dollar career with his million-dollar cocaine habit. His drug dependency not only cost him his fast-lane lifestyle, but also landed him in jail, bereft of dignity, friends, and even the Super Bowl rings he cherished. It is from this abyss that he began to piece together his life.

129. Hill, Robert A., and Barbara Bair,* eds. *Marcus Garvey: Life and Lessons: A Centennial Companion to the Marcus Garvey Universal Negro Improvement Association Papers.* Berkeley: University of California Press, 1987.

130. Himes, Chester B. *My Life of Absurdity: The Autobiography of Chester Himes.* 1st ed. Garden City, N.Y.: Doubleday and Co., 1976.

131. ————. *The Quality of Hurt: The Autobiography of Chester Himes.* Garden City, N.Y.: Doubleday and Co., 1972. Reprint. New York: Paragon House, 1990.

132. Hodges, Willis Augustus. *Free Man of Color: The Autobiography of Willis Augustus Hodges.* Edited with an introduction by

Willard B. Gatewood, Jr.** Knoxville: University of Tennessee Press, 1982.

This is the first publication of Willis Augustus Hodges's (1815–1890) autobiography in book form. It provides a rare look at the life of a "free man of color" (1815–1890) during an important period in history. Includes bibliography and index.

133. Holley, Joseph Winthrop. *You Can't Build a Chimney from the Top: The South Through the Life of a Negro Educator.* New York: William–Frederick Press, 1948.

134. Hughes, Langston. *The Big Sea: An Autobiography.* 1st ed. New York: Hill and Wang, 1963. Reprint. New York: Thunder's Mouth Press, 1986.

135. ———. *Famous Negro Heroes of America.* Illustrated by Gerald McCann.* 1958. Reprint. New York: Dodd, Mead and Co., 1966.

136. ———. *I Wonder as I Wander: An Autobiographical Journey.* New York: Rinehart, 1956. Reprint. New York: Thunder's Mouth Press, 1986.

137. Hughes,* William Hardin, and Frederick D. Patterson, eds. *Robert Russa Moton of Hampton and Tuskegee.* Chapel Hill: University of North Carolina Press, 1956.

138. Hull, Gloria T. *Color, Sex, and Poetry: Three Women Writers of the Harlem Renaissance.* Bloomington: Indiana University Press, 1987.

139. Hurston, Zora Neale. *Dust Tracks on a Road: An Autobiography.* 1942. Reprint. Philadelphia: J. B. Lippincott Co., 1971.

The author—a novelist, folklorist, anthropologist, and daughter of the Harlem Renaissance—provides an account of her rise from childhood poverty in the rural South to a place of prominence in the pantheon of American writers.

140. Jackson, Andrew Stonewall. *Gentleman Pimp: An Autobiography.* Los Angeles: Holloway House, 1973.

141. Jackson, Mahalia, with Evan McLeod Wylie.* *Movin' On Up.* 1st ed. New York: Hawthorn Books, 1966.

This work is the autobiography of a gospel singer, Mahalia Jackson. It describes her life from childhood in New Orleans to international fame.

142. Jackson, Reggie, with the assistance of Mike Lupica.** *Reggie: The Autobiography.* New York: Villard, 1984.

The author of this autobiography offers observations from his experience in baseball. For example, he points out that Charles O. Finley was so stingy that in 1975, after the Oakland A's had won their third World Series in a row, Jackson played with a year-old jersey and three-year-old uniform pants. The book is full of comments that have helped make Jackson a familiar face on the sports page.

143. Johnson, Earvin (Magic), and Richard Levin.** *Magic.* New York: Viking Press, 1983.

144. Johnson, James Weldon. *Along This Way: The Autobiography of James Weldon Johnson.* New York: Viking Press, 1933.

James Weldon Johnson traces his own life, successes, and failures from as far back as his childhood in Haiti. He details specific turning points in his life, such as his escapades in Paris, his times at Atlanta University, and his participation in such political actions as protest marches. He also gives a rare personal insight into James Weldon Johnson, the man. The text is replete with photographs illustrating his historical prominence.

145. ———. *The Autobiography of an Ex-Colored Man.* Boston: Sherman, French and Co., 1912. Reprint. New York: Alfred A. Knopf, 1927.

146. Johnson, Robert E. *Bill Cosby: In Words and Pictures.* Chicago: Johnson and Johnson Publishing Co., 1986.

The author, associate publisher of *Jet* and confidant of the comedian, tells the story of the private and public man behind the star of one of America's most successful television programs. Johnson follows Cosby from a Philadelphia housing project to the apex of the entertainment world. In the course of this journey, he takes the reader behind the scenes and headlines. For example, there are candid photographs of the comedian with his wife, Camille, and the five Cosby children. There are also revealing analyses of the cultural and political activities of Bill Cosby.

147. Johnson, Timothy V. *Malcolm X: A Comprehensive Annotated Bibliography.* New York: Garland Publishing Co., 1986.

148. Jones, Lawrence Clifton. *Piney Woods and Its Story.* New York: Fleming H. Revell Co., 1922.

The personal life experiences of a man who dedicated himself to the education of his people in remote, but recognized, Piney Woods. Jones traces the influences that caused him to travel his particular road of giving aid to and uplifting the situation of his people. Many photographs illustrate the text and fully exemplify each path taken by the author as he embarked on his pilgrimage through life.

149. King, Martin Luther, Sr., with Clayton Riley.* *Daddy King: An Autobiography.* New York: William Morrow and Co., 1980.

Describes King's life as father of the eminent Martin Luther King, Jr., and as pastor of the famed Ebenezer Baptist Church in Atlanta, Georgia. Includes a foreword by Benjamin E. Mays and an introduction by Andrew J. Young. It also includes an index.

150. Lacy, Leslie Alexander. *Native Daughter.* New York: Macmillan Co., 1974.

In 1970 Leslie Lacy published *The Rise and Fall of a Proper Negro: An Autobiography.* The present work, *Native Daughter,* is also autobiographical.

151. ————. *The Rise and Fall of a Proper Negro: An Autobiography.* New York: Macmillan Co., 1970.

152. Latta, Morgan London. *The History of My Life and Work.* Raleigh, N.C.: Author, 1903.

153. LeFlore, Ron, with Jim Haskins. *Breakout: From Prison to the Big Leagues.* New York: Harper and Row, 1978.

LeFlore tells how he learned to play baseball in prison and subsequently became the centerfielder for the Detroit Tigers.

154. Lester, Julius. *All Is Well: An Autobiography.* New York: William Morrow and Co., 1976.

An autobiographical work in which Lester tells of his experiences from childhood. His experiences as a black writer are striking, and there are inclusions of various articles written by him. The last part of the book comprises a diary of a trip made across the country and provides some insights into the places visited.

155. ————. *Lovesong: Becoming a Jew.* New York: Henry Holt and Co., 1988.

This autobiographical odyssey begins with a black southern childhood in the 1940s; continues through Fisk University, the civil rights movement, and the New York intellectual scene of the late 1960s; and ends with Lester, as a forty-nine-year-old professor at the University of Massachusetts at Amherst. It captures his experiences—as a minister's son who converted to Judaism, as a black man twice married to white women, as the father of two children, and as a prolific writer—and his attitude toward his ethnic and religious background.

156. Lewis, Davis Levering. *King: A Biography of Martin Luther King, Jr.* 2d ed. Urbana: University of Illinois Press, 1978.

157. Lewis, Selma S., and Marjean G. Kremer,* *The Angel of Beale Street: A Biography of Julia Ann Hooks.* Vol 1. Memphis, Tenn.: St. Luke's Press, 1986.

158. Lightfoot, Sara Lawrence. *Balm in Gilead: Journey of a Healer.* Reading, Mass.: Addison–Wesley Publishing Co., 1988.

This book is Sara Lawrence Lightfoot's biography of her mother, brown–skinned Margaret Morgan Lawrence, who was born in Mississippi in 1914. There she lived a privileged life and met and married her light–skinned husband (1938), a Morehouse student, before moving to New York, where she earned a medical degree. Lightfoot explains what every black American knows, lives with, and yet hopes that white people somehow do not suspect—that light skin is prized and dark skin is despised by black people and that this distorts black women's self–image. Lightfoot speaks openly of the anger and even madness that stem from racial dynamics manifested within families and from plain human cruelties from which black people are not exempt.

159. Logan, Rayford Whittingham, ed. *W. E. B. DuBois: A Profile.* New York: Hall and Wang, 1971.

The introduction, in conjunction with the brief but informative biography, is an excellent explanation of DuBois. Contributors such as August Meier, William Ferris, and Francis Broderick permit a view of the political nature and career of DuBois, the eminent figure of Afro–American history.

160. Logan, Rayford Whittingham, and Michael R. Winston, eds. *Dictionary of American Negro Biography.* 1st ed. New York: W. W. Norton and Co., 1982.

Over a decade in preparation, this book is a comprehensive biographical dictionary with more than 700 entries spanning three centuries of American history. Many experts from diverse fields contributed to the book, often revealing facts that are largely unknown to the general public. The contributions of these scholars were edited by Rayford W. Logan and Michael R. Winston. The end product is a compilation of lives—cowboys, explorers, and sea captains, along with well–known scientists, athletes and artists—as varied and complex as the history they helped to make.

161. Louis, Joe, with Edna Rust and Art Rust, Jr. *Joe Louis: My Life.* 1st ed. New York: Harcourt Brace Jovanovich, 1978.

162. Lynch, John Roy. *Reminiscences of an Active Life: The Autobiography of John Roy Lynch.* Edited and with an introduction by John Hope Franklin. Chicago: University of Chicago Press, 1970.

John R. Lynch, the first black to preside over a national convention of the Republican party, recalls his life (1847–1939). Born into slavery in Louisiana, he grew up in Mississippi and at age twenty–one was appointed justice of the peace. A year later, he was elected to the Mississippi legislature. Among other things, Congressman Lynch was elected to the House of Representatives on three separate occasions—in 1873, 1875, and 1881. Much of his earlier work, *The Facts of Reconstruction,* can be found in this book.

163. Lynk, Miles Vandahurst. *Sixty Years of Medicine; or, The Life and Times of Dr. Miles V. Lynk, an Autobiography.* Memphis, Tenn.: Twentieth Century Press, 1951.

164. Makeba, Miriam, with James Hall.* *Makeba: My Story.* New York: New American Library, 1988.

This book begins with Makeba's birth in South Africa and ends with the death of her only child, a daughter Bongi, in 1986. It tells about her life defined by personal tragedy springing from political sources, her exile, her convulsive career, her five failed marriages, her contractual cervical cancer, and the loss of her daughter due to madness. What keeps her going is her music. She writes, "Already I have discovered that music is a type of magic. It can do all sorts of things. It can make sad people happy. It can make dull people sit up and pay attention. I know what it does to me. . . . It is as if I am possessed. . . . Who can keep us down as long as we have our music?"

165.   Manning, Kenneth R. *Black Apollo of Science: The Life of Ernest Everett Just.* New York: Oxford University Press, 1983.

A detailed story of the life of Ernest Everett Just, the prominent marine biologist, substantiated with photos and facts about his family background, upbringing, education, work, travels, marriage, and death. The book also contains a list of publications by Just, a glossary of manuscript citations, and an index.

166.   Matney, William C., Jr., ed. *Who's Who Among Black Americans.* Vol. 1, *1975-76.* Northbrook, Ill.: Who's Who Among Black Americans Inc., Publishing Company, 1976. Reprint. Lake Forest, Ill.: Educational Communications, 1985.

This valuable volume includes approximately 10,000 biographical entries of Afro-Americans who have made names for themselves in America over the years, their selections being "based on one characteristic: reference value." The blacks sketched herein include leading executives and officials in government, business, education, religion, journalism, and medicine. The book also contains a glossary of abbreviations, a sample biography keyed to data, and cross-indexes by geographical location and career cluster groups.

167.   Mays, Benjamin Elijah. *Born to Rebel.* New York: Charles Scribner's Sons, 1971.

This autobiography is dedicated to young people today who cannot have any idea about early black-white relations in the South. It tells of one man's determination to preserve his pride and dignity in a hostile society, and of his arduous attempt to become educated against almost overwhelming odds. Pictures of the author at different periods in his life, appendixes, and an index are included. The appendixes include the "Eulogy at the Funeral Services of Martin Luther King, Jr., at Morehouse College, Atlanta, Georgia, April 9, 1968."

168. McKay, Nellie Y. *Jean Toomer, Artist: A Study of His Literary Life and Work, 1894-1936.* Chapel Hill: University of North Carolina Press, 1984.

169. McNeil, Genna Rae. *Groundwork: Charles Hamilton Houston and the Struggle for Civil Rights.* Philadelphia: University of Pennsylvania Press, 1983.

The core of this book—winner of the 1984 American Bar Association Silver Gavel Award—is an account of Houston's educational work at Howard University, his landmark civil rights cases, and his leadership. It documents his contributions to the struggle for civil rights and, in particular, his pivotal role in the effort to integrate American schools. In addition to Houston's personal and professional papers and correspondence, McNeil reviewed records of organizations with which Houston was affiliated, and the papers of people who knew him, and interviewed his family, friends, colleagues, critics and admirers. Includes appendixes, a selected bibliography, notes, and indexes.

170. Moody, Anne. *Coming of Age in Mississippi.* New York: Dial Press, 1968.

171. Morgan, Gordon Daniel. *Poverty Without Bitterness: Black Life in Central Arkansas.* Jefferson City, Mo.: New Scholars Press, 1969.

172. Moton, Robert Russa. *Finding a Way Out: An Autobiography.* Garden City, N.Y.: Doubleday and Co., 1920. Reprint. College Park, Md.: McGrath Publishing Co., 1969.

The author begins this autobiography with some references to his roots in Africa. He traces his ancestry from his grandmother's great-grandfather, who was taken as a slave and

brought to America. His story is written with the view that, in
spite of all the hardships endured by his ancestors as slaves, the
Afro–American has survived the ordeal "with much to his credit
and with great many advantages over his condition when he
entered the relationship." Moton also traces his life experiences
as a small boy on a plantation to his eventual evolution as an
accomplished man training and encouraging his people to have
greater fortitude.

173. Murray, Pauli. *Proud Shoes: The Story of an American Family.*
New York: Harper & Brothers, 1956. Reprint. New York:
Harper and Row, 1978.

This autobiographical memoir, reissued in 1978, is the first
volume of Murray's autobiography. Born in Baltimore, Maryland,
she traces her roots back to North Carolina, where she grew up.
Several years after graduating from Hunter College in New York
City, Murray was denied admission to the University of North
Carolina because of her race. After graduating first in her class
from Howard University Law School, she was denied admission
to Harvard for graduate study in law—because of her sex.
Adversity did not stop her. In 1965, some time after she earned
her master's in law from Berkeley, Murray earned a doctorate in
law from Yale Law School. At age sixty–two she entered the
seminary and, in 1977, became the nation's first black woman
Episcopal priest.

174. ———. *Song in a Weary Throat: An American Pilgrimage.*
New York: Harper and Row, 1987.

Completed just before Murray's death in 1985, this book is
the second autobiography (*Proud Shoes* is the first) of a
granddaughter of a slave, an early civil rights activist, feminist
(one of the founding members of the National Organization for
Women), poet, lawyer, educator, and the first black American
woman to become an Episcopal priest (in 1977).

175. Nazel, Joseph [Dom Gober, pseud.; and Joyce Lezan, pseud.]
     Richard Pryor: The Man Behind the Laughter. Los Angeles:
     Holloway House Publishing Co., 1981.

176. Owens, Jesse, with Paul G. Neimark.* *Jesse: A Spiritual
     Autobiography.* Plainfield, N.J.: Logos International, 1978.

177. Parks, Gordon. *A Choice of Weapons.* New York: Harper and
     Row, 1965.

     This book is by a black man who survives America. Parks
     tells of his personal fight against poverty and racial bigotry, but
     he does so in such a way that it leaves his readers viewing this
     as the story of all black men. The book opens with a scene of
     death in a gas chamber and continues to emphasize death as a
     motif. By allowing this and other deaths to speak for themselves,
     Parks shows how life in Afro–America is a constant battle with
     death and violence.
         Parks tells of being thrown out into the winter streets of
     Minneapolis at age sixteen, having to sleep in trolley cars,
     working in a brothel, peddling dope in New York, and rising to
     become a successful photographer. To him the question is not
     whether to fight but rather the choice of weapons. Herein lies the
     difference between life and death.

178. Payne, Daniel Alexander. *Recollections of Seventy Years.*
     Nashville: Publisher House of the A.M.E. Sunday School
     Union, 1888. Reprint. New York: Arno Press and the New
     York Times, 1969.

     This is the autobiography of the first Afro–American college
     president (Wilberforce University, 1863). Payne discusses not
     only his childhood, youth, and marriages, but also the important
     issues of his time. He attempts to keep life in its historical
     perspective by dealing with his work in the abolitionist
     movement, the African Episcopal church, and the black education
     movement. Included also are his trips to Canada and Europe. In
     addition to the introduction by Francis J. Grinke and the preface

by Benjamin Quarles, there are photos of several Afro–American religious leaders of the times.

179. Perinbam, B. Marie. *Holy Violence: The Revolutionary Thought of Frantz Fanon: An Intellectual Biography.* Washington, D.C.: Three Continents Press, 1982.

180. Poindexter, Hildrus A. *My World of Reality: An Autobiography.* Detroit: Balamp Publishing, 1973.

"This is a succinct story of one Negro farm boy from the West Tennessee delta who wanted to become a doctor and did." In addition to his work at Howard University, Poindexter shares his experiences while serving in various foreign countries.

181. Poitier, Sidney. *This Life.* New York: Alfred A. Knopf, 1980.

Poitier tells of his premature birth (at less than three pounds) on February 20, 1927, in Miami, Florida, and of his subsequent life experiences. From three months of age until he was eleven, Poitier lived with his family on Cat Island in the Bahamas. Then they moved to Nassau, where his home was a stone hut with a thatched roof. The youngest of seven children, Poitier attended school for only a year and a half. His days were spent roaming the island playing with turtles, catching fish, and swimming. At age fifteen he was sent to Miami, where he lived until the early 1940s when he left for New York. There he slept on newspaper on the roof of a building until he had saved some money from his dish–washing job. The book is filled with anecdotes and portraits of his romance with Diahann Carroll, his two marriages, his six children (all girls), and his friendship with Harry Belafonte. There is also a section devoted to his lengthy analysis. This work won the Coretta Scott King Award in 1981.

182. Powell, A. Clayton. *Against the Tide: An Autobiography.* New York: R. R. Smith, 1938. Reprint. New York: Arno Press, 1980.

A. Clayton Powell (1863–1953), the father of former New York Cong. Adam Clayton Powell, Jr., tells his life experiences. Born in Virginia, the elder Powell worked his way through school and eventually became pastor of the Abyssinian Baptist Church in New York—one of the most celebrated Afro–American congregations in the world.

183. Powell, Adam Clayton, Jr. *Adam by Adam: The Autobiography of Adam Clayton Powell, Jr.* New York: Dial Press, 1971.

In this autobiography, Adam Clayton Powell, Jr., talks about his life experiences. Born in New York City in 1908, he began his career as a "radical" crusader for reform early in life by organizing demonstrations against racial discrimination in Harlem during the depression. He succeeded his father as pastor of the Abyssinian Baptist Church in 1937, won a seat on the New York City Council in 1941, and was elected to Congress in 1945.

184. Quarles, Benjamin. *Lincoln and the Negro.* New York: Oxford University Press, 1962.

185. ———, ed. *Frederick Douglass.* Washington, D.C.: Associated Publishers, 1948. Reprint. Englewood Cliffs, N.J.: Prentice–Hall, 1968.

This is the life of the famous abolitionist told in his own words and in those of his contemporaries. The view of modern scholars is also given.

186. Rampersad, Arnold. *The Life of Langston Hughes.* Vol. 1, *1902–41.* New York: Oxford University Press, 1986.

Rampersad details the early life of one of America's most important black poets. Through psycho–literary probing, he reveals the genesis of Langston Hughes's poetic development as well as the turmoil and achievements of the poet's incredibly productive life. Using Hughes's two autobiographies—*The Big Sea* and *I Wonder as I Wander*—as well as papers from the collections of Countee Cullen, Alain Locke, Carl Van Vechten, and Claude McKay, and information from a variety of other sources (including surviving observers of the period), Rampersad reconstructs Hughes's complex life. Plotting the significant events from infancy to adulthood, Rampersad establishes a clear time line, filling the chronology with family, friends, and encouraging teachers, and moving from Hughes's place of birth through his nomadic childhood and adulthood.

187.   ————. *The Life of Langston Hughes.* Vol. 2, *1941–1967, I Dream a World.* New York: Oxford University Press, 1989.

In this second volume of Hughes's biography, Rampersad shows Hughes during his lowest ebb—ill and being attacked by the Left and the Right. He shows that in the years that follow, Hughes regains his standing and compiles a massive body of work that includes radio scripts, plays, poems, songs, novels, and short stories.

188.   Reddick, Lawrence Dunbar. *Crusader Without Violence: A Biography of Martin Luther King, Jr.* New York: Harper and Row, 1959.

189.   Redford, Dorothy Spruill, with Michael D'Orso.* *Somerset Homecoming: Recovering a Lost Heritage.* 1st ed. Introduction by Alex Haley. New York: Doubleday and Co., 1988.

190.   Reynolds, Barbara A. *And Still We Rise: Interviews with 50 Black Achievers.* Washington, D.C.: USA Today Books/Gannett New Media, 1988.

This book presents conversations with fifty black role models from a variety of fields. Included are Maya Angelou, Bill Cosby, Angela Davis, Mary Futtrell, Coretta Scott King, Cicely Tyson, Harold Washington, and Roosevelt "Rosey" Grier. This diverse group of achievers share their insights and offer examples for the many formulas of success.

191. ————. *Jesse Jackson: America's David.* Washington, D.C.: JFJ Associates, Publishers, 1985.

This book, which is a tenth-year anniversary reprint of *Jesse Jackson: The Man, the Movement, and the Myth* (1975), provides a rare glimpse of Jesse Jackson from his birth through his run for president of the United States. Reynolds states that "Jackson has grown from an ego-centered missionary forever self-testing his own somebodiness to an inspired visionary offering new hopes and ranges of possibilities for the despised, neglected, abused, and maligned in the United States and abroad." Appendixes include A: "Operation PUSH Convening Board of Directors"; B: "The Kingdom Theory"; C: "National Tea Company Review of Covenant with Operation Breadbasket"; D: "Covenant Between Miller Brewing Company and PUSH"; E: "Black Expo '71 – Audit Report"; and F: "PUSH Audit Report." Also includes photographs and an index.

192. Robeson, Paul. *Here I Stand.* New York: Othello Associates, 1958. Reprint. Boston: Beacon Press, 1988.

With a new introduction by Northwestern University historian Sterling Stuckey, this book, first published in 1958, is the story of the famous "Robeson of Rutgers," an all-time All-American football superstar who gained international renown as a concert singer and actor in starring roles on stage and screen. Robeson was blacklisted during the McCarthy era for his outspoken criticism of racism in the United States, for his enthusiasm for African independence, and for his fascination with the Soviet Union.

193. Robinson, John Roosevelt. *I Never Had It Made: The Autobiography of Jackie Robinson.* As told to Alfred Duckett.* New York: J. P. Putnam's Sons, 1972.

Winner of the Coretta Scott King Award in 1973, this autobiography by John (Jackie) Robinson, among other things, talks about the adversity Robinson encountered as the first black to play major league baseball.

194. ————. *Jackie Robinson, My Own Story.* As told to Wendell Smith.* Foreword by Branch Rickey.** New York: Greenberg, 1948.

John Roosevelt (Jackie) Robinson tells the story of his life and of his historic crossing of baseball's color line.

195. Robinson, Smokey, with David Ritz.** *Smokey: Inside My Life.* New York: McGraw-Hill, 1989.

A former member of the Miracles, founded in 1957, Robinson, one of Motown's most successful and exciting singers and songwriters, tells his story which includes the loss of his mother when he was ten; his friendships with other stars—Diana Ross, Michael Jackson, Marvin Gaye, Aretha Franklin, Stevie Wonder, and the legendary boss Berry Gordy; his cocaine addiction; and the extramarital affairs that cost him his marriage. The book includes photos, records, selected songs of Smokey Robinson, and an index.

196. Rowan, Carl Thomas. *South of Freedom.* New York: Alfred A. Knopf, 1952.

This work is a stirring personal report of a trek through the segregated South.

197. Rowan, Carl Thomas, with Jackie Robinson. *Wait Till Next Year: The Life Story of Jackie Robinson.* New York: Random House, 1960.

198. Russell, Bill. *Go Up for Glory.* As told to William McSweeny.* New York: Coward-McCann, 1966. Reprint. New York: Coward, 1980.

199. Scott, EdRoyal. *Profiles of Black Achievers, 1930–1950.* Los Angeles: Authors Unlimited, 1988.

200. Seale, Bobby. *A Lonely Rage: The Autobiography of Bobby Seale.* New York: New York Times Books, 1978.

201. Sellers, Cleveland, with Robert L. Terrell. *The River of No Return: The Autobiography of a Black Militant and the Life and Death of SNCC.* New York: William Morrow and Co., 1973.

202. Sewell, George Alexander. *Mississippi Black History Makers.* Jackson: University Press of Mississippi, 1977.

    The belief that blacks in Mississippi have suffered more than and are inferior to blacks elsewhere in the United States is one that some people have held for a long time. Sewell's book reflects the fact that a great many well-known blacks are natives of Mississippi. With an introduction by Margaret Walker, this book focuses on native black Mississippians who are successful singers, educators, civil rights leaders, journalists, and ministers, in addition to other careers. The book contains information on Lerone Bennett, Jr., James Earl Jones, Richard Wright, Fannie Lou Hamer, B. B. King, and others. It also includes pictures, notes, and a biographical montage.

203. Shakur, Assata. *Assata: An Autobiography.* Westport, Conn.: Lawrence Hill and Co., 1987.

    A Member of the Black Panther party, Shakur, aka JoAnne Chesimard, recounts the formative experiences that led her to embrace a life of activism. She discusses racism, J. Edgar Hoover's campaign to defame black nationalist organizations, her incarceration, and her eventual escape to Cuba.

204. Shockley, Ann Allen, and Sue P. Chandler. *Living Black American Authors: A Biographical Directory.* New York: R. R. Bowker Co., 1973.

    This work not only identifies contemporary black American authors but also provides information about their background and work. The book includes, according to its definition of the word *author*, people who have written books and also those who have published anthologies, newspapers, journals, or periodicals. Also included are listed editors of works, and authors of plays, television scripts, and filmstrips. The list of black publishers in the book provides information on the names and addresses of some of the most active firms that have been publishing or reprinting the works of black authors. The title index lists, alphabetically, all books mentioned in the bibliography sections, giving for each book the name of the author, and the date and the name of the publisher, but not necessarily the original publisher.

205. Sinnette, Elinor Des Verney. *Arthur Alfonso Schomburg, Black Bibliophile & Collector: A Biography.* New York: New York Public Library; Detroit: Wayne State University Press, 1989.

This work deals with the Puerto Rican–born Schomburg, the black book collector whose private collection forms the core of the New York Public Library's Schomburg Center for Research in black culture.

206. Smith, Benjamin Julian. *Dedicated . . . Committed: The Autobiography of Bishop Benjamin Julian Smith.* Nashville: Hemphill Press, 1978.

207. Spellman, Cecil Lloyd. *Rough Steps on my Stairway: The Life of a Negro Educator.* 1st ed. New York: Exposition Press, 1953.

In an autobiography narrating the life of a teacher in southern black colleges, Spellman chronicles various events that occurred in the first half of the nineteenth century, which he refers to as the "Modern Renaissance Period." He explains that World War I had various effects on the economic, social, and cultural conditions that developed. The latter section of the book demonstrates some difficulties encountered by black students attempting to survive in predominantly black colleges.

208. Spradling, Mary (Louis) Mace. *In Black and White: Afro-Americans in Print: A Guide to Afro Americans Who Have Made Contributions to the USA from 1619 to 1969.* Kalamazoo, Mich.: Kalamazoo Library System, 1971.

209. Starks, John Jacob. *Lo These Many Years: An Autobiographical Sketch.* Columbia, S.C.: State College, 1941.

This autobiography is an unaffected recounting of the events that molded the character of the author. The book relates the course of Starks's life from Seneca to Morris College in Atlanta, Georgia.

210. Sterling, Dorothy. *Black Foremothers: Three Lives.* Old Westbury, N.Y.: Feminist Press, 1979.

211. ————. *Captain of the Planter: The Story of Robert Smalls.* Illustrated by Ernest Crichlow.* Garden City, N.Y.: Doubleday and Co., 1958.

212. ————. *The Making of an Afro-American: Martin Robinson Delany, 1812-1885.* 1st ed. Garden City, N.Y.: Doubleday and Co., 1971.

213. Sterling, Dorothy, and Benjamin Quarles. *Lift Every Voice: The Lives of Booker T. Washington, W. E. B. DuBois, Mary Church Terrell, and James Weldon Johnson.* Garden City, N.Y.: Doubleday and Co., 1965.

214. Sterling,* Philip, and Rayford Whittingham Logan. *Four Took Freedom: The Lives of Harriet Tubman, Frederick Douglass, Robert Smalls, and Blanche K. Bruce.* Garden City, N.Y.: Doubleday and Co., 1967.

Bibliographical portraits of four famous Negro Americans who escaped the slavery into which they were born to further the fight for freedom and equality: Tubman (1815?-1913), Douglass (1817?-1895), Smalls (1839-1915), and Bruce (1840-1898).

215. Stewart, Ruth Ann. *Portia: The Biography of Portia Washington Pittman.* Garden City, N.Y.: Doubleday and Co., 1977.

This intimate biography of Booker T. Washington's only daughter focuses on Pittman's remarkable life as well as on that of her father.

216. Stingley, Darryl, with Mark Mulvoy.* *Darryl Stingley: Happy to Be Alive.* New York: Beaufort Books, 1983.

Stingley, former wide receiver for the New England Patriots, describes his life since being paralyzed in a football game against the Oakland Raiders.

217. Stone, Donald P. *Fallen Prince: William James Edwards, Black Education, and the Quest for Afro-American Nationality.* Snow Hill, Ala.: The Snow Hill Press, 1990.

In this biography of his maternal grandfather, William James Edwards, Stone tells of Edwards's heroic rise from abject poverty to establish Snow Hill Institute in 1893 for former bondspeople and their progeny in the midst of pervasive oppression in the Gulf Coastal Plain of western Alabama. The biography is set within the period of Booker T. Washington's leadership and the Tuskegee Program, which was the model for Snow Hill Normal and Industrial Institute.

218. T, Mr. *Mr. T: The Man with the Gold: An Autobiography.* New York: St. Martin's Press, 1984.

Born Lawrence Tureaud in 1952 but changed his name in 1972 to Mr. T, the author shares his life experiences before and after he became a nationally known television star.

219. Tarry, Ellen. *The Third Door: The Autobiography of an American Black Woman.* New York: O. McKay Co., 1955. Reprint. Westport, Conn.: Negro Universities Press, 1971.

In this autobiographical work of an Afro-American woman, Tarry tells of the joys and struggles of a young black woman growing up in the South into recognition as a writer. The book also sheds light on social and political conditions existing during her time.

220. Taulbert, Clifton L. *Once Upon a Time When We Were Colored.* 1st ed. Tulsa, Okla.: Council Oak Books, 1989.

221. Taylor, Lawrence, with David Falkner.** *LT: Living on the Edge.* New York: Warner Books, 1987.

Lawrence (LT) Taylor talks about his childhood in Williamsburg, Virginia; his college days at the University of North Carolina in Chapel Hill; his pro debut as NFL Rookie of the Year; his linebacking role behind the New York Giants' Super Bowl-winning 1986–1987 season; his bout with substance abuse; and generally his life in the fast lane. "I drink too much, I party too much, I drive too fast, and I'm hell on quarterbacks. It's always been that way." Includes sixteen pages of photographs and his 1981–1986 game-by-game statistics.

222. Terrell, Mary Church. *A Colored Woman in a White World.* Washington, D.C.: Ransdell, 1940. Reprint. Salem, N.H.: Ayer Co., 1986.

Born the daughter of Robert R. Church, Sr., a pioneer Memphis businessman who reportedly was the South's first black millionaire, Terrell presents her activities and experiences. She relates her life in Tennessee, in Ohio, and in Europe, as well as in Washington, D.C. A feminist and activist, she founded a women's club in Washington and engaged in battles to eliminate segregation.

223. Thomas, Will. *The Seeking.* New York: A. A. Wyn, 1953.

224. Thompson, Era Bell. *American Daughter.* Chicago: University of Chicago Press, 1946. Reprint. St. Paul: Minnesota Historical Society Press, 1986.

In this autobiography, Era Bell Thompson describes the experiences of her North Dakota girlhood: busting broncos with her brothers, making friends with Norwegian and German neighbors, selling furniture in her father's store in Mandan, working her way through college in Grand Forks, and facing the bias without the support of a large black community.

225. Thorpe, Earl Endris. *The Old South: A Psychohistory.* Durham, N.C.: Seeman Printery, 1972. Reprint. Westport, Conn.: Greenwood Press, 1979.

This book uses primary source material—such as George Fitzhugh's famous book, *Cannibals All*—in an attempt to account for the sometimes irrational political activity of some Southerners in the antebellum era. Thorpe also discusses the uses of psychohistory in exploring other aspects of black history.

226. Thurman, Howard. *With Head and Heart: The Autobiography of Howard Thurman.* 1st ed. New York: Harcourt Brace Jovanovich, 1979.

227. Travis, Dempsey J. *"Harold," The People's Mayor: The Authorized Biography of Mayor Harold Washington.* Chicago: Urban Research Press, 1989.

This biography of the late Harold Washington, the first black mayor of Chicago (1983–1987), provides an inside view of Chicago's political machine and Washington's relationship to it.

228. Troup, Cornelius V. *Distinguished Negro Georgians.* Dallas: Royal Publishing Co., 1962.

A compilation of biographies of over one hundred living blacks from the state of Georgia who have made outstanding achievements in various fields of endeavor. A listing of biographies of deceased Georgian blacks of eminence is included.

229. Vivian, Octavia. *Coretta: The Story of Mrs. Martin Luther King, Jr.* Philadelphia: Fortress Press, 1970.

Autobiographies and Biographies   51

230. Washington, Booker T. *Up From Slavery: An Autobiography*. New York: Doubleday, Page and Co., 1902. Reprint. New York: Doubleday and Co., 1963.

In this autobiography, Washington tells of being born into slavery, of walking five hundred miles to attend the Hampton Norman and Agricultural Institute in Virginia, of gaining entrance through his good job of sweeping and dusting a recitation room, of his becoming the principal of a new school in Alabama called Tuskegee Institute, of his emphasis on a vocational curriculum, and of his serving as an unofficial ambassador to resolve racial tensions with reason rather than revolt. Washington often stated that his most important life goals were to improve the educational and living standards of his people and to cultivate the relationship between blacks and whites.

231. Waters, Ethel, with Charles Samuels. *His Eye Is on the Sparrow: An Autobiography*. Garden City, N.Y.: Doubleday, 1951. Reprint. Westport, Conn.: Greenwood Press, 1978.

232. White, Walter Francis. *A Man Called White: The Autobiography of Walter White*. Bloomington: Indiana University Press, 1948.

An autobiography of a blue-eyed, blonde, white-skinned black man who refused to "pass." Walter White, assistant secretary of the N.A.A.C.P. until his death, recounts the tales and history of "Jim Crowism," lynching, extreme racial and religious prejudice, southern politics, and northern racism in America during the 1920s-1950s.

233. Wilkins, Roger W. *A Man's Life: An Autobiography*. New York: Simon and Schuster, 1982.

234. Wilkins, Roy, with Tom Mathews.* *Standing Fast: The Autobiography of Roy Wilkins*. New York: Viking Press, 1982.

235. Williams, John Alfred. *The Most Native of Sons: A Biography of Richard Wright.* Garden City, N.Y.: Doubleday and Co., 1970.

236. Wilson, Mary, with Patricia Romanowski* and Ahrgus Juilliard.* *Dreamgirl: My Life as a Supreme.* New York: St Martin's Press, 1986.

   Dreamgirl is the Cinderella story of three girls from the Brewster Projects of Detroit who'd originally been turned down by Berry Gordy because his record company already had enough "girl groups" with the Marvellettes and Martha and the Vandellas. In this book, based on the diary that she kept during her years with the Supremes, Wilson details Ross's rise to superstardom and Florence Ballard's fall from fame and fortune to the welfare roll and finally to a mysterious death in 1976 at age thirty–two. Cindy Birdsong replaced Ballard when Ballard was kicked out in 1967, and Jean Terrell replaced Diana Ross when Ross left the group in 1970. Wilson discusses how Motown treated its stars, and talks about her life after the Supremes. Includes a Supremes itinerary, a discography, and an index.

237. Winfield, Dave, with Tom Parker.** *Winfield: A Player's Life.* New York: W. W. Norton and Co., 1988.

   This book is about how Winfield was inspired to achieve by his mother's struggle as a single parent, how his wildness as a young man landed him in jail and changed his life for the better, how he found a father figure in a Jewish businessman, how he was led to form the Winfield Foundation for disadvantaged children, how he became embroiled in a legal feud with George Steinbrenner, and much more.

238. Wright, Richard. *Black Boy: A Record of Childhood and Youth.* 1945. Reprint. Philadelphia: Harper and Row, 1969.

   Wright, in this autobiography, tells us what he thought and felt as a black boy in the Jim Crow South.

239. X, Malcolm, with Alex Haley. *The Autobiography of Malcolm X.* New York: Grove Press, 1966.

In sensitive but power–evoking words, Malcolm tells of his life in Lansing, Boston, and Harlem. The early scenes are filled with the awe of a son for his father. Then the insulting life of being a welfare family following the assassination of his father is told in clear and bitter tones. Malcolm tells of his being "educated" in the streets of Boston and Harlem. His life of stealing, peddling dope, running numbers, and pimping are discussed openly, as are his prison life and conversion to Islam. The book, written with the assistance of Alex Haley, covers Malcolm's life with the Nation of Islam, his breakaway, and his establishment of the Organization of Afro–American Unity. In the epilogue, Alex Haley discusses the events preceding and following Malcolm's assassination. The book ends with an essay by Ossie Davis.

240. Young, Tommie Morton. *African–American Genealogy: Exploring and Documenting the Black Family.* Clarksville, Tenn.: Josten's Publishers, 1982.

CHAPTER 2

BIBLIOGRAPHIES AND LIBRARY SCIENCE

241. Addo, Linda D. *The Negro in American History: A Selected Bibliography.* Greensboro, N.C.: Greensboro Tri-College Consortium, 1970.

242. Allen, Walter R., Richard Allyn English, and Jo Anne Hall, eds. *Black American Families, 1965–1984: A Classified, Selectively Annotated Bibliography.* Westport, Conn.: Greenwood Press, 1986.

     "This summary of the research record on black American families includes more than 1,100 citations."

243. Bailey, Pearl. *Hurry Up, America, & Spit.* New York: Harcourt Brace Jovanovich, 1976.

244. Baker, Augusta. *The Black Experience in Children's Books.* Cover design by Ezra Jack Keats.** New York: New York Public Library, 1971.

     Baker published this work in 1957, 1961, and 1963 under the title, *Books about Negro Life for Children.* The 1974 edition was published by Barbara Rollock.

245. Bellman,** Richard Earnest, and David Harold Blackwell. *On Games Involving Bluffing.* Santa Monica, Calif.: Rand Corp., 1950.

246. Blassingame, John W., and Mae G. Henderson, eds. *Antislavery Newspapers and Periodicals.* 5 vols. Vols. 3–5 edited by John W. Blassingame, Mae G. Henderson, and Jessica M. Dunn.* Boston: G. K. Hall, 1980, 1984.

247. Butler, Frieda R. *A Resource Guide on Black Aging.* Washington, D.C.: Institute for Urban Affairs and Research, Howard University, 1981.

248. Caliver, Ambrose, and Ethel G. Green, comps. *Education of Negroes: A 5-Year Bibliography, 1931–1935.* Washington, D.C.: U.S. Government Printing Office, 1937.

249. Chapman, Dorothy Hilton. *Index to Poetry by Black American Women.* Westport, Conn.: Greenwood Press, 1986.

250. Clark, Barbara Randall. *Reflections.* Orangeburg, S.C.: Williams Associates, 1982.

251. Daniel, Walter C. *Black Journals of the United States.* Westport, Conn.: Greenwood Press, 1982.

252. Darden, Joseph Turner. *The Ghetto: A Bibliography.* Monticello, Ill.: Council of Planning Librarians, 1977.

The preface to this bibliography contains a working definition of the ghetto and pinpoints its attributes. The bibliography itself, while not annotated, is selective, listing only those works focusing primarily on the ghetto. Included also is a table on "Trends in Ghetto Studies." The bibliography is organized around eight major themes, including "The Concept and Origin of the Ghetto," "The Changing Population of the Ghetto: Ethnic Ghetto U.S. Racial Ghetto," "The Spatial Diffusion of the Ghetto," and "The Economy of the Ghetto."

253. Davis, Lenwood G., comp. *The Black Aged in the United States: A Selectively Annotated Bibliography.* 2d ed., rev. and updated. Westport, Conn.: Greenwood Press, 1989.

Besides a substantial increase in the number of citations, this revised edition of the 1980 publication deals with new issues of immediate relevance, such as AIDS, the effects of prison life, the gay lifestyle, adoption, abuse of the aged, and sickle cell anemia.

254. ———, comp. *Black Businesses, Employment, Economics, and Finance in Urban America: A Research Bibliography.* Monticello, Ill.: Council of Planning Librarians, 1974.

255. ———, comp. *The Black Family in the United States: A Revised, Updated, Selectively Annotated Bibliography.* Westport, Conn.: Greenwood Press, 1986.

Davis has added many new references, sources, articles, and dissertations on the black family in the United States to this revised and updated version of his previously published work. He addresses several important topics pertinent to black family life that were not fully developed in the earlier volume, such as abortion, adoption, aging, racism, and sickle cell disease, among others.

256. ———, comp. *The Black Family in Urban Areas in the United States: A Bibliography of Published Works on the Black Family in Urban Areas in the United States.* 2d ed. Monticello, Ill.: Council of Planning Librarians, 1973.

A bibliography of material relating to the black family life and child-rearing practices in the urban areas of New York City, Chicago, Philadelphia, Cleveland, Washington, D.C., Los Angeles, Newark, Detroit, and San Francisco. The bibliography comprises government documents, reports, pamphlets, and articles. It also includes books.

257. ————, comp. *A History of Blacks in Higher Education, 1875–1975: A Working Bibliography.* Monticello, Ill.: Council of Planning Librarians, 1975.

258. Davis, Lenwood G., with Marsha L. Moore. *Joe Louis: A Bibliography of Articles, Books, Pamphlets, Records, and Archival Materials.* Westport, Conn.: Greenwood Press, 1983.

259. Davis, Lenwood G., and Janet L. Sims, eds. *Black Artists in the United States: An Annotated Bibliography of Books, Articles, and Dissertations on Black Artists, 1779–1979.* Westport, Conn.: Greenwood Press, 1980.

   This annotated bibliography covers the whole range of black art from anonymous slave artisans, through early black artists such as Scipio Moorhead, Joshua Johnston, and Henry O. Tanner, to the many black painters and sculptors of today. Works by and about pioneering black historians, such as James A. Porter and Alain Locke, are included. Special attention is paid to articles in scholarly journals as well as articles in popular magazines. Includes an appendix cataloging black art in the National Archives, and a subject index.

260. ————, comps. *The Black Family in the United States: A Selected Bibliography of Annotated Books, Articles, and Dissertations on Black Families in America.* Westport, Conn.: Greenwood Press, 1978.

   The first comprehensive annotated work on the black family, this book examines the historical role of the black family through a variety of significant materials. It contains author and keyword indexes.

261. ————, comps. *Marcus Garvey: An Annotated Bibliography.* Westport, Conn.: Greenwood Press, 1980.

   This is a comprehensive, annotated bibliography of writings by and about Marcus Garvey, founder of the Universal Negro

Improvement Association (U.N.I.A.). In addition to listing all of Garvey's own works, this volume lists books, articles, dissertations, chapters in books, and theses about Garvey. The Constitution of the U.N.I.A. is reprinted in its entirety.

262. Davis, Lenwood G., and George H. Hill, with Janie Miller Harris, comps. *A Bibliographical Guide to Black Studies Programs in the United States: An Annotated Bibliography.* Westport, Conn.: Greenwood Press, 1985.

Compiled with the assistance of Janie Miller Harris, this book is a compilation of information about black studies programs, departments, institutions, and centers, as well as about the discipline itself. Works by both black and white writers are covered. Included in this resource guide is an index listing authors, joint authors, and editors.

263. Davis, Lenwood G., and Janet L. Sims-Wood, with Marsha L. Moore. *The Ku Klux Klan: A Bibliography.* Westport, Conn.: Greenwood Press, 1984.

This volume lists books, pamphlets, journal articles, theses, and dissertations on the Ku Klux Klan. It includes official documents of the Klan, government documents on the Klan, speeches of elected public officials concerning the Klan, and articles from the official Klan publication, *The Kourier Magazine*. Materials on Klan activities in various countries are also included, as well as information on KKK publications, estimated KKK membership, the Klansman's creed, and a listing of manuscript and archival materials located throughout the country. The materials are listed state by state. Includes a comprehensive author and subject index.

264. Davis, Nathaniel, ed. *Afro-American Reference: An Annotation Bibliography of Selected Resources.* Westport, Conn.: Greenwood Press, 1985.

265. Gandy, Oscar H., Jr., William Rivers,** Susan Miller,** et al.** *Media and Government: An Annotated Bibliography.*

Stanford, Calif.: Institute for Communication Research, 1975.

266. Gibson,** Gail S., and Ashton F. E. Gibbons. *Hypertension Among Blacks: An Annotated Bibliography.* American Heart Association Monograph, no. 85. Dallas: American Heart Association, 1982.

267. Guzman, Jessie Parkhurst. *George Washington Carver: A Classified Bibliography.* Tuskegee, Ala.: Dept. of Records and Research, Tuskegee Institute, 1954.

This is a bibliography of books, pamphlets, sketches, articles, and some newspaper references written about the life and work of the agricultural scientist, George Washington Carver.

268. Hatch, James Vernon, and Omanii Abdullah, eds. *Black Playwrights, 1823-1977: An Annotated Bibliography of Plays.* New York: R. R. Bowker Co., 1977.

269. Hill, George H. *Black Business and Economics: A Bibliography.* New York: Garland Publishing, Inc., 1985.

270. Howard, Elizabeth Fitzgerald. *America as Story: Historical Fiction for Secondary Schools.* Chicago: American Library Association, 1988.

271. Hudson, Theodore R. *A LeRoi Jones (Amiri Baraka) Bibliography: A Keyed Research Guide to Works by LeRoi Jones and to Writing About Him and His Works.* Washington, D.C.: Privately published, 1971.

272. Jackson, Irene Viola, comp. *Afro-American Religious Music: A Bibliography and a Catalogue of Gospel Music.* Westport, Conn.: Greenwood Press, 1979.

273. Jackson, Miles Merrill, Jr., ed. *Comparative and International Librarianship: Essays on Themes and Problems.* Westport, Conn.: Greenwood Press, 1970.

An aid to librarians and students, this five-part book contains original essays on the problems, progress, and prospects for librarianship. Besides development in this country, the book includes library developments that have taken place worldwide. Part 4 consists of essays on national libraries and bibliographies in the U.S.S.R., Latin America, and Africa. The appendix contains tabular data on the books in the libraries of Africa, the U.S.S.R., and Latin America. It shows the republic or country, the name of the library, the year founded, and the number of books.

274. ————, ed. *International Handbook of Contemporary Developments in Librarianship.* Westport, Conn.: Greenwood Press, 1981.

275. Jackson, Miles Merrill, Jr., Mary W. Cleaves, and Alma Long Gray, comps. *Bibliography of Materials by and About Negro Americans for Young Readers.* Washington, D.C.: U.S. Office of Education, 1967.

276. Jackson, Miles Merrill, Jr., with Mary W. Cleaves and Alma Long Gray, comps. *A Bibliography of Negro History and Culture for Young Readers.* Pittsburgh: Published for Atlanta University by the University of Pittsburgh Press, 1968.

A graded and annotated list of books and other materials by and about Afro-Americans for children from preschool through senior high school. It includes all fields of literature. Special attention has been focused on multimedia materials: films, recordings, pictures, and other aids. Each entry contains complete biographical information about author, title, publisher, copyright date, and price.

277. Jackson,* Sidney L., Eleanor B. Herling,* and Elonnie Junius Josey, eds. *A Century of Service: Librarianship in the United States and Canada.* Chicago: American Library Association, 1976.

This book celebrates a century of library service, honoring librarianship as a profession and libraries as important instruments of education in a broad review of their accomplishments, failures, advances, and present prospects in both the United States and Canada. The author discusses four basic topics: (1) the efforts of librarians to serve the public; (2) the concern of librarians with equal rights for disadvantaged minorities; (3) library personnel, their problems, and importance; and (4) the national libraries of the United States and Canada.

278.   Jenkins, Betty Lanier, Lorna Kent,* and Jeanne Perry,* eds. *Kenneth B. Clark: A Bibliography.* 1st. ed. New York: Metropolitan Applied Research Center, 1970.

This bibliography of Dr. Kenneth B. Clark's work from 1936 to 1970—compiled by the Metropolitan Applied Research Center—includes books, magazines, newspaper articles, chapters in books, speeches, television and radio interviews, testimonies, roundtable discussions, book reviews, and some unpublished letters.

279.   Johnson, Harry Alleyn, ed. *Ethnic American Minorities: A Guide to Media and Materials.* New York: R. R. Bowker Co., 1976.

280.   Josey, Elonnie Junius, ed. *The Black Librarian in America.* Metuchen, N.J.: Scarecrow Press, 1970.

The twenty-five essays written for this book examine the multifaceted role of the black librarian in America and all the issues raised by that role. The book discusses library education and the various federal, state, and city agencies involved directly or indirectly in library services.

281.   ———, ed. *New Dimensions for Academic Library Service.* Metuchen, N.J.: Scarecrow Press, 1975.

The twenty-five essays written especially for this book focus on different perspectives of librarians, information scientists, and educators. The main topics addressed in this four-part book are the academic library as a vital component of higher learning; special problems confronting academic librarians; new approaches in solving academic library problems; and the three Rs system and the academic library community. In the final section, the editor discusses future trends in academic libraries. Each essay contains its own list of references.

282. ————, ed. *What Black Librarians Are Saying*. Metuchen, N.J.: Scarecrow Press, 1972.

All twenty-seven essays in this eight-part book discuss various aspects of librarianship in relation to problem areas in the black community. Part 1 defines the black librarian and distinguishes between the roles of a professional and an advocate. Other sections examine academic libraries, intellectual freedom, the needs of black communities for information, views of library education, and library schools and black people.

283. Josey, Elonnie Junius, and Kenneth Eugene Peeples, Jr., eds. *Opportunities for Minorities in Librarianship*. Metuchen, N.J.: Scarecrow Press, 1977.

This career book encourages young people from minority groups to consider entering the library profession. Essays are written by twenty distinguished librarians from a variety of backgrounds, including Charles Townley, a native American; Lillian Lopez, a Puerto Rican; Roberto Cabello-Argandona, a Chicano; and C. K. Huang and Janet M. Suzuki, Asian-Americans. Divided into six parts, this book concentrates on six minority groups and their careers as librarians.

284. Joyce, Donald Franklin. *Blacks in the Humanities, 1750-1984: A Selected Annotated Bibliography*. Westport, Conn.: Greenwood Press, 1986.

285. ————. *Gatekeepers of Black Culture: Black-Owned Book Publishing in the United States, 1817-1981*. Westport, Conn.: Greenwood Press, 1983.

Black businessmen and cultural entrepreneurs have been active in book publishing since 1817 when the African Methodist Episcopal Church established the A.M.E. Book Concern in Philadelphia. Joyce, coordinator of the Downtown Library of Tennessee State University, traces the growth and development of these publishers. His book, based on original research and interviews with publishing executives, is a ground-breaking study of an almost neglected, but extremely fascinating, area of American book publishing. "Most Black book publishers," he writes, "are small book publishers [who face] many of the same problems as other small book publishers. Black book-publishing executives and Black librarians, however, suggest in the scant literature available that Black book publishers also face unique problems related to acquiring capital, to gaining experience and expertise in book publishing, and to getting their books reviewed by major white reviewing media." Despite these problems, Joyce concludes, "Black book publishing in the United States will continue to grow [and] the Black book-publishing industry will, like the Black recording segment of the American recording industry, command a greater share of the Black business market."

286. Low, W. Augustus, and Virgil A. Clift, eds. *The Encyclopedia of Black America.* New York: McGraw Hill, 1981.

287. McPherson, James M., et al.,* eds. *Blacks in America: Bibliographical Essays.* Garden City, N.Y.: Doubleday and Co., 1971.

This valuable book combines narrative, interpretative, and bibliographical information to create a contemporary guide to Afro-American history and culture. It includes one hundred topics from the origins of Afro-Americans and slavery to the urban ghettos of 1970. Annotated references on the most important aspects of black American history are included. Topic summaries and study questions, with a discussion of the major books, articles, and printed primary sources, provide valuable research information.

288. Newby, James Edward. *Black Authors and Education: An Annotated Bibliography of Books.* Washington, D.C.: University Press of America, 1980.

This annotated bibliography of books on education and education policy by black authors includes over 230 entries and covers the period from the 1800s to 1980. Besides a preface, it includes an author index and a title index.

289. Page, James Allen. *Selected Black American Authors: An Illustrated Bio-Bibliography.* Boston: G. K. Hall and Co., 1977.

This work includes 453 authors—novelists, poets, essayists, playwrights, historians, social scientists, theologians, and others—whose works have been published from colonial times to the present. Each entry contains data grouped into the following major categories: biographical–personal, career–professional, writings, honors and awards, memberships, and sources. Also includes photographs of 285 authors, title and subject indexes, and a bibliography of sources.

290. Page, James Allen, and Jae Min Roh,** comps. *Selected Black American, African, and Caribbean Authors: A Bio-Bibliography.* Rev. and expanded. Littleton, Colo.: Libraries Unlimited, Inc., 1985. Originally published as *Selected Black American Authors: An Illustrated Bio-Bibliography.* Boston: G. K. Hall and Co., 1977.

291. Parks, Arnold G. *Urban Education: An Annotated Bibliography.* Saratoga, Calif.: Century Twenty One Publishers, 1981.

292. Porter, Dorothy Burnett. *The Negro in the United States: A Selected Bibliography.* Washington, D.C.: Library of Congress, 1970.

293. ———. *North American Poets: A Bibliographical Check List of Their Writings, 1760–1944.* Hattiesburg, Miss.: The Book Farm, 1945.

This selective bibliography arose out of the demands for lists of books that could be used to support the study of black history and culture in high schools and universities. Invaluable to researchers, educators, and librarians, it covers areas of race relations, social conditions, history, and the lives of famous blacks. The section on fiction identifies novels and short stories written by representative black authors.

294. Ratteray, Joan D. *The Testing of Cultural Groups: A Paradigmatic Analysis of the Literature on Testing and a Proposition.* Santa Monica, Calif.: Rand Corp., 1974.

295. Rollins, Charlemae Hill, ed. *We Build Together: A Reader's Guide to Negro Life and Literature for Elementary and High School Use.* 3d ed. Champaign, Ill.: National Council of the Teachers of English, 1963.

This bibliography defines criteria for selecting literature depicting minorities in a positive light. Contributors include Augusta Baker and others.

296. Rollock, Barbara. *Black Authors and Illustrators of Children's Books: A Biographical Dictionary.* New York: Garland Publishing, Inc., 1988.

Rollock provides biographical sketches of 115 authors and illustrators who published works in the United States, but who may live and work not only in this country but also in Canada, African countries, the Caribbean, or other parts of the world. She also includes sketches individuals no longer living. Besides basic biographical data on each subject, she lists their books, including many works that have had short publication lives. Included are a preface, introduction, bibliography, general index, and photographs of some authors and artists.

297. Shockley, Ann Allen. *A History of Public Library Service to Negroes in the South, 1900-1955.* Dover: Delaware State College, 1959.

This study of the Southeast and Southwest reveals that there was an uneven, sporadic, and slow development of public library service to blacks in these regions. Shockley argues that this was due to social attitudes, economy, and the South's segregation system.

298. Sims–Wood, Janet L. *Marian Anderson: An Annotated Bibliography and Discography.* Westport, Conn.: Greenwood Press, 1981.

This annotated bibliography catalogs materials on every facet of Anderson's life and career. Arranged topically, the book includes personal data as well as information about dramatic events in her life: her White House appearances, Metropolitan Opera debut (the first by a black), foreign tours, and the famous DAR controversy. Information about Marian Anderson's activities as a United Nations delegate and her public activities during World War II are also documented. The bibliography includes sections on awards and honors, manuscript holdings, and a discography of her recordings.

299. ————. *The Progress of Afro-American Women: A Selected Bibliography and Resource Guide.* Westport, Conn.: Greenwood Press, 1980.

This bibliography covers a wide range of topics on American black women, particularly in the twentieth century. Books and articles on black women in medicine, politics, journalism, science, the theater, religion, and other fields are listed, as well as special periodical issues and publications dealing with black family life, sexual discrimination, blacks in the suffrage movement, and so on. There are also sections devoted to autobiographies and biographies, and recollections of female slaves. The bibliography includes information on various black women's organizations, special collections on black women, and an extensive subject index.

300. Sinnette, Elinor Des Verney, W. Paul Coates, and Thomas C. Battle, eds. *Black Bibliophiles and Collectors: Preservers of*

Black History. Washington, D.C.: Howard University Press, 1990.

Divided into eight parts, this book is the outgrowth of a conference, "Black Bibliophiles and Collectors: A National Symposium," held November 29–30, 1983, at Howard University. The objectives of the conference were to identify black collectors and bibliophiles and to produce a national directory; to document the nature and scope of the collecting efforts of these bibliophiles and collectors; to provide information about collectors and their experience in collecting; to discuss the roles played by bibliophiles and collectors in preserving black history; and to disseminate information presented at the symposium through a publication of selected presentations. Contributors include Thomas C. Battle, Dorothy Porter Wesley, Tony Martin, Elinor Des Verney Sinnette, Robert Hill, Jessie Carney Smith, Betty M. Culpepper, Paul Robeson, Jr., and Michael R. Winston. Includes a gallery of bibliophiles, biographies of contributors, and an index.

301. Teague, Bob. *Live and Off-Color: News Biz.* New York: A and W Publishers, 1982.

302. Thorpe, Earl Endris. *Black History and the Organic Perspective: An Essay to Introduce the Directory and Bibliography No. 870–872.* Monticello, Ill.: Council of Planning Librarians, 1975.

303. Turner, Darwin T. *Afro-American Writers.* New York: Appleton-Century-Crofts, 1970.

This bibliography serves as a guide to drama, fiction, poetry, and library scholarship of Afro-Americans. It includes references to such related topics as the historical and sociological backgrounds of black literature, art, music, journalism, and folklore. It also includes critical studies of the uses of Africans and Afro-Americans as characters in American literature.

304. Turner, Patricia. *Afro-American Singers: An Index and Preliminary Discography of Long-Playing Records of Opera, Choral Music, and Song.* Minneapolis: Challenge Production, 1977.

305. Walton, Hanes, Jr. *The Study and Analysis of Black Politics: A Bibliography.* Metuchen, N.J.: Scarecrow Press, 1973.

306. Washington, Valora, and Velma D. LaPoint. *Black Children and American Institutions: An Ecological Review and Resource Guide.* New York: Garland Publishing, Inc., 1988.

This reference book, which contains essays, a reference list, and annotated bibliographies, offers a comprehensive cultural, historical, and ecological approach to understanding the black child's development from infancy to adolescence. Includes a general introduction, subject index, and author index.

307. Williams, R. Ora. *American Black Women in the Arts and Social Sciences: A Bibliographic Survey.* 1973. Rev. and expanded ed. Metuchen, N.J.: Scarecrow Press, 1978.

This volume compiles over twelve hundred entries of work by American black women in the arts and social sciences. Included are movies, tapes, and recordings based on works written by black women, as well as interesting portrait photographs of some contributors.

308. Work, Monroe Nathan, ed. *A Bibliography of the Negro in Africa and America.* New York: Argosy-Antiquarian Ltd., 1965.

This volume contains references relating to many phases of black life today, including the conditions that affect this life as well as anthropological and historical influences. References are based on two main categories: (1) the black man in Africa, and (2) the black man in America.

309. Young, Glenell S., and Janet L. Sims-Wood, comps. *The Psychology and Mental Health of Afro-American Women:*

A Selected Bibliography. Resources on Afro-American Women. Temple Hills, Md.: Afro-Resources Inc., 1984.

This selected bibliography includes citations on nearly every aspect of the developmental and life-changing processes affecting Afro-American women. Topics include adolescent behavior, fear of success, father absence, mother/daughter relationships, mother/son relationships, male/female relationships, relationships with other females, health, deviant behavior, and so forth. The authors grouped the entries according to books and pamphlets, articles in books, journal articles, master's theses, and doctoral dissertations. Includes author and subject indexes.

CHAPTER 3

EDUCATION

310. Abramowitz, Elizabeth A. *Equal Educational Opportunity for Blacks in U.S. Higher Education: An Assessment.* Washington, D.C.: Howard University Press, 1976.

Prepared at the Institute for the Study of Educational Policy, Howard University, this book examines academic year 1973 and is a comprehensive treatment of black progress in higher education. Chapter 1 deals with problems of the data on blacks in college; chapter 2 examines access, distribution, and persistence of blacks in college; chapter 3 discusses barriers to equal educational opportunity for blacks; chapter 4 shows the impact of higher education on black income; and chapter 5 discusses federal policies related to equal educational opportunity.

Appendixes A through G include "Federal Higher Education Legislation," "Survey of National Data Collectors," "Enrollment in Selected Institutions," "Graduate and Professional School Enrollment," "College Cost," "Income Redistribution," and "References," respectively.

311. ————. *Equal Educational Opportunity: More Promise Than Progress.* Washington, D.C.: Howard University Press, 1978.

This volume, prepared at the Institute for the Study of Educational Policy, Howard University, expands the 1976 report. It describes the trends in academic year 1974 that forecast diminishing progress toward equality of educational opportunity. Includes appendixes, notes, and an index.

312. Adair, Alvis V. *Desegregation: The Illusion of Black Progress.* Washington, D.C.: University Press of America, 1984.

The author contends that desegregation legislation has proven to be a hindrance to the educational advancement of black schoolchildren. He argues that desegregation is destroying the black's most vital institutional base, the educational partnership between black elementary and secondary schools and black colleges. Adair maintains that desegregation without equitable allocation of tax dollars is as unconstitutional as segregation. He suggests a policy of equity for blacks and proposes the following: more equitable allocation of tax dollars for black institutions rather than the closing and demoting of black schools; more black models in the schools rather than elimination of black principals and teachers; either real integration via quotas, if necessary, or separation without isolation and without legal barriers to social interaction. Includes a glossary of terms and concepts, a subject/author index, and a note about the author.

313. Adams, Effie Kaye. *Experiences of a Fulbright Teacher.* Boston: Christopher Publishing Co., 1956.

This work describes Adams's travel and educational experiences in Pakistan as both an educator and a student. The book assumes the form of a diary into which dates and the experiences of the educator are duly recorded. This autobiography is interspersed with episodes of the author's experiences in other parts of Asia, in addition to Africa and Europe.

314. ———. *Tall Black Texans: Men of Courage: A Relevant Reading Work–Text with Comprehension, Vocabulary, and Study Skills Exercises.* Dubuque, Iowa: Kendall/Hunt Publishing Co., 1972.

315. Alexander,* David M., A. P. Johnston,* and Houston Conley, eds. *Legal Rights of Teachers and Students.* Gainesville, Fla.: Maxwell–King Co., 1974.

"In part, a compilation of major addresses delivered to a conference on school law held in November 1973 in Blacksburg, Virginia."

316. Andersen,** Charles J., Deborah J. Carter, and Andrew G. Malizio,** comps. *1989–1990 Fact Book on Higher Education.* New York: American Council on Education, Macmillan, 1989.

With over 180 tables covering eight major subject areas, this new edition of the *Fact Book* offers a one–stop source of answers to hundreds of questions about higher education. For example, which jobs will have the largest growth by the year 2000? Which states are least affected by the decline in the college–age population?

317. Anderson, James Douglas. *The Education of Blacks in the South, 1860–1935.* Chapel Hill: University of North Carolina Press, 1988.

Drawing on extensive primary sources, Anderson places black education in a political, cultural, and economic context and provides critical analyses of the conflicting goals of various philanthropic groups, the importance of Hampton and Tuskegee institutes as models of black education, and various attempts to frustrate efforts of ex–slaves to create an educational system that would support and extend their emancipation. Includes illustrations, a bibliography, and an index.

318. Anthony, Earl. *The Time of the.Furnaces: A Case Study of Black Student Revolt.* New York: Dial Press, 1971.

A case study of black student revolt beginning at North Carolina Agricultural and Technical College in 1960 and proceeding through the major college revolts at San Fernando

Valley State in 1968. Anthony considers the effects of these revolts on college curricula, racial makeup of faculty, and educational opportunities for blacks during the period when revolutionaries continued to be prosecuted.

319. Arnez, Nancy Levi. *The Besieged School Superintendent: A Case Study of School Superintendent–School Board Relations in Washington, DC, 1973–1975*. Washington, D.C.: University Press of America, 1981.

A case study of Barbara Sizemore's public school superintendency in Washington, D.C., this volume examines the relationship between Sizemore and her school board in an attempt to provide insights applicable to other urban school systems.

320. ———. *Teaching the Inner-City Child*. Morristown, N.J.: Silver Burdett, 1973.

Ethnic groups have pushed for their children to be taught solely by members of their group. This push came from the black quarter in the 1960s. Arnez believes that teachers in inner-city schools have consistently tried to impose their values and ideas on the children of ethnic groups, without adequately understanding the culture of these children. This handbook offers insights to help the prospective teacher understand the lifestyle of inner-city children. It discusses undergraduate programs that prepare prospective teachers to teach "standardized" American English, and provides suggestions and classroom techniques for better teaching.

321. Bacote, Clarence A. *The Story of Atlanta University: A Century of Service, 1865–1965*. Atlanta, Ga.: Atlanta University, 1969.

This book discusses the various reigns of administrators dating from 1867 up to 1966, including extracurricular activities, student life, and academic and physical developments during the postwar period.

322. Ballard, Allen B. *The Education of Black Folk: The Afro-American Struggle for Knowledge in White America.* New York: Harper and Row, 1973.

Ballard traces the white fear of black education to slavery's need for docile and illiterate creatures. He discusses the struggle of men like Woodson, Washington, and DuBois to foster black education. He also analyzes the strengths and weaknesses of black colleges, the bitter experience of blacks on white campuses, racism implicit in curricula and textbooks, the campus rebellions, and the rise of the Third World forces. An administrator on a predominantly white campus, he criticizes educational leaders for creating an undereducated class in public schools, for patronizing black students by not taking them seriously as human beings or as students, and for setting and implementing low standards.

323. Banks, James A. *Multiethnic Education: Theory and Practice.* 2d ed. Boston: Allyn and Bacon, 1988.

Banks substantially revised and reorganized this second edition and divided it into five parts. Part 1 discusses "History, Goals, and Practices"; part 2 deals with "Conceptual Issues"; part 3 examines "Philosophical Issues"; part 4 discusses "The Curriculum"; and part 5 analyzes "Teaching and Instruction." The book describes actions that educators can take to institutionalize educational programs and practices related to ethnic and cultural diversity. Includes a "multiethnic education inventory" and an index.

324. ———. *Teaching Strategies for Ethnic Studies.* 3d ed. Boston: Allyn and Bacon, 1984.

This teaching guide provides strategies, concepts, and resources for teaching comparative ethnic studies. Various chapters examine the historical perspective and teaching strategies for each major American ethnic group. Appendixes include Ethnic Groups in American History: "A Chronology of Key Events," "Selected Films and Filmstrips on American Ethnic Groups," "Ethnic Periodicals: A Selected List," and "The

Multiethnic Education Program Evaluation Check list." Includes an index.

325.   ————. *Teaching Strategies for the Social Studies: Inquiry, Valuing, and Decision Making.* 2d ed. Reading, Mass.: Addison–Wesley Publishing Co., 1977.

The text is primarily concerned with the methods of teaching social sciences at the elementary and junior high school level. Its arrangement reflects Banks theory of social studies: that individuals must learn the skills of decision making, which will in turn help in their personal lives and help the society as a whole. The author's illustrations and arrangement of topics are clear and make a useful guide for beginning teachers.

326.   ————. *Teaching the Black Experience: Methods and Materials.* Belmont, Calif.: Fearon Pitman Publishers, 1970.

An aid to teachers interested in methods, resources, and strategies for teaching the black experience. This book highlights different approaches to effective teaching of race relations and the black experience in North America. The last chapter is an annotated bibliography of resources for teaching the black experience.

327.   ————, ed. *Education in the 80's: Multiethnic Education.* Washington, D.C.: National Education Association, 1981.

328.   ————, ed. *Teaching Ethnic Studies: Concepts and Strategies.* Washington, D.C.: National Council for the Social Studies, 1973.

Rejecting the racism and complacency of the dominant American society, this guide for teachers and students covers a variety of sensitive problems, from bilingualism to culture differences of various ethnic groups, that call for special teaching strategies.

329. Banks, James A., with Ambrose A. Clegg, Jr.** *Teaching Strategies for the Social Studies: Inquiry, Valuing, and Decision-Making.* 3d ed. White Plains, N.Y.: Longman, 1985.

The central thesis of the third edition remains that social studies should help students develop the ability to make reflective decisions to solve personal problems and shape public policy through intelligent citizen action. Beginning with the idea that decision making can be taught, the authors identify the three main components: (1) scientific knowledge, (2) value analysis and clarification, and (3) development of a course of action through a synthesis of knowledge and values. They then provide multiple strategies for teaching these skills to elementary and junior high school students. Includes an index.

330. Banks, James A., and William W. Joyce.** *Teaching Social Studies to Culturally Different Children.* Reading, Mass.: Addison-Wesley Publishing Co., 1971.

This book focuses on the teaching skills, knowledge, and attitudes that are helpful in making social studies relevant and exciting for Afro-American, Mexican-American, Puerto Rican-American, American Indian, and other children who come from a culture of poverty. It explores (1) the basic problems in teaching social studies, (2) classroom strategies for teachers of culturally deprived students, and (3) curriculum and other subjects more meaningful for poor and alienated children.

331. Banks, James A., and Cherry A. McGee Banks, eds. *Multicultural Education: Issues and Perspectives.* Boston: Allyn and Bacon, 1989.

This book has six parts. Part 1 examines issues and concepts; part 2 deals with social class and religion; part 3 discusses gender; part 4 addresses ethnicity and language; part 5 examines exceptionality; and part 6 deals with school reform. Also included are an appendix—multicultural resources—a glossary, and an index.

332. Banks, James A., and Jean D. Grambs,** eds. *Black Self-Concept: Implications for Education and Social Science.* New York: McGraw–Hill, 1972.

This book is the outgrowth of a conference held in September 1963 at Tufts University. The purpose of the conference was to explore the various dimensions of black self-concept, and to delineate ways in which the school could enhance the self–images of black children and thereby increase their academic achievement and emotional growth. Position papers are by James A. Banks, Jean Dresden Grambs, Cynthia N. Shepard, Donald H. Smith, Alvin F. Poussaint, Carolyn Atkinson, Bradbury Seasholes, Nancy L. Arnez, James A. Goodman, and Barbara Sizemore. Their different ideas serve to stimulate actions on the part of educators about the school's role in enhancing the self–perceptions and identities of black youth.

333. Banks, James A., and James Lynch,** eds. *Multicultural Education in Western Societies.* New York: Praeger Publishers, 1986.

This book features contributors who are veterans in the field and who offer a range of perspectives from many different nations and cultures. They also offer rigorous analysis and discussion of the issues and problems in multicultural education, avoiding the kind of rhetoric frequently found in the literature in this field; discussion and analysis of antiracist education and the racist paradigm; a comprehensive index; and annotated bibliographies after each chapter that describe related key books and references.

334. Baptiste, H. Prentice, Jr. *Multicultural Education: A Synopsis.* 2d ed., rev. Washington, D.C.: University Press of America, 1979.

335. Beckham, Barry, ed. *The Black Student's Guide to Colleges.* 2d ed. Providence, R.I.: Beckham House, 1984.

336. ――――, ed. *The College Selection Workbook.* 2d ed. Providence, R.I.: Beckham House, 1987.

337. Bell, Derrick Albert, Jr., ed. *Shades of Brown: New Perspectives on School Desegregation.* New York: Teachers College Press, Columbia University, 1980.

In these provocative essays, noted educators, lawyers, and civil rights advocates analyze why many of the nation's minority children are still trapped in inferior schools more than twenty-five years since the *Brown* decision. The authors challenge the assumption that effective education can only be achieved through school integration, whether by busing or by other racial balance remedies. Instead, the book outlines guidelines for better schools for all children, especially those who have been the victims of race and class discrimination. Includes bibliographical references and index.

338. Black, Luther H. *Prescriptions for Adult Education and Secondary Education.* Detroit: Harlo Press, 1974.

339. Blackwell, James Edward. *Access of Black Students to Graduate and Professional Schools.* Atlanta, Ga.: Southern Education Foundation, 1975.

Blackwell examines factors that help and hinder black students applying to graduate and professional schools. He also provides information on scholarships and financial aid programs.

340. ――――. *Mainstreaming Outsiders: The Production of Black Professionals.* Bayside, N.Y.: General Hall, 1981.

This is a study of the successes and failures of the collective efforts employed to help black Americans enter the mainstream. Those efforts are placed in the historical context of precedents established during Reconstruction, and transformed by post–*Plessy v. Ferguson* events and by the legal assaults on the philosophy of "separate but equal." This book has two essential features. First, it is a trend analysis of access, enrollment, and graduation of black students. Second, it assembles in one place pertinent data on its subject, which makes it easy to render comparisons across disciplines or fields of study. Includes indexes, tables, and bibliography.

341.   ————. *The Participation of Blacks in Graduate and Professional Schools: An Assessment.* Atlanta, Ga.: Southern Education Foundation, 1977.

The author analyzes the participation rates of blacks in professional schools of law, dentistry, and medicine, as well as the distribution of blacks in journalism and allied health in relation to manpower needs and projections through 1985. Sources of financial aid and school admission policies are also given some attention.

342.   Bloom,** Benjamin S., Allison Davis, and Robert E. Hess.** *Compensatory Education for Cultural Deprivation.* New York: Holt, Rinehart and Winston, 1965.

Following the Civil Rights Act of 1964, the federal government began to sponsor a variety of programs to make up educational losses suffered by the underprivileged in the United States before the 1960s. This book describes various federally funded programs—including Head Start, tutorial programs, school reorganization, guidance and counseling, and bilingual education—designed to overcome shortcomings in learners and to raise their achievement levels.

343.   Bond, Horace Mann. *Black American Scholars: A Study of Their Beginnings.* Detroit: Balamp Publishing, 1972.

This study is a follow-up to *The Search for Talent.* Correlating genetic and neo-Darwinian theories, it examines the socioeconomic background of scholars all over the world. Its aim is to show the equalitarian nature of human ability.

344.   ————. *Education of the Negro in the American Social Order.* 2d ed. New York: Octagon Books, 1970.

Bond describes the effects of racial segregation on the educational process for blacks and makes an analogy with the suppression of other groups in world history. He also discusses blacks' awareness of their mistreatment by American political and social institutions, and their willingness to articulate dissatisfaction.

345. ———. *Negro Education in Alabama: A Study in Cotton and Steel.* Washington, D.C.: Associated Publishers, 1939.

This study discusses public education for black children of Alabama, with particular emphasis on the social and economic influences on segregated schools. Cotton and steel—two symbols of life in Alabama—were, of course, the most important of these influences. *Cotton* brought the two races to Alabama, and determined their distribution in the state and the relationship between social and economic classes among white persons. *Steel* is a symbol of change and has dissolved the political combinations in the state, dug up and replanted hundreds of thousands of families, white and black, and concentrated populations and wealth in areas that in 1860 were little more than wilderness.

346. ———. *The Search for Talent.* Cambridge: Harvard University Press, 1959.

This short book describes private and public schemes to identify and help talented young people by means of scholarships, loans, federal aid to education, football and basketball scholarships, and standardized tests. It analyzes drawbacks in methods of selection and compares the American and European educational systems.

347. Bonner, Mary Winstead. *Educators' Diagnostic Guidebook and Reference Manual for Problems in Reading.* Emporia, Kans.: Emporia State University Press, 1978.

The title of this book describes its purpose: to help teachers diagnose reading disabilities by using a competency–based approach, which should be used with other materials and textbooks. Bonner gives detailed procedures for identifying obstacles that prevent progress and for establishing an individual program in reading diagnosis and remediation. The manual also can be used for planning workshops in diagnostic reading. Bonner discusses various tests for recording reading performance, such as the Wechsler Intelligence Scale for Children, the Gates–MacGinitie Reading Test, and the Schoolfield's Articulation Test.

348.   ————. *Study Guide and Resource Manual for Introduction to Exceptional Children.* Emporia, Kans.: Emporia State University Press, 1974.

349.   Bontemps, Arna Wendell. *Young Booker: Booker T. Washington's Early Days.* New York: Dodd, Mead and Co., 1972.

This book traces the events of Booker T. Washington's youth and early career that were the driving force behind his determination to help educate his people.

350.   Bowles,** Frank, and Frank DeCosta. *Between Two Worlds: A Profile of Negro Higher Education.* New York: McGraw–Hill, 1971.

This book describes and analyzes the present condition of historically black colleges. Topics discussed include (1) the origins and development of educational institutions, (2) the limitations of these institutions, (3) the groups of schools that now enroll black students, (4) the broad picture of black higher education, (5) comparisons between historically white colleges and historically black colleges, and (6) the future of black colleges.

351.   Boyd, William M. *Desegregating America's Colleges: A Nationwide Survey of Black Students.* New York: Praeger Publishers, 1974.

This survey on black students was conducted during the 1972–1973 academic year at forty predominantly white institutions of higher learning. Boyd notes relationships between diverse characteristics and backgrounds of the black student and the selected institution. He suggests new perspectives on issues confronting the black student on the desegregated campus.

352. Boyer, James B. *Teaching the Economically Poor (the Disadvantaged): Poverty and Learning Relationships.* Manhattan, Kans.: James B. Boyer and AG Press, 1979.

353. Boyer, James B., and Joe L. Boyer. *Curriculum Desegregation in Public School: An Action Manual.* Columbia, Mo.: MCEEO, 1975.

354. ————, eds. *Curriculum and Instruction After Desegregation: Form, Substance, and Proposals.* Manhattan, Kans.: AG Press, 1975.

355. Brawley, Benjamin Griffith. *Doctor Dillard of the Jeanes Fund.* New York: Fleming H. Revell Co., 1930.

Dr. James Hardy Dillard has been closely identified with the educational boards in the South. This biography recounts the way he and others attacked the problem of relations between Anglo-Saxons and blacks in the United States. It describes his lifelong devotion to two objectives: the educating of the American black, and the creation of a better understanding between blacks and whites. Dillard's greatest achievement is perhaps the Jeanes teachers fund, organized first in America "to help the little country schools" and to create jobs for black teachers in the South. These teachers, in turn, improved the health conditions and provided instructions in activities of daily living for their black pupils.

356. ————. *History of Morehouse College.* Atlanta, Ga.: Morehouse College Press, 1917. Reprint. College Park, Md.: McGrath Publishing Co., 1970.

Morehouse College in Atlanta, Georgia was operated by the American Baptist Home Mission Society of New York for the education of black men. This book highlights the efforts of the northern missionary activities to relieve the unorganized conditions in education in the South soon after the Civil War. The author pays tribute to some early presidents of the college and, to present a total picture, gives some insight into changes in student life since the college began.

357.   Brawley, James Philip. *The Clark College Legacy: An Interview History of Relevant Education 1869 to 1975.* Princeton, N.J.: Princeton University Press, 1977.

Clark University in Atlanta, later called Clark College, is remarkable for the commitment it has made to programs relevant to blacks since it was founded in 1869. This book traces this commitment and the part played by Clark University in the movement of the Freedman's Aid Society of the Methodist Episcopal church. Brawley writes from four decades of personal and intimate involvement with the college as a teacher, dean, president and president emeritus, and member of the board of trustees.

358.   ————. *Two Centuries of Methodist Concern: Bondage, Freedom, and Education of Black People.* 1st ed. New York: Vantage Press, 1974.

A comprehensive study of the Methodist church and its role in the social and educational progress of blacks in the United States. The first two parts of the book examine the church's role during slavery and emancipation, and its work with the Freedman's Aid Society up to 1916. The remainder of the book evaluates the church's contribution to the founding of black colleges.

359.   Brazziel, William F. *Quality Education for All Americans: An Assessment of Gains of Black Americans with Proposals for Progressive Development in American Schools and Colleges for the Next Quarter–Century.* Washington, D.C.: Howard University Press, 1974.

This book describes the strides blacks have made in their drive toward quality education, and the interrelationship between education and economic well–being. It examines different kinds of schooling, including networks of metropolitan colleges and cradle schools. Brazziel recommends specific ways in which business, government, schools, and the black community itself can continue the momentum toward better education for blacks. He strongly urges adoption of more accurate methods of testing minority students and evaluating the work of the schools. Brazziel uses the past as a springboard for future hopes for quality education for all blacks in the next quarter–century.

360. Britts, Maurice W. *Blacks on White College Campuses.* Minneapolis: Challenge Production, 1975.

This study concerns itself specifically with the special Metropolitan Teacher Education Program Selection inaugurated for nonwhite students in the summer of 1968 at Concordia College, St. Paul, Minnesota. Unfortunately, the program revealed the lack of skill and foresight with which many predominantly white institutions of higher education have handled the needs of the large number of minority students that they massively recruited for their campuses. This study focuses on the attempts of the Concordia College administration to carry out the teacher education program.

361. Brookover,** Wilbur P., and Charles H. Beady, Jr. *School Social Systems and Student Achievement: Schools Can Make a Difference.* New York: Praeger Publishers, 1979.

362. Brooks, Charlotte Kendrick. *They Can Learn English.* Belmont, Calif.: Wadsworth Publishing Co., 1973.

Brooks believes that if some students coming out of our schools have not learned to speak and write English fluently and correctly, it is not because they cannot learn. Rather, they have not been properly taught. This book provides practical teaching methods that can be helpful not only to English teachers, but to parents and college students as well. It focuses on literature, reading, language, and composition.

363. Brooks, George Washington. *History of the Tennessee Education Congress, 1923-1967.* Washington, D.C.: National Education Association, 1975.

364. Brooks, Lyman Beecher. *Upward: A History of Norfolk State University.* Washington, D.C.: Howard University Press, 1983.

This book details the history of Norfolk State University from its founding in 1935. Lyman B. Brooks was president of Norfolk State University from 1938, and this volume recites his leadership through his retirement in 1975, noting that the university grew from a junior college division of Virginia Union University to a university in its own right. Includes photographs.

365. Brown, Charles Allen. *The Origin and Development of Secondary Education for Negroes in the Metropolitan Area of Birmingham, Alabama.* Birmingham, Ala.: Commercial Printing Co., 1959.

This book investigates the background of secondary education in Birmingham, Alabama, with attention to Afro-American enrollments, courses of study, the qualifications of the teachers, and school funding. The appendix includes additional information about the purpose of secondary education, and various letters about the author's research.

366. Brown, Donna B. *Learning Disabilities for the Classroom Teacher.* Chicago: Follett Educational Corp., 1972.

367. Brown, Hugh Victor. *E-Qual-ity Education in North Carolina Among Negroes.* Raleigh, N.C.: Irving-Swain Press, 1964.

Written in the early 1960s, this book explains how equal education in North Carolina and elsewhere has proven costly because it has remained segregated, a fact that, from the beginning of black education, has plagued the consciences of the liberal elements. Brown discusses how liberal elements in North Carolina began the long road toward equality from March 1866 to the 1960s. He emphasizes both the programs, blacks are shunted into, such as industrial education, and the promotion of inequality.

368. ————. *A History of the Education of Negroes in North Carolina.* Raleigh, N.C.: Irving Swain Press, 1961.

This history was the outgrowth of the North Carolina Newbold conference at Shaw University, which met to set the stage for many "next steps" in the saga of black racial equality. This book recounts the early history of education for blacks in North Carolina, from the religious instructions of slaves, their industrial and practical training, and the era of John Chavis, through the influence of Afro-Americans in the State Department and the recent development of industrial and vocational education. It also discusses the influence of philanthropic individuals and organizations, such as the Slater Fund, the Jeanes Fund, Southern Education Board, and General Education Board in the education of North Carolina blacks.

369. Brown, Thomas J. *Teaching Minorities More Effectively: A Model for Educators.* Washington, D.C.: University Press of America, 1986.

Brown aims to enhance the academic achievement and opportunity for minorities. He argues that the cycle of minority underachievement continues because minority students are taught less effectively than their white middle-class counterparts. He contends that because minorities are expected to achieve less, they are provided with fewer opportunities to engage actively in structured learning experiences. He concludes that four variables are integral to improving minority education: motivation, classroom behavior, student/teacher interaction, and evaluation.

370. Bryant, Spurgeon Quinton. *Why I Don't Like Bussing.* New York: Vantage Press, 1973.

Bryant uses busing to illustrate one of the primary forms of racial discrimination that has dominated American life ever since slaves were imported from Africa. In the early days of education, busing was for whites only; black students walked. Busing thus represents an important part of the network of injustices imposed upon blacks, a conflict in which both black and white children are caught. Bryant writes from personal experiences and observations of discrimination, segregation, and injustices.

371. Bullock, Henry Allen. *A History of Negro Education in the South: From 1619 to the Present.* Cambridge: Harvard University Press, 1967. Reprint. New York: Praeger Publishers, 1970.

Bullock traces the history of Afro–American education from 1619 to the present. Seeking to explain the educational and social revolutions in American race relations today, Bullock turns to a model of conflict–unintention–accommodation. He selects strategic periods in American history and attempts to identify the "direct intention" and "inherent conflicts" in relations between blacks and whites. He then explores the unintended and contrary interracial practices resulting from this interaction. In each period, blacks and whites learn to accommodate each other on new and higher levels.

372. Burrell, Leon F., and Zacharie J. Clements.** *A Survival Kit for Brothers & Sisters Going to Grey Colleges: The Way to Make It Through Higher Education.* White Plains, N.Y.: Weilen Press, 1973.

In an intimate "big brother" style, Burrell and Clements speak to black students at white colleges. The book offers study skill techniques, verbal skill suggestions, and general academic improvement ideas. A useful book, not only for students but also for administrators, faculty, and staff who would like to enhance their understanding of minorities and the difficulties minorities encounter while attending predominantly white institutions.

373. Burrell, Leon F., and Timothy S. Knowles. *Perception of Administrators and Minority Students of Minority Student Experience on Predominantly White Campuses.* Barre, Vt.: Northlight Studio Press, 1979.

374. Burrell, Natelkka E. *Katrina Stands Alone.* Washington, D.C.: Review and Herald Publishing Association, 1988.

375. Butler, Addie Louise Joyner. *The Distinctive Black College: Talladega, Tuskegee, and Morehouse.* Metuchen, N.J.: Scarecrow Press, 1977.

376. Caldwell, Dista H. *The Education of the Negro Child.* New York: Carlton Press, 1961.

Originally written as a master's thesis and slightly revised, this book is primarily concerned with how integration or the maintenance of separate schools affects the quality of Afro–American primary and secondary education, and with the impact of segregation upon the moral, mental, and social development of the Afro–American. The author weighs both sides of the argument and concludes that voluntary separate schools are recommended, as a temporary measure, on all educational levels except perhaps nursery school and college. She feels that Afro–Americans can best fulfill themselves and their goals, ideals, and needs, and gain a better perspective of life if they first attend a voluntary separate school that will teach them self–respect, self–acceptance, self–reliance, a sense of value, and a true knowledge of the contribution of the black race to mankind.

377. Caliver, Ambrose. *A Background Study of Negro College Students.* Washington, D.C.: U.S. Government Printing Office, 1933. Reprint. Westport, Conn.: Negro Universities Press, 1970.

This book is based on questionnaires sent in the early 1930s to ninety–five colleges located in seventeen states to create an accurate personal profile of black college freshmen and their family histories (number of children, previous college graduates, income, and home life).

378.   ————. *Education of Negro Teachers.* Washington, D.C.: U.S. Government Printing Office, 1933. Reprint. Westport, Conn.: Negro Universities Press, 1970.

A progress report made to the U.S. Office of Education on the state of black teacher education in the early 1930s. It notes the need for improvement as well as the progress that has been made in solving some complex problems in educating black teachers. The study surveys elementary, secondary, and college teachers, and takes into account their degrees, writings, tenure, sex, marital status, salary, and so on.

379.   ————. *National Survey of the Higher Education of Negroes: A Summary.* Washington, D.C.: U.S. Government Printing Office, 1943.

This survey describes the social and economic conditions of higher education for blacks in the 1940s. It urges the passage of federal legislation and makes suggestions for federal government participation in developing high–grade university education for both races. Responsibility for reform is given to the federal government.

380.   ————. *A Personnel Study of Negro College Students.* New York: Columbia University, 1931. Reprint. Westport, Conn.: Negro Universities Press, 1970.

This study, undertaken at Fisk University, explores the ways in which education can best serve the needs of the individual and of society. It analyzes the academic progress of black college students in relation to their social, economic, and intellectual backgrounds, and it shows how an understanding of this relationship will help in counseling black students.

381.   ————. *Secondary Education for Negroes.* Washington, D.C.: U.S. Government Printing Office, 1932.

This work is the result of a three-year study conducted by the Department of Education on secondary education for blacks: its organization, curriculum (including some of the more fundamental subjects), extra-curriculum, the pupil population, administrative and supervisory problems, personnel, and activities.

382. ————. *Vocational Education and Guidance of Negroes: Report of a Survey Conducted by the Office of Education.* Washington, D.C.: U.S. Government Printing Office, 1938. Reprint. Westport, Conn.: Negro Universities Press, 1970.

This statistical report surveys the effects of technological growth and social and economic changes on blacks in the first quarter of the century. What is needed, it suggests, is a new equilibrium between education and occupation for blacks. This survey investigates the opportunities and facilities for vocational education and guidance of Afro-Americans in rural and urban communities.

383. Cameron, Howard K., Charles Alexander Asbury, Winifred F. Cameron, et al. *Professional Roles of Urban School Psychology.* Washington, D.C.: Bureau of Educational Research, Howard University, 1982.

This monograph—the first in a series to be published by the Bureau of Educational Research—sets out to provide information that would serve to thwart any potential conflict resulting from perceptual differences in school psychologists' role expectations. The central investigation is the perceptions of the Pupil Personnel Services team members regarding what the urban school psychologists' role should be. The study seeks answers to a number of related questions: (1) Are there significant differences among members of the Pupil Personnel Services team in their perception of what professional role(s) of urban school psychologists should be? (2) Do urban school psychologists generally agree on what their professional roles in the schools should be? (3) Do black and white school psychologists indicate different preferences for how certain professional roles in the school are performed?

384. Campbell, Thomas Monroe. *The Movable School Goes to the Negro Farmer.* Tuskegee: Tuskegee Institute Press, 1936.

This semiautobiographical sketch begins with Campbell's early life in Georgia and his later efforts to work his way through the school under Booker T. Washington. Then the federal government chose Campbell to operate the first Movable School, a program begun at Tuskegee Institute. The rest of the book outlines the purpose and results of this type of education for rural people, discusses its present scope and influence in this country and abroad, and presents a brief on the future of black rural life.

385. Carter, Vertie L. *Arkansas Baptist College: A Historical Perspective, 1884–1982.* Houston, Tex.: D. Armstrong Company, 1981.

386. Cary, Willie Mae. *Worse Than Silence: The Black Child's Dilemma.* New York: Vantage Press, 1976.

Worse Than Silence demonstrates how the black child's value system affects the child's motivation, disciplines, and his general involvement at school. Cary presents various teaching strategies that have been shown to be effective over the years, and argues that the black child can be taught but must first be induced to settle down to the business of learning in the classroom.

387. Castaneda,** Alfredo, Richard L. James, and Webster Robbins.** *The Educational Needs of Minority Groups.* Lincoln, Nebr.: Professional Educators Publications, 1974.

This book consists of three essays on educational and other needs of Mexican–Americans, black Americans, and native Americans. The essays were contributed by three scholars, themselves members of these three minority groups, who have bridged the gaps between the dominant society and their own societies. This book is useful for those who seek a better understanding of minorities' problems.

388. Cheek, James Edward. *Higher Education's Responsibility for Advancing Equality of Opportunity and Justice.* Washington, D.C.: Institute for the Study of Educational Policy, Howard University, 1977.

Presented at the Institute for the Study of Educational Policy's invitational conference, "Advancing Equality of Opportunity: A Matter of Justice," held May 17, 1977, this work examines three themes: (1) the close relationship between knowledge and power and between ideas and action, (2) the ways in which universities have evolved historically from "ivory towers" of knowledge to influential factors in the practical application of that knowledge, and (3) how advancing equality of opportunity and justice for black Americans is within the purview of modern universities. This work also contains a foreword by Kenneth Tollett, director of the institute.

389. Cheers, Arlynne Lake, and Lamore J. Carter. *Teaching and Learning in the Model Classroom: The Conditions, Relationships, and Instructional Specifics.* New York: Exposition Press, 1974.

This book presents a three–phase teaching–learning sequence. The first phase treats the teacher's efforts to communicate to the learner attainable goals and a rationale for seeking to attain them. The second phase involves showing a student appropriate approaches to the task and providing the student with a thought model. The final phase includes all of the behaviors through which the teacher communicates his or her evaluations of the student's efforts to achieve. The book also includes a list of suggested readings and an index.

390. Clark, Felton Grandison. *The Control of State–Supported Teacher–Training Programs for Negroes.* New York: Bureau of Publications, Teachers College, Columbia University, 1934. Reprint. New York: AMS Press, 1972.

This book, published in the 1930s, is divided into two parts. The first analyzes state institutions designed to train black teachers. The second presents, experts who make recommendations for the proper functioning of the institutions.

391. Clark, Kenneth Bancroft, and Lawrence Plotkin.** *The Negro Student at Integrated Colleges.* New York: The National Scholarship Service and Fund for Negro Students, 1963.

An interesting study of the lives of 509 black students who received financial aid from the National Scholarship Service and Fund for Negro Students. The major findings concern college performance, college experiences, and postcollege adjustment.

392. Clark, Reginald M. *Family Life and School Achievement: Why Poor Black Children Succeed or Fail.* Chicago: University of Chicago Press, 1983.

In intimate portraits of ten black families in Chicago, Clark makes a case for the importance of family culture and interaction to academic achievement among schoolchildren. Visiting the homes of the well–to–do, welfare recipients, one- and two-parent families, and high and low achievers, Clark observed the quality of home life, noting how family habits and interactions affect school success identifying and what characteristics of family life provide children with the essential "school survival skills." Clark offers specific suggestions and strategies for use by teachers, parents, school administrators, and social service policymakers.

393. Clift, Virgil A., Archibald W. Anderson,** and Gordon H. Hullfish,** eds. *Negro Education in America: Its Adequacy, Problems, and Needs.* New York: Harper and Row, 1962.

This collection of essays by famous black educators examines the many problems blacks in the United States have in satisfying their right to equal education. Using sociological, anthropological, and psychological data, the essays trace the historical development of these problems. Changes and future directions for black education are also discussed.

394. Clifton, Fred J. *Darl.* New York: Third Press, 1973.

Using the unusual and interesting format of a series of letters between a fictitious student (Darl) and his English teacher, Clifton reveals the subtle prejudices and misunderstandings that exist between people of different races and social classes. Gradually, a sense of mutual understanding and respect develops between Darl and his teacher. The author implies that given a line of communication, others can also experience such understanding and respect. There is a lot of subtle humor, which adds enjoyment to the reading but does not take away from the serious message of the book.

395. Coger, Rick. *Developing Effective Instructional Systems.* North Quincy, Mass.: Christopher Publishing House, 1975.

Written both as a guide to prospective and practicing teachers and as a supplementary text for education courses, this book explores and analyzes various instructional systems. It is also designed as a supplementary text for courses in education. At the beginning of each chapter, the author presents questions as an aid in identifying the major problem area focused on in that chapter. At the end of chapters 1 through 7, he provides examples from representative subject fields. Work sheets are located after each sample topic to help teachers design instructional systems.

396. Collins, Marva, and Civia Tamarkin.* *Marva Collins' Way.* Los Angeles: Tarcher, 1982.

This book gives the story of the life and times of one of America's most outspoken and controversial educators. It tells how she left the Chicago public school system and started her own school, and how she instilled a love for learning and self–respect in her students.

397. Colson, Edna Meade. *An Analysis of the Specific References to Negroes in Selected Curricula for the Education of Teachers.* New York: Bureau of Publications, Teachers

College, Columbia University, 1940. Reprint. New York: AMS Press, 1972.

Starting with the assumption that the United States is a democracy and that a democracy uses its educational system as one way of solving its problems, Colson then argues that schools "should develop those understandings, attitudes, and abilities in children which make for the solution of these problems." For the schools to be able to do this, she maintains, teachers must be made aware of the problems.

After giving a comprehensive description of the "Negro Problem" in America, Colson then examines the degree and quality of the study of blacks in the curricula of teacher education. Chapter 2 discusses provisions for the study of blacks in elementary school courses of study, and chapter 3 discusses blacks in the curricula of teachers' colleges. Numerous tables are included, together with an extensive bibliography.

398. Comer, James Pierpoint. *School Power: Implications of an Intervention Project.* New York: Free Press, 1980.

This book demonstrates the effect of psychological, social, and institutional forces on the performance of administrators, teachers, parents, and students in schools. It shows how a university, a public school system, and parents worked together to move problem schools to an acceptable level of social and academic achievement.

399. Conley, Houston, Judith Bailey,** Georgia Eugene, et al. *Contingency Planning for a Unitary School System: A Process Guide for School Desegregation.* Nashville: McQuiddy Printing Co., 1977.

This document is designed to help provide contingency plans for a unitary school system in communities where desegregation is being carried out. It examines school personnel, students, ·community and human relations departments, and other relevant issues in the effort to show that barriers to equal educational opportunities for black children *can* be eliminated. The other coauthors are June Key** and Bernard Minnis.

400. Cordasco,** Francesco, Maurie Hillson,* and Henry Allen Bullock, eds. *The School in the Social Order: A Sociological Introduction to Educational Understanding.* Scranton, Penn.: Intext Publisher, 1970. Reprint. Washington, D.C.: University Press of America, 1981.

This volume of readings puts the educator in touch with the wisdom derived from the sociologist's objective studies of the conditions and social life of people as they relate to and are connected with the educational environments of America. A society has many social systems. The editors perceive each system as a formal organization, a configuration of differentiated and coordinated human activities, that seeks, through a complex of available resources, to socialize youths according to specifications shaped by the dominant value system of the general society.

401. Cox, George O. *Education for the Black Race.* 2d ed. New York: African Heritage Studies Publishers, 1976.

402. Cozart, Leland Stanford. *A History of the Association of Colleges and Secondary Schools, 1934-1965.* Charlotte, N.C.: Heritage Printers, 1967.

403. ————. *A Venture of Faith: Barber-Scotia College 1867-1967.* Charlotte, N.C.: Heritage Printers, 1976.

This book relates the history of Barber-Scotia College during the first century of its service to contemporary issues. This college, which originated after the Civil War, was created for southern Afro-American girls by the Presbyterian church. The author discusses the different purposes and programs of Barber-Scotia and the calibre of the people who presided over the college. The book is highlighted by photographs.

404. Crawford, George Williamson. *The Talladega Manual of Vocational Guidance.* Talladega, Ala.: Talladega College, 1937.

This book, published in 1937, is addressed to students attending black colleges in the United States. The book is arranged in three sections. The first describes the aims and objectives of vocational guidance, with particular reference to black colleges. The second deals with a selection of careers, which were moderately open to young black students in the 1930s, with emphasis on appropriate college courses relevant to such careers. The final section contains additional information that may be very helpful in previewing occupational fields.

405. Cross, Dolores E., Gwendolyn C. Baker, and Lindley J. Stiles,** eds. *Teaching in a Multi-Cultural Society.* New York: Free Press, 1977.

These essays discuss a variety of educational issues, including the student as immigrant, the intellectual strengths of minority children, and language arts in a multicultural society. This is a helpful book for meeting the demands of teaching in a contemporary, multicultural society.

406. Culp, Daniel Wallace, ed. *Twentieth Century Negro Literature: or, a Cyclopedia of Thought on the Vital Topics Relating to the American Negro by One Hundred of America's Greatest Negroes.* Naperville, Ill.: J. L. Nichols and Co., 1902.

When it was published, early in the century, this volume sought to enlighten uniformed whites on the intellectual ability of the Afro-American, to enumerate the contributions of Afro-Americans to American society, and to enlighten Afro-American youth on various ethical, political, and sociological questions arising from the race problem. The list of contributors is long and impressive. The book contains many pertinent topics but pays particular attention to the education of the Afro-American.

407. Cyphert,* Frederick Ralph, and Ernest Spaights, eds. *An Analysis and Projection of Research in Teacher Education.* Columbus: Ohio State University Research Foundation, 1964.

    This work—supported by the Cooperative Research Project no. F–015 of the Office of Education, U.S. Department of Health, Education, and Welfare—includes papers presented at a conference held at Columbus, Ohio, March 29, 1964, through April 3, 1964.

408. Dabney, Lillian Gertrude. *The History of Schools for Negroes in the District of Columbia, 1807–1947.* Washington, D.C.: Catholic University of America Press, 1949.

    Originally a doctoral dissertation, this book gives a detailed history of black education in the District of Columbia through the Second World War. It covers all levels of schooling from nursery through college, and examines the public, private, and parochial schools that existed in the District, as well as various societies concerned with the education of blacks. The author provides numerous tables and detailed illustrations of the subject matter.

409. Daniel, Walter Green. *The Reading Interests and Needs of Negro College Freshmen Regarding Social Science Materials.* New York: Bureau of Publications, Teachers College, Columbia University, 1942.

    Daniel conducted this study of entering college freshmen in fall of 1939 and 1940 while he was at Howard University. It examines their needs, interests, and abilities in the social sciences. Daniel discusses methods and findings, and suggests ways of promoting general and cultural reading.

410. Dansby, B. Baldwin. *A Brief History of Jackson College: A Typical Story of the Survival of Education Among Negroes in the South.* Jackson, Miss.: Jackson College, 1953.

The history of Jackson College, formerly known as Natchez Seminary, begins after the Civil War and proceeds into the 1930s. Various churches, such as the Baptist and the Methodist, saw the dire need for educating blacks in the South and fanatically strove to meet this need. Jackson College was a result of their endeavor. This book highlights several prominent people who associated with the college.

411.   Davidson, Edmonia White. *Family and Personal Development in Adult Basic Education: Curriculum Guide and Resource Units.* Washington, D.C.: National University Extension Association, 1971.

This work was funded by a grant from the Education Office, U.S. Department of Health, Education, and Welfare, in a national effort to find ways of eliminating adult illiteracy in the United States. In this volume, Davidson extensively analyzes low–income family structure on the premise that teachers of adult illiterates should enrich their understanding of their students.

412.   ————. *Operation COPE: Family Learning Center Handbook with Mothers Who Are Heads of Households.* Washington, D.C.: National Council of Negro Women, 1975.

Operation COPE, established by the National Council of Negro Women, is an experimental project that established two family learning centers in Washington, D.C., from July 1, 1973, to June 30, 1975. The project was designed to serve the needs of low–income mothers who were educationally disadvantaged (had less than eight years of schooling, as measured by standardized tests) and were heads of households. This handbook provides information about procedures used in parent–child, academic, vocational, and community programs, in staff development, with the advisory committee and volunteers.

413.   Davis, Allison. *Social Class Influences upon Learning.* Cambridge: Harvard University Press, 1948.

In this work, Davis discusses the concept of socialization of children and examines certain differences among social classes and cultural groups in the United States. He discusses the cultural definitions of what constitutes the "good" and the "bad" of the middle and lower social classes, and examines the impact of these differences on the learning abilities of the children.

414. Davis, Arthur, Jr. *Racial Crisis in Public Education: A Quest for Social Order.* 1st ed. New York: Vantage Press, 1975.

415. Dawson, Martha Eaton, and Mary Christian. *The Nuts and Bolts of Elementary Education.* Chicago: Science Research Associates, 1968, [1969].

This work comprises twenty of Dawson's and Christian's letters published biweekly, October 7, 1968, through June 30, 1969, and bound together.

416. Delaney, William H. *Learn by Doing: A Projected Educational Philosophy in the Thought of Booker T. Washington.* New York: Vantage Press, 1974.

An informative evaluation of Booker T. Washington's philosophical approach to education: education for the good of life and social significance. Washington believed that for education to be worthwhile it should enable the individual to develop the will and capacity to enrich the whole life of the community by his or her personal character and attitudes as well as by economic endowment. Delaney also gives a biographical sketch of Washington to enhance the reader's understanding of Washington's philosophy.

417. Della-Dora,** Delmo, and James E. House, eds. *Education for an Open Society.* Washington, D.C.: Association for Supervision and Curriculum Development, 1974.

A discussion of the prospects for an open society in which all people, including ethnic minorities and the aged, are equally and properly represented. The discussion centers around four essential questions: (1) How open is the society presently? (2) Have educational institutions promoted or inhibited the growth of an open society? (3) Can power be exercised in the society to create or maintain openness? (4) What can be suggested to aid the United States in becoming a truly open society? James A. Banks and Barbara A. Sizemore are among the many contributors to this work.

418. Derbigny, Irving Antony. *General Education in the Negro College.* Stanford, Calif.: Stanford University Press, 1947. Reprint. Westport, Conn.: Negro Universities Press, 1969.

This book is the result of field work study conducted by the author during the school year 1942–1943. It describes the general education programs of twenty black colleges during that period and compares their general education programs with those of other American colleges. On the basis of these comparisons, Derbigny suggests ways in which improvements can be made.

419. Dilworth, Mary Elizabeth, with V. Y–Tessa Perry.* *Teacher's Totter: A Report on Teacher Certification Issues.* Washington, D.C.: Institute for the Study of Educational Policy, Howard University, 1984.

Divided into eight chapters—"Teacher Training Development," "History of Black Teachers," "Accountability," "Tests," "Status Report," "Responses," "Supply, Demand and Other Considerations," and "Findings, Conclusions and Recommendations"—this monograph focuses on issues pertinent to new teacher certification requirements while giving special attention to the dilemma of black colleges and their graduates. It indicates that the overemphasis on teacher certification tests promises to persist, and that black teacher training institutions have no alternative but to adjust their curricula and programs in a manner that will substantially improve the performance of their students. Includes a selected bibliography, appendixes, and an index.

420. DuBois, W. E. B. *The Economic Value of Negro Education.* Washington, D.C.: U.S.A. Chamber of Commerce, 1916.

421. DuBois, W. E. B., and Augustus Granville Dill, eds. *The Common School and the Negro American: Report of a Social Study Made by Atlanta University Under the Patronage of the Trustees of the John F. Slater Fund.* Atlanta, Ga.: The Atlanta University Press, 1911.

The authors trace the development of the Afro–American common schools and discuss general conditions in the schools, such as poor teaching facilities, unqualified and incompetent teachers and superintendents, teachers' salaries, poor enrollment of pupils, and poor financial support. Based on their findings, the authors project a grim outlook for the schools.

422. Duncan, Lionel Sebastian. *Plato to IBM: Development of Computer Assisted Instruction as a Medium of Instruction.* Washington, D.C.: Bond Publishing Co., 1980.

423. Edwards, Harry. *Black Students.* New York: Free Press, 1970.

The author gives a historical account of the black student movement in the United States. He describes the goals, philosophies, and directions of the movement in different stages, and the forces and personalities that have helped to shape it. He also discusses the relationship that black students have with the black community at large, with American colleges and universities, and with white liberal student coalitions. He advocates the development of black curricula at all levels in the American educational system as a means of combating institutionalized racism in American education.

424. Edwards, Norma S. *A Special Delivery: A Manual for Teachers of Children.* Washington, D.C.: ICAY Publishing Co., 1977.

This well–illustrated manual is written for teachers who work with children who have learning problems. The structure of the book follows the pattern of oral communication, beginning with the phoneme–grapheme association and leading eventually to a discussion of written communication. The book includes various classroom techniques and a reading series that can be made to suit individual children.

425. Edwards, Thomas Bentley. *Attitudes of High School Students as Related to Success in School.* Berkeley: University of California Press, 1958.

This work is based on research done in the late 1950s on the attitudes of high school students toward their school subjects. The study was undertaken with the aim of improving science education by devising ways to "identify and attract students with potential gifts in this area." Attitudes toward the entire range of academic studies are reviewed. Attitudes favorable to the study of science were compared with attitudes favorable to the study of the humanities, and with attitudes of students showing no inclination toward academic studies, in order to measure the strength of attitudes favorable to science study.

426. ————. *The Regional Project in Secondary Education: Evaluation of a Program of Cooperative Curriculum Development.* Berkeley: University of California Press, 1956.

The Regional Project in Secondary Education (RPSE) is discussed and evaluated in eight sections. Section 2 describes a number of programs similar in nature and philosophy, and notes the need for careful evaluation of these studies. Section 4 describes the method of the RPSE, its history, its finances, and its organization. Sections 5 and 6 tell the story of RPSE in the eighteen participating schools. Section 7 presents and analyzes additional data, and the final section gives summaries and conclusions.

427. Edwards, Thomas Bentley, and Alan B. Wilson,* *A Study of Some Social and Psychological Factors Influencing Educational Achievement.* Berkeley: University of California Press, 1961.

The data in this study of the elementary school children in Berkeley, California, are derived from a study conducted in the spring of 1959. Using this data, the authors were able to determine the differences in social composition of various elementary schools. The data showed a clear relationship between certain familiar social backgrounds and academic achievement and aspirations. They also suggest ways in which different school milieux might modify this relationship. Chapters 2 and 5 analyze the effects of the social factors upon the achievement and educational aspirations of sixth-grade boys. The remaining chapters concern an analysis of the joint effects of background, situational factors, and psychological variables.

428. Edwards, Thomas Bentley, and Frederick Wirt,* eds. *School Desegregation in the North: The Challenge and the Experience.* San Francisco: Chandler Publishing Co., 1967.

This book contains case studies of how ten communities, four near New York City and six in California, responded to the challenge of de facto segregation. Using interdisciplinary techniques, the first two chapters put forward a model of political decisionmaking and summarize the social and psychological consequences of various ways of grouping children for instructional purposes. The third chapter explores the relationship between segregation and the aspirations of schoolboys. The book includes notes on the chapters.

429. Elam, Julia C., ed. *Blacks on White Campuses: Proceedings of a Special NAFEO Seminar.* Washington, D.C.: University Press of America, 1983.

This work is a collection of essays developed from a special seminar by the same name as part of the Seventh National Conference on Blacks in Higher Education, held in Washington, D.C., in March of 1982, and sponsored by the National Association for Equal Opportunity (NAFEO). The recurring theme is that black professionals as well as students socialize little with their white counterparts and are generally isolated from the mainstream of campus activities. The proceedings argue that blacks should actively seek involvement in all campus and professional activities, including campuswide committees and national organizations in their disciplines. The appendix contains a map of black junior, four-year, graduate and professional institutions enrolling in excess of two hundred thousand students.

430. Elliott,** Peggy G., and Robert E. Mays. *Early Field Experiences in Teacher Education.* Bloomington, Ind.: Phi Delta Kappa Educational Foundation, 1979.

431. Ellis, Mary Jackson. *Teaching Resources for the Kindergarten – Primary Teacher.* Minneapolis: T. S. Denison and Co., 1960.

432. Ellis, Mary Jackson, and Joy Ellis Bartlett.* *The Kindergarten Log.* 1955. Reprint. Minneapolis: T. S. Denison and Co., 1977.

433. Ellis, Mary Jackson, Pearl K. Esko,* and Robert Kane.* *First Grade Log.* Minneapolis: T. S. Denison and Co., 1962.

434. Epps, Edgar G., ed. *Black Students in White Schools.* Worthington, Ohio: Charles A. Jones, 1972.

This collection of seven essays by outstanding black educators deals with the rising population of black students attending white colleges and universities in the United States. These students usually differ from the majority of white students in socioeconomic background, career plans, and patterns of behavior. Consequently, the contributors focus on the various problems that black students experience while attending these institutions.

435. ———, ed. *Cultural Pluralism.* Berkeley: McCutchan Publishing Corp., 1974.

One of four in a series called "Contemporary Issues" presented by the National Society for the Study of Education, this book examines cultural pluralism and its relation to equality in education. Various authors speak out in favor of both cultural pluralism in education and the goals implied by it. The article by Barbara A. Sizemore discusses four important points surrounding the issue of cultural pluralism in America: (1) the meaning of culture, pluralism, and related concepts; (2) the values emanating from the culture; (3) the educational system produced by this value system; and (4) a model for change.

436. Evans, Zelia Stephens. *Tricks of the Trade for Teachers of Language Arts.* New York: Exposition Press, 1974.

437. Everett, Faye Philip. *Adventures in Educational Progress.* Boston: Meador Publishing Company, 1945.

438. Farmer, Marjorie. *Career Education and the Teaching of English.* Columbus: National Center for Research in Vocational Education, Ohio State University, 1980.

439. Fisher,* Margaret Barrow, and Jeanne L. Noble. *College Education as Personal Development.* Englewood Cliffs, N.J.: Prentice–Hall, 1960.

This interesting book introduces concepts related to the student's personal development during college. The book is divided into three parts. Part 1 concentrates on understanding oneself, part 2 focuses on the role of the student, and part 3 emphasizes choices and values. The book, which contains a comprehensive section of notes on the various chapters, should prove most helpful to current and prospective college students.

440. Fisher,* Richard I., and William E. Sims. *Educational Psychology for the Secondary School Teacher.* Lexington, Mass.: Ginn Custom Publishing Co., 1980.

441. Fleming, Jacqueline. *Blacks in College: A Comparative Study of Students' Success in Black and in White Institutions.* San Francisco: Jossey–Bass, 1984.

The author examines a major study on the intellectual and personal development of blacks in black and white colleges to assess which kinds of colleges better serve blacks. Using a wide range of measures—including academic achievement, social adjustment, self–concept, levels of stress, assertiveness, competitive performance, vocational interest, and black identity—she reveals that white colleges, despite generally superior facilities and resources, may be less supportive of black students' personal, social, and cognitive development than black colleges.

442. Fleming, John E. *The Lengthening Shadow of Slavery: A Historical Justification for Affirmative Action for Blacks in Higher Education.* Washington, D.C.: Howard University Press, 1976.

The author chronicles key factors in the black experience that impeded or enhanced the struggle for educational equality. The eras of slavery, the Revolutionary War, post–Civil War, "Jim Crowism," and the present are examined. Fleming argues persuasively for affirmative action for blacks in higher education.

443. Fleming, John E., Gerald R. Gill, and David H. Swinton. *The Case for Affirmative Action for Blacks in Higher Education.* Washington, D.C.: Howard University Press, 1976.

This book is an attempt to answer controversial questions about the legality and viability of affirmative action programs. Part 1 provides background to affirmative action and discusses past efforts by blacks to obtain equal educational opportunities. Part 2 briefly examines current affirmative action programs, and part 3 deals with the current position of black faculty members. Fleming argues that it is the responsibility of the federal government, through its various agencies, to enforce affirmative action programs "at all levels of society." Historical documents and executive orders in the appendixes should prove useful to researchers.

444. Foster, Marcus A. *Making Schools Work: Strategies for Changing Education.* Philadelphia: Westminster Press, 1971.

Written from a sociological perspective, this work discusses the various facets of school life, both positive and negative, and ways of making schools live up to their primary function of educating students. Part 1 considers the reevaluation of institutional goals; part 2 looks at the uses of crisis situations to yield positive outcomes; part 3 discusses the changes that schools in trouble can expect to undergo; and part 4 looks at the opportunities that arise out of a complex educational system.

445. Franklin, Vincent P. *The Education of Black Philadelphia: The Social and Educational History of a Minority Community, 1900–1950.* Philadelphia: University of Pennsylvania Press, 1979.

This book is a forcefully argued account of the impact of white racism and discriminatory policies on black education during the twentieth century. Includes illustrations, an epilogue, appendixes ("Committees Working with Black Migrants to Philadelphia," and "Black Enrollment in the Philadelphia Public Schools, 1920–1940"), notes, a selected bibliography, and an index.

446. Franklin, Vincent P., and James Douglas Anderson, eds. *New Perspectives on Black Educational History.* Boston: G. K. Hall and Co., 1978.

This book is a collection of essays in Afro–American educational history. The essays are detailed accounts of specific educational issues and problems facing minorities, viewed within the larger social, political, and economic context of American society. The editors primarily undertake to provide new perspectives on previously documented historical accounts of black education by citing specific works and giving brief critiques on them. Some of the authors reviewed are Carter G. Woodson, Horace Mann Bond, and W. E. B. DuBois. The issues covered by the essays include Quaker beneficence and black control, the

Hampton model of normal school industrial education, a case study on Fisk University, the transformation of Howard University School of Law, and an historical perspective on the desegregated school, among others.

447. Froe, Otis D., and Otyce B. Froe.* *The Easy Way to Better Grades.* 2d ed. New York: Arco Publishing Co., 1959.

Addressed to both full- and part-time students and is applicable at both the high school and college level, this book is designed to help students develop the skill necessary for succeeding in school. Practical methods of study and learning are discussed and suggested. Note especially the thirty principles of study and learning that preface the text, as well as section 3, which deals with the planning of a study-recreation-work-rest schedule. The text abounds with illustrations and exercises.

448. Froe, Otis D., and Maurice A. Lee.** *How to Become a Successful Student.* New York: Arco Publishing Co., 1959.

This book is designed to help students succeed in school. A practical guide to methods of study and learning, it discusses study techniques, effective reading and listening, notetaking, quizzes and examinations, and how to make the fullest use of educational resources and facilities. A useful guide for all students.

449. Gallot, Mildred B. G. *A History of Grambling State University.* Lanham, Md.: University Press of America, 1985.

This book traces the emergence and establishment of Grambling State University as one of the nation's best-known black institutions. It reveals the ongoing problems the university faces, including disparities in funding between black and white institutions, discontent among blacks, and opposition from whites. It also provides an insight into the unique personalities and philosophies of the three university presidents who have shaped the institution.

450. Gardner, William E. *Reducing Aspiration Conflict Among Minority Youth*. Ardmore, Pa.: Resources for Human Development Inc., 1982.

451. Garibaldi, Antoine M., ed. *Black Colleges and Universities: Challenges for the Future*. New York: Praeger Publishers, 1984.

This volume focuses on those institutions established primarily for the education of blacks, although in most cases their charters were not exclusionary. The study asks how effective black colleges have been—and will be—in producing leaders for the black community. What has the role of these colleges been in the past, and what should it be in the future? How can black colleges meet the changing needs of today's society? What are the external factors influencing the direction these schools will take in the years to come?

452. Gary, Lawrence E., and Aaron Favors, eds. *Restructuring the Educational Process: A Black Perspective*. Washington, D.C.: Institute for Urban Affairs and Research, Howard University, 1975.

This book is the result of a workshop sponsored jointly by Howard University's Institute for Urban Affairs and Research, Center for the Study of Handicapped Children and Youth, School of Education, and Institute for Child Development and Family Life. Three broad areas discussed are Afro–American lifestyles and educational development, policy and organizational development in education, and curriculum and student development.

453. Gayles, Anne Richardson, ed. *Instructional Planning in the Secondary School: Selected Readings*. New York: David McKay Co., 1973.

Designed for prospective high school teachers, this book explores the importance of instructional planning, the relationship between culture and educational processes fundamental to learning and teaching, guidelines for achieving a continuous process in instructional planning, and other related topics. A text of special interest to the student–teacher.

454. Gayles, Anne Richardson, and Larney G. Rackley. *Proven and Promising Educational Innovations in Secondary Schools.* New York: Simon and Schuster, 1976.

This work is geared toward "putting educational theory into practice in a practical method." It will prove useful in college and university classes and seminars that relate to innovations in secondary education. It is hoped that this book will motivate school officials to experiment with different teaching strategies and thus increase their effectiveness.

455. Gentry, Atron A., et al. *Urban Education: The Hope Factor.* Philadelphia: W. B. Saunders, 1972.

456. Gifford, Bernard R., ed. *Test Policy and Test Performance: Education, Language, and Culture.* Norwell, Mass.: Kluwer Academic Publishers, 1989.

This book, the second of a two–volume set, contains papers prepared for presentation at a conference, that was held at the University of California at Berkeley, December 11–13, 1986. It provides a further review of testing policy and offers guidance for future testing policies. Includes index.

457. Giles, Raymond H., Jr. *Black Studies in Public Schools.* New York: Praeger Publishers, 1974.

Details the goals, instructional materials, and teacher preparation of twenty–five black studies programs in large urban school districts of eleven northern, midwestern, and western states. It outlines the educational objectives of these programs, and shows how these programs originated, how they operate, and how each district measures the effectiveness of its own program.

458. ————. *The West Indian Experience in British Schools: Multi-Racial Education and Social Disadvantage in London.* London: Heinemann Educational Publishers Ltd, 1977.

This book describes the special educational needs of West Indian pupils in socially disadvantaged areas, as perceived by their teachers. The author has edited tape-recorded interviews with directors and teachers from seventeen schools to provide a fascinating account of the many different assumptions related to the special needs of West Indians pupils, and the teaching strategies designed to address them in multiracial schools. He offers analysis of the various issues and concerns that are raised in the interviews and concludes that, while schools and their neighborhoods are very diverse, there is still an urgent need for broad policy guidelines for minority groups.

459. Glasgow, Ann Duncan. *Black Leadership in Urban Schools: A Focus on the Nation's Capital.* Framingham, Mass.: Wellesley Press, 1974.

This book publishes research on how black high school principals in Washington, D.C. perceive their own leadership behavior. The study does not report any significant differences between the self-perceptions of black and white principals. It also shows that black principals see themselves as competent for leadership roles in professional staffed organizations.

460. Godwin, Winfred L. *The Academic Common Market.* Atlanta, Ga.: Southern Regional Educational Board, 1975.

461. Godwin, Winfred L., and Peter B. Mann,* eds. *Higher Education: Myths, Realities, and Possibilities.* Atlanta, Ga.: Southern Regional Educational Board, 1972.

462. Godwin, Winfred L., and James Lorenzo Wattenbarger,* eds. *The Community College in the South: Progress and Prospects.* Daytona, Fla.: Southern Work Conference, 1962.

463. Goodwin, Bennie Eugene. *The Emergence of Black Colleges: An Introduction to the Origins of Black Institutions of Higher Learning in the United States.* Jersey City, N.J.: Goodpatrick Publishers, 1974.

   This book gives a brief introduction to the origin of predominantly black institutions of higher education. Included is a list of black colleges, universities, and other institutions of higher education, as well as their controllers, locations and founding dates.

464. Gordon, Edmund Wyatt, and Doxey A. Wilkerson. *Compensatory Education for the Disadvantaged; Programs and Practices: Preschool Through College.* New York: College Entrance Examination Board, 1966.

   This book presents a critical evaluation of compensatory educational programs for disadvantaged children of all races and national origins. In addition, it focuses on such important issues as the reasons for compensatory education, the recruitment of teachers, preparation and in-service training, curriculum innovation, the role of the parents and the community, and the recent inadequate approach to the education of disadvantaged children. On the basis of these variables, the authors discuss the challenges for the future.

465. Grady,** Michael K., and Charles Vert Willie. *Metropolitan School Desegregation: A Case Study of Saint Louis.* Bristol, Ind.: Wyndham Hall Press, 1986.

   Sponsored by the Danforth Foundation, this study was undertaken to examine the nature and implications of the Voluntary Transfer Program in the St. Louis area.

466. Grant, Carl A. *Bringing Teaching to Life: An Introduction to Education.* Boston: Allyn and Bacon, 1982.

   This book offers frameworks for thinking through problems related to education. According to Grant, it is designed to help the student become a "teacher" and not a babysitter or crowd-control employee for a school system. It does not offer recipes or guarantees for such concerns as discipline. The author uses interviews, cartoons, topical essays, photographs, and various exhibits to "bring teaching to life." Acceptance and appreciation of human diversity as it relates to age, class, handicap, race, and sex are integrated throughout the chapters and photographs.

467. ―――, ed. *Preparing for Reflective Teaching.* Boston: Allyn and Bacon, 1984.

Divided into five chapters, this book is designed to help the reader think reflectively and critically about teaching. Each chapter is preceded by a discussion and questions pertaining to the several articles in the chapter, many of which were written especially for this book in response to the invitation: "If you had only five or ten minutes to talk with a group of prospective teachers about your area of interest, what would you say?"

468. ―――, ed. *Sifting and Winnowing: An Exploration, the Relationship Between Multi-Cultural Education and CBTE.* Madison: University of Wisconsin Teacher Corps Associates, 1975.

469. Grant, Carl A., and Christine E. Sleeter.** *After the School Bell Rings.* Philadelphia: The Falmer Press, 1986.

Situated within the camp of conflict theory, this three-year ethnographic study analyzes the daily reality of school life for teachers, students, and administrators in a desegregated and mainstreamed junior high school. It also analyzes ways in which the school perpetuates social inequality based on race, social class, gender, and handicap, and also ways in which such inequalities are challenged. Includes a plan for action, a bibliography, a subject index, and an author index.

470. ―――. *Turning on Learning: Five Approaches for Multicultural Teaching Plans for Race, Class, Gender, and Disability.* Columbus, Ohio: Merrill Publishing Co., 1989.

For student teachers and students in practicum courses, this text contains forty–eight lesson plans that cover a variety of subject areas and grade levels, 1–12, as well as ten action research activities that investigate the various dimensions of teaching, such as learning styles and textbook analysis. Includes an index.

471.   Green, Robert Lee. *The Urban Challenge: Poverty and Race.* Chicago: Follett Publishing Co., 1977.

A survey of the current state of urban problems and recommendations for specific solutions. The author looks into all aspects of the urban challenge, including unemployment, housing, health care, education, welfare, law enforcement, finance, and power.

472.   ————, ed. *Racial Crisis in American Education.* Chicago: Follett Publishing Co., 1969.

The various papers in this book examine such issues in urban schools as curriculum, language, community control, teacher training, compensatory education, and separatism. The main theme is that minority children can learn and that it is up to the school system to adopt methods that will be successful in teaching all students.

473.   Green, Robert Lee, with Frances S. Thomas,* eds. *Metropolitan Desegregation.* New York: Plenum Press, 1985.

With the assistance of Frances S. Thomas, Green describes and analyzes the New Castle County (Wilmington), Delaware, desegregation experience. In his introductory chapter, he sketches the history of school desegregation and suggests that segregated schooling tends to be inferior schooling. Includes bibliographies and index.

474.   Green, Robert Lee., et al.* *The Educational Status of Children During the First School Year Following Four Years of Little or No Schooling.* East Lansing: School for Advanced Studies

Research Services, College of Education, Michigan State University, 1966.

The study in this monograph, a follow–up study of school–deprived black children in Prince Edward County, Virginia, October 1966, was undertaken to determine the effects of a short period of formal education on a sample of children from a private school system known as the Prince Edward County Free School Association. These children were previously deprived of formal education due to the closing of the public schools in the county. It was found that resumed formal education brought significant gains in measured intelligence to the sample. There was also a slight increase in measured achievement. Levels of educational and occupational aspiration, it was found, were related to schooling. The students displayed favorable attitudes toward their resumed schooling.

475. ————, et al.* *The Educational Status of Children in a District Without Public Schools.* East Lansing: Bureau of Educational Research, College of Education, Michigan State University, 1964.

This monograph, the results of a cooperative research project, investigates the backgrounds of the adult and nonadult Afro–American members of the Prince Edward County, Virginia, community and merges this formation with tests and interviews done at a later date. The project addresses the role of formal education in our society. There are two parts to this study. In the first phase, parents and guardians of school–aged children are questioned to determine the number of children, their ages, their educational levels, the types of schools they have attended, and the related experiences they have had in the last four years. The second phase focuses on the effects of the school closing on the educational and social life of the Afro–American community. Chapter 5 deals with conclusions.

476. Greene, Harry Washington. *Holders of Doctorates Among American Negroes: An Educational and Social Study of Negroes Who Have Earned Doctoral Degrees in Course,*

1876–1943. Boston: Meador Publishing Co, 1946. Reprint. Newton, Mass.: Crofton, 1974.

A documented survey of Afro–American holders of doctorates during the inquiry period of 1876–1943. It examines the Afro–American doctorates' output, achievement, occupational status, and affiliation with professional and learned societies. Factors prohibiting creative scholarship among black men and women who have earned doctoral degrees are also touched upon in this informative survey.

477. Gurin,** Patricia, and Edgar G. Epps. *Black Consciousness, Identity, and Achievement: A Study of Students in Historically Black Colleges.* New York: John Wiley and Sons, 1975.

Based on a series of studies conducted on black college campuses from 1964–1970, the book focuses on the consciousness, identity, and achievement of the black student on the black campus. The aspects of (1) individual achievement goals, (2) collected achievements as expressed through social action, and (3) the relationship between the previous two and how each is influenced by precollege family and demographic background, personal motivation, and the students' environment are dealt with in great depth and in a scholarly manner. Special attention is given to the concept of group as contrasted with individually oriented motivation among black students.

478. Guthrie,** James W. and Rodney J. Reed. *Educational Administration and Policy: Effective Leadership for American Education.* Englewood Cliffs, N.J.: Prentice–Hall, 1986.

479. Hale–Benson, Janice E. *Black Children: Their Roots, Culture, and Learning Styles.* Rev. ed. Baltimore, Md.: Johns Hopkins University Press, 1986.

This updated edition with a new preface and epilogue by the author draws on the fields of anthropology, sociology, history, and psychology to explore the effects of black American culture on a child's intellectual development. As black children are acculturated at home and in the black community, Hale–Benson argues, they develop cognitive patterns and behaviors that can prove to be incompatible with the school environment. This book proposes curricular reforms that would allow black children to pursue their strengths and succeed in school and in the workplace.

480. Halliburton, Warren Jennings, and Erwin Goss,* eds. *America's Color Caravan.* New York: Educational Reading Aids Corp., 1971.

481. Hankerson, Henry Edward. *Promoting Pre–School Curriculum and Teaching.* Bristol, Ind.: Wyndham Hall Press, 1987.

This book combines curriculum and instruction, and bridges the gap from theory to practice. It is a fundamental resource and action guide for caregivers. It addresses questions such as "How do children's learning styles influence curriculum?" "How do children learn?" How can we tell when teaching, learning, and curriculum are operating together?"

482. Hankins, Lela Ruth. *Biology: A Problem Solving Approach.* New York: Carlton Press, 1970.

This book stresses an inquiry approach for teaching biology to non–science majors for the purposes of general education. Includes syllabus, laboratory experiments, other student activities, and a bibliography.

483. Harper, Frederick Douglas. *Black Students: White Campus.* Washington, D.C.: APGA Press, 1975.

This seventy–two–page book is designed to be a supplementary textbook for counselors and personnel administrators. The author combines both research and case studies to present a comprehensive view of the challenges faced by black students on predominantly white campuses. The references presented at the end of each chapter are extensive and provide good sources for further research in this area.

484.   Harris, Marquis Lafayette. *The Voice in the Wilderness.* Boston: Christopher Publishing House, 1941.

Harris offers a critical evaluation of higher education in this society. He stresses the importance of religious conviction and sensitivity in elementary and secondary teachers, and discusses Afro–American social philosophy.

485.   Harris,* Norene, Nathaniel Jackson, and Carl E. Rydingsword.* *The Integration of American Schools: Problems, Experiences, Solutions.* Boston: Allyn and Bacon, 1975.

The authors, writing in an open and lively style, describe and analyze the effects of desegregation and integration in public education. Based upon personal experiences, interviews, newspaper articles, speeches, and insight, this collection of essays focuses on issues such as busing; what happens when black and white children are grouped together and why; and how to establish quality education for blacks in integrated settings. Each section include a bibliography to facilitate further exploration of the subject matter.

486.   Harris, William McKinley, Sr. *A Design for Desegregation Evaluation.* Washington, D.C.: University Press of America, 1976.

Motivated by Afro–Americans' demand to know the impact desegregated schools have on their community, the author argues for the adoption of the Urban Dynamics model to evaluate the impact of desegregation in Seattle public schools. Includes footnotes and a bibliography.

487.   Haskins, James. *Diary of a Harlem Schoolteacher.* New York: Grove Press, 1969. Reprint. New York: Stein and Day, 1979.

In describing his experience as a Harlem schoolteacher, Haskins gives a brief personality profile of his students, many of whom live in substandard housing and areas infested with drug addicts. The present educational system, Haskins argues, has not been effective in meeting the needs of these students. He suggests that America's educational institutions need to be restructured and reorganized.

488. —————, ed. *Black Manifesto for Education.* New York: William Morrow and Co., 1973.

In this book, eminent black educators respond to the white diagnosis of the educational problems of black children. This diagnosis has led to faulty prescriptions, such as compensatory education. The educators maintain that the problems encountered by black children in the public schools do not rest with the children, their families, or their backgrounds. Instead, they attribute the problem to the school itself, its basic structure, and the educational process. Divergent views about the solutions to the problems are offered.

489. Hawley,** Willis D., Robert L. Crain,** Christine H. Rossell,** et al. *Strategies for Effective Desegregation: Lessons from Research.* Lexington, Mass.: Lexington Books, 1983.

The authors—one black and five nonblacks—analyze effective school desegregation strategies, which include pupil assignments, parent and community involvement, in-service training, and administration. The impact of desegregation on housing, curriculum, personnel, and discipline is also documented and discussed. Includes notes, tables, bibliography, and index. The other coauthors are Mark A. Smylie,** Ricardo R. Fernandez,** and William T. Trent.

490. Haynes, Carrie Ayers. *Good News on Grape Street: The Transformation of a Ghetto School.* New York: Citation Press, 1975.

The story of the transformation of a "demoralized" ghetto school in Watts (Grape Street School) into a model learning environment with open classrooms, integrated curriculum, cross-age grouping, and staff–in service training programs. Under the administrative leadership of Carrie Ayers Haynes, principal of the school, this successful transition awarded Grape Street School much attention in such media as *Newsweek,* the *Christian Science Monitor,* and *National Educational Television.*

491. Haynes, Leonard L., III., ed. *A Critical Examination of the Adams Case: A Source Book.* Washington, D.C.: Institute for Services to Education 1978.

This book details the history of the *Adams v. Richardson* (1973) case, a class action suit filed by the National Association for the Advancement of Colored People (NAACP) against the Department of Health, Education, and Welfare (HEW), alleging defaults on the part of HEW in its duty to enforce Title VI of the 1964 Civil Rights Act. The defaults concern ten cases in which southern and border states were operating dual systems of education. Haynes's editing and presentation of the legal documents are particularly effective.

492. Heilman,** Arthur W., and Elizabeth Ann Holmes. *Really Reading.* Columbus, Ohio: Charles E. Merrill Co., 1976.

This book draws together a variety of word roots, phrase reading, vocabulary, and conceptual knowledge useful to students. The companion workbook is designed for a developmental reading skills program, effective in enhancing independent reading skills as well as in supplementing standard curriculum through individualized instruction.

493. ————. *Smuggling Language into the Teaching of Reading.* Columbus, Ohio: Charles E. Merrill Co., 1972.

Why are so many children not learning to read? This text demonstrates different skills and methods for making reading meaningful to children. One technique is to "smuggle" language into reading and make it as attractive as possible. Each chapter contains actual exercises as examples of how child participation in language can be an incentive to reading.

494. Henderson, George. *America's Other Children: Public Schools OutSide Suburbia.* 1st ed. Norman: University of Oklahoma Press, 1971.

Focusing on rural schools and small communities, the author attempts to bridge the gap between rural and urban schools. "Problems of Disadvantaged Youth, Urban and Rural," "The School of Appalachia," "What Migrant Farm Children Learn," and "The Desegregation of Southern Schools: A Psychiatric Study" are among the fifty-one articles. The book is divided into six parts with an introduction to each part.

495. ————. *Introduction to American Education: A Human Relations Approach.* Norman: University of Oklahoma Press, 1978.

This is an up-to-date review of the major sociocultural forces affecting American education. It is interdisciplinary in its approach and draws from sociology, psychology, and anthropology in addition to studies in the field of education. The author emphasizes current problems in planning curricula for today's students, placing special emphasis on human rights issues: racism, sexism, cultural pluralism, and student rights. Separate chapters are dedicated to drug and alcohol abuse. This book provides data, techniques, and strategies for the improvement of school conditions.

496. ————, ed. *Education for Peace: Focus on Mankind.* Washington, D.C.: Association for Supervision and Curriculum Development, 1973.

Presupposing a need for greater commitment to peace, this book includes literacy references and statistical data that can present a framework for improving the effectiveness of educators for peace. The book discusses the implications for education making a comprehensive study of relationships between man and his total environment, among other issues. The four appendixes present data on the human crisis, a teacher's guide, a selected bibliography on international education, additional resources and consortium on peace research, and information on education and development.

497. Henderson, George, and Robert F. Bibens.** *Teachers Should Care: Social Perspectives of Teaching.* New York: Harper and Row, 1970.

This book contains information and teaching techniques useful to both students and teachers. It discusses the importance of grade transfers; the way school records affect reputations; parent–teacher conferences; discipline; and goals for better human relations.

498. Hendrick,** Irving G., and Reginald Lanier Jones, eds. *Student Dissent in the Schools.* Boston: Houghton Mifflin Co., 1972.

This book examines the relationship between activist students and personnel in public secondary schools. The final chapter, "Directions for the Future," should prove most helpful to educators.

499. Hesburgh,** Theodore Martin, Paul A. Miller,* and Clifton R. Wharton. *Patterns for Lifelong Learning.* San Francisco: Jossey–Bass, 1973.

This volume grew out a project conducted at the University of Notre Dame by several task forces on continuing education and the authors. The major sections are entitled "Continuing Education and the Future," "Universities and the Learning Society," and "The Lifelong University." An attempt to present broad effective educational ideas and systems, this book is of great value to educators and the general public.

500. Hill,** Beverly, Rick Coger, and Tony Kwak.** *Instructional Development: The Process and the Profession.* Milwaukee, Wis.: Health Sciences Communication Association, 1978.

501. Hill, Johnny R. *A Study of the Public-Assisted Black College Presidency.* New York: Carlton Press, 1974.

502. Hohenshil,** Thomas H., and Johnnie Harris Miles, eds. *School Guidance Services: A Career Development Approach.* Dubuque, Iowa: Kendall/Hunt Publishing Co., 1976.

503. Holley, Joseph Winthrop. *Education and the Segregation Issue: A Program of Education for the Economic and Social Regeneration of the Southern Negro.* New York: William–Frederick Press, 1955.

   Holley discusses the historical and philosophical implications of state–supported education for blacks in a segregated milieu, and argues that economic and social regeneration of blacks must begin in the earliest years of education.

504. Holmes, Dwight Oliver W. *The Evolution of the Negro College.* College Park, Md.: McGrath Publishing Co., 1934. Reprint. New York: Arno Press, 1969.

   Using primary sources, Holmes examines the conditions under which black colleges were founded and studies the agencies primarily responsible for their development. The manuscript was Holmes's doctoral dissertation, completed at Teachers College, Columbia University.

505. Holtzclaw, William Henry. *The Black Man's Burden.* New York: Neal Publishing Co., 1915. Reprint. New York: Haskell House, 1971.

   This autobiography of the formal principal of Utica Normal and Industrial Institute is written in a series of autobiographical sketches, along with essays and articles the author published. It tells the story of rural life as experienced by most southern blacks. It is also the story of the black colleges and institutions that developed to meet the needs of these black people. The book is addressed not only to blacks but also to whites in the hopes that the two races may come to know each other more intimately. An introduction by Booker T. Washington and several photos of Utica and prominent people of the time are included.

506. Hudson, Herman C., ed. *How to Make It in College.* Bloomington: Indiana University Press, 1976.

A useful guide for college students, this book provides basic facts about dormitories, dating, drugs, I.Q. tests, program planning, effective study procedures, financial aid, counseling, and tutorial services. Included also are student exercises on budget making, term paper preparation, and techniques for job interviews. Real–life problems are illustrated through biographical sketches of students.

507. Hunte, Christopher Norman. *The Development of Higher Education in the West Indies.* 1st ed. Birmingham, Ala.: Banner Press, 1978.

508. Hunter, William Andrew, ed. *Multicultural Education Through Competency–based Teacher Education.* Washington, D.C.: American Association of Colleges for Teacher Education, 1974.

This book provides a social and historical view of education with an emphasis on multicultural education; it examines multicultural education from a black perspective and looks at some native American views on this topic. Finally, the book provides a cross–cultural approach to multicultural education and examines what our next steps in this area will be.

509. Hurst, Charles G. *Passport to Freedom, Education, Humanism, and Malcolm X.* Hamden, Conn.: Linnet Books, 1972.

To counteract the effects of racism on black youths in America, the educational structure has to be revitalized to meet the needs of black American youth. Malcolm X College, inspired by the humanistic message of Malcolm X on education for blacks, is presented as an example of how creative efforts on the part of competent persons can help to produce an environment suitable for developing human potential.

510. Jackson, Edward Merica. *Black Education in Contemporary America: A Crisis in Ambiguity.* Bristol, Ind.: Wyndham Hall Press, 1986.

This work includes topics such as "Black and White Colleges" and "The Rise of Multi–Cultural Education and the Decline of Black Studies." It argues that black Americans in higher education are currently enduring a crisis of identity brought on by the ambiguities of conflicting pressures and expectations of the present political economy and its blatant but hidden racism.

511. Jackson, John Henry. *History of Education from the Greeks to the Present Time.* Denver: Western Newspaper Union, 1903.

The author covers the development of education over a period of 2,000 years, beginning with the Greeks. He also includes biographical data on such noted black educators as Booker T. Washington, Richard Wright, Peter Clark, and Lucy Moten.

512. Jackson–Coppin, Fanny. *Reminiscences of School Life and Hints on Teaching.* Philadelphia: A. M. E. Book Concern, 1913. Reprint. New York: Garland Publishing, Inc., 1987.

513. Jahannes, Ja Arthur. *Postdoctoral Study in the U.S. 1977–78: A Guide to Institutions and Agencies Offering Postdoctoral Studies.* Hampton, Va.: Institute of Postdoctoral Study, 1978.

514. James, Richard L., and Ray Brown,* eds. *Emerging Concepts for Collaboration: Selected Papers.* Washington, D.C.: Association of Teacher Educators, 1975.

515. Jenkins, Martin D. *The Morgan State College Program: An Adventure in Higher Education.* Baltimore, Md.: Morgan State College Press, 1964.

Written by Martin D. Jenkins, former president of Morgan State, in collaboration with Albert N. Whiting and others, this work consists of "a portion of the President's Annual Report to the Board of Trustees for 1962–63." It contains a "description of what was at the time the most comprehensive compensatory education program in American higher education."

516. Johnson, Charles Spurgeon. *Education and the Cultural Crisis.* New York: Macmillan Co., 1951.

Johnson focuses upon cultural aspects of education found in schools. He argues that our schools tend to support the dominant cultural pattern of education while ignoring other cultural patterns. He recommends ways of counterbalancing this bias.

517. ———. *The Negro College Graduate.* Chapel Hill: University of North Carolina Press, 1938. Reprint. College Park, Md.: McGrath Publishing Co., 1969.

This book publishes the results of a study conducted by the General Education Board on the objective records of college and professionally trained blacks in the United States from 1826–1936. Its statistical data cover the number, distribution, and occupational adjustment of black graduates of colleges, professional, and vocational schools.

Johnson analyzes in detail the particular social factors that influence the number and status of black graduates. He also examines existing educational methods and aims in higher education and suggests educational modifications. He lists producers and distributors of multimedia materials on Afro-Americans and the peoples of Africa.

518. Johnson, Harry Alleyn. *Multimedia Materials for Afro-American Studies: A Curriculum Orientation and Annotated*

Bibliography of Resources. New York: R. R. Bowker Co., 1971.

This volume discusses ways of relating new technological and educational media to the ghetto youth and of integrating black studies, especially Afro-American history, into the curriculum. It also explores the sociological and psychological needs of ghetto youth.

519. Johnson, Kenneth R. *Teaching the Culturally Disadvantaged: A Rational Approach*. Palo Alto, Calif.: Science Research Associates, 1970.

Johnson's primary concern is to provide teachers of culturally disadvantaged children with some meaningful guides in this area. His suggestions are stimulating and useful.

520. Johnson, Roosevelt, ed. *Black Agenda for Career Education*. Columbus, Ohio: ECCA Publications, 1974.

In this anthology scholars and thinkers, including William F. Brazziel, Melvin Sikes, and Joseph Discon, discuss pertinent issues surrounding career education. References are made to evaluation and career education, the development of institutional goals in a public school system, and adaptation of the career education concept to correctional settings.

521. ―――, ed. *Black Scholars on Higher Education in the 70's*. Columbus, Ohio: ECCA Publications, 1974.

This collection of articles by the author and other prominent blacks in higher education addresses diverse issues, ranging from compensatory programs for blacks to higher education for black inmates. This book is of special interest to policymakers in the areas of student development, research, administration, and personnel development.

522. Johnson, Simon Otis. *Better Discipline: A Practical Approach*. Springfield, Ill.: Charles C. Thomas, 1980.

Designed to be an aid to teachers, principals, and others, this book discusses some of the major causes of classroom problems, as well as suggestions for eliminating them. Chapters 3 and 5 are devoted to suggestions, activities, and tips that can be used to prevent discipline problems, and ways to eliminate them if they are already present. Chapter 4 reflects discipline as it relates to minority groups. In this book, a minority means a black person in a school or community. Chapter 5 focuses on games and activities as a means of preventing disruptive behavior. There are fifteen activities; each is outlined in terms of objectives, materials, procedures, evaluation, and follow–up.

523.   ————. *Good Morning Mrs. "B"*. Dubuque, Iowa: Kendall/Hunt Publishing Co., 1973.

Based on his own experiences as a principal in an integrated school system, Johnson has given us what is really a novel about a new teacher's first year working with students from different cultural backgrounds. Somewhat inept, Mrs. "B" allows one student to disrupt the entire class and follows his edicts without being aware that she is doing so. Unfortunately, it is very difficult for Mrs. "B" to see the need to change her teaching style. The book illustrates that although need for a change in teaching styles may be obvious to many others, it does not occur unless the teacher sees a need for it.

524.   ————. *Multicultural Elementary Classrooms*. Dubuque, Iowa: Kendall/Hunt Publishing Co., 1972.

This book serves as a guide for both current and prospective teachers in the following respects: (1) to help them develop curricula for children in a multicultural setting, (2) to make them aware of barriers to effective teaching and learning brought on by their lack of understanding of cultural differences among children and between themselves and children, and (3) to set forth paradigms of value in resolving classroom problems. The book depicts five classroom situations familiar to most teachers and suggests solutions to them. It also includes a rating scale of ten teaching characteristics with a general explanation of each. This is intended to motivate the teacher to seek additional help in the areas he or she identifies as weak.

525. Johnson, Sylvia T. *The "Measurement Mystique": Issues in Selection for Professional Schools and Employment.* Occasional paper of the Institute for the Study of Educational Policy, no. 02. Washington, D.C.: Institute for the Study of Educational Policy, Howard University, 1979.

Do the selection methods used by schools accurately predict performance in the first and second years of school? Can these methods determine the calibre of the applicant upon completion of school? According to Johnson, tests are necessary, but educational and vocational decisions cannot depend entirely on them since the tests do not accurately assess the aptitude of all students, especially minority students. Inspired by the *Bakke* (1978) case, Johnson carefully discusses the admissions criteria of various medical schools: GPAs, MCAT scores, faculty recommendations, socioeconomic and demographic ratings, and other factors such as personality and direction of interest. She examines the origins and identification of test bias in the United States, and recommends modifications in selection procedures for professional schools.

526. Johnston, Gladys Styles, and Carol Camp Yeakey, eds. *Research and Thought in Administrative Theory: Developments in the Field of Educational Administration.* Washington, D.C.: University Press of America, 1986.

This compilation of essays represents an intellectual dialogue among scholars who pioneered the theory movement in educational administration that began in the 1950s. It explores how the movement revolutionized the field with its new emphasis on theory and research. Essays by noted organizational theorists provide a provocative synthesis of more than thirty-three years of research, and constitute a comprehensive account of the evolving issues in the field of educational administration.

527. Jones, Edward Allen. *A Candle in the Dark: A History of Morehouse College.* Valley Forge, Pa.: Judson Press, 1967.

The story of Morehouse College is the story of higher education for many Afro–Americans in the deep South, and of the social, political, and economic difficulties they faced and continue to face. This history can boast of its success in creating men of worth and psychological freedom, who have contributed significantly to their environment. The book concludes with a list of Morehouse graduates who have earned doctorates. Included are photographs of presidents of Morehouse College and of some of the buildings and social events relating to the college.

528. Jones, Faustine Childress. *A Traditional Model of Educational Excellence: Dunbar High School of Little Rock, Arkansas.* Washington, D.C.: Howard University Press, 1981.

This book explores the success of a southern black public high school. Spanning twenty–five years, 1930–1955, this study evaluates the results of questionnaires, examines school records, and presents interviews with alumni and faculty for the ingredients that have produced remarkably successful graduates. Jones reveals the high level of cooperation among the community, administrators, teachers, and students, and the efforts of teachers to foster positive self–images in their students. She concludes that the Paul Laurence Dunbar High School in Little Rock, Arkansas, is an important and viable model for public school systems. The data are supported by appendixes that profile the alumni, the curriculum, and the school.

529. Jones, Gilbert Haven. *Education in Theory and Practice.* Boston: R. G. Badger, 1919.

This book discusses various theoretical and practical aspects of traditional education systems, including the concept of education, the nature and objectives of education, and methodology.

530. Jones, Leon. *From Brown to Boston: Desegregation in Education, 1954–1974.* 2 vols. Metuchen, N.Y.: Scarecrow Press, 1979.

This two–volume work comprises literature on desegregation in education covering the period from the historic *Brown* decision in 1954 to the *Milliken v. Bradley* ruling in 1974 and the Boston busing crisis of the same year. In addition to a foreword by Roy Wilkins, volume 1 contains an introduction that represents the author's "views on the issues and the problems of school desegregation" during the twenty–year period under consideration. The bulk of the volume consists of a bibliography of summarized articles and books pertaining to school desegregation. Volume 2 contains summaries of legal cases reported in *Race Relations Law Survey.* Appendixes containing *Brown, Milliken,* and indexes are also included. Together, the two volumes include "over 5000 summary statements" covering more than 2,000 pages.

531. Jones, Lewis Wade, and Herman Hodge Long. *The Negotiation of Desegregation in Ten Southern Cities.* Nashville: Race Relations Department of the American Missionary Association, United Church Board for Homeland Ministries at Fisk University, 1965.

532. Jones, Reginald Lanier. *New Directions in Special Education.* Boston: Allyn and Bacon, 1970.

A collection of essays on trends and developments in special education for teachers in special education, administrators, and counselors, as well as a textbook in advanced courses in the education and psychology of exceptional children. This four–part book presents teaching methods and readings on curriculum and teaching, technology, and federal programs concerned with the exceptional child.

533. ———, ed. *Black Adult Development and Aging.* Berkeley: Cobb and Henry, 1989.

534. ———, ed. *Problems and Issues in Education of Exceptional Children.* Boston: Houghton Mifflin Co., 1971.

     Essays on the controversial issues and problems pertaining to the education of exceptional children. The volume also covers the field of handicapped children.

535. ———, ed. *Psychoeducational Assessment of Minority Group Children: A Casebook.* Richmond, Calif.: Cobb and Henry, 1988.

536. Jones, Reginald Lanier, and Donald L. Macmillan,** eds. *Special Education in Transition.* Boston: Allyn and Bacon, 1974.

     This collection of articles explores new perspectives in the area of special education. Various authorities focus on a wide range of issues, such as alternative curricula, the use and abuse of educational categories, "tracking," and the integration of exceptional children into regular classes.

537. Joyce,** William W., and James A. Banks, eds. *Teaching the Language Arts to Culturally Different Children.* Reading, Mass.: Addison–Wesley Publishing Co., 1971.

538. Kimmons, Willie James. *Black Administrators in Public Community Colleges: Self–Perceived Role and Status.* New York: Carlton Press, 1977.

     How do black educators see themselves and their positions of authority in local colleges? Kimmons examines the personal and professional backgrounds of black administrators and brings out some interesting findings. The black administrators generally felt their salaries were below average when compared with those of administrators in predominantly white institutions. The social perspective this study presents is good food for thought, and indeed, all aspects touched upon in these pages are worthy of consideration.

539. Knox, Ellis O. *Democracy and the District of Columbia Public Schools: A Study of Recently Integrated Public Schools.* Washington, D.C.: Judd and Detweiler, 1957.

A 1957 study of the integration of District of Columbia public schools. Knox describes the inequities of segregated schools, the D.C. public school testing program, health hazards, and the effects of accelerated migration on D.C. public schools.

540. Kunjufu, Jawanza. *Children Are the Reward of Life: Parent/Teacher Guidelines for Maximizing Black Children's Potential.* 2d ed. Chicago: Afro-Am Publishing Co., 1982.

541. ————. *Countering the Conspiracy to Destroy Black Boys.* 1st ed. Chicago: Afro-Am Publishing Co., 1984.

Choosing to concentrate on Afro-American boys because he feels that the Afro-American males pose the greatest threat to white supremacy, Kunjufu describes how these boys are systematically programmed for failure so that, when they become adults, they pose little danger to the status quo. He divided the book into four chapters--"The Conspiracy to Destroy Black Boys," "Fourth-Grade Failure Syndrome," "Male Seasoning," and Counter-Conspiracy Strategies." He contends that there are many contributors to the conspiracy, ranging from those who are more obvious to the less visible and silent partners who, through their indifference, perpetuate white racism and white male supremacy. According to Kunjufu, this passive group of conspirators consist of parents, educators, and white liberals who deny being racist but, through their silence, allow institutional racism to continue. The public school is cited as the most flagrant institution. He suggests more Afro-American male teachers be assigned to the primary grades, particularly fourth grade, where many boys begin to exhibit signs of intellectual retrogression. Also he believes in a strong principal, a strong family unit, and a more concerned and aroused community to correct the dehumanization of Afro-American boys.

542. ———. *Developing Positive Self-Images and Discipline in Black Children.* 1st ed. Chicago: African American Images, 1984.

543. ———. *A Talk with Jawanza: Critical Issues in Educating African American Youth.* 1st ed. Chicago: African American Images, 1989.

In this work, written in a question–and–answer format, Kunjufu calls for revamping culturally insensitive curricula, and for recruiting trained teachers who can function within the expectations of an Afrocentric educational environment and who have higher academic expectations of black youth. He stresses the need to increase the number of black male teachers, particularly at the elementary school level.

544. Lawrence, Margaret Morgan. *The Mental Health Team in the Schools.* New York: Behavioral Publications, 1971.

545. Lemelle, Tilden J., and Wilbert J. Lemelle. *The Black College: Strategy for Achieving Relevancy.* New York: Praeger Publishers, 1969.

Particular areas of interest in this study include the development of black colleges; an ideology for black educational development; a design for institutional administration, faculty, and student reevaluation and renewal; the problem of support for black colleges; the future of black colleges and their effects on the black community and on black/white relations; and the influence of education in black colleges on a pluralistic democracy.

546. Lewis, James, Jr. *Administering the Individualized Instruction Program.* West Nyack, N.Y.: Parker Publishing Co., 1971.

Lewis focuses on individualized instruction as a way of making the education process more effective and relevant to the concerns of special students. He takes into account differences in levels of ability, rates of learning, and learning goals.

Understanding these differences is important to reforming liberal education.

547. ――――. *Appraising Teacher Performance.* West Nyack, N.Y.: Parker Publishing Co., 1973.

In this book, Lewis examines the necessity for teacher appraisals, alternative approaches (as well as his own), and ways of carrying out his learning–centered approach and appraisal. Lewis devotes several chapters to personal and professional skills and objectives, and to the use of motivation and perception for improving teacher performance.

548. ――――. *The Tragedies in American Education.* New York: Exposition Press, 1971.

According to Lewis, the tragedy in American education is the public educational system, which perpetuates an outdated curriculum and an antique teacher–training system. Other ills, says Lewis, are the lack of federal and state financial support and a dearth of effective parental involvement in the schools. The greatest tragedy, Lewis believes, is the effect all this has on the child.

549. Lightfoot, Sara Lawrence. *The Good High School: Portraits of Character and Culture.* New York: Basic Books, 1983.

Winner of the 1984 American Educational Research Association Book Award, this book describes how six high school cultures emerge as an expression not only of educational aims but also of cultural aspirations of subcultures within the society. The six high schools are George Washington Carver High School in Atlanta; John F. Kennedy High School in the Bronx, New York; Highland Park High School in Chicago; Brookline High School in Brookline, Massachusetts; St. Paul's in Concord, New Hampshire; and Milton Academy, near Boston.

550. ――――. *Worlds Apart: Relationships Between Families and Schools.* New York: Basic Books, 1978.

This volume explores the complex relationship between American families and schools—its conflicts, tensions, and harmonies. Lightfoot brings in diverse viewpoints, including those of institutions, social structures, teachers, and parents. She views the present state of the school–family relationship in terms of its roots in the sociopolitical and cultural history of America. Lightfoot offers suggestions for the direction our educational institutions might take in the future.

551. Logan, Rayford Whittingham. *Howard University: The First Hundred Years 1867–1967.* New York: New York University Press, 1969.

Logan discusses the growth and development of this institution during the administration of Mordecai W. Johnson (1926–1960). It was during this time that Howard University was awarded full accreditation. Logan also gives us brief biographies of many faculty and graduates who attained prominence in local, national, and international affairs, including Charles H. Houston, William H. Hastie, James Nabrit, and Ralph J. Bunche. Of particular interest is Logan's discussion of Howard University's involvement in international activities and civil rights movements (1867–1967).

552. Lomotey, Kofi. *African–American Principals: School Leadership and Success.* Westport, Conn.: Greenwood Press, 1989.

553. ———, ed. *Going to School: The African–American Experience.* Albany: State University of New York, 1990.

554. Lyda, Wesley J., and Napoleon William.* *Who's Who Among Negro Principals, Jeanes Curriculum Directors, and State Instructional Consultants in Georgia, 1954–1964.* Dallas: Royal Publishing Co., 1964.

555. Lynk, Miles Vandahurst. *The Afro–American School Speaker and Gems of Literature for School Commencements, Literary Circles, Debating Clubs, and Rhetoricals Generally.* Jackson, Tenn.: M. V. Lynk Publishing House, 1896.

556. Marfo, Kofi, Sylvia Walker, and Bernard Charles, eds. *Childhood Disability in Developing Countries: Issues in Habilitation and Special Education.* New York: Praeger Publishers, 1986.

This three-part book represents an effort to raise awareness about the magnitude of the childhood disability problem in developing countries and to provide some insights into how several dimensions of the problem are being addressed in different parts of the developing world. Part 1 deals with issues and research related to incidence, prevention, early detection, and habilitation. Part 2 concerns issues related to the education and training of disabled children. Part 3 focuses on social-psychological considerations, including a cross-cultural study of attitudes toward mentally retarded persons, using samples from Canada, Kenya, Barbados, Scotland, Peru, and Sierra Leone.

557. Martinez, Maurice M., Jr., and Josepha M. Weston,* eds. *School and Community Issues and Alternatives.* Dubuque, Iowa: Kendall/Hunt Publishing Co., 1976.

558. Maupin, Madeline Taylor. *Peer Group Counseling Policies and Human-Relations Workshops Procedures.* Louisville, Ky.: Printing Needs-Lincoln Foundation, 1975.

This book surveys procedures for conducting peer group counseling and student human relations workshops. It includes letters of recommendation and various forms used to implement successful guidance programs. Student comments before and after workshop experiences, newspaper stories, and pictures are also included. The material in this book is the result of actual guidance experiences tried and evaluated in a predominantly black, inner-city secondary school.

559. May, Lola June. *Teaching Mathematics in the Elementary School.* New York: Macmillan Co., 1970.

In this book Lola June May discusses the link between content and method in mathematics, and suggests imaginative ways of teaching mathematics in elementary school. She emphasizes student involvement and includes a helpful glossary.

560. ———. *Teaching Mathematics in the Elementary School.* 2d ed. New York: Free Press, 1974.

The author demonstrates how teachers in elementary school can present math to their pupils in an interesting way. In this second edition, she devotes chapter 1 to the role of the teacher and includes up-to-date material on teaching the metric system.

561. Mayberry, Claude, Jr., ed. *Urban Education: The City as a Living Curriculum.* Alexandria, Va.: Association for Supervision and Curriculum Development, 1980.

562. Mayer,** Robert R., Charles Edward King, Anne Border-Patterson, et al.** *The Impact of School Desegregation in a Southern City.* Lexington, Mass.: D. C. Heath and Co., 1974.

563. Mays, Robert E. *Supervising Student Teachers: A Practical Approach.* Dubuque, Iowa: Kendall/Hunt Publishing Co., 1978.

This handbook gives a general overview of teacher education at Indiana State University in Evansville. It outlines the roles of each member of a supervisory team, and discusses the limitations and responsibilities imposed by legal requirements and policy. The appendix presents evaluation and other special forms.

564. ———, comp. *Opening the Public School Curriculum.* Dubuque, Iowa: Kendall/Hunt Publishing Co., 1976.

This book, designed for teachers of graduate and undergraduate courses, is divided into three parts: "Openness in the Classroom," "The Nature of Openness," and "Now and Beyond." Many noteworthy advocates of open education have contributed articles. In the first selection, Ronald Baret argues for a philosophical commitment to the assumptions of open education. Other articles discuss operating principles of the open classroom and the complex nature of educational change. The book also reviews selected literature on open education.

565. McAllister, Jane Ellen. *Training of Negro Teachers in Louisiana.* New York: Columbia University, 1929.

This ninety–five–page text is based on a 1929 survey of black teacher training agencies in the state of Louisiana, including Southern University, Leland, and Straights colleges. McAllister discusses factors affecting the program, such as the supply and demand of black teachers. She evaluates the agencies and recommends remedial measures.

566. McKinney, Richard Ishmael. *Religion in Higher Education Among Negroes.* New Haven: Yale University Press, 1945.

McKinney examines the history of the relationship between religion and higher education for blacks in the United States; the attitudes of eighteen presidents of black colleges toward religion in higher education during the 1940–1941 school year; the extent of religion in curricula; and student attitudes toward religion. The appendix includes all the colleges that contributed in some form to the study. An extensive bibliography is provided for those interested in further research in this area.

567. McKinney, Theophilus Elisha, ed. *Higher Education Among Negroes.* Charlotte, N.C.: Johnson C. Smith University, 1932.

A collection of addresses delivered at the twenty–fifth anniversary of the presidency of Dr. Henry Lawrence McCrorey of Johnson C. Smith University by such notables as Carter G. Woodson and Mary McLeod Bethune. The speakers discuss Afro–American education in the twenty–five years prior to 1932, the situation in 1932, and what education would probably be like in the next twenty–five years. Contemporary scholars of Afro–American higher education will be interested in comparing their projections, made sixty years ago, with what has actually taken place in the decades since the thirties.

568. McLemore, William Prince. *Foundations of Urban Education.* Washington, D.C.: University Press of America, 1977.

569. ———, ed. *Social Studies Strategies for Today's Learners.* New York: MSS Information Corp., 1976.

570. Mercer, Walter Alexander. *Humanizing the Desegregated School: Guide for Teachers and Teacher Training.* New York: Vantage Press, 1973.

This book is particularly pertinent to students in elementary and secondary teacher training institutions. It looks at the difficulties of desegregating southern schools, and at the effects of training programs, desegregation of teachers, and relationships between the teacher and the principal.

571. ———. *Teaching in the Desegregated School: Guide to Intergroup Relations.* New York: Vantage Press, 1971.

Many books have been written on the education of black and white Americans. This book looks at teacher education in desegregated schools. Mercer tries to make teachers aware of their importance in molding young minds and of the harmful effect of holding prejudices, whether conscious or not, against the ethnic cultures of their students.

572. Meredith, James Howard. *Three Years in Mississippi.* Bloomington: Indiana University Press, 1966.

Meredith gives an account of his experiences as the first Afro–American to enter the University of Mississippi. He tells how he survived in an environment of hate and violence under the protection of U.S. marshals.

573. Miller, Lamar P., ed. *Equality of Educational Opportunity: A Hand–book for Research.* New York: AMS Press, 1974.

This compilation is designed to inspire more research in equality of educational opportunity. Material is presented in two historical frameworks: first, the history of American education, through which equality can be achieved; and, second, the development of educational research in the United States. The editors argue that complex problems remain to be solved.

574. ————, ed. *The Testing of Black Students: A Symposium.* Englewood Cliffs, N.J.: Prentice–Hall, 1974.

The symposium begins with the assumption that the most controversial and complex issue affecting the education of minorities in America today is the role of educational and psychological testing. The ten contributors review specific issues connected with testing, such as "The Latent Functions of Intelligence Testing in the Public Schools" (by Jane Mercer) and the heredity versus environment issue (by Lawrence Plotkin). Questions raised include how tests predict and measure school achievement, what the situational effects of testing are, and to what extent tests should be diagnostic or evaluative.

575. Mohr, Paul B. *A Cross–Cultural Program for Attitude Modification of White Students on a Predominantly Black University Campus; A Research Monograph.* Tallahassee: Florida A & M University, 1975.

576. Mohr, Paul B., Lillie S. Davis,* and Joshua Williams.* *Competency–based Teacher Education: Organization, Operation, Management.* Tallahassee: School of Education, Florida A & M University, 1973.

577. Moore, Bradley George. *Fifteen Methods of Teaching Secondary School Subjects.* New York: Carlton Press, 1983.

578. ————. *Great Teachers: Their Philosophic Thoughts Applied to Formal Education: Studying the Characteristics of Great Teachers Through the Ages.* New York: Carlton Press, 1980.

Summary, questions for consideration and discussion, suggested assignments, and selected readings at the end of each chapter enhance this work. Includes an index.

579. Moore, William, Jr. *Against the Odds.* 1st ed. San Francisco: Jossey–Bass, 1970.

The subject of this book is the so–called high–risk or marginal student, and the difficulties that student faces in a community college. Both the high–risk student and the two–year college, which often has the reputation of being a "remedial learning situation," are struggling with what might be called a crisis of identity. Little research has been done on the characteristics of the marginal students. But we know that faculty members at two–year colleges are often torn between adjusting the curriculum to accommodate the high–risk students and upholding the academic standards of the institution, which sometimes means expelling the ill–equipped students.

580. ———. *Blind Man on a Freeway.* San Francisco: Jossey–Bass, 1971.

Moore examines the crucial problems and issues facing the two–year college administrator and advocates more effective training for that professional educator. He discusses the effect of emerging groups such as militants, minorities, and the educationally disadvantaged students on the campus community. He also touches upon collective bargaining problems.

581. ———. *Community College Response to the High–Risk Student: A Critical Reappraisal.* Washington, D.C.: American Association of Community and Junior Colleges, 1976.

Community colleges claim success in remediating high–risk students so that these students can make normal academic progress. Appraising this claim, Moore points up the lack of hard evidence supporting it and contends that the problem of the poor academic achiever remains even beyond the community college.

Moore suggests that community colleges reevaluate their policies on the achievement problem and take a new and closer look at their general response to high-risk students.

582. Moore, William, Jr., and Lonnie H. Wagstaff. *Black Educators in White Colleges: Progress and Prospects.* 1st ed. San Francisco: Jossey-Bass, 1974.

The book is based on a survey of black faculty and administrators in white colleges and universities that included responses from both black and white faculty administrators and university heads. The book is a provocative and enlightening survey of the problems and prospects of the black educators and administrators on the white campus.

583. Morris, Lorenzo. *Elusive Equality: The Status of Black Americans in Higher Education.* Washington, D.C.: Institute for the Study of Educational Policy, Howard University Press, 1979.

This study investigates the effectiveness of national policy in advancing equal opportunity for black Americans in higher education. Research focusing on the early seventies, including much conducted by the Institute for the Study of Educational Policy, under whose auspices this study was conducted, concludes that blacks made considerable progress toward gaining racial parity with other Americans in higher education. However, the data on the status of blacks from 1975 through 1977 show that progress in all areas of higher education slowed down, and in areas such as professional education, it came to a standstill. Includes an appendix, notes, a general bibliography, and a selected annotated bibliography on black student attrition publications since 1970.

584. Moseley, Clifton L. *The Torch Glows.* New York: Carlton Press, 1966.

This study, undertaken in DeSoto County, Mississippi, covers a twenty-year period. Beginning with historical sketches of DeSoto County, Moseley then discusses the educational background of blacks in the county and one of the county's important institutions, the Baptist Industrial School. Moseley also discusses educational principles and policies in a segregated school system, and examines such issues as faculty, students, testing, and the classroom. The book is illustrated with pictures of the school.

585. Muhammad, Farid I. *Islamic Social and Educational Issues.* Chicago: World Community of Islam in the West, 1977.

Muhammad argues that Al–Islam, in general, and the Islamic education, in particular, can improve the state of the Bilalian (black) community of North America. Each chapter begins with a brief history, followed by an analysis of why secular and non–Islam societies have failed to improve the situation, and finally why Al–Islam is the best alternative. Underlying Muhammad's arguments is the assumption that no distinction should be made between secular and religious education. "The educational system, as viewed from an Islamic social context," says Muhammad, "has a primary responsibility in facilitating the careful cultivation and natural growth of [the] moral and spiritual quality of man."

586. Nabrit, Samuel M., and Julius Samuel Scott, Jr. *Inventory of Academic Leadership: An Analysis of the Board of Trustees of Fifty Predominantly Negro Institutions.* Atlanta, Ga.: Southern Fellowship Fund, 1969.

587. Napper, George. *Blacker Than Thou: The Struggle for Campus Unity.* Grand Rapids, Mich.: William B. Eerdmans Publishing Co., 1973.

This book examines the political world of the black college students analyzes their situations in predominantly white institutions of higher learning, and presents a new perspective on student unrest during the black student movement. Topics covered include the politics of becoming black, how to get it together at Berkeley, and the relationship between black men and women.

Napper speaks directly from his own experiences as a black administrator at the University of California at Berkeley.

588. Nettles, Michael Terrael, with A. Robert Theony,** eds. *Toward Black Undergraduate Student Equality in American Higher Education.* Westport, Conn.: Greenwood Press, 1988.

This book addresses some of the issues of equity and equality for black undergraduates in higher education during the latter years of the twentieth century. It provides analyses of black students' experiences and performances at predominantly white colleges as well as at black colleges, and it examines the role of federal and state governments and private interest groups in achieving equity for blacks in higher education.

589. Newby, James Edward. *Teaching Faculty in Black Colleges and Universities: A Survey of Selected Social Science Disciplines, 1977–1978.* Washington, D.C.: University Press of America, 1982.

"Drawing upon a survey designed to assess the degree of client–centered undergraduate teaching goals in American black colleges and universities, the results reported here look at the teaching faculty in psychology, economics, political science, sociology, and education. Results include the ethnic composition of the surveyed faculty, their sex, age, highest degree earned, employment status, principal activity, publications, and results of the goals analysis. Text reprints the survey instrument and related methodological information." This work includes appendixes, notes, references, selected bibliography, and index.

590. Newton, Eunice Sheed. *The Case for Improved College Teaching: Instructing High–Risk College Students.* New York: Vantage Press, 1982.

This book gives an instructional model designed by the author for both theoretical and practical programs and geared to maximize facilitation of increased learning competencies of high–risk college students. It draws on existing prototype instructional models of private traditional, land–grant state colleges and universities, junior and community colleges, and historically black colleges and universities and uses features consistent with her design. An attempt is made to redefine the purpose of education in relation to what is practical and realistic in a society in which a large number of high–risk students are from minority groups and low socioeconomic backgrounds. A section for appendixes outlines a syllabus in "Basic English/Threshold Level," "Divided Reading Activity," and "Levels and Dimensions of Reading Comprehension Applicable to all Types of Discourse."

591.   Newton, James E. *A Curriculum Evaluation of Black Studies in Relation to Student Knowledge of Afro–American History and Culture.* San Francisco: R and E Research Associates, 1976.

Newton evaluates the effectiveness of black studies in teaching Afro–American history and culture. Newton uses ninety–two male and female undergraduate students, and two samples consisting of the black studies curriculum group and the traditional curriculum group. He provides an inventory of Afro–American knowledge, with questions to test the reader's familiarity with Afro–American history and culture.

592.   Neyland, Leedell Wallace, and John W. Riley.* *The History of Florida Agricultural and Mechanical University.* Gainesville: University of Florida Press, 1963.

Neyland and Riley trace the history of A & M University from its founding seventy–five years ago to what they describe as its present–day success as a career school. The text includes illustrations and appendixes, with lists of former graduates who later obtained terminal degrees, as well as those who became successful in the sports arena.

593.   Noble, Jeanne L. *The Negro Woman's College Education.* New York: Bureau of Publications, Teachers College, Columbia University, 1956. Reprint. New York: Garland Publishing, Inc, 1987.

Prepared under the auspices of the Commission on the Education of Women of the American Council on Education, this book is the result of a 1956 study of black women with four or more years of college education. The history of black education, the demographic data, and the motivations for this education, as well as types of education sought and received by black women are discussed. Noble's discussion of educational priorities and the benefits of education for women is clearly a product of the fifties. But although dated, the text explores areas that are still relevant to black women (and men) today.

594. Ogbu, John U. *Minority Education and Caste: The American System in Cross–Cultural Perspective.* New York: Academic Press, 1978.

595. Ongiri, David O. *School and Home Communications: A Guide for Parents and Teachers.* Lancaster, N.Y.: Forry and Hacker, 1973.

596. ————, ed. *Three–Dimensional Approach to Teaching in the Urban Schools: The Child, the School, the Community.* New York: Simon and Schuster, 1972.

597. Ornstein,** Allen C., Daniel U. Levine,** and Doxey A. Wilkerson. *Reforming Metropolitan Schools.* Pacific Palisades, Calif.: Goodyear Publishing Co., 1975.

The central question of this book is whether public schools are providing adequate education for economically deprived children who attend schools in predominantly low–income urban areas. The major issues, each treated in a separate chapter, are compensatory education, educational accountability, decentralization and community control, and desegregation.

598. Payne, Charles Ray. *Multi–Cul: Programs for the Preparation of Teachers for Multi–Cultured Secondary Schools.* Muncie, Ind.: Ball State University Faculty Publication 1976.

In this brief discussion of the teacher education program at Ball State University (Muncie, Indiana), Payne demonstrates the success of the program in training teachers to be more effective in multicultural classrooms.

599.   Payne, Charles Ray, and Dennis Redbury,** eds. *Multi-Cultural Education Clinic Papers.* Muncie, Ind.: Ball State University Teachers College Publication, 1976.

This book examines various aspects of multicultural education, such as programs and curriculum. It studies blacks and other minorities in American schools and provides an interesting summary of the 1975 conference on multicultural education.

600.   Payne,** James S., Edward A. Polloway,** James E. Smith, Jr., et al.** *Strategies for Teaching the Mentally Retarded.* 2d ed. Columbus, Ohio: Charles E. Merrill Co., 1981.

With coauthors Edward A. Polloway,** James E. Smith, Jr., Ruth Ann Payne,** and others, James S. Payne,** divides this text into three units. Using PL 94-142 (the Education for All Handicapped Children Act of 1975) as the focal point, Unit 1 presents some introductory information on teaching and on retarded learners. Unit 2, "Strategies of Organization," deals with diagnostic prescriptive teaching, learning through the presentation of antecedent and consequent stimuli, arranging the classroom environment, and the importance of scheduling. Unit 3, "Common Content of Teaching," is primarily concerned with teaching methods in specific instructional areas.

601.   Perry, Cereta, and Clark E. Moustakas.** *Learning To Be Free.* Englewood Cliffs, N.J.: Prentice-Hall, 1973.

Self-awareness, understanding feelings, and being responsible are a few of the characteristics that Perry and Moustakas focus on as essential to a child's education. In addition, they stress the importance of aspirations, self-respect, and self-pride for black children. For example, the section entitled "Encounters in Learning" includes the "Black ABC's."

"A" is for afro, "B" is for beautiful, and "C" is for cool. Each letter has a corresponding sentence that has some meaning for the black child. A picture is also included, along with teaching suggestions on the reverse side of each alphabet.

602.   Perry, Thelma Davis. *History of the American Teachers Association.* Washington, D.C.: National Education Association, 1975.

Perry describes the subtle methods used by a group of black teachers to undermine the racist educational system. The book deals with the successes and failures of the group as a whole, and includes speeches, papers, quotations of the American Teachers Association, and state bulletins and periodicals. The appendix has descriptions of outstanding past presidents.

603.   Picott, John Rupert. *History of the Virginia Teachers Association.* Washington, D.C.: National Educational Association, 1975.

The Virginia Teachers Association rose to national recognition as one of the most effective forces for educational reform in Virginia. This history traces the association from its inception as a source of Afro–American school leaders to its coalition with the more broadly based Virginia Education Association. The policies of the organization are included, together with profiles of a few of its outstanding leaders and personalities. There are numerous photographs.

604.   ————. *A Quarter Century of the Black Experience in Elementary and Secondary Education, 1950–1975.* Washington, D.C.: Author, 1976.

A short history of black education at the elementary and secondary levels. This book discusses the values of these school systems in the context of American educational goals, which are often middle class and oblivious to the needs of blacks. Key issues discussed are desegregation, busing, government and education, black studies, black English, and, of course, testing. The text includes photographs of some prominent black

individuals and offers projections for the future of black
education up to the year 2000.

605. Pilgrim, David, ed. *Deception by Stratagem: Segregation in
Public Higher Education.* Bristol, Ind.: Wyndham Hall
Press, 1985.

This book is a collection of papers written by black
scholars—sociologists, historians, political scientists, and
educators. Each contributor, drawing from the existing literature
in his or her field and from original research, addresses the issue
of what it means to be black in America in 1985. Includes a
bibliography.

606. Prator, Ralph. *The College President.* Washington, D.C.: Center
for Applied Research in Education, 1963.

607. Price, Linda Whitson. *The Implications of Existential Psychology
for the Black Experience with Application to Education.* Palo
Alto, Calif.: R and E Research Associates, 1982.

According to Price, the present investigation was inspired
because of the need for a viable educational alternative for black
students. The study is descriptive and the philosophical
orientation is existentialism. Existentialism is recommended as an
essential alternative that fosters healthy identity formation for
black Americans. A "must," she contends, for a better
understanding.

608. Pruitt, Anne S. *New Students and Coordinated Counseling.*
Atlanta, Ga.: Institute for Higher Educational Opportunity,
Southern Regional Education Board, 1973.

In this report on coordinated counseling in traditionally black
colleges, Pruitt conducts the case study of a new student on a
predominantly white campus. The report argues for a coordinated
counseling program, and discusses traditionally black colleges in
terms of staffing patterns, relationships between coordinated
counseling programs, and other units of the institution. The report

aims to increase the effectiveness of black colleges in serving the needs of their students. Includes diagrams.

609.   ———, ed. *In Pursuit of Equality in Higher Education.* Dix Hills, N.Y.: General Hall, 1987.

This compilation is a response to events in the states affected by the *Adams's* case and the litigation concerning violations of Title VI of the Civil Rights Act of 1964. It is organized around five major themes: "Access and Progression: Determinants of Success," "Aspirations and Career Choices of Black Students," "Social and Psychological Dimensions of the Learning Environment: Experiences of Blacks on College Campuses," "The Significance of Financial Aid for Black Students in Higher Education," and "Employment of Blacks in Predominantly White Institutions." Gail Thomas, James Blackwell, Edgar Epps, and William and Marian Brazziel are among the twenty contributors.

610.   Ragan,* William Burke, and George Henderson. *Foundations of American Education.* New York: Harper and Row, 1970.

Designed primarily for the first-year education student, this text focuses on the factors and forces in society that affect American education. Attention is also directed to the problem of the poor, innovative programs, new perspectives in human growth and learning, and lastly, to projections of changes likely to occur in the future. As background material, this text is of general interest to social science students.

611.   Ramsey,** Patricia G., Edwina Battle Vold, and Leslie R. Williams.** *Multicultural Education: A Source Book.* New York: Garland Publishing Co., 1989.

This work is a comprehensive review of the resources in multicultural education published from 1976–1986. It covers a wide range of topics, including evolving philosophies and policies; related research in child development; multicultural

programs, curricula, and teaching strategies; and philosophical
and practical implications for teacher education.

612. Reed, Rodney J. *Characteristics of Teachers: A Survey Tool for
Policy–Making: A Descriptive Study in Liberia.* Berkeley:
Berkeley Center for Research and Development in Higher
Education, University of California, 1975.

613. —————. *Peer Tutoring Programs for the Academically Deficient
Student in Higher Education.* Berkeley: Berkeley Center for
Research and Development in Higher Education, University
of California, 1974.

614. Rembert, Emma White. *Alternative Strategies: Reading in the
Elementary School.* Dubuque, Iowa: Kendall/Hunt Publishing
Co., 1976.

This work presents a coordinated set of nine modules
designed as a course guide for teachers. It contains competencies
to be developed, trainee tasks, enabling activities, and suggested
instructional resources for each module. It also contains
references for teacher study, a selected list of teaching material
for pupils, and a list of tests useful for developing diagnostic
shells.

615. Richardson, Joe Martin. *A History of Fisk University,
1865–1946.* University, Ala.: University of Alabama Press,
1980.

616. Richmond, Mossie J., Jr. *Issues in Year–Round Education.* North
Quincy, Mass.: Christopher Publishing House, 1977.

This book attempts to resolve the wide range of difficulties
relating to year–round education. Richmond identifies extended
school, year or year–round school programs in the United States,
and discusses the rationale for the extended school year, problems
in administration, sources of additional revenue, and community
acceptance of these programs.

617. Robinson, Kitty Kidd, and Ethel J. Greene.* *Putting It All Together: Skills and Activities for the Elementary Child.* Washington, D.C.: University Press of America, 1977.

618. Rodgers, Frederick A. *The Black High School and Its Community.* Lexington, Mass.: D. C. Heath and Co., 1975.

619. ————. *Curriculum and Instruction in the Elementary School.* New York: Macmillan Co., 1975.

Rodgers's major concerns are the social and educational indicators of trends, developments and conditions in society, the elementary school as an institution, curricula and structures to attain set objectives, specific aspects of instructional programs in elementary settings, instructional support systems, and problems likely to confront the elementary school of the near future. Even experienced teachers, administrators, and supervisors of elementary schools are likely to find that this volume contains useful information on effective ways of contributing to the social and educational experience of students.

620. Samuda, Ronald J., and Sandra L. Woods,* eds. *Perspectives in Immigrant and Minority Education.* Washington, D.C.: University Press of America, 1983.

An anthology that deals with the vital matter of how non–English–speaking ethnic minorities and their teachers communicate in an environment that promotes learning. Further, it discusses prospects for applying these methods of communication in areas other than education. The anthology is based largely on studies of how faculties respond to new opportunities for service that have been generated by the refugee influx in southeast Florida.

621. Saylor,** John Galen, and Joshua L. Smith, eds. *Removing Barriers to Humaneness in the High School.* Washington, D.C.: Association for Supervision and Curriculum Development, National Education Association, 1971.

This collection of essays aims to improve the quality of education in the American secondary schools by suggesting ways of overcoming some of the barriers to freedom and humanity.

622. Scott, Hugh Jerome. *The Black School Superintendent: Messiah or Scapegoat?* Washington, D.C.: Howard University Press, 1980.

The black school superintendent is a new personality in America's educational system. Scott focuses on seven black superintendents and the situation in which they find themselves, on the job and in the community. The book takes us to the heart of urban education, with its many challenges to policy–making and the problems accompanying the breakdown of urban centers.

623. Scott, John Irving Elias. *The Education of Black People in Florida.* Philadelphia: Dorrance Publishing Co., 1974.

624. ———. *Finding My Way.* Boston: Meador Publishing Co., 1949.

This book is designed to prepare freshmen for college life. Scott discusses study skills, writing term papers, selecting the right vocation, and preparing for and taking examinations, as well as other problems frequently encountered by college freshmen. Students will find much of the information still applicable in this day.

625. ———. *Getting the Most out of High School.* 2d ed. New York: Oceana Publications, 1967.

Scott speaks candidly about the meaning and advantages of a secondary school education and about the unfortunate consequences of *not* grasping this opportunity. He traces the development of the high school and its relation to governmental agencies.

626. ————. *Living with Others: A Foundation Guidance Program for Junior High and Upper Elementary Grades.* Boston: Meador Publishing Co., 1939.

Designed for use in upper elementary and junior high schools, this book reviews the aims of education and presents teaching modules built around seven cardinal principles of education.

627. ————. *Negro Students and Their Colleges.* Boston: Meador Publishing Co., 1949.

This book, consisting of three parts, is primarily addressed to black secondary students. In the first part the author cites various reasons for attending college. Part 2 consists of demographical data on various black colleges and includes a curriculum. The third part contains data on black enrollment and on graduates of nonblack institutions.

628. Sedlacek,** William E., and Glenwood C. Brooks, Jr. *Racism in American Education: A Model for Change.* Chicago: Nelson–Hall, 1976.

The authors show that most of the minority groups in America—Afro–Americans, American Indians, Mexican–Americans, and Puerto Ricans—have suffered from discrimination and racism in education. They suggest ways of eliminating this "institutional" racism. Presented in a workshop format, the book contains a comprehensive bibliography and an appendix of information on minorities in American society.

629. Sewell, George Alexander, and Cornelius V. Troup. *Morris Brown College: The First Hundred Years, 1881–1981.* Atlanta, Ga.: Morris Brown College, 1981.

630. Shabazz, Abdul-Alin. *Fundamentals of Islamic Education.* Chicago: World Community of Islam in the West, 1977.

Based on articles published in *Muhammad Speaks* (now called *The Bilalian News*), this book deals with the development of a system of education for Islamic schools in the Muslim community in America. Shabazz discusses general issues such as the purpose of education, as well as specific topics such as education in prisons and adult education. The introduction and epilogue by Farid Muhammad contain the main thesis of the book—namely, that education must be ideologically oriented if it is to be useful in developing the World Community of Islam in the West.

631.   Shade, Barbara J. Robinson, ed. *Culture, Style, and the Educative Process.* Springfield, Ill.: Charles C. Thomas Publishers, 1989.

632.   Sherriffs, Alex C., and Kenneth Bancroft Clark. *How Relevant Is Education in America Today?* Washington, D.C.: American Enterprise Institute for Public Policy Research, 1970.

This book consist of two lectures delivered during the Rational Debate Seminar in Washington, D.C., in 1970, which was sponsored by the American Enterprise Institute. Also included are the rebuttals and finally the discussion session. A timely and enlightening discourse, which merits the attention of educators, parents, and students alike.

633.   Sims, William E. *Political Education in Black and White: A Case Study.* Washington, D.C.: University Press of America, 1976.

634.   Sims, William E., and Bernice Bass de Martinez. *Perspectives in Multicultural Education.* Washington, D.C.: University Press of America, 1981.

What constitutes a good, multicultural education? What can make it easier for teachers to understand and relate positively to the culturally diverse learner? What should teachers know and experience to make them responsive to this complex challenge? This volume addresses these and other questions.

635. Sizemore, Barbara A. *The Ruptured Diamond: The Politics of the Decentralization of the District of Columbia Public Schools.* Washington, D.C.: University Press of America, 1984.

Using the "Rational Actor Model," the "Organizational Process Model," and the "Political Bargaining Model," Sizemore discusses the politics of decentralization of the Washington, D.C., public school system. She concluded that the entire conflict over decentralization and radical curriculum change was merely a shadow of the struggle with Congress over popular sovereignty in the District.

636. Slaughter, Diana T., and Deborah Jean Johnson, eds. *Visible Now: Blacks in Private Schools.* Westport, Conn.: Greenwood Press, 1988.

With a foreword by James P. Comer, this book looks at all aspects of the educational experiences of black children in private and parochial schools, and explores the implications of private schooling for educational policy and future research. The editors' introduction provides an overview of the educational situation of black children, focusing on the relationships between the children, their families, and academic achievement in their schools. The organization of the volume reflects the diversity of private schools attended by black children.

637. Slaughter, John, Richard Lapchick,* Ernest L. Boyer,** eds. *Ethics in College Sports.* New York: American Council on Education: Macmillan Co., 1989.

In these fourteen chapters, the contributors—college presidents, athletic directors, coaches, and journalists—attempt to clarify such issues as recruiting, drug abuse, and the proper role of academics, and offer solutions to the crisis surrounding veracity in college sports.

638. Sleeter,** Christine E., and Carl A. Grant. *Making Choices for Multicultural Education: Five Approaches to Race, Class, and Gender.* Columbus, Ohio: Merrill Publishing Co., 1988.

While examining the goals and assumptions related to diversity in the classroom and the implications of these assumptions for actual teaching practice, this text also offers a way of thinking about race, culture, language, class, gender, and disability. Includes an index.

639. Smith, Cynthia J., ed. *Advancing Equality of Opportunity: A Matter of Justice.* Washington, D.C.: Institute for the Study of Educational Policy, Howard University, 1978.

Are all affirmative action programs guilty of reverse discrimination? This and other questions dealing with the advancement of equality in America are addressed in these articles, originally presented at a conference held in Washington, D.C., in May 1977. An introduction by Faustine Jones gives the reader a framework for the various papers presented. Among the contributors are Kenneth Tollett, Charles Hamilton, and other noted figures from government, academia, and the media.

640. Smith, Ed Calvin. *Black Students in Interracial Schools: A Guide for Students, Teachers, and Parents.* Garrett Park, Md.: Garrett Park Press, 1980.

641. Smith, Elsie J. *Counseling the Culturally Different Black Youth.* Columbus, Ohio: Charles E. Merrill Co., 1973.

Smith emphasizes "action–oriented counseling techniques" over talk in dealing with black youths and discusses the counselor's relationship to the families of the black students counseled. Smith explores a number of prominent issues, assumptions, and barriers related to counseling culturally different black youths, including the role of educational counseling in vocational guidance and development. She also discusses some counseling theories and their relevance to the black student, the counselor in the 1970s, and representative cases for discussion. The book also includes a bibliography.

642. Smith, Ida Ragins, and Marvin Farbstein,* eds. *Educational Psychology and Teaching.* New York: Selected Academic Readings, 1968.

643. Smith, James Wesley. *Who's Who Among Virginia State Graduates.* Petersburg, Va.: Virginia State University, 1982.

644. Smith, Willy DeMarcell, and Eva Wells Chunn, eds. *Black Education: A Quest for Equity and Experience.* New Brunswick, N.J.: Transaction Publishers, 1989.

Originally published as a special issue of the *Urban League Review,* Summer 1987, Winter 1987–1988, this collection of essays provides a portrait of black education in transition. The twenty–five essays are assembled under "Editors Preamble," "Commentaries," Perspectives and Analysis," "Selected Issues," "Spectrum on Desegregation," "Strategies for Academic Excellence," and "Special Reports." Contributors include John E. Jacob, Charles Willie, James Comer, and Joyce Ladner.

645. Smitherman, Geneva. *Talkin' & Testifyin': The Language of Black America.* Boston: Houghton Mifflin Co., 1977.

Blacks and whites in the United States sometimes seem to speak different languages, and misunderstandings are bound to result. From African villages to Motown, from the sacred to the secular, the author draws on black culture in examining black speech. She illustrates her theories with the words of Frederick Douglass, Curtis Mayfield, W. E. B. DuBois, Claude Brown, Isaac Hayes, Richard Wright, and others. She offers as a remedy specific public policy suggestions that recognize the validity of and use black English, such as a reading/language program that aims at fluency in both dialects.

646. Sommerville, Joseph C., and Linda L. Brucklacher.** *Selected Group Analyses of Administrative Field Experience Problems.* Toledo, Ohio: University of Toledo, 1973.

This book describes the experiences of participants in the Administrative Field Experience Program at the University of Toledo. Problems commonly plaguing administrators and supervisors are analyzed. These include instructional leadership, philosophy and policy–making, school community relations, and routine administrative functions. The document is designed to serve as a resource and guide for administrative internship seminars.

647. Sommerville, Joseph C., and Robert Thiede.** *Contemporary Administrative and Supervisory Challenges: Analysis of Interesting Problems.* Toledo, Ohio: University of Toledo, 1976.

This work, according to the authors, grew out of the corporate efforts of many individuals and evolves from numerous different school environments. Students, practitioners, and professors responded to each problem presented. Concepts, skills, and techniques that the students acquire in academic training are related to specific challenges that confront them in their field experiences. Several alternative approaches are considered for solving the problems. Although the publication does not offer definite solutions to administrative problems, it does provide many tested approaches that are valuable to those who are faced with the challenges of school administration and supervision.

648. Sowell, Thomas. *Affirmative Action Reconsidered. Was It Necessary in Academia?* Washington, D.C.: American Enterprise Institute for Public Policy Research, 1975.

This study accomplishes four major tasks: (1) it distinguishes between the basic concepts of affirmative action and many of the laws that arose out of the affirmative action label; (2) it measures the magnitude of the problem that affirmative action programs were meant to either solve or lessen; (3) it considers the results of these programs; and (4) it weighs the implications of affirmative action policies for those directly involved as well as for the general public. Vast literature on such areas as education, employment, pay, and promotion is drawn upon in the study.

649. ———. *Black Education: Myths and Tragedies.* New York: David McKay Co., 1972.

The author presents the experiences of the Afro–American student on both black and white college campuses, and discusses widespread academic policies such as the so–called intelligence testing that tend to perpetuate myths and tragedies in the education of blacks. Sowell has proposals for solving some of these problems. His personal experiences as a student and educator on various college campuses (Cornell, Howard, Harvard) make for a powerful and provocative presentation of the black educational experience in America today.

650. ———. *Education: Assumptions Versus History: Collected Essays.* Stanford, Calif.: Hoover Institution Press, 1986.

This book consists of the collected papers of Thomas Sowell dating from 1966 through 1981. Subjects range from the elementary school to the university, and from the educational insights of Thorstein Veblen to the contemporary controversy over affirmative action. The central theme of the essays is that we cannot educate on the basis of assumptions but must test even our most cherished beliefs against the historical and contemporary evidence. Heterogeneous as these writings are—ranging from essays to scholarly studies to testimony and interchanges with congresspeople—their repeated theme is the extent to which the various "innovations" and buzzwords of education have ignored evidence on their validity or lack of validity.

651. Spaights, Ernest, Jean C. Waterland,* and Penny McGovern.* *Techniques for Teaching Disadvantaged Youth.* Washington, D.C.: Educational Systems Corp., 1968.

652. Spiva, Ulysses Van. *Leadership Plus Administration in School Management.* Birmingham, Ala.: Banner Press, 1978.

This book reveals the inner dynamics of successful school management and shows how they can be used to resolve key issues facing the schools today. Topics include school finance, corporal punishment, Title IX programs, alternative schools, women in school administration, legal rights and responsibilities of students, behavioral objectives, and personnel development.

653.   ————. *Legal Outlook: A Message to College and University People.* Saratoga, Calif.: Century Twenty One Publishers, 1981.

This handbook contains more than fifty legal decisions that affect the people who live, work, and study at institutions of higher education around the country. It is written in simple and easy–to–read language, and can be read and enjoyed by students, faculty, and administrators who may be too busy to search through countless volumes to gain insight into contemporary court cases that directly affect the operation of colleges and universities.

654.   Spivey, Donald. *The Politics of Miseducation: The Booker Washington Institute of Liberia, 1919–1984.* Lexington: University Press of Kentucky, 1986.

Spivey's depiction of the rise of industrial schooling in the United States and its projection abroad as an elite plan to maintain the status quo of power becomes stronger and stronger as the details accumulate. He focuses specifically on the subject of industrial education for blacks in Liberia. In his account, he reveals the operation of elite power in the historical development of one foundation's educational institution abroad.

655.   ————. *Schooling for the New Slavery: Black Industrial Education, 1868–1915.* Westport, Conn.: Greenwood Press, 1978.

This is the story of the role industrial education played in the resubjugation of black Americans. Spivey begins his analysis with the role of the Freedmen's Bureau and other agencies in the birth of industrial education. He notes that although northerners like Samuel Chapman Armstrong, founder of the Hampton Normal Institute in Hampton, Virginia, were responsible for the "uplift" of blacks, their real concerns were bringing order and stability to war–ravaged areas and reconciling the North and South. To return blacks to a productive and subservient role, Armstrong and his pupil, Booker T. Washington, stressed practical teaching of physical skills.

656. Spruill, Albert W. *The Historic Tour of N.C. A and T State University.* Greensboro, N.C.: Coleman Printing Company (Private), 1982.

657. Stent, Madelon Delany, and Frank Brown. *Minorities in U.S. Institutions of Higher Education.* New York: Praeger Publishers, 1977.

The book reviews minority college enrollment and educational attainment in the United States. Data on all major minority groups are listed separately by institutional type and control. Distinctions are also made between lower– and upper–division enrollment, and among various fields and major professional student populations.

658. ———. *Minority Access and Achievement in Higher Education.* New York: Praeger Publishers, 1982.

With a foreword by Patricia Graham, this book provides a comprehensive review and analysis of minority enrollment and achievement in institutions of higher education. It presents and analyzes data on enrollment and earned degrees for American Indians, Afro–Americans, Asians, and Hispanic Americans by type of institution, including undergraduate, graduate, and professional schools. Stent and Brown also review existing and ongoing studies of affirmative action, recruitment, financial aid, and special admissions, and pay particular attention to the implications of important Court decisions.

659. Stent, Madelon Delany, William R. Hazard,** and Harry N. Rivlin,** eds. *Cultural Pluralism in Education: A Mandate for Change.* New York: Appleton–Century–Crofts, 1973.

This work contains a wealth of information on cultural pluralism in education and in the community. Essays are contributed by respected scholars in the field of education. Rather than tending toward the old direction of the melting pot theory, they propose a different kind of cultural pluralism in education by suggesting we eliminate the present dichotomy between culture as taught in schools and culture as it exists in the community. Their recommendations are stimulating and insightful.

660. Stevens, Joseph H., Jr., and Edith W. King.* *Administering Early Childhood Education Programs.* New York: Little, Brown and Co., 1976.

661. Strain, Lucille B. *Accountability in Reading Instruction.* Columbus, Ohio: Charles E. Merrill Co., 1976.

This book, addressed mainly to teachers of reading instruction, is in three major parts: (1) a description of the major aspects of accountability, with applications to reading instructions; (2) a review of some basic procedures in reading instructions; and (3) a description of some reading skills and concepts. The text includes a glossary of the educational terms used throughout, as well as a sample plan for reading instruction.

662. Strickland, Arvarh E., Jerome R. Reich,** and Edward L. Biller.** *Building the United States.* New York: Harcourt Brace Jovanovich, 1971.

663. Sullivan,** Dorothy D., Beth Davey,** and Dolores Pawley Dickerson. *Games as Learning Tools: A Guide for Effective Use.* Paoli, Pa.: Instructo/McGraw–Hill, 1978.

This book is the result of the authors' commitment to the concept that "classroom learning should and can be a positive experience for kids." Games, they argue, can contribute to this experience, and they proceed to show just the kinds of games that can be designed and implemented in the classroom. The material comes from practical classroom and clinical usage, and can be adapted to suit individual classroom situations.

664. Tate, Elfleda Jackson. *Teaching the Disadvantaged: A Teacher's Manual*. Mountain, N. Dak.: Peek Publications, 1971.

This book, a practical guide for teachers of disadvantaged children, describes disadvantaged learners and recommends methods, materials, and content to help eradicate their deficits. Tate suggests ways to eliminate the trying situations that tend to defeat teachers of the disadvantaged. The emphasis is mainly on the lower–class Afro–American child. In the first part, Tate suggests ways of making elementary school curricula—particularly reading, social studies, and health education—more relevant to black children. In the second part, she examines the problems of discipline, classroom control, and the influence of black power on schoolchildren. Tate illustrates her suggestions with specific lesson plans.

665. Taylor, Ruth Sloan. *Teaching in the Desegregated Classroom*. West Nyack, N.Y.: Parker Publishing Co., 1974.

This study examines practical techniques, both tried and untried, for teaching in the desegregated classroom. It offers guidelines for assessing teacher values and developing positive activities for the students. Taylor suggests ways of improving student–to–student communication and incorporating minority group contributions into the curriculum. She gives methods of evaluating student progress, selecting the right materials and activities, and maintaining good after–classroom relationships among the students. Chapter 10 consists of twenty select questions and pertinent answers to the first nineteen of these questions on the subject of teaching in the desegregated classroom. The twentieth question is of particular interest, as only the reader can answer it.

666. Thomas, Gail Elaine. *Black Students in Higher Education: Conditions and Experiences in the 1970s*. Westport, Conn.: Greenwood Press, 1981.

These twenty–eight essays represent the findings of specialists—lawyers, doctors, research scientists, and college professors and administrators—on the special problems of black higher education in their areas of expertise. Individual articles treat the aspirations and achievements of black students in the 1970s; their successes and failures in medicine, law, and engineering; the implications of the *Bakke* decision and other court cases; the importance of testing to black students' careers; and many other topics. Includes an index.

667. Thompson, Cleopatra Davenport. *The History of the Mississippi Teachers Association.* Washington, D.C.: NEA, Teachers' Rights Commission and the Mississippi Education Association, 1973.

668. Thompson, Daniel Calbert. *Private Black Colleges at the Crossroads.* Westport, Conn.: Greenwood Press, 1974.

This study presents some of the issues that arise in the survival of black colleges and universities, against a background of the rapidly changing American society and the rising expectations of black youth. Thompson asks whether black colleges are fulfilling their traditional goals, and he takes a look at their students, faculty, curriculum, and economic status. He then questions whether these institutions are worth saving.

669. Timmons, Eleanor Lewis. *Teaching English.* 1st ed. New York: Vantage Press, 1958.

In this book, an experienced teacher gives constructive advice to the beginning teacher, particularly the teacher of English.

670. Tollett, Kenneth S. *Black Colleges as Instruments of Affirmative Action.* Washington, D.C.: Institute for the Study of Educational Policy, Howard University, 1982.

With a foreword by Morris T. Keeton and Stephen J. Wright, this book is divided into three major sections: "The Constitutionalization of Racism and the Counter Attack," "The Situation of Blacks: The Legacy of Slavery and Jim Crowism," and "The Supreme Court Action and Black Colleges." Tollett concludes that affirmative action is needed to compensate for the injustices suffered by blacks in the past, and that the black college is an instrument of affirmative action because it is more responsive to oppression and the disadvantages of blacks. Includes a bibliography and an index.

671. Turner, Bridges Alfred. *From a Plow to a Doctorate—So What?* Hampton, Va.: Author, 1945.

Using his own college experiences, Turner describes the difficulties encountered by blacks as they seek higher education. His main purpose, however, is to propose a plan for raising money for black scholarships. The plan is essentially to collect one dollar from at least 1 million people and then to invest funds to be used for scholarships for selected students. The end of the text includes a question sheet on the plan to be mailed back to the author for an assessment of his plan's feasibility.

672. Vincent, Charles. *A Centennial History of Southern University and A&M College, 1880–1980.* Baton Rouge, La.: Southern University, 1981.

673. Vontress, Clemmont E. *Counseling Negroes.* Boston: Houghton Mifflin Co., 1971.

The author addresses himself to the specific problems and concerns faced in the counseling of adolescent blacks, in preparation for college, in adulthood, and in the use of testing. The first section explores special tactics for counseling blacks. A very informative monograph.

674. Walker, James E., and Thomas M. Shea.* *Behavior Management: A Practical Approach for Educators.* 4th ed. Columbus, Ohio: Merrill Publishing Co., 1988.

This text presents the behavior management field from four points of view: psychodynamic, biophysical, environmental, and behavioral. Theoretical background is combined with numerous case studies and actual examples of behavior management, which gives preservice teachers, in–service teachers, parents, and paraprofessionals a practical guide for applying behavior management techniques in special education and regular education settings and at home. Quizzes and skill–building projects are presented at the end of every chapter. Bibliographies, references, and lists of related journals and texts are also included.

675.   Walker, Mae, ed. *Education of the Afro–American in America.* Washington, D.C.: University Press of America, 1976.

676.   Wallace, Walter L. *Student Culture: Social Structure and Continuity in a Liberal Arts College.* Chicago: Aldine Publishing Co., 1966.

This study concerns itself with the phenomenon of assimilation or socialization as it occurs on the campus of a small midwestern liberal arts college. Socialization, Wallace argues, occurs at a faster rate than was believed by many social scientists. His conclusions center around a new social psychological technique. He uses a variation of the sociometric techniques to characterize the interpersonal environments of each student in the midwestern college. Included in appendix 4 are questionnaires to study the interests and attitudes of college students.

677.   Walton, Sidney F., Jr. *The Black Curriculum: Developing a Program in Afro–American Studies.* East Palo Alto, Calif.: Nairobi, 1969.

A proposal for an academic paradigm exclusively designed for black individuals. The author discusses issues, past and present, confronting black students caught up in white America's educational system. At issue are various aspects of racism and an evaluation of the Afro–American Studies Program at Merritt College in Oakland, California. The author also presents guidelines for developing relevant curriculum for blacks at all educational levels—elementary, secondary, and higher education. He also discusses the role of black educators.

678. Washington, Booker T. *My Larger Education: Being Chapters from My Experience.* New York: Doubleday, Page and Co., 1911.

679. ————. *The Story of My Life and My Work.* Original pen drawings by Frank Beard.* Naperville, Ill.: J. L. Nichols and Co., 1900. Reprint. Westport, Conn.: Negro Universities Press, 1969.

680. ————. *Working with the Hands: Being a Sequel to "Up From Slavery," Covering the Author's Experience in Industrial Training at Tuskegee.* New York: Doubleday, Page and Co., 1904.

In this sequel to *Up from Slavery*, Washington articulates his philosophy on the values of industrial training and the methods employed to develop it. He stresses that the objectives of education should be to upgrade the living conditions of its graduates or at least to make life more endurable for them. He strongly attacks the view that being educated means being free from hard work. While he stresses the need for industrial training, he maintains that this must be in conjunction with moral, religious, and mental education. The book is based on the vocational training for blacks as developed and instituted at Tuskegee Institute.

681. ————, ed. *Tuskegee and Its People: Their Ideals and Achievements.* New York: Appleton and Co., 1905. Reprint. Freeport, N.Y.: Books for Libraries Press, 1971.

682. Washington, Valora, and Ura Jean Oyemade. *Project Head Start: Past, Present, and Future Trends in the Context of Family Needs.* New York: Garland Publishing, Inc., 1987.

This guide presents an ecological and historical analysis of the program to determine how well Project Head Start has met the changing needs of the children and families it serves. Topical chapters present original essays, reference lists, and annotated bibliographies, addressing many important factors and issues as they relate to Project Head Start. Includes subject and author indexes.

683. Watson, Bernard C. *In Spite of the System: The Individual and Educational Reform.* Cambridge, Mass.: Ballinger Publishing Co., 1974.

The first half of this book is devoted to a discussion of the impact of education on society, public policy, and education, and an analysis of Christopher Jencks' *Inequality.* Watson also discusses the structural context of schools—the principal's role, decentralization, and community control. Watson includes biographies of three individuals whose dynamic contributions in the field of education identify them as outstanding leaders.

684. Webster, Staten Wentford. *Discipline in the Classroom: Basic Principles and Problems.* San Francisco: Chandler Publishing Co., 1968.

Designed primarily for teachers, the book outlines in two parts the basic principles of classroom control while presenting in the latter part some very interesting test cases with both analyses and proposed solutions.

685. ————. *The Education of Black Americans.* New York: Intext Educational Publishers, 1974.

This book is divided into two parts, with the first giving a historical and contemporary outline of blacks in America and the second dealing mainly with the sociological aspects of blacks and education in the United States. The book primarily concerns the education of economically and socially disadvantaged blacks. It provides interesting data concerning the socioeconomics and value systems of low–income blacks subjected to a white–oriented system.

686. ———, ed. *The Disadvantaged Learner: Knowing, Understanding, Educating: A Collection of Original and Published Articles.* San Francisco: Chandler Publishing Co., 1966.

This book describes the disadvantaged learner, presents that learner's educational problems, and provides a guideline to circumventing these problems. Designed as a reference for those concerned with urban education.

687. Wesley, Charles Harris. *The History of Alpha Phi Alpha: A Development in Negro College Life.* Washington, D.C.: Howard University Press, 1929. Reprint. Chicago: Foundation Publishers, 1981.

Alpha Phi Alpha is the oldest Afro–American male college fraternity. This book, published in the thirties, considers the potential values of Afro–American college life, especially in a select group like this. Based on the documentation from primary sources, this history is a useful tool in the study of race history and Afro–American college life. Inside are graphic representations of some of the symbols of the fraternity, along with pictures of outstanding members of the fraternity.

688. Whiting, Helen Adele. *Primary Education.* 2d ed. Boston: Christopher Publishing House, 1927.

A methods book containing model lesson plans and activities. The first part discusses general methods such as questioning and story telling, while the latter part deals with more specific areas of methodology, such as math and music.

689. Wilcox, Preston. *Education for Black Humanism: A Study of Approaching It.* New York: Afram Associates, 1969.

First, this work discusses teaching for black humanism; it then presents the role of black revolutionary intellectuals in search of black humanism. Mentioned are the efforts of Malcom

X, Martin Luther King, Jr., Marcus Garvey, Frank Fanon, Eldridge Cleaver, and Harold Cruse.

690.   ————. *Integration or Separation in Education: K–12.* New York: Afram Associates, 1969.

The primary subject dealt with in this research paper is the issue of educational integration, segregation, and separation. Wilcox discusses the outcomes of integrated school systems and the black–controlled school movement. He provides evidence supporting the notion that educating for humanism is far more relevant than the issue of integrated or separatist education.

691.   Wilkerson, Doxey A. *Special Problems of Negro Education.* Washington, D.C.: U.S. Government Printing Office, 1939.

This book is the result of research done in 1937 by the staff of the advisory committee established to investigate public education in eighteen states that, at that time, required complete school segregation on all levels. Data used are primarily official publications and records for the years 1933 through 1936. The author focuses on the external aspects of public education, such as the presence or absence of schools; their physical plant and resources; the attendance of children in the school; the number, qualifications, and salaries of teachers; pupil transportation; and financial support. Consideration is given to public elementary and secondary schools, to institutions of higher learning, and to auxiliary educational programs (e.g., public library services, vocational education, and rehabilitation services for the physically handicapped).

692.   Wilkinson,* Louise Cherry, and Cora Bagley Marrett, eds. *Gender Influences in Classroom Interaction.* Orlando, Fla.: Academic Press, 1985.

693.   Williams, Eric Eustace. *Education in the British West Indies.* Port of Spain, Trinidad: Guardian Commercial Printery, 1950.

This book calls for the creation of a university for West Indian students throughout the Caribbean. It is directed at educators and administrators in the hope that they would see the need for such an institution. Various forms of education at different levels are analyzed with a view to expanding the existing system to include a university system. An official report on higher education in British colonies is included to reinforce arguments for the establishment of a university that would meet the needs of all students.

694. Williams, John B., III., ed. *Desegregating America's Colleges and Universities: Title VI Regulation of Higher Education.* New York: Teachers College Press, Columbia University, 1988.

This volume addresses a significant set of public policy interventions aimed at remedying the crisis of decreased black participation in the higher education arena. The research–based essays identify effectiveness problems associated with government efforts to compel public institutions of higher learning to admit more black students and to hire more black faculty and administrators. They explore alternative means of accomplishing these goals and describe potentially more successful approaches for government action. Contributors include John B. Williams III, Barbara Newell, Lary Leslie, Raymond Burse, James E. Blackwell, Charles V. Willie, and Edgar G. Epps.

695. Williams, Lucius L., and Jerome Kaplan.** *Student's Self-Directing Computational Guide I.* New York: Random House, 1974.

This computational guidebook consists of mathematical exercises to be used to review basic skills. Because of the model examples, "Quick Check" sections, and answer sections, the guidebook can be used with the aid of a teacher or independently. *Guide I* contains practice exercises on whole numbers, fractions, and decimals that include practice in adding, subtracting, multiplying, and dividing.

696. ————. *Student's Self–Directing Computational Guide II*. New York: Random House, 1974.

Like *Guide I, Guide II* consists of mathematical exercises to be used to review basic skills, and can be used with the aid of a teacher or independently. It contains practice exercises on whole numbers, integers, rational numbers (fractions and decimals in both positive and negative form), equations, proportions, and percentages. Again, practice in adding, subtracting, multiplying, and dividing is included.

697. Williams, Robert L. *Cross–Cultural Education: Teaching Toward a Planetary Perspective*. Washington, D.C.: National Education Association, 1977.

698. ————. *Educational Alternatives for Colonized People: Models for Liberation*. Port Washington, N.Y.: Kennikat Press, 1974.

The strength of this book—with a foreword by Nathan Wright, Jr.—lies in the educational alternatives proposed, with detailed carefully worked out models for their implementation. This book is recommended for upper–level undergraduates and beginning graduate students in teacher–education programs.

699. Williams, William Taylor B. *Duplication of Schools for Negro Youth*. Lynchburg, Va.: J. P. Bell Co., 1914.

The author emphasizes the need for greater efficiency in the school systems in the South. There should be a concerted effort to prevent the unwise use of means and efforts of other people, and a reduction of "rivalries, divisions, jealousies, and other evils" resulting from unnecessary duplication of southern schools for blacks (i.e., segregated schools). Williams lists fifty instances of misappropriation of funds and efforts in the duplication of these schools. The book includes charts and tables of these fifty duplicated schools.

700.   ————. *Report on Negro Universities in the South.* New Orleans: Tulane University Press, 1913.

This pre–World War I study of black universities in the South was undertaken to determine the nature of the work of the black universities at that time. The data were collected from twenty–two reputable black colleges with campuses scattered over ten southern states and the District of Columbia. The work done by these universities covers every phase of education from the lowest elementary school grade up to college work. Areas investigated were length of terms, college entrance requirements, courses of study, administration instruction, and relative costs of college departments. The author also lists Howard, Fisk, Virginia Union, Atlanta, Shaw, and Wiley as the six best black universities in the South. There are tables in the book drawn to represent the different areas studied.

701.   Willie, Charles Vert. *Effective Education: A Minority Policy Perspective.* Westport, Conn.: Greenwood Press, 1987.

This book analyzes the ways in which majority and minority interests interact in the educational system. It outlines the concepts, goals, and policies of effective educational environments, and examines teaching and learning strategies for diversified groups of students. The work begins with an examination of the excellence movement in American education, and then analyzes alternative trends through which, by accepting adequacy rather than insisting on excellence, minority groups can be included in the educational process. Includes an index.

702.   ————. *The Ivory and Ebony Towers: Race Relations and Higher Education.* Lexington, Mass.: Lexington Books, 1981.

Willie proposes that the primary goal of higher education should be to endow its students with a deep sense of community in order to enable them to make future political and moral decisions. To promote this goal, he analyzes the advantages for both minority and majority populations of a diversified student body. He includes practical suggestions for the recruitment, admission, and retention of minority students.

703.   ————. *The Sociology of Urban Education: Desegregation and Integration.* Lexington, Mass.: Lexington Books, 1978.

The author holds the view that because the United States is essentially urban, its educational system must be essentially urban as well. He then shows that pluralism is the essence of an urban society. The educational system can meet the needs of contemporary America only by educating students for life in a pluralistic community and developing in them a sense of community among heterogeneous and diversified people. This is to be achieved through a conceptual approach to desegregation and integration, rather than through the trial and error techniques that have prevailed.

The book is divided into four parts. Part 1 discusses urban education issues; part 2, education planning and policy making; part 3, desegregating elementary and secondary schools; and part 4, integrating colleges and universities.

704.   ————, ed. *School Desegregation Plans That Work.* Westport, Conn.: Greenwood Press, 1984.

In this practical analysis of desegregation planning, the author discusses a series of school desegregation plans that work. Three of the plans are court ordered and one is community initiated. Of the four plans presented, one or more may be adapted to a number of local situations. The value of this book in planning is that it presents desegregation ideas that have been tested in specific cities such as Atlanta, Boston, Milwaukee, and Seattle.

Willie discusses the implications of various plans, including those that show how cities may prevent violence and foster a sense of community. The association, if any, between white flight and the kind of plan a community adopts is analyzed. The study concludes that there is no association between the kind of desegregation plan implemented and the rate of white migration from the cities.

705. Willie, Charles Vert, with Jerome Beker.* *Race Mixing in the Public Schools.* New York: Praeger Publishers, 1973.

Willie examines the bases for success and failure in integrated education by exploring integration situations in two elementary schools and two junior high schools. The purpose of the study is to discover patterns of social adjustment in young children.

706. Willie, Charles Vert, and Ronald R. Edmonds, eds. *Black Colleges in America: Challenge, Development, Survival.* New York: Teachers College Press, Columbia University, 1978.

This book contains papers presented at the Black College Conference held at Harvard Graduate School of Education in March and April 1976. The sixteen papers are presented in three parts. Part 1 deals with the history and purpose of black colleges; part 2 deals with the administration, financing, and governance of black colleges; and part 3 deals with teaching and learning. Each part is preceded by an overview that sets a frame of reference for the papers presented in that section. The authors describe this work as "a serious effort to lay before the public an analysis of what black colleges and universities do for themselves and for the nation." The papers are varied and reflect the diversified backgrounds of their contributors, who include such notables as Benjamin E. Mays, Samuel DuBois Cook, and Daniel C. Thompson.

707. Willie, Charles Vert, and Arline Sakuma McCord.* *Black Students at White Colleges.* New York: Praeger Publishers, 1972.

Originally a study of white colleges in upper New York State, the authors examine, from the students' point of view, the still little-explored area of black students on predominantly white college campuses. The reader will find the authors' methodology and conclusions of special interest.

708. Willie, Charles Vert, and Inabeth Miller,** eds. *Social Goals and Educational Reform: American Schools in the Twentieth Century.* Westport, Conn.: Greenwood Press, 1988.

This collection provides a multidisciplinary perspective on the development of educational policy and practice in the United States during the twentieth century. It presents education as a complex social structure and process that has changed through the years and that defies simplistic solutions. By reviewing competing theories of education, the editors promote an analytical framework that welcomes educational conflict as creative and beneficial.

709. Wilson, Charles H., Sr. *Education for Negroes in Mississippi Since 1910: An Historical Approach.* Boston: Meador Publishing Co., 1947.

A well-documented treatise of the elementary, secondary, and postsecondary educational institutions in Mississippi for the Afro-American from 1910 to 1947. The author includes chapters on Afro-American teachers, the general high school curriculum, and the financing of these schools, as well as on industrial, vocational, religious, athletic, and music education in the state.

710. Wilson, George D. *A Century of Negro Education in Louisville, Kentucky.* Louisville, Ky.: Louisville Municipal College, 1900.

711. Wilson, Thomasyne Lightfoot. *Toward Equitable Education for Multicultural Consciousness for Early Childhood: A Bicentennial Revolution?* Redwood City, Calif.: Ujamaa Educational Publishers, 1976.

712. ————. *Toward Viable Directions in Postsecondary Education: Nontraditional/Unconventional Education Through a "Community-Family" Context.* San Francisco: Sapphire Publishing Co., 1976.

This book puts forward some viable directions for secondary education. The author finds that prospects for equality in postsecondary education are good. She argues, however, that postsecondary education should include the whole community, and that the values, goals, processes, and assessments of and for education should come from the "realities" of nontraditional students and not simply from the "privileged." The book contains several schemes, diagrams, and tables, and also an appendix containing an evaluative instrument for educational programs.

713. Woodard, Samuel L., ed. *Reducing Stress on Black Administrators.* New York: Vantage Press, 1978.

Comprises papers presented at a conference on "Creative Leadership" sponsored by Howard University. Part 1, by James P. Comer, and part 2, by Maurice C. Woodard and Charles W. Harris, contain analyses of the pressure–building situations faced by most administrators, and by black administrators in particular. The third and last part consists of exercises for administrators to reduce stress using the transactional analysis approach.

714. Woodson, Carter Goodwin. *The Education of the Negro Prior to 1861: A History of the Education of the Colored People of the United States from the Beginning of Slavery to the Civil War.* New York: G. P. Putnam's Sons, 1915.

Focusing on the education of the Afro–American in the antebellum period, the author starts from the inception of slavery when education was denied the Afro–American. The history of the antebellum covers two periods. The first extends from the time slavery was introduced to the climax of the insurrectionary movement in about 1835. The second extends from the time when the industrial revolution changed slavery from a patriarchal to an economic institution and when intelligent blacks, encouraged by abolitionists, made so many attempts to organize servile insurrections that the pendulum began to swing the other way.

The early advocates of the education of blacks were in three classes: masters who desired to increase the economic efficiency of their labor supply; sympathetic persons who wished to help the oppressed; and, zealous missionaries who taught the slaves the English language so they might learn the principles of the Christian religion.

715. ————. *The Mis–Education of the Negro*. Washington, D.C.: Associated Publishers, 1933.

Woodson, who was the founder of the *Journal of Negro History*, describes the blighting effects the American educational system has had on blacks. He argues that the aim of education was "to transform the Negro," not to develop him through the study of his own culture and history. Woodson says much to encourage the teaching of black history and culture in the schools and to develop the student's ability to *think*.

716. Woolfolk, E. Oscar, ed. *Curriculum Change in Black Colleges: A Report on the Cooperative Academic Planning Curriculum Development Conference*. Washington, D.C.: Institute for Services to Education, 1972.

This book is the result of the "Curriculum Change in Black Colleges" conference held in 1972. It includes the presentations of the various speakers and selected excerpts from the discussions. The speakers represent faculty and staff from twenty–five black colleges and include such people as Elias Blake, Harold Delaney, and Edward Brantley. Topics discussed include forging new directions in black colleges, deparochializing general education, introducing nontraditional study, and implementing curriculum change.

717. ————, ed. *Focus on Curriculum Change in Black Colleges II: A Report on the Cooperative Academic Planning Curriculum Development Workshop*. Washington, D.C.: Institute for Services to Education, 1972.

This book is a report on the second workshop held by the Cooperative Academic Planning Program and consists of papers presented in the five plenary sessions (part 1), synopses of four educational systems that address themselves to the educational needs of students at black colleges (part 2), and summaries of curriculum documents prepared by each team.

The contributing speakers, experts from various black colleges as well as from the broader higher education community, include such notables as George Owens, Albert Berrian, Renee Westcott, and Joseph Katz. Topics discussed include the black college as a manpower resources delivery system, an academic skills center, and the developmental perspective in higher education.

718. Woolfolk, E. Oscar, and Roosevelt Calbert.* *Curriculum Change in Black Colleges IV: A Report on Two Cooperative Academic Planning Curriculum Development Workshops.* Washington, D.C.: Institute for Services to Education, 1973.

Contains the proceedings of two workshops: the December 4–6, 1972, orientation workshop for over fifty consortial schools, and the June 4–13, 1973, summer workshop in Dallas, Texas, for the same colleges and universities. Topics include "Past Goals, Present Mission and Future Prospects for Our Colleges and Universities," "Freshmen Interdisciplinary Program at Fisk University," "Performance–based Instructional Programs: A Realistic Approach Toward Developing and Implementing," "The Black College in Transition," and "Academic Skills Center." In addition, abstracts of curriculum documents are included. Elias Blake, Jr., Hugh Gloster, and Broadus N. Butler are among the contributors.

719. Woolfolk, E. Oscar, and Sherman Jones.* *Planning the Academic Program.* Washington, D.C.: Institute for Services to Education, 1973.

The monograph presents the results of the work by the Office of Cooperative Academic Planning with a number of traditional black colleges over a period of two years. The first part is a conceptual framework for academic planning; the second part concerns curricular analysis. The bibliography offers a wealth of references for those in education interested in the area of curriculum development and academic planning.

720. Woolfolk, E. Oscar, and Joel O. Nwagbaraocha,* eds. *Curriculum Change in Black Colleges III: A Report on Two Cooperative Academic Planning Curriculum Development Workshops.* Washington, D.C.: Institute for Services to Education, 1973.

The papers contained in this book are the result of two workshops held in Atlanta, Georgia, by the Office of Cooperative Academic Planning in cooperation with its consortial colleges. These workshops were held in 1972 and 1973, and reflect an attempt by black colleges to effect programs that deal with problems in America today. Contributors in this volume include Margaret Alexander, James Parker, Eddie Martin, and Lillie Davis. Topics discussed include humanities with a black focus, development of urban–related programs in black colleges, and accelerated curricular change on black campuses.

721. Woolfolk, George Ruble. *Prairie View: A Study in Public Conscience, 1878–1946.* New York: Pageant Press, 1962.

722. Wright, Nathan, Jr., ed. *What Black Educators Are Saying.* New York: Hawthorn Books, 1970.

A collection of essays contributed by prominent educators, such as C. Eric Campbell and Preston Wilcox. The anthology is divided into five parts: the black educator, the white establishment, the university scene, the educational redefinition, and community involvement and action.

A section containing brief introductions of the contributors is also contained in the volume. Collectively, these educators present substantial insight into the critical issues faced by blacks in all aspects of education.

723. Wright, Richard Robert. *A Brief Historical Sketch on Negro Education in Georgia.* Savannah, Ga.: Robinson Printing House, 1894.

A brief but informative record of Afro–American education in Georgia from the times of clandestine "school" meetings to the founding of such prominent universities as Morris Brown, Spelman, and Clark. The monograph tells of the influences of the various denominations and missionaries in establishing a formidable educational system. A review of the public schools in major cities, of the quality of education, and of the students contribute to this excellent chronicle of the history of education for the Afro–American in Georgia.

724. Wynn, Cordell. *Multicultural Education Through Competency–based Teacher Education.* Washington, D.C.: U.S. Office of Education, 1974.

725. Young,** Beverly Sue, Mary Hilton Appleberry,** and Odis Odean Rhodes. *Reading How and Why.* Dubuque, Iowa: Kendall/Hunt Publishing Co., 1976.

Reading How and Why, a handbook on reading, offers the typical classroom teacher concrete and practical suggestions on teaching techniques and materials in specific areas of reading instruction.

726. Young,** Ethel, and Natelkka E. Burrell. *Forward March.* Mountain View, Calif.: Pacific Press, 1963.

This book is designed for the fifth–grade reading level and includes many interesting short stories as well as a useful glossary. A booklet of tests is also available for this book, which was developed by the Department of Education General Conference of Seventh–Day Adventists. In the same series there are other readers for the different levels.

CHAPTER 4

FINE ARTS, ENTERTAINMENT, AND SPORTS

727. Aaron, Henry, with Joel Cohen.** *Hitting the Aaron Way.* Englewood Cliffs, N.J.: Prentice-Hall, 1974.

The most effective techniques in hitting a baseball are described by Henry Aaron, a National League batting champion and a home run king—he surpassed Babe Ruth's home run record.

728. Abdul, Raoul. *Blacks in Classical Music: A Personal History.* New York: Dodd, Mead and Co., 1977.

This work discusses blacks in classical music from the eighteenth century to the present day. It includes composers, singers, operas and opera companies, keyboard artists, instrumentalists, conductors, orchestras, choruses, and critics.

729. Archer, Leonard Courtney. *Black Images in the American Theatre: NAACP Protest Campaign—Stage, Screen, Radio, and Television.* Brooklyn, N.Y.: Pageant-Poseidon, 1973.

730. Ashe, Arthur R., Jr., with Kip Branch,* Ocania Chalk, et al.* *A Hard Road to Glory: A History of the African–American Athlete.* 3 vols. New York: Warner Books, 1988.

Written with the assistance of Kip Branch,* Ocania Chalk, and Francis Harris,* Arthur Ashe's three–volume work examines the history of black athletes in America. Each volume treats major sports in separate chapters. The first volume deals with black athletes from 1619–1918, the second covers the period from 1918–1946, and the third encompasses the period since 1946.

731. Baker, David N., Lida M. Belt,* and Herman C. Hudson, eds. *The Black Composer Speaks.* Metuchen, N.J.: Scarecrow Press, 1978.

732. Baraka, Imamu Amiri. *Black Music.* New York: William Morrow and Co., 1967. Reprint. Westport, Conn.: Greenwood Press, 1980.

This work comprises a collection of articles on jazz written after 1961. Provides an analysis of the music and its environment.

733. ————. *Blues People: Negro Music in White America.* New York: William Morrow and Co., 1963. Reprint. Westport, Conn.: Greenwood Press, 1980.

734. Barrow, Joe Louis, Jr., and Barbara Munder.** *Joe Louis: 50 Years an American Hero.* New York: McGraw–Hill, 1988.

This book describes both the background and the exciting action of the "Brown Bomber's" most famous bouts. The narrative is enhanced by recollections of people who knew him, fought him, and or were influenced by him—siblings, former wives, boyhood friends, trainers, opponents (including Max Schmeling and Billy Conn), sportswriters, politicians, and many others. Includes a foreword by Arthur R. Ashe, Jr., Joe Louis's complete professional boxing record, and a bibliography.

735. Bartley, Lua Stewart. *A Brief History of the Division of Health, Physical Education, and Recreation at Florida A & M University from 1918 Through 1978 (60 yrs).* Tallahassee: Florida A & M University, 1979.

Noting that the first physical education facility at Florida Agriculture and Mechanical University was a sand tennis court erected in 1901, the author traces the development of the physical education program by discussing it in terms of "Conception," "Embryo," "Burping," "Crawling," "Standing," "Toddling," and "Walking." Bartley also includes tabular data about students and teachers, the curriculum for majors in health and physical education, and the curriculum for graduate students in physical education.

736. Baylor, Don, with Claire Smith.* *Don Baylor: Nothing but the Truth, A Baseball Life.* New York: St. Martin's Press, 1989.

737. Bogle, Donald. *Black Arts Annual.* New York: Garland Publishing, Inc., 1989.

This book presents the contributions of black artists during the 1987–1988 season in dance, literature, theater, film, television, popular music, jazz and classical music, painting and sculpture, and photography. Each section is written by an expert in the field and includes an essay that surveys the year's events and pinpoints new trends, issues, and ideas.

738. ————. *Blacks in American Film and Television: An Encyclopedia.* New York: Garland Publishing, Inc., 1988.

This book, written by a leading expert on blacks in American popular culture, is divided into three sections. The first section consists of short articles on the representative films that feature black performers who were important in black film history from *The Birth of a Nation* (1915) to *She's Gotta Have It* (1986). The second section reviews in detail those television shows from "Beulah" (1950) to the present sitcoms and dramas with significant black participation. The third section provides short critical biographies of the blacks who have left their mark on motion pictures and television in the United States. Includes a subject index.

739.   ————. *Brown Sugar: Eighty Years of America's Black Female Superstars.* 1st ed. New York: Harmony Books, 1980.

740.   ————. *Toms, Coons, Mulattoes, Mammies, and Bucks: An Interpretive History of Blacks in American Films.* New York: Viking Press, 1973.

741.   Carew, Rod. *Rod Carew's Art and Science of Hitting.* New York: Viking Press, 1986.

742.   Coleridge–Taylor, Samuel. *Twenty-Four Negro Melodies.* Boston: O Ditson Co., 1905. Reprint. New York: Da Capo Press, 1980.

743.   Cooper, T. G., and Carole Singleton. *On Stage in America.* Bristol, Ind.: Wyndham Hall Press, 1986.

Covering "Theatre as Art," "Theatre in America," "The Organized Theatre," "Theatre and Stage," and "The Actor and the Stage," two distinguished actor/playwright/directors provide an introductory text to the theater for beginning students. They include a glossary and an expansive bibliography.

744.   Cornelius, James. *Drama in Bahamas: The Story of Muhammad Ali's Last and Greatest Fight.* Atlanta, Ga.: General Publishing Co., 1985.

Cornelius recounts how he became the promoter of the "Drama in Bahamas" fight between Muhammad Ali and Trevor Berbick, who took Larry Holmes fifteen rounds in Las Vegas in a losing effort. He tells how Ali at age thirty–nine wanted to "rumble" but could not obtain a boxing license in the United States, and how he, while undergoing personal financial problems, evading the FBI, and fighting Don King, managed to bring the ten–round fight to fruition in Nassau on December 11, 1981. This book provides a brief glimpse into the dog–eat–dog world of boxing, "the most brutal sport known to man."

745. Curry, George. *Jake Gaither, America's Most Famous Black Coach.* New York: Dodd, Mead and Co., 1977.

746. Dandridge, Dorothy, and Earl Conrad.* *Everything and Nothing: The Dorothy Dandridge Tragedy.* New York: Abelard–Schuman, 1970.

747. Davis, Howard. *Contributions of Blacks to the Physical Education Profession.* Birmingham, Ala.: Alabama Center for Higher Education 1978.

748. Davis, Sammy, Jr., Jane Boyar,** and Burt Boyar.** *Why Me? The Sammy Davis, Jr., Story.* New York: Farrar, Straus and Giroux, 1989.

From ages three until sixteen, Davis performed a song–and-dance act with his father and his "Uncle" Will Mastin in the world of Negro vaudeville. In this book, he looks back on his career and his obsession with super–stardom, an obsession intensified by the fear that he would lose his appeal and, that age would cut him down. Includes photographs.

749. ———. *Yes I Can.* New York: Farrar, Straus and Giroux, 1965.

This book looks at the famous entertainer's bumpy road to stardom and his development as a person.

750. Devall, William Sigure, Jr. *Junior High School Art Curriculum.* Washington, D.C.: University Press of American, 1980.

751. Dunham, Katherine. *Dances of Haiti.* Photographs by Patricia Cummings. Los Angeles: Center for Afro–American Studies, UCLA, 1983.

This work is a revision of the author's thesis on the subject. Includes bibliographical references.

752. Ellington, Duke (Edward Kennedy). *Music Is My Mistress.* Garden City, N.Y.: Doubleday and Co., 1973. Reprint. New York: Da Capo Press, 1976.

753. Ellington, Mercer, and Stanley Dance.* *Duke Ellington in Person: An Intimate Memoir.* Boston: Houghton Mifflin Co., 1978. Reprint. New York: Da Capo Press, 1979.

754. Fax, Elton C. *Black Artists of the New Generation.* New York: Dodd, Mead and Co., 1977.

755. Fisher, Miles Mark, Sr. *Negro Slave Songs in the United States.* New York: Citadel Press, 1953.

The present work is a revision of the author's doctoral dissertation, "The Evolution of Slave Songs of the United States," at the University of Chicago. Not only does Fisher condense the discussion of black folk songs as folk music and as proof of various theories about blacks, but he also adds analyses of a number of well-known antebellum spirituals. As decoded by Fisher, the spirituals reveal data respecting their authors, dates, places of origin, plans for escape, and protests against slavery.

756. Fletcher, Tom. *One Hundred Years of the Negro in Show Business.* New York: Burdge, 1954. Reprint. New York: Da Capo Press, 1984.

757. Gayle, Addison, Jr. *The Black Aesthetic.* Garden City, N.Y.: Doubleday and Co., 1972.

This anthology, the first major study of the approaches to a black aesthetic, includes thirty-three essays on black arts. Black writers offer theoretical interpretations of black aesthetics and its implications in music, poetry, drama, and fiction. Includes an index and biographies.

758. George, Nelson. *The Death of Rhythm and Blues.* New York: Pantheon Books, 1988.

759. ————. *Where Did Our Love Go? The Rise and Fall of the Motown Sound.* 1985. Reprint. New York: St. Martin's Press, 1987.

This book discusses the legendary Motown and its stars, including Smokey Robinson and Diana Ross. It includes a foreword by Quincy Jones, an extensive discography, and an index.

760. Gibson, Bob, with Phil Pepe.* *From Ghetto to Glory: The Story of Bob Gibson.* Englewood Cliffs, N.J.: Prentice-Hall, 1968.

761. Gillespie, Dizzy, and Al Fraser.** *To Be or Not—To Bop: Memoirs.* New York: Doubleday and Co., 1979. Reprint. New York: Da Capo Press, 1985.

762. Green, Mildred Denby. *Black Women Composers: A Genesis.* Boston: Twayne Publishers, 1983.

763. Green, Tina Sloan, Carole A. Oglesby,** Alpha Vernell Alexander, et al.* *Black Women in Sport.* Reston, Va.: Aahperd Publications, 1981.

In this five-chapter book, the authors discuss black women in sports. The five chapters are "Myths and Realities of Black Women in Sport," "Her Story of Black Sportswomen," "Real Problems and Real Solutions," "Cross-Cultural Study: Nigerian Women in Sport," and "Towards a Better Day." Nikki Franke* is the fourth author.

764. Griese,** Bob, and Gale Sayers. *Offensive Football.* Edited by Bill Bondurant.* New York: Atheneum Publishers, 1972.

765. Handy, William Christopher, ed. *Blues: An Anthology: Complete Words and Music of 53 Great Songs.* A. & C. Boni, 1926. Reprint. New York: Da Capo Press, 1985.

766. Harrison, Daphne. *Black Pearls: Blues Queens of the 1920s.* New Brunswick, N.J.: Rutgers University Press, 1988.

Harrison focuses on four blues queens: Alberta Hunter, Sippie Wallace, Victoria Spivey, and Edith Wilson. She spent a year listening to their original recordings, reviewing newspaper accounts of their performances, and interviewing three of them before all four died. She finds the blues rooted in spirituals, which explore the misery of oppression.

767. Haskins, James. *Break Dancing.* Minneapolis: Lerner Publications Co., 1985.

"Presents a history of break dancing, instructions for break dance steps, and profiles of some of today's famous performers."

768. ————. *Gambling: Who Really Wins?* New York: Franklin Watts, 1979.

769. ————. *Snow Sculpture and Ice Carving.* New York: Macmillan Co., 1974.

It was the Dartmouth College students of the early 1920s who first discovered the enormous creative potential of snow sculpture. In this book, Haskins uses illustrations to demonstrate techniques for "Working with Snow" and "Working with Ice." The snow games are of particular interest to young readers.

770. Haskins, Jim, with Kathleen Benson.** *The Stevie Wonder Scrapbook.* New York: Grosset and Dunlap, 1978.

771. Henderson, Edwin Bancroft. *The Black Athlete: Emergence and Arrival.* 1st ed. New York: Publishers Co., 1968. Reprint. Cornwells Heights, Pa.: Publishers Agency, 1979.

772. ————. *The Negro in Sports.* 1939. Reprint. Washington, D.C.: Associated Publishers, 1949.

773. Higgins,* Chester, Jr., and Orde Coombs. *Drums of Life: A Photographic Essay on the Black Man in America.* Garden City, N.Y.: Anchor Press, 1974.

774. Hinton, Milt, with David G. Berger.* *Bass Line: The Stories and Photographs of Milt Hinton.* Philadelphia: Temple University Press, 1988.

Known as the "dean of bass players," Hinton outlines his fifty-year career and presents his nearly two Hundred photographs of the musicians and singers who have been his colleagues and friends. He tells of his early days with Cab Calloway's orchestra and his work as a studio musician as he provides a look at the world of jazz musicians. Includes discography and index.

775. Holiday, Billie, with William F. Dufty.* *Lady Sings the Blues.* Garden City, N.Y.: Doubleday and Co., 1956. Reprint. New York: Avon Books, 1976.

776. Horne, Lena, with Richard Schickel.* *Lena.* 1st ed. Garden City, N.Y.: Doubleday and Co., 1965.

The life story of a well-known artist, with emphasis on her career in the entertainment field.

777. Hughes, Langston. *The First Book of Jazz.* Pictures by Cliff Roberts.* Music selected by David Martin.* New York: Franklin Watts, 1955.

778. ————. *The First Book of Rhythms.* Pictures by Robin King.* New York: Franklin Watts, 1954.

779. Hughes, Langston, and Milton Meltzer,* eds. *Black Magic: A Pictorial History of the Negro in American Entertainment.* Englewood Cliffs, N.J.: Prentice-Hall, 1967.

Presented in this book is a panorama of black actors, singers, musicians, comedians, dancers, and composers from slave days to the present.

780. Jackson, Irene Viola, ed. *More Than Dancing: Essays on Afro-American Music and Musicians.* Westport, Conn.: Greenwood Press, 1985.

Prepared under the auspices of the Center for Ethnic Music, Howard University, this book includes essays on Afro-American music, bibliographies, a discography, and an index.

781. ――――, ed. *More Than Drumming: Essays on African and Afro-Latin American Music and Musicians.* Westport, Conn.: Greenwood Press, 1985.

782. Jackson, Michael. *Moonwalk.* 1st ed. New York: Doubleday and Co., 1988.

This autobiography narrates the personal recollections of pop music superstar Michael Jackson. Jackson offers a rare peek into his closely guarded private life, as he writes about a variety of subjects, from family and friends to plastic surgery. This book contains nearly one hundred photographs.

783. Jackson, Michael, with David Newman.* *Moonwalker: The Storybook.* Illustrated with scenes from the screenplay by David Newman.* Garden City, N.Y.: Doubleday and Co., 1988.

This is a seventy-page companion volume to entertainer Michael Jackson's "Moonwalker" video. Written by Michael Jackson and screenwriter David Newman,* it is the story of three children who help Michael prevent an evil genius from ruining the lives of children all over the world.

784. Johnson, James Weldon, and John Rosamond Johnson, eds. *The Book of American Negro Spirituals.* New York: Viking Press, 1925; 1969. Reprint. New York: Da Capo Press, 1977.

785. Jules-Rosette, Bennetta. *The Message of Tourist Art: An African Semiotic System in Comparative Perspective.* New York: Plenum Publishing Corporation, 1984.

786. King, Woodie, Jr. *Black Theatre, Present Condition.* New York: National Theatre Touring Circuit, 1981.

787. Lester, Julius, and Pete Seeger.* *The 12-String Guitar as Played by Leadbelly: An Instruction Manual.* New York: Oak Publications, 1965.

This work consists of song transcripts by Jerry Silverman* and Julius Lester, photographic selections and arrangements by Julius Lester, and a cover design by Ronald Clyne.*

788. Lewis, David Levering. *When Harlem Was in Vogue.* 1st ed. New York: Alfred A. Knopf, 1981.

789. Locke, Alain LeRoy. *The Negro and His Music.* Washington, D.C.: The Associates in Negro Folk Education, 1936. Reprint. Port Washington, N.Y.: Kennikat Press, 1968.

790. Long, Richard A. *The Black Tradition in American Dance.* London: Prion, 1989.

791. Lovinggood, Penman. *Famous Modern Negro Musicians.* Brooklyn, N.Y.: Press Forum Co., 1921. Reprint. New York: Da Capo Press, 1978.

792. Mapplethorpe, Robert. *Black Book.* New York: St. Martin's Press, 1986.

793. Mays, Willie. *Willie Mays: My Life in and out of Baseball, As Told to Charles Einstein.*** Rev. ed. New York: E. P. Dutton and Co., 1972.

794. Mays, Willie, with Maxine Berger.* *Willie Mays: "Play Ball!"* Introduction by Joe Garagiola.** New York: Julian Messner, 1980.

795. Mays, Willie, and Jeff Harris.* *Danger in Centerfield.* Larchmont, N.Y.: Argonaut Books, 1963. Reprint. New York: J. Lowell Pratt and Co., 1964.

796. McFerrin, Bobby. *Don't Worry, Be Happy.* New York: Delacorte Press, 1988.

   This little book consists of the complete, illustrated (by Bennett Carlson*) lyrics to the song, "Don't Worry, Be Happy," along with more than twenty new verses created exclusively for this book. The song won a Grammy Award in 1989.

797. Mitchell, Lofton. *Black Drama: The Story of the American Negro in the Theatre.* New York: Hawthorn Books, 1967.

   Mitchell offers a historical perspective of the Afro-American in the theater, spanning several generations. He studies the black pioneers who opposed the minstrels, the Harlem theater movements, the Off-Broadway developments, and the plays of James Baldwin, LeRoi Jones, and Lorraine Hansberry. Included are also several interviews with these authors as well as with important black stars such as Sidney Poitier.

798. Molette, Carlton W., and Barbara J. Molette. *Black Theatre: Premise and Presentation.* Bristol, Ind.: Wyndham Hall Press, 1986.

799. Moutoussamy-Ashe Jeanne. *Viewfinders: Black Women Photographers.* New York: Dodd, Mead and Co., 1986.

800. Murray, Albert. *Stomping the Blues.* New York: McGraw-Hill, 1976. Reprint. New York: Da Capo Press, 1989.

   This book is a history and criticism of blues music. It won the Deems Taylor Award as best music book of the year from the American Society of Composers and Publishers. Includes an index.

801. Page, James Allen. *Black Olympian Medalists*. Littleton, Colo.: Libraries Unlimited, 1990.

802. Parks, Gordon. *To Smile in Autumn: A Memoir*. New York: W. W. Norton and Co., 1979.

803. Patterson, Lindsay, comp. *Anthology of the Afro-American in the Theatre: A Critical Approach*. Rev. ed. Cornwell Heights, Pa.: Publishers Agency, 1976.

 Divided into thirteen sections, this book includes such work as *The Tattered Queens*, by Ruby Dee. Includes biographies, a bibliography, and an index.

804. ————, comp. *Black Films and Film-Makers: A Comprehensive Anthology from Stereotype to Superhero*. New York: Dodd, Mead and Co., 1975.

805. ————, comp. *The Negro in Music and Art*. 1st ed. New York: Publishers Co., 1967.

806. Pearson, Preston. *Hearing the Noise: My Life in the NFL*. 1st ed. New York: William Morrow and Co., 1985.

 This is the story of Preston Pearson's life in the National Football League. Includes an index.

807. Pfaff, Françoise. *The Cinema of Ousmane Sembene, A Pioneer of African Film*. Westport, Conn.: Greenwood Press, 1984.

808. ————. *Twenty-Five Black African Filmmakers: A Critical Study, with filmography and Bio-Bibliography*. Westport, Conn.: Greenwood Press, 1988.

 This book could be described as a guide to the creative offerings of a select group of black African filmmakers—twenty-three males and two females from thirteen countries, whose films have earned international exposure. Entries include eight filmmakers from Senegal, four from the Ivory Coast, two each from Cameroon and Niger, and one each from Burkina Faso, Ethiopia, Gabon, Ghana, Mali, Mauritania, Nigeria, and South Africa.

809. Porter, James Amos. *Modern Negro Art.* New York: The Dryden Press, 1943. Reprint. New York: Arno Press, 1969.

Porter discusses the important artists and artisans who worked before the Harlem Renaissance, and the impact of "the New Negro Movement" on those artists and artisans. He includes eighty–five halftone plates; works by Edmonia Lewis, Henry O. Tanner, Patrick Reason, Jacob Lawrence, Mata Warrick Fuller, and Archibald Motley are among them.

810. Reed, Ishmael, and Al Young, eds. *Yardbird Lives!* 1st Evergreen ed. New York: Grove Press, 1978.

811. Richardson,** John Adkins, Floyd W. Coleman, and Michael J. Smith.** *Basic Design: Systems, Elements, Applications.* Englewood Cliffs, N.J.: Prentice–Hall, 1984.

812. Robinson, Frank, with Al Silverman.** *My Life is Baseball.* 1968. Reprint. Garden City, N.Y.: Doubleday and Co., 1975.

813. Robinson, John Roosevelt. *Baseball Has Done It.* Edited by Charles Dexter.* 1st ed. Philadelphia: J. B. Lippincott Co., 1964.

814. Sample, Johnny, with Fred J. Hamilton* and Sonny Schwartz.* *Confessions of a Dirty Ballplayer.* New York: Dial Press, 1970.

815. Sayers, Gale, with Al Silverman.** *I Am Third.* Introduction by Bill Cosby. New York: Viking Press, 1970.

816. Smith, Willie (the Lion), with George Hoefer.* *Music on My Mind: The Memoirs of an American Pianist.* New York: Doubleday and Co., 1964. Reprint. New York: Da Capo Press, 1978.

This work by Willie (The Lion) Smith with George Hoefer* includes a foreword by Duke Ellington and a new introduction by John S. Wilson.* It also includes bibliographical references and an index.

817. Snowden, Frank M., Jr. *The Image of the Black in Western Art: From the Pharoahs to the Fall of the Roman Empire.* Vol. 1. New York: William Morrow and Co., 1976.

818. Southall, Geneva H. *Blind Tom: The Post-Civil War Enslavement of a Black Musical Genius.* Minneapolis: Challenge Production, 1979.

The first volume of a projected three-volume series, this book focuses on Thomas Greene Wiggins (Blind Tom), a black musician who lived from 1849-1908 and, according to Southall, was maliciously maligned in music histories. She looks at his life within the context of the politics of slavery and the social conditions prevailing in the South from 1849 to 1864. Through research and literary work, Southall establishes Wiggins's exceptional talents, training, and public successes. She asserts that contemporary reviews, announcements, and other writings about him reflect the sociopolitical events of his day.

819. ————. *The Continuing "Enslavement" of Blind Tom, the Black Pianist-Composer (1865-1887).* Vol 2. Minneapolis: Challenge Production, 1983.

820. Southern, Eileen Jackson. *The Music of Black Americans: A History.* 1st ed. New York: W. W. Norton and Co., 1971.

This history of black American music, a unique blend of African and European musical traditions, is useful as a college text in showing the development of this music from colonial to modern times and its relationship to traditional western music. Southern traces the social, political, and economic influences on the peculiar development of black American music. She emphasizes black musicians in the antebellum period through the early twentieth century.

821. ————, ed. *Readings in Black American Music.* 1st. ed. New York: W. W. Norton and Co., 1971.

This anthology includes "authentic contemporary documents" illustrating the history of black American music from the seventeenth century to contemporary times. The readings were selected according to their relevance to the history of music. Also included are comments by nonmusicians with keen insight into the power and significance of black music. Biographical information precedes each document, and wherever possible, the author includes the complete text of a selection.

822. Stewart, Rex. *Jazz Masters of the Thirties.* New York: Macmillian Co., 1972. Reprint. New York: Da Capo Press, 1982.

823. Story, Rosalyn M. *And So I Sing: African–American Divas of Opera and Concert.* New York: Warner Books, 1990.

824. Tatum, Jack, with Bill Kushner.* *They Call Me Assassin.* New York: Everest House Publishers, 1979.

825. Thomas, Duane, and Paul Zimmerman.* *Duane Thomas and the Fall of America's Team.* New York: Warner Books, 1988.

Named Rookie of the Year by the news service, Thomas and his coauthor Zimmerman explain what happened to him and to his football career. They also examine the reasons the Dallas Cowboys have fared so poorly during the late 1980s. Thomas, who grew up in the black ghetto of Dallas, was drafted in the first round by the Cowboys and after two years was traded to the San Diego Chargers. He later played briefly with the Washington Redskins, followed by a brief stint in Hawaii with the World Football League.

826. Walker, David Anthony, and Jim Haskins. *Double Dutch.* Hillside, N.J.: Enslow Publishers, 1986.

827. Warner, Malcolm–Jamal, with Daniel Paisner.* *Theo and Me: Growing Up Okay.* New York: E. P. Dutton and Co., 1988.

Warner, one of America's most popular teenage television actors, uses excerpts from his fan mail as a jumping–off point to discuss troublesome aspects of adolescence, including family life, schooling, dating, race relations, and drugs. Examples are drawn from his own experiences on and off the set of "The Cosby Show," in which he plays Theo Huxtable. The book includes a foreword by Bill Cosby, photos, a chapter on "Where to Go for Help," and an afterword by Alvin F. Poussaint.

828. Waters, Ethel. *To Me It's Wonderful.* With an introduction by Eugenia Price* and Joyce Blackburn.* New York: Harper and Row, 1972.

829. Webb, Spud, with Reid Slaughter.** *Flying High.* New York: Harper and Row, 1988.

Winner of an NBA Slam Dunk Championship, 5'6" Anthony Spud Webb shares his highs and lows. For example, he was initially kept off his high school varsity basketball team because he was too short. Later, when he was given a chance, he took that team to the play–offs. He talks about his dedication to the game and about the people who helped him. Includes photographs and a foreword by Julius Erving.

830. Wharton, Dolores Duncan. *Contemporary Artists of Malaysia: A Biographic Survey.* New York: Asia Society, 1971.

This biographical study of leading Malaysian artists is based on a detailed questionnaire completed by each artist. The focus is more upon the personality of the artist than upon his or her work. A "descriptive sketch," together with a photograph, prefaces each artist's biography. Included in the text is a collection of illustrations.

831. Willis–Thomas, Deborah. *Black Photographers, 1840–1940: An Illustrated Bio–Bibliography.* New York: Garland Publishing, Inc., 1985.

 Willis–Thomas presents the lives and work of about sixty–five nineteenth– and twentieth–century Afro–American photographers. Includes indexes.

832. ————. *An Illustrated Bio–Bibliography of Black Photographers, 1940–1988.* New York: Garland Publishing, 1988.

 This work is a sequel to the author's earlier book, *Black Photographers, 1840–1940: An Illustrated Bio–Bibliography.* It treats the work of contemporary black photographers in the United States. Includes an index.

833. Woll, Allen. *Black Musical Theatre: From Coontown to Dreamgirls.* Baton Rouge: Louisiana State University Press, 1989.

834. Young, Al. *Bodies and Soul: Musical Memoirs.* Berkeley: Creative Arts Book Co., 1981.

835. ————. *Kinds of Blues: Musical Memoirs.* San Francisco: Creative Arts Book Co., 1984.

836. ————. *Things Ain't What They Used To Be: Musical Memoirs.* Berkeley: Creative Arts Book Co., 1987.

CHAPTER 5

HISTORY

837. Akpan, Moses E. *African Goals and Diplomatic Strategies in the United Nations: An In-Depth Analysis of African Diplomacy.* North Quincy, Mass.: Christopher Publishing House, 1976.

838. Allen, Robert L. *Black Awakening in Capitalist America: An Analytical History.* Garden City, N.Y.: Doubleday, 1969.

The author focuses on the American power elite and the underdeveloped Third World at home. Includes an index and a bibliography.

839. Austin, Lettie J., Lewis H. Fenderson, and Sophia P. Nelson, eds. *The Black Man and the Promise of America.* Glenview, Ill.: Scott, Foresman and Co., 1970.

840. Avery, Burniece. *Walk Quietly Through the Night and Cry Softly.* Detroit: Balamp Publishing, 1977.

In this work, her first book, Avery—a playwright, director, and actress—tells the story of her own family, starting around 1911 in York, Alabama, and of their experiences over the next fifty-six years through Virginia, Ohio, Kentucky, and finally Detroit. Includes bibliography and index.

841. Bailey, Minnie Thomas. *Reconstruction in Indian Territory: A Story of Avarice, Discrimination, and Opportunism.* Port Washington, N.Y.: Kennikat Press, 1972.

This book is a historical narrative of the significant political, economic, and educational efforts toward reconstruction made by the Five Civilized Tribes in Indian Territory from 1865 to 1877. It also provides a comprehensive scholarly synthesis of reconstruction efforts collectively and within the individual Indian nations of Seminole, Creek, Choctaw, Chickasaw, and Cherokee. An analysis of the role of the U.S. government in Indian reconstruction is also examined. Includes a map of the five Indian nations, a bibliography, and an index.

842. Ballard, Allen B. *One More Day's Journey: The Making of Black Philadelphia.* Philadelphia: Institute for the Study of Human Issues, 1987.

843. ————. *One More Day's Journey: The Story of a Family and a People.* New York: McGraw–Hill, 1984.

This is the story of a family and a people who migrated to Philadelphia in the early years of the twentieth century.

844. Baraka, Imamu Amiri. *Raise, Race, Rays, Raze: Essays Since 1965.* New York: Vintage Books, 1972.

845. Barbour, Floyd B., ed. *The Black Seventies.* Boston: Porter Sargent Publishers, 1970.

The contributors of essays to this collection attack the racism of American educational, cultural, and political institutions, and expose what they take to be the purely mythical notion that America is a melting pot in which black and white culture will blend and become indistinguishable. Typical of the point of view expressed in this collection is the remark by H. Rap Brown: "Our will to live must no longer supersede our will to fight, for our fighting will determine if our race shall live. To desire freedom is not enough. We must move from resistance to aggression, from revolt to revolution."

846. Bennett, Lerone, Jr. *Confrontation: Black and White*. Chicago: Johnson Publishing Co., 1965.

Bennett provides a historical record of black protest, struggle, and revolution from the seventeenth century to the present with major emphasis on Booker T. Washington, W. E. B. DuBois, Marcus Garvey, and Martin Luther King, Jr.

847. Berry, Leonidas H. *I Wouldn't Take Nothin' for My Journey: Two Centuries of an Afro–American Minister's Family*. Chicago: Johnson Publishing Co., 1981.

Berry, a famous physician, author, and researcher, writes a narrative biography of his family across six generations, and documents the impact of the AME and other black churches upon the cultural development of the black family. The book includes fifty–six illustrations, a bibliography and an index.

848. Berry, Mary Frances, and John W. Blassingame. *Long Memory: The Black Experience in America*. New York: Oxford University Press, 1982.

Two well–known authors have put this book together around themes that reveal the complexities of the black experience in this country. Subjects include family and church, sex and racism, politics, education, criminal justice, black nationalism, and the history of black military service. The authors trace black cultural continuity to its African origin through the survival of folk tales, proverbs, names, beliefs, and musical motifs. The bibliographical appendix covers thirty–two pages.

849. Blake, Clarence Napoleon, and Donald F. Martin. *Quiz Book on Black America*. Boston: Houghton Mifflin Co., 1976.

Who was the first black doctor in the United States? Who invented the baby carriage? Who was the first black college president in America? In what film did black composer Isaac Hayes win an Academy Award for best musical score? This book answers these and over one hundred other questions on topics pertaining to blacks, including medicine, movies, education, religion, inventions, horse racing, court cases, publishing, and labor. A suggested reading list and index are included.

850. Blakely, Allison. *Russia and the Negro: Blacks in Russian History and Thought.* Washington, D.C.: Howard University Press, 1986.

This book investigates the historic relationship between blacks and Russia's attempt to capture the world's black masses. It explores and features epic black figures who range from the legendary military hero Abram Hannibal and his great–grandson to such Afro–Americans as novelist Richard Wright and Paul Robeson. Other included luminaries are Ira Aldridge, U.S.–born Shakespearean actress; W. E. B. DuBois, sociologist; Claude McKay, Jamaican–born poet and journalist; George Padmore, Trinidadian politician; and Richard T. Greener, Harvard graduate and lawyer. Blakely exmines those talented blacks who were greeted in the highest circles of Soviet hierarchy while being rejected by segments of their own government in the United States. Includes a bibliography and an index.

851. Blassingame, John W. *Black New Orleans, 1860–1880.* Chicago: University of Chicago Press, 1973.

In this new approach to an old topic, Blassingame examines the social and economic aspects of black New Orleans during Reconstruction. He pays attention to education, religion, social and economic activities and to family life, and provides statistical data on birth rates, family structure, the value of property held by blacks, and distribution of occupations. Includes illustrations.

852. ————. *The Slave Community: Plantation Life in the Antebellum South.* 2d ed. New York: Oxford University Press, 1979.

Diverging from traditional histories of Afro-American slaves, Blassingame analyzes the life of the slave and brings psychological insights to bear upon personal records left by slaves themselves. Using such primary sources as white autobiographies, plantation records, agricultural journals, and travel accounts to get further insight into the life of the slave, Blassingame dispels several myths and stereotypes of blacks.

In 1979 he revised and enlarged the 1972 edition. Expanded essays discuss the culture and family while examining such historical phenomena as the origin of the blues in slave secular music, and the impact of Africa and white churches on sexual attitudes, child rearing, wedding ceremonies, familial roles, and language.

853. ———, ed. *New Perspectives on Black Studies.* Urbana: University of Illinois Press, 1971.

This collection of essays by sixteen writers, including Genovese, Hare, Fischer, and Blassingame, discusses black studies programs in some North American colleges. Several essays look at definitions of black studies and ask what function Afro-American education should play in the undergraduate curriculum.

854. ———, ed. *Slave Testimony: Two Centuries of Letters, Speeches, Interviews, and Autobiographies.* Baton Rouge: Louisiana State University Press, 1977.

This work recreates the private and interpersonal life of the slave through letters written by slaves between 1736 and 1864, together with speeches and interviews conducted by journalists, scholars, and government officials between 1827 and 1938. These documents were discovered in manuscripts, collections, vertical files, scrapbooks, newspapers, rare books, and state federal government archives; all contain some black testimony on slavery.

855. Blockson, Charles. *Pennsylvania Black History.* Philadelphia: Portfolio Associates, 1975.

856. Bontemps, Arna Wendell. *Free At Last: The Life of Frederick Douglass.* New York: Dodd, Mead and Co., 1971.

857. Brawley, Benjamin Griffith. *A Short History of the American Negro.* New York: Macmillan Co., 1913.

This book begins with a definition of the term *Negro* and then proceeds to give a history of blacks in the Americas. Topics discussed are the social and economic aspects of slavery, slavery as an institution, the revolution, epoch missionary endeavors, Tuskegee Institute, the black church, the black soldier, and, finally, black achievements in the arts and sciences. It contains an index and bibliography.

858. ————. *A Social History of the American Negro: Being a History of the Negro Problem in the U.S., Including a History and Study of Liberia.* New York: Macmillan Co., 1921.

Brawley examines the social history of Afro–America from the first black explorers and indentured servants to the era of the "Negro problem" in the twentieth century. The book documents of the initiation of black enslavement in the Old as well as the New World, the black–American Indian affiliation, and the seeds of black awareness. With objectivity and a balanced presentation, Brawley recounts the reactions and counterreactions of blacks and whites to real and imagined racial fears.

859. Broudy,* Eric, Warren Jennings Halliburton, and Laurence Swinburne.* *They Had a Dream: True Stories About Blacks in America and their Achievements.* New York: Pyramid Books, 1969.

860. Brown, Roscoe Conkling, Jr., with Mathias Freese* and Mae G. Henderson. *The Black Experience.* New York: Hearne Brothers, 1972.

A historical guide reflecting the heritage of black people in Africa, the Caribbean, and the United States. The material comprises both geographical and cultural insights to reinforce the history presented. The relationship between the history of Africa and the development of Afro-Americans is also examined. Particular eras are elaborated on with special reference to the various personalities outstanding during them. The text is excellent for students in history as well as geography, and includes numerous maps and illustrations.

861. Browne, Robert S., and Robert J. Cummings, eds. *The Lagos Plan of Action Versus the Berg Report: Contemporary Issues in African Economic Development.* Lawrenceville, Va.: Brunswick Publishing Co., 1984.

This 216-page monograph, developed under the auspices of the Howard University African Studies and Research Program, deals with contemporary economic development issues involving Africa. Presents problems, issues, and proposed solutions.

862. Bryant, Henry A., Jr., ed. *Black Politics and Race: A Contemporary Reader of Racism and Black Politics.* Washington, D.C.: University Press of America, 1979.

863. Campbell, Bebe Moore. *Sweet Summer: Growing Up With & Without My Dad.* New York: G. P. Putnam's Sons, 1989.

864. Carew, Jan Rynveld. *Fulcrums of Change.* Trenton, N.J.: Africa World Press, Inc., 1988.

In this collection of essays, Carew expounds on the history, politics, racism, and varying cultures of the Third World. He also includes visions of future promise.

865. Carruthers, Jacob H. *Essays in Ancient Egyptian Studies.* Los Angeles: Timbuktu Publishers, 1984.

866. ———. *The Irritated Genie: An Essay on the Haitian Revolution.* Chicago: The Kemetic Institute, 1985.

867. Chambers, Lucille Arcola, ed. *America's Tenth Man: A Pictorial Review of One-Tenth of a Nation, Presenting the Negro Contribution to American Life Today.* New York: Twayne Publishing Co., 1957.

This compilation presents an overview of the American black in his efforts American in every sense. It includes photographs and biographies of over 1,000 distinguished blacks who have contributed to American life.

868. Chrisman, Robert, and Nathan Hare, eds. *Contemporary Black Thought: The Best from Black Scholars.* Indianapolis: Bobbs–Merrill Co., 1973.

An anthology of writings by eminent black authors on pressing issues of race relations in the areas of culture, family, politics, and economics. Various points of view emerge from the book, rather than a unilateral perspective.

869. Clark, Kenneth Bancroft. *Dark Ghetto: Dilemmas of Social Power.* New York: Harper and Row, 1965.

Kenneth Clark spent two years as project consultant for and chairman of the board of directors of Harlem Youth Opportunities Unlimited. As an "involved observer," he analyzes the black power structure and dissects the effectiveness of civil rights strategies. Clark offers his insights and comprehension of the ghetto to outsiders.

870. ————. *The Negro Protest: James Baldwin, Malcolm X, Martin Luther King Talk with Kenneth B. Clark.* Boston: Beacon Press, 1963.

871. Clark, Kenneth Bancroft, Julian Bond, and Richard G. Hatcher. *The Black Man in American Politics: Three Views.* Washington, D.C.: Metropolitan Applied Research Center for the Institute for Black Elected Officials, 1969.

Three prominent black men present their views of blacks in the American political scene. Julian Bond contributes a brief history of blacks elected to public office in the South; Richard Hatcher recounts experiences as councilman and mayor of Gary, Indiana; and Kenneth Clark writes of the challenges confronting black elected officials. These speeches were originally presented at the Institute for Black Elected Officials.

872.   Clarke, John Henrik, ed. *Harlem: A Community in Transition.* 2d ed. New York: Citadel Press, 1969.

Clarke traces many different aspects of Harlem life throughout its history and highlights famous personages, such as Marcus Garvey, whose fame was first proclaimed by Harlem.

873.   ———, ed. *Harlem, U.S.A.: The Story of a City Within a City Told by James Baldwin* . . . [et al.] Berlin: Seven Seas, 1964.

In this work, James Baldwin, who turned to writing after an early career as a boy preacher in Harlem's storefront churches, talks about the community ("city") in which he grew up. "The contents of this book, in part, have been taken from various issues of *Freedomways.*"

874.   Clarke, Nina L., and Lillian B. Brown. *History of the Black Public Schools of Montgomery County, Maryland 1872–1961.* New York: Vantage Press, 1978.

Former teachers and principals of the Montgomery County school system, the authors have meticulously compiled the history of public schools in that county. They show that the education of slaves and free blacks was not illegal in Maryland, and report that the first school for black children in Montgomery County was Sharp Street School at Sandy Springs. The book also contains photographs of the early black schools and students, as well as an appendix, a bibliography, and an index. The appendix includes a listing of black teachers in Montgomery County from 1876 to 1920, "firsts" in Montgomery County public schools for blacks, and a text of the U.S. Supreme Court's opinion in the *Brown II* (1955) case, as well as the attorney general's opinion.

875. Clarke, Robert Lewis, ed. *Afro-American History: Sources for Research.* Washington, D.C.: Howard University Press, 1981.

This book, volume 12 in the National Archives series on American historiography, is a look at the government's role in shaping the black experience in America through its own military, diplomatic, presidential and domestic records. Contributors to this volume include Alex Haley, John Blassingame, Mary Frances Berry, Andrew Billingsley, and Harold T. Pinkett.

876. Cleaver, Eldridge. *Soul on Ice.* New York: McGraw-Hill, 1968.

Writing in Folsom State Prison, Cleaver, in a series of essays and vignettes, gives his philosophy and position on issues ranging from the black man's stake in Vietnam to his reason for being in prison, or "on ice." An interpretation of the interrelationships of the black male, white female, white male, black female is elucidated in the chapter titled "Primeval Mitosis."

877. Cleveland, Edward Earl. *No Stranger Now.* Mountain View, Calif.: Pacific Press, 1972.

878. Coombs, Orde, ed. *Is Massa Day Dead? Black Moods in the Caribbean.* Garden City, N.Y.: Anchor Books, 1974.

879. Crockett, Harry J., and Jerome L. Schulman,* eds. *Achievement Among Minority Americans: A Conference Report.* Cambridge, Mass.: Schenkman Publishing Co., 1973.

This book arose from the efforts of a research community to exclude white middle-class bias in its studies on achievement among minority Americans. Topics discussed include definition of achievement, current knowledge regarding achievement in the United States, determinants of achievement among adults, potential differences in achievement associated with familiar variations among diverse groups, and action–intervention programs to affect achievement.

880. Crogman, William Henry. *Talks for the Times.* Atlanta, Ga.: Atlanta Press of Franklin Prtg. and . . . , 1896. Reprint. Freeport, N.Y.: Books for Libraries Press, 1971.

In these public addresses, the nineteenth–century thinker William Crogman promoted the welfare and advancement of his peoples. Some of the topics included are "Effects of Christian Education" and "The Negro Needs and the Negro Problem." In "Negro Education—Its Helps and Hinderances," delivered before the National Teachers' Association at Madison, Wisconsin, in 1884, Crogman enumerates the particulars of southern education at that time and exhorts blacks to continue their drive for education.

881. Cromwell, Adelaide M., ed. *Dynamics of the African Afro-American Connection: From Dependency to Self-Reliance.* Washington, D.C.: Howard University Press, 1987.

This book presents the proceedings of a seminar in Monrovia, which looked at the means of improving communication between Africans and Afro-Americans. At this seminar, the University of Liberia and the University of Sierra Leone through Fourah Bay College joined Boston University.

882. Cruse, Harold. *The Crisis of the Negro Intellectual.* New York: William Morrow and Co., 1967.

Working from Milton Gordon's hypothesis that "intellectuals in the United States interact in such patterned ways as to form at least the elementary structure of a subsociety of their own, and that this subsociety is the only one in American life in which people of different ethnic backgrounds interact in primary group relations with considerable frequency and with relative comfort and ease," Cruse attempts to determine whether black intellectuals, who he believes are not fully integrated, measure up to the complex problem of being spokesmen on behalf of their ethnic group—the black masses. Thus, he claims, two aspects of black reality demand closer examination and analysis: black ethnic group consciousness and the "new" black intellectual class that has emerged as of the late 1950s and 1960s. Includes bibliography and index.

883.   Daise, Ronald. *Reminiscences of Sea Island Heritage.* 2d ed. Orangeburg, S.C.: Sandlapper Publishing, 1987.

Daise documents the lifestyle, superstitions, and folklore of St. Helena Island, one of the sea islands off the coast of South Carolina. Includes photos of the early 1800s–1900s.

884.   Daniels, Douglas Henry. *Pioneer Urbanites: A Social and Cultural History of Black San Francisco.* Philadelphia: Temple University Press, 1980.

Daniels shows that blacks became prominent as prize-fighters, vice entrepreneurs, and entertainers; some achieved a quieter economic security by running boardinghouses or by "hustling," inventing extra services they could perform in addition to their regular jobs. Blacks took pride in their newspapers and social events, and posed for portraits in elegant finery. This is a pioneering work in a new area of study—western ethnic communities. In addition to traditional sources, Daniels uses interviews with a number of the old black families to enrich his account of life in the Bay Area and especially to explain the psychology of "coping" with discrimination.

885.   Darden, Joseph Turner. *Afro-Americans in Pittsburgh: The Residential Segregation of a People.* Lexington, Mass.: D. C. Heath and Co., 1973.

This book explores the causes and extent of segregation in Pittsburgh in the period between 1930 and 1970, and examines how patterns of segregation have changed during this time. The book contains demographic charts, graphs, and a selected bibliography.

886. Davis, Allison, and John Dollard.** *Children of Bondage: The Personality Development of Negro Youth in the Urban South.* New York: Harper and Row, 1940. Reprint. New York: Harper Torchbook, 1964.

Selecting from their case studies of thirty Afro–American children between the ages of twelve and sixteen living in the Deep South, Davis and Dollard describe the socialization of eight black teenagers.

887. Davis, John Preston, ed. *The American Negro Reference Book.* Englewood Cliffs, N.J.: Prentice–Hall, 1966.

This single volume summarizes outstanding aspects of Afro–American life, past and contemporary, with emphasis on blacks in the social sciences and humanities. It is extremely helpful to the researcher since it contains footnotes, bibliographical references, and a full cross–referenced index.

888. Davis, Lenwood G. *Black–Jewish Relations in the United States, 1752–1984: A Selected Bibliography.* Westport, Conn.: Greenwood Press, 1984.

889. Davis, Lenwood G., and George H. Hill. *Blacks in the American Armed Forces, 1776–1983: A Bibliography.* Westport, Conn.: Greenwood Press, 1985.

890. Davis, Marianna White, ed. *Contributions of Black Women to America.* Vols. 1 and 2. Columbia, S.C.: Kenday Press, 1982.

Covering two hundred years (1776–1977) of the contributions of black women to this nation, this work consists of two volumes. Volume 1 covers the arts, media, business, law, and sports; volume 2 covers civil rights, politics and government, education, medicine, and sciences. Both volumes contain pictures, bibliographies, introductory essays, and an index for each subject area.

891. Delany, Martin Robison. *The Condition, Elevation, Emigration, and Destiny of the Colored People of the United States.* 1852. Reprint. New York: Arno Press and The New York Times, 1969.

With an introduction by Benjamin Quarles, this book deals with (1) the status and the treatment of blacks in America; (2) the achievements of blacks as soldier, farmer, artisan, businessman, writer, and professional; and (3) an analysis of possible solutions to the predicament of black Americans. Includes an appendix.

892. Dewart, Janet, ed. *The State of Black America 1988.* New York: National Urban League, 1988.

An official report of the National Urban League, this edition includes articles on "Black Enrollment in Higher Education," by Niara Sudarkasa; "Tomorrow's Teachers," by Bernard C. Watson; "Civil Rights and the Future of the American Presidency," by Dianne M. Pinderhughes; "The Psychology of Race," by Price M. Cobbs; "The Black Family," by Charles V. Willie; "Black Youth at Risk," by Bruce R. Hare; "Crime in the Black Community," by Lee P. Brown; "Blacks in the Military," by Alvin J. Schexnider; and "The Economic Status of Blacks," by David H. Swinton.

893. Dorsey, James W. *Up South: Blacks in Chicago's Suburbs, 1719-1983.* Bristol, Ind.: Wyndham Hall Press, 1986.

Dorsey explores the unique systems of slavery and indentured servitude in Illinois. The underground railroad routes and stations are highlighted with substantial illustrations taken from a collection of antique photographs of blacks just before and after the turn of the century. An analysis of North Chicago provides a deeper understanding of black history and urban social relations and development, not only in Chicago but throughout urban America. Includes notes.

894. Drake, John Gibbs St. Clair, and Horace R. Cayton. *Black Metropolis: A Study of Negro Life in a Northern City.* New York: Harcourt, Brace and Co., 1945.

Combining sociological and anthropological perspectives, this book discusses three major issues concerning blacks in the city of Chicago: the relationship between blacks and whites; the way of life blacks have developed as a result of their separate, subordinate status; and the impact of the groups upon the personalities and institutions of Chicago blacks.

895. DuBois, Shirley Lola Graham. *There Was Once a Slave . . . The Heroic Story of Frederick Douglass.* New York: Julian Messner, 1947.

896. DuBois, W. E. B. *Black Reconstruction in America: An Essay Toward a History of the Part Which Black Folk Played in the Attempt to Reconstruct Democracy in America, 1860–1880.* New York: Harcourt, Brace and Company, 1935. Reprint. Cleveland, Ohio: World, Meridian, 1962.

This book tells the story of transplanting millions of Africans to the New World, of their bondage for four centuries, of their freedom in the nineteenth century and the attempt through them to reconstruct the basis of American democracy from 1860–1880. The book also presents and interprets those twenty years of fateful history with special reference to the efforts and experiences of blacks themselves. It includes a bibliography and an index.

897. ———. *Dusk of Dawn: An Essay Toward an Autobiography of a Race Concept.* New York: Harcourt Brace Jovanovich, Inc., 1940. Reprint. New Brunswick, N.J.: Transaction Publishers, 1984.

With a new introduction by Irene Diggs, this work explores the phenomenon of race through DuBois's own experience for, as DuBois states, "In my life the chief fact has been race." This book traces the development of DuBois's lifelong concern with the problem of race: how nonwhites might be openly and effectively admitted into the freedom of democracy.

898.   ————. *The Gift of Black Folk: The Negroes in the Making of America.* Boston: Stratford Co., 1924. Reprint. New York: Washington Square Press, 1970.

This early twentieth–century document describes many different contributions blacks have made to American society. DuBois discusses Afro–American literature, folklore, and music as example of these contributions, and, he cites the black spiritual as an example of the faith, hope, and tolerance of a people.

899.   ————. *John Brown.* Philadelphia: G. W. Jacobs and Co., 1909. Reprint. Northbrook, Ill.: Metro Books, 1972.

In this book—first published in 1909 and reprinted in 1962 by International Publishers and in 1972 by Metro Books—DuBois defends John Brown from charges of being a fanatic, freak, or traitor. He provides the reader with insight into the motives of this strong abolitionist.

900.   ————. *The Philadelphia Negro: A Social Study.* 1899. Reprint. Philadelphia: University of Pennsylvania, 1973.

This was the first sociological study of Afro–Americans and is still valuable for its insights.

901.   ————. *The Souls of Black Folk: Essays and Sketches.* Chicago: A. C. McClurgand Co., 1903. Reprint. New York: Penguin Books, 1989.

DuBois gives us his vision of the inner life and qualities of the black man as he searches to find himself in America. In addition, DuBois discusses the cultural and economic and social conditions of the black man in turn–of–the–century America.

902.   ————. *The Suppression of the African Slave-Trade to the United States of America, 1638-1870.* New York: Russell and Russell, Inc., 1898. Reprint. New York: Schocken Books, 1969.

With a new introduction by A. Norman Klein* and the "Apologia" of the author, dated 1954, this book presents the efforts made in the United States to limit and suppress the trade in slaves between Africa and America. For example, chapter 2 presents the attitude of the planting, farming, and trading groups of colonies toward the slavetrade; chapter 3 also focuses on the farming colonies, while chapter 4 discusses the trading colonies. Chapter 5 deals with the period of the revolution, 1774–1787, while chapter 6 talks about the Federal Convention in 1787 and indicates that slavery occupied no prominent place in the convention called to remedy the defects of the Confederation.

Chapter 7 covers Toussaint L'ouverture and the anti–slavery effort (1787–1806), while the period of attempted suppression (1807–1825), the international status of the slavetrade (1783–1862), the rise of the cotton kingdom (1820–1850), the movement against the slave–trade law (1850–1870), and the essentials in the struggle are discussed in chapters 8 through 12, respectively. Includes an apologia.

903. Dunham, Katherine. *Island Possessed.* Garden City, N.Y.: Doubleday, 1969.

904. ————. *Katherine Dunham's Journey to Accompong.* Drawings by Ted Cook.* New York: H. Holt and Company, 1946. Reprint. Westport, Conn.: Negro Universities Press, 1971.

This book discusses the culture of the Maroons—descendents of fugitive slaves of the seventeenth and eighteenth centuries—of Accompong, Jamaica. It describes the Maroons's hunting and farming economy, which is based on African patterns, as well as their raids on British plantations.

905. Dunnigan, Alice Allison, ed. *A Fascinating Story of Black Kentuckians: Their Heritage and Traditions.* Lexington, Ky.: University of Kentucky Press, 1982.

906. Durham, John Stephens. *To Teach the Negro History: A Suggestion.* 1897. Reprint. Philadelphia: David McKay, 1987.

907. Dyson, Walter. *Howard University, The Capstone of Negro Education, A History: 1867–1940.* Washington, D.C.: The Graduate School, Howard University, 1941.

This work is a souvenir of the seventy–fifth anniversary of the founding of Howard University. Written by Dyson, a former professor of history at the university, it covers the period of March 2, 1867, to March 2, 1942. Includes an index.

908. Earley, Charity Adams. *One Woman's Army: A Black Officer Remembers the WAC.* College Station: Texas A & M University Press, 1989.

909. Edwards, Vetress Bon. *Go South with Christ: A Study in Race Relations.* 1st ed. New York: Exposition Press, 1959.

A look at the problem of race relations in the South from a religious perspective. The situation of blacks in the South in the first half of this century is compared with the time of Christ, and the contradictions of southern society and its treatment of the Afro–American are contrasted with the humanitarian doctrines of Christianity. This book challenges its readers to recognize and correct wrongdoings against humankind, especially the black man.

910. Engs, Robert Francis. *Freedom's First Generation: Black Hampton, Virginia, 1861–1890.* Philadelphia: University of Pennsylvania Press, 1979.

911. Epps, Edgar G., ed. *Race Relations: Current Perspectives.* Cambridge, Mass.: Winthrop Publishers, 1973.

The text concentrates on race relations between blacks and whites in America, although nonblack minorities are also discussed. Race relations are viewed from theoretical, institutional, political, and sociological perspectives. The latter two perspectives may be of special interest to educators and students alike for a stimulating discussion of blacks in America.

912. Faggett, Harry Lee. *Blacks and Other Minorities in Shakespeare's England: Study Guide and Workbook; Exercises in Reading, Writing, Discussion, and Research.* Prairie View, Tex.: Prairie View Press, 1971.

913. Farmer, James. *Lay Bare the Heart: An Autobiography of the Civil Rights Movement.* New York: Arbor House, 1985.

Written in an autobiographical style, Farmer, founder of the Congress of Racial Equality (CORE), shares his memories of the organization and its activities, Rosa Parks and the initiation of the civil rights movement, the death of Malcolm X, and other civil rights events. He also discusses his youth and the psychological mayhem of being a preacher's son, the founding of CORE, and his acceptance of a top position at the U.S. Department of Health, Education, and Welfare.

As one of the Big Six of the black leadership cadre of the 1950s and 1960s, Farmer provides illuminating personal portraits of Martin Luther King, Jr., John F. Kennedy, and Lyndon B. Johnson. He also chillingly analyzes the "cannibalizing of the movement," and the civil rights setbacks of the 1970s and 1980s.

914. Favors,* John S., and Kathryne Favors. *White Americans Who Cared.* Oakland, Calif.: Jonka Enterprises, 1974.

915. Fax, Elton C. *Through Black Eyes: Journeys of a Black Artist to East Africa and Russia.* New York: Dodd, Mead and Co., 1974.

916. Fields, Alonzo. *My 21 Years in the White House.* New York: Coward-McCann, 1961.

917. Fields, Barbara Jeanne. *Slavery and Freedom on the Middle Ground: Maryland During the Nineteenth Century.* New Haven: Yale University Press, 1985.

918. Fishel, Leslie H., Jr., and Benjamin Quarles. *The Negro American: A Documentary History.* New York: William Morrow and Co., 1968.

This work comprise excerpts from court decisions, statutes, speeches, memoirs, eyewitness accounts, and other documents detailing the history of blacks in America.

919. Fleming,* Daniel, Paul Slayton, Jr.,* and Edgar A. Toppin. *Virginia History and Government: 1850 to the Present.* Morristown, N.J.: Silver Burdett Co., 1986.

920. Ford, Nick Aaron. *Black Studies: Threat-or-Challenge.* Port Washington, N.Y.: Kennikat Press, 1973.

Based on personal interviews with administrators, teachers, and students, as well as on brochures, catalogs, and questionnaires, this book discusses black studies—the relatively new field in American education.

921. Forman, James. *The Making of Black Revolutionaries: A Personal Account.* New York: Macmillan Co., 1972. Reprint. Washington, D.C.: Open Hand, 1985.

Forman, who served as executive secretary of the Student Nonviolent Coordinating Committee, talks about his life and about his role in SNCC during the civil rights movement.

922. Fowler,* David H., Jacquelyn Slaughter Haywood, and others, eds. *In Search of America: Community, National Identity, Democracy.* New York: Dryden Press, 1972.

923. Franklin, Jimmie Lewis. *The Blacks in Oklahoma.* 1st ed. Norman: University of Oklahoma Press, 1980.

924. ———. *Journey Toward Hope: A History of Blacks in Oklahoma.* 1st ed. Norman: University of Oklahoma Press, 1982.

925. Franklin, John Hope. *The Emancipation Proclamation.* Garden City, N.Y.: Doubleday and Co., 1969.

Franklin describes events leading up to the proclamation and its subsequent national and international impact. Includes notes, sources, and an index.

926. ————. *The Free Negro in North Carolina, 1790–1860.* Chapel Hill: University of North Carolina Press, 1943.

Franklin examines the frustrating legal status of the Afro–American—neither slave nor full citizen—in the antebellum South, with reference to the black man's economic, social, and religious life from the years 1790 to 1860. Based on primary sources, such as county records, papers of the state legislature and Supreme Court, private letters, diaries, and newspapers of the time, this book is a helpful reference book on relations between black minorities and the dominant white society.

927. ————. *A Southern Odyssey: Travelers in the Antebellum North.* Baton Rouge: Louisiana State University Press, 1976.

A comprehensive work about the South's views and attitudes about the North. Some of the South's seasoned travelers even bore seeds of distrust, an atmosphere unsuitable for reasonable discourse. Included is an album of southern travel illustrating outstanding sceneries visited by the southern traveler in New York.

928. Franklin, John Hope, and Alfred A. Moss, Jr. *From Slavery to Freedom: A History of Negro Americans.* 6th ed. 1947. Reprint. New York: Alfred A. Knopf, 1987.

Initially published in 1947, this sixth edition extends its coverage to include the vast number of revolutionary changes that have taken place in recent years. This is a comprehensive overview of the history of Afro–Americans, from their origins in Africa through their struggle up from slavery in the West Indies, Latin America, and the United States.

929. Franklin, Vincent P. *Black Self–Determination: A Cultural History of the Faith of the Fathers*. Westport, Conn.: Lawrence Hill and Co., 1984.

This work is an examination of the "core values" of the Afro–American experience.

930. Fuller, Chet. *I Hear Them Calling My Name: A Journey Through the New South*. Boston: Houghton Mifflin Co., 1981.

Fuller, a native Atlanta newsman, tells of his journey through five southeastern states—North Carolina, South Carolina, Georgia, Alabama, and Mississippi—to evaluate changes in the lives of poor blacks. A college graduate and winner of newspaper awards, Fuller set forth wearing work clothes to hunt jobs in large and small cities and to live with poor families in rural shanties. His experiences in those states indicate clearly that despite the war on poverty, many blacks are still in dire straits.

931. Fuller, Thomas Oscar. *Pictorial History of the American Negro . . . A Story of Progress and Development Along Social, Political, Economic, Educational, and Spiritual Lines*. Memphis, Tenn.: Pictorial History, Inc., 1933.

Written in the 1930's, this book begins with the beauty of unspoiled nature and the life of the black man in Africa, then traces his development through all the important stages of American life. Chapter eight concentrates on the schools, highlighting the education of the black American from slavery to the twentieth century.

932. Gary, Lawrence E., ed. *Social Research and the Black Community: Selected Issues and Priorities*. Washington, D.C.: Institute for Urban Affairs and Research, Howard University, 1974.

This is a selection of papers presented at a workshop on "Developing Research Priorities for the Black Community." The workshop was conducted with the view of making black social scientists more active in defining the research strategies for "solving the problems and developing the resources of the black community." The first three parts discuss the functional significance of social research in the black community, black family life and socialization in the black community, and the criminal justice system as it affects blacks. Part 4 focuses on human resource development and techniques for assessing human and societal growth and development. Each paper includes references.

933. Gayle, Addison, Jr. *The Black Situation.* New York: Horizon Press, 1970.

Using an autobiographical approach, the author portrays the black situation as one of rage, hurt, and determination to overcome the racism in the dominant society. He investigates religion and the black situation, black fathers and their sons, and revolutionary philosophy.

934. Gifford, Bernard R., ed. *History in the School: What Shall We Teach?* New York: Macmillan Co., 1988.

935. Giles, Raymond H., Jr. *Pride and Power: From Watts to Mexico City.* Columbus, Ohio: American Education Publications, 1971.

A chronicle of the struggles and achievements of today's black American, this book focuses on voter registration in the South, breaking out of the ghetto in the North, and other consciousness–raising factors leading to such historical incidents as the Watts riots in 1965 and the raising of clenched fists at the Olympic games in Mexico City in 1968. The book is the last in the series, *The Black Experience in America.*

936. Gordon, Asa Hines. *The Georgia Negro: A History.* Ann Arbor: Edwards Brothers, 1937.

Written in the late 1930s, this volume seeks to fill the gap in the history of blacks in Georgia that was omitted by other pre-

World War II history books on Georgia. Written and arranged to be used as a supplementary text, it includes pictures and illustrations, as well as discussions about Georgia blacks who have attained some prominence in and out of the state.

937. ————. *Sketches of Negro Life and History in South Carolina.* 2d ed. New York: W. B. Conkey, 1929. Reprint. Columbia, S.C.: University of South Carolina Press, 1971.

In this book Gordon gives us insight into the numerous struggles of the black man in South Carolina, from the inception of slavery to the present day.

938. Grant, Nancy L. *TVA and Black Americans: Planning for the Status Quo.* Philadelphia: Temple University Press, 1989.

939. Green, Robert L. *Daring Black Leaders.* Milwaukee, Wis.: Franklin Press, 1974.

This work is a series of brief biographies (seven books) on the following black leaders: Barbara Jordan (1936–), Julian Bond (1940–), John W. Porter (1931–), Coretta Scott King (1926–), Darmon Jerome Keith (1922–), Clifton Reginald Wharton, Jr. (1926–), and Charles Evers (1923–).

940. Greene, Lorenzo Johnston. *The Negro in Colonial New England, 1620–1776.* 1942. Reprint. New York: Columbia University Press, 1966.

Covering a period of approximately 150 years and embracing all the colonies, the author traces the history of blacks in New England from 1620 to 1776. Heavily substantiated with articles, documents, records, dates, statistics, reminiscences, and citations from the law (then existent in New England), the record compiled by Greene is a detailed historical account of the role of blacks in colonial New England.

The book begins with a survey of New England's slave trade and the sale of blacks in its slave markets. It proceeds into a detailed discussion about the social repercussions of the slavery system and the conflict between the Puritan philosophy and the philosophy of slavery. Finally, Greene discusses the life and legal status of free blacks and closes with a summary of the issues covered. The book contains a bibliography, an index, and appendixes. The appendixes include the distribution of blacks, an account of burial and baptisms, and a list of 162 leading slaveholding families in colonial New England.

941. Greene, Lorenzo Johnston, Gary R Kremer,** and Antony F. Holland. *Missouri's Black Heritage.* St. Louis, Mo.: Forum Press, 1980.

942. Greene, Robert Ewell. *Black Defenders of America, 1775–1973: A Reference and Pictorial History.* Chicago: Johnson Publishing Co., 1974.

The author, a U.S. Army major and director of the U.S. Army Europe Race Relations School, presents a history of black participation in America's military—the army, navy, marines, and air force. The book is divided into ten chapters, each dealing with the period of a particular war, from the American Revolution to the involvement in the Vietnam conflict. There are two appendixes concerned with milestones in black presence in the various services. The book also includes a bibliography, an index, and hundreds of photographs.

943. Guthrie, Robert V., ed. *Being Black: Psychological–Sociological Dilemmas.* San Francisco: Canfield Press, 1972.

Guthrie has collected essays by various authors—psychiatrists, psychologists, and sociologists. They deal with concepts of race, psychosocial aspects of racism, regional discrimination, concepts of the soul, and the generation gap.

944. Guzman, Jessie Parkhurst. *Crusade for Civic Democracy: The Story of the Tuskegee Civil Association, 1941–1970.* 1st ed. New York: Vantage Press, 1984.

945. ————. *Some Achievements of the Negro Through Education.*
2d ed., Rev. Tuskegee, Ala.: Department of Records and
Research, Tuskegee Institute, 1951.

The author examines the contributions of various
blacks—including such notables as Ralph J. Bunche, Charles S.
Johnson, Thurgood Marshall, and Marian Anderson—in the
realms of academics, politics, sports, and the fine arts.

946. Gwaltney, John Langston. *Drylongso: A Self-Portrait of Black
America.* New York: Random House, 1980.

Gwaltney collected for this portrait forty-two personal
narratives from black people in a dozen northeastern urban black
communities. Most of the narratives are provided by his friends
and relatives and by their friends and relatives. They constitute
most of the "drylongso," or ordinary folk, whose lives are
characterized by work. They recount childhoods spent hauling
wood, shelling peas, emptying bedpans, and waiting on white
folks. In general, they indicate that blacks are foreigners in their
own country, and that the behavior of whites makes it hard for
blacks to exist and get ahead in the world.

947. Halliburton, Warren Jennings, with Ernest Kaiser. *Harlem: A
History of Broken Dreams.* New York: Doubleday and Co.,
1974.

948. Halliburton, Warren Jennings, and William Loren Katz.**
*American Majorities and Minorities: A Syllabus of United
States History for Secondary Schools.* New York: Arno
Press, 1970.

949. Hamilton, Charles V., ed. *The Black Experience in American
Politics.* New York: G. P. Putman's Sons, 1973.

These essays discuss various aspects of the black experience
in American politics and day-to-day problems facing black
people. The book is divided into three parts: "The Search for
Culturally Relevant and Adaptive Programs," "Crisis Orientation,"

and "Focus on the Federal Government." Its focus is on present-day America, though some of the writings take a perspective from the 1850s. The editor contends that the political thought of black Americans has been "overwhelmingly problem–solving and action–oriented." This edition bears testimony to that.

950. Hansberry, Lorraine. *The Movement: Documentary of a Struggle for Equality.* New York: Simon and Schuster, 1964.

This book consists entirely of photographs that illustrate the turbulent black–white relationship of the early 1960s. Beside each particular set of photographs are either historical quotes or descriptive phrases outlining the events depicted. Note especially the book's natural progression from the black experience in the South to that experience in the North.

951. Hare, Nathan. *The Black Anglo–Saxons.* New York: Marzani and Munsell, 1965. Reprint. New York: Collier Books, 1970.

In this book, Hare, a black sociologist, dissects middle–class Afro–American society and aims to expose Afro–Americans who abandon their cultural heritage for unsatisfactory white norms.

952. Harris, Joseph Earl. *The African Presence in Asia: Consequences of the East African Slave Trade.* Evanston, Ill.: Northwestern University Press, 1971.

This book is a study of African migration to and settlement in parts of Asia. It notes that the paramount cause of the slave trade was the demand of Arabs and Europeans who were determined to initiate and maintain the trade with or without African assistance. It highlights the presence of Africans in Asian history and the achievements made by Malik Ambar and others of African heritage. Includes an appendix, a bibliographical essay, and an index.

953. ———. *Repatriates and Refugees in a Colonial Society: The Case of Kenya.* Washington, D.C.: Howard University Press, 1987.

This book examines the impact of the slave trade on East Africa, with a focus on two Kenyan settlements—the ex–slave communities at Freetown and Rabai. It shows the extent to which repatriates (including ex–slaves), refugees, and religious converts to Christianity contributed to Kenyan society. In tracing the specific identities of the slaves, the actual volume of slave trade in East Africa, and repatriate settlement patterns, Harris establishes the linkages between the slave trade as a dispersal mechanism and repatriation. He studied the history of three generations of prominent repatriate families to measure the returnees' impact as agents of social and cultural change. Includes index and bibliography.

954.   ———, ed. *Global Dimensions of the African Diaspora.* Washington, D.C.: Howard University Press, 1982.

This is a collection of papers from the international conference held at Howard University's Blackburn Center in August 1979. The conference brought together more then 130 scholars from around the world to assess the state and study of the diaspora. Contributors include Elliott Skinner, George Shepperson, Okon Edet Uya, Darwin Turner, Trevor Purcell, St. Clair Drake, Lawrence Levine, and Michel Fabre.

955.   ———, ed. *The William Leo Hansberry African History Notebook.* Vol. 2, *Africa and Africans As Seen by Classical Writers.* Washington, D.C.: Howard University Press, 1977.

Acknowledged by many in the United States to be the father of African studies, William L. Hansberry laid the foundation for the systematic study of Africa history, culture, and politics. These essays taken from his private papers reflect his interpretation of comments by classical writers about Africa and Africans. Hansberry analyzes the references to Africa and its inhabitants in the writings of Hesiod, Aeschylus, Apollonius, Virgil, Homer, and others. The work also includes a map of the Near East and the Nile Valley in ancient times.

956. ———, ed. *The William Leo Hansberry African History Notebook.* Vol. 1, *Pillars in Ethiopian History.* Washington, D.C.: Howard University Press, 1974.

Taken from William Leo Hansberry's private papers, the four essays in volume 1, better described as narrative histories, decipher and remove from the entanglement of myth, legend, and spurious historical documentation the pillars of Ethiopia's unity. The four histories focus upon the towering figures in and epochs of Ethiopia's vital heritage—the Queen of Sheba, the origins and development of Ethiopian Christianity, medieval international relations, and Ezana the Great.

957. Harris, Leonard, ed. *Philosophy Born of Struggle: Anthology of Afro-American Philosophy from 1917.* Dubuque, Iowa: Kendall/Hunt Publishing Co., 1983.

This book includes works by Alain L. Locke, Robert C. Williams, Angela Y. Davis, Lucius T. Outlaw, Maulana Karenga, William R. Jones, Houston A. Baker, Jr., and Leonard Harris.

958. Harris, William Hamilton. *The Harder We Run: Black Workers Since the Civil War.* New York: Oxford University Press, 1982.

The book is divided into three sections. The first section covers the period from the end of the Civil War through 1925. Much of the discussion focuses on black agricultural workers in the South and their dispersal into southern industry during the rise of the New South. The second section covers the Brotherhood of Sleeping Car Porters; the Great Depression, during which black workers suffered proportionately; and World War II. This section also deals with the postwar years up to 1956. The final section concentrates on black workers in the period of the civil rights movement and affirmative action, particularly the 1960s and 1970s. It was a time of growing militancy among black workers, especially those in the industrial unions, and a period of increased black unemployment due in part to pressure from accelerated automation and, generally unstable economy.

959. Harris, William Henry. *Colored Girls and Boys: Inspiring United States History and a Heart to Talk About White Folks.* Allentown, Pa.: Searle and Dressler Co., 1921.

Harris attempted to make up for the total lack of material on black history in pre-World War II history books by writing about Afro-Americans. He begins with 1619 and the arrival of the first Africans to Virginia, and then proceeds to discuss such things as the underground railway, the various wars, black organizations and black achievements in the arts and sciences. The book is written in a very warm and informal style, with bits of poetry dispersed throughout.

960. Harris, William McKinley, Sr. *Black Community Development.* San Francisco: R and E Research Associates, 1976.

Focusing on blacks in urban ghettoes, this study contends that community development as practiced in the larger society is, to some degree, inappropriate for constructive social change in the urban black ghetto. Harris argues for alternative forms of community development in the ghetto, urging unity of thought and action as prerequisites to successful action.

961. Haskins, James. *The Cotton Club.* New York: Random House, 1977. Reprint. New York: New American Library, 1984.

This book led to the movie of the same name and provided work for more black actors, actresses, dancers, and technicians than any film in American cinema history. Includes foreword, index, and over 125 photos.

962. ————. *The Creoles of Color of New Orleans.* New York: Thomas Y. Crowell Co., 1975.

A refreshing discussion of the Creoles of New Orleans. Haskins provides a working definition of the term *Creole.* He traces the history of the Creoles from the founding of the town in the 1700s by the French through the eighteenth, nineteenth, and twentieth centuries, with a discussion of the effects of advanced technology on present–day Creoles. In the last section Haskins discusses Creole contributions to American life and culture. Chapter 9 contains details concerning Creole education.

963. ————. *Leaders of the Middle East.* Hillside, N.J.: Enslow Publishers, 1985.

964. ————. *The Statue of Liberty: America's Proud Lady.* Minneapolis: Lerner Publications Co., 1986.

965. ————. *The War and the Protest: Vietnam.* Garden City, N.Y.: Doubleday and Co., 1970.

This discussion of the hotly protested U.S. involvement in the Vietnam War contains views of such notable opponents to that involvement as Julian Bond, Martin Luther King, Jr., and Benjamin Spock.

966. ————, ed. *The Filipino Nation: A Concise History of the Philippines.* 3 vols. New York: Grolier, 1982.

967. Haskins, Jim, and Kathleen Benson.** *The 60s Reader.* New York: Viking Kestrel, 1988.

968. Hatch, Rodger D., and Frank E. Watkins, eds. *Straight from the Heart: Jesse L. Jackson.* Philadelphia: Fortress Press, 1987.

This compilation of thirty–six sermons, speeches, eulogies, essays, and interviews is divided into seven sections: political progressive, human rights advocate, preacher, comforter, evangelist for educational excellence, peacemaker, corporate and cultural critic.

969. Henderson, Lenneal J., Jr., ed. *Black Political Life in the United States: A Fist as the Pendulum.* San Francisco: Chandler Publishing Co., 1972.

This analogy presents the views of black scholars on black political life past, present, and future in the United States. Noted contributors include Chuck Stone and Nathan Hare as well as the editor, Lenneal Henderson, Jr. This informative text is an excellent supplement in political science and related courses of study.

970. Higgins,* Chester, Jr., and Orde Coombs. *Some Time Ago: A Historical Portrait of Black Americans from 1850–1950.* Garden City, N.Y.: Anchor Press/Doubleday and Co., 1980.

971. Hill, Robert A., ed. *The Marcus Garvey and Universal Negro Improvement Association Papers.* Vol. 1, *1916–1919.* Berkeley: University of California Press, 1983.

972. ————, ed. *The Marcus Garvey and Universal Negro Improvement Association Papers.* Vol. 2, *1919–1920.* Berkeley: University of California Press, 1983.

973. ————, ed. *The Marcus Garvey and Universal Negro Improvement Association Papers.* Vol. 3, *1920–1921.* Berkeley: University of California Press, 1984.

974. ————, ed. *The Marcus Garvey and Universal Negro Improvement Association Papers.* Vol. 4 *1921–1922.* Berkeley: University of California Press, 1985.

975. ————, ed. *The Marcus Garvey and Universal Negro Improvement Association Papers.* Vol. 5, *1922–1924.* Berkeley: University of California Press, 1987.

The fifth volume of this monumental series chronicles another stormy period in the history of Marcus Garvey and the Universal Negro Improvement Association. It opens in the aftermath of the tumultuous 1922 convention, when opposition was increasing from black leaders outside the UNIA. The "Garvey Must Go" campaign and the U.S. government's charges of mail fraud put ever-increasing pressure on Garvey. Illustrated with photographs and documents, it includes bibliographical references and an index.

976. Himes, Joseph Sandy. *Racial and Ethnic Relations.* Dubuque, Iowa: William C. Brown Co., 1974.

An interesting study of the effects of race and ethnicity on members of groups designated as "dominant" and "minority," and of changing relations between these groups. The book is a good introduction to the field of racial and ethnic relations. Contains a glossary of terms.

977. ————. *Racial Conflict in American Society.* Columbus, Ohio: Charles E. Merrill Co., 1973.

This study of the racial conflicts of the late 1950s and the early 1960s examines the progression from "nonviolent to violent" modes of protest used by blacks in the United States. Viewing the conflict from a sociological perspective, Himes sees racial confrontation as one of several forms of group conflict and postulates theories on the evolution, function, and institutionalization of racial conflict.

978. Hine, Darlene Clark. *When the Truth Is Told: A History of Black Women's Culture and Community in Indiana, 1875–1950.* Indianapolis: National Council of Negro Women, 1981.

979. ————, ed. *The State of Afro–American History: Past, Present, and Future.* Baton Rouge: Louisiana State University Press, 1986.

This compilation is based on proceedings of a conference on the study and teaching of Afro–American history.

980. Holland, Jerome H. *Black Opportunity.* New York: Weybright and Talley, 1969.

Holland argues that new job opportunities have been opened to blacks and that to qualify for these new jobs, blacks must receive "more and better education and training." *Black Opportunity* is a positive and promising message to blacks on how they should avail themselves of educational opportunity.

981. Holt, Thomas C. *Black over White: Negro Political Leadership in South Carolina During Reconstruction.* Urbana: University of Illinois Press, 1977.

This revised version of the author's thesis at Yale University describes and analyzes various facets of black political leadership in South Carolina after the Civil War. Includes a bibliography and an index.

982. Hornsby, Alton, Jr. *The Black Almanac: From Involuntary Servitude (1619–1860) to the Age of Disillusionment (1964–1973).* 2d ed. Woodbury, N.Y.: Barron's Educational Series, 1975.

Contains important biographical data, significant events, laws, court decisions, programs, manifestos, and data on important institutions as they affect black Americans. The book is divided into the ten most significant periods in Afro–American history since slavery. Also included is a selected bibliography on the period covered.

983. ————. *The Negro in Revolutionary Georgia.* Atlanta, Ga.: Georgia Department of Education, 1977.

984. ————, ed. *In the Cage: Eyewitness Accounts of the Freed Negro.* Chicago: Quadrangle Books, 1971.

985. Huggins, Nathan Irvin. *Black Odyssey: The Afro–American Ordeal in Slavery.* New York: Pantheon Books, 1977. Reprint. New York: Vintage Books, 1979.

This is a concise, provocative account of the enslavement of Africans and their experience as slaves in America.

986. ————. *W. E. B. DuBois: Writings.* New York: Library of America, 1986.

With the publication of his collected *Writings*, DuBois becomes the first black writer included in *The Library of*

America, the collected works of America's foremost authors. This work is one of some thirty volumes already in print in this series. DuBois wrote or edited thirty-six books and numerous essays, articles, and pamphlets. Each selection in *Writings* provides valuable insight into the man and his works. Nathan Huggins, who selected and annotated the material—1,334 pages—is director of the W. E. B. DuBois Institute at Harvard.

987. Hughes, Langston. *The First Book of the West Indies.* Pictures by Robert Bruce.* New York: Franklin Watts, 1956.

988. Hurston, Zora Neale. *Tell My Horse.* New York: J. B. Lippincott Co., 1938. Reprint. Berkeley: Turtle Island, 1981.

Hurston tells us about superstitions and the voodoo ceremonies that she studied in the 1930s on a field trip to Haiti and Jamaica. Includes illustrations.

989. ————. *Voodoo Gods: An Inquiry into Native Myths and Magic in Jamaica and Haiti.* London: J. M. Dent and Sons, 1939. Originally published as *Tell My Horse* (New York: J. B. Lippincott Co., 1938).

990. Hutchins, Fred Lew. *What Happened in Memphis.* Kingsport, Tenn.: Author, 1965.

991. Hylton, Patrick C. *The Struggle of the Caribbean People (1492–1984): An Introduction.* Washington, D.C.: Billpops Publishers, 1984.

992. Ingle, Edward. *The Negro in the District of Columbia.* Baltimore, Md.: Johns Hopkins Press, 1893.

This book is the result of an eighteen-month investigation of the conditions in the District of Columbia during the early 1890s for the already established freed black community and for the newly freed slaves. It is well documented with newspaper articles, quotations of prominent citizens, and firsthand accounts of blacks living in the District at the time.

993. Jackson, Jacquelyne Johnson. *Black Women: Their Problems and Power.* Woodbury, N.Y.: Barron's Educational Series, 1974.

994. Jacques–Garvey, Amy, comp. *Philosophy and Opinions of Marcus Garvey, or, Africa for the Africans.* Centennial ed. New York: The Universal Publishing House, 1923. Reprint. Dover, Mass.: Majority Press, 1986.

      In addition to Marcus Garvey's comments on a wide variety of subjects—from the philosophy of Booker T. Washington to slavery, world disarmament, education, and miscegenation—this work includes Garvey's most famous speeches, trial transcripts, address to the jury at the close of his trial, messages from prison, letter to his wife requesting that she publish his manuscript, and other documents. It also includes photographs, such as a picture of his wife, Amy Jacques Garvey.

995. James, Felix. *The American Addition: History of a Black Community.* Washington, D.C.: University Press of America, 1978.

996. Jenkins, William Sumner. *Pro–Slavery Thought in the Old South.* Gloucester, Mass.: P. Smith, 1960.

      This is an historical overview of the origin of slavery in America. Jenkins discusses in detail the development of proslavery thought in the South; theories as to the nature, moral, and philosophy of slavery and a slave society; the relation of slavery to government; and the ethnological justification of slavery.

997. Johnson, Charles Spurgeon. *The Economic Status of Negroes.* Nashville: Fisk University Press, 1933.

998. ———. *The Negro in American Civilization.* New York: H. Holt and Company, 1930.

999. ———. *Patterns of Negro Segregation.* New York: Harper and Brothers, 1943.

A discussion of the social dynamics surrounding the various patterns of Afro-American segregation, including descriptions of the patterns themselves and the behavioral responses to them. Both segregation and discrimination are viewed and analyzed in the light of the social norms that first brought them into being. The Carnegie Corporation requested the study as a guide to its own activities and to others concerned about race relations.

1000. ————. *Shadow of the Plantation.* 1934. Reprint. Chicago: University of Chicago Press, 1966.

Writing in the 1930s, Johnson discusses the persisting influence of slavery on the day-to-day existence of Afro-American families in Macon County, Alabama.

1001. ————. *Statistical Atlas of Southern Counties: Listing and Analysis of Socio-Economic Indices of 1104 Southern Counties.* Chapel Hill: University of North Carolina Press, 1941.

1002. Johnson, Charles Spurgeon, et al.* *To Stem This Tide: A Survey of Racial Tension Areas in the United States.* Chicago: The Pilgrim Press, 1943. Reprint. New York: AMS Press, 1969.

This survey of racial tension areas in the United States focuses on the impact of the two world wars on black and white relations. The authors have traced an interesting and contrasting pattern of prejudice and discrimination during and after World Wars I and II. The study was sponsored by the Julius Rosenwald Fund of Chicago and was made by the Institute of Social Studies at Fisk University under the direction of Johnson.

1003. Johnson, Charles Spurgeon, Elizabeth L. Allen, Horace Mann Bond, et al.* *Into the Mainstream: A Survey of Best Practices in Race Relations in the South.* Chapel Hill: University of North Carolina Press, 1947.

Programs in employment, education, religion, and housing designed specifically to improve the situation of blacks in the

South are discussed by humanitarians from both a theoretical and a practical standpoint. The text includes discussions of the opposition to various policies, that were designed for the benefit of blacks and were regarded as controversial at the time. Chapter 6 examines the ways in which various organizations from schools to Boy Scouts and Girl Scouts can contribute to the molding of attitudes that may greatly assist in solving the problem of race relations in the South. The additional coauthors are Margaret McCulloch,* and Alma Forrest Polk.*

1004.   Johnson, Edward Augustus. *History of Negro Soldiers in the Spanish–American War and Other Items of Interest.* Raleigh, N.C.: Capital Printing Co., 1899.

A historical look at the nineteenth–century Afro–American in his role as an American soldier fighting in the Spanish–American War, and the effects of this role on him and on race relations at home. Johnson notes the value of the black soldier to America's success in the war, and—in a discussion particularly relevant in the aftermath of Vietnam—he discusses the ill-treatment of Afro–Americans at home despite their seeming importance as a needed fighting force for America. A few illustrations are included in the text.

1005.   ———. *Light Ahead for the Negro.* New York: Grafton Press, 1904. Reprint. New York: AMS Press, 1975.

This book illustrates nonviolent approaches to race relations through the story of Irene, a woman who befriends blacks by performing actions beneficial to their existence as free men. Through benevolence such as hers, America could become a country of true liberty for both blacks and whites.

1006.   ———. *A School History of the Negro Race in America from 1619 to 1890: Combined with the History of the Negro Soldiers in the Spanish–American War, Also a Short Sketch of Liberia. Part One.* Raleigh, N.C.: Edwards & Broughton, 1890, rev. 1911. Reprint. New York: AMS Press, 1969.

This history textbook is a useful tool in teaching American history to black children. The emphasis falls on the contributions of blacks to the history of North America. Johnson begins from the earliest origins of the black race in Africa and then connects the Africans to America by investigating the Atlantic slave trade and slavery in the colonies of North America. He then traces the development of blacks over the years, looking at them and at their determined bid for freedom. The book also goes into the history of black soldiers in the Spanish–American War.

1007. Johnson, James Weldon. *Black Manhattan.* New York: Alfred A. Knopf, 1930. Reprint. Salem, N.H.: Ayer Co., 1988.

1008. Jones, Adrienne Lash. *Jane Edna Hunter: A Case Study of Black Leadership, 1910–1950.* Brooklyn, New York: Carlton Publishers, 1990.

1009. Jordan, June Meyer. *Civil Wars.* Boston: Beacon Press Books, 1981.

1010. ————. *On Call: Political Essays.* Boston: South End Press, 1985.

1011. Karenga, Maulana, and Jacob H. Carruthers, eds. *Kemet and the African Worldview: Research, Rescue, and Restoration.* Los Angeles: University of Sankore Press, 1986.

1012. Katz,** William Loren, and Warren Jennings Halliburton. *A History of Black Americans.* New York: Harcourt Brace Jovanovich, 1973.

This book is a comprehensive, well–illustrated history of black Americans; of the slave trade in the Spanish, Dutch, French, and English colonies; and, finally, of the experience of black Americans on the frontier, in the Far West, the North, and the South, and at important historical moments such as the Civil War, the Age of Reform, and the civil rights revolution.

1013. Kilson, Martin. *Political Change in a West African State: A Study of the Modernization Process in Sierra Leone.* Cambridge: Harvard University Press, 1966.

1014. Kincaid, Jamaica. *A Small Place.* New York: Farrar, Straus, Giroux, 1988.

1015. King, Coretta Scott. *My Life with Martin Luther King, Jr.* 1st ed. New York: Rinehart and Winston, 1969.

   A heartwarming account of the life and work of Martin Luther King, Jr., as seen through the eyes of his wife. Contains pictures of some memorable and historic occasions.

1016. Kletzing,* Henry F., and William Henry Crogman. *Progress of a Race, or, the Remarkable Advancement of the Afro-American, from the Bondage of Slavery, Ignorance, and Poverty, to the Freedom of Citizenship, Intelligence, Affluence, Honor and Trust.* Atlanta, Ga.: J. L. Nichols and Co., 1897. Reprint. New York: Negro Universities Press, 1969.

   This history concentrates on the progress of the Afro-American from bondage to present times. It presents the Afro-American in different stages of development—for example, in moral and social advancement, and in industries. A large portion of the book focuses on educational improvement and on the different aspects that have to be dealt with before such improvement can be achieved. Includes black-and-white photographs of famous Afro-Americans and an introduction by Booker T. Washington.

1017. Ladner, Joyce A. *Tomorrow's Tomorrow: The Black Woman.* Garden City, N.Y.: Doubleday and Co., 1971.

   Ladner provides both a historical and a contemporary perspective of such issues as racial oppression, self-concept, and social and economic conditions as they relate to primarily low-income black girls growing up in the city.

1018. ————, ed. *The Death of White Sociology*. New York: Vintage
Books, 1973.

Noted black social scientists such as Nathan Hare, Kenneth
Clark, and E. Franklin Frazier, who contributed to this collection,
believe that the social norms postulated by sociologists studying
white culture cannot be unequivocally applied to blacks. Attempts
to apply them in the past have contributed to institutional racism
and the sociological victimization of blacks. A provocative and
enlightening look at sociology, and a must for all black educators
and students in this and related fields.

1019. Lee, Andrea. *Russian Journal*. 1st ed. New York: Random
House, 1981.

1020. Lester, Julius. *Revolutionary Notes*. New York: Richard Baron
Publishing Co., 1969.

1021. ————. *Search for the New Land: History as Subjective
Experience*. New York: Dial Press, 1969.

Lester uses a unique form and style—that of a private
journal—to recreate historical moments. Taking articles from
newspapers and magazines, he has rearranged them in poetic
form, transforming impersonal historical events into personal, live
experience. He includes one of his own poems, which tells of his
experiences in Vietnam.

1022. ————, ed. *The Seventh Son: The Thoughts and Writings of
W. E. B. DuBois*. 2 vols. New York: Random House, 1971.

This section of DuBois's editorials, which originally
appeared in *The Crisis* during the years DuBois was editor, are
arranged by theme and subject matter, chronologically within
each section.

1023. Littleton, Arthur C., and Mary W. Burger,* eds. *Black
Viewpoints*. New York: New American Library, 1971.

This book presents major aspects of the black movement. It also talks about the aspirations and frustrations, and victories and defeats of the contemporary black man. Thirty–one outstanding blacks present their views on programs and strategies for the black movement. The essays differ widely in emphasis, vocabulary, and style, but they share common thoughts and themes.

1024.   Locke, Alain LeRoy, and Bernhard J. Stern,* eds. *When People Meet: A Study in Race and Culture Contacts.* Rev. ed. New York: Hinds, Hayden and Eldredge, 1946.

1025.   Logan, Rayford Whittingham. *The African Mandates in World Politics.* Washington, D.C.: Public Affairs Press, 1948.

1026.   ———. *Haiti and the Dominican Republic.* New York: Oxford University Press, 1968.

1027.   ———. *The Negro and the Post–War World: A Primer.* Washington, D.C.: Minorities Publishers, 1945.

1028.   ———. *The Negro in American Life and Thought: The Nadir, 1877–1901.* New York: Dial Press, 1954.

1029.   ———. *The Negro in the United States: A Brief History.* New York: Van Nostrand Co., 1957.

This work is divided into two parts. Part 1 comprises seven chapters: "Slavery and Emancipation, 1619–1865"; "Reconstruction, 1865–1877"; "From Reconstruction to the Nadir, 1877–1901"; "From the Nadir to World War I"; "From World War I to World War II"; "World War II and the Cold War"; "Conclusion." Part 2 consists of "Documents," including the Emancipation Proclamation (January 1, 1863), several amendments to the U.S. Constitution, several court cases, and executive orders. A selected bibliography and an index are also included.

1030. —————. *The Negro in the United States*. Vol. 1, *A History to 1945—From Slavery to Second-Class Citizenship*. New York: Van Nostrand Reinhold Co., 1970.

This revised and expanded version of Logan's earlier text (1957) includes new materials and interpretations of Afro-American history through 1945; a second volume by Logan and Michael Winston covers Afro-American history from 1945 to 1971. Volume 1 examines the Civil Rights acts of 1866, 1870, and 1871; the militant views of Booker T. Washington prior to his 1895 Atlanta address and again after 1901; It discusses the events leading to the establishment of the NAACP; and, with an entire chapter on World War II, the struggle to establish training camps for black military aviators. It also includes documents, a bibliography, and an index.

1031. Logan, Rayford Whittingham, and Michael R. Winston. *The Negro in the United States*. Vol. 2, *The Ordeal of Democracy*. New York: Van Nostrand Reinhold Co., 1971.

Beginning with 1945, this second volume chronicles the Afro-American's more recent attempts to attain first-class citizenship. It also discusses the conflicting currents of black identity, self-determination, and integration in the black American freedom movement. Includes documents to illustrate the changes in the period since World War II, a selected bibliography, and an index.

1032. Lomax, Louis E. *The Negro Revolt*. New York: New American Library, 1962.

Lomax looks at the extensive changes in methods and ideas of American blacks of the 1960s, in contrast to their tactics of the 1950s, for dealing with racism and discrimination. He offers a brief history of the earliest blacks to reach the American shores, the pre-civil rights forerunners, and discusses at length the civil rights movement and the growth of the black Muslims.

1033. Long, Herman Hodge, and Charles Spurgeon Johnson. *People v Property: Race Restrictive Covenants in Housing.* Nashville: Fisk University Press, 1947.

Long and Johnson provide a comprehensive study of racial segregation and the problems encountered by blacks and other disadvantaged minority groups in acquiring property. The study includes maps, graphs, and tables.

1034. Lyles, Carl C., Sr. *Lyles Station: Yesterday and Today.* Evansville: University of Southern Indiana, 1984.

The author provides the history of an all-black community in Indiana. He shows its origin, development, and prospects for the future. Includes illustrations, a bibliography, and an index.

1035. Lynch, Hollis Ralph. *Edward Wilmot Blyden: Pan-Negro Patriot, 1832-1912.* New York: Oxford University Press, 1970.

1036. ―――, ed. *Black Africa.* New York: Arno Press, 1973.

1037. ―――, ed. *Black Spokesman: Selected Published Writings of Edward Wilmot Blyden.* London: Case, 1971.

1038. ―――, ed. *Selected Letters of Edward Wilmot Blyden.* Millwood, N.Y.: KTO Press, 1978.

1039. Lynch, John Roy. *The Facts of Reconstruction.* New York: The Neale Publishing Company, 1913. Reprint. New York: Arno Press, 1968.

Born a slave in 1847, Lynch, one of twenty-two blacks to serve in Congress between 1870 and 1901, deals with the "facts" of Reconstruction. He also includes personal descriptions of his life, experiences, and conversations with important lawmakers, including the president of the United States. James M. McPherson wrote a new preface for this edition.

1040. Lynk, Miles Vandahurst. *The Black Troopers; or, The Daring Heroism of the Negro Soldiers in the Spanish-American War.* Jackson: M. V. Lynk Publishing House, 1899. Reprint. New York: AMS Press, 1971.

1041. ———. *The Negro Pictorial Review of the Great World War: A Visual Narrative of the Negro's Glorious Part in the World's Greatest War.* Memphis, Tenn.: Twentieth Century Art Co., 1919.

1042. Major, Geraldyn Hodges, with Doris E. Saunders. *Black Society.* Chicago: Johnson Publishing Co., 1976.

Using numerous photographs, Major (with Saunders) traces the development of the black aristocracy, which she contends is based on birth. A member of the aristocracy for over eighty years, she provides a genealogy of some of the "first families" of black America, and describes the role played and contributions made by the black upper-class in American history. Early black elites include Phillis Wheatley, Crispus Attucks, and Richard Allen; among the more contemporary elites are Andrew Young, Maynard Jackson, and Eunice W. Johnson.

1043. McAdoo, Harriette Pipes, and John Lewis McAdoo, eds. *Black Children: Social, Educational, and Parental Environments.* Beverly Hills, Calif.: Sage Publications, 1985.

In this collection of empirical research, the editors state that to be fully functional, Afro-American children must develop the skills to do well simultaneously in two different cultures, both black and nonblack. Consequently, they develop a duality for their existence. This volume explores the meaning of this duality in four distinct environments—socioeconomic, educational, parental, and internal. The complex resulting picture explodes many of the myths that surround black childhood development. For example, although it is generally assumed that the harsh socioeconomic realities faced by most black children reduce their sense of self-worth, the studies in this collection show that black children have about the same distribution of self–esteem as other children; they just derive their self esteem from different sources.

1044. McGuire, Phillip. *Taps for a Jim Crow Army: Letters from Black Soldiers in World War II.* With a foreword by Benjamin Quarles. Santa Barbara, Calif.: ABC–Clio, 1983.

1045. McKay,** John P., Bennett D. Hill, and John Buckler.** *A History of World Societies.* Boston: Houghton Mifflin Co., 1984.

1046. McNeil, Genna Rae, and Michael R. Winston, eds. *Historical Judgements Reconsidered: Selected Howard University Lectures in Honor of Rayford W. Logan.* Washington, D.C.: Howard University Press, 1988.

Presents a collection of thirteen lectures selected from the annual Rayford W. Logan Lecture Series at Howard University. It marks the seventy–fifth anniversary of the university's Department of History, in which Logan worked for many years.

1047. Micheaux, Oscar. *The Conquest: The Story of a Negro Pioneer, by the Pioneer.* Lincoln, Nebr.: The Woodruff Press, 1913. Reprint. Miami, Fla.: Mnemosyne Publishing Co., 1969.

1048. Miller, Abie. *The Negro and the Great Society.* 1st ed. New York: Vantage Press, 1965.

1049. Miller, Kelly. *An Appeal to Conscience: America's Code of Caste a Disgrace to Democracy.* New York: Macmillan Co., 1918. Reprint. New York: Arno Press and the New York Times, 1969.

This interesting appeal to white America's conscience to treat blacks as equals is as timely now as when it was first written a half–century ago. Using the American democratic creed for a foundation, Miller emphasizes the loyalty and patriotism of Afro–Americans and calls for a redress of grievances. He compares the position of blacks in the early 1900s with that of the Belgian victims during the German invasion, and says this position reflects poorly on whites' ability to live according to the American creed. Areas covered by the book include race contact, lawlessness, segregation, patriotism, and righteousness.

1050. ————. *Race Adjustment and the Everlasting Stain.* 1908; 1924. Reprint. New York: Arno Press, 1968.

This collection of essays by the author concerns many issues that relate to the Afro-American since World War I. Several of these essays deal with issues of education, including school segregation and the responsibility of the federal government for black education. Other issues relate to lynching and radicalism among blacks. Letters and commentaries are dedicated to personalities such as Abraham Lincoln and Lloyd George.

1051. Miller, Loren. *The Petitioners: The Story of the Supreme Court of the United States and the Negro.* New York: Pantheon Books, 1966.

This work is a historical review of the changing relationship between the U.S. Supreme Court and the Afro-American, as reflected in individual court cases.

1052. Moore, William, Jr. *The Vertical Ghetto: Everyday Life in an Urban Project.* New York: Random House, 1969.

This captivating and educational book confronts the reader with the hardships of ghetto life. The author describes the problems of survival, race, class, and self-identity. He examines education and attempts to outline future programs to alleviate these problems.

1053. Morgan, Gordon Daniel. *African Vignettes: Notes of an American Negro Family in East Africa.* Jefferson City, Mo.: New Scholars Press, 1967.

1054. ———. *Marianna: A Sociological Essay on an Eastern Arkansas Town.* Jefferson City, Mo.: New Scholars Press, 1973.

1055. Morgan, Kathryn L. *Children of Strangers: The Stories of a Black Family.* Philadelphia: Temple University Press, 1980.

1056. Morris, Aldon D. *The Origins of the Civil Rights Movement: Black Communities Organizing for Change.* New York: Free Press, 1984.

For this book, the American Sociological Association awarded Morris the 1986 "Distinguished Contribution to Scholarship" prize for the best book published that year in the field of sociology. In part, the book was written to dispel the myth that blacks were apathetic and disorganized prior to early bus boycotts and lunchroom sit-ins, and that they owed their success to white northerners who joined the cause. He contends that organized protest against white domination has always been a cornerstone of the black experience.

1057. Mosley, Charles C. *The Negro in Mississippi History.* Jackson, Miss.: Hederman Brothers, 1950. Reprint. Jackson, Miss.: Percy Brothers, 1969.

1058. Moss, Alfred A., Jr. *The American Negro Academy: Voices of the Talented Youth.* Baton Rouge: University of Louisiana Press, 1981.

The author discusses the leadership, activities, and legacy of a learned society: the American Negro Academy.

1059. Moton, Robert Russa. *What the Negro Thinks.* 1929. Reprint. Garden City, N.Y.: Doubleday and Co., 1942.

1060. Moutoussamy-Ashe, Jeanne. *Daufuskie Island: A Photographic Essay.* With a foreword by Alex Haley. Columbia: University of South Carolina Press, 1982.

1061. Murray, Albert. *South to a Very Old Place.* New York: McGraw-Hill, 1971.

Nominated for a National Book Award, this book tells of Murray's trip back to his boyhood home in Alabama. It also reveals his college days at Tuskegee.

1062. Newton, James E., and Ronald L. Lewis,** eds. *The Other Slaves, Mechanics, Artisans, and Craftsmen.* Boston: G. K. Hall and Co., 1978.

This book focuses on the use of the slave in business and industry in the Old South. Part 1 focuses on the skilled slaves in industry. Newton, for example, indicates that tobacco factories relied on slave labor almost exclusively. Hemp and salt industries also relied heavily on slave labor. Part 2 concentrates on the plantation slaves' desire to be hired in the cities and industries to secure the privileges, social opportunities, rewards, and freedom, which they could not enjoy on the plantation. Part 3 highlights slave artisans and craftsmen, who represented a privileged echelon in the slave community.

1063. Neyland, Leedell Wallace. *Twelve Black Floridians.* Tallahassee: Florida A and M University Foundation, Inc., 1970

This text, designed mainly for junior and senior high school students, looks at the lives of twelve black Floridians whose service to their state contributed significantly to its growth and development. Neyland gives biographical sketches of the lives and major contributions of blacks who have given fifteen or more years of dedicated service. A sketch of each person discussed prefaces his or her biography.

1064. Painter, Nell Irvin. *Exodusters: Black Migration to Kansas After Reconstruction.* New York: Alfred A. Knopf, 1977. Reprint. Lawrence: University Press of Kansas, 1986.

1065. Parker, Marjorie H. *Alpha Kappa Alpha: In the Eye of the Beholder.* 3d ed. Washington, D.C.: Alpha Kappa Alpha Sorority, 1978.

Designed to preserve the heritage of the organization and thus have the history become a legacy for those who will come afterwards, this book discusses the founding of Alpha Kappa Alpha at Howard University—the first black sorority; presents the structure, membership, and leadership; and describes the sorority's participation in community service projects. The appendixes include national meetings, honorary members, and past national officers.

1066. Parker, Robert, with Richard Rashke.* *Capitol Hill in Black and White.* 1st ed. New York: Dodd, Mead and Co., 1986.

This is an "inside" story by the former maitre d' of the Senate Dining Room—Robert Parker.

1067. Parks, David. *GI Diary.* New York: Harper and Row, 1968. Reprint. Washington, D.C.: Howard University Press, 1984.

This diary of a black GI reveals the inherent racism of America, both at home and abroad, during the Vietnam War. The author gives the reader a running account of life in Vietnam over a two-year period, portraying the fear, the insanity, the insensitivity, and the brutality.

1068. Perkins, Hattie Logan. *Humanities: Lecture–Discussion Syllabus.* 1st ed. Sherman Oaks, Calif.: Banner Books International, 1977.

1069. Pinkney, Alphonso. *Red, Black, and Green: Black Nationalism in the U.S.* New York: Cambridge University Press, 1976.

Pinkney's book traces the path formed by black nationalism from 1963–1973. He begins with a discussion of black nationalist ideology, including its religion and culture, and ends with a look at the direction that black nationalism is now taking. Chapter 9 discusses educational nationalism as an outcome of black nationalism. Included in this chapter is "a note on the blackening of Howard University."

1070. Ploski, Harry A., and Roscoe Conkling Brown, Jr., eds. *The Negro Almanac*. 1st ed. New York: Bellwether Publishing Co., 1967.

This almanac contains a wealth of information on the history and culture of blacks in the United States and the rest of the world. It focuses on the role and contributions of the Afro-American in the settlement of the United States and on contemporary American society and culture. Biographical information on outstanding blacks from all stations of life, as well as statistical information in the form of tables, charts, and graphs, is also included.

1071. Plummer, Brenda Gayle. *Haiti and the Great Powers, 1902–1915*. Baton Rouge: Louisiana State University Press, 1988.

1072. Porter, Dorothy Burnett, ed. *Negro Protest Pamphlets*. New York: Arno Press, 1969.

This collection contains some of the rarest protest pamphlets of the pre–Civil War period. Protesters include Absalom Jones, Richard Allen, Daniel Coker, Nathaniel Paul, William Hamilton, Hosea Easton, and William J. Watkins.

1073. Poussaint, Alvin F. *Why Blacks Kill Blacks*. New York: Emerson Hall, 1972.

Written in an informal, relaxed style, the essays in this book examine such controversial topics as black power, black suicide, and black sexuality. Poussaint attempts to answer such questions as why blacks kill other blacks, what black parents should tell their children, and how white parents can raise prejudice-free children. Of special interest is the section on black self-hatred, which is written in the form of a discussion between Poussaint and Jesse Jackson.

1074.   Proctor, Samuel Dewitt. *The Young Negro in America, 1960–1980.* New York: Associated Press, 1966.

The author looks toward 1980 as the year for evaluating how far the young black has come and how far there is yet to go on the road to equality. The young black has already set a pace. Can it be sustained in upcoming decades? What will happen if it is sustained? These are questions posed by Proctor.

1075.   Quarles, Benjamin. *Black Mosaic: Essays in Afro–American History and Historiography.* Amherst: University of Massachusetts Press, 1988.

1076.   ———. *The Negro in the American Revolution.* Chapel Hill: University of North Carolina Press, 1961.

This book tells of the activities of blacks on the battlefronts and behind the lines. A battle narrative is not presented in any detail because, according to Quarles, the War of Independence, unlike the Civil War, did not have all–black units; hence the military history of the black soldier in the revolutionary war is one with the general history of the American soldier in action. Except at the battle of Rhode Island, in which the Rhode Island regiment of predominantly black composition took part, the black soldier of the revolutionary war does not stand out as a racial entity. The book contends that blacks saw only limited military service until the third year of the war. The negative attitudes toward enlisting blacks sprang from a reluctance to deprive a master of his chattel. Quarles, however, shows that these fears were put into the background and blacks mustered in.

1077.   ———. *The Negro in the Civil War.* Boston: Little, Brown, 1953. Reprint. New York: Da Capo Press, 1988.

1078.   ———. *The Negro in the Making of America.* Rev. and expanded. New York: Macmillan Co., 1969.

This account of the influence of dynamic black personalities on American history chronicles the black man's role in American life from the arrival of the first blacks in 1619 to the end of the Nixon era. It includes his role in plantation life, his participation in the American Revolution and the Civil War, and his struggle for equality.

1079. Redding, J. Saunders. *An American in India: A Personal Report on the Indian Dilemma and the Nature of Her Conflicts.* 1st ed. Indianapolis: Bobbs–Merrill, 1954.

1080. Richard, Henry J. *Topics in Afro–American Studies.* Buffalo, N.Y.: Black Academy Press, 1971.

1081. Richardson, Marilyn, ed. *Maria W. Stewart, America's First Black Woman Political Writer: Essays and Speeches.* Bloomington: Indiana University Press, 1987.

1082. Robinson, Armstead L., Craig C. Foster,* and Donald H. Ogilvie,* eds. *Black Studies in the University: A Symposium.* New Haven: Yale University Press, 1969.

Resulting from a symposium on Afro–American studies presented at Yale University in November 1967 by the school's Black Student Alliance, the text consists of a collection of edited presentations by both black and white scholars trained in Afro–American studies. Among the contributors are Alvin Poussaint, McGeorge Bundy, and Nathan Hare. The question–and–answer component of the symposium adds an additional dimension to the work.

1083. Robinson, Robert, with Jonathan Slevin.* *Black on Red: A Black American's 44 Years Inside the Soviet Union.* Washington, D.C.: Acropolis, 1988.

This is an autobiography of a Jamaican–born, naturalized American depicting life in the Soviet Union. Robinson had accepted a Soviet agency's 1930 offer of an annually renewable contract to work in the new Stalingrad tractor factory at twice his salary, as well as the prospect of professional advancement in an environment free of the racism he experienced as the only black mechanical engineer in Henry Ford's River Rouge.

1084.   Rogers, Joel A. *World's Great Men of Color.* Vol. 1. Edited by John Henrik Clarke. New York: Macmillan Publishing Co., 1972.

The anthropologist and historian J. A. Rogers was one of the first black scholars to reject and explode the racist myth that blacks played only minor roles in world history. Devoting more than a half century to careful research on the lives of hundreds of African and Asian statesmen, warriors and artists who achieved distinction in every part of the world and in every period of history, Rogers succeeded, with this book, in reclaiming for black history such figures as Aesop, Cleopatra, and the Mahdi.

1085.   ———. *World's Great Men of Color.* Vol. 2. Edited by John Henrik Clarke. New York: Macmillan Publishing Co., 1972.

The second volume of Rogers's monumental survey focuses on the outstanding blacks of Europe, the United States, South and Central America, and the West Indies, and details the enormous contributions made to world history by men such as Marcus Garvey and Frederick Douglass, as well as by many individuals not commonly known to have been of black ancestry, such as Robert Browning, Alexandre Dumas, and Aleksandr Pushkin.

1086.   Rout, Leslie B., Jr. *The African Experience in Spanish America, 1502 to the Present Day.* New York: Cambridge University Press, 1976.

1087.   Rustin, Bayard. *Down the Line: The Collected Writings of Bayard Rustin.* Chicago: Quadrangle Books, 1971.

In his essays, Rustin examines the ebb and flow of the movement for black rights—from violence to nonviolence, from hope to despair, from integration to separation and back again.

He pinpoints the real problems in American society to be those of employment, wages, housing, health, and education. Rustin urges nonviolence, integration, and coalition policies as the only viable solutions. He criticizes black studies programs for encouraging separation, which he sees as part of the vicious cycle.

1088. Salley, Columbus. *Accent African Fashions.* New York: Col–Bob Associates, 1975.

"Purpose is to show that Africa is part of contemporary life and fashions and to show the sources of inspiration African dress and fashions have on contemporary black designers."

1089. Saunders, Doris E., ed. *The Ebony Handbook.* Chicago: Johnson Publishing Co., 1974.

1090. ———, ed. *The Kennedy Years and the Negro: A Photographic Record.* Chicago: Johnson Publishing Co., 1964.

1091. Scott, Emmett Jay, and Lyman Beecher Stowe.** *Booker T. Washington, Builder of Civilization.* Garden City, New York: Doubleday, Page and Co., 1916. Reprint. New York: Kraus Reprint Co., 1972.

1092. Seale, Bobby. *Seize the Time: The Story of the Black Panther Party and Huey P. Newton.* New York: Random House, 1970.

This is the story of the Black Panthers by one of its main leaders. The origin of the Black Panther party is presented in some depth, together with party policies. The history chronicles the rise of the Black Panthers to prominence as the self–imposed party of black America. Details of Panther activities in their struggle for the recognition of the black man as a part of American society are included. More interesting, though, are the personal insights to the character at the core of the Black Panther party.

1093. Shockley, Grant Sneed. *Understanding the New Generation in Africa: The Guide for Teachers and Leaders.* New York: Friendship Press, 1971.

Shockley presents a guide for teachers and others who are interested in planning activities of an Afrocentric nature. Activities are divided according to age group, and all agelevels are included.

1094. Simms, Ruth P. *Urbanization in West Africa: A Review of Current Literature.* Evanston, Ill.: Northwestern University Press, 1965.

1095. Sims, William E. *Black Studies: Pitfalls and Potential.* Washington, D.C.: University Press of America, 1978.

A systematic and dispassionate discussion of black studies programs in American higher education since 1968, focusing on administrative structure, responsibilities, directorates, budgeting, faculty and student relations, profits, curriculum, and future needs.

1096. Smith, Ed Calvin. *Where to, Black Man: An American Negro's African Diary.* Chicago: Quadrangle Books (The New York Times) 1967.

This book is based on the diary Smith kept while he served with the Peace Corps in Ghana for two years. It is a vivid and forthright account of what transpired in his mind as he observed closely the political and social conditions of the then emerging African nation. It also relates how he evaluated these events from the perspective of a black American who had dreamed of finding a sense of fulfillment and belonging in an African nation, having experienced poverty, segregation, and racism growing up in Greensboro, Alabama. Alternating between moods of elation, anger, humor, sarcasm, and frustration, Smith describes his journey as leading to a personal discovery of a new meaning and understanding of his earlier desired brotherhood with his African ancestry.

1097. Smith, James Wesley. *Goldwater and the Republic That Was.* New York: Carlton Press, 1965.

1098. Smith, Roland McFatridge, Eugene D. Levy,** and Martha H. Brown. *Faces of America: A History of the U.S.* New York: Harper and Row, 1982.

1099. Snowden, Frank M., Jr. *Before Color Prejudice: The Ancient Views of Blacks.* Cambridge: Harvard University Press, 1983.

This book traces the image of blacks as seen by whites from Egyptian to Roman times. It explores the rationale for the attitude toward blacks during that period. It also shows that the very striking similarities in the total picture that emerges from an examination of the basic sources—Egyptian, Greek, Roman, and early Christian—point to a highly favorable image of blacks. Finally, Snowden concludes that it is difficult to say with certainty what conditions may have been most influential in forming the attitude of the ancient world toward blacks, and that the onus of intense color prejudice cannot be placed upon the shoulders of the ancients.

1100. ————. *Blacks in Antiquity: Ethiopians in the Greco-Roman Experience.* Cambridge: Harvard University Press, 1970.

The term *Ethiopian* is used in this book in the same way that the Greeks and Romans used it. It refers to dark- and black-skinned Africans. A result of extensive research, the book focuses on the Ethiopian from the Homeric period to the age of Justinian. In addition, it reflects what knowledge the Greeks and Romans had of the Ethiopians, as well as what attitude the early Christians had about them. The book also contains 120 illustrations of blacks depicted in ancient art objects.

1101. Sowell, Thomas. *Ethnic America: A History.* New York: Basic Books, 1981.

Sowell traces the history of nine American ethnic groups—the Irish, the Germans, the Jews, the Italians, the Chinese, the Japanese, the Afro-Americans, the Puerto Ricans, and the Mexicans—to explain their varied experiences in adapting to American society. He examines American immigrants according to skills, age, IQ, location, time of arrival, imported culture, and other differences and similarities.

1102.   ————. *Race and Economics.* New York: David McKay Co., 1975.

In discussing the historical relationship between race and economics, Sowell analyzes the distinctive features and historical background of ethnic groups in the United States, and compares these groups with each other and with the American mainstream. He discusses the economics of race from the viewpoint of market and government, and he makes projections about future educational and economic trends for ethnic groups.

1103.   ————, ed. *American Ethnic Groups.* Washington, D.C.: The Urban Institute, 1978.

This volume is a product of a study of American ethnic groups that was conducted at the Urban Institute from 1972 to 1975 under the direction of Thomas Sowell. Of the dozen or more groups that were examined, six were selected for special emphasis in this volume: those with black, Chinese, Japanese, Irish, Italian, or Jewish backgrounds. One of the chief concepts implicit in this study is that the evolution of minority immigrant groups proceeds in parallel continual, during the course of which each group experiences similar developments, although not necessarily at the same time, with the same intensity, or in exactly the same way. Includes notes and an index.

1104.   Spellman, Cecil Lloyd. *Elm City, A Negro Community in Action.* Tallahassee: Florida A. and M. College, 1947.

Research and old census records provide much of the information about the early history and development of the area around Wilson, North Carolina, of which the village of Elm City is the center. This study provides a detailed account of the profile of that community.

1105. Staples, Robert E. *The Black Woman in White America: Sex, Marriage, and the Family.* Chicago: Nelson–Hall Publishers, 1973.

The author explores some of the socioeconomic dilemmas for the black woman in a white–oriented, male–dominated society. He examines such areas as prostitution, motherhood, and the feminist movement.

1106. Starling, Marion Wilson. *The Slave Narrative: Its Place in American History.* 2d ed. Boston: G. K. Hall, 1981. Washington, D.C.: Howard University Press, 1988.

In this work, first published in 1981, the accounts of slavery are unveiled against a backdrop of American history and extend from the early 1700s to the emancipation of the slaves in 1865. This volume also explores the influence of firsthand accounts in spawning the genre of slavery novels typified by Harriet Beecher Stowe's *Uncle Tom's Cabin*, and it establishes the narrative's significance for literary research. Includes an index.

1107. Sterling, Dorothy. *We Are Your Sisters: Black Women of the 19th Century.* New York: W. W. Norton and Co., 1984.

1108. ———, ed. *Speak Out in Thunder Tones: Letters and Other Writing by Black Northerners, 1787–1865.* Garden City, N.Y.: Doubleday and Co., 1973.

1109. ———, ed. *The Trouble They Have Seen: Black People Tell the Story of Reconstruction.* 1st ed. Garden City, N.J.: Doubleday and Co., 1976.

1110. Strickland, Arvarh E., and Jerome R. Reich.** *The Black American Experience: From Slavery Through*

Reconstruction. New York: Harcourt Brace Jovanovich, 1974.

1111.   Taylor, Alrutheus Ambush. *The Negro in the Reconstruction of Virginia.* Washington, D.C.: The Association for the Study of Negro Life and History, 1926. Reprint. New York: Russell and Russell, 1969.

This study of the role played by blacks in the reconstruction of Virginia parallels a similar study of the reconstruction of South Carolina. This study confronts the common assumption that since Virginia had fewer blacks than South Carolina, its patterns of reconstruction differed; it shows that blacks did not figure much in the government of Virginia and so, like to their counterparts in South Carolina, they too struggled through education, labor, and the church to remain above the status of serf.

1112.   Taylor, Arnold H. *Travail and Triumph: Black Life and Culture in the South Since the Civil War.* Westport, Conn.: Greenwood Press, 1976.

1113.   Taylor, Clyde R., ed. *Vietnam and Black America: An Anthology of Protest and Resistance.* New York: Doubleday/Anchor Press, 1973.

Eminent black intellectuals, including Julian Bond, Nathan Hare, Martin Luther King, Jr., and Samuel Yette, contribute essays, speeches, poems, short stories, and editorials expressing their opposition to the Vietnam conflict. A list of contributors, their accomplishments, and their published works is included.

1114.   Terry, Wallace, ed. *Bloods: An Oral History of the Vietnam War by Black Veterans.* New York: Random House, 1984.

This book, edited by Terry, is a self–portrait by twenty black veterans who symbolize the large number of blacks who shouldered a disproportionate share of the burden of the Vietnam War. Among the twenty "bloods" (as blacks called themselves) who relate their war and postwar experiences in this book are enlisted men, noncommissioned officers, commissioned officers, airmen, sailors, soldiers, marines, those with urban backgrounds, those with rural backgrounds, those for whom the war had a devastating impact, and those for whom the war basically was an opportunity to advance in a career. All twenty had won a badge of courage in combat. They talk about fighting two wars: Vietnam and racism.

1115. Thomas, Charles W., ed. *Boys No More: A Black Psychologist's View of Community.* Beverly Hills, Calif.: Glencoe Press, 1971.

While viewing Afro-America as a subculture, Thomas maintains that any program aimed at creating an antiracism pressure group on the larger American society must have an effective strategy that is consistent with the values, beliefs, and mores of the Afro-American subculture. He argues persuasively that "since the dominant institution is business, the forces for change must be socio-economic and political rather than moral." Each of nine essays by different authors examines some aspect of black consciousness. Topics include "The Changing Image of the Black American," by Robert Williams, and "White Racism: Its Roots, Form and Function," by James Comer.

1116. Thompson, Daniel Calbert. *The Negro Leadership Class.* Englewood Cliffs, N.J.: Prentice-Hall, 1963.

The text is the result of a study that focuses on New Orleans from 1940 to 1960 as a "typical" Southern city. It examines the evolution of factors and conditions that gave rise to and affected the characteristics of black leadership there. In a direct, candid style, Thompson examines the city, its systems, and racial politics. Includes a foreword by Martin Luther King, Jr.

1117. Thompson, Era Bell. *Africa, Land of My Fathers.* 1st ed. Garden City, N.Y.: Doubleday and Co., 1954.

1118. Thornton, J. Mills. *Politics and Power in a Slave Society: Alabama, 1800–1860.* Baton Rouge: Louisiana State University Press, 1981.

1119. Thorpe, Earl Endris. *African Americans and the Sacred: Spirituals, Slave Religion, and Symbolism.* Durham, N.C.: Harrington Publication, 1982.

The author uses the lyrics of the "sorrow songs" as a vehicle to study the significance of myths, symbols, and ritual—"the sacred"—in Afro–American religious thought; to argue his "conviction that African Americans have been and are uniquely a people committed to nonrepression—to the sacred"; and to explore the ways in which Christian eschatology has symbolized the black experience.

1120. ———. *Black Historians: A Critique.* New York: William Morrow and Co., 1971. Originally published as *Negro Historians in the United States* (1958).

In his study of black historians, Thorpe delineates four historical periods. The first, "The Beginning School," covers the period from 1800 to 1896. The second, "The Middle Group," covers the period from 1896 to 1930; the third, "The Modern Layman," which Thorpe considers an adjunct of the Middle Group, spans the period from 1896 through the 1960s; and the last group, "The New School," covers the general period from about 1930 to 1960. He evaluates the contributions of historians in each period, using such criteria as their background and training in historical methodology, their philosophical depth and the soundness of their historical interpretations, their objectivity, and the impact of their work. Includes a selected bibliography and an index.

1121. ———. *The Central Theme of Black History.* Durham, N.C.: Seeman Printery, 1969.

This is a discussion on the field of black historiography, the theory and philosophy of Afro–American history. Thorpe writes about the progress of American blacks while stressing the need for more historical material on the subject. He examines some themes in black history and gives biographies of those who have contributed to black historiography. Particularly interesting chapter is chapter 8, which raises questions about how white teachers should approach black history.

1122. ————. *The Desertion of Man: A Critique of Philosophy of History.* Baton Rouge, La.: Ortlieb Press, 1958.

1123. ————. *Eros and Freedom in Southern Life and Thought.* Durham, N.C.: Seeman Printery, 1967.

This volume gives another view of the history of the American South. Thorpe is reacting against how some history books portray the leaders of the Old South as being inhumane. He also believes that black-white relations in America have never been as bad as some historians have contended. In chapter 3, "Psychoanalysis and Negro Studies," Thorpe suggests some reasons why psychoanalysis and black studies should be joined.

1124. ————. *The Mind of the Negro: An Intellectual History of Afro-Americans.* Baton Rouge: Ortlieb Press, 1961. Reprint. Westport, Conn.: Greenwood Press, 1970.

The relationship between Afro-Americans and the dominant Anglo culture is unique, Thorpe argues, in that the chattel slavery, segregation, and discrimination suffered by blacks are not associated with other ethnic groups. As a result, the intellectual history of blacks is also unique. Thorpe thoroughly examines the historical development of the Afro-American's pattern of thought, with special emphasis on emancipation and the American system. The text is very detailed, covering a period that ranges from the days of slavery to the mid-twentieth century.

1125. Tolson, Arthur L. *The Black Oklahomans: A History, 1541-1972.* New Orleans: Edwards Printing Co., 1974.

1126. Toppin, Edgar Allan. *A Biographical History of Blacks in America Since 1528*. 1969. Reprint. New York: David McKay Co., 1971.

This book grew out of an educational television course taught by Toppin and a series of his newspaper articles. The first fourteen chapters give a history of black Americans from an African background to the era of civil rights, with suggestions for additional readings, both in general works and reading on specific aspects of black history. The last section of the book consists of biographies of notable black Americans.

1127. ————. *The Black American in United States History*. Boston: Allyn and Bacon, 1973.

1128. ————. *Blacks in America: Then and Now*. Boston: Christian Science Publishing Society, 1969.

1129. ————. *A Mark Well Made: The Negro Contribution to American Culture*. Chicago: Rand McNally and Co., 1967.

1130. Toppin, Edgar Allan, and Lavinia Dobler.* *Pioneers and Patriots: The Lives of Six Negroes of the Revolutionary Era*. New York: Doubleday and Co., 1965.

1131. Toppin, Edgar Allan, and Carol Drisko.* *The Unfinished March: The Negro in the United States, Reconstruction to World War I*. New York: Doubleday and Co., 1967.

1132. Travis, Dempsey J. *An Autobiography of Black Chicago*. Chicago: Urban Research Institute, 1981.

This book is an autobiography supplemented by historical and economic analyses. A unique feature of the volume is a series of interviews with contemporary educators, activists, and community leaders.

1133. Turner, Ethel Marie. *A Negro History Compendium*. Cheyney, Pa.: Cheyney State College, 1971.

1134. Turner, Glennette Tilley. *The Underground Railroad in DuPage County, Illinois.* 1980. Reprint. Wheaton, Ill.: Newman Educational Publishers, 1986.

1135. Van Sertima, Ivan. *Egypt Revisited.* 2d ed. New Brunswick, N.J.: Transaction Publishers, 1989.

1136. ————. *They Came Before Columbus.* New York: Random House, 1976. Reprint. New York: Vintage Books, 1989.

Using facts of navigation and shipbuilding; the sources of latitudinal and longitudinal coordinates; cultural analogies only found in America and Africa; African languages and the transportation of plants, cloths, and animals from Africa to the Americas; diaries, letters, and journals of the explorers themselves, as well as other sources, Van Sertima builds his pyramid of evidence of the presence and legacy of black Africans in pre–Columbian America, and their impact on the civilization they found here. Includes notes and an index.

1137. Walker, David, and Henry Highland Garnet. *Walker's Appeal in Four Articles (David Walker).* An Address to the Slaves of the United States of America (Henry Highland Garnet), 1829. New York: Hill and Wang, Inc., 1965. Reprint. New York: Arno Press, 1969.

This volume consist of *Walker's Appeal in Four Articles*, with a brief sketch of his life by Henry Highland Garnet. It also contains Garnet's Address to the Slaves of the United States of America. Both men called for the abolition of slavery and massive slave resistance. "If any single event may be said to have triggered the Negro revolt, it is the publicaton of David Walker's *Appeal to the Coloured Citizens of the World* in September, 1829." Includes a new preface by William Loren Katz.**

1138. Walker, Juliet E. K. *Free Frank: A Black Pioneer on the Antebellum Frontier.* Lexington: University Press of Kentucky, 1983.

1139. Washington, Booker T. *The Story of the Negro: The Rise of the Race from Slavery.* New York: Doubleday, Page, 1909.

1140. Weatherford,** Willis Duke, and Charles Spurgeon Johnson. *Race Relations: Adjustment of Whites and Negroes in the U.S.* Boston: D. C. Heath and Co., 1934. Reprint. New York: Negro Universities Press, 1969.

   Written in the 1930s, this book uses historical, sociological, and statistical data to demonstrate the falsehood of certain generalizations about whites and blacks. The text is divided into three parts: part 1 discusses the philosophy of race relations; part 2 looks back at Afro-American slavery; and part 3 reviews race relations at the present time.

1141. Webster, Staten Wentford. *Knowing and Understanding the Socially Disadvantaged Ethnic Minority Groups.* Scranton, Pa.: InText Educational Publishers, 1972.

   This book provides an understanding and knowledge of the backgrounds, problems, and lifestyles of five ethnic minorities: black Americans, Mexican-Americans, Puerto Rican-Americans, American Indians, and Japanese- and Chinese-Americans. Webster selected these groups because of their high visibility among the socially disadvantaged and because their fight for civil and economic rights has had a decided impact on American society. The book includes photographs and interviews with a noted member of each group, as well as a selection of essays on each group by various knowledgeable personalities.

1142. Wesley, Charles Harris. *Neglected History: Essays in Negro History by a College President.* Wilberforce, Ohio: Central State College Press, 1965. Reprint. Washington, D.C.: Association for the Study of Negro Life and History, 1969.

1143. Wesley, Charles Harris, and Patricia W. Romero.* *Negro Americans in the Civil War: From Slavery to Citizenship.* 2d ed. New York: Publishers Co., 1970.

1144. Weston, Rubin Francis. *Racism in U.S. Imperialism: The Influence of Racial Assumption on American Foreign Policy, 1893–1946.* Columbia: University of South Carolina Press, 1972.

Weston traces the influences of racism on American foreign policy, beginning with the imperialist campaign in 1893 that marks the U.S. acquisition of Hawaii. The author discusses American imperialism and its effects in the Philippine Islands; Cuba; Puerto Rico, where the dilemma of statehood or dependence is still being played out; and U.S. imperial relations to Hispaniola.

1145. Wilkinson, Doris Yvonne, ed. *Black Revolt: Strategies of Protest.* Berkeley, Calif.: McCutchan Publishing Co., 1969.

This collection of essays, which focuses on black strategies for counteracting racist attitudes and policies, was designed to enhance our understanding of black–white relations. It is an excellent supplement in courses of sociology, history, and Afro–American studies. Exercises are included at the end of the text to stimulate classroom discussion.

1146. Williams, Chancellor. *The Destruction of Black Civilization: Great Issues of Race from 4500 B.C. to 2000 A.D.* Rev. ed. Chicago: Third World Press, 1987.

Included among the fifteen chapters of this work are "Egypt: The Rise and Fall of Black Civilization" and "Organizing a Race for Action." Also included are notes, a selected bibliography, and an index.

1147. Williams, Eric Eustace. *From Columbus to Castro: The History of the Caribbean, 1492–1969.* New York: Vintage Books, 1983.

Written in 1970, this landmark work by the late prime minister of Trinidad—popular statesman, author of the classic

Capital and Slavery—illuminates a profoundly important but neglected and misrepresented area of the world.

1148.   Williams, George Washington. *History of the Negro Race in America from 1619 to 1880: Negroes as Slaves, as Soldiers, and as Citizens.* 2 vols. New York: G. P. Putnam's Sons. 1883.

Williams—the first black member of the Ohio legislature and former judge advocate of the Grand Army of the Republic of Ohio—details the history of blacks from their initial arrival in 1619 to 1880. Volume 1 addresses the period 1619–1800, and volume 2 embraces the period 1800–1880.

1149.   Williams, John Alfred. *Africa: Her History, Lands, and People, Told with Pictures.* 1965. Reprint. New York: Cooper Square Publishers, 1973.

1150.   Williams, Lorraine Anderson, ed. *Africa and the Afro-American Experience.* Washington, D.C.: Howard University Press, 1977.

This collection of essays by eight renowned black historians is intended to bring to widespread public knowledge the intriguing history of Africa and the Afro-American experience, as well as to lend support to the need for African studies. It is a tribute to Leo William Hansberry, who once taught at Howard University and was one of the first to relate Africa to the black experience in America. The text includes an essay by Hansberry, plus biographical data on the contributors and a bibliography for each essay.

1151.   Williams, Melvin D. *On the Street Where I Lived.* New York: Holt, Rinehart and Winston, 1981.

One in a series of case studies in cultural anthropology, this book provides an ethnographic account of a black neighborhood in Pittsburgh—Belmar. The author examines the daily living conditions in the neighborhood, as well as the character and behavior of the people who live there. Having been a resident of Belmar himself, Williams states that, for the most part, he interviewed his neighbors. The book covers various topics as they relate to the lifestyle of the people in Belmar, including landlords and tenants, verbal communication, activities, and household styles. The book also includes references, pictures, and a listing of case studies in contemporary American culture.

1152. Winston, Michael R. *The Howard University Department of History, 1913-1973.* Washington, D.C.: Department of History, Howard University, 1973.

1153. Wood, Forrest G. *Black Scare: The Racist Response to Emancipation and Reconstruction.* Berkeley: University of California Press, 1968.

A history of white backlash during the period of emancipation and reconstruction following the Civil War. Wood sees the Civil War and Reconstruction as leading to the destructive forms of racism that are permeating American society to this day. A few plates depicting early racist attitudes are included.

1154. ———. *The Era of Reconstruction 1863-1877.* New York: Thomas Y. Crowell Co., 1975.

In *The Era of Reconstruction*, Wood again addresses the issues of Reconstruction and its relation to the Civil War, to the U.S. Congress, and to the racist attitudes of the era. The book concludes with a bibliographical essay.

1155. Woodson, Carter Goodwin. *Negro Makers of History.* Washington, D.C.: Associated Publishers, 1958.

1156. ———. *The Rural Negro.* Washington, D.C.: Association for the Study of Negro Life and History, Inc., 1930. Reprint. New York: Russell and Russell, 1969.

1157.   ————. *The Story of the Negro Retold.* Washington, D.C.: Associated Publishers, 1935.

1158.   Woodson, Carter Goodwin, and Charles Harris Wesley. *The Negro in Our History.* 12th ed. 1962. Reprint. Washington, D.C.: Associated Publishers, 1972.

1159.   Woolfolk, George Ruble. *The Cotton Regency: The Northern Merchants and Reconstruction, 1865–1880.* New York: Twayne Publishers, 1958. Reprint. New York: Octagon Books, 1979.

1160.   ————. *The Free Negro in Texas, 1800–1860: A Study in Cultural Compromise.* Ann Arbor, Mich.: University Microfilms International, 1976.

1161.   Wright, Nathan, Jr. *Let's Face Racism.* New York: Thomas Nelson, 1970.

One in a series of books sponsored by the Youth Research Center, Inc., this book focuses on the very real concerns, problems, aspirations, and goals of today's youth. It deals with the relationship of racism to religion and the effects of racism on personality. It argues that "overcoming racism in our religious life will give a continuous sense of challenge and adventure."

1162.   ————. *Let's Work Together.* New York: Hawthorn Books, 1968.

Wright makes the point that before blacks and whites can work together, they have to resolve their own problems. He focuses on three types of racial problems: those that blacks must solve for themselves, those that whites must solve, and those that require cooperation between blacks and whites. In the chapter called "Making Educational Changes," he argues that the present educational system should be redirected toward meeting new needs in a period of rapidly accelerating change.

1163. Wright, Richard. *12 Million Black Voices*. New York: Viking Press, 1941. Reprint. New York: Thunder's Mouth Press, 1988.

This work combines Wright's prose with photographs selected (by Edwin Rosskam,* the photographic editor) from the Farm Security Administration files compiled during the Great Depression. The work reveals the history of black oppression in America.

1164. Yette, Samuel F., and Frederick Walton Yette. *Washington and Two Marches 1963 and 1983: The Third American Revolution*. Silver Spring, Md.: Cottage Books, 1984.

This work is a commemorative pictorial with more than 140 photographs of two of the major demonstrations of our times. The photographs are the work of Samuel F. Yette and his son, Frederick Walton Yette.

1165. Young, Richard P., ed. *Roots of Rebellion: The Evolution of Black Politics and Protest Since World War II*. New York: Harper and Row, 1970.

These essays trace the development of black protest from the 1940s, when Jim Crow practices were the rule even in the North and when most blacks played roles of accommodation, to the present period of black pride and rebellion against the status quo. Contributors include sociologists, political scientists, psychologists, and psychiatrists, both black and white, as well as leading figures of the "Negro Revolution" and the contemporary black revolutionary movement. Part 1 outlines recent changes in white attitudes and behavior toward black Americans; part 2 focuses on the economic profile of blacks; part 3 explains the development of black pride; and parts 4 and 5 trace the development of conventional black politics and protest since World War II.

CHAPTER 6

JUVENILE LITERATURE

1166. Abdul, Raoul. *Famous Black Entertainers of Today.* New York: Dodd, Mead and Co., 1974.

The author presents intimate portraits of eighteen noted figures in the world of entertainment, many of them based on personal interviews. Includes Alvin Ailey, Martina Arroyo, Alex Bradford, James DePriest, Gloria Foster, Aretha Franklin, Micki Grant, Ellis Haizlip, James Earl Jones, Arthur Mitchell, Carman Moore, Ron O'Neal, Diana Ross, Cicely Tyson, Melvin Van Peebles, Ben Vereen, Andre Watts, and Flip Wilson. Also includes an introduction, photographs, and an index.

1167. ————, comp. *The Magic of Black Poetry.* Illustrated by Dane Burr. New York: Dodd, Mead and Co., 1972.

Compiled for young readers with commentaries by Abdul, this work is a collection of poetry written by black people all over the world. Many are prominent living poets. The book makes the reader cognizant that blacks are part of an international culture rich with poetic treasures, and that they express themselves in many languages. Includes a section describing the poets.

1168.   Achebe, Chinua, and John Iroaganachi.* *How the Leopard Got His Claws.* Illustrated by Per Christiansen.* New York: Third Press, 1973.

1169.   Adams, Russell L. *Great Negroes Past and Present.* Illustrated by Eugene Winslow. 3d ed. Chicago: Afro-Am Publishing Co., 1969. Reprint. Sacramento: California State Department of Education, 1973.

This book presents brief biographies of great blacks, past and present. It is divided into twelve chapters: "Our African Heritage," "Early American History," "From the Civil War Forward," "Science and Industry," "Business Pioneers," "Religion," "Leaders and Spokesmen," "Education," "Literature," "The Theater," "Music," and "Visual Art." This third edition has been revised, updated, and expanded to broaden its use as a supplementary text for the primary and secondary grades.

1170.   Alexander, Rae Pace, and Julius Lester, eds. *Young and Black in America.* New York: Random House, 1970.

A collection of self-descriptive essays about black people whose contributions have been outstanding. Introductory notes accompany each essay.

1171.   Allen, Samuel, comp. *Poems from Africa.* Illustrated by Romare H. Bearden. New York: Thomas Y. Crowell Co., 1973.

1172.   Arkhurst, Joyce. *The Adventures of Spider: West African Folk Tales.* Illustrated by Jerry Pinkney. Boston: Little, Brown and Co., 1964.

In these stories from Liberia and Ghana, Spider is a clever, mischievous character who usually outwits his foes, but sometimes he catches himself. Foods, occupations, and some of the customs are described.

1173.   ———. *More Adventures of Spider.* New York: Scholastic, 1971.

1174. Ashe, Arthur R., Jr., with Louie Robinson, Jr. *Getting Started in Tennis.* 1st ed. New York: Atheneum Publishers, 1977.

"A Wimbledon champion instructs beginning players in the mechanics, rules, strategy, and etiquette of tennis." Includes photographs by Jeanne Moutoussamy.

1175. Baker, Augusta. *The Golden Lynx.* Philadelphia: J. B. Lippincott Co., 1960.

1176. ————. *The Talking Tree.* Philadelphia: J. B. Lippincott Co., 1955.

1177. ————, ed. *The Young Years: Anthology of Children's Literature.* New York: Parents Magazine Press, 1950.

1178. Baker, Augusta, and Ellin Greene. *Storytelling, Art and Technique.* New York: R. R. Bowker Co., 1977.

1179. Baldwin, James. *Little Man, Little Man: A Story of Childhood.* Illustrated by Yoran Cazac.** New York: The Dial Press, 1976.

It is about the coming of age in Harlem of boys named WT and TJ, about the surface incidents of daily life that mask a menace in the Harlem streets that is external.

1180. Bambara, Toni Cade. *Gorilla, My Love.* New York: Vintage Books, 1981.

This collection of stories by one of America's leading black writers has been recognized as "among the best portraits of black life to have appeared."

1181. ————. *The Salt Eaters.* 1st ed. New York: Random House, 1980.

1182.   ———. *The Seabirds Are Still Alive: Collected Stories*. 1st ed. New York: Random House, 1977. Reprint. New York: Vintage Books, 1982.

1183.   ———, ed. *Tales and Stories for Black Folks*. Garden City, N.Y.: Zenith Books, 1971.

This anthology aims to present history and culture to youth. Written in first person, the first section of the book, "Our Great Kitchen Tradition," encourages the reader to remember that African heritage is preserved through oral history or stories usually told in the kitchen. The author believes it is important for young people to learn to listen to and to be proud of elders who tell family stories. The second section, "Rapping About Story Forms," contains poems and short stories, and explains the importance of the African fable.

1184.   Banks, James A., and Cherry A. McGee Banks. *March Toward Freedom: A History of Black Americans*. Palo Alto, Calif.: Fearon Publishers, 1970.

This volume, written for teenagers, traces the history of the black American's struggle for freedom. The authors begin with the black man's life in Africa, and then discuss his conditions under slavery and various phases of his experience in post–Civil War America. Chapters 4 and 7 focus on the black man's involvement in the Civil War and World War II. Chapters 8 and 9 discuss heightened attempts in the 1950s and 1960s to obtain more freedom. The final chapter pays tribute to outstanding black Americans. (Also see second edition, Fearon Publishers, 1974.)

1185.   Barrett, Joyce Durham. *Willie's Not the Hugging Kind*. Illustrated by Pat Cummings. New York: Harper and Row, 1989.

"Willie's best friend Jo–Jo thinks hugging is silly, so Willie stops hugging everybody but he soon misses giving and getting hugs from his family."

1186. Baugh, Dolores M., and Marjorie P. Pulsifer.* *Bikes.* San Francisco: Chandler Publishing Co., 1964. Reprint. New York: Noble and Noble Publishers, 1970.

This is one of several books in the Chandler Reading Program series. Others include *Let's See the Animals, Bikes, Let's Take a Trip, Trucks and Cars to Ride,* and *Swings.*

1187. ————. *Let's Go!* New York: Noble and Noble Publishers, 1970.

1188. ————. *Let's See the Animals.* New York: Noble and Noble Publishers, 1970.

1189. ————. *Let's Take a Trip.* New York: Noble and Noble Publishers, 1970.

1190. ————. *Supermarket.* New York: Noble and Noble Publishers, 1970.

1191. ————. *Swings.* New York: Noble & Noble Publishers, 1970.

1192. ————. *Trucks and Cars to Ride.* New York: Noble and Noble Publishers, 1970.

1193. Bearden, Romare H., and Henry Henderson. *Six Black Masters of American Art.* Garden City, N.Y.: Doubleday/Zenith, 1972.

1194. Bennett, Lerone, Jr. *Before the Mayflower: A History of Black America.* 6th ed. 1962. Reprint. Chicago: Johnson Publishing Co., 1987.

A history of black Americans from their roots in Africa to their experiences in North America, this book deals with the inception of slavery and with segregation in contemporary times. First published in 1962 and continuously updated in succeeding years, this book now in its sixth revised edition, contains new and expanded material in every chapter and a section on black pioneers and black firsts. It also provides a detailed bibliography of relevant sources.

1195. ————. *Black Power U.S.A.: The Human Side of Reconstruction 1867–1877.* 1st ed. Chicago: Johnson Publishing Co., 1967.

1196. ————. *The Challenge of Blackness.* Chicago: Johnson Publishing Co., 1972.

The theme in this collection of essays and speeches by Bennett is the challenge of blacks to obtain political, economic, and cultural power. Essentially the challenge is much more than the surface struggle over integration and segregation; these conditions merely symbolize what is at the core of the problem—a need to reassess black and white cultural identities. The white person's identity cannot be evaluated or described independently of the black person's identity; they are inextricably related.

1197. ————. *Pioneers in Protest.* Chicago: Johnson Publishing Co., 1968.

1198. ————. *The Shaping of Black America.* Illustrated by Charles White. Chicago: Johnson Publishing Co., 1975.

This book grew out of Bennett's earlier publication, *Before the Mayflower.* The difference between the two books is that *The Shaping of Black America* is a developmental history rather than a chronological one. The book is divided into two parts: "Foundations" and "Directions." "Foundations" treats the first generation of Afro–Americans as well as the relationship between blacks and Indians. "Directions" is mainly concerned with the history of black labor and capital. In addition, the book contains several illustrations of Afro–Americans, and an appendix that contains statistical charts about the black population in cities with 100,000 or more blacks, the "Ten Leading Metropolitan Areas for Black-owned Firms," and the "Ten Leading Industries for Black-owned Firms."

1199. ————. *Wade in the Water: Great Moments in Black History.*
1st ed. Chicago: Johnson Publishing Co., 1979.

Fifteen dramatic episodes in black history, that have
provided turning points in the shaping of the two Americas, the
black and the white. The reader will feel the complete meaning
of the black tradition as summed up in the spiritual "Wade in the
Water."

1200. ————. *What Manner of Man: A Biography of Martin Luther
King, Jr., 1929-1968.* 4th rev. ed. Chicago: Johnson
Publishing Co., 1976.

An insight into the personality of Dr. Martin Luther King,
Jr., this biography covers King's development from his youth
through manhood and his emergence as a national leader. This
edition also includes an extra chapter on the events of Dr. King's
last fateful weeks. The title of the book and the names of the
chapters are of symbolic significance. The book is also well
illustrated, with pictures of Dr. King in different stages of his
career.

1201. Bible, Charles. *Hamdaani: A Traditional Tale from Zanzibar.*
New York: Holt, Rinehart and Winston, 1977.

1202. ————. *Jennifer's New Chair.* New York: Holt, Rinehart and
Winston, 1978.

1203. Bond, Jean Carey. *A Is for Africa.* New York: Franklin Watts,
1969.

1204. ————. *Brown Is a Beautiful Color.* New York: Franklin
Watts, 1969.

1205. Bontemps, Arna Wendell. *Chariot in the Sky: A Story of the
Jubilee Singers.* Rev. ed. New York: Holt, Rinehart and
Winston, 1971.

Eleven black students form a singing group and tour the
world in an attempt to save their college from financial ruin.

1206. ————. *Famous Negro Athletes.* New York: Dodd, Mead and Co., 1964.

1207. ————. *Golden Slippers: An Anthology of Negro Poetry for Young Readers.* New York: Harper and Row, 1941.

1208. ————. *Lonesome Boy.* Boston: Houghton Mifflin Co., 1955.

1209. ————. *Mr. Kelso's Lion.* Philadelphia: J. B. Lippincott Co., 1970.

1210. ————. *One Hundred Years of Negro Freedom.* New York: Dodd, Mead and Co., 1961. Rev. ed. Westport, Conn.: Greenwood Press, 1980.

Bontemps, using biographical material, provides an account of Afro-American history from Frederick Douglass to 1960.

1211. ————. *The Story of George Washington Carver.* Illustrated by Harper Johnson. New York: Grosset and Dunlap, 1954.

1212. ————. *Story of the Negro.* 5th ed. Illustrated by Raymond Lufkin.* New York: Alfred A. Knopf, 1969.

1213. ————. *We Have Tomorrow.* Illustrated with photographs by Marian Palfi.* 1945. Reprint. Boston: Houghton Mifflin Co., 1960.

1214. ————, ed. *American Negro Poetry.* New York: Hill and Wang, 1963.

This assorted collection of poetry extends across many years. Biographical descriptions of the poets are included.

1215. ————, ed. *Hold Fast to Dreams: Poems Old and New.* Chicago: Follett Publishing Co., 1969.

1216. Bontemps, Arna Wendell, and Jack Conroy.* *The Fast Sounder Hound.* Illustrated by Virginia Lee Burton.* Rev. ed. Boston: Houghton Mifflin Co., 1970.

Chagrined that the hound Sooner continually outruns his trains, the roadmaster pits Sooner's speed against that of his fastest train, the Cannon Ball.

1217. Bontemps, Arna Wendell, and Langston Hughes. *Popo and Fifina: Children of Haiti.* Illustrated by E. Simms Campbell.* New York: Macmillan Co., 1932.

1218. Boyd, Candy Dawson. *Breadsticks and Blessing Places.* New York: Macmillan Co., 1987.

1219. ———. *Charlie Pippin.* New York: Macmillan Co., 1987.

Spunky eleven–year–old Charlie hopes to understand her rigid father by finding out everything she can about the Vietnam War, the war that let him survive but killed his dreams.

1220. ———. *Circle of Gold.* New York: Scholastic, 1984.

In this novel—Boyd's first, and a Coretta Scott King Award Honor Book—ten–year–old Mattie copes with the loss of her father and the mixed feelings toward her mother, who is under pressure to support the family.

1221. ———. *Forever Friends.* New York: Puffin Books, 1986.

Originally published under the title *Breadsticks and Blessing Places,* which was a 1985 Booklist Editor's Choice, this work is about a twelve–year–old black girl whose preparation for the prestigious King's Academy entrance exam is disrupted when her best friend is killed.

1222. Breinburg, Petronella. *Doctor Shawn.* With illustrations by Errol Lloyd. New York: Thomas Y. Crowell Co., 1975.

Originally published under title *Doctor Sean.* A little boy and his sister play at being doctor and nurse.

1223. ————. *Legends of Suriname.* Illustrations by Art Derry.* London: New Beacon Books, 1971.

1224. ————. *My Brother Sean.* With illustrations by Errol Lloyd. London: Bodley Head, 1973. Reprint. Harmondsworth: Puffin, 1978.

1225. ————. *One Day, Another Day.* Illustrated by Mary Dinsdale.* Basingstoke: Macmillan and Co., 1977.

1226. ————. *Sally–Ann in the Snow.* With illustrations by Ossie Murray.* London: Bodley Head, 1977.

1227. ————. *Sean's Red Bike.* Illustrated by Errol Lloyd. London: Bodley Head, 1975.

1228. ————. *Shawn Goes to School.* Illustrated by Errol Lloyd. New York: Thomas Y. Crowell Co., 1973.

1229. ————. *Tiger, Paleface, and Me.* Pictures by Richard Rose.* London: Macmillan and Co., 1979.

1230. ————. *Tiger, Tinker, and Me.* New York: Macmillan Co., 1974.

1231. ————. *Us Boys of Westcroft.* London: Macmillan and Co., 1975.

1232. ————. *What Happened at Rita's Party.* With pictures by Jim Russell.* Harmondsworth: Kestrel Books, 1976.

1233. Brooks, Gwendolyn. *Bronzeville Boys and Girls.* Illustrations by Ronni Salbert. New York: Harper and Brothers, 1956. Reprint. Eau Claire, Wis.: E. M. Hale, Brothers, 1968. Reprint. New York: Harper and Row, 1970.

This is a book of poems about and dedicated to the children of Bronzevilles across the country, but it expresses the emotions and thoughts of all city children.

1234. —————. *The Tiger Who Wore White Gloves: or, What You Are You Are.* Illustrated by Timothy Jones.* Chicago: Third World Press, 1974.

1235. Brown, Kay. *Beauty and the Beast.* Retold by Kay Brown. Illustrated by Gerry A. Embleton.* New York: Derrydale Books, 1978.

"Through her capacity to love, a kind and beautiful maid releases a handsome prince from the spell which has made him an ugly beast."

1236. —————. *Hansel and Gretel.* Retold by Kay Brown. Illustrated by Gerry A. Embleton.* New York: Derrydale Books, 1979.

"A retelling of the tale of two children, lost in the woods, who came upon a gingerbread house inhabited by a wicked witch."

1237. —————. *Jack and the Beanstalk.* Retold by Kay Brown, and Illustrated by Gerry A. Embleton.* New York: Derrydale Books, 1978.

"A boy climbs to the top of a giant beanstalk where he uses his quick wits to outsmart an ogre and make his and his mother's fortune."

1238. —————. *Knock Ten: A Novel of Mining Life.* Sydney: Wentworth Books, 1976.

1239. —————. *The Pied Piper of Hamelin.* Retold by Kay Brown. Illustrated by Gerry A. Embleton.* New York: Derrydale Books, 1979.

"The pied piper pipes the village free of rats and when the villagers refuse to pay him for the service, he pipes away their children."

1240. ———. *Pinocchio.* Retold by Kay Brown. Illustrated by Gerry A. Embleton.* New York: Derrydale Books, 1979.

"In Geppetto's hand a piece of wood that talks becomes a living mischievous marionette and eventually, after many trials and errors, a real boy."

1241. ———. *Red Riding Hood.* Retold by Ian Paul Robinson. Illustrated by Gerry A. Embleton.* New York: Derrydale Books, 1979.

"A little girl meets a wolf in the forest on her way to visit her grandmother."

1242. ———. *Sleeping Beauty.* Retold by Kay Brown. Illustrated by Gerry A. Embleton.* New York: Derrydale Books, 1979.

"Enraged at not being invited to the princess' christening, the 13th fairy casts a spell that dooms the princess to sleep for 100 years."

1243. ———. *Snow White and the Seven Dwarfs.* Illustrated by Gerry A. Embleton.* New York: Derrydale Books, 1979.

"Retells the tale of the beautiful princess whose lips were red as blood, skin was white as snow, and hair was black as ebony."

1244. ———. *Willy's Summer Dream.* New York: Harcourt Brace Jovanovich, 1989.

1245. Brown, Virginia Suggs. *Hidden Lookout.* New York: McGraw–Hill, 1965.

1246. ———. *Out Jumped Abraham.* New York: McGraw–Hill, 1967.

1247. ———. *Watch Out For C.* New York: McGraw–Hill, 1965.

1248. ———. *Who Cares?* New York: McGraw–Hill, 1965.

1249. Bryan, Ashley. *The Adventures of Aku.* New York: Atheneum Publishers, 1976.

1250. ———. *Beat the Story Drum, Pum–Pum.* New York: Aladdin Books, 1987.

Five traditional Nigerian tales include "Hen and Frog," "Why Bush Cow and Elephant and Bad Friends," "The Husband Who Counted the Spoonfuls," "Why Frog and Snake Never Play Together," and "How Animals Got Their Tails." This work, authored and illustrated by Bryan, was a 1980 American Library Association Notable Book and won the Coretta Scott King Award in 1981 for its illustrations.

1251. ———. *Black American Spirituals.* Vol. 2, *I'm Going to Sing.* New York: Atheneum Publishers, 1982.

1252. ———. *Black American Spirituals.* Vol. 1, *Walk Together Children.* New York: Atheneum Publishers, 1974.

This book of songs (music is included with the words) presents familiar and lesser–known spirituals, including "Walk Together Children," "Little David Play on Your Harp," "I've Got Shoes," and others. It was a 1974 American Library Association Notable Book.

1253. ———. *The Cat's Purr.* New York: Atheneum Publishers, 1985.

Cat and Rat are friends, but when Rat tricks Cat and plays a special cat drum that only cats may play, Cat winds up swallowing the drum, and that is how he got his purr.

1254. ———. *The Dancing Granny.* New York: Aladdin Books, 1977.

This book, retold and illustrated by Bryan, comes from "He Sings to Make the Old Woman Dance" (Antigua, English Antilles). In Elsie Clews Parsons,* *Folk–Lore of the Antilles, French and English*, part 2 (New York: American Folk–Lore Society, 1936), p. 314.

1255. ————. *Lion and the Ostrich Chicks and Other African Tales.* New York: Atheneum Publishers, 1986.

This book includes four traditional tales told by the Hausa, Angolan, Masai, and Bushmen people of Africa.

1256. ————. *The Ox of the Wonderful Horns, and Other African Folktales.* New York: Atheneum Publishers, 1971.

Folktales include ananse, the spider in search of a fool; frog and his two wives; elephant and frog go courting; tortoise, hare, and the sweet potatoes; and the ox of the wonderful horns.

1257. Burroughs, Margaret Taylor G. *Jasper the Drummin' Boy.* Illustrated by Ted Lewin.* Rev. ed. Chicago: Follett Publishing Co., 1970.

All Jasper's problems seem to stem from his strong desire to be a famous drummer like his grandfather and from his mother's equally strong determination to make him a concert pianist.

1258. ————, comp. *Did You Feed My Cow? Street Games, Chants, and Rhymes.* Illustrated by Joe E. De Velasco.* Rev. ed. Chicago: Follett Publishing Co., 1969.

Seventy–six chants and rhymes used and adapted by American children for jumping rope, bouncing balls, or just fun.

1259. Caines, Jeannette Franklin. *Abby.* Illustrated by Steven Kellogg.** New York: Harper, 1973. Reprint. New York: Trophy, 1984.

1260. ————. *Chilly Stomach.* Illustrated by Pat Cummings. New York: Harper, 1986.

1261. ————. *Daddy.* Illustrated by Ronald Himler.* New York: Harper, 1977.

A child of separated parents describes the special activities she shares with her father on Saturdays.

1262. ————. *I Need a Lunch Box.* Pictures by Pat Collins.* New York: Harper and Row, 1988.

A little boy yearns for a lunch box, even though he hasn't started school yet.

1263. ————. *Just Us Women.* Illustrated by Pat Cummings. 1st ed. New York: Harper and Row, 1982. Reprint. New York: Trophy, 1984.

A young girl and her favorite aunt share the excitement of planning a very special car trip for just the two of them.

1264. ————. *Window Wishing.* Illustrated by Kevin Brooks.* New York: Harper and Row, 1980.

Grandma Meg, who wears sneakers all the time and leads a very active life, demonstrates her love for her grandchildren. When they visit her, she takes them fishing and "window wishing" (her name for window shopping).

1265. Campbell, Barbara. *A Girl Called Bob, A Horse Named Yoki.* New York: Dial Press, 1982.

1266. Carew, Jan Rynveld. *Black Midas.* Adapted for schools by Sylvia Wynter. Illustrated by Audrey Williams. London: Longman, 1969.

1267. ————. *Children of the Sun.* New York: Little, Brown and Co., 1978.

1268. ———. *Rope the Sun.* New York: Third Press, 1973.

1269. ———. *The Third Gift.* Illustrated by Leo Dillon and Diane Dillon.** Boston: Little, Brown and Co., 1977.

1270. ———. *The Twins of Ilora.* Boston: Little, Brown and Co., 1977.

1271. Carter, Mary Kennedy. *Count on Me.* New York: American Book Company, 1970.

1272. ———. *On to Freedom.* New York: Hill and Wang, 1970.

1273. Cartey, Wilfred G. *The West Indies: Islands in the Sun.* Nashville: Thomas Nelson, 1967.

1274. Chase–Riboud, Barbara. *Sally Hemings: A Novel.* New York: Viking Press, 1979.

1275. Chestnutt, Charles Waddell. *Conjure Tales.* Retold by Ray Anthony Shepard.* Illustrated by John Ross* and Clare Romano.* New York: Dell Publishing Co., 1978.

Stories include "Poor Sandy," "The Conjurer's Revenge, "The Gray Wolf's Haint," "Master James' Nightmare," "The Goophered Grapevine," "Hot–Foot Hannibal," and "Sister Becky's Child."

1276. ———. *The Conjure Woman.* New York: Houghton, Mifflin Co., 1899. Reprint. Ann Arbor, Mich.: University of Michigan Press, 1969.

Stories include "The Goophered Grapevine," "Po' Sandy," "Mars Jeems's Nightmare," "The Conjurer's Revenge," "Sis' Becky's Pickaninny," "The Gray Wolf's Ha'nt," and "Hot–Foot Hannibal."

1277. Childress, Alice. *A Hero Ain't Nothin' but a Sandwich.* New York: Avon/Flare Books, 1973.

The life of a thirteen-year-old Harlem youth, Benjie, on his way to becoming a confirmed heroin addict is seen from his viewpoint and from that of several people around him.

1278. ————. *Let's Hear It for the Queen.* New York: Coward, 1976.

1279. ————. *Rainbow Jordan.* New York: Coward, McCann and Geoghegan, 1981.

Her mother, her foster guardian, and fourteen-year-old Rainbow comment on the state of things as she prepares to return to a foster home for yet another stay.

1280. ————. *A Short Walk.* New York: Coward, McCann and Geoghegan, 1979.

1281. ————. *When the Rattle Snake Sounds.* New York: Coward, 1975.

1282. Clapp, Ouida H. *Holt English.* New York: Holt, Rinehart and Winston, 1984.

1283. Clements,** Zacharie J., and Leon F. Burrell. *Profiles: A Collection of Short Biographies.* New York: Globe Book Co., 1975.

This collection of biographies of great Americans is for juvenile readers. Questions are provided at the end of the stories. There is also a section called "Reading First Aid," which can help in answering the reading questions. The book provides explanations and sample exercises as an aid to the student.

1284. Clifton, Lucille. *All Us Come Cross the Water.* Pictures by John Steptoe. New York: Holt, Rinehart and Winston, 1973.

This is a story of a young black boy's search for his heritage, his country of origin. Ujamaa learns that all black people come from across the water.

1285. ————. *Amifika.* Illustrated by Thomas DiGrazia.* New York: E. P. Dutton, 1977.

Fearful that his father won't remember him after being away in the army, little Amifika looks for a place to hide.

1286. ————. *The Black BC's.* Illustrated by Don Miller. 1st ed. New York: Dutton, 1970.

This ABC book presents a concept for each letter. It gives a short verse for the letter, which helps the young reader fill in some of the concepts of black pride and history.

1287. ————. *The Boy Who Didn't Believe in Spring.* Illustrated by Brinton Turkle.* 1973. Reprint. New York: E. P. Dutton, 1988.

In this illustrated book, King Shavazz and his friend Tony, two young boys, go in search of Spring.

1288. ————. *Don't You Remember?* Illustrated by Evaline Ness.* New York: E. P. Dutton, 1973.

Until her birthday, Desire Mary Tate, a four–year–old black girl, is convinced that everyone makes promises to her that only she remembers.

1289. ————. *Everett Anderson's 1 2 3.* Illustrated by Ann Grifalconi.* New York: Holt, Rinehart and Winston, 1977.

As a small boy's mother considers remarriage, he considers the numbers one, two, three: sometimes they're lonely, sometimes crowded, but sometimes just right.

1290. ————. *Everett Anderson's Christmas Coming.* 1st ed. New York: Holt, Rinehart and Winston, 1971.

1291. ————. *Everett Anderson's Friend.* New York: Holt, Rinehart and Winston, 1976.

1292. ————. *Everett Anderson's Goodbye.* Illustrated by Ann Grifalconi.* 1st ed. New York: Holt, Rinehart and Winston, 1983.

1293. ————. *Everett Anderson's Nine Month Lag.* New York: Holt, Rinehart and Winston, 1978.

1294. ————. *Everett Anderson's Year.* Illustrated by Ann Grifalconi.* New York: Holt, Rinehart and Winston, 1974.

Even though his father has left them, Everett's mother manages well. Although he, too, is coping well, Everett loves his father and misses him.

1295. ————. *Generations: A Memoir.* 1st ed. New York: Random House, 1976.

1296. ————. *Good, Says Jerome.* Illustrated by Stephanie Douglas. New York: E. P. Dutton and Co., 1973.

A little black boy, Jerome, worries about moving to a new place, having a new teacher, and many other things, but his older sister, Janice Marie, allays his fears.

1297. ————. *Good Times: Poems.* New York: Random House, 1969.

1298. ————. *Good Woman: Poems and a Memoir, 1969–1980.* 1st ed. Brockport, N.Y.: BOA Edition, 1987.

1299. ————. *The Lucky Stone.* Illustrated by Dale Payson. New York: Delacorte Press, 1979.

1300. ————. *My Brother Fine with Me.* Illustrated by Moneta Barnett. New York: Holt, Rinehart and Winston, 1970.

1301. ————. *My Friend Jacob.* Illustrated by Thomas DiGrazia.* New York: Dutton, 1980.

This story describes the relationship between an eight–year–old black child, Sam, and his fourteen–year–old white, mentally disabled friend, Jacob.

1302. ———. *Some of the Days of Everett Anderson.* Illustrated by Evaline Ness.* New York: Henry Holt and Co., 1970.

These poems tell all about six–year–old Everett Anderson, who lives in Apartment 14A. Everett Anderson is a fictitious character who could be any child who ever played in the rain, was afraid of the dark, felt lonely, or wondered about the stars.

1303. ———. *Sonora Beautiful.* With drawings by Michael Garland.* New York: E. P. Dutton, 1981.

1304. ———. *The Times They Used To Be.* Illustrated by Susan Jeschke.* New York: Holt, Rinehart and Winston, 1974.

A young black girl relates the adventures of the summer her Uncle Sunny died and her best friend "broke out in sin" because she wasn't saved.

1305. Cornish, Sam. *Grandmother's Pictures.* Illustrated by Jeanne Johns.* Scarsdale, N.Y.: Bradbury Press, 1976.

1306. ———. *Your Hand in Mind.* San Diego: Harcourt Brace Jovanovitch, 1970.

1307. Crews, Donald. *Bicycle Race.* New York: Greenwillow Books, 1985.

1308. ———. *Carousel.* New York: Greenwillow Books, 1982.

1309. ———. *Flying.* New York: Greenwillow Books, 1986.

An airplane takes off, flies, and lands after having passed over cities, country areas, lakes, and more.

1310. ———. *Freight Train.* New York: Greenwillow Books, 1978.

1311. ————. *Harbor.* New York: Greenwillow Books, 1982.

1312. ————. *Light.* New York: Greenwillow Books, 1981.

1313. ————. *Parade.* New York: Greenwillow Books, 1983.

1314. ————. *School Bus.* New York: Greenwillow Books, 1984.

1315. ————. *Trucks.* New York: Greenwillow Books, 1980.

1316. ————. *We Read: A to Z.* New York Greenwillow Books, 1984.

1317. Cummings, Pat Marie. *C.L.O.U.D.S.* Illustrated by the author. 1st ed. New York: Lothrop, Lee and Shepard Books, 1986.

   Chuku, the angel, is given a job of painting the skies of New York City, an assignment he approaches with reluctance but grows to love.

1318. ————. *Jimmy Lee Did It.* New York: Lothrop, Lee and Shepard Books. 1985.

   Artie keeps telling his sister that the messes all over their house are the work of the elusive Jimmy Lee.

1319. Davis, Ossie. *Escape to Freedom: A Play About Young Frederick Douglass.* New York: Viking Press, 1978.

1320. ————. *Langston: A Play.* New York: Delacorte Press, 1982.

   A play based on the life of Langston Hughes by the author of *Purlie.* This description of Hughes also includes some of his writing.

1321. Dee, Ruby. *Two Ways to Count to Ten: A Liberian Folktale.* Retold by Ruby Dee. Illustrated by Susan Meddaugh.* New York: Henry Holt and Co., 1988.

"A retelling of a traditional African tale in which King Leopard invites all the animals to a spear–throwing contest whose winner will marry his daughter and succeed him as King."

1322. DeVeaux, Alexis. *Don't Explain: A Song of Billie Holiday.* New York: Harper and Row, 1980.

"Presents a prose poem recounting the life of the American jazz singer affectionately known as Lady Day."

1323. ————. *An Enchanted Hair Tale.* Illustrated by Cheryl Hanna.* New York: Harper and Row, 1987.

"Sudan suffers from the general ridicule of his strange-looking hair, until he comes to accept and enjoy its enchantment."

1324. ————. *Na–Ni.* A story and pictures by Alexis DeVeaux. 1st ed. New York: Harper and Row, 1973.

"A little girl living in a New York City ghetto imagines all the wonderful things she'll be able to do with the bicycle her mother promised to buy."

1325. ————. *Spirits in the Street.* Drawings by the author. 1st ed. Garden City, N.Y.: Anchor Press, 1973.

1326. Diop, Birago. *Jojo.* New York: Third Press, 1970.

1327. ————. *Mother Crocodile = Maiman–Caiman.* Translated by Rosa Guy. Illustrated by John Steptoe. New York: Delacorte Press, 1981.

Because Mother Crocodile tells stories of the past, the little crocodiles choose to believe she is crazy. When it is almost too late, they learn otherwise.

1328. Dodson, Owen. *Boy at the Window: A Novel.* New York: Farrar, Straus, 1951. Reprint. Chatham, N.J.: Chatham Bookseller, 1972.

1329. DuBois, Shirley Lola Graham. *The Story of Phillis Wheatley.* Illustrated by Robert Burns.* New York: 1949. Reprint. New York: Julius Messner, 1969.

In this biography of a great black female personality, the author portrays the true humanness of a woman whose entire life was filled with love for her people and a desire to see them free from slavery. Dubois makes sure to include the fact that her subject was one of those unfortunates sold off the block. The material is divided into stanzas as a tribute to Phillis Wheatley's poetic genius. An illustration prefaces each chapter.

1330. Dunbar, Paul Laurence. *Little Brown Baby.* New York: Dodd, Mead and Co., 1940.

1331. Edwards, Audrey, with Gary Wohl.* *Muhammad Ali, the People's Champ.* New York: Franklin Watts, 1977.

1332. ————. *The Picture Life of Bobby Orr.* New York: Franklin Watts, 1976.

1333. ————. *The Picture Life of Muhammad Ali.* New York: Franklin Watts, 1976.

1334. ————. *The Picture Life of Stevie Wonder.* New York: Franklin Watts, 1977.

1335. Egypt, Ophelia Settle. *James Weldon Johnson.* New York: Thomas Y. Crowell Co., 1974.

1336. Emecheta, Buchi. *The Moonlight Bride.* New York: George Braziller, 1983.

Two Nigerian girls overhear some elders making secret preparations for a marriage.

1337. ————. *Nowhere to Play.* Illustrated by Peter Archer.* London: Allison and Busby, 1980; Distributed by Schocken Books.

A group of schoolchildren have difficulty finding a safe place to play during the summer vacation. Based on a story by the author's twelve-year-old daughter, Christy.

1338. ————. *Titch the Cat.* Illustrations by Thomas Joseph.* London: Allison and Busby, 1979.

This story is based on one by Emecheta's eleven-year-old daughter, Alice.

1339. ————. *The Wrestling Match.* 1980. Reprint. New York: George Braziller, 1983.

Sixteen-year-old Okei, left an orphan after the Nigerian civil war, engages in a wrestling match to prove to his critical uncle and aunt that he is not as idle and worthless as they think.

1340. Evans, Mari. *I Look at Me.* Chicago: Third World, 1974.

1341. ————. *J. D.* Garden City, N.Y.: Doubleday and Co., 1973.

1342. ————. *Jim Flying High.* Illustrated by Ashley Bryan. Garden City, N.Y.: Doubleday and Co., 1979.

1343. ————. *Rap Stories.* Chicago: Third World, 1974.

1344. Fax, Elton C. *Contemporary Black Leaders.* New York: Dodd, Mead and Co., 1970.

1345. ————. *Garvey: Story of a Pioneer Black Nationalist.* New York: Dodd, Mead and Co., 1972.

1346. ————. *Seventeen Black Artists.* New York: Dodd, Mead and Co., 1971.

1347. ————. *West African Vignettes.* New York: Dodd, Mead and Co., 1963.

1348. Feelings, Muriel. *Jambo Means Hello: Swahili Alphabet Book.* Illustrated by Tom Feelings. New York: Dial Press, 1974.

Each illustrated letter has a word and its definition, followed by a more complete explanation of the customs associated with the word.

1349. ————. *Moja Means One: The Swahili Counting Book.* New York: Dial Press, 1971.

This book attempts to teach Afro-American boys and girls how to count in Swahili and simultaneously to add to their knowledge of Africa. This is done subtly by associating the color red with the Swahili word and the English word that designates the number. Also included is a note on the language of Swahili and some biographical information on the author and her former husband, Tom Feelings, who illustrated the book.

1350. ————. *Zamani Goes to Market.* Illustrated by Tom Feelings. New York: Seabury Press, 1970.

Inspired by the Feelings' visit with a Kenyan family, this book is the story of Zamani (the real name of the Feelings' son), who is old enough to accompany his father and brothers to market.

1351. Feelings, Tom. *Black Pilgrimage.* New York: Lothrop, Lee and Shepard Co., 1972.

This autobiographical work, illustrated by the author, recounts in a stirring manner Feelings' childhood in a black community in Brooklyn, New York, and his struggle as a black artist to gain some recognition and get a regular job. The book tells of his growing success and of his visit to Africa.

1352. Feelings, Tom, and Eloise Greenfield. *Daydreamers.* New York: Dial Press, 1981.

1353.   Ferguson, Amos, and Eloise Greenfield. *Under the Sunday Tree.* 1st ed. New York: Harper and Row, 1988.

A collection of poems and paintings that evoke life in the Bahamas. Paintings are by Ferguson and poems are by Greenfield.

1354.   Fields, Julia. *The Green Lion of Zion Street.* Illustrated by Jerry Pinkney. New York: Macmillian Co., 1988.

This is the author's first book for children. The story is about a group of children who, while waiting for the school bus on a foggy morning, become bored and go across a high bridge where, way up above, a green, green lion crouches, fog–shrouded. They imagine it will roar out loud and maybe start to move. They run but return to look again and find that the fog is gone, the lion is only a lion of stone, and they have missed the bus.

1355.   Flournoy, Valerie R. *The Best Time of Day.* New York: Random House, 1978.

1356.   ———. *The Patchwork Quilt.* Illustrated by Jerry Pinkney. New York: Dial Press, 1985.

This work won a Christopher Award, the Ezra Jack Keats,** and New Writer Award. Pinkney's illustrations won the 1986 Coretta Scott King Award.

1357.   ———. *The Twins Strike Back.* New York: Dial Press, 1980.

1358.   Fufuka, Karama. *My Daddy is a Cool Dude and Other Poems.* Illustrated by Mahiri Fufuka.* New York: Dial Press, 1975.

1359.   Gilpin,* Sandra, and Kay Brown. *How to Make Animal Models.* London: Studio Vista, 1975.

1360.   Giovanni, Nikki. *Ego–Tripping and Other Poems for Young People.* Illustrated by George Ford, Jr. New York: Lawrence Hill and Co., 1973.

1361. ———. *Spin a Soft Black Song: Poems for Children*. Illustrated by George Martins.* 1971. Reprint. New York: Hill and Wang, 1985.

This book includes a wide variety of poetry—sad poems; happy poems; poems about dreams, mommies, haircuts, and basketball—and all of them share the one common thread of being for and about black children.

1362. Goss, Linda, and Clay Goss. *The Baby Leopard: "How and Why" Story*. With illustrations by Suzanne Bailey–Jones* and Michael R. Jones.* New York: Bantam Books, 1989.

"An original story inspired by a West African folktale about how the leopard got its spots after ignoring a warning to be careful around fire."

1363. Graham, Lorenz. *God Wash the World and Start Again*. New York: Thomas Y. Crowell Co., 1971.

1364. ———. *Hungry Catch the Foolish Boy*. Illustrated by James Brown, Jr. New York: Thomas Y. Crowell Co., 1973.

This illustrated account of the Prodigal Son is retold here in Liberian English.

1365. ———. *John Brown: A Cry for Freedom*. New York: Thomas Y. Crowell Co., 1980.

While not portraying him as a saint, this biography of John Brown shows him as having deep religious convictions about freeing slaves, rather than the view taken by some historians that he was a wild, insane brute.

1366. ———. *North Town*. New York: Thomas Y. Crowell Co., 1965.

1367. ———. *Return to South Town*. New York: Thomas Y. Crowell Co., 1976.

1368. ———. *Song of the Boat.* New York: Thomas Y. Crowell Co., 1975.

1369. ———. *Whose Town?* New York: Thomas Y. Crowell Co., 1969.

In this sequel to *North Town* and *South Town*, which also tell about David Williams and the struggles that his family endures, a series of tragic events threaten to prevent eighteen-year-old David from fulfilling his desire to go to medical school after college.

1370. Graham, Shirley Lola. *Booker T. Washington: Educator of Hand, Head, and Heart.* New York: Julian Messner, 1955.

1371. ———. *Julius K. Nyerere: Teacher of Africa.* New York: Julian Messner, 1975.

1372. ———. *Paul Robeson: Citizen of the World.* New York: Julian Messner, 1955.

1373. Greenfield, Eloise. *Africa Dream.* Illustrated by Carole Byard. New York: John Day Co., 1977.

A black child's dreams are filled with the images of the people and places of Africa. This book won the 1978 Coretta Scott King Award.

1374. ———. *Bubbles.* Washington, D.C.: Drum and Spear Press, 1972.

1375. ———. *Darlene.* Illustrated by George Ford.* New York: Methuen, 1980.

Once she starts having fun with her uncle and cousin, a young girl, who is confined to a wheelchair, is no longer anxious to go home.

1376. ————. *First Pink Light.* Illustrated by Moneta Barnett. New York: Thomas Y. Crowell Co., 1976.

A little black boy determines to stay up all night so he can welcome his father home in the morning. Selected as a "Classroom Choice" by a joint committee of the International Reading Association and the Children's Book Council.

1377. ————. *Good News.* Illustrated by Pat Marie Cummings. New York: Coward-McCann, 1977.

1378. ————. *Grandmama's Joy.* Illustrated by Carole Byard. New York: Philomel Books, 1980.

A little girl tries to cheer up her despondent grandmother by reminding her of some very important things.

1379. ————. *Grandpa's Face.* Illustrated by Floyd Cooper.* New York: Philomel Books, 1988.

Seeing her beloved grandfather making a mean face while he rehearses for one of his plays, Tamika becomes afraid that someday she will lose his love and he will make that mean face at her.

1380. ————. *Honey, I Love and Other Love Poems.* Pictures by Diane Dillon** and Leo Dillon. New York: Thomas Y. Crowell Co., 1978.

Designated a Notable Children's Book by the American Library Association, this forty-eight-page book includes "I Look Pretty," "Riding on the Train," "Harriet Tubman," and "By Myself." The sixteen poems tell of love and the simple joys of everyday life, seen through the eyes of a child playing with a friend, skipping rope, riding on a train, or keeping Mama company till Daddy gets back.

1381. ————. *Little.* New York: Thomas Y. Crowell Co., 1979.

1382.   ————. *Mary McLeod Bethune.* Illustrated by Jerry Pinkney. New York: Thomas Y. Crowell Co., 1978.

This biography of Mary McLeod Bethune (1875–1955), who made numerous contributions to education for Afro–Americans, was a runner–up for the Coretta Scott King Award.

1383.   ————. *Me and Neesie.* Illustrated by Moneta Barnett. New York: Thomas Y. Crowell Co., 1975.

In this story, Janelle tells what happens to her invisible friend, Neesie, when Aunt Bea comes to visit. It was designated Notable Children's Books by the American Library Association.

1384.   ————. *Paul Robeson.* Illustrated by George Ford, Jr. New York: Thomas Y. Crowell Co., 1975.

This winner of the 1976 Jane Addams Book Award is a biography of Paul Robeson (1898–1976), who became a famous singer, actor, and spokesman for equal rights for black people.

1385.   ————. *Rosa Parks.* Illustrated by Eric Marlow. New York: Thomas Y. Crowell Co., 1973.

This is a brief biography of the black woman sometimes known as the mother of the civil rights movement for her part in precipitating the Montgomery bus boycott. It won the first Carter G. Woodson Award, given by the National Council for the Social Studies.

1386.   ————. *She Come Bringing Me That Little Baby Girl.* Illustrated by John Steptoe. Philadelphia: J. B. Lippincott Co., 1974.

A child's disappointment and jealousy over a new baby sister are dispelled as he becomes aware of the importance of his new role as a brother. This volume was designated Notable Children's Books by the American Library Association.

1387. ————. *Sister.* Drawings by Moneta Barnett. New York: Thomas Y. Crowell Co., 1974. Reprint. New York: Harper and Row, 1987.

"After her father dies of a heart attack, a young black girl watches her sister withdraw from her and her mother." This novel for children approaching the teenage years was named one of the *New York Times'* Best Books of 1974.

1388. ————. *Talk About a Family.* Philadelphia: J. B. Lippincott Co., 1978.

1389. Greenfield, Eloise, with Lessie Jones Little. *Childtimes: A Three Generation Memoir.* 1st ed. New York: Thomas Y. Crowell Co., 1979.

Written with her mother, Lessie Jones Little, these are the childhood memoirs of three black women—Eloise's grandmother, mother, and Eloise herself—who grew up between the 1880s and 1950s. With material by Pattie Ridley Jones, drawings by Jerry Pinkney, and photos from the authors' family albums.

1390. Greenfield, Eloise, with Alesia Revis.* *Alesia.* New York: Philomel Books, 1981.

1391. Griffin, Judith Berry. *The Magic Mirrors.* Illustrated by Ernest Crichlow. New York: Coward–McCann, 1971.

1392. ————. *Nat Turner.* New York: Coward–McCann, 1971.

1393. ————. *Phoebe and the General.* Illustrated by Margot Tomes.* New York: Coward–McCann, 1971.

1394. Grimes, Nikki. *Growin'.* Illustrated by Charles Lilly. New York: Dial Press, 1977.

1395. ————. *Something on My Mind.* Illustrated by Tom Feelings. New York: Dial Press, 1978.

1396. Guirma, Frederic. *Princess of the Full Moon.* New York: Macmillan Co., 1970.

1397. ————. *Tales of Mogho: African Stories from Upper Volta.* New York: Macmillan Co., 1971.

1398. Guy, Rosa. *And I Heard a Bird Sing.* New York: Delacorte Press, 1987.

Eighteen–year–old Imamu's newlyfound contentment with his job and the apartment he shares with his frail mother is shattered when he is inadvertently drawn into the sinister events taking place in a wealthy household where he has been delivering groceries.

1399. ————. *Bird at My Window.* 1st ed. Philadelphia: J. B. Lippincott Co., 1965.

An account of the effects of Harlem's ghetto life upon a young man.

1400. ————. *The Disappearance.* New York: Delacorte Press, 1979.

An American Library Association Best Book for Young Adults and a *New York Times* Outstanding Book of the Year. The disappearance of the seven–year–old daughter of a Brooklyn family casts suspicion on a juvenile offender from Harlem, who has recently come to live with them.

1401. ————. *Edith Jackson.* New York: Viking Press, 1978.

1402. ————. *The Friends.* New York: Holt, Rinehart and Winston, 1973.

This is the tragic story of a West Indian family—the Cathy family—that lives in Harlem. The mother dies of breast cancer; the father is stern and harsh in his bereavement; two daughters—Phyllisia and Ruby—are victimized at school; a friend of Phyllisia is looked down upon by both her and her father.

1403. ————. *A Measure of Time.* 1st. ed. New York: Holt, Rinehart and Winston, 1983.

1404. ————. *Mirror of Her Own.* New York: Delacorte Press, 1981.

1405. ————. *My Love, My Love, or, The Peasant Girl.* 1st ed. New York: Holt, Rinehart and Winston, 1985.

1406. ————. *New Guys Around the Block.* New York: Delacorte Press, 1983.

Harlem teenager Imamu Jones, repainting his mother's apartment and hoping to help her overcome her alcoholism, is troubled as he begins to suspect that one of his friends may be guilty of a series of burglaries and other crimes.

1407. ————. *Paris, Pee Wee, and Big Dog.* Illustrated by Caroline Binch.* New York: Delacorte Press, 1984.

When his mother goes off to work one Saturday, ten-year-old Paris and two friends spend the day on the streets of New York having fun and some hair-raising adventures, too.

1408. ————. *Ruby.* New York: Viking Press, 1976.

1409. ————, ed. *Children of Longing.* Introduction by Julius Lester. New York: Holt, Rinehart and Winston, 1971.

1410. Hall, Carol. *Northern J. Calloway Presents: I Been There.* Illustrated by Sammis McLean.** Garden City, N.Y.: Doubleday and Co., 1977.

1411. Halliburton, Warren Jennings. *The Picture Life of Jesse Jackson.* 2d ed. 1972. Reprint. New York: Franklin Watts, 1984.

1412. Hamilton, Virginia. *Anthony Burns: The Defeat and Triumph of a Fugitive Slave.* New York: Alfred A. Knopf, 1988.

"A biography of the slave [Anthony Burns, 1834–1862] who escaped to Boston in 1854, was arrested at the instigation of his owner, and whose trial caused a furor between abolitionists and those determined to enforce the Fugitive Slave Acts." Includes a bibliography and an index.

1413. ———. *Arilla Sun Down*. New York: Greenwillow Books, 1976. Reprint. New York: Dell Publishing Co., 1979.

"Young girl, half black and half Indian, lives in a small town where her life evolves around family, school, and friends."

1414. ———. *The Bells of Christmas*. Illustrated by Lambert Davis.* San Diego: Harcourt Brace Jovanovich, 1989.

"Twelve–year–old Jason describes the wonderful Christmas of 1890 that he and his family celebrate in their home in Springfield, Ohio."

1415. ———. *Dustland*. 1st ed. New York: Greenwillow Books, 1980.

In this second volume of a trilogy—the first is *Justice and Her Brothers*, the third is *The Gathering*—four children, all prossessing extraordinary mental powers, are projected far into the future to a bleak region called Dustland.

1416. ———. *The Gathering*. New York: Greenwillow Books, 1981.

In this volume, the third in a trilogy, Justice and her brothers, the first of a new race with extraordinary powers, return to Dustland to destroy the force that retards the growth of their advanced civilization.

1417. ———. *The House of Dies Drear*. Illustrated by Eros Keith.* New York: Macmillan Co., 1968. Reprint. New York: Collier Books, 1984.

"A family of five moves into an enormous house once used as a hiding place for runaway slaves. Mysterious sounds and events and discoveries of secret passageways make the family believe they are in grave danger." Hamilton is the recipient of the Edgar Allan Poe Award for the best juvenile mystery for this title.

1418. ————. *Jahdu.* 1st ed. New York: Greenwillow Books, 1980.

"When his Shadow steals his magic dust, Jahdu must try to recover it." Includes pictures by Jerry Pinkney.

1419. ————. *Junius Over Far.* 1st ed. New York: Harper and Row, 1985.

"After his grandfather leaves his family and returns to a dangerous situation on his home island in the Caribbean, fourteen-year-old Junius decides to follow him in search of his lost heritage."

1420. ————. *Justice and Her Brothers.* New York: Greenwillow Books, 1978.

This is the first volume in a trilogy; the second volume is *Dustland,* and the third is *The Gathering.*

1421. ————. *A Little Love.* New York: Putnam Publishing Group, 1984. Reprint. New York: Berkley Publishing Corp., 1985.

"Though she has been raised lovingly by her grandparents, a black teenager goes in search of her father." A Coretta Scott King Honor Book.

1422. ————. *M. C. Higgins, the Great.* New York: Macmillan Co., 1974. Reprint. Santa Barbara, Calif.: ABC-CLIO, 1988.

"As a slag heap, the result of strip mining, creeps closer to his house in the Ohio hills, fifteen-year-old M. C. is torn between trying to get his family away and fighting for the home they love." Large print edition.

1423. ————. *The Magical Adventures of Pretty Pearl.* New York: Harper and Row, 1983.

"Pretty Pearl, a spirited young African god child eager to show off her powers, travels to the New World where, disguised as a human, she lives among a band of free blacks who have created their own separate world deep inside a vast forest."

1424. ————. *The Mystery of Drear House: The Conclusion of the Dies Drear Chronicle.* New York: Greenwillow Books, 1987. Reprint. New York: Collier Books, 1988.

"A black family living in the house of long–dead abolitionist Dies Drear must decide what to do with his stupendous treasure, hidden for one hundred years in a cavern near their home."

1425. ————. *Paul Robeson: The Life and Times of a Free Black Man.* New York: Harper and Row, 1974. Reprint. New York: Dell Publishing Co., 1979.

A biography of Paul Robeson (1898–1976), which gives extensive treatment to his career as an actor and singer. A brief history of his parents and marital relationship is discussed. Little mention is made of his political activities. Includes a bibliography and an index.

1426. ————. *The People Could Fly: American Black Folktale.* Illustrated by Leo Dillon and Diane Dillon.** New York: Alfred A. Knopf, 1985.

"Retold Afro–American folktale of animals, fantasy, the supernatural, and desire for freedom, born of the sorrow of the slaves, but passed on in hope." Hamilton won the 1986 Coretta Scott King Award for this work.

1427.   ————. *The Planet of Junior Brown*. New York: Macmillan Co., 1971. Reprint. Boston: G. K. Hall and Co., 1988.

"Already a leader in New York's underground world of homeless children, Buddy Clark takes on the responsibility of protecting the overweight, emotionally disturbed friend with whom he has been playing hooky from eighth-grade all semester."

1428.   ————. *Sweet Whispers, Brother Rush*. New York: Philomel Books (Putnam), 1982.

"Fourteen-year-old Tree, resentful of her working mother who leaves her in charge of a retarded brother, encounters the ghost of her dead uncle and comes to a deeper understanding of her family's problems." A Newbery Honor Book, *Sweet Whispers* also won the *Boston Globe*–Horn Book Award and the 1983 Coretta Scott King Award.

1429.   ————. *Time-Ago Lost: More Tales of Jahdu*. Illustrated by Ray Prather. New York: Macmillan Co., 1973.

In this book, Mama Luka, Lee Edward's baby sitter, tells him tales about Jahdu, who runs through a magical world. Mama Luka has learned that her building is to be torn down, and she knows she will soon have to move from her "tight little room in a fine good place called Harlem." But once Mama Luka reaches into the air to "catch" a Jahdu story, the encroaching world is closed out and magic prevails. Lee Edward learns sadly that things must change, but he finds comfort in the knowledge that wherever Mama Luka lives, he will be able to visit her, and he knows too that wherever she is, there will be Jahdu.

1430.   ————. *The Time-Ago Tales of Jahdu*. Illustrated by Nonny Hogrogian.* New York: Macmillan Co., 1969.

"Mama Luka of Harlem had told Lee Edward many stories about Jahdu, including a story with a strong taste, a heavy story, and a story full of mischief, but not until the cool and fresh story does Jahdu assume even temporary identity."

1431.   ————. *A White Romance.* New York: Philomel Books, 1987.

"As her all–black high school becomes more racially mixed, Talley befriends a white girl who shares her passion for running and becomes romantically involved with a drug dealer."

1432.   ————. *Willie Bea and the Time the Martians Landed.* 1st ed. New York: Greenwillow Books, 1983.

"In October of 1938, on their farm homestead in Ohio, a black family is caught up in the fear generated by the Orson Wells' `Martians have landed' broadcast."

1433.   ————. *Zeely.* Illustrated by Symeon Shimin. New York: MacMillan, 1967. Reprint. New York: Aladdin Books, 1986.

In this story, "Geeder's summer at her uncle's farm is made special because of her friendship with a very tall, composed woman who raises hogs and who closely resembles the magazine photograph of a Watusi queen."

1434.   ————, ed. *The Writings of W. E. B. DuBois.* New York: Thomas Y. Crowell Co., 1975.

"A selection of essays, articles, speeches, and excepts from other writings by W. E. B. DuBois recording his views on a variety of social injustices." Includes a bibliography and an index.

1435.   Hansen, Joyce W. *The Gift–Giver.* Boston: Clarion Books, 1980.

1436.   ————. *Home Boy.* Boston: Clarion Books, 1982.

1437.   ————. *Out from This Place.* New York: Walker and Co., 1989.

The year she is in fifth grade, Doris meets a special friend in her Bronx neighborhood. This story won the Spirit of Detroit Award and was designated Notable Children's Trade Book in the field of social studies in 1980.

1438. ————. *Which Way Freedom?* New York: Walker and Co., 1986.

1439. ————. *Yellow Bird and Me.* Boston: Clarion Books, 1986.

1440. Haskins, James. *Andrew Young: Man with a Mission.* New York: Lothrop, Lee and Shepard Co., 1979.

Using a historical approach, Haskins traces the life of Andrew Young from his birth in New Orleans through his role as student, clergyman, civil rights advocate, U.S. congressman, and U.S. ambassador to the United Nations.

1441. ————. *Barbara Jordan: Speaking Out.* New York: Dial Press, 1977.

1442. ————. *Black Music in America: A History Through Its People.* 1st ed. New York: Thomas Y. Crowell Co., 1987.

This book surveys the history of black music in America, from early slave songs through jazz and the blues to soul, classical music, and current trends.

1443. ————. *Count Your Way Through the Arab World/China/Japan/Russia.* Minneapolis: Carolrhoda Books, 1987.

A four-book series for children introducing them to Arabic, Chinese, Japanese, and Russian. Won the Alabama Library Association Award.

1444. ————. *James Van DerZee: The Picture-Takin' Man.* New York: Dodd, Mead and Co., 1979.

1445.   ————. *The New Americans: Cuban Boat People*. Hillside, N.J.: Enslow Publishers, 1982.

1446.   ————. *The Picture Life of Malcolm X*. New York: Franklin Watts, 1975.

1447.   ————. *The Story of Stevie Wonder*. New York: Lothrop, Lee and Shepard Co., 1976. Reprint. London: Panther, 1978.

The book looks at the life of Stevie Wonder and describes him as a talented blind composer, singer, and pianist. Haskins traces the youth of the child prodigy up to and including his success in the music world. Stevie Wonder is portrayed as an individual who, constantly aware of his worth, went on to win ten Grammy Awards by 1976. The text includes several photographs and is excellent for juvenile readers. It won the Coretta Scott King Award in 1977.

1448.   Haskins, Jim, with Kathleen Benson.** *Space Challenger: The Story of Guion Bluford: An Authorized Biography*. Minneapolis: Carolrhoda Books, 1984.

1449.   Hayden, Robert Carter. *Eight Black American Inventors*. Reading, Mass.: Addison–Wesley Publishing Co., 1972.

Although not always officially recognized, blacks have contributed a great many inventions to this country. This work treats the contributions of Garrett A. Morgan, Lewis Temple, Frederick McKinley Jones, Jan E. Matzeliger, Lewis H. Latimer, Elijah McCoy, Norbert Rillieux, and Granville T. Woods. These men created inventions that not only benefited the people of their time, but continue to be useful today. For example, Matzeliger created the shoe–lasting machine, a machine that would sew the uppers to the soles of shoes. He did something no one else had been able to do, and he provided an effective way of completing a task that was previously done by hand. In addition to the biographical information on the inventors, there is a photograph of each one.

1450. ————. *Seven Black American Scientists.* Reading, Mass.: Addison–Wesley Publishing Co., 1970.

A must for anyone interested in the contributions of black science, this book focuses on the lives and work of seven black American scientists: Dr. Charles R. Drew, Dr. Daniel Hale Williams, Benjamin Banneker, Charles Henry Turner, Ernest E. Just, Matthew A. Henson, and George Washington Carver. These men made great achievements; for example, Dr. Hale performed the first open heart surgery. The book also includes photographs of each scientist, as well as a glossary of scientific terms used in the book.

1451. Hayden, Robert Carter, and Jacqueline Harris.* *Nine Black American Doctors.* Reading, Mass.: Addison–Wesley Publishing Co., 1976.

The major focus of this book is on the lives and work of nine American doctors who have made contributions during the twentieth century and whose medical careers cover various fields. Included are Solomon Carter Fuller, William A. Hinton, Louis T. Wright, William Montague Cobb, Arthur C. Logan, Daniel A. Collins, Jane C. Wright, Eugene W. Adams, and Angella D. Ferguson. Dr. Hinton devoted much of his life to the treatment of syphilis; Dr Logan practiced in Harlem; and Dr. Ferguson is a sickle cell researcher. Hayden shows how to make their various contributions, the doctors had to struggle and remain determined.

1452. Hopkins, Lee Bennett, comp. *Don't You Turn Back: Poems.* Woodcuts by Ann Grifalconi.* New York: Alfred A. Knopf, 1969.

Forty–five poems chosen from the work of the black poet, Langston Hughes, by Harlem fourth graders.

1453. Howard, Elizabeth Fitzgerald. *Chita's Christmas Tree.* Illustrated by Floyd Cooper.* New York: Bradbury Press, 1989.

"Papa and Chita leave downtown Baltimore in a buggy to find a Christmas Tree in the Deep Woods."

1454. ————. *The Train to Lulu's.* Illustrated by Robert Casilla.* New York: Bradbury Press, 1988.

1455. Howard, Moses Leon. *The Human Mandolin.* Illustrated by Barbara Morrow.* New York: Holt, Rinehart and Winston, 1974.

The old musician puts into the mandolin the most beautiful and joyous sounds he can find.

1456. ————. *The Ostrich Chase.* Illustrated by Barbara Seuling.* New York: Holt, Rinehart and Winston, 1974.

Although the women are forbidden to participate in the hunt, a young Bushman girl is determined to realize her dream of hunting an ostrich.

1457. Howard, Vanessa. *A Screaming Whisper.* Photographs by J. Ponderhughes.* New York: Holt, Rinehart and Winston, 1972.

1458. Hudson, Cheryl Willis. *Afro-Bets 123 Book.* Orange, N.J.: Just US Books, 1987.

1459. ————. *Afro-Bets ABC Book.* Orange, N.J.: Just US Books, 1987.

1460. Hudson, Wade, and Valerie Willis Hudson. *Afro-Bets Book of Black Heroes from A to Z: An Introduction to Important Black Achievers for Young Readers.* Orange, N.J.: Just US Books, 1988.

From the actor Ira Aldridge (1805-1867) to the African warrior Shaka Zulu (1787-1828), the black heroes are from the past and from the present.

1461. Hughes, Langston. *Black Misery*. Port Washington, N.Y.: Paul S. Eriksson Publisher, 1969.

> While creating the present volume, Hughes died in 1967. The book was published in 1969 by Arna Bontemps and George Houston Bass as executors of Langston Hughes's estate. Illustrated by Arouni, this final work is more than humor, more than satire, even more than its laughter. It is black children growing up.

1462. ———. *The Dream Keeper and Other Poems*. Illustrated by Helen Sewell.* 1932. Reprint. New York: Alfred A. Knopf, 1986.

> Selected by the author for young readers, this is a collection of fifty-nine poems, including lyrical poems, songs, and blues, many exploring the black experience.

1463. ———. *Famous American Negroes*. New York: Dodd, Mead and Co., 1954.

1464. ———. *Famous Negro Music Makers*. 1955. Reprint. New York: Dodd, Mead and Co., 1966.

1465. ———. *The First Book of Africa*. Rev. and rewritten. 1960. Reprint. New York: Franklin Watts, 1964.

1466. ———. *The First Book of Negroes*. Pictures by Ursula Koering.* New York: Franklin Watts, 1952.

1467. ———. *Jazz*. 3d ed. Updated and expanded by Sandford Brown.* New York: Franklin Watts, 1982. Originally published as *The First Book of Jazz*.

> An introduction to jazz, this piece of juvenile literature focuses on the historical development of jazz and on famous performers. Includes an index.

1468. ————. *Not Without Laughter.* New York: Alfred A. Knopf, 1930. Reprint. New York: Collier Books, 1985.

With an introduction by Arna Bontemps, this—Hughes's first novel—is a poignant story of a black boy growing to manhood in a small Kansas town during the Depression.

1469. Hughes, Langston, Milton Meltzer,* and C. Eric Lincoln. *A Pictorial History of Black Americans.* 5th ed., rev. New York: Crown Publishers, 1984.

1470. Hunter, Kristin. *Boss Cat.* Illustrated by Harold Franklin.* New York: Charles Scribner's Sons, 1971.

Tyrone's mother objects strenuously to the new cat despite its acceptance by other family members.

1471. ————. *Guests in the Promised Land.* New York: Charles Scribner's Sons, 1973.

1472. ————. *Lou in the Limelight.* New York: Charles Scribner's Sons, 1981.

1473. ————. *The Soul Brothers and Sister Lou.* New York: Charles Scribner's Sons, 1968.

Lauretta (Sister Lou) and Fess are members of a neighborhood club. Their reactions to the killing of an innocent black youth by a white policeman bring them into direct conflict.

1474. Jackson, Jesse J. *Anchor Man.* Illustrated by Doris Spiegel.* New York: Harper and Row, 1947.

1475. ————. *Call Me Charley.* Illustrated by Doris Spiegel.* New York: Harper and Row, 1945.

Jackson's first book for children is a large-type edition of the story of a twelve-year-old black boy who moves into an all-white suburban neighborhood where his parents work for a doctor and who must prove himself before the board of education will let him remain in school.

1476. ———. *Charley Starts from Scratch.* New York: Harper and Row, 1958.

A story of human determination, endeavor, and success. The author shows how, confronted by a hostile environment, one can still manage to break clean with courage and effort.

1477. ———. *The Fourteenth Cadillac.* New York: Doubleday and Co., 1972.

1478. ———. *Make a Joyful Noise Unto the Lord! The Life of Mahalia Jackson, Queen of Gospel Singers.* New York: Thomas Y. Crowell Co., 1974.

Illustrated with photos, this is a biography of the famous gospel singer, Mahalia Jackson (1911–1972), who hoped, through her art, to break down some of the barriers between black and white people.

1479. ———. *Queen of Gospel Singers.* New York: Thomas Y. Crowell Co., 1974.

1480. ———. *Room for Randy.* Illustrated by Frank Nicholas.* New York: Friendship Press, 1957.

1481. ———. *The Sickest Don't Always Die the Quickest.* Garden City, N.Y.: Doubleday and Co., 1971.

The book describes the events in the life of a twelve–year–old black youth when he discovers he has many unanswered questions concerning his church and the people he knows.

1482. ———. *Tessie.* Illustrated by Harold Laymont James.* New York: Harper and Row, 1968.

This is a novel of one young girl's struggles, disappointments, and triumphs. It tells of her attempts to reconcile two worlds—Harlem and an exclusive private high school in New York—after she wins a scholarship and becomes that high school's first black student. The resultant trauma and confusions are resolved in *Tessie*.

1483. Jackson, Jesse J., and Elaine Landau.* *Black in America: A Fight for Freedom*. New York: Julian Messner, 1973.

This is a history of blacks in America from their days as slaves to their present–day status. The book chronicles their long struggle up from slavery and includes details on segregation laws and Reconstruction, as well as an index of some outstanding black Americans. The text is illustrated with numerous photographs and is excellent for juvenile readers.

1484. Johnson, Angela. *Do Like Kyla*. Illustrated by James Ransome.* New York: Orchard Books, 1990.

"A little girl imitates her big sister Kyla all day, until in the evening Kyla imitates her."

1485. ———. *Tell Me a Story, Mama*. Pictures by David Soman.* New York: Orchard Books, 1989.

"A young girl and her mother remember together all the girl's favorite stories about her mother's childhood."

1486. ———. *When I Am Old with You*. Illustrated by David Soman.* New York: Orchard Books, 1990.

"A child imagines being old with Grandaddy and joining him in such activities as playing cards all day, visiting the ocean, and eating bacon on the porch."

1487. Johnson, James Weldon. *God's Trombones*. Illustrated by Aaron Douglas.* New York: Viking Press, 1927.

1488. Johnson, James Weldon, with John Rosamond Johnson. *Lift Every Voice and Sing.* Illustrated by Mozelle Thompson. New York: Hawthorn Books, 1970.

1489. Jordan, June Meyer. *Dry Victories.* New York: Holt, Rinehart and Winston, 1972.

Two young black boys examine the Reconstruction and civil rights eras and the effect these periods have had on the lives of their people. Includes pertinent documents and photographs.

1490. ————. *Fannie Lou Hamer.* Illustrated by Albert Williams. New York: Thomas Y. Crowell Co., 1972.

A brief biography of one of the first black organizers of voter registration in Mississippi.

1491. ————. *His Own Where.* New York: Thomas Y. Crowell Co., 1971.

1492. ————. *Kimako's Story.* Illustrated by Kay Burford.* Boston: Houghton Mifflin Co., 1981.

A little girl, Kimako Anderson, almost eight years old, describes her life in the city where she works poetry puzzles indoors and has outdoor adventures with the dog that she is taking care of for a friend.

1493. ————. *New Life: New Room.* Illustrated by Ray Cruz.* New York: Thomas Y. Crowell Co., 1975.

Encouraged by Father, three children move into and decorate their own room while Mother is in the hospital having a new baby sister.

1494. ————. *Who Look at Me.* New York: Thomas Y. Crowell Co., 1969.

A poem exploring the condition, feelings, and ideas of blacks in a white society. Illustrated by reproductions of paintings depicting the life of blacks in America throughout history.

1495. Jordan, June Meyer, and Terri Bush,* comps. *The Voice of the Children.* New York: Holt, Rinehart and Winston, 1970.

Twenty black and Puerto Rican children write their poetic impressions of growing up in the ghettos of America.

1496. Kirpatrick, Oliver Austin. *Naja the Snake and Mangus the Mongoose.* Garden City, N.Y.: Doubleday and Co., 1970.

1497. Kunjufu, Jawanza. *Lessons From History: A Celebration in Blackness.* Illustrated by Yaounde Olu* and Cornell Barnes.* 1st elementary ed. Chicago: African American Images, 1987.

"Surveys the history and civilization of Africa and the culture and contributions of blacks both there and in America."

1498. ————. *Lessons from History: A Celebration in Blackness.* Illustrated by Yaounde Olu* and Cornell Barnes.* 1st junior–senior high ed. Chicago: African American Images, 1987.

"Surveys the history and civilization of Africa and the culture and contributions of blacks both there and in America."

1499. ————. *To Be Popular or Smart: The Black Peer Group.* 1st ed. Chicago: African American Images, 1988.

1500. Lacy, Leslie Alexander. *Black Africa on the Move.* New York: Franklin Watts, 1969. Reprint. London: Franklin Watts, 1972.

This book describes the history, people, and culture of Africa south of the Sahara Desert, with emphasis on the continuing struggle for a completely independent Africa. Includes maps, illustrations, and index.

1501.   ————. *Cheer the Lonesome Traveler: The Life of W. E. B. DuBois.* Illustrated by James Barkley.* New York: Dial Press, 1970.

This is a biography of the black sociologist, activist, author who devoted most of his life (1868–1963) to gaining equality for blacks.

1502.   Lawrence, Jacob. *Harriet and the Promised Land.* New York: Simon and Schuster, 1968.

1503.   Lester, Julius. *Black Folktales.* Illustrated by Tom Feelings. New York: Grove Press, 1969.

The tales in this book are told in villages of Africa, in the South, and in black sections of cities—on the street corners, stoops, and porches, and in barbershops, bars, and wherever else in America black people gather.

1504.   ————. *The Knee–High Man and Other Tales.* Illustrated by Ralph Pinto.* New York: Dial Press, 1972.

Retells six tales from American black folk literature: "Why the Waves Have Whitecaps," "Mr. Rabbit and Mr. Bear," "Why Dogs Hate Cats," "The Farmer and the Snake," "What is Trouble?" and "The Knee–High Man."

1505.   ————. *Long Journey Home: Stories from Black History.* New York: Dial Press, 1972.

With these accounts of many lesser–known people, Lester demonstrates that many black people were the source of their own freedom, that they played a role in maintaining the underground railroad, and that they did not always rely on the kindness and help of white people.

1506.   ———. *More Tales of Uncle Remus: Further Adventures of Brer Rabbit, His Friends, Enemies, and Others.* New York: Dial Books, 1988.

The author retells the classic Afro–American tales. Illustrated by Jerry Pinkney.

1507.   ———. *The Tales of Uncle Remus: The Adventures of Brer Rabbit.* Illustrated by Jerry Pinkney. New York: Dial Press, 1987.

1508.   ———. *This Strange New Feeling.* New York: Dial Press, 1982.

Three love stories that reflect the human spirit. Ras and Sally fell in love before they could stop themselves. Maria thought Forrest was too good for her until he bought her freedom. William and Ellen knew the only way to be free was through a dangerous masquerade that could separate them forever.

1509.   ———, ed. *To Be a Slave.* Illustrated by Tom Feelings. New York: Dial Press, 1968. Reprint. New York: Scholastic, 1986.

This is a compilation, selected from various sources and arranged chronologically, of the reminiscences of slaves and ex-slaves about their experiences from the time they left Africa through the Civil War and into the early twentieth century. *To Be a Slave*, Lester's first children's book, was a Newbery Honor Book in 1969 and winner of the 1968 Nancy Bloch Award.

1510.   Lewin, Hugh. *Jafta.* Pictures by Lisa Kopper.* Minneapolis: Carolrhoda Books, 1983.

Jafta describes some of his everyday feelings by comparing his actions with those of various African animals.

1511. Little, Lessie Jones, and Eloise Greenfield. *I Can Do It by Myself.* Illustrated by Carole Byard. New York: Thomas Y. Crowell Co., 1978.

"Donny is determined to buy his mother's birthday present all by himself, but he meets a scary challenge on the way home."

1512. Lloyd, Errol. *Nini at Carnival.* Illustrated by Errol Lloyd. New York: Thomas Y. Crowell Co., 1978.

1513. Lynch, Lorenzo. *The Hot Dog Man.* Indianapolis: Bobbs–Merrill Co., 1970.

1514. Magubane, Peter. *Black Child.* New York: Alfred A. Knopf, 1982.

Magubane won the 1983 Coretta Scott King Award for his illustrations in this book.

1515. Mathis, Sharon Bell. *The Hundred Penny Box.* Illustrated by Leo Dillon and Diane Dillon.** New York: Viking Press, 1975.

Michael's love for his great–great–aunt, who lives with them, leads him to intercede with his mother, who wants to toss out all her old things.

1516. ————. *Listen for the Fig Tree.* New York: Viking Press, 1984.

A sixteen–year–old black girl's first celebration of Kwanza gives her a sense of the past and the strength to deal with her troubled mother and her own blindness. The black community is very supportive of her.

1517. ————. *Ray Charles.* Illustrated by George Ford, Jr. New York: Thomas Y. Crowell Co., 1973.

For this work, both the author and the illustrator won the Coretta Scott King Award in 1974.

1518. ————. *Sidewalk Story.* Illustrated by Leo Carty. New York: Viking Press, 1971. Reprint. New York: Puffin Books (Viking Penguin Inc.), 1986.

When her best friend, Tanya, is evicted from her apartment, a nine–year–old black girl, Lilly Etta Allen, decides to do something about the situation. She contacts a sympathetic reporter and saves the day.

1519. ————. *Teacup Full of Roses.* New York: Viking Press, 1972.

In this black family, Joe's decision to leave home is prompted by despair over his mother's blindness to his younger brother's talents and his older brother's drug addiction.

1520. McCannon, Dinga. *Peaches.* New York: Lothrop, Lee and Shepard Co., 1974.

1521. McCarthy,* Agnes, and Lawrence Dunbar Reddick. *Worth Fighting For: A History of the Negro in the United States During the Civil War and Reconstruction.* Illustrated by Colleen Browning.* Garden City, N.Y.: Doubleday and Co., 1965.

This book relates the deeds and accomplishments of Afro–Americans during and after the Civil War, particularly in the army and in Congress.

1522. McKissack, Fredrick, and Patricia C. McKissack. *Abram, Abram, Where Are We Going?* Illustrated by Joe Boddy.* Elgin, Ill.: Chariot Books, 1984.

"Recounts the Biblical stories about Abraham and how he became the father of many nations."

1523. ————. *We Are Not Afraid, Elijah's God Is Great!* Illustrated by Joe Boddy.* Elgin, Ill.: Chariot Books, 1986.

"A retelling of the Old Testament story about the prophet Elijah and his deeds."

1524. McKissack, Patricia C. *Flossie and the Fox.* Pictures by Rachel Isadora.* New York: Dial Books for Young Readers, 1986.

A wily fox, notorious for stealing eggs, meets his match when he encounters a bold little girl in the woods who insists upon proof that he is a fox before she will be frightened.

1525. ————. *Mirandy and Brother Wind.* Illustrated by Jerry Pinkney. New York: Alfred A. Knopf, 1988.

This book won the 1989 Coretta Scott King Award for Pinkney's illustrations.

1526. ————. *Monkey–Monkey's Trick.* Illustrated by Paul Meisel.* New York: Random House, 1988.

"A greedy hyena's mean tricks on monkey–monkey eventually backfire when his victim finds out how he is being deceived."

1527. ————. *Nettie Joe's Friends.* Illustrated by Scott Cook.* New York: Alfred A. Knopf, 1989.

"Nettie Jo desperately needs a needle to sew a new dress for her beloved doll, but the tree animals she helps during her search do not seem inclined to give her their assistance in return."

1528. McKissack, Patricia C., and Fredrick McKissack. *All Paths Lead to Bethlehem.* Illustrated by Kathryn E. Shoemaker.* Minneapolis: Augsburg Publishing House, 1987.

1529. ————. *The Big Bug Book of Counting.* Illustrated by Bartholomew.* St. Louis, Mo.: Milliken Publishing Co., 1987.

1530. ————. *The Big Bug Book of Opposites.* Illustrated by Bartholomew.* St. Louis, Mo.: Milliken Publishing Co., 1987.

1531. ————. *The Big Bug Book of Places to Go.* Illustrated by Bartholomew.* St. Louis, Mo.: Milliken Publishing Co., 1987.

1532. ————. *The Big Bug Book of the Alphabet.* Illustrated by Bartholomew.* St. Louis, Mo.: Milliken Publishing Co., 1987.

1533. ————. *The Big Bug Book of Things to Do.* Illustrated by Bartholomew.* St. Louis, Mo.: Milliken Publishing Co., 1987.

1534. ————. *Bugs!* Illustrated by Clovis Martin.* Chicago: Childrens Press, 1988.

"Simple text and illustrations of a variety of insects introduce the numbers one through five."

1535. ————. *The Children's ABC Christmas.* Illustrated by Kathy Rogers.* Minneapolis: Augsburg Publishing House, 1988.

"Based on a typical, chaotic Christmas pageant, the story of Jesus' birth unfolds from A to Z." "Twenty-six young performers present an event from the Christmas story."

1536. ————. *Cinderella.* Illustrated by Tom Dunnington.* Chicago: Childrens Press, 1985.

"An easy-to-read retelling of Cinderella's trip to a ball at the palace."

1537. ————. *The Civil Rights Movement in America from 1865 to the Present.* Chicago: Childrens Press, 1987.

1538.   ―――――. *Constance Stumbles.* Illustrations by Tom Dunnington.*
Chicago: Childrens Press, 1988.

"Despite many setbacks, a little girl is determined to learn
to ride a bicycle."

1539.   ―――――. *Country Mouse and City Mouse.* Retold by Patricia C.
McKissack and Fredrick McKissack. Illustrated by Anne
Sikorski.* Chicago: Childrens Press, 1985.

"An easy–to–read retelling of the well–known fable about
two mice and the discovery they make."

1540.   ―――――. *Frederick Douglass: the Black Lion.* Chicago:
Childrens Press, 1987.

"Describes the life and work of the man who escaped
slavery to become an orator, writer, and leader in the anti–slavery
movement of the nineteenth century."

1541.   ―――――. *God Made Something Wonderful.* Illustrated by Ching.*
Minneapolis: Augsburg Publishing House, 1989.

1542.   ―――――. *Hooray! Hooray! David Is the One.* Illustrated by Joe
Boddy.* Elgin, Ill.: Chariot Books, 1986.

"A retelling of the Bible stories relating how David rose
from being a shepherd boy to the king of Israel."

1543.   ―――――. *The King's New Clothes.* Illustrated by Gwen
Connelly.* Chicago: Childrens Press, 1987.

"An easy–to–read retelling of the vain king's experience
with two deceitful tailors."

1544.   ―――――. *The Little Red Hen.* Illustrated by Dennis Hockerman.*
Chicago: Childrens Press, 1985.

"An easy-to-read retelling of the traditional tale about the little red hen and her lazy friends."

1545. ————. *A Long Hard Journey: The Story of the Pullman Porter.* New York: Walker, 1989.

"A chronicle of the first black-controlled union, made up of Pullman porters, who after years of unfair labor practices staged a battle against a corporate giant resulting in a 'David and Goliath' ending."

1546. ————. *Messy Bessey.* Illustrated by Richard Hackney.* Chicago: Childrens Press, 1987.

1547. ————. *Messy Bessey's Closet.* Illustrated by Richard Hackney.* Chicago: Childrens Press, 1989.

"Messy Bessey learns a lesson about sharing when she cleans out her closet."

1548. ————. *My Bible ABC Book.* Illustrated by Reed Merrill.* Minneapolis: Augsburg Publishing House, 1987.

1549. ————. *Oh, Happy, Happy Day! A Child's Easter in Story, Song, and Prayer.* Illustrated by Elizabeth Swisher.* Minneapolis: Augsburg Fortress, 1989.

1550. ————. *A Real Winner.* Illustrated by Quentin Thompson* and Ken Jones.* St. Louis, Mo.: Milliken Publishing Co., 1987.

"What do you do if the neighborhood bully keeps pushing you around? Chip and his friends think the way to win is to push back, but Chip's father teaches his son what it is to be a real winner."

1551. ————. *Taking a Stand Against Racism and Racial Discrimination.* New York: Franklin Watts, 1990.

"Examines racism and racial discrimination in the United States, and the individuals and organizations who have acted against it."

1552. ————. *Tall Phil and Small Bill.* Illustrated by Kathy Mitter.* St. Louis, Mo.: Milliken Publishing Co., 1987.

"What if you could change places with somebody and live as they live? Would it be better or worse than home?"

1553. ————. *The Three Bears.* Retold by Patricia C. McKissack and Fredrick McKissack. Illustrated by Virginia Bala.* Chicago: Childrens Press, 1985.

"An easy–to–read retelling of the encounter a family of bears has with a tired and hungry little girl."

1554. ————. *Three Billy Goats Gruff.* Retold by Patricia McKissack and Fred McKissack. Illustrated by Tom Dunnington.* Chicago: Childrens Press, 1987.

"An easy–to–read retelling of the fairy tale about three clever goats and a nasty troll."

1555. ————. *A Troll in a Hole.* Illustrated by Bartholomew.* St. Louis, Mo.: Milliken Publishing Co., 1989.

1556. ————. *The Ugly Little Duck.* Illustrated by Peggy Perry Anderson.* Chicago: Childrens Press, 1986.

"An easy–to–read retelling of the fairy tale in which an ugly duckling spends an unhappy year ostracized by other animals before he grows into a beautiful swan."

1557. ————. *When Do You Talk to God? Prayers for Small Children.* Illustrated by Gary Gumble.* Minneapolis: Augsburg Publishing House, 1986.

1558.   Mendez, Phil. *The Black Snowman*. Illustrated by Carole Byard. New York: Scholastic, 1989.

        "Through the powers of a magical dashiki, a black snowman comes to life and helps young Jacob discover the beauty of his ' black heritage as well as his own self-worth."

1559.   Meriwether, Louise M. *Daddy was a Number Runner*. Englewood Cliffs, N.J.: Prentice-Hall, 1970. Reprint. New York: Feminist Press at the City University of New York, 1986.

1560.   ————. *Don't Ride the Bus on Monday: The Rosa Parks Story*. Illustrated by David Scott Brown.* Englewood Cliffs, N.J.: Prentice-Hall, 1973.

        "A brief biography of the Alabama black woman whose refusal to give up her seat on the bus marked the beginning of the civil rights movement."

1561.   ————. *The Freedom Ship of Robert Smalls*. Illustrated by Lee Jack Morton.* Englewood Cliffs, N.J.: Prentice-Hall, 1971.

        "A brief biography of the slave who escaped to freedom with his family and other runaway slaves on a captured Confederate gunboat."

1562.   ————. *The Heart of Man: Dr. Daniel Hale Williams*. Illustrated by Floyd Sowell.* Englewood Cliffs, N.J.: Prentice-Hall, 1972.

        "A brief biography of the black surgeon who performed the first successful heart operation in 1893." Williams's life expanded the period 1856-1931.

1563.   Millender, Dharathula [Hood]. *Crispus Attucks, Boy of Valor*. Indianapolis: Bobbs-Merrill Co., 1965.

1564.   ————. *Louis Armstrong, Young Music Maker*. Indianapolis: Bobbs-Merrill Co., 1972.

1565. ———. *Martin Luther King, Jr., Boy with a Dream.* Indianapolis: Bobbs–Merrill Co., 1969.

1566. Miller, Melba. *The Black is Beautiful Beauty Book.* Illustrated by Lorenzo Lynch. Englewood Cliffs, N.J.: Prentice–Hall, 1974.

1567. Moore, Carmen Leroy. *Somebody's Angel Child: The Story of Bessie Smith.* New York: Thomas Y. Crowell Co., 1969.

1568. Moore, Emily R. *Just My Luck.* New York: E. P. Dutton, 1982.

1569. ———. *Something to Count On.* New York: E. P. Dutton, 1982.

1570. Morninghouse, Sundaira. *Nightfeathers.* Illustrated by Jody Kim. 1st ed. Seattle, Wash.: Open Hand Publishing, 1989.

1571. Muhammad, Fonda K. *Ramadan: Through the Eyes of a Child.* Jersey City, N.J.: New Mind Productions, 1989.

1572. Murphy, Beatrice M., comp. *Today's Negro Voices: An Anthology by Young Negro Poets.* New York: Julian Messner, 1970.

In this analogy, young Afro–Americans—thirty years old and under—are given a forum and a listening audience. The racial orientations of these young poets are evident in these seventy-five poems, which speak of racial pride, a determination to change the status quo, militancy, and hatred. Underlying the rage, however, is a sense that these young poets are waiting for help from someone who cares. For grades 7 and up. Includes biographical notes on each poet.

1573. Musgrove, Margaret. *Ashanti to Zulu: African Traditions.* Illustrated by Leo Dillon and Diane Dillon.** New York: Dial Press, 1977.

Using many native words, this book describes aspects of life and the traditions of many African tribes. It was a Caldecott Honor Book.

1574.   Myers, Walter Dean. *The Black Pearl and the Ghost.* New York: Viking Press, 1980.

1575.   ———. *Crystal.* New York: Viking Press, 1987.

1576.   ———. *Fallen Angels.* New York: Scholastic, 1988.

"Seventeen–year–old Richie Perry, just out of high school, enlists in the Army in the summer of 1967 and spends a devastating year on active duty in Vietnam." Myers won the 1989 Coretta Scott King Award for this work.

1577.   ———. *Fast Sam, Cool Clyde, and Stuff.* New York: Viking Press, 1975.

A young black boy in New York City recollects the adolescent years. The language is that of the city.

1578.   ———. *Fly Jimmy Fly!* Illustrated by Moneta Barnett. New York: G. P. Putnam's Sons, 1974.

1579.   ———. *Hoops.* New York: Dell Publishing Co., 1983.

Hoops, an American Language Association Best Book for Young Adults, captures growing up on the streets of Harlem, where basketball is presented as one of the ghetto games and as one way for kids to build confidence, trust, and friendship.

1580.   ———. *It Ain't All for Nothin'.* New York: Viking Press, 1978.

1581.   ———. *The Legend of Tarik.* New York: Scholastic, 1982.

1582.   ———. *Me, Mop, and the Moondance Kid.* Illustrated by Rodney Pate.* New York: Delacorte Press, 1988.

Although adoption has taken them out of the institution where they grew up, eleven-year-old T.J. and his younger brother Moondance remain involved with their friend Mop's relentless attempts to become adopted herself and to wreak revenge on their baseball rivals, the obnoxious Eagles.

1583. ————. *Motown and Didi: A Love Story.* New York: Viking Penguin, 1984. Reprint. New York: Dell Publishing Co., 1987.

Myers' main characters, Motown and Didi, deal with love and a sense of space and hope against a backdrop of junkies, threats, danger, and death in the streets of Harlem.

1584. ————. *Mr. Monkey and the Gotcha Bird.* New York: Delacorte Press, 1984.

1585. ————. *The Outside Shot.* New York: Dell Publishing Co., 1987.

When Jonnie Jackson leaves Harlem for a basketball scholarship to a midwestern college, he knows he must keep his head straight and record clean. He has one year to learn how to make it as a college man. It's his outside shot at a bright future. Does he have what it takes? This book is a sequel to *Hoops.*

1586. ————. *Scorpions.* 1st ed. New York: Harper and Row, 1988.

After reluctantly taking on leadership of the Harlem gang, the Scorpions, Jamal finds that his enemies treat him with respect when he acquires a gun—until tragedy occurs.

1587. ————. *Tales of a Dead King.* New York: William Morrow and Co., 1983.

1588. ————. *Where Does the Day Go?* Illustrated by Leo Carty. New York: Parents Magazine Press, 1969.

Several children tell what they think happens to the day when night arrives.

1589. ———. *Won't Know Till I Get There.* New York: Viking Press, 1981.

1590. ———. *The Young Landlords.* New York: Viking Press, 1979.

1591. Nagenda, John. *Mukasa.* Illustrated by Charles Lilly. New York: Macmillian Co., 1973.

Although his ancestors have always been goatherders, a young Ugandan boy's mother is determined to send him to school.

1592. Nagenda, Musa [Moses Leon Howard]. *Dogs of Fear: A Story of Modern Africa.* Pictures by Floyd Sowell.* New York: Holt, Rinehart and Winston, 1972.

To prove to his father that the European school has not made him cowardly, a thirteen-year-old African boy goes alone at night to kill three wild dogs that attacked their goats.

1593. Neal, Annie W. *Where's Geraldine?* Illustrated by Charles Shaw. Philadelphia: J. B. Lippincott Co., 1978.

1594. Oliver, Elizabeth Murphy. *Black Mother Goose Book.* Illustrated by Thomas A. Stockett. 2d ed. Brooklyn, N.Y.: Dare Books, 1981.

"A collection of well-known nursery rhymes illustrated with black children. Includes some Swahili vocabulary."

1595. Palmer, Cyril Everard. *Baba and Mr. Big.* Indianapolis: Bobbs-Merrill Co., 1972.

1596. ———. *Big Doc Bitteroot.* Indianapolis: Bobbs-Merrill Co., 1968.

1597. ———. *The Cloud with the Silver Lining*. Indianapolis: Bobbs–Merrill Co., 1966.

1598. ———. *A Cow Called Boy*. Indianapolis: Bobbs–Merrill Co., 1972.

1599. ———. *The Sun Salutes You*. Indianapolis: Bobbs–Merrill Co., 1970.

1600. Patterson, Lillie G. *Coretta Scott King*. Champaign, Ill.: Garrard Publishing Co., 1977.

1601. ———. *David, the Story of a King*. Nashville: Abingdon Press, 1985.

1602. ———. *Dr. Martin Luther King, Jr.: Man of Peace*. Illustrated by Victor Mays.* Champaign, Ill.: Garrard Publishing Co., 1969.

1603. ———. *Frederick Douglass: Freedom Fighter*. Champaign, Ill.: Garrard Publishing Co., 1965.

1604. ———. *Sequoyah: The Cherokee Who Captured Words*. Champaign, Ill.: Garrard Publishing Co., 1975.

1605. ———. *Sure Hands, Strong Heart: The Life of Daniel Hale Williams*. Nashville: Abingdon Press, 1981.

1606. Payton, Vanessa. *All-American Girl*. New York: Silhouette Books, 1983.

1607. Petry, Ann Lane. *The Drugstore Cat*. Illustrated by Susanne Suba.* New York: Thomas Y. Crowell Co., 1949.

1608. ———. *Harriet Tubman: Conductor on the Underground Railroad*. New York: Thomas Y. Crowell Co., 1955.

1609. ———. *Legend of the Saints*. Illustrated by Anne Rockwell.* New York: Thomas Y. Crowell Co., 1970.

1610.   ———. *Tituba of Salem Village.* New York: Thomas Y. Crowell Co., 1964.

Petry recreates the superstition and intolerance surrounding seventeenth–century Tituba and her husband from the time they were sold in Barbados.

1611.   Prather, Ray. *Anthony and Sabrina.* New York: Macmillan Co., 1973.

Two black children—a brother and sister—visit their grandmother's farm in Florida.

1612.   ———. *Double Dog Dare.* New York: Macmillan Co., 1975.

1613.   ———. *New Neighbors.* New York: McGraw–Hill, 1975.

1614.   ———. *No Trespassing.* New York: Macmillan Co., 1974.

1615.   ———. *The Ostrich Girl.* New York: Charles Scribner's Sons, 1978.

1616.   Robinet, Harriette Gillem. *Jay and the Marigold.* Illustrated by Trudy Scott.* Chicago: Childrens Press, 1976.

This is the story of a young boy who, born with cerebral palsy, watched a flower grow in spite of its handicap. This shows him that he too can grow and blossom.

1617.   ———. *Ride the Red Circle.* Illustrated by David Scott Brown.* Boston: Houghton Mifflin Co., 1980.

In this story, Jerome, who has been crippled since the age of two, struggles to realize his dream of riding a cycle.

1618.   Robinson, Adjai. *Femi and Old Grandaddie.* Illustrated by Jerry Pinkney. New York: Coward, 1972.

1619. ———. *Kasho and the Twin Flutes.* Illustrated by Jerry Pinkney. New York: Coward, 1973.

1620. ———. *Singing Tales of Africa.* Illustrated by Christine Price.* New York: Charles Scribner's Sons, 1974.

1621. ———. *Three African Tales.* Illustrated by Carole Byard. New York: G. P. Putnam's Sons, 1979.

1622. Robinson, Jackie. *Jackie Robinson's Little League Baseball Book.* Englewood Cliffs, N.J.: Prentice-Hall, 1972.

1623. Robinson, Louie, Jr. *Arthur Ashe, Tennis Champion.* Garden City, N.Y.: Doubleday and Co., 1967.

1624. Rollins, Charlemae Hill. *Black Troubador: Langston Hughes.* Chicago, Ill.: Rand McNally and Co., 1970.

1625. ———. *Christmas Gif'.* Chicago: Follett Publishing Co., 1963.

1626. ———. *Famous American Negro Poets.* New York: Dodd, Mead and Co., 1965.

1627. ———. *Famous Negro Entertainers of Stage, Screen, and TV.* New York: Dodd, Mead and Co., 1967.

1628. ———. *They Showed the Way: Forty American Negro Leaders.* New York: Thomas Y. Crowell Co., 1964.

1629. Ruffin, Reynold. *My Brother Never Feeds the Cat.* New York: Charles Scribner's Sons, 1979.

1630. Salkey, Andrew. *Earthquake.* New York: Oxford University Press, 1965.

1631. ———. *Hurricane.* New York: Oxford University Press, 1964.

1632. ———. *Jonah Simpson.* New York: Oxford University Press, 1969.

1633. Sanchez, Sonia. *The Adventures of Fathead, Smallhead, and Squarehead.* Illustrated by Taiwo DuVall.* New York: Third Press, 1973.

The adventures of three friends prove that "slow is not always dumb, and fast is not always smart."

1634. ———. *It's a New Day: Poems for Young Brothers and Sistuhs.* 1st ed. Detroit: Broadside Press, 1971.

1635. ———. *A Sound Investment: Short Stories for Young Readers.* Illustrated by Larry Crowe. Chicago: Third World Press, 1980.

1636. Shearer, John. *Billy Jo Jive and the Midnight Voices.* Illustrated by Ted Shearer. New York: Delacorte Press, 1982.

1637. ———. *I Wish I Had an Afro.* New York: Cowles Book Co., 1970.

1638. ———. *Little Man in the Family.* New York: Delacorte Press, 1972.

1639. Sherlock, Philip. *Anansi, the Spider Man.* New York: Thomas Y. Crowell Co., 1954.

1640. ———. *Iguana's Tail: Crick Crack Stories from the Caribbean.* New York: Thomas Y. Crowell Co., 1969.

1641. ———. *West Indies Folk Tales.* New York: Oxford University Press, 1966.

1642. Sherlock, Philip, with Hilary Sherlock. *Ears and Tails and Common Sense: More Stories from the Caribbean.* New York: Thomas Y. Crowell Co., 1974.

1643. Slaton, William, and Nellie Slaton. *Bacteria and Viruses: Friends or Foes?* Englewood Cliffs, N.J.: Prentice–Hall, 1965.

1644. Steptoe, John. *Baby Say.* New York: Lothrop, Lee and Shepard Co., 1988.

A baby and big brother figure out how to get along. Includes illustrations.

1645. ————. *Birthday.* New York: Holt, Rinehart and Winston, 1972.

Javaka is the firstborn in an idealized black community where all the people are loving and joyful. It is his birthday, so there is a celebration. Includes illustrations.

1646. ————. *Daddy Is a Monster . . . Sometimes.* New York: Lothrop, Lee and Shepard Co., 1980.

1647. ————. *Jeffrey Bear Cleans Up His Act.* New York: Lothrop, Lee and Shepard Co., 1982.

1648. ————. *Marcia.* New York: Viking Press, 1976.

1649. ————. *Mufaro's Beautiful Daughters.* New York: Lothrop, Lee Shephard Co., 1987.

1650. ————. *My Special Best Words.* New York: Viking Press, 1974.

1651. ————. *Stevie.* New York: Harper and Row, 1969.

Robert's mother takes care of Stevie while Stevie's mother works. Robert resents Stevie's demanding, babyish ways. But when Stevie and his parents move away, Robert remembers the good things about Stevie and misses him. Written in black dialect and illustrated by the author.

1652. ————. *The Story of Jumping Mouse: A Native American Legend.* New York: Lothrop, Lee and Shepard Co., 1984.

1653. ————. *Train Ride.* New York: Harper and Row, 1971.

Written in black English, this is the story of a group of black children who decide to take a train ride from Brooklyn, where they live, uptown to Times Square. They have a terrific time, return home late, and are punished. Includes illustrations.

1654. ———. *Uptown.* New York: Harper and Row, 1970.

Two young boys, Dennis and John, discuss what they will be when they grow up. They discuss clothing, junkies, black pride, hippies, and karate. Includes illustrations.

1655. Sterling, Dorothy. *Forever Free.* Illustrated by Ernest Crichlow. Garden City, N.Y.: Doubleday and Co., 1963.

1656. ———. *Freedom Train: The Story of Harriet Tubman.* Illustrated by Ernest Crichlow. Garden City, N.Y.: Doubleday and Co., 1963.

1657. ———. *Mary Jane.* Illustrated by Ernest Crichlow. New York: Scholastic, 1959.

1658. Sutherland, Efua. *Playtime in Africa.* Photographs by Willis E. Bell.* New York: Atheneum Publishers, 1962.

1659. Tarry, Ellen. *Young Jim: The Early Years of James Weldon Johnson.* New York: Dodd, Mead and Co., 1967.

This is a biography of James Weldon Johnson, who contributed in various ways to the culture and civic life of America. The book includes information on Johnson's early life and experiences as he progressed through different stages of development. Included also is a picture of a poetical composition in his handwriting, taken from an original collection in his notebook now being preserved at Yale University.

1660. Tate, Eleanora E. *Just an Overnight Guest.* New York: Dial Press, 1980.

Just an Overnight Guest became the basis for a film produced by Phoenix Film, Inc. The film was named to the Selected Films for Young Adults 1985 list by the Young Adults Committee of the America Library Association.

1661. ————. *The Secret of Gumbo Grove.* New York: Bantam Books, 1987.

"Peer and family relations, including sibling rivalry, are masterfully blended to create a warm, humorous, and wonderful story centered around an intellectually curious and spirited black girl."

1662. Taylor, Mildred D. *The Friendship.* Illustrated by Max Ginsburg.** New York: Dial Press, 1987.

1663. ————. *The Gold Cadillac.* Pictures by Michael Hays.* New York: Dial Press, 1987.

Two black girls living in the North are proud of their family's beautiful new Cadillac until they take it on a visit to the South and encounter racial prejudice for the first time.

1664. ————. *Let the Circle Be Unbroken.* New York: Dial Press, 1981.

This book is the third in the series about the Logan family, and a sequel to *Roll of Thunder, Hear My Cry.* Cassie is now older, and her bold family is struggling to stay together against overwhelming odds. This book was a finalist for the 1982 American Book Award, and it was awarded the American Library Association Best Book of the Year. It also won the 1982 Coretta Scott King Award.

1665. ————. *Roll of Thunder, Hear My Cry.* Frontispiece by Jerry Pinkney. New York: Dial Press, 1976.

A black family living in the South during the 1930s is faced with prejudice and discrimination, which the children don't understand. This book won the Newbery Award for 1976.

1666.   ————. *Song of the Trees.* Illustrated by Jerry Pinkney. New York: Dial Press, 1975.

During the Depression, a rural black family deeply attached to the forest on their land in Mississippi tries to save it from being cut down by an unscrupulous white man. The first book in a trilogy. Won the Jane Addams Children's Book Award and the Council of Interracial Books Award in the African American category. Also a *New York Times* Outstanding Book of the Year in 1975.

1667.   Teague, Bob. *Adam in Blunderland.* Illustrated by Floyd Sowell. Garden City, N.Y.: Doubleday and Co., 1971.

Blaming adults for the evils of their society, an Afro–American boy, a Chinese boy, and a Puerto Rican girl wish themselves to a land populated exclusively by kids, only to find it plagued by the same evils for which they must now accept responsibility.

1668.   ————. *Agent K–13, the Super–Spy.* Illustrated by Geoffrey Moss. Garden City, N.Y.: Doubleday and Co., 1974.

"K–13, the best spy in the secret service, must retrieve the deadly Crumble–Bomb from the world's greediest man who is holding it for ransom."

1669.   ————. *Super–Spy K–13 in Outer Space.* Illustrated by Sammis McLean. Garden City, N.Y.: Doubleday and Co., 1980.

"The best spy in the secret service must foil exiles from Planet X who plan to invade the earth."

1670. Thomas, Dawn C. *A Bicycle from Bridgetown.* Illustrated by Don Miller. New York: McGraw-Hill, 1975.

1671. Thomas, Ianthe. *Eliza's Daddy.* Illustrated by Moneta Barnett. 1st ed. San Diego: Harcourt Brace Jovanovich, 1976.

Eliza wonders what her daddy's daughter in his new marriage is like. She works up the courage to ask to visit his new home.

1672. ————. *Hi, Mrs. Mallory!* Illustrated by Ann Toulmin-Rothe.* New York: Harper and Row, 1979.

1673. ————. *Lordy, Aunt Hattie.* Pictures by Thomas DiGrazia.* 1st ed. New York: Harper and Row, 1973.

Set in the Deep South, this story finds Jeppa Lee engaged in conversation with her Aunt Hattie. By finding out what kind of day it is, as well as what kind of day it isn't, Jeppa Lee concludes it must be summer.

1674. ————. *My Street's a Morning Cool Street.* Pictures by Emily A. McCully.* 1st ed. New York: Harper and Row, 1976.

While on his way to school, a young black boy observes the early morning sights and sounds that give life to his busy street.

1675. ————. *Walk Home Tired, Billy Jenkins.* Pictures by Thomas DiGrazia.* 1st ed. New York: Harper and Row, 1974.

Even though he is tired, a little city boy, Billy Jenkins, takes a special walk home from the playground with his imaginative friend. The book includes illustrations of the people and the city.

1676. ————. *Willie Blows a Mean Horn.* Pictures by Ann Toulmin-Rothe.* New York: Harper and Row, 1981.

A young boy adores his jazz musician father and contemplates becoming a performer himself.

1677.   Thomas, Joyce Carol. *Black Child.* Illustrated by Tom Feelings. New York: Zamani Productions, 1981.

1678.   ———. *Blessing: Poems.* 1st ed. Berkeley: Jocato Press, 1975.

1679.   ———. *Bright Shadow.* New York: Avon Books, 1983.

    Abyssinia Jackson must learn to cope with tragedy when peace is shattered in her Oklahoma countryside and her boyfriend Carl Lee disappears.

1680.   ———. *The Golden Pasture.* New York: Scholastic, 1986.

    This is a story of a boy, Carl Lee Jefferson, who spends his summer with his grandfather. When he finds a magnificent Appaloosa horse hidden in a golden pasture, Carl Lee knows he must ride Cloudy. But how can he train a horse who's as wild as the pasture he lives in?

1681.   ———. *Marked by Fire.* New York: Avon/Flare Books, 1982.

    In this first novel by Thomas, her character Abby, born in an Oklahoma cotton field in the wake of a tornado, learns the secrets of folk medicine from the healer, Mother Barker, as she grows up. She emerges as a young woman who faces pain, laughter, anguish, and joy with the dignity of her heritage and the determination of her spirit. This work won the American Book Award.

1682.   ———. *Water Girl.* New York: Avon Books, 1986.

1683.   Walker, Alice. *Langston Hughes, American Poet.* Illustrated by Don Miller. New York: Crowell Junior Books, 1974.

    This biography tells of Langston Hughes youth and the problems he had because of his father's negative attitudes.

1684.   ———. *To Hell with Dying.* Illustrated by Catherine Deeter.* New York: Harcourt Brace Jovanovich, 1988.

The author relates how old Mr. Sweet, though often on the verge of dying, could always be revived by the loving attention that she and her brother gave him.

1685. Walter, Mildred Pitts. *Because We Are.* New York: Lothrop Lee and Shepard Co., 1983.

1686. ————. *Brother to the Wind.* Illustrated by Diane Dillon** and Leo Dillon. New York: Lothrop Lee and Shepard Books, 1985.

With the help of Good Snake, a young African boy gets his dearest wish.

1687. ————. *The Girl on the Outside.* New York: Lothrop, Lee and Shepard Co., 1982.

A fictional recreation of the 1957 integration of Little Rock's Central High School, focusing on the experiences of two female students—one white, the other black.

1688. ————. *Have a Happy.* Illustrated by Carole Byard. New York: Lothrop, Lee and Shepard Books, 1989.

"Upset because his birthday falls on Christmas and will therefore be eclipsed as usual, and worried that there is less money because his father is out of work, eleven–year–old Chris takes solace in the carvings he is preparing for Kwanzaa, the Afro–American celebration of their cultural heritage."

1689. ————. *Justin and the Best Biscuit in the World.* Illustrated by Catherine Stock.* New York: Lothrop, Lee and Shepard Co., 1986.

Suffering in a family full of females, ten–year–old Justin feels that cleaning and keeping house are women's work, until he spends time on his beloved grandfather's ranch. This book won the 1987 Coretta Scott King Award.

1690.   ———. *Lillie of Watts: A Birthday Discovery.* Illustrated by Leonora E. Prince.* Los Angeles: Ward Ritchie Press, 1969.

During a weekend following a miserable birthday, things go from bad to worse for an eleven–year–old black girl living in Watts when she loses a valuable cat temporarily entrusted to her family's care. This is the author's first book.

1691.   ———. *Lillie of Watts Takes a Giant Step.* Illustrated by Bonnie Helene Johnson.* Garden City, N.Y.: Doubleday and Co., 1971.

Lillie's first year at Pelham Junior High in Watts is exciting, but she faces a difficult decision when the African Culture Club tries to get Malcolm X's birthday declared a holiday.

1692.   ———. *Mariah Loves Rock.* New York: Bradbury Press, 1988.

As fifth grade comes to an end, Mariah, who idolizes a famous rock star, experiences many misgivings, as does every member of her family, about the arrival of a half–sister who is coming to live with them.

1693.   ———. *My Mama Needs Me.* Illustrated by Pat Cummings. New York: Lothrop, Lee and Shepard Co., 1983.

Jason wants to help but isn't sure that his mother needs him at all after she brings home a new baby from the hospital. Cummings won the 1984 Coretta Scott King Award for her illustrations.

1694.   ———. *Trouble's Child.* New York: Lothrop, Lee and Shepard Co., 1985.

Martha longs to leave her island home off the Louisiana coast and go to high school, where she can learn more than the ways of her midwife grandmother so that perhaps someday she can broaden the lives of the superstitious villagers.

1695. Walton, Darwin McBeth. *What Color Are You?* Photos by Hal Franklin.* Chicago: Johnson Publishing Co., 1973.

This juvenile literature describes the purpose of skin and the cause of various skin colors. It discusses the fact that skin color has no effect on basic human needs and feelings.

1696. White, Edgar B. *Children of Night.* New York: Lothrop, Lee and Shepard Co., 1974.

1697. ————. *Omar at Christmas.* Illustrated by Dindga McCannon. New York: Lothrop, Lee and Shepard Co., 1973.

1698. ————. *Sati the Rastafarian.* Illustrated by Dindga McCannon. New York: Lothrop, Lee and Shepard Co., 1973.

1699. Wilkinson, Brenda Scott. *Ludell.* New York: Harper and Row, 1975.

This book received the Best Children's Book Award 1975. In it, a young black girl experiences the pleasure and pain of growing up during the 1950s in a small Georgia town.

1700. ————. *Ludell and Willie.* New York: Harper and Row, 1977.

As Ludell and Willie prepare to graduate from their high school in a small southern town, they experience events that alter their plans for the future. An American Library Association Best Book for Young Adults, 1977.

1701. ————. *Ludell's New York Time.* New York: Harper and Row, 1980.

Ludell moves from Georgia to New York City during spring of her senior year and struggles to adjust to life in Harlem.

1702. ————. *Not Separate, Not Equal.* New York: Harper and Row, 1987.

Marlene, one of a group of six blacks to integrate a Georgia public high school in the mid–sixties, experiences hatred and racism as well as the beginnings of the civil rights movement.

1703. Williams–Garcia, Rita. *Blue Tights.* 1st ed. New York: E. P. Dutton and Co., 1988.

"Growing up in a city neighborhood, fifteen–year–old Joyce, unsure of herself and not quite comfortable with her maturing body, tries to find a place to belong and a way to express herself through dance."

1704. Williamson, Mel, and George Ford, Jr. *Walk On.* Illustrated by George Ford, Jr. New York: Third Press, 1972.

1705. Wilson, Beth. *Giants for Justice.* San Diego: Harcourt, 1978.

1706. ————. *Great Minu.* Chicago: Follett, 1974.

1707. ————. *Martin Luther King, Jr.* New York: Putnam, 1971.

1708. ————. *Muhammad Ali.* New York: Putnam, 1974.

1709. ————. *Stevie Wonder.* New York: Putnam, 1979.

1710. Wilson, Johnniece Marshall. *Oh, Brother.* New York: Scholastic, 1988.

Alex's older brother bullies him, taking his bicycle and his money, until Alex discovers a way to stand up for himself. This is Wilson's first novel.

1711. Woodson, Carter Goodwin. *African Heroes and Heroines.* Washington, D.C.: Associated Publishers, 1948.

1712. ————. *African Myths.* Rev. ed. Washington, D.C.: Associated Publishers, 1948.

1713. Woodson, Jacqueline. *Last Summer with Maizon.* New York: Delacorte Press, 1990.

1714. Yarbrough, Camille. *Cornrows.* Illustrated by Carole Byard. New York: Coward, McCann and Geoghegan, 1979.

"As they braid the children's hair into cornrows, Mama and Great-Grammaw tell the children of the meaning of the designs of the cornrows. They present some of the tradition of African-American history." Byard won the 1980 Coretta Scott King Award for her illustrations.

1715. ————. *A Little Tree Growing in the Shade.* New York: Putnam, 1987.

1716. Young, Andrew Sturgeon N. *Black Champions of the Gridiron: Leroy Keys and O. J. Simpson.* San Diego: Harcourt, 1969.

1717. ————. *The Mets from Mobil: Tommie Agee, Cleon Jones.* New York: Harcourt, 1970.

1718. Young, Bernice Elizabeth. *Harlem: The Story of a Changing Community.* New York: Julian Messner, 1972.

Young gives the history of Harlem from early Dutch times to the present. Shows its transition.

1719. ————. *The Picture Story of Frank Robinson.* New York: Julian Messner, 1975.

1720. ————. *The Picture Story of Hank Aaron.* New York: Julian Messner, 1974.

1721. Young, Margaret Buckner. *The First Book of American Negroes.* New York: Franklin Watts, 1966.

A pictorial history of blacks in America for juvenile readers who wish to learn more about blacks in America, past and present. The topics include education, employment, housing, culture, and civil rights. The Afro-American depicted by Young has made giant steps forward since slavery but must continue making substantial progress to be truly accepted as an American citizen.

1722. ———. *The Picture Life of Martin Luther King, Jr.* New York: Franklin Watts, 1968.

This forty-five-page book for juveniles portrays in large bold print and numerous explicit photographs the life story of a dynamic leader of Afro-American people. While the text is predominantly pictorial, with only essentials of the subject's life being included, it nonetheless projects the inner dynamism that was Dr. King's.

CHAPTER 7

LANGUAGE and LITERATURE

1723. Abrahams, Peter. *A Wreath for Udomo.* New York: Alfred A. Knopf, Inc., 1956. Reprint. New York: Collier Books, 1971.

1724. Abramowitz,* Jack, and Warren Jennings Halliburton. *Pathways to the World of English.* 5 books. New York: Globe Book Co., 1973.

Five books comprise this title: Book 1A, *Searching for Identity*; Book 1B, *Searching for Values*; Books 1A and 1B, *Teaching Guide for Books 1A and 1B*; Book 2A, *Knowing Ourselves and Others*; and Book 2B, *Gaining Insights.*

1725. Adams, William. *Afro-American Authors.* Boston: Houghton Mifflin Co., 1972.

This book is a documentary of the life and works of noted black writers. For each writer, the book includes a photo, a brief life history, a major speech/public address and/or major publication(s). Writers include Claude McKay, W. E. B. DuBois, Langston Hughes, Richard Wright, Gwendolyn Brooks, Medger Evers, James Baldwin, and Martin Luther King, Jr.

1726. Adams, William, Peter Conn, and Barry Slepian, eds. *Afro-American Literature.* Vol. 4, *Nonfiction.* Boston: Houghton Mifflin Co., 1970.

This book is a collection of excerpts from the works of noted black authors, including Frederick Douglass, Booker T. Washington, W. E. B. DuBois, Dick Gregory, Malcolm X, Claude Brown, Martin Luther King, Jr., James Farmer, Eldridge Cleaver, and Bob Teague. A photo and a brief autobiography of each author precede each excerpt. The excerpts are grouped under five chapters: "Early Spokemen," "Black Identity," "Black Experience," "Civil Rights," and "New Directions." Every excerpt is followed by questions designed to generate further discussion.

1727. ———, eds. *Afro-American Literature.* Vol. 1, *Fiction.* Boston: Houghton Mifflin Co., 1970.

This book is a collection of short fiction stories by black writers. It contains a photo and a brief annotation about each contributing author. All the stories are grouped under four chapters: "The Family," "Black Soldiers: The War Within," "On Being Black," and "Man Alone." Each story is followed by questions designated "For Discussion." Contributors include Ann Petry, Ralph Ellison, Gwendolyn Brooks, Cyrus Cotter, W. E. B. DuBois, Charles L. Russell, Frank London Brown, Langston Hughes, William Melvin Kelley, James Baldwin, Junius Edwards, and John Oliver Killens.

1728. Addo, Peter Eric Adotey. *Ghana Folk Tales: Ananse Stories from Africa.* 1st ed. New York: Exposition Press, 1968.

1729. Amos, W. J. *Borderline: The Case of Too Many Graves, A Novel.* Los Angeles: Holloway House Publishing Co., 1988.

In this novel, Cal Robbins's accidental discovery of buried treasure in New Mexico unleashes a nightmare of mistaken identity, murder, and mayhem. It is the story of a man teased and trapped by circumstances beyond his control.

1730. ———. *M. I. A.: Saigon.* Los Angeles: Holloway House Publishing Co., 1986.

In telling the story of a black GI who turned up missing in action in Vietnam, Amos reveals how many American soldiers were seduced by the attraction of quick riches to be gained in such illegal activities as prostitution, selling narcotics, and even intercepting arms bound for the South Vietnamese and selling them to the Vietcong. He tells what it is like to be trapped in Vietnam.

1731. Andrews, Malachi, and Paul T. Owens.* *Black Language*. Los Angeles: Seymour-Smith Publishers, 1973.

1732. Angelou, Maya. *And Still I Rise*. 1st ed. New York: Random House, 1978.

1733. ————. *I Swore I'd Never Lose It Again*. Garden City, N.Y.: Doubleday and Co., 1984.

1734. ————. *Just Give Me a Cool Drink of Water 'fore I Diiie: The Poetry of Maya Angelou*. New York: Random House, 1971.

1735. ————. *Maya Angelou: Poems*. New York: Bantam Books, 1981.

1736. ————. *Mrs. Flowers: A Moment of Friendship*. Minneapolis: Redpath Press, 1986.

1737. ————. *Now Sheba Sing the Song*. 1st ed. New York: E. P. Dutton/Dial Books, 1987.

1738. ————. *Oh Pray My Wings Are Going to Fit Me Well*. 1st ed. New York: Random House, 1975.

1739. ————. *Shaker, Why Don't You Sing?* New York: Random House, 1983.

1740. Ansa, Tina McElroy. *Baby of the Family*. 1st. ed. San Diego: Harcourt Brace Jovanovich, 1989.

"Set in a small Georgia town in the placid 1950s, this is a wholly original portrait of everyday black life as seen through the comings and goings of one affluent family."

1741. Arnez, Nancy Levi. *Daniel Defoe: Moll Flanders.* New York: Barnes and Noble, 1969.

1742. Asante, Molefi Kete. *African and African American Communication Continuities.* Buffalo: Council on International Studies, State University of New York, 1975.

This essay investigates the structure of Afro–American English and provides evidence that it "derived from the genius of West African languages." Focusing on a combination of classes of sounds, units of meaning, and syntax behaviors, rather than on any single one of these simple lexical factors frequently used by early American scholars, Asante outlines the complex verbal behaviors that constitute what survives of African communication in Afro–American speech. He argues that it is in the "communicative style" of Afro–Americans that their essential Africanness can be ascertained. Notes are included.

1743. ————. *The Afrocentric Idea.* Philadelphia: Temple University Press, 1987.

The author seeks both to render a critique of Western theorizing about discourse by revealing its cultural presuppositions and its narrow empirical limitations, and simultaneously to posit in its stead an indigenous "African" theory of discourse.

1744. ————. *Afrocentricity: The Theory of Social Change.* Buffalo, N.Y.: Amulefi Publishing Company, 1980.

This book advocates the need for an Afrocentric philosophy among Afro–Americans who are victims of Eurocentricity. It examines the future of an African cultural system, African ways, and the values obtained from the experiences of Afro–Americans.

It also discusses Nija, Kawaida, and Mfundalai, and includes a glossary and subject index.

1745. Asante, Molefi Kete, and Jerry K. Frye.** *Contemporary Public Communication Applications.* New York: Harper and Row, 1977.

This text contains "innovative concepts, recent research findings, multiracial and multinational illustrations and references, and an emphasis on communication for effective human interaction." It focuses on pluralistic and multinational features of modern societies, and includes a glossary of authors, experiences, concepts, and examples. There are also references to a number of outstanding public addresses and exemplary speeches.

1746. Asante, Molefi Kete, and Abdulai S. Vandi, eds. *Contemporary Black Thought: Alternative Analysis in Social and Behavioral Sciences.* Beverly Hills, Calif.: Sage Publications, 1980.

Representing the best tradition of fair and open analysis and evaluation, the contributors present alternative views to the Eurocentric conceptualization of the behavioral and social sciences. Together they help to counteract the prevalent and erroneous model that depicts Europe as teacher and the African world as pupil.

1747. Asante, Molefi Kete, Eileen Newmark,** and Cecil A. Blake, eds. *Handbook of Intercultural Communication.* Beverly Hills, Calif.: Sage Publications, 1979.

This volume comprises six parts: theoretical considerations, conceptual framework, issues in intercultural communications, general problems and data, research in specific cultures, and practical applications: training methods. Interdisciplinary and intercultural in scope, it addresses the critical issues confronting researchers and theorists of intercultural communication. It includes bibliographical references and information about the contributors.

1748. Aubert, Alvin. *Against the Blues: Poems*. 1st ed. Detroit: Broadside Press, 1972.

1749. ————. *Feeling Through: New Poems*. New York: Greenfield Review Press, 1975.

1750. Awkward, Michael. *Inspiriting Influences: Tradition, Revision, and Afro-American Women's Novels*. New York: Columbia University Press, 1989.

1751. Bailey, Pearl. *Duey's Tale*. New York: Harcourt Brace Jovanovich, 1975.

   "An allegorical tale of a maple seed, a bottle, and a log." Won the Coretta Scott King Award in 1976.

1752. Baker, Houston A., Jr. *Afro-American Poetics: Revisions of Harlem and the Black Aesthetic*. Madison: University of Wisconsin Press, 1988.

1753. ————. *Black Literature in America*. New York: McGraw-Hill, 1971.

1754. ————. *Blues, Ideology, and Afro-American Literature: A Vernacular Theory*. Chicago: University of Chicago Press, 1984.

   Baker's study of Richard Wright rescues Wright from the social realist stigma put on him by heirs apparent Ralph Ellison and James Baldwin, and it locates in his language a liberating critique of bourgeois Western literary practices.

1755. ————. *The Journey Back: Issues in Black Literature and Criticism*. Chicago: University of Chicago Press, 1980.

1756. ————. *Long Black Song: Essays in Black American Literature and Culture*. Charlottesville: University Press of Virginia, 1972.

1757. ―――――. *Modernism and the Harlem Renaissance.* Chicago: University of Chicago Press, 1987.

Baker positions the Harlem Renaissance in a movement predating the 1920s, when Afro-Americans embraced the task of self-determination and in so doing gave forth a distinctive form of expression that is reflected in twentieth century Afro-American arts. Includes photographs.

1758. ―――――. *Singers of Daybreak: Studies in Black American Literature.* Washington, D.C.: Howard University Press, 1974.

This volume includes six essays that examine such disparate writers as James Weldon Johnson, Malcolm X, Paul Laurence Dunbar, Gwendolyn Brooks, George Cain, Richard Wright, Ralph Ellison, and Jean Toomer. Baker has written a new introduction that assesses the unifying aspects of the book.

1759. Baker, Houston A., Jr., and Patricia Redmond,** eds. *Afro-American Literary Style in the 1990s.* Chicago: University of Chicago Press, 1989.

This volume—the result of a three-day conference in 1987 sponsored by the Albert M. Greenfield professorship and the University of Pennsylvania's Center for the Study of Black Literature and Culture—assesses the state of Afro-American literary study and projects a vision of that study for the coming decade. It treats such issues as genre, theory, and performance. Each essay is followed by a response from one or more contributors. Includes an index.

1760. Baldwin, James. *Amen Corner: A Play.* 1968. Reprint. New York: Dial Press, 1971.

1761. ―――――. *Another Country.* New York: Dial Press, 1962.

1762. ―――――. *Blues for Mister Charlie: A Play.* New York: Dial Press, 1964.

1763.   ———. *Giovanni's Room: A Novel.* New York: Dial Press, 1956.

1764.   ———. *Go Tell It on the Mountain.* New York: Alfred A. Knopf, 1953. Reprint. New York: New American Library, 1963.

In an enthralling but honest manner, James Baldwin tells the story of a family's survival in Harlem. Life's primary objective, as pursued by the characters, is to combat the imperatives of their existence as they search for salvation through religious conviction.

1765.   ———. *Going to Meet the Man.* New York: Dial Press, 1965. Reprint. New York: Dell Publishing Co., 1976.

This collection of Baldwin's short fiction deals with the following circumstances: a young girl tries to accept the departure of her lover; a Negro entertainer who has received much recognition in Europe faces the prospect of returning to the United States; a young man who has achieved middle–class status has to adjust to his brother's life of jazz, dope addiction, and prison; a white policeman in a southern town recalls the mutilation and lynching of a Negro.

1766.   ———. *If Beale Street Could Talk.* New York: Dial Press, 1974.

1767.   ———. *Just Above My Head.* London: Michael Joseph, 1979.

1768.   ———. *The Price of the Ticket: Collected Nonfiction, 1948–1985.* 1st ed. New York: St. Martin's Press, 1985.

This book presents Baldwin's best nonfiction works and is a major literary and autobiographical statement of the twentieth century. The book contains the full text of *The Fire Next Time*, *No Name in the Street*, and *The Devil Finds Work*, along with dozens of other pieces, including those found in *Notes of a Native Son* and *Nobody Knows My Name*. In this work, Baldwin continues his exploration of the price black and white Americans have paid to survive in America.

1769. ———. *Tell Me How Long the Train's Been Gone: A Novel.* New York: Dial Press, 1968.

1770. Baraka, Imamu Amiri. *The Dead Lecturer: Poems.* New York: Grove Press, 1964.

1771. ———. *Dutchman and the Slave: Two Plays.* New York: William Morrow and Co., 1964.

1772. ———. *The System of Dante's Hell.* New York: Grove Press, 1965.

1773. ———, ed. *The Moderns: An Anthology of New Writing in America.* London: MacGibbon and Kee, 1965.

1774. Baraka, Imamu Amiri, and Amina Baraka, comps. *Confirmation: An Anthology of African American Women.* 1st ed. New York: William Morrow and Co., 1983.

1775. Barksdale, Richard, and Kenneth Kinnamon, eds. *Black Writers of America: A Comprehensive Anthology.* New York: Macmillan Co., 1972.

Divided into six parts, this book is a comprehensive collection of Afro-American literature from the eighteenth century to the present. The sections are entitled "The Eighteenth-Century Beginnings," "The Struggle Against Slavery and Racism: 1800-1860," "The Black Man in the Civil War: 1861-1865," "Reconstruction and Reaction: 1865-1915," "Renaissance and Radicalism: 1915-1945," and "The Present Generation: Since 1945." The sections contain generous selections of autobiographies, essays, speeches, letters, political pamphlets, histories, journals, and folk literature, as well as poems, plays, and stories. Some of the many notable black writers included are Phillis Wheatley, Benjamin Banneker, Frederick Douglass, Nat Turner, Paul Laurence Dunbar, Booker T. Washington, Langston

Hughes, Marcus Garvey, Margaret Walker, Malcolm X, and Mari E. Evans. Wherever feasible, the authors have presented complete works of these black writers rather than fragments. Introductions, headnotes, bibliographies, and indexes are included.

1776. Barrett, Lindsay. *Song for Mumu.* London: Longman, 1967. Reprint. Washington, D.C.: Howard University Press, 1974.

This story tells of the loves and death of the young girl Mumu. Filled with folklore and legend, it is set in a Caribbean countryside, that has been spoiled by slavery, and in the city, a place without love.

1777. Beck, Robert [Iceberg Slim, pseud.]. *Airtight Willie & Me.* Los Angeles: Holloway House Publishing Co., 1987.

1778. ————. *Long White Con.* Los Angeles: Holloway House Publishing Co., 1987.

1779. ————. *Mama Black Widow.* Los Angeles: Holloway House Publishing Co., 1969.

1780. ————. *The Naked Soul of Iceberg Slim.* Los Angeles: Holloway House Publishing Co., 1971.

1781. ————. *Pimp: The Story of My Life.* Los Angeles: Holloway House Publishing Co., 1969.

1782. ————. *Trick Baby.* Los Angeles: Holloway House Publishing Co., 1967.

1783. Beckham, Barry. *My Main Mother.* New York: Walker and Co., 1969.

1784. ————. *Runner Mack.* New York: William Morrow, 1972. Reprint. Washington, D.C.: Howard University Press, 1982.

This is the story of Henry Adams, a confused and unthinkable bumbler who comes of age when he meets Runner

Mack. Henry Adams lives his life in dreamlike fashion and eventually learns, through Runner Mack, about blackness, struggle, liberation, white hate, distrust, and, ultimately, manhood.

1785. Bellegarde, Ida Rowland. *Easy Steps to a Large Vocabulary: A Practical Approach to Individualized Self-Study: A Successfully Proven Method in a Self-Help Program.* Pine Bluff, Ark.: Bell Enterprises, 1971.

1786. ————. *Easy Steps to Correct Speech: A Mini-Book for Self-Improvement.* 3d ed. Detroit: Harlo Press, 1971.

This small handbook is designed primarily for individuals who frequently use substandard English. Proper usage of certain common expressions and pronunciations can be achieved in a pleasurable way using the techniques outlined. Drills involve some specific consonant combinations and troublesome endings for improved articulation and more effective speech power in communication.

1787. ————. *Easy Steps to Good Grammar: A Mini-Book for Self-Improvement.* Detroit: Harlo Press, 1972.

1788. ————. *Haiku Reflections.* Pine Bluff, Ark.: Bell Enterprises, 1978.

1789. ————. *Idylls of the Season.* Pine Bluff, Ark.: Bell Enterprises, 1978.

1790. ————. *Lisping Leaves.* Rev. ed. Pine Bluff, Ark.: Bell Enterprises, 1976.

1791. ————. *Little Stepping Stones to Correct English.* Pine Bluff, Ark.: Bell Enterprises, 1977.

1792. ————. *Little Stepping Stones to Correct Speech: A New Way to Study Your ABC's.* Detroit: Harlo Press, 1973.

1793. Bellegarde, Ida Rowland, and Peter E. Lopez.* *Pasaderitas Hacia El Ingles Correcto: Un Mini-libro par El Mejoramiento Personal.* Pine Bluff, Ark.: Bell Enterprises, 1977.

1794. Berry, Faith. *Langston Hughes: Before and Beyond Harlem.* Westport, Conn.: Lawrence Hill and Co., 1983.

In this biography Berry has probed deeply into the poet's complex personality and has shed light on significant areas of the Harlem Renaissance—the widespread homosexuality among many of the stalwarts of the Renaissance and the relationship between black Renaissance figures and their white patrons, particularly the white Park Avenue benefactor, Charlotte Mason. Includes bibliographical references and an index.

1795. Bertrand, Yolande. *Borrowed Moments.* Los Angeles: Holloway House Publishing Co., 1984.

1796. ———. *Come September.* Los Angeles: Holloway House Publishing Co., 1984.

1797. ———. *Dark Road Home.* Los Angeles: Holloway House Publishing Co., 1984.

1798. ———. *A Play for Love.* Los Angeles: Holloway House Publishing Co., 1983.

1799. Black, Luther H. *This Life.* New York: Vantage Press, 1968.

1800. Blaine, Laurence. *Sweet Street Blues.* Los Angeles: Holloway House Publishing Co., 1978.

1801. Bogus, S. Diane. *Her Poems: An Anniversaric Chronology.* Inglewood, Calif.: W. I. M. Publications, 1980.

1802. ———. *I'm Off to See the Goddam Wizard, Alright!* Inglewood, Calif.: W. I. M. Publications, 1971.

This is a book of poems about black people and some of the misconceptions and fantasies they have. Bogus suggests that fantasies—Never Never Land, Wonderland, fairy godmothers, and the land of Oz—are responsible for blacks not loving themselves. She contends that "the wizard is any and all myths perpetrated by white people and tenaciously, without any question, adhered to by blacks." Black Americans will grow strong when the wizard is "found out."

1803. ————. *Sapphire's Sampler: An Anthology of Poetry, Prose, and Drama.* Inglewood, Calif.: W. I. M. Publications, 1982.

This two-hundred-page collection of poems, stories, essays, and plays by Bogus deals with different aspects of her being a human, a black, a woman, and a proclaimed lesbian. Most of the material directly addresses homosexuality, but there are also many selections that make a statement about American society and its ability to repress individual thought and persecute those who are different. Includes illustrations by Naeemah Shabazz.

1804. ————. *Woman in the Moon.* Stamford, Conn.: Soapbox Publishing Co., 1977. Reprint. Inglewood, Calif.: W. I. M. Publications, 1979.

This book of poems is divided into four parts. Part 1, "Woman in the Moon," focuses on women. Part 2, "Of the Birds and the Be's," addresses love and loving. Parts 3 and 4 treat "Persona" and "Consciousness," respectively. Illustrations by Pat King are included, along with a note about the author.

1805. Boles, Robert. *Curling: A Novel.* Boston: Houghton Mifflin Co., 1968.

1806. ————. *The People One Knows: A Novel.* Boston: Houghton Mifflin Co., 1964.

1807. Bontemps, Arna Wendell. *Black Thunder.* Boston: Beacon Press, 1936.

This is the story of an unsuccessful slave insurrection in Richmond, Virginia, in 1800. The protagonist, Gabriel Prosser, is an illiterate slave who feels that it is his responsibility to lead his fellow slaves to freedom.

1808. ————. *The Old South; "A Summer Tragedy" and Other Stories of the Thirties.* New York: Dodd, Mead and Co., 1973.

1809. ————, ed. *The Harlem Renaissance Remembered: Essays.* 1st ed. 1972. Reprint. New York: Dodd, Mead and Co., 1984.

1810. Boone, Mark Allen. *Reunion.* Los Angeles: Holloway House Publishing Co., 1989.

This novel tells the story of two friends and of one man's determination to find his origin. This story of friendship goes beyond family; it is the kind of friendship that lives forever. Levi Merriweather and Wesley Luckett are such friends. They share everything, even the same woman. When they grow apart, something happens that brings them back together.

1811. Boulware, Marcus Hanna. *Jive and Slang of Students in Negro Colleges.* Hampton, Va.: Marcus Hanna Boulware, 1947.

Boulware defines and describes "jive" and "slang" terms used on college campuses. He then suggests that this so–called `hip' language aids `jitterbugs' in expressing their emotions when their limited vocabularies fail.

1812. ————, ed. *The Oratory of Negro Leaders, 1900–1968.* Westport, Conn.: Negro Universities Press, 1969.

Boulware vividly examines the nature of the orator and the role he played in the history and progress of black America. He includes brief historical records of how each black orator influenced his or her environment, and the entire black population, where applicable. All the orators examined are categorized according to the historical, political, or religious framework within which they lived and carried out their duties.

The categories cover the Era of Booker T. Washington, the period of Marcus Garvey, the leaders of the NAACP, public addresses of black women, labor leaders, and church and pulpit oratory. The appendixes include a list of leading orators documented from newspaper speeches, and another list of orators tabulated from questionnaires. This work also includes a bibliography, an index, and a foreword by Alex Haley.

1813. Boyd, Sue Abbott. *Aftermaze.* Fort Smith, Ark.: Pioneer Press, 1977.

1814. ———. *How It Is.* Homestead, Fla.: Olivant Press, 1968.

1815. ———. *Poems by Blacks.* Vol. 2. Fort Smith, Ark.: South and West, 1972.

1816. Bradley, David. *The Chaneysville Incident.* New York: Harper and Row, 1981. Reprint. London: Serpent's Tail, 1986.

1817. ———. *South Street.* New York: Charles Scribner's Sons, 1986.

1818. Brawley, Benjamin Griffith. *The Negro Genius: A New Appraisal of the Achievement of the American Negro in Literature and Fine Arts.* 1937. Reprint. New York: Dodd, Mead and Co., 1966.

Starting from the premise that every race has its peculiar genius, Brawley argues that the genius of blacks is artistic but will express itself only after blacks have passed through their period of suffering. He also emphasizes that there is "no connection between primitive African art and that of the Negro in America today [1937]." After laying this philosophical foundation, Brawley begins to discuss the lives and works of famous black women and men in America. He starts with the slave narratives of Gustavus Vassa and proceeds through the works of such well-known people as Marian Anderson, Frederick Douglass, and W. E. B. DuBois. He deals with such themes as the maturing of black literature, protest and vindication, and realism in black art.

1819.   ———. *The Negro in Literature and Art in the United States.* New York: Duffield and Company, 1930. Reprint. New York: AMS Press, 1971.

This is an attempt to place black writers and their work in a historical framework. Brawley discusses the work of writers, musicians, and artists such as Frederick Douglass, Paul Laurence Dunbar, W. E. B. DuBois, and Phillis Wheatley, but his primary interest is in their biography. In the appendix he discusses such topics as blacks in American fiction and blacks in contemporary literature. The book also includes portraits of each person.

1820.   ———. *Paul Laurence Dunbar: Poet of His People.* Chapel Hill: University of the North Carolina Press, 1936. Reprint. Port Washington, N.Y.: Kennikat Press, 1967.

1821.   ———, ed. *Early Negro American Writers: Selections with Biographical and Critical Introductions.* Chapel Hill: University of North Carolina Press, 1935. Reprint. New York: Dover Publications, 1970.

This is a collection of biographical sketches and illustrative pieces of literary work produced by early black American writers prior to and during the Civil War. Among others, contributions by Jupiter Hammon, Phillis Wheatley, and Gustavus Vassa are included. This book serves as a valuable source for scholars interested in the field of black history in the United States.

1822.   Brehan, Delle. *Kicks is Kicks.* Los Angeles: Holloway House Publishing Co., 1970.

1823.   Brooke, Amos. *Black in a White Paradise.* Los Angeles: Holloway House Publishing Co., 1978.

1824.   ———. *Doing Time.* Los Angeles: Holloway House Publishing Co., 1977.

1825.   ———. *The Last Toke.* Los Angeles: Holloway House Publishing Co., 1977.

1826. Brooks, Charlotte Kendrick. *Impact on Reading*. New York: Holt, Rinehart and Winston, 1979.

This work covers grades seven through twelve and includes teacher's guides. Book A, *Circles*; Book B, *Mirrors And Windows*; Book C, *Blue Notes, Bright Notes*; Book D, *Searching*; Book E, *Conflict*; Book F, *Dreams and Danger*.

1827. ————, ed. *African Rhythms: Selected Stories and Poems*. New York: Pocket Books, 1974.

This anthology contains stories and poems by Africans about the history and spirit of Africa. The circular relationship of past and present is the central theme, and most of the selections also reflect the idea of unity of family, clan, tribe, or community.

Creation—how, when, and why things were created—is the theme of the stories and poems in part 1. Part 2 focuses on the contemporary struggle for self–identity, and part 3 represents a synthesis of the old and the new. There are also three photographic essays on culture and traditions in Africa, living Africa, and the children of Africa. Biographical data on contributing authors and a glossary of important terms are also included.

1828. ————, ed. *The Outnumbered: Stories, Essays, and Poems About Minority Groups by America's Leading Writers*. New York: Delacorte Press, 1967.

This book describes the many obstacles faced by America's racial, religious, and ethnic minorities throughout our history and the strategies used to overcome those obstacles. This book should be of particular interest to (1) those students with limited knowledge about minority groups other than their own, (2) the Anglo majority, and (3) the minorities whose forefathers' stories are shared in this collection.

1829. Brooks, Gwendolyn. *Aloneness*. Detroit: Broadside Press, 1971.

1830. ———. *Annie Allen.* New York: Harper, 1949. Reprint. Westport, Conn.: Greenwood Press, Inc., 1971.

> This is Brooks's second book and the one for which she won the Pulitzer Prize in 1950. She was the first black to receive this award.

1831. ———. *Beckonings: Poems.* Detroit: Broadside Press, 1975.

1832. ———. *Blacks.* Chicago: The David Co., 1987.

> Brooks, the Pulitzer Prize winner, furnishes new poems and the complete texts of classic works, including *A Street in Bronzeville, Annie Allen, The Bean Eaters, In the Mecca, Riot,* and *Maud Martha.*

1833. ———. *Family Pictures.* Detroit: Broadside Press, 1970.

1834. ———. *Maude Martha.* New York: Harper and Row, 1953.

> The story in this novel is a series of episodes in the life of a black girl, Maude Martha. Maude is not pretty like her sister, and she is concerned about being able to keep her handsome husband.

1835. ———. *The Near–Johannesburg Boy, and Other Poems.* Chicago: David Co., 1986.

1836. ———. *Selected Poems.* 1st ed. New York: Harper and Row, 1963.

1837. ———. *A Street in Bronzeville.* New York: Harper, 1945.

> This book of verses is a prize winner from the Mid–West Writers' Conference.

1838. ———. *To Disembark.* Chicago: Third World Press, 1981.

1839. ———. *The World of Gwendolyn Brooks.* New York: Harper and Row, 1971.

1840. ———, comp. *A Broadside Treasury.* 1st ed. Detroit: Broadside Press, 1971.

1841. ———, comp. *Jump Bad: A New Chicago Anthology.* 1st ed. Detroit: Broadside Press, 1971.

1842. Brown, Frank London. *The Myth Maker: A Novel.* Chicago: Path Press, 1969.

1843. ———. *Turmbull Park: A Novel.* Chicago: Regnery, 1959.

1844. Brown, Lloyd Wellesley. *Bits of Ivory: Narrative Techniques in Jane Austen's Fiction.* Baton Rouge: Louisiana State University Press, 1973.

In this critique of the narrative style of Jane Austen, the author explores Austen's use of symbolism, dialogue, parody, and imagery in her novels. In doing this, Brown pays particular attention to Austen's most notable works, *Sense and Sensibility* and *Pride and Prejudice.*

1845. ———, ed. *The Black Writer in Africa and the Americas.* Los Angeles: Hennessey and Ingalls, 1973.

This is a collection of papers presented at the Fourth Annual Conference on Comparative Literature in April 1970 under the sponsorship of the University of Southern California. The papers are pan–African and include discussions of the United States, Latin America, Africa, and the Caribbean. One paper making a plea for pan–Africanism argues that the new creativity emerging in each of these regions is not accidental; rather, it is the result of the movement for pan–Africanism. Notable authors discussed include Frantz Fanon, Ralph Ellison, W. E. B. DuBois, and Richard Wright.

1846.   Brown, Sterling Allen. *Collected Poems*. 1st ed. New York: Harper and Row, 1980.

1847.   ————. *The Negro in American Fiction*. Port Washington, N.Y.: Kennikat Press, 1968.

Said to be the first full-length presentation of this subject, this book is a survey of blacks in American fiction, both as character and as author. It is divided into twelve chapters and addresses the period between 1789 and 1936. It provides a penetrating analysis of what social factors and attitudes lay behind the various schools and periods and of how stereotypes evolved at the dictates of social policy. When slavery was being attacked, for example, southern authors countered with the contented slave; when cruelties were mentioned, they dragged forward the comical and happy-hearted black.

1848.   ————. *Southern Road, Poems by Sterling A. Brown*. Boston: Beacon Press, 1974.

"Sterling Brown's cultural contributions touched a broad range of people, places and years. He is perhaps best known as a writer. *Southern Road*, a collection of his poetry, was one of the first works to honor the implicit dignity of Afro-American folk. It has been a source of inspiration to countless poets."

1849.   Brown, Sterling Allen, Arthur P. Davis, and Ulysses Lee, eds. *The Negro Caravan: Writings by American Negroes*. New York: Arno Press. 1941. Reprint. Salem, N.H.: Ayer Co., 1987.

1850.   Brown, William Wells. *Clotel, or, The President's Daughter*. London: Partridge and Oakey, 1853. Reprint. New York: Arno Press, 1969.

Published a year after *Uncle Tom's Cabin*, this novel, the first in America by a black man, shows what slave life was like. The title of this antislavery novel refers to the report that Thomas

Jefferson had a slave wife and children. Brown used the novel as a weapon against chattel slavery.

1851. Brown–Guillory, Elizabeth. *Their Place on the Stage: Black Women Playwrights in America.* Westport, Conn.: Greenwood Press, 1988.

1852. ————, ed. *Wines in the Wilderness: Plays by African American Women from the Harlem Renaissance to the Present.* Westport, Conn.: Greenwood Press, 1990.

1853. Bullock, Clifton. *Baby Chocolate and Other Short Stories: Aspects of the Black Experience.* New York: William–Frederick Press, 1975.

1854. ————. *The Master Plan: A Novel.* Hicksville, N.Y.: Exposition Press, 1979.

1855. Burke, Carolyn M. *Afraid of the Dark.* Detroit: Heirloom Books, 1984.

1856. ————. *Cactus in Bloom.* N.p. 1983.

1857. ————. *Watercolor.* Detroit: Heirloom Books, 1985.

1858. ————, ed. *Energies: Americanfolk Poetry.* Detroit: Heirloom Books, 1984.

1859. ————, ed. *Heirloom Poetry Sample.* Detroit: Heirloom Books, 1985.

1860. ————, ed. *Stained Glass.* Detroit: Heirloom Books, 1986.

1861. Butcher, Margaret Just. *The Negro in American Culture: Based on Materials Left by Alain Locke.* 2d ed. New York: Alfred A. Knopf, 1972.

This book traces the historical patterns of the folk and formal contributions of Afro–Americans to American culture.

Butcher analyzes the impact of Afro–American culture, which affects the "changing morals and ideological context of American literature and art." The emphasis is on trends and types rather than on individual artists and authors. The book includes a postscript written in 1972 and also some biographical information on the author.

1862.   Butcher, Philip, ed. *The Ethnic Image in Modern American Literature, 1900–1950.* 2 vols. Washington, D.C.: Howard University Press, 1984.

A sequel to *The Minority Presence in American Literature, 1600–1900,* this two–volume collection of fiction and poetry constitutes a comprehensive and significant survey of American literature and social history over a fifty–year span. The collection contains more than two hundred works of poetry, drama, fiction, and nonfiction that depict the realities, as well as stereotypes, of ethnic participation in American culture. It compares survival in the North with survival in the South. Includes an index.

1863.   ———, ed. *The Minority Presence in American Literature, 1600–1900: A Reader and Course Guide.* 2 vols. Washington, D.C.: Howard University Press, 1977.

Written for readers interested in American life and literature and in the role and status of minorities in the development of this nation, as well as for college students studying these areas, this collection includes contributions by people such as Walt Whitman, James P. Beckwourth, Oliver Wendell Holmes, Charles W. Chesnutt, Booker T. Washington, Ralph Waldo Emerson, and Paul Laurence Dunbar. The articles are presented in chronological order, and each author's work is followed by a study guide. In addition to black Americans and American Indians, other minority groups such as Japanese, Chinese, Ethiopians, and Italians are explored. Includes a selected bibliography (reference books, anthologies, background, and articles in periodicals) and an index.

1864. ———, ed. *The William Stanley Braithwaite Reader*. Ann Arbor, Mich.: University of Michigan Press, 1972.

1865. Cain, George. *Blueschild Baby*. New York: McGraw–Hill, 1970. Reprint. New York: Ecco Press, 1987.

1866. Carn, John Benjamin. *Death and Duplicity*. Los Angeles: Holloway House Publishing Co., 1989.

1867. ———. *Stressed Out: A Novel*. Indianapolis: African Visions Small Press, 1988.

1868. ———. *Vietnam Blues*. Los Angeles: Holloway House Publishing Co., 1988.

1869. Cartey, Wilfred G. *Black Images*. New York: Teachers College Press, 1970.

Cartey "presents and analyzes some of the principal ways in which the black man has been portrayed in poetry, tracing his literary evolution from the image of slave to one of human distinction." One unusual quality of the book is Cartey's attempt to match the language and style of his analysis to the rhythm, feeling, and intention of the poetry being discussed. Topics include the derogative treatment of blacks in literature and history, Afro–Antillean poetry, Afro–Cuban poetry, and negritude. The book includes excerpts from the works of such varied writers as Nicolas Guillen, Arna Bontemps, Palis Matoe, and W. E. B. DuBois.

1870. Cartier, Xam W. *Be-Bop, Re-Bop*. New York: Ballantine Books, 1987.

1871. Casmier, Adam A., and Sally Souder,* eds. *Coming Together: Modern Stories by Black and White Americans*. Encino, Calif.: Dickenson Publishing Co., 1972.

1872.   Cassata,** Mary B., and Molefi Kete Asante. *Mass Communication: Principles and Practices.* New York: Macmillan Co., 1979.

The authors present critical insights into how communication creates, animates, and influences human societies. They discuss international news–gathering agencies, satellite systems, the relationship of minorities to the media, and regulatory agencies, as well as models and theories of mass communication. Unique to this volume is a chronology, within a historical perspective, of mass communication from the early fifteenth century to 1975, followed by a summary of significant events. A code of ethics and a glossary of terms are included in the appendixes.

1873.   ————, eds. *The Social Uses of Mass Communication.* Buffalo: Communication Research Center, State University of New York at Buffalo, 1977.

Growing out of a conference entitled "The Social Uses of Mass Communication," this collection of papers includes, in addition to an introduction by the authors, papers with such titles as "Institutional Forces and the Mass Media," "Cultural Aspects of Mass Media," "Woman as Tool: A Metaphor of Mass Media," "Mass Communicated Images and Racial Minorities," "Functional and Behavioristic Measures of the Mass Media," and "Communications Media and Attitudinal and Social Change." These papers provide insight into the dynamics of that technological marvel—mass media.

1874.   Cat,* Christopher, and Countee Cullen. *The Lost Zoo.* New York: Harper and Brothers, 1940. Reprint. Chicago: Follett Publishing Co., 1969.

These poems for the young, illustrated by Joseph Low, "explain why one will not find such animals as the Wakeupworld, the Squilililigee, the Sleepamitemore, and the Treasuretit in any zoo we know."

1875. ————. *My Lives and How I Lost Them.* Illustrated by Rainey Bennett.* New York: Harper and Brothers, 1942. Reprint. Chicago: Follett Publishing Co., 1971.

Now in his ninth life, a cat reminisces about adventures in the previous eight.

1876. Chase–Riboud, Barbara. *Echo of Lions: A Novel.* New York: William Morrow and Co., 1989.

This story relates the kidnapping, capture, and escape of Cinque, a well–to–do African rice planter. Along with adding fictionalized accounts of the political maneuvering that went on in the background, Chase–Riboud narrates on Cinque's misguided voyage, his capture off Long Island, and various trials.

1877. Chesley, Donald. *Black Vendetta.* Los Angeles: Holloway House Publishing Co., 1982.

Charlie Anderson, a Vietnam veteran, had only one reason to return to Washington after his discharge from the Army: to search for his lost love, Joyce. Her abrupt disappearance had first hurt and puzzled, then angered him. He was determined to find her, no matter what the cost, and his search led him through the streets of hell, an underworld of blackmail, kidnapping, drugs, and prostitution.

1878. ————. *The Marrow of Tradition.* 1901. Reprint. Ann Arbor: University of Michigan Press, 1969.

A novel of racial conflict that results in the Wilmington race riot of 1898.

1879. Childress, Alice, ed. *Black Scenes.* Garden City, N.Y.: Doubleday and Co., 1971.

Childress provides scenes from plays by black writers dealing with the black experience.

1880. Christian, Barbara. *Black Feminist Criticism: Perspectives on Black Women Writers*. Elmsford, N.Y.: Pergamon Press, 1985.

1881. ———. *Black Women Novelists: The Development of a Tradition, 1892–1976*. Westport, Conn.: Greenwood Press, 1980.

1882. Church, Vivian. *Colors Around Me*. Illustrated by Sherman Beck. Chicago: Afro-Am Publishing Co., 1971.

Explains the meaning of the words *Black, Negro,* and *Afro-American* and describes the varied hues a black child can be.

1883. Clarke, John Henrik, ed. *American Negro Short Stories*. 1st ed. New York: Hill and Wang, 1966.

Stories and excerpts from novels by authors ranging from DuBois to Baldwin. Much of this writing deals with civil rights and the yearning for identity and freedom.

1884. Clay, Stanley Bennett. *Diva*. Los Angeles: Holloway House Publishing Co., 1988.

This story is about Ida Lake, known as "The Diva" to her millions of fans when she reigned as Hollywood's black singing sensation of the 1940s. After the suspicious deaths of the husband she adored and the daughter she worshipped, and victimized by the Red Scare of the 1950s, Ida took refuge abroad. Two decades later, she is cajoled into a comeback as the star of a Broadway musical. But tragedy shadows Ida Lake once again as a mysterious web of intrigue, sex scandal, and murder envelops the show.

1885. Clifton, Lucille. *Good News About Earth: New Poems*. 1st ed. New York: Random House, 1972.

1886. ———. *Next: New Poems*. Brockport, N.Y.: BOA Editions, 1987. Distributed by Bookslinger.

1887. ———. *An Ordinary Woman.* New York: Random House, 1974.

1888. ———. *Two-Headed Woman.* Amherst: University of Massachusetts Press, 1980.

1889. Clifton, Lucille, Amma Khalil, and Audre Lorde, eds. *Hoo-doo 5, Special Women's Issue.* DeRidder, La.: Energy BlackSouth Press, 1976.

1890. Cobb, Martha Kendrick. *Harlem, Haiti, and Havana: A Comparative Critical Study of Langston Hughes, Jacques Roumain, Nicolas Guillen.* Washington, D.C.: Three Continents Press, 1979.

Cobb points to the inherent similarities and relatedness of the philosophical viewpoints of Hughes, Roumain, and Guillen, as articulated in their literature. She examines folk songs and tales, forms of African heritage, as tenets of an enduring black spirit that refuses to be totally imprisoned by the larger society. She then presents a comparative literary inquiry into these forms that provide an awareness of black traditions and characterize black literature. The book constitutes a valuable source, demonstrating the use of the arts (specifically poetry) as a vehicle for black cultural communication and understanding, despite the language differences—English, French, and Spanish—of the poets. The selective bibliography contains biographies, critiques, and the histories of the three poets.

1891. Cogdell, Roy Thomas, and K. Sitaram.** *Foundations of Intercultural Communication.* Columbus, Ohio: Charles E. Merrill Co., 1976.

This interesting book about intercultural communication represents a new direction in the art and process of human interaction. The authors compare and contrast the cultures of Japan, China, India, Africa, and other nations, as well as the minority groups within the United States. They evaluate the cultural contributions of ethnic groups to American society.

1892. Colter, Cyrus. *The Amoralists & Other Tales: Collected Stories.* New York: Thunder's Mouth Press, 1988.

1893. ————. *The Beach Umbrella.* Iowa City: University of Iowa Press, 1970.

1894. ————. *A Chocolate Soldier: A Novel.* New York: Thunder's Mouth Press, 1988.

1895. ————. *The Hippodrome: A Novel.* Chicago: Swallow Press, 1973.

1896. ————. *Night Studies.* Chicago: Swallow Press, 1979.

1897. ————. *The Rivers of Eros.* Chicago: Swallow Press, 1972.

1898. Cook, Mercer. *Five French Negro Authors.* Washington, D.C.: Associated Publishers, 1943.

1899. Cook, Mercer, and Stephen E. Henderson. *The Militant Black Writer in Africa and the United States.* Madison: University of Wisconsin Press, 1969.

Expanded versions of two papers delivered at a symposium at the University of Wisconsin in Madison, August 8-9, 1968.

1900. Coombs, Orde, comp. *We Speak as Liberators: Young Black Poets; An Anthology.* New York: Dodd, Mead and Co., 1970.

1901. ————, comp. *What We Must See: Young Black Storytellers: An Anthology.* New York: Dodd, Mead and Co., 1971.

This work includes "Rites Fraternal," by J. Barber; "Second Line/Cutting the Body Loose," by V. Ferdinand; "Etta's Mind," by L. Gant; "Cheesy, Baby!" by R. E. Holmes; "The Blue of Madness," by A. Kemp; "Waiting for Her Train," by A. M. Lee, among others.

1902. Cortez, Jayne. *Coagulations: New and Selected Poems.* New York: Thunder's Mouth Press, 1984.

1903. ———. *Firespitter.* New York: Bola Press, 1982.

1904. ———. *Mouth on Paper.* New York: Bola Press, 1977.

1905. ———. *Scarifications.* 2d ed. New York: Bola Press, 1978.

1906. Cosby, Bill. *Time Flies.* 1st ed. Garden City, N.Y.: Doubleday and Co., 1987.

In this work, Cosby—an actor, teacher, and father of five—talks about aging and tries to face approaching fifty years of age without flinching.

1907. Costello, Bagz. *Where Have All the Little Girls Gone?* Los Angeles: Holloway House Publishing Co., 1987.

1908. Crawford, Samuel D., and Robert H. Bentley.** *Black Language Reader.* Glenview, Ill.: Scott, Foresman and Co., 1973.

This is a collection of essays on the language of black people in America. Their language is viewed within the context of the total black experience. The various dialects of black language are examined as well to point out the profound differences between them and standard or "white" English. The essays are based on both personal experience and case studies.

1909. Cromwell,* Otelia, Lorenzo Dow Turner, and Eva B. Dykes,* eds. *Readings from Negro Authors, for Schools and Colleges, with a Bibliography of Negro Literature.* New York: Harcourt Brace Jovanovich, 1931.

This collection is the result of the editors' commitment to their students: "To teach them to read thoughtfully and with appreciation, to form in them a taste for good reading, and to teach them how to find books that are worthwhile." These classic works of black authors are divided into five sections—poetry, stories, one–act plays, essays, and public addresses—with an introduction to each section. Suggestions for study, biographical sketches, a bibliography, and an index of authors and titles are included.

1910.   Cullen, Countee. *The Black Christ & Other Poems.* New York: Harper and Brothers, 1929.

1911.   ————. *Color.* New York: Harper and Brothers, 1925. Reprint. New York: Arno Press, 1969.

This book, Cullen's first collection of poems, won the Harmon Foundation's Award for literature, awarded by the NAACP for "distinguished achievement in literature by a Negro."

1912.   ————. *Copper Sun.* New York: Harper and Brothers, 1927.

1913.   ————. *The Medea and Some Poems.* New York: Harper and Brothers, 1935.

1914.   ————. *On These I Stand: An Anthology of the Best Poems of Countee Cullen.* New York: Harper and Brothers, 1947.

1915.   ————. *One Way to Heaven.* New York: Harper and Brothers, 1932. Reprint. New York: AMS Press, 1975.

1916.   ————, ed. *Caroling Dusk: An Anthology of Verse by Negro Poets.* New York: Harper and Brothers, 1927. Reprint. New York: Harper and Row, 1974.

"The biographical notices carried with these poems have been written by the poets themselves save in three cases."

1917.   Curry, Gladys J., ed. *Viewpoints from Black America.* Englewood Cliffs, N.J.: Prentice–Hall, 1979.

This anthology of prose writings by black writers of diverse backgrounds includes vital topics of American life and culture, such as education, assimilation, literature and language, the arts, religion, and politics. Through this variety in content, the author hopes to acquaint her readers with the diverse thinking of blacks over the past few years.

1918. Davis, Arthur Paul. *From the Dark Tower: Afro-American Writers 1900 to 1960.* Washington, D.C.: Howard University Press, 1974.

Designed to be an aid to students of Afro-American literature, this book is divided into two parts: "The New Negro Renaissance (1900-1940)" and "Towards the Mainstream (1940-1960)." The first part includes such notable authors as Langston Hughes, Alain LeRoy Locke, James Weldon Johnson, and Sterling A. Brown. Richard Wright, James Baldwin, and Gwendolyn Brooks are some of the reputable writers in the second part. The book also includes "A Selective Bibliography," which contains works by and about black writers.

1919. Davis, Arthur Paul, and J. Saunders Redding, comps. *Cavalcade: Negro American Writers from 1760 to the Present.* Boston: Houghton Mifflin Co., 1971.

This two volume edition of *Cavalcade*, the classic anthology of Afro-American writings, goes beyond the period of the original volume (1760 to 1954) to include writers of the sixties, seventies, and eighties (1954 to the present). Spanning the pioneer writers, the freedom fighters, the New Negro Renaissance and beyond, it includes poems, essays, short stories, and excerpts from novels, autobiographies, and plays.

1920. Davis, Arthur Paul, and Michael W. Peplow,* eds. *The New Negro Renaissance: An Anthology.* New York: Holt, Rinehart and Winston, 1975.

1921. Davis, Charles Twitchell. *Black Is the Color of the Cosmos: Essays on Afro-American Literature and Culture, 1942-1981.* Edited by Henry Louis Gates, Jr. New York: Garland Publishing, Inc., 1982. Reprint. Washington, D.C.: Howard University Press, 1989.

1922. Davis, George. *Coming Home.* New York: Random House, 1972. Reprint. Washington, D.C.: Howard University Press, 1984.

Three Air Force pilots, two black and one white, and the effect of war on their lives are at the center of the novel *Coming Home.* It is a book about lust, passion, greed, and racism. This novel is rich in its treatment of the impact of the Indo–Chinese conflict (1961–1975), upon which the very seam of man's capacity to love, trust and care. The strains of war, the blind ambitions, and lust all become looming figures in the lives of three men whose friendship unravels as the novel unfolds.

1923. Davis, Marianna White. *Beyond the Basics: A Rhetoric Reader.* 1st ed. Columbia, S.C.: ABC Development Corporation, 1975.

A textbook of freshman English, this book contains several examples of what is considered good writing, together with exercises in interpreting and selecting passages. Writing assignments at the end of the book are designed to test students' reading and writing skills. This is a helpful book to be used by both students and teachers of English.

1924. ———. *Transformational Grammar and Written Sentences.* New York: Mouton and Company, 1973.

This is a study involving the direct instruction of one hundred concept lessons of transformational generative grammar that the researcher designed for fifty students in experimental groups. This study has implications for linguistic theory of composition in elementary and secondary schools, and for the teaching of students with inhibited language habits.

1925. Davis, Marianna White, and Albert Berrian. *Strategies for Language Acquisition.* Washington, D.C.: Institute for Services to Education, 1977.

1926. Davis, Nolan. *Ain't Got Time to Die.* Los Angeles: Holloway House Publishing Co., 1971.

1927. Davis, Thulani. *Playing the Changes.* Middletown, Conn.: Wesleyan University Press, 1985. Distributed by Harper and Row, 1985.

1928. DeCarava, Roy, and Langston Hughes. *The Sweet Flypaper of Life.* New York: Hill and Wang, 1955. Reprint. Washington, D.C.: Howard University Press, 1984.

First published in 1955, this volume of photography by DeCarava and prose by Hughes weaves a poignant story of Sister Mary Bradley's ordinary life in Harlem.

1929. DeCosta-Willis, Miriam, and Fannie Mitchell Delk, eds. *Homespun Images: An Anthology of Black Memphis Writers and Artists.* Memphis, Tenn.: LeMoyne-Owen College, 1989.

1930. DeCoy, Robert H. *Cold Black Preach.* Los Angeles: Holloway House Publishing Co., 1971.

1931. Dee, Ruby. *My One Good Nerve: Rhythm, Rhymes, Reasons.* Chicago: Third World Press, 1986.

A collection of "bits, pieces, poems and short stories" by the multitalented Ruby Dee, with an introduction by Ossie Davis.

1932. Delany, Samuel R. *Babel-17.* New York: Ace Books, 1966.

1933. ————. *The Ballad of Beta-2.* New York: Ace Books, 1965.

1934. ————. *City of a Thousand Suns.* New York: Ace Books, 1965.

1935. ————. *Empire Star.* New York: Ace Books, 1966.

1936. Dillard, Joey Lee. *Black English: Its History and Usage in the United States.* New York: Random House, 1972.

This is an interesting attempt to investigate the important ways in which black English differs from other varieties of

American English. Dillard maintains that differences from other English dialects are traceable to normal historical factors, specifically to language–contact phenomena associated with the West African slave trade and with European maritime expansion in general, and to survivals from West African languages. After examining the unique black English language patterns and their structure and historical origins, Dillard investigates their impact on today's established academic system.

1937.   Dillard, John Milton, and Robert R. Reilly,** eds. *Systematic Interviewing: Communication Skills for Professional Effectiveness.* Columbus, Ohio: Charles E. Merrill Co., 1988.

Through a combination of narratives, case studies, examples, and illustrations, this text examines theories and techniques that are fundamental to all interviewing. It then shows how specific techniques apply to particular groups of individuals, settings, and issues. An appendix contains statements of ethical principles from representative professional organizations, including the NASW, the AACD, and the APA.

1938.   Dove, Rita. *Fifth Sunday: Stories.* 1st ed. Lexington: University of Kentucky, 1985.

1939.   ———. *Grace Notes: Poems.* 1st ed. New York: W. W. Norton and Co., 1989.

1940.   ———. *Museum: Poems.* 1st ed. Pittsburgh: Carnegie–Mellon University Press, 1983.

1941.   ———. *Thomas and Beulah: Poems.* 1st ed. Pittsburgh: Carnegie–Mellon University Press, 1986.

1942.   ———. *The Yellow House on the Corner: Poems.* 2d ed. Pittsburgh: Carnegie–Mellon University Press, 1989.

1943.   DuBois, W. E. B. *Mansart Builds a School.* Book 2, *The Black Flame.* New York: Mainstream Publishers, 1959. Reprint. Millwood, N.Y.: Kraus–Thomson Organization, 1976.

1944. ————. *The Ordeal of Mansart.* Book 1, *The Black Flame.* New York: Mainstream Publishers, 1957. Reprint. Millwood, N.Y.: Kraus–Thomson Organization, 1976.

1945. ————. *Worlds of Color.* Book 3, *The Black Flame.* New York: Mainstream Publishers, 1961. Reprint. Millwood, N.Y.: Kraus–Thomson Organization, 1976.

1946. Duke, Romare [Robert Fleming]. *Hot Snake Nights.* Los Angeles: Holloway House, 1985.

1947. Dumas, Glenda. *The Rootworker: A Novel.* Los Angeles: Holloway House Publishing Co., 1983.

1948. Dumas, Henry. *Play Ebony: Play Ivory.* Edited by Eugene B. Redmond.* New York: Random House, 1974.

This work contains posthumously published poems that reveal the life of Henry Dumas (1934–1968).

1949. ————. *Poetry for My People.* Edited by Hale Chatfield* and Eugene B. Redmond.* Carbondale: Southern Illinois University Press, 1971.

1950. Dunbar, Paul Laurence. *The Complete Poems of Paul Laurence Dunbar.* 1913. Reprint. New York: Dodd, Mead and Co., 1980.

1951. ————. *Candle-Lightin' Time.* Illustrated with photos by Hampton Institute Camera Club and decorations by Margaret Armstrong.* New York: Dodd, Mead, 1901. Reprint. New York: AMS Press, 1972.

1952. ————. *Howdy, Honey, Howdy.* Illustrated with photos by Leigh Richmond Miner.* New York: Dodd, Mead, 1905. Reprint. New York: AMS Press, 1972.

1953.   ————. *I Greet the Dawn: Poems.* Selected, illustrated, and with an introduction by Ashley Bryan. 1st ed. New York: Atheneum Publishers, 1978.

1954.   ————. *The Life and Works of Paul Laurence Dunbar.* Naperville, Ill.: J. L. Nichols and Co., 1907.

1955.   ————. *The Love of Landry.* New York: Dodd, Mead and Co., 1900. Reprint. Bound Brook, N.J.: Literature House, 1970.

A romantic novel in which Mildred Osbourne travels to the West and falls in love with a cowboy.

1956.   ————. *Lyrics of Love and Laughter.* New York: Dodd, Mead and Co., 1907.

1957.   ————. *Lyrics of Lowly Life.* New York: Dodd, Mead and Co., 1896. Reprint. Secaucus, N.J.: Citadel Press, 1984.

1958.   ————. *Lyrics of the Hearthside.* New York: Dodd, Mead and Co., 1899. Reprint. New York: AMS Press, 1972.

1959.   ————. *The Paul Laurence Dunbar Reader: A Selection of the Best of Paul Laurence Dunbar's Poetry and Prose.* New York: Dodd, Mead and Co., 1975.

1960.   ————. *Poems of Cabin and Fields.* New York: Dodd, Mead and Co., 1899. Reprint. New York: AMS Press, 1972.

1961.   ————. *The Strength of Gideon and Other Stories.* Illustrated by E. W. Kemble.* New York: Dodd, Mead and Co., 1900. Reprint. New York: Arno Press, 1969.

Written by one of the most popular black poets of the early twentieth century, this collection of short stories represents the broad scope of Dunbar's view. Some are typical plantation stories designed to promote blacks and others are humorous anecdotes, but most are stories of social criticism. A new preface by Darwin T. Turner is included.

1962. ————. *When Malindy Sings.* Illustrated with photos by the Hampton Institute Camera Club and decorations by Margaret Armstrong. New York: Dodd, Mead, 1903. Reprint. New York: AMS Press, 1972.

1963. Dunham, Katherine. *Kasamance: A Fantasy.* Illustrated by Bennie Arrington* after original drawings by John Pratt.* New York: Odarkai Books, 1974.

1964. Durr,* William K., Vivian O. Windley, and Kay S. Earnhardt,* comps. *Impressions.* Boston: Houghton Mifflin Co., 1976.

This book attempts to make English an exciting and meaningful subject for sixth-grade students. It contains short stories, poems, articles, skill lessons, jokes, and book lists. The wide range of authors reflects an earnest attempt by the authors to include as many of the subcultures of America, Europe, and Africa as possible. The result is not only a book that builds better English skills, but also one that offers a lot of cultural information about people around the world. Also included are bibliographical data on the various authors, pictures, a glossary, and a pronunciation key.

1965. Durr,* William K., Vivian O. Windley, and Anne A. McCourt,* comps. *Medley.* Boston: Houghton Mifflin Co., 1976.

This is a delightful collection of short stories and poems for the fourth-grade reader. Each story reflects cultures of the many varied and exciting ethnic groups that make up America. In addition to the short stories and poems, there are lessons that cover such useful skills as recognizing important story elements and distinguishing between fact and opinion. A glossary is also included, together with a pronunciation key. The book is beautifully illustrated and should appeal to young readers.

1966. Durr,* William Kirtley, Vivian O. Windley, Anne A. McCourt.* *Teacher's Guide for Medley.* Boston: Houghton Mifflin Co., 1979.

1967.   Edwards, Junius. *If We Must Die.* Garden City, N.Y.: Doubleday and Co., 1963. Reprint. Washington, D.C.: Howard University Press, 1985.

Originally published in 1963, this book chronicles a day in the life of a young black man who, recently home from the war, attempts to carry out his mother's wish for him to register and vote. Through the degradation of one young black man, this novel speaks to the struggle for dignity in a world dominated by white brutality and inhumanity.

1968.   Elder, Lonne, III. *Ceremonies in Dark Old Men.* New York: Farrar, Straus and Giroux, 1969.

1969.   Ellison, Ralph. *Going to the Territory: The American Dream and the Black Artist.* 1st ed. New York: Random House, 1986.

In this collection of sixteen essays, Ellison continues his analysis of American culture. For him American culture is a vibrant melting pot, and he believes his role as a novelist/critic, is to identify the contributions of Afro–Americans to this American melange. Generally, the essays concentrate on unraveling the complex skein of American interactions to find the black threads. Some of the sixteen essays are adapted from lectures and interviews or previously published essays on literature and culture.

1970.   ———. *The Invisible Man.* New York: Signet Books, 1947. Reprint. New York: Vintage Books, 1972.

In this story, which is considered a classic, the protagonist, a black man, gropes for meaning, for a way of becoming visible. This searing record of a black man's journey through contemporary America won Ellison the National Book Award.

1971.   ———. *Shadow and Act.* New York: Random House, 1964.

Ellison's essays deal with the themes of literature and folklore, Afro–American musical expression (with emphasis on jazz and the blues), and the relationship between the Afro-American subculture and North America as a whole.

1972. Emecheta, Buchi. *Adah's Story: A Novel.* London: Allison and Busby, 1983.

1973. ————. *The Bride Price: A Novel.* New York: George Braziller, 1976. Reprint. Oxford: Oxford University Press, 1989.

1974. ————. *Destination Biafra: A Novel.* London: Allison and Busby, 1982. Distributed by Schocken Books.

1975. ————. *Double Yoke.* 1st ed. New York: George Braziller, 1983.

1976. ————. *The Joys of Motherhood: A Novel.* 1st ed. New York: George Braziller, 1979.

1977. ————. *A Kind of Marriage.* London: Macmillan and Co., 1986.

1978. ————. *Rape of Shavi.* New York: George Braziller, 1985.

1979. ————. *Second-Class Citizen.* London: Allison and Busby, 1974. Reprint. New York: George Braziller, 1983.

1980. ————. *The Slave Girl: A Novel.* 1977. Reprint. New York: George Braziller, 1980.

1981. Evans, Mari. *I Am a Black Woman.* New York: William Morrow and Co., 1970.

This book contains fifty poems written by Evans. Many originally appeared in such magazines and anthologies as *The Negro Digest; American Negro Poetry*, edited by Arna Bontemps; and *Black Voices*, edited by Abraham Chapman. The title poem, "I Am a Black Woman," originally appeared in *The Negro Digest.* Evans's works include such poems as "If There Be

Sorrow," "The Silver Cell," "I Can No Longer Sing," "In the Wake of My Departed," "Escape," and "The Great Civil Rights Law."

1982.   ———, ed. *Black Women Writers (1950–1980): A Critical Evaluation.* 1st ed. Garden City, N.Y.: Anchor Press/Doubleday and Co., 1984.

This source book describes the aspirations and methodology of fifteen leaders of the new wave of black literature. Edited by Mari Evans, it contains an autobiographical statement from each writer and critical analyses of styles and themes. Among the women cited are Toni Cade Bambara, Toni Morrison, Gwendolyn Brooks, Sonia Sanchez, Alice Walker, Margaret Walker, and Maya Angelou.

1983.   ———, ed. *Black Women Writers: Arguments and Interviews.* 1st ed. London: Pluto Press, 1984.

1984.   Faggett, Harry Lee. *Lines to a Little Lady: From Someone Who Begs to Be Remembered.* 2d ed. Ardmore, Pa.: Dorrance and Company, 1977. Reprint. Orangeburg: Communications Center, South Carolina State College, 1987.

1985.   Faggett, Harry Lee, and Nick Aaron Ford, eds. *Best Short Stories by Afro–American Writers, 1925–1950.* Boston: Meador Press, 1950. Reprint. Millwood, N.Y.: Kraus Reprint Co., 1977.

Covering the time span between 1925 and 1950, this book contains a collection of short stories taken from the Afro–American newspapers. This book is divided into five parts: "Of Human Relations," "Of Crime and Punishment," "Of Loyalty and Patriotism," "Of Love and Romance," and "Of Sunshine and Shadow." Some of the stories included in the first part are "Let the Church Roll On," by Nick Aaron Ford; "The Red Hat," by Martha Brown; and "I Shall Not Be Moved," by Ollie Stewart.

1986. Fairbairn, Ann. *That Man Cartwright: A Novel*. New York: Crown Publishers, 1970.

1987. Farmer, Marjorie, ed. *Consensus and Dissent: Teaching English Past, Present, and Future*. Urbana, Ill.: National Council of Teachers of English, 1986.

1988. Ferguson, Ira Lunan. *The Biography of G. Wash Carter, White: Life Story of a Mississippi Peckerwood, Whose Short Circuit Logic Kept Him Fantastically Embroiled*. San Francisco: Lunan–Ferguson Library, 1969.

1989. Finney, Nikky. *On Wings Made of Gauze*. New York: William Morrow and Co., 1985.

1990. Fisher, Rudolph. *The Walls of Jericho*. New York: Alfred A. Knopf, 1928. Reprint. New York: Arno Press, 1969.

In this novel the author, widely published throughout the twenties, writes about Harlem life—the black folk life, the uncomprehending white philanthropist, the honest and put–upon black, as well as the educated avant–garde black—during the Harlem Renaissance. He includes "An Introduction to Contemporary Harlemese."

1991. Fleming, Mickey C. *About Courage*. Los Angeles: Holloway House Publishing Co., 1989.

1992. Flemns,* Delois M., and Rita Dandridge Simons. *Relevant Expository Techniques and Programmed Grammar*. Dubuque, Iowa: Kendall/Hunt Publishing Co., 1971.

1993. Foster, Frances Smith. *Witnessing Slavery: The Development of the Ante–bellum Slave Narratives*. Westport, Conn.: Greenwood Press, 1979.

1994. Franklin, J. E. *Black Girl: From Genesis to Revelations*. Washington, D.C.: Howard University Press, 1977.

This volume contains a lengthy commentary on the way in which *Black Girl*, a now famous play, was conceived and on the experiences of a young writer's first encounter with New York. The general reader, as well as those involved in the arts, will gain insights into what goes on behind the scenes in the theater, television, and film industries.

1995. Fuller, Charles. *A Soldier's Play: A Play.* 1st ed. New York: Hill and Wang, 1982.

1996. Gaines, Ernest J. *A Gathering of Old Men.* 1st ed. New York: Alfred A. Knopf, 1983.

In his new novel, Gaines uses a murder on a farm to explore changing race relations in the South. The novel begins as Beau Boutan, a white Cajun farmer, is shot to death on a Louisiana farm. Candy Marshall, the headstrong white overseer, confesses to the murder; so do a dozen aged black farmers. In questioning the suspects, Maples, the Old South sheriff, discovers suddenly that he can no longer physically intimidate the blacks for whom a whole lifetime of oppression has burst forth in a final act of courage and defiance. The violent climax of this book symbolizes the struggle between two cultures for possession of the New South.

1997. ————. *Of Love and Dust.* New York: Dial Press, 1967. Reprint. New York: W. W. Norton and Co., 1979.

1998. Galloway, Phyllis Hyacinth. *Mechanics and Conventions in Formal Writing.* Landover, Md.: Bond Publishing Co., 1985.

Designed to be used with four cassettes, this book is concerned only with formal writing. It is not concerned with creative writing nor with the stimulation of ideas. It is based on remediation through the application of established traditions and grammar rules. Includes exercises and an index.

1999. Gandy, Oscar H., Jr. *Beyond Agenda Setting: Information Subsidies and Public Policy.* Norwood, N.J.: Ablex Publishing Corp., 1982.

This book concerns sources and their use by journalists and other gatekeepers, and also explains how to deliver information subsidies to participants in the policy process. It enumerates how sources enter into an exchange of values with journalists: it states that they reduce the cost of news work to increase their control over news content. It focuses primarily on the subsidy or cost-reduction aspects of the production of influence through information.

2000. ————, ed. *Communications: A Key to Economic and Political Change.* Washington, D.C.: Howard University Center for Communications Research, 1987.

2001. Gandy, Oscar H., Jr., Paul Espinosa,** and Janusz A. Ordover,** eds. *Proceedings from the Tenth Annual Telecommunications Policy Research Conference.* Norwood, N.J.: ABLEX Publishing Corp., 1982.

These proceedings, which grew out of a conference held in Annapolis, Maryland, examine some important issues in telecommunications policy. In the three plenary sessions and eighteen different panels, conferees focus their discussions on broadcasting, cable, common carrier regulation, and the Third World nations.

2002. Gates, Henry Louis, Jr. *Figures in Black: Words, Signs, and the "Racial" Self.* Fair Lawn, N.J.: Oxford University Press, 1986.

2003. ————. *The Signifying Monkey: A Theory of Afro-American Literary Criticism.* Fair Lawn, N.J.: Oxford University Press, 1988.

2004. ————, ed. *"Race," Writing, and Difference.* Chicago: University of Chicago Press, 1985.

This work addresses the question, "What importance does 'race' have as a meaningful category in the study of literature and the shaping of critical theory?" The papers in this volume reveal a variety of critical approaches through which one may discuss the complex interplay among race, writing, and difference. The papers illustrate that neither literature nor its critical theories are color-blind, neutral, apolitical, or universal. The book includes illustrations, notes, and an index.

2005. Gayle, Addison, Jr. *Black Expression: Essays by and About Black Americans in the Creative Arts.* New York: Weybright and Talley, 1969.

2006. ————. *Claude McKay: The Black Poet at War.* 1st ed. Detroit: Broadside Press, 1972.

Included in this critique of McKay's poetry are useful biographical data on the Jamaican poet himself. Poems discussed in the book are "Flame-Heart," "Harlem Shadows," "To the White Friends," and "If We Must Die."

2007. ————. *The Way of the New World: The Black Novel in America.* 1st ed. Garden City, N.Y.: Anchor Press, 1975.

2008. ————, ed. *Bondage, Freedom and Beyond: The Prose of Black Americans.* Garden City, N.Y.: Zenith Books, 1971.

Gayle illustrates the richness and variety of black prose, using essays and newspaper and magazine articles written by historic and contemporary black men and women. Prose samples from three eras—slavery, the Civil War and Reconstruction, and the twentieth century—are placed in historical perspective. Among the contributing authors are Josephine Brown, Frederick Douglass, Marcus Garvey, Ralph Ellison, Malcolm X, and Martin Luther King, Jr. The book contains bibliographical data for each contributing author and a useful index.

2009. Gibson, Donald B. *The Fiction of Stephen Crane.* Carbondale: Southern Illinois University Press, 1968.

2010. ————. *The Politics of Literary Expression: A Study of Major Black Writers.* Westport, Conn.: Greenwood Press, 1981.

2011. ————. *The Red Badge of Courage: Redefining the Hero.* Boston: Twayne Publishers, 1988.

2012. ————, ed. *Five Black Writers: Essays on Wright, Ellison, Baldwin, Hughes, and Le Roi Jones.* New York: New York University Press, 1970.

2013. ————, ed. *Modern Black Poets: A Collection of Critical Essays.* Englewood Cliffs, N.J.: Prentice–Hall, 1973.

2014. Gibson, Donald B., and Carol Anselment,** eds. *Black and White: Stories of American Life.* New York: Washington Square Press, 1971.

2015. Gilmer, J. Lance. *Hell Has No Exit.* Los Angeles: Holloway House Publishing Co., 1976.

2016. ————. *Hell Is Forever.* Los Angeles: Holloway House Publishing Co., 1977.

2017. Giovanni, Nikki. *Black Feeling, Black Talk.* 3d ed. Detroit: Broadside Press, 1970.

2018. ————. *Black Feeling, Black Talk, Black Judgement.* New York: William Morrow and Co., 1970.

2019. ————. *Black Judgement.* Detroit: Broadside Press, 1968.

2020. ————. *Cotton Candy on a Rainy Day: Poems.* New York: William Morrow and Co., 1978.

2021. ————. *My House: Poems.* 1972. Reprint. New York: Morrow Quill Paperbacks, 1983.

2022. ————. *Night Comes Softly: An Anthology of Black Female Voices.* Newark, N.J.: Medic Press, 1970.

2023.   ————. *Recreation.* 1970. Reprint. Detroit: Broadside Press, 1973.

2024.   ————. *Sacred Cows and Other Edibles.* 1st ed. New York: William Morrow and Co., 1988.

Topics in this collection of articles that have been previously published in various publications—*Essence, Boston Globe, USA Today*—include tennis, termites, black political leaders, the profession of writing, game shows, odes to fellow writers, the proper celebration of holidays, and literary politics.

2025.   ————. *Those Who Ride the Night Winds.* New York: William Morrow and Co., 1983.

2026.   ————. *Vacation Time: Poems for Children.* 1st ed. New York: William Morrow and Co., 1980.

Includes twenty–two poems on a variety of topics. Illustrated by Marisabina Russo.

2027.   ————. *The Women and the Men.* New York: William Morrow and Co., 1975.

2028.   Giovanni, Nikki, and Margaret Walker. *A Poetic Equation: Conversations Between Nikki Giovanni and Margaret Walker.* Rev. ed. Washington, D.C.: Howard University Press, 1983.

This book presents an intense conversation between two significant literary figures—Nikki Giovanni and Margaret Walker. As these two women cover a wide spectrum of issues—Vietnam, racial struggle, the sexes, violence, literature—their commitments, philosophies, and attitudes ring forth, often divergent. Highly opinionated, they compare the sixties, which shaped Giovanni's sensibilities, with the thirties and forties, which molded Walker's thinking. In this revised edition, new material projects the uninhibited dialogue into the eighties and beyond.

2029. Gober, Dom [Joseph Nazel]. *Black Cop.* Los Angeles: Holloway House Publishing Co., 1974.

2030. Goines, Donald [Al C. Clark, pseud.]. *Black Gangster.* Los Angeles: Holloway House Publishing Co., 1977.

2031. ———. *Black Girl Lost.* Los Angeles: Holloway House Publishing Co., 1973.

2032. ———. *Crime Partners.* Los Angeles: Holloway House Publishing Co., 1974.

2033. ———. *Cry Revenge.* Los Angeles: Holloway House Publishing Co., 1974.

2034. ———. *Daddy Cool.* Los Angeles: Holloway House Publishing Co., 1974.

2035. ———. *Death List.* Los Angeles: Holloway House Publishing Co., 1974.

2036. ———. *Dopefiend.* Los Angeles: Holloway House Publishing Co., 1971.

2037. ———. *Eldorado Red.* Los Angeles: Holloway House Publishing Co., 1974.

2038. ———. *Inner City Hoodlum.* Los Angeles: Holloway House Publishing Co., 1975.

2039. ———. *Kenyatta's Escape.* Los Angeles: Holloway House Publishing Co., 1974.

2040. ———. *Kenyatta's Last Hit.* Los Angeles: Holloway House Publishing Co., 1975.

2041. ———. *Never Die Alone.* Los Angeles: Holloway House Publishing Co., 1974.

2042.   ————. *Street Players.* Los Angeles: Holloway House Publishing Co., 1973.

2043.   ————. *Swamp Man.* Los Angeles: Holloway House Publishing Co., 1974.

2044.   ————. *White Man's Justice: Black Man's Grief.* Los Angeles: Holloway House Publishing Co., 1973.

2045.   ————. *Whoreson: The Story of a Ghetto Pimp.* Los Angeles: Holloway House Publishing Co., 1972.

2046.   Golden, Marita. *A Woman's Place.* Garden City, N.Y.: Doubleday and Co., 1986.

2047.   Goodwin, Bennie Eugene. *Beside Still Waters.* Pittsburgh: Williams Press, 1973.

2048.   Gordon, Ethel. *The Chaperone.* New York: Coward McCann and Geoghegan, 1973. Reprint. New York: Dell Publishing Co., 1974.

2049.   Goss, Clay. *Homecookin': Five Plays.* Washington, D.C.: Howard University Press, 1974.

These five plays—*Oursides, Andrew, Homecookin', Of Being Hit,* and *Mars: Monument to the Last Black Eunuch*—are part of the cycle the author calls Homecookin'. The plays dramatize the lives of black people who try to transcend their limited environments.

2050.   Graham, Maryemma, ed. *Complete Poems of Frances E. W. Harper.* New York: Oxford University Press, 1988.

2051.   Grant, J. Jason. *Bitch.* Los Angeles: Holloway House Publishing Co., 1979.

2052.   ————. *Coal.* Los Angeles: Holloway House Publishing Co., 1978.

2053. Green, Joseph E. *Pseudo Cool.* Los Angeles: Holloway House Publishing Co., 1988.

This novel is about five black seniors at a prestigious California university. Each has got a secret: one sells herself to pay the expensive tuition; one drinks heavily and sleeps with white girls to deny his blackness; another is gay and living in the closet; and two believe they were responsible for a friend's death. They discover that what's important is not always who you are, but who you appear to be.

2054. Green, Robert W. *The Ebony Tree and the Spirit of Christmas.* Illustrated by Al Kaiser.* 1st ed. Hicksville, N.Y.: Exposition Press, 1975.

In this story, a tiny ebony tree seed from faraway Africa and a small black boy find each other on a ship bound for a new land. The little boy keeps the seed and in time finds a place to plant and nurture it—on a Christmas tree plantation.

2055. Gregory, Dick. *From the Back of the Bus.* Edited by Bob Orden.* Photographs by Jerry Yulsman.* New York: E. P. Dutton, 1962. Reprint. New York: Avon Books, 1966.

Afro–Americans, segregation, anecdotes, facetiae, satire, etc. With an introduction by Hugh M. Hefner.**

2056. ————. *What's Happening?* 1st ed. New York: E. P. Dutton, 1965.

2057. Gregory, Dick, and James R. McGraw.* *Up from Nigger.* New York: Stein and Day, 1976.

2058. Haley, Alex. *A Different Kind of Christmas.* 1st ed. New York: Doubleday and Co., 1988.

For readers of all ages, this book is a story about a young southerner who becomes an agent for the underground railroad and helps mastermind the escape of slaves from his father's plantation on Christmas Eve.

2059. Hall, William S., and Roy O. Freedle.* *Culture and Language: The Black American Experience.* New York: Halsted Press, 1975.

This book interprets black American language in terms of interacting cultural forces, self–concept, and intellectual functioning. The black American culture is treated as a subculture of the larger "wholistic" American culture.

2060. Halliburton, Warren Jennings. *Cry Baby!* New York: McGraw–Hill, 1968.

2061. ————. *The Heist.* New York: McGraw–Hill, 1968.

2062. ————. *Some Things That Glitter.* New York: McGraw–Hill, 1970.

2063. Hansberry, Lorraine. *A Raisin in the Sun: A Drama in Three Acts.* New York: Random House, 1959.

2064. ————. *The Sign in Sidney Brustein's Window: A Drama in Three Acts.* New York: Random House, 1965.

This is Hansberry's last play, giving a revealing picture of the stresses of contemporary American society.

2065. Harper, Frederick Douglas. *Poems on Love and Life.* Alexandria, Va.: Douglass Publishers, 1985.

2066. Harper, Michael S. *Dear John, Dear Coltrane: Poems.* Pittsburgh: University of Pittsburgh Press, 1970. Reprint. Urbana: University of Illinois Press, 1985.

2067. ————. *Images of Kin: New and Selected Poems.* Urbana: University of Illinois Press, 1977.

2068. ————, ed. *The Collected Poems of Sterling A. Brown*. New York: Harper and Row, 1983.

This book contains over one hundred poems, including "Old Man Buzzard," "Johnny Thomas," "Bessie," "Mecca," "Revelations," and "Southern Road." This collection illustrates the range of Brown's poetic contribution. Many of the poems have never before been gathered together in book form. Includes a bibliography.

2069. Harper, Michael S. and Robert Burns Stepto, eds. *Chant of Saints: A Gathering of Afro-American Literature, Art, and Scholarship*. Urbana: University of Illinois Press, 1979.

2070. Harris, Charlie Avery. *Black and Deadly*. Los Angeles: Holloway House Publishing Co., 1989.

2071. ————. *Broad Players*. Los Angeles: Holloway House Publishing Co., 1975.

2072. ————. *Con Man*. Los Angeles: Holloway House Publishing Co., 1978.

2073. ————. *Fast Track*. Los Angeles: Holloway House Publishing Co., 1978.

2074. ————. *Macking Gangster*. Los Angeles: Holloway House Publishing Co., 1976.

2075. ————. *Whore-Daughter*. Los Angeles: Holloway House Publishing Co., 1976.

2076. Harris, Randolph. *Trickshot: The Story of a Black Pimp*. Los Angeles: Holloway House Publishing Co., 1974.

2077. Haskins, James. *Black Theater in America*. New York: Thomas Y. Crowell Co., 1982.

2078. ⸻. *Jokes from Black Folks.* Garden City, N.Y.: Doubleday and Co., 1973.

In this analogy of Afro–American jokes centering around seven different themes, the jokes reflect the moods of blacks under varying circumstances, with some indicating the desire of blacks to make their tough existence tolerable by humor.

2079. Haskins, James, and Hugh F. Butts. *The Psychology of Black Language.* New York: Barnes and Noble, 1973.

This book explores the roots of black verbal behavior, from its African origin to the psychology of oppression, the development of verbal behavior among blacks during infancy and childhood, and the evolution of various dialects among blacks. This book draws on psychology, sociology, anthropology, history, and politics in its discussion of black language. It also provides tests, a helpful glossary of selected terms, and a selected bibliography.

2080. Hatch, James Vernon, comp. *Black Theater, U.S.A.: Forty-five Plays by Black Americans, 1847–1974.* New York: Free Press, 1974.

Plays in this volume include *The Amen Corner*, by James Baldwin; *Walk Hard*, by Abram Hill; *Star of the Morning*, by Loften Mitchell; *Limitations of Life*, by Langston Hughes; *Fly Blackbird*, by C. Bernard Jackson; *The Slave*, by Imamu Amiri Baraka; *The Owl Answers*, by Adrienne Kennedy; *The Drinking Gourd*, by Lorraine Hansberry; and *Native Son*, by Richard Wright.

2081. Hawkins, Odie. *The Busting Out of an Ordinary Man.* Los Angeles: Holloway House Publishing Co., 1985.

2082. ⸻. *Chicago Hustle.* Los Angeles: Holloway House Publishing Co., 1987.

2083. ———. *Chili: Memoirs of a Black Casanova.* Los Angeles: Holloway House Publishing Co., 1985.

2084. ———. *My Menfriends.* Los Angeles: Holloway House Publishing Co., 1989.

2085. ———. *Scars and Memories.* Los Angeles: Holloway House Publishing Co., 1987.

2086. ———. *Secret Music: A Book.* Los Angeles: Holloway House Publishing Co., 1988.

2087. ———. *Sweet Peter Deeder.* Los Angeles: Holloway House Publishing Co., 1979.

2088. Hayes, Leola G. *Come and Get It: Reading for Information Through Recipes.* Hicksville, N.Y.: Exposition Press, 1976.

2089. Henderson, Stephen E., comp. *Understanding the New Black Poetry: Black Speech and Black Music as Poetic References.* New York: William Morrow and Co., 1972.

This work is divided into three sections: "Pre-Harlem Renaissance and Soul-Field"; "The Harlem Renaissance and Afterward, Soul-Field"; and "The New Black Consciousness, The Same Difference." It includes less-known and well-known black writers as well as biographical notes.

2090. Hernton, Calvin C. *The Coming of Chronos to the House of Nightsong: An Epical Narrative of the South.* New York: Interim Books, 1964.

2091. ———. *Medicine Man: Collected Poems.* New York: Reed, Cannon and Johnson, 1976.

2092. ———. *Scarecrow.* 1st ed. Garden City, N.Y.: Doubleday and Co., 1974.

2093. ————. *The Sexual Mountain and Black Women Writers: Adventures in Sex, Literature, and Real Life.* 1st ed. New York: Anchor Press, 1987.

2094. Hill, Roy L. *Rhetoric of Racial Revolt.* Denver: Golden Bell Press, 1964.

2095. Himes, Chester B. *All Shot Up.* New York: Berkley Publishing Corp., 1960.

2096. ————. *The Big Gold Dream.* New York: Avon Book Division, Hearst Corp., 1960. Reprint. Harmondsworth: Penguin Books, 1976.

2097. ————. *Black on Black: Baby Sister and Selected Writings.* London: Joseph, 1975.

2098. ————. *Blind Man with a Pistol.* New York: William Morrow and Co., 1969.

2099. ————. *A Case of Rape.* New York: Targ Editions, 1980. Reprint. Washington, D.C.: Howard University Press, 1984.

A Case of Rape is the story of four black men residing in Paris who are charged with the rape and murder of a wealthy, middle-aged American divorcée. It blends a provocative fictional account and a biting critique of society.

2100. ————. *Cast the First Stone: Novel.* New York: Coward-McCann, 1952.

2101. ————. *Cotton Comes to Harlem.* New York: G. P. Putnam's Sons, 1965. Reprint. New York: Vintage Books, 1988.

In this novel, Grave Digger Jones and Coffin Ed Johnson are black detectives in Harlem trying to solve the Reverend Deke O'Malley case. O'Malley is a pastor of Ham Church and leader of the Back to Africa Movement. After the pastor collects $87,000, it is stolen by masked white gunmen and a murder is committed. The dominant evidence is a bale of cotton. Other characters in the novel include Lieutenant Anderson, Colonel Calhoun, O'Malley's girlfriend Iris, Billie the dancer, and a street person named Uncle Bud. Uncle Bud finds the bale of cotton. Himes carries the reader through various adventures with these characters.

2102. ————. *The Crazy Kill.* New York: Avon Books, 1959.

2103. ————. *For Love of Imabelle.* Greenwich, Conn.: Fawcett Publications, 1957.

2104. ————. *The Heat's On.* New York: Allison and Busby, 1986.

2105. ————. *Hot Day, Hot Night.* New York: New American Library, 1975. Originally published as *Blind Man with a Pistol.*

2106. ————. *If He Hollers, Let Him Go.* Garden City, N.Y.: Doubleday and Co., 1945. Reprint. New York: Thunder's Mouth Press, 1986.

Using the 1940s as its setting, this novel is a history of black workers in a transitional period, when the demand for labor in a war economy opened new doors to employment for Afro–Americans. Its main character, Bob Jones, a defense worker in Los Angeles during World War II, tells of racial antagonism.

2107. ————. *Lonely Crusade.* New York: Alfred A. Knopf, 1947. Reprint. New York: Thunder's Mouth Press, 1986.

2108. ————. *Pinktoes.* New York: G. P. Putnam's Sons/Stein and Day, 1965. Reprint. New York: Dell Publishing Co., 1969. Reprint. Chatham, N.J.: Chatham Bookseller, 1975.

2109. ————. *The Primitive.* New York: New American Library, 1955.

2110. ————. *The Real Cool Killers.* New York: Avon, 1959. Reprint. New York: Vintage Books, 1988.

2111. ————. *Run Man, Run.* New York: Dell Publishing Co., 1969.

2112. ————. *The Third Generation.* 1st ed. Cleveland, Ohio: World Publishing Co., 1954.

2113. Hogue, W. Lawrence. *Discourse and the Other: The Production of the Afro-American Text.* Durham, N.C.: Duke University Press, 1986.

2114. Holmes, Butch. *Black Rage.* Los Angeles: Holloway House Publishing Co., 1975.

2115. ————. *Sunday Hell.* Los Angeles: Holloway House Publishing Co., 1982.

2116. Hoskins, Thurman. *Cannibals.* Los Angeles: Holloway House Publishing Co., 1988.

This novel is about the struggle of two hobos—yesteryear's homeless.

2117. ————. *Rip & Run.* Los Angeles: Holloway House Publishing Co., 1989.

"Calvin and Holly wanted to live like bad, bad street dudes. Problem was, they couldn't do anything, anything, right. Or without getting caught at it." Their attention span was about zero except when it came to women. They wanted to become the Vice Lords of Ohio. But Ohio already had several of those. Their own neighborhood had one: Robert Earl.

2118. Hudson, Herman C., and Maurice L. Imhoot.** *From Paragraph to Theme: Understanding and Practice.* New York: Macmillian Co., 1972.

2119. Hudson, Theodore R. *From LeRoi Jones to Amiri Baraka: The Literary Works.* Durham, N.C.: Duke University Press, 1973.

2120. Hudson, Theodore R., and Kimberley W. Benston,** eds. *Imamu Amiri Baraka (Leroi Jones): A Collection of Critical Essays.* Englewood Cliffs, N.J.: Prentice-Hall, 1978.

2121. Hudson, Theodore R., and James Vinson, eds. *Contemporary Poets.* 3d & 4th eds. New York: St. Martin's Press, 1985.

2122. Hughes, Langston. *Ask Your Mama: 12 Moods for Jazz.* 1961. Reprint. New York: Alfred A. Knopf, 1971.

2123. ———. *The Best of Simple.* Illustrated by Bernhard Nast.* 1961. Reprint. New York: Hill and Wang, 1964.

2124. ———. *Five Plays.* Edited with an introduction by Webster Smalley.* 1963. Reprint. Bloomington: Indiana University Press, 1972.

2125. ———. *Freedom's Plow.* New York: Musette Publishers, 1943.

2126. ———. *The Langston Hughes Reader.* 1958. Reprint. New York: George Braziller, 1971.

2127. ———. *Laughing to Keep from Crying.* 1st ed. New York: Holt, 1952. Reprint. Mattituck, N.Y.: Aeonian Press, 1976.

2128. ———. *Montage of a Dream Deferred.* 1st ed. New York: Holt, 1951.

2129. ———. *The Negro Mother, and Other Dramatic Recitations.* Decorations by Prentiss Taylor.* New York: Golden Stair Press, 1931. Reprint. Salem, N.H.: Ayer Co., 1987.

2130. ———. *One-Way Ticket.* 1st ed. Illustrated by Jacob Lawrence.* New York: Alfred A. Knopf, 1949.

2131. ———. *The Panther and the Lash: Poems of Our Times.* 1967. Reprint. New York: Alfred A. Knopf, 1985.

The famous black American poet's last collection: seventy poems selected by Hughes shortly before his death in 1967.

2132. ———. *Scottsboro Limited: Four Poems and a Play in Verse.* Illustrations by Prentiss Taylor.* New York: Golden Stair Press, 1932.

2133. ———. *Selected Poems of Langston Hughes.* 1959. Reprint. New York: Alfred A. Knopf, 1988.

Poems selected by Hughes, including some that had previously been only privately published as well as his most famous poems.

2134. ———. *Shakespeare in Harlem.* Drawings by E. McKnight Kauffer.* 1942. New York: Alfred A. Knopf, 1947.

2135. ———. *The Simple Omnibus.* Mattituck, N.Y.: Aeonian Press, 1978.

2136. ———. *Simple Speaks His Mind.* New York: Simon and Schuster, 1950. Reprint. Mattituck, N.Y.: Aeonian Press, 1976.

2137. ———. *Simple Stakes a Claim.* New York: Rinehart, 1957.

2138. ———. *Simple Takes a Wife.* New York: Simon and Schuster, 1953. Reprint. Mattituck, N.Y.: Aeonian Press, 1976.

2139. ———. *Simple's Uncle Sam.* 1965. Reprint. New York: Hill and Wang, 1968.

2140. ———. *Something in Common, and Other Stories.* New York: Hill and Wang, 1963.

2141. ————. *Tambourines to Glory: A Novel.* 1958. Reprint. New York: Hill and Wang, 1970.

2142. ————. *The Ways of White Folks.* 1934. Reprint. New York: Alfred A. Knopf, 1979.

2143. ————. *The Weary Blues.* 1926. Reprint. New York: Alfred A. Knopf, 1947.

2144. ————, ed. *An African Treasury: Articles, Essays, Stories, Poems by Black Africans.* New York: Crown Publishers, 1960. Reprint. New York: Pyramid Books, 1965.

2145. ————, ed. *The Best Short Stories by Black Writers: The Classical Anthology from 1899 to 1967.* Boston: Little, Brown and Co., 1967. Originally published as *The Best Short Stories by Negro Writers.*

2146. ————, ed. *The Best Short Stories by Negro Writers: An Anthology from 1899 to the Present.* 1st ed. Boston: Little, Brown and Co., 1967.

2147. ————, ed. *The Book of Negro Humor.* New York: Dodd, Mead and Co., 1966.

Included in this collection are the comics, comedians such as Jackie Mabley, Pigmeat Markham, Cassius Clay, and Dick Gregory, who take the essence of Negro folk humor and bring it to the forefront. Hughes includes jokes and jive from minstrel days to the be-bop era; dialect tales of Deep Dixie; and the works of such modern authors as James Baldwin, Richard Wright, and Martin Luther King, Jr. The fourteen sections of this book also contain nonsense verses, ballads and songs, stanzas of the blues, poetry, Harlem party cards, and tales from the world of jazz.

2148. ————, ed. *New Negro Poets, U.S.A.* 1964. Reprint. Bloomington, Ind.: Indiana University Press, 1966.

2149. ————, ed. *Poems from Black Africa.* 1963. Reprint. Bloomington, Ind.: Indiana University Press, 1966.

This anthology of African literature brings African achievements to American readers. It includes works from thirty-six poets of ten African countries. Most works have a modern style mixed with Western and tribal influences. Some countries represented are Ethiopia, Southern Rhodesia, Sierra Leone, Madagascar, Nigeria, Kenya, Senegal, Ghana, South Africa, and Liberia. The book is divided into four categories: the French-speaking poets, the oral traditionals, the English–speaking poets, and the Portuguese–speaking poets. It includes biographical notes on each author.

2150. Hughes, Langston, and Arna Wendell Bontemps, eds. *The Book of Negro Folklore.* 1958. Reprint. New York: Dodd, Mead and Co., 1983.

This volume contains selections from the folklore of blacks in the United States, ranging from antebellum days to the present, and originating on the plantation, in New Orleans, Chicago, and Harlem. Included are animal tales and rhymes (such as those of Brer Rabbit), games, spirituals, and blues, as well as gospel songs, jazz, and jive. Early slave memories, accounts of hoodoo, and ghost stories are also included.

2151. Hughes, Langston, and Arna Wendell Bontemps, eds. *The Poetry of the Negro, 1746–1970: An Anthology.* Rev. and updated ed. Garden City, N.Y.: Doubleday and Co., 1970.

2152. Hughes, Langston, and Mercer Cook. *Masters of the Dew.* New York: Reynal and Hitchcock, 1947.

2153. Hull, Gloria T. *Healing Heat: Poems, 1973–1988.* 1st ed. Illustrated by Michele Gibbs.* Latham, N.Y.: Kitchen Table, Women of Color Press, 1989.

2154. ————, ed. *The Works of Alice Dunbar–Nelson.* New York: Oxford University Press, 1988.

2155. Hunter, Kristin. *God Bless the Child.* New York: Charles Scribner's Sons, 1964. Reprint. Washington, D.C.: Howard University Press, 1986.

The novel tells of the driven life, irrepressible spirit, and early, tragic death of a black woman, Rosie Fleming. Her reckless pursuit of a better life for her family, fueled by an obsessive ambition for wealth, proves to be her undoing. The victims of greed in this novel are forced to realize the deep-seated truth—that material possessions in and of themselves cannot satisfy the deeper longings of the human spirit for inner peace.

2156. ————. *The Lakestown Rebellion.* New York: Charles Scribner's Sons, 1978.

2157. Hurston, Zora Neale. *The Gilded Six-Bits: Love Is Fragile.* Illustrated by Etienne Delessert* designed by Rita Marshall.* Minneapolis: Redpath Press, 1986.

2158. ————. *I Love Myself When I Am Laughing . . . And Then Again When I Am Looking Mean and Impressive: A Zora Neale Hurston Reader.* Edited by A. Walker. Old Westbury, N.Y.: Feminist Press, 1979.

2159. ————. *Jonah's Gourd Vine.* 1934. Reprint. With a new introduction by Larry Neal. Philadelphia: J. B. Lippincott Co., 1971.

2160. ————. *Moses, Man of the Mountain.* Philadelphia: J. B. Lippincott Co., 1939. Reprint. Urbana: University of Illinois Press, 1984.

"In this novel the Moses of the Old Testament and the Moses of Negro myth, legend, and song are superimposed to create a new 'reading' of the Exodus story. Hurston focuses foremost upon Moses himself, his transformation from privileged Egyptian prince into the Great Emancipator, his evolving awareness of and identification with the enslaved Jews, and his parallel growth in mystical knowledge and power."

2161. ———. *Mules and Men.* Philadelphia: J. B. Lippincott Co., 1935. Reprint. Bloomington: Indiana University Press, 1978.

This book contains many types of tales, including myths devised to explain the mysteries of nature and life (such as why the rabbit has a short tail, why some people are black), imaginative stories about how to defeat the devil or win a loved one, and anecdotes that condemn American injustice toward blacks. The author also introduces the reader to the realm of hoodoo, or voodoo, and its practitioners.

2162. ———. *Seraph on the Suwanee: A Novel.* New York: Charles Scribner's Sons, 1948. Reprint. New York: AMS Press, 1974.

2163. ———. *Their Eyes Were Watching God: A Novel.* Philadelphia: J. B. Lippincott Co., 1937. Reprint. Urbana: University of Illinois Press, 1978.

This semiautobiographical novel is an example of a woman's search for self-expression in Afro-American literature.

2164. Jackman, Oliver. *Saw the House in Half: A Novel.* Washington, D.C.: Howard University Press, 1974.

This novel explores the West Indian dilemma of living between cultures. The search for self-realization by central character Sinclair Brathwaite differs greatly from the exploits of his countryman Dacosta Payne, a shrewd calculating entrepreneur and symbolic inhabitant of the "house sawed in half."

2165. Jackson, Blyden. *Operation Burning Candle: A Novel.* New York: Third Press, 1973.

2166. —————. *The Waiting Years: Essays on American Negro Literature.* Baton Rouge: Louisiana State University Press, 1976.

Jackson begins with an introductory autobiographical essay. He takes an integrationist stand as he focuses on Afro–American literature, and in the last chapter, "A Survey Course in Negro Literature," he puts forward the crucial need for consensus in the teaching of Afro–American literature.

2167. Jackson, Blyden, and Louis D. Rubin, Jr.* *Black Poetry in America: Two Essays in Historical Interpretation.* Baton Rouge: Louisiana State University Press, 1974.

The first of two essays in this book is by Louis Rubin and concerns the elementary problem of language in Afro–American poetry as Afro–American poets search for a form to explain themselves and their total experience. The second essay, by Blyden Jackson, takes a perspective from the Harlem Renaissance and shows how Afro–American poets have explored the different, modern Afro–American experiences. Both essays together offer an analysis of the principal directions of Afro–American poetry for the past two centuries and trace its development today.

2168. Jackson, Edward Merica. *American Slavery and the American Novel, 1852–1977.* Bristol, Ind.: Wyndham Hall Press, 1987.

Covering Harriet Beecher Stowe, William Wells Brown, Mark Twain, Margaret Walker, Nat Turner, William Melvin Kelley, Ernest J. Gaines, and Alex Haley, Jackson provides insights into the interplay between black history and American literature.

2169. Jahannes, Ja Arthur. *The Poet's Song.* 1st ed. Hampton, Va.: Hampton Institute Press, 1981.

2170. Jeffers, Lance. *Grandsire: Poems.* Detroit: Lotus Press, 1979.

2171.   Jefferson, Roland S. *The Secret Below 103rd Street.* Los Angeles: Holloway House Publishing Co., 1976.

2172.   Jemie, Onwuchekwa. *Langston Hughes: An Introduction to the Poetry.* New York: Columbia University Press, 1976.

2173.   Jenkins, Lee Clinton. *Faulkner and Black–White Relations: A Psychoanalytic Approach.* New York: Columbia University Press, 1981.

2174.   Johnson, Charles Richard. *The Sorcerer's Apprentice.* New York: Penguin Books, 1987.

2175.   Johnson, Charles Spurgeon. *Ebony and Topaz, a Collectanea.* New York: Opportunity, National Urban League, 1927. Reprint. Freeport, N.Y.: Books for Libraries Press, 1971.

2176.   Johnson, James Weldon, ed. *The Book of American Negro Poetry.* Rev. ed. 1931. San Diego: Harcourt Brace Jovanovich, 1983.

2177.   Jones, Edward Allen, comp. *Voices of Negritude: The Expression of Black Experience in the Poetry of Senghor, Cesaire, and Damas.* Valley Forge, Pa.: Judson Press, 1971.

2178.   Jones, Gayl. *Corregidora.* New York: Random House, 1975. Reprint. Boston: Beacon Press, 1986.

2179.   ———. *Eva's Man.* New York: Random House, 1976. Reprint. Boston: Beacon Press, 1987.

2180.   ———. *The Hermit–Woman: Poems.* Detroit: Lotus Press, 1983.

2181.   ———. *Song for Anninho.* 1st ed. Detroit: Lotus Press, 1981.

2182.   ———. *White Rat: Short Stories.* New York: Random House, 1977.

2183. ———. *Xarque and Other Poems.* Detroit: Lotus Press, 1985.

2184. Jones, Jesse B., III *Midnight's Daughter.* Los Angeles: Holloway House Publishing Co., 1981.

2185. ———. *The Predator.* Los Angeles: Holloway House Publishing Co., 1982.

2186. Jones, LeRoi. *Tales.* New York: Grove Press, 1976.

Sixteen stories ranging from the narrative to the expressionistic vignette, depicting moods of bitter wit and aggression.

2187. Jones, LeRoi, and Larry Neal, eds. *Black Fire: An Anthology of Afro-American Writing.* New York: William Morrow and Co., 1968.

The essays, poetry, drama, and stories in this volume are the works of approximately seventy young black writers, including LeRoi Jones (Imamu Amiri Baraka) and Larry Neal.

2188. Jones-Jackson, Patricia. *When Roots Die: Endangered Traditions on the Sea Islands.* Athens: University of Georgia Press, 1987.

This book tells of the lives and literature of the Sea Island blacks—the free descendants of slaves from Barbados and West Africa—who, from their earliest time in America, have drawn on a distinctive culture and spoken a Creole language known as Gullah in South Carolina and Geechee in Georgia. This Creole language, developed by the slaves on the Sea Islands and in the South Carolina and Georgia low country, and the way of life associated with it are threatened by increased contact with the mainland. According to Charles Joyner, who wrote the foreword, "this book is an act of cultural conservation." It is the first book-length treatment of the contemporary Gullah language and culture that would engage both the scholar and the nonlinguists and nonfolklorists. Includes photos, appendixes, notes, selected bibliography, and an index.

2189. Jordan, June Meyer. *Living Room: New Poems.* New York: Thunder's Mouth Press, 1985.

2190. ————. *New Days: Poems of Exile and Return.* New York: Emerson Hall, 1974.

2191. ————. *Passion: New Poems, 1977–1980.* Boston: Beacon Press, 1980.

2192. ————. *Some Changes.* New York: E. P. Dutton and Co., 1971.

2193. ————. *Things That I Do in the Dark: Selected Poetry.* New York: Random House, 1977. Reprint. Boston: Beacon Press, 1981.

2194. ————, comp. *Soulscript: Afro–American Poetry.* 1st ed. Garden City, N.Y.: Doubleday and Co., 1970.

2195. Kelley, William Melvin. *Dancers on the Shore.* New York: Doubleday, 1964. Reprint. Washington, D.C.: Howard University Press, 1984.

This book is a collection of sixteen short stories, the themes of which include love, fear, anger, hate, despair, loneliness, and hope. These short stories depict the lives of desperate, lonely, and marginal people. Many of the main characters appear in several stories, thus weaving a delicate thread throughout the collection.

2196. ————. *Dem.* 1st ed. Garden City, N.Y.: Doubleday and Co., 1967.

2197. ————. *A Different Drummer.* Garden City, N.Y.: Doubleday and Co., 1962. Reprint. Garden City, N.Y.: Anchor Books, 1969.

2198.   ————. *A Drop of Patience.* Garden City, N.Y.: Doubleday and Co., 1965. Reprint. Chatham, N.J.: Chatham Bookseller, 1973.

2199.   ————. *Dunfords Travels Everywheres.* 1st ed. Garden City, N.Y.: Doubleday and Co., 1970.

2200.   Kendrick, Dolores. *Now Is the Thing to Praise: Poems.* Detroit: Lotus Press, 1984.

2201.   ————. *Through the Ceiling.* 2d ed. London: Paul Breman Limited, 1975.

2202.   Killens, John Oliver. *And Then We Heard the Thunder.* 1st ed. New York: Alfred A. Knopf, 1962. Reprint. Washington, D.C.: Howard University Press, 1983.

This book is a story of the black American GI's bloody encounter with racism and hatred during World War II. The novel unfolds in four arrangements: "The Planting Season," "Cultivation," "Lightning–Thunder–Rainfall," and "The Crop." These sections represent the four periods of change experienced by the book's main character throughout the war.

2203.   ————. *The Cotillion, or, One Good Bull is Half the Herd.* New York: Trident Press, 1971. Reprint. New York: Ballantine Books, 1988.

A novel of romance, a plea for black power, a parable, a comedy, and a blistering putdown of whites.

2204.   ————. *Great Gittin' Up Morning.* Garden City, N.Y.: Doubleday and Co., 1972.

2205.   ————. *A Man Ain't Nothin' but a Man: The Adventures of John Henry.* Boston: Little, Brown and Co., 1975.

This book retells the life of the legendary steel driver of early railroad days, who challenged the steam hammer to a steel-driving contest.

2206. ————. *'Sippi.* New York: Trident Press, 1967. Reprint. New York: Thunder's Mouth Press, 1988.

Set against a background of southern civil rights, this novel explores the black man's realization that he is his own salvation.

2207. ————. *Slaves.* New York: Pyramid Publications, 1969.

2208. ————. *Youngblood.* New York: Dial Press, 1954. Reprint. Athens: University of Georgia Press, 1982.

A black family in Georgia answers the question, "How do you live in a white man's world?" Foreword by Addison Gayle, Jr.

2209. Kincaid, Jamaica. *Annie John.* New York: Farrar, Straus and Giroux, 1985.

2210. ————. *At the Bottom of the River.* New York: Farrar, Straus and Giroux, 1983.

2211. King, Woodie, Jr., ed. *Black Short Story Anthology.* New York: Columbia University Press, 1972.

A collection of work that reflects the struggle of the late 1950s and early 1960s, this book includes short stories by Langston Hughes, James Baldwin, Nikki Giovanni, and Imamu Amiri Baraka (LeRoi Jones). The introduction to the book treats the sixties from a literary perspective. During the sixties, the black man seemed to be reaching out to other black people through his work.

2212. ————, ed. *Black Spirits: A Festival of New Black Poets in America.* 1st ed. New York: Random House, 1972.

2213. ———, ed. *The Forerunners: Black Poets in America.* Washington, D.C.: Howard University Press, 1980.

With an introduction by Addison Gayle, Jr., and a preface by Dudley Randall, this work highlights selected works of sixteen "poets who came to prominence, mainly after the Renaissance years, and who bridged the gap between poets of the twenties and those of the sixties and seventies." The poets include Samuel Allen, Russell Atkins, Arna Bontemps, Gwendolyn Brooks, Sterling Brown, Margaret Burroughs, Margaret Danner, Frank Marshall Davis, Owen Dodson, Robert Hayden, Lance Jeffers, Oliver La Grone, Naomi Long Madgett, Dudley Randall, Margaret Walker, and Jay Wright. They provide personal statements about poetry, about themselves, and about the future.

2214. King, Woodie, Jr., and Ron Milner, eds. *Black Drama Anthology.* New York: Columbia Press, 1972. Reprint. New York: New American Library, 1986.

2215. Knuckles, Jeffery. *Private Conversations: A Novel.* Los Angeles: Holloway House Publishing Co., 1989.

2216. Lacey, Henry Clark. *To Raise, Destroy, and Create: The Poetry, Drama, and Fiction of Imamu Amiri Baraka (LeRoi Jones).* Troy, N.Y.: Whitston Publishing Co., 1981.

2217. Lakin, Mattie Temple T. *Portico of the Temple.* 2d ed. Gastonia, N.C.: Minges Printers, 1970.

2218. Lamming, George. *The Emigrants.* London: Joseph, 1954. Reprint. New York: McGraw–Hill, 1955.

2219. ———. *In the Castle of My Skin.* New York: McGraw–Hill, 1953. Reprint. Essex, England: Longman, 1986.

2220. ———, comp. *Cannon Shot and Glass Beads: Modern Black Writing.* London: Pan Books, 1974.

2221. Lane, Pinkie Gordon. *I Never Scream: New and Selected Poems.* Detroit: Lotus Press, 1985.

2222. ———. *The Mystic Female: Poems.* 1st ed. Fort Smith, Ark.: South and West, 1978.

2223. ———. *Wind Thought: Poems.* Fort Smith, Ark.: South and West, 1972.

2224. ———, ed. *Poems by Blacks.* Vol. 3. Fort Smith, Ark.: South and West, 1975.

2225. Lee, Andrea. *The Lady Cavaliers.* New York: Dell Publishing Co., 1979.

2226. ———. *Sarah Phillips.* New York: Random House, 1984.

2227. Lester, Julius. *Do Lord Remember Me.* New York: Holt, Rinehart and Winston, 1985.

This adult novel is an intense and passionate story of family, politics, and religion. Told in the space of one man's last day on earth, the novel focuses on the memories of Rev. Joshua Smith, a singing evangelist, who had conducted revivals in most American states, the West Indies, and South America. Lester calls his novel "a book of memories," and he introduces us—through the scenes crowding Reverend Smith's mind—to "remembrances of a people, imperfect and brave, who create their history with a faith that makes miracles." From segregation through the civil rights movement, Reverend Smith keeps the faith of his fathers and mothers.

2228. ———. *Two Love Stories.* New York: Dial Press, 1972.

2229. ———. *Who I Am.* New York: Dial Press, 1974.

2230. Lezan, Joyce [Joseph Nazel]. *Heartbeat.* Los Angeles: Holloway House Publishing Co., 1983.

2231. ———. *Lover's Holiday.* Los Angeles: Holloway House Publishing Co., 1983.

2232. ———. *Spring Embrace.* Los Angeles: Holloway House Publishing Co., 1983.

2233. ———. *Summer Blues.* Los Angeles: Holloway House Publishing Co., 1984.

2234. Little, Lessie Jones. *Children of Long Ago.* Pictures by Jan Spivey Gilchrist. New York: Philomel Books, 1988.

    Poems reflecting simpler days, with grandmothers who read aloud and children who walked barefoot on damp earth and picked blackberries for their paper dolls to eat.

2235. Locke, Alain LeRoy, and Montgomery Gregory, eds. *Plays of Negro Life: A Source-Book of Native America Drama.* New York: Harper, 1927. Reprint. Westport, Conn.: Negro Universities Press, 1970.

2236. Lomax,** Allan, and Raoul Abdul, eds. *Three Thousand Years of Black Poetry.* New York: Dodd, Mead and Co., 1984.

2237. Lomax, Louis E. *To Kill a Black Man.* Los Angeles: Holloway House Publishing Co., 1987.

2238. Long, Richard A., and Eugenia W. Collier, eds. *Afro-American Writing: An Anthology of Prose and Poetry.* New York: New York University Press, 1972. 2d and enl. ed. University Park: Pennsylvania State University Press, 1985.

2239. Lorde, Audre. *From a Land Where Other People Live.* 1st ed. Detroit: Broadside Press, 1973.

2240. ———. *New York Head Shop and Museum.* 1974. Detroit: Broadside Press, 1975.

2241. ———. *Our Dead Behind Us: Poems.* New York: W. W. Norton and Co., 1986.

2242. ———. *Sister Outsider: Essays and Speeches.* Tramansburg, N.Y.: The Crossing Press, 1984.

2243. MacCann, Donnarae, and Gloria Woodard, eds. *The Black American in Books for Children: Readings in Racism.* 2d ed. Metuchen, N.J.: Scarecrow Press, 1985.

2244. Madhubuti, Haki R. *Earthquakes and Sunrise Missions: Poetry and Essays of Black Renewal 1973–1983.* Chicago: Third World Press, 1984.

2245. ———. *Killing Memory, Seeking Ancestors.* Detroit: Lotus Press, 1987.

2246. ———. *We Walk the Way of the New World.* Detroit: Broadside Press, 1970.

2247. Major, Clarence. *Black Slang: A Dictionary of Afro-American Talk.* London: Routledge and Kegan Paul, 1971.

2248. ———. *Such Was the Season: A Novel.* San Francisco: Mercury House, 1987.

2249. ———. *Surfaces and Masks: A Poem.* Minneapolis: Coffee House Press, 1988.

2250. ———. *Swallow the Lake.* Middletown, Conn.: Wesleyan University Press, 1970.

2251. ———. *Symptoms & Madness: Poems.* New York: Corinth Books, 1971.

2252. ———. *The Syncopated Cakewalk.* New York: Barlenmir House, 1974.

2253. Makward,* Edris, and Leslie Alexander Lacy, comps. *Contemporary African Literature.* New York: Random House, 1972.

2254. Marshall, Paule. *Brown Girl, Brownstones.* New York: Avon, 1959. Reprint. New York: Feminist Press, 1981.

2255. ————. *The Chosen Place, The Timeless People.* New York: Harcourt, Brace and World, 1969. Reprint. New York: Vintage Books, 1984.

2256. ————. *Praisesong for the Widow.* New York: G. P. Putnam's Sons, 1983. Reprint. New York: E. P. Dutton and Co., 1984.

This is the story of the spiritual transformation of a sixty-two-year-old widow, Avey Johnson. It is, on one level, a metaphor for the possibility of change and renewal of which all women and men are capable, no matter what their age.

2257. ————. *Reena and Other Stories.* New York: Feminist Press, 1984.

2258. ————. *Soul Clap Hands and Sing.* New York: Atheneum Publishers, 1961. Reprint. Washington, D.C.: Howard University Press, 1988.

This quartet of short stories describes the despair of four middle-aged or elderly men who failed to love, care deeply, or share intimately. In each tale, a woman precipitates a confrontation in which the man is given the opportunity to surmount his indifference of fear and attempt to love or care. The stories are set in the tropical climes of Barbados, Brazil, and British Guiana, as well as in the city and suburbs of Brooklyn, New York.

2259. Mataka, Laini. *Never As Strangers.* Baltimore, Md.: W. M. DuForcelf, 1988.

2260.   McDowell, Deborah E., and Arnold Rampersad, eds. *Slavery and the Literary Imagination*. Baltimore, Md.: Johns Hopkins University Press, 1989.

2261.   McElroy, Colleen J. *Bone Flames: Poems*. Middletown, Conn.: Wesleyan University Press, 1987.

2262.   ―――――. *Jesus and Fat Tuesday and Other Short Stories*. Berkeley: Creative Arts Book Co., 1987.

2263.   ―――――. *Lie and Say You Love Me: Poems*. Tacoma, Wash.: Circinatum Press, 1981.

2264.   ―――――. *Looking for a Country Under Its Original Name: Poems*. Yakima, Wash.: Blue Begonia Press, 1984.

2265.   ―――――. *The Mules Done Long Since Gone*. Seattle, Wash.: Harrison–Madrona Center, 1972.

2266.   ―――――. *Music from Home: Selected Poems*. Carbondale: Southern Illinois University Press, 1976.

2267.   ―――――. *Queen of the Ebony Isles*. Middletown, Conn.: Wesleyan University Press, 1984.

2268.   McKay, Claude. *Banjo: A Story Without a Plot*. New York: Harper and Brothers, 1929. Reprint. New York: Harcourt Brace Jovanovich, 1970.

2269.   ―――――. *Home to Harlem*. New York: Harper and Brothers, 1928. Reprint. Boston: Northeastern University Press, 1987.

2270.   ―――――. *A Long Way from Home*. New York: L. Furman, 1937. Reprint. New York: Arno Press, 1969.

In this work, Jamaican–born McKay tells the story of his life and his struggles to become a recognized poet, a goal which he had started toward after writing his first verse at the age of ten in Jamaica. He describes his literary mentors, the scenes and people of the Harlem Renaissance, and his trips to various countries, including Russia.

2271. ————. *Selected Poems*. With an introduction by John Dewey** and a biographical note by Max Eastman.** New York: Bookman Associates, 1953.

2272. McKay, Nellie Y., comp. *Critical Essays on Toni Morrison*. Boston: G. K. Hall and Co., 1988.

2273. McMillan, Terry. *Disappearing Acts*. New York: Viking Press, 1989.

2274. ————. *Mama*. Boston: Houghton Mifflin Co., 1987.

Set in the industrial town of Point Haven, Michigan, during the 1960s and 1970s, this is the story of Mildred Peacock, a mother of five, black, and fed up with poverty and the jealous rampages of her husband, Crook. When Crook runs over her foot with his 1959 Mercury, she finally kicks him out to raise her kids on her own.

2275. Melham, D. H. *Gwendolyn Brooks: Poetry and the Heroic Voice*. Lexington: University Press of Kentucky, 1987.

Although Gwendolyn Brooks is a major American poet—the first black to win a Pulitzer Prize—she has received far less critical attention than her peers. Melham, a poet and critic, deplores this literary oversight and builds on the critical foundation of black writers. The result is a comprehensive biocritical study that traces the development of Brooks's poetry over four decades, from such early works as *A Street in Bronzeville* and the Pulitzer Prize–winning *Annie Allen*, to the more recent *In the Mecca*, *Riot*, and *To Disembark*. The author also examines the biographical, historical, and literary roots of the Illinois poet laureate's art; her birth in Topeka, Kansas; her upbringing in Chicago; her support of the black liberation struggle; her work on behalf of young poets, and her influence on black letters.

2276.   Micheaux, Oscar. *The Case of Mrs. Wingate*. 6th ed. New York: Book Supply Co., 1945. Reprint. New York: AMS Press, 1975.

2277.   ————. *The Homesteader: A Novel*. Illustrated by W. M. Farrow.* Sioux City, Iowa: Western Book Supply Co., 1917. Reprint. College Park, Md.: McGrath Publishing Co., 1969.

2278.   ————. *The Masquerade, an Historical Novel*. New York: Book Supply Co., 1947. Reprint. New York: AMS Press, 1975.

2279.   ————. *The Story of Dorothy Stanfield, Based on a Great Insurance Swindle, and a Woman!* New York: Book Supply Co., 1946.

2280.   ————. *The Wind from Nowhere*. New York: Book Supply Co., 1941. Reprint. Freeport, N.Y.: Books for Libraries Press, 1972.

2281.   Miller, E. Ethelbert. *Where Are the Love Poems for Dictators?* Washington, D.C.: Open Hand Publishing, 1986.

2282.   Miller, May. *The Clearing and Beyond*. 1st ed. Washington, D.C.: Charioteer Press, 1974.

2283.   ————. *Dust of Uncertain Journey*. Detroit: Lotus Press, 1975.

2284.   ————. *Halfway to the Sun*. Washington, D.C.: Washington Writers' Publishing House 1981.

2285.   ————. *Into the Clearing*. Washington, D.C.: Charioteer Press, 1959.

2286.   ————. *Not That Far*. San Luis Obispo, Calif.: Solo Press, 1973.

2287.   ————. *Poems*. Thetford, Vt.: Cricket Press, 1962.

2288. ———. *The Ransomed Wait: Poems.* Detroit: Lotus Press, 1983.

2289. Millican, Arthenia Bates. *The Deity Nodded.* Detroit: Harlo Press, 1973.

2290. ———. *Seeds Beneath the Snow: Vignettes from the South.* 1969. Reprint. Washington, D.C.: Howard University Press, 1975.

This book is a refreshing approach to black life in the rural South. With simplicity, wit, and insight, the author presents twelve short stories about the people and life she knew so well.

2291. ———. *Such Things from the Valley.* Norfolk, Va.: Millican, 1977.

2292. Morrison, Toni. *Beloved.* New York: Alfred A. Knopf, 1987.

The recipient of the 1988 Pulitzer Prize for fiction, this novel, set in post–Civil War Ohio, is the story of Sethe, an escaped slave who lives in a small house on the edge of town with her daughter, Denver; her mother–in–law, Baby Suggs; and a disturbing, mesmerizing intruder who calls herself Beloved. Sethe's struggle to prevent Beloved from gaining full possession of her and to cast off the legacy of her past is the center of this novel.

2293. ———. *The Bluest Eye.* New York: Holt, Rinehart and Winston, 1970. Reprint. New York: Washington Square Press, 1972.

This is a story about Pecola Breedlove, a young black girl who yearns so deeply for the blue eyes of a little white girl that she comes to believe she has them and ultimately goes insane.

2294. ———. *Song of Solomon.* New York: New American Library, 1978.

The recipient of the 1978 National Book Critics Circle Award for fiction, this novel spans four generations of black life in America and centers on Macon Dead, Jr., the son of the richest black family in a midwestern town, as he explores the essence of family bond and conflict.

2295. ———. *Sula.* 1st ed. New York: Alfred A. Knopf, 1974.

The story of the friendship between two black women, Sula and Nel, who share everything until Sula leaves their small Ohio town for the city, and, ten years later upon her return, of how and why that friendship is destroyed.

2296. ———. *Tar Baby.* 1st ed. New York: Alfred A. Knopf, 1981.

Set on a Caribbean island, this story explores a whole spectrum of emotions underlying the relationships between black men and women and black and white people as seen through the lives of a white millionaire couple and their black servant couple.

2297. Morse, L. C. *Sundial.* Boston: Stonehill Press, 1986.

Against the backdrop of Howard University in the late sixties and early seventies, Morse's novel follows the lives of four students—William Christopher Bennett III, Lisa Brevard, Hugo Mackey, and Ronald Maxwell—as they experience love, friendship, the death of peers, and the loss of innocence while coming of age. Omega Psi Phi fraternity life on the campus is depicted through the eyes of Chris Bennett, a third-generation Howardite.

2298. Motley, Willard. *Let No Man Write My Epitaph.* New York: Random House, 1958.

2299. ———. *Let Noon Be Fair: A Novel.* London: Longman, 1966.

2300. ———. *We Fished All Night.* New York: Appleton-Century-Crofts, 1951.

2301. ————, ed. *The Diaries of Willard Motley.* Ames: Iowa State University Press, 1979.

2302. Muller,* Gilbert H., and John Alfred Williams, comps. *The McGraw-Hill Introduction to Literature.* New York: McGraw-Hill, 1985.

2303. Murphy, Beatrice M. *Love Is a Terrible Thing.* New York: Hobson Book Press, 1945.

2304. ————, ed. *Ebony Rhythm: An Anthology of Contemporary Negro Verse.* Freeport, N.Y.: Books for Libraries, 1948. Reprint. Great Neck, N.Y.: Granger Book Company, 1982.

2305. ————, ed. *Negro Voices.* Illustrations by Clifton Thompson Hill. New York: H. Harrison, 1938.

2306. Murphy, Beatrice M., and Nancy Levi Arnez. *The Rocks Cry Out.* Detroit: Broadside Press, 1969.

This collection of poetry addresses the theme of what it is like to be black in America.

2307. Murray, Albert. *The Hero and the Blues.* Columbia: University of Missouri Press, 1973.

Contains the Paul Anthony Brick lectures, "originally presented at the University of Missouri, Columbia, in the form of three public lectures on October 7, 8, and 9, 1972."

2308. ————. *Train Whistle Guitar.* New York: McGraw-Hill, 1974. Reprint. Boston: Northeastern University Press, 1989.

In this novel the young protagonist learns from a cast of characters who include a twelve-string guitar player, Luzana Cholly, and a piano player, Stagolee Dupas. The book won the Lillian Smith Award of the Southern Regional Council.

2309. Murray, Pauli. *Dark Testament and Other Poems*. Norwalk, Conn.: Silvermine, 1970.

2310. Naylor, Gloria. *Linden Hills*. New York: Ticknor and Fields, 1985. Reprint. New York: Penguin Books, 1986.

In this novel, the residents of Linden Hills fight to maintain and improve their upper- and middle-class social status. Naylor depicts the bourgeoisie as a people who are drowning in their own miasma. *Linden Hills* is her second work of fiction. Her first is *The Women of Brewster Place*, which won an American Book Award in 1983.

2311. ————. *Mama Day*. New York: Vintage Books, 1988.

2312. ————. *The Women of Brewster Place*. New York: Viking Press, 1982.

This is Naylor's first work of fiction, which won an American Book Award in 1983. It derives its power from strongly drawn portraits of contemporary black women, an interesting blend of the poor and middle class united by race, sex, and displacement in American society.

2313. Nazel, Joseph [Dom Gober, pseud.; and Joyce Lezan, pseud.] *Billion Dollar Death*. Los Angeles: Holloway House Publishing Co., 1974.

2314. ————. *The Black Exorcist*. Los Angeles: Holloway House Publishing Co., 1974.

2315. ————. *Black Fury*. Los Angeles: Holloway House Publishing Co., 1976.

2316. ————. *The Black Gestapo*. Los Angeles: Holloway House Publishing Co., 1975

2317. ————. *Black Is Back*. New York: Pinnacle Books, 1974.

2318. ———. *Black Prophet.* Los Angeles: Holloway House Publishing Co., 1976.

2319. ———. *Death for Hire.* Los Angeles: Holloway House Publishing Co., 1986.

2320. ———. *Delta Crossing.* Los Angeles: Holloway House Publishing Co., 1984.

2321. ———. *Every Goodbye Ain't Gone.* Los Angeles: Holloway House Publishing Co., 1982.

2322. ———. *Finders Keepers, Losers Weepers: A Novel.* Los Angeles: Holloway House Publishing Co., 1987.

2323. ———. *Foxtrap: A Novel.* Los Angeles: Holloway House Publishing Co., 1986.

In this story—now a motion picture starring Fred Williamson—Fox, the international private eye, is hired to find a beautiful woman and follow a cold trail that leads him to the glamour capitals of Europe where, it seems, everyone who has ever known Susan keeps turning up murdered.

2324. ———. *The Golden Shaft.* Los Angeles: Holloway House Publishing Co., 1974.

2325. ———. *The Iceman: Canadian Kill.* Los Angeles: Holloway House Publishing Co., 1974.

2326. ———. *The Iceman: Spinning Target.* Los Angeles: Holloway House Publishing Co., 1974.

2327. ———. *Killer Cop.* Los Angeles: Holloway House Publishing Co., 1975.

2328. ———. *Satan's Master.* Los Angeles: Holloway House Publishing Co., 1974.

2329. ————. *The Shakedown.* Los Angeles: Holloway House Publishing Co., 1975.

2330. ————. *Slick Revenge.* Los Angeles: Holloway House Publishing Co., 1974.

2331. ————. *Street Wars: A Novel.* Los Angeles: Holloway House Publishing Co., 1987.

2332. ————. *Sunday Fix.* Los Angeles: Holloway House Publishing Co., 1974.

2333. ————. *Uprising.* Los Angeles: Holloway House Publishing Co., 1987.

2334. ————. *Wolves of Summer.* Los Angeles: Holloway House Publishing Co., 1984.

2335. Neal, Larry. *Black Boogaloo: Notes on Black Liberation.* San Francisco: Journal of Black Poetry Press, 1969.

2336. ————. *Hoodoo Hollerin' Bebop Ghosts.* Washington, D.C.: Howard University Press, 1974.

This collection of poems is a comment upon almost every level of black consciousness. As Neal says "I've tried to select poems for this volume in which the polemic and poetic merge into an organic, personal statement."

2337. Norton, Kimberly. *Love's Silken Web.* Los Angeles: Holloway House Publishing Co., 1984.

2338. ————. *Passion's Surrender.* Los Angeles: Holloway House Publishing Co., 1983.

2339. ————. *Snowfire.* Los Angeles: Holloway House Publishing Co., 1983.

2340. O'Daniel, Therman B., ed. *James Baldwin: A Critical Evaluation.* Washington, D.C.: Howard University Press, 1977.

The first comprehensive study of Baldwin's prolific career, these essays critically examine Baldwin the novelist, essayist, short story writer, playwright, scenarist, and conversationalist.

2341. ————, ed. *Jean Toomer: A Critical Evaluation.* Washington, D.C.: Howard University Press, 1988.

The third in a series of comprehensive studies of major twentieth–century Afro–American writers issued under the auspices of the College Language Association, this book follows the format of the two previous volumes on Langston Hughes and James Baldwin. Its purpose is the same: to present an in–depth and broad critical treatment of the author and his works. This volume contains over forty essays contributed by thirty–nine authors, as well as an extensive bibliography.

2342. ————, ed. *Langston Hughes, Black Genius: A Critical Evaluation.* New York: William Morrow and Co., 1971.

2343. O'Meally, Robert G. *The Craft of Ralph Ellison.* Cambridge: Harvard University Press, 1980.

2344. ————, ed. *New Essays on Invisible Man.* New York: Cambridge University Press, 1988.

2345. ————, ed. *Tales of the Congaree.* Chapel Hill: University of North Carolina Press, 1987.

2346. Paquet, Sandra Pouchet. *The Novels of George Lamming.* London: Heinemann, 1982.

2347. Pasteur, Alfred B., and Ivory L. Toldson. *The Roots of Soul: The Psychology of Black Expressiveness: An Unprecedented and Intensive Examination of Black Folk Expressions in the Enrichment of Life.* Garden City, N.Y.: Anchor Press/Doubleday and Co., 1982.

Written by two psychologists, this book is an analytical examination of black folk expressions. According to the authors, there are five aspects of black expressiveness: depth of feeling, naturalistic attitudes, stylistic renderings, poetic and prosaic vernacular, and expressive movement. These aspects, they say, "overlay each other and act in combination to produce wonderful expressions of the soul." The book is designed "to raise questions and offer tentative answers that are in the process of becoming."

2348. Patterson, Lindsay, comp. *Black Theater: A 20th Century Collection of Works of Its Best Playwrights.* New York: Dodd, Mead and Co., 1971.

2349. ———, comp. *An Introduction to Black Literature in America, from 1746 to the Present.* 1st ed. New York: Publishers Co., 1968.

2350. ———, comp. *A Rock Against the Wind: Black Love Poems: An Anthology.* New York: Dodd, Mead and Co., 1973.

2351. Patterson, Orlando. *An Absence of Ruins.* London: Hutchinson, 1967.

2352. ———. *The Children of Sisyphus.* London: New Authors Limited, 1964. Reprint. London: Longman, 1982.

2353. ———. *Die the Long Day.* New York: William Morrow and Co., 1972.

2354. Paznik–Bondarin,* Jane, and Milton Baxter. *Write and Write Again: A Worktext with Readings.* New York: Macmillan Co., 1987.

2355. Pennington, Dorothy L., and Jon A. Blubaugh.** *Crossing Difference—Interracial Communication.* Columbus, Ohio: Charles E. Merrill Co., 1976.

This text—one of eight books in the Interpersonal Communication Series—begins with the premise that everyone, regardless of desire, participates in some form of interracial communication. Using a cross-difference model, the authors present methods of communicating that transcend racial assumptions, language differences, and values and beliefs, and explain sociological phenomena associated with interracial communication.

2356. Perry, Margaret. *A Bio-Bibliography of Countee P. Cullen, 1903-1946.* Westport, Conn.: Greenwood Press, 1971.

In this interesting attempt to merge the man and the poet, Perry sketches Cullen the man and discusses both his famous and his less-known poetry. In the first part of the book, she surveys contemporary reviews of Cullen's work. Part 2 includes bibliographies of Cullen's major writings, writings about Cullen, and anthologies in which Cullen's works have appeared. The book contains a title and name index.

2357. ————. *Silence to the Drums: A Survey of the Literature of the Harlem Renaissance.* Westport, Conn.: Greenwood Press, 1976.

This survey examines the new directions and dimensions of the black creative writers whose works appeared regularly during the 1920s and 1930s, the period of the Harlem Renaissance. Perry shows that these writers were searching for roots and glorification of blackness, as well as simply relating their own experiences. The epilogue offers an overview of this period of black literature.

2358. Peterson, Carla L. *The Determined Reader: Gender and Culture in the Novel from Napoleon to Victoria.* New Brunswick, N.J.: Rutgers University Press, 1986.

2359. Petry, Ann Lane. *Country Place.* Boston: Houghton Mifflin, 1947. Reprint. Chatham, N.J.: Chatham Bookseller, 1971.

2360. ————. *The Narrows.* Boston: Houghton Mifflin Co., 1953. Reprint. Boston: Beacon Press, 1988.

2361. ———. *The Street.* Boston: Houghton Mifflin Co., 1946. Reprint. London: Virago, 1986.

2362. Pickens, William Garfield, ed. *Trends in Southern Sociolinguistics: Selected Writings.* Atlanta, Ga.: Pickens, 1975.

Papers selected from the Morehouse College Conference on Urban Linguistics and Speech, April 17–18, 1972.

2363. Polite, Carlene Hatcher. *The Flagellants.* New York: Farrar, Straus and Giroux, 1967.

2364. ———. *Sister X and the Victims of Foul Play.* New York: Farrar, Straus and Giroux, 1975.

2365. Priestley, Eric. *Raw Dog.* Los Angeles: Holloway House Publishing Co., 1985.

2366. Pryse,* Marjorie, and Hortense Jeanette Spillers, eds. *Conjuring: Black Women, Fiction, and Literary Tradition.* Bloomington: Indiana University Press, 1985.

2367. Pugh, Charles. *The Griot: A Novel.* Los Angeles: Holloway House Publishing Co., 1986.

The Griot is a story about the extraordinary relationship between an old man "the griot," a Zulu storyteller and keeper of tribal tradition) and a young boy growing up in a Chicago ghetto. As the years pass, the Griot become something of a Ninji figure to the boy, teaching him a form of self-discipline and self-defense as practiced by his people in Africa for centuries.

2368. Rampersad, Arnold. *Melville's Israel Potter: A Pilgrimage and Progress.* Bowling Green, Ohio: Bowling Green University Popular Press, 1969.

2369. Ray, David, and Robert M. Farnsworth.* *Richard Wright: Impressions and Perspectives.* Ann Arbor: University of Michigan Press, 1973.

A collection of critical essays, biographical sketches and memoirs, a bibliographical essay, and a posthumously published essay by Wright.

2370. Readus, James–Howard. *The Big Hit.* Los Angeles: Holloway House Publishing Co., 1975.

2371. ———. *Black Renegades.* Los Angeles: Holloway House Publishing Co., 1976.

2372. ———. *The Death Merchants.* Los Angeles: Holloway House Publishing Co., 1974.

2373. Redding, J. Saunders. *Stranger and Alone: A Novel.* 1st ed. New York: Harcourt, Brace and World, 1950. Reprint. Boston: Northeastern University Press, 1989.

2374. ———. *To Make a Poet Black.* Chapel Hill: University of North Carolina Press, 1939. Reprint. New York: McGraw–Hill Publishing Co., 1968; Ithaca, N.Y.: Cornell University Press, 1988.

2375. Reed, Ishmael, ed. *God Made Alaska for the Indians: Selected Essays.* New York: Garland Publishing, Inc., 1982.

Collection of recent essays ranging from a description of the Ali–Spinks fight to an analysis of contemporary poetry. The title essay is a detailed account of the struggle involving Indians and conservationists over Alaskan land. Other titles include "Black Macho, White Macho: The Stale Drama" and "Black Irishman."

2376. ———, ed. *New and Collected Poems.* New York: Atheneum Publishers, 1988.

This is a compilation of three previously published volumes as well as recently composed works by the novelist, essayist, and playwright Ishmael Reed.

2377. ————. *Reckless Eyeballing.* New York: St Martin's Press, 1986.

A fierce and funny novel about sexual and racial politics, written in a style designed to provoke, edify, entertain, and outrage.

2378. Render, Sylvia Lyons. *Charles W. Chesnutt.* Boston: Twayne Publishers, 1980.

Criticism and interpretation of Charles Waddell Chesnutt (1858–1932).

2379. ————, ed. *The Short Fiction of Charles W. Chesnutt.* 1974. Reprint. Washington, D.C.: Howard University Press, 1981.

This volume contains all but four of Chesnutt's pieces of short fiction, excluding the sixteen tales and short stories in *The Conjure Woman* and those in *The Wife of His Youth and Other Stories of the Color Line*, both previously published. The anecdotes have never been published prior to this volume, and the tales and short stories appear for the first time in book form.

2380. Richardson, Craig. *Deep Woods.* Los Angeles: Holloway House Publishing Co., 1984.

2381. Richardson, Marilyn, and Janice H. Mikesell,* eds. *Women Houses & Homes: An Anthology of Prose, Poetry, and Photography.* Brookings, S.Dak.: UNI Press, 1988.

2382. Richardson, Willis, and May Miller, eds. *Negro History in Thirteen Plays.* Washington, D.C.: Associated Publishers, 1935.

2383. Riley, Cole [Robert Fleming]. *Rough Trade*. Los Angeles: Holloway House Publishing Co., 1987.

2384. Rive, Richard. `Buckingham Palace,' District Six*. New York: Random House, 1986.

2385. Rodgers, Carolyn M. *The Heart As Evergreen*. Garden City, N.Y.: Doubleday and Co., 1978.

2386. ———. *How I Got Ovah*. Garden City, N.Y.: Doubleday and Co., 1976.

Contains poetry expressing powerful, loving, and humorous reflections on the author's black womanhood. Includes an introduction by Gwendolyn Brooks.

2387. Russell, Charlie London. *A Birthday Present for Katheryn Kenyatta*. New York: McGraw–Hill, 1970.

2388. ———. *Five on the Black Hand Side: A Play in Three Acts*. New York: Third Press, 1969.

2389. Salaam, Kalamu Ya. *The Blues Merchant: Songs (Poems) for Blackfolk*. New Orleans: Blkartsouth, 1969.

2390. ———. *Revolutionary Love: Poems & Essays*. New Orleans: Ahidiana–Habari 1978.

2391. Sanchez, Sonia. *A Blues Book for Blue Black Magical Women*. 1st ed. Detroit: Broadside Press, 1974.

2392. ———. *Generations: Poetry, 1969–1985*. London: Karnak House, 1986.

2393. ———. *Home Coming: Poems*. Introduction by Don L. Lee. Detroit: Broadside Press, 1969.

2394. ———. *Homegirls and Handgrenades: A Collection of Poetry and Prose*. New York: Thunder's Mouth Press, 1984.

2395. ————. *I've Been a Woman: New and Selected Poems.* Sausalito, Calif.: Black Scholar Press, 1980.

2396. ————. *Love Poems.* New York: Third Press, 1973.

2397. ————. *Under a Soprano Sky.* Trenton, N.J.: Africa World Press, 1987.

2398. ————, ed. *We Be Word Sorcerers: 25 Stories by Black Americans.* New York: Bantam Books, 1974.

2399. Sanders, Dori. *Clover.* Chapel Hill, N.C.: Algonquin Books of Chapel Hill, 1990.

"After her father dies within hours of being married to a white woman, a ten-year-old black girl learns with her new mother to overcome grief and to adjust to a new place in their rural black South Carolina community."

2400. Sandle, Floyd L. *The Negro in the American Educational Theater: An Organizational Development, 1911–1964.* Ann Arbor, Mich.: Edwards Brothers, 1964.

2401. Sarden, Claudia. *The Memoirs of Dolly: A High School Graduate.* Los Angeles: Holloway House Publishing Co., 1987.

2402. Schwarz-Bart, Simone. *Between Two Worlds: A Novel.* Translated from the French by Barbara Bray.* New York: Harper and Row, 1981.

2403. Sekora,* John, and Darwin T. Turner, eds. *The Art of Slave Narrative: Original Essays in Criticism and Theory.* Macomb: Western Illinois University, 1982.

2404. Shange, Ntozake. *Betsey Brown.* New York: St. Martin's Press, 1985.

2405. ————. *A Daughter's Geography.* New York: St. Martin's Press, 1983.

These poem maps challenge the expanding horizons of the black imagination today, from the indigo mood of Harlem's streets to the sun-drenched colors of the Caribbean, from passionate songs of pain and outrage to the tipsy cakewalks of love's exhilaration.

2406. ————. *For Colored Girls Who Have Considered Suicide/When the Rainbow Is Enuf: A Choreopoem.* New York: Macmillan Co., 1977. Reprint. New York: Bantam Books, 1986.

2407. ————. *From Okra to Greens: A Different Kinda Love Story: A Play with Music and Dance.* New York: S. French, 1985.

2408. ————. *From Okra to Greens: Poems.* St. Paul: Coffee House Press, 1984.

2409. ————. *Nappy Edges.* New York: St. Martin's Press, 1978.

"The roots of your hair/what turns back when we sweat, run, makelove, dance, get afraid, get happy: the tell-tale signs of living." Poetry.

2410. ————. *A Photograph: Lovers in Motion: A Drama.* New York: S. French, 1981.

2411. ————. *Ridin' the Moon in Texas: Word Paintings.* New York: St. Martin's Press, 1987.

2412. ————. *Sassafrass.* San Lorenzo, Calif.: Shameless Hussy Press, 1976.

"This is the first section of a four-part novel dealing with the lives of different women in the same family. The next three sections will be published by Heirs in San Francisco and Shameless Hussy."

2413. ————. *Sassafrass, Cypress, and Indigo: A Novel.* New York: St. Martin's Press, 1982.

2414. ————. *See No Evil: Prefaces, Essays, & Accounts, 1976–1983.* San Francisco: Momo's Press, 1984.

2415. ————. *Spell #7: A Theater Piece in Two Acts.* New York: S. French, 1981.

2416. ————. *Three Pieces.* New York: St. Martin's Press, 1981.

2417. Sharp, Saundra. *From the Windows of My Mind: Poems.* New York: Togetherness Productions, 1970.

2418. ————. *In the Midst of Change: Poems.* Photos by Chester Higgins, Jr., Cornell Norris, and Ronald St. Clair. 2d ed. New York: Togetherness Productions, 1972.

2419. Sheffey, Ruthe T., and Eugenia W. Collier, eds. *Impressions in Asphalt: Images of Urban America in Literature.* New York: Charles Scribner's Sons, 1969.

2420. Smith, Arthur Lee, Jr. *The Break of Dawn.* Philadelphia: Dorrance and Co., 1964.

This book contains fifty poems by the author, including "Visions of Tomorrow," "Advice from King," "Sisyphus," "Concerning Freedom," "Soul," "Black Man's Theme," "Shall I Not Speak," "Africa," "Peace," "The Death of a System," "Four Young Philomels," "Death of Medgar Evers," and "In Memory of John Kennedy."

2421. ————. *Rhetoric of Black Revolution.* Boston: Allyn and Bacon, 1969.

The author discusses the origin, strategies, themes, and audience of the black revolutionary rhetoric. Noting that the authentic rhetoric of black America has always been militant and revolutionary, Smith includes sample speeches by Charles Lenox

Remond, Frederick Douglass, Adam Clayton Powell, Franklin Florence, Eldridge Cleaver, and Bobby Seale. This is a useful book for those who seek a better understanding of the rhetoric of black revolution and its subtleties.

2422. ————. *Towards Transracial Communication.* Los Angeles: UCLA Afro-American Studies Center, 1970.

This monograph, the first in a series of papers published by the UCLA Afro-American Studies Center, examines communication between various racial/ethnic groups within the context of existing communication theory, which is "insensitive to the demands of situational pluralism." Directions in transracial communication, the importance of race and culture in verbal interaction, and the structure of transracial communication are discussed. A bibliography and index are included.

2423. ————. *Transracial Communication.* Englewood Cliffs, N.J.: Prentice-Hall, 1973.

Within the purview of current communication theory, Smith shows how communication is patterned in interracial situations and how it may impede cross-cultural interaction, particularly in the area of elocution. He includes a discussion of black idioms, the function of black language, and the effects of classism and sexism as well as racism on our interpersonal interaction. In addition to the author's suggestions, the lists of objectives at the beginning of each chapter are invaluable.

2424. ————, ed. *Language, Communication, and Rhetoric in Black America.* New York: Harper and Row, 1972.

This collection of twenty-nine articles by Smith and other scholars in the field addresses the place of language and communication in black society. It is divided into five parts: "Black Language," "Language and Ethnicity," "Rhetorical Case Studies," "Criticisms and Social Change," and "Social and Historical Dimensions," and included is an introduction to each part. Collectively, these essays support the premise that blacks in

America have developed "peculiar modes of inventing and organizing language and communication."

2425. Smith, Arthur Lee, Jr., and Stephen Robbs,** eds. *The Voice of Black Rhetoric: Selections.* Boston: Allyn and Bacon, 1971.

Spanning more than 140 years, this collection includes some of the most notable speeches by politicians, educators, preachers, legislators, and movement leaders dealing with a variety of subjects. Included are David Walker, Henry Highland Garnet, Eldridge Cleaver, Benjamin E. Mays, Malcolm X, Charles Lenox Remond, Martin Luther King, Jr., H. Rap Brown, and Robert C. Weaver.

2426. Smith, Arthur Lee, Jr., Deluvina Hernandez,** and Anne Allen.** *How to Talk "With" People of Other Races, Ethnic Groups, and Cultures.* Los Angeles: Trans–Ethnic Foundation, 1971.

The authors analyze various research studies to determine how stereotyped images of various racial/ethnic groups develop and how these false images impede interracial and interpersonal communication. They summarize their findings and provide guidelines to effective transracial communication.

2427. Springs, John B., III. *Kansas: A Novel.* Los Angeles: Holloway House Publishing Co., 1984.

2428. ———. *Mink: A Novel.* Los Angeles: Holloway House Publishing Co., 1985.

2429. ———. *The Pocket: A Novel.* Los Angeles: Holloway House Publishing Co., 1985.

2430. Stadley, Quandra Prettyman, ed. *Out of Our Lives: A Collection of Contemporary Black Fiction.* 1975. Reprint. Washington, D.C.: Howard University Press, 1981.

This work features short stories by seventeen of the most outstanding contemporary fiction writers, including Toni Cade Bambara, Darrell Gray, Albert Murray, Louise Meriwether, Deloris Harrison, and LeRoi Jones. It presents a wide variety of subjects, locales, and styles.

2431. Stepto, Robert Burns. *From Behind the Veil: A Study of Afro-American Narrative.* Urbana: University of Illinois Press, 1979.

2432. Stetson, Erlene LaQuetta, ed. *Black Sister: Poetry by Black American Women 1746–1980.* Bloomington: Indiana University Press, 1981.

2433. Stewart, Rae Shawn. *Dying Is So Easy.* Los Angeles: Holloway House Publishing Co., 1984.

2434. ———. *Gotta Pay to Live.* Los Angeles: Holloway House Publishing Co., 1985.

2435. ———. *Treat Them Like Animals.* Los Angeles: Holloway House Publishing Co., 1982.

2436. Stone, Chuck. *King Strut.* Indianapolis: Bobbs–Merrill Co., 1970.

2437. Strickland, Dorothy S., ed. *Listen Children: An Anthology of Black Literature.* Toronto: Bantam Books, 1982. Reprint. New York: Bantam Skylark Books, 1986.

This book contains more than twenty pieces of literature by such authors as Gwendolyn Brooks, Langston Hughes, Kristin Hunter, Alice Childress, Virginia Hamilton, and Stevie Wonder.

2438. Tarry, Ellen. *Hezekiah Horton.* New York: Viking Press, 1942.

2439. ———. *Janie Belle.* New York: Garden City Publishing Co., 1940.

2440. Tarry, Ellen, and Marie Hall Ets.* *My Dog Rinty.* New York: Viking Press, 1946.

2441. Tate, Claudia. *Black Women Writers at Work.* New York: Continuum, 1983.

This book is collection of interviews with fourteen major black women writers—Maya Angelou, Toni Cade Bambara, Gwendolyn Brooks, Alexis DeVeaux, Nikki Giovanni, Kristin Hunter, Gayl Jones, Audre Lorde, Toni Morrison, Sonia Sanchez, Ntozake Shange, Alice Walker, Margaret Walker, and Sherley Anne Williams. Claudia Tate orchestrates the interviews which blend personal histories and literary reflections.

2442. ————. *The Climate of Candor: A Novel of the 1970s.* New York: Pageant Press, 1961.

2443. Thomas, Charles Cyrus. *A Black Lark Caroling.* Dallas: Kaleidograph Press, 1936.

2444. Thomas, Joyce Carol. *Bittersweet: Poems.* San Jose, Calif.: Firesign Press, 1973.

2445. ————. *Crystal Breezes: Poems.* 1st ed. Berkeley: Firesign Press, 1974.

2446. ————. *Journey.* New York: Scholastic, 1988.

Meggie spearheads an investigation into the mysterious disappearances and murders of young people in her town, discovering a plot to rob others of their youth in a horrifying way.

2447. Thurman, Wallace. *Infants in the Spring.* 1932. Reprint. Carbondale: Southern Illinois University Press, 1979.

Thurman was one of the Harlem Renaissance writers, and this novel satirizes the role of black writers and artists during that period.

2448.   Tinker, Barbara Wilson. *When the Fire Reaches Us.* New York: William Morrow and Co., 1970.

2449.   Troupe, Quincy, and Rainer Schulte,* eds. *Giant Talk: An Anthology of Third World Writers.* New York: Random House, 1975.

This important volume of literature offers a clear yet broad definition of the term *Third World.* Striving to be comprehensive in recognition of the incredible volume, wealth, and range of Third World literature, this book is also concerned with an arrangement of the selections that reveals the uniqueness of this literature. A bibliography and biographical notes on Third World writers are included.

2450.   Turner, Darwin T. *In a Minor Chord: Three Afro–American Writers and Their Search for Identity.* Carbondale: Southern Illinois University Press, 1971.

Turner traces the careers of Jean Toomer (1894–1967), Countee Cullen (1903–1946), and Zora Neale Hurston (1901–1960). He also deals with the difficulties black writers have had in gaining recognition and acceptance.

2451.   ———. *Katharsis.* Wellesley, Mass.: Wellesley Press, 1964.

2452.   ———, ed. *Black American Literature: Essays, Poetry, Fiction, Drama.* Columbus, Ohio: Charles E. Merrill Co., 1970.

"A composite of three volumes, previously published separately in 1969, and a new section on drama." Includes bibliographical references.

2453.   ———, ed. *Black American Literature: Fiction.* Columbus, Ohio: Charles E. Merrill Co., 1969.

This work includes "Po Sandy," by C. W. Chesnutt; "The Modification of the Flesh," by P. L. Dunbar; "Mr. Cornelius Johnson, Office–seeker," by P. L. Dunbar; "Fern," by J. Toomer;

"Cordelia the Crude," by W. Thurman; "Sweat," by Z. Hurston; "Thank You, M'am," by L. Hughes; "Last Whiping," by L. Hughes; "Christmas Song," by L. Hughes; "The Man Who Was Almost a Man," by R. Wright; "My Brother Went to College," by F. Yerby; "Mister Toussan," by R. Ellison; "The Man Child," by J. Baldwin; "The Only Man on Liberty Street," by W. M. Kelley; "Debut," by K. Hunter. It also includes a bibliography.

2454. ——, ed. *Black American Literature: Poetry.* Columbus, Ohio: Charles E. Merrill Co., 1969.

2455. ——, ed. *Black Drama in America: An Anthology.* Greenwich, Conn.: Fawcett Publications, 1971.

This work includes a critical introduction by D. T. Turner; "The Chip Woman's Fortune," by Willis Richardson; "Emperor of Haiti," by Langston Hughes; "Our Lan,'" by T. Ward; "Bayou Legend," by O. Dodson; "Take a Giant Step," by L. Peterson; "Earth and Stars," by R. Edmonds; "Purlie Victorious," by O. Davis; "The Toilet," by L. Jones (Imamu Amiri Baraka); "We Righteous Bombers," by K. B. Bass, Jr. It also includes a bibliography.

2456. ——, ed. *Black Literature: Essays.* Columbus, Ohio: Charles E. Merrill Co., 1969.

2457. ——, ed. *Cane: An Authoritative Text, Backgrounds, Criticisms.* New York: W. W. Norton and Co., 1988.

2458. ——, ed. *The Wayward and the Seeking: A Collection of Writings by Jean Toomer.* Washington, D.C.: Howard University Press, 1980.

With an introduction by Turner, this collection reveals Jean Toomer's intellectual and psychological development prior to the publication of *Cane,* which instantly made Toomer a major figure of the Harlem Renaissance.

2459. Turner, Darwin T., and Jean M. Bright, eds. *Images of the Negro in America.* Boston: D. C. Heath and Co., 1965.

2460. Turner, Darwin T., Jean M. Bright, and Richard Wright, comps. *Voices from the Black Experience: African and Afro-American Literature.* Lexington, Mass.: Ginn and Co., 1972.

2461. Turner, Glennette Tilley. *Surprise for Mrs. Burns.* Chicago: Albert Whitman, 1971.

When they discover she is leaving, Mrs. Burns's class decides to give her a party.

2462. Turner, Lorenzo Dow. *Africanisms in the Gullah Dialect.* Chicago: University of Chicago Press, 1949. Reprint. New York: Arno Press, 1969.

Turner refutes the assumption that the peculiarities of the Gullah dialect spoken by many blacks in coastal South Carolina and Georgia are traceable almost entirely to the British dialects of the seventeenth and eighteenth centuries and to a form of "baby talk" adopted by slave masters to facilitate oral communication between themselves and slaves. His investigation, which extended over fifteen years, shows that Gullah, a Creolized form of English, contains survival from many African languages spoken by slaves. These Africanisms can be observed in the sounds, syntax, morphology, intonation, and methods used to form words, as well as in the vocabulary of the Gullah dialect. Turner outlines the most important Africanisms and their equivalents in the West African languages. The book includes an appendix, bibliography, notes, and index.

2463. ————. *Anti-Slavery Sentiment in American Literature Prior to 1865.* Washington, D.C.: Association for the Study of Negro Life and History, 1929. Reprint. Port Washington, N.Y.: Kennikat Press, 1966.

Using novels, poems, short narratives, plays, essays, magazine and newspaper articles, and a selected number of orations, letters, diaries, journals, sermons, and books of travel, Turner traces the growth of antislavery sentiment prior to 1865 and indicates that it was influenced by the "spirit of the time." The time span is divided into five periods: 1641 to 1808, when the Slave–Trade Act abolished slavery; 1808 to 1831, when William Lloyd Garrison published *The Liberator*; 1831 to 1850, when the Fugitive Slave Act was passed; 1850 to 1861, when the Civil War began; and 1861 to 1865, when it ended. Turner provides various reasons—moral, religious, social, economic, sentimental, and political—for the antislavery sentiment.

2464.   Vandi, Abdulai S. *A Model of Mass Communications and National Development: A Liberian Perspective.* Washington, D.C.: University Press of America, 1979.

This study was designed to review the use of mass media in community education in both advanced (United States, Canada, Japan) and developing (El Salvador, India, Ivory Coast) countries to ascertain basic principles that could be used in developing mass media in community education programs in Liberia.

2465.   Vernon, William Tecumseh. *The Upbuilding of a Race; or, The Rise of a Great People, a Compilation of Sermons, Addresses, and Writing on Education, the Race Question and Public Affairs.* Quindaro, Kans.: Industrial Student Printers, 1904.

2466.   Wade–Gayles, Gloria Jean. *No Crystal Stair: Visions of Race and Sex in Black Women's Fiction.* New York: Pilgrim Press, 1984.

2467.   Walker, Alice. *The Color Purple.* 1st ed. New York: Harcourt Brace Jovanovich, 1982.

2468.   ————. *Good Night Willie Lee, I'll See You in the Morning: Poems.* New York: Dial Press, 1979. Reprint. San Diego: Harcourt Brace Jovanovich, 1984.

2469. ———. *Horses Make a Landscape Look More Beautiful: Poems.* San Diego: Harcourt Brace Jovanovich, 1984.

2470. ———. *In Love and Trouble: Stories of Black Women.* New York: Harcourt Brace Jovanovich, 1974.

2471. ———. *In Search of Our Mothers' Gardens.* New York: Harcourt Brace Jovanovich, 1983.

2472. ———. *Meridan.* San Diego: Harcourt Brace Jovanovich, 1976. Reprint. Santa Barbara, Calif.: ABC–Clio Information Services, 1987.

2473. ———. *Revolutionary Petunias and Other Poems.* San Diego: Harcourt Brace Jovanovich, 1973.

The winner of the Pulitzer Prize and the American Book Award for fiction, this story is told by Celie, the main character, through letters to God and to her sister, Nettie. It shows how Celie survived with very little and how she learned to ask for more—to laugh, to play, and to love.

2474. ———. *The Temple of My Familiar.* New York: Harcourt Brace Jovanovich, 1989.

Written by the Pulitzer Prize–winning author of *The Color Purple*, this story is a "romance of the last 500,000 years." Central to the story are two marriages in crisis and a third that has long since shaken down. Miss Celie and Miss Shug of *The Color Purple* are among the many characters.

2475. ———. *The Third Life of Grange Copeland.* 1st ed. New York: Harcourt Brace Jovanovich, 1970.

2476. ———. *You Can't Keep a Good Woman Down: Stories.* New York: Harcourt Brace Jovanovich, 1981.

2477. Walker, Margaret. *For My People.* New York: Arno Press, 1968. Reprint. Salem, N.H.: Ayer Co., 1987.

2478. ———. *Jubilee.* Boston: Houghton Mifflin, 1966. Reprint. Chicago: Third World Press, 1972.

Based on the true story of her great–grandmother, Walker depicts black life in Georgia before, during, and after the Civil War. Vyry, the main character of the novel, is the daughter of the white plantation owner and his black (slave) mistress. Born into slavery, Vyry, who works in the "big" house, overcomes the hardships of slavery and blooms into a strong beautiful woman. Margaret Walker received the Houghton Mifflin Literary Fellowship Award for this novel.

2479. ———. *Prophets of a New Day.* Detroit: Broadside Press, 1970.

2480. ———. *Richard Wright: Daemonic Genius: A Portrait of the Man, A Critical Look at His Work.* New York: Warner Books, 1988.

Divided into five parts, related to five periods of his life, this biography of Wright by one of his contemporaries provides a synthesis of Wright's life and his works. Includes an index.

2481. Wall, Cheryl A., ed. *Essays on Criticism, Theory, and Writing by Black Women.* New Brunswick, N.J.: Rutgers University Press, 1989.

2482. Wallace, Susan J. *Bahamian Scene.* Philadelphia: Dorrance and Co., 1970.

2483. Warbash, Denver. *Execution by Choice.* Los Angeles: Holloway House Publishing Co., 1985.

2484. Washington, Mary Helen, ed. *Black–Eyed Susans: Classic Stories By and About Black Women.* Garden City, N.Y.: Doubleday and Co., 1975.

This book contains stories by Jean Wheeler Smith, Toni Morrison, Gwendolyn Brooks, Louise Meriwether, Toni Cade

Bambara, Alice Walker, and Paule Marshall. Introduction is by Mary Helen Washington.

2485.   ————, ed. *Invented Lives: Narratives of Black Women 1860-1960*. Garden City, N.Y.: Doubleday and Co., 1987.

2486.   ————, ed. *Midnight Birds: Stories of Contemporary Black Women Writers*. Garden City, N.Y.: Doubleday and Co., 1980.

2487.   Waters, Elroy. *Stack A Dollar*. Los Angeles: Holloway House Publishing Co., 1979.

2488.   Webb, Frank J. *The Garies and their Friends*. New York: G. Routledge, 1857. Reprint. New York: Arno Press, 1969.

First published in 1857, this novel, the second by an American black, depicts the plight of free blacks in pre-Civil War Philadelphia. It is the story of two families, the Ellises, a dark group, and the Garies, a "mixed" family consisting of a wealthy white southerner, his mulatto wife, and their two children. Includes a preface by Harriet Beecher Stowe** and a new preface by Arthur P. Davis.

2489.   Wheatley, Phillis [*afterwards* Mrs. John Peters. ca. 1753-1784]. *The Poems of Phillis Wheatley, As They Were Originally Published in London, 1773*. Philadelphia: Republished by R. R. and C. C. Wright, 1909.

This work has subsequently been edited with an introduction by Julian Dewey Mason, Jr.,** and published by the University of North Carolina Press, 1966, 1989.

2490.   Whitaker, Ginger. *The Dowry: A Novel*. Los Angeles: Holloway House Publishing Co., 1989.

Carrie Brown is young and beautiful, and a mystery the townspeople can't figure out. For Jimmy, she is the answer to the age-old gnawing in his heart. He will do anything to have Carrie

Brown, even buy her. But what Jimmy ends up paying and what Carrie ends up getting are not what either had expected.

2491. White, Edgar B. *Underground: Four Plays.* New York: William Morrow and Co., 1970.

2492. White, Oscar, and Sonia Martin.** *Learning English as a Second Language for Secondary Schools and Continuing Education.* 4 vols. Dobbs Ferry, N.Y.: Oceana Publications, 1976.

2493. White, Walter Francis. *The Fire in the Flint.* New York: Alfred A. Knopf, 1924. Reprint. New York: Negro Universities Press, 1969.

2494. ————. *Flight.* New York: Alfred A. Knopf, 1926. Reprint. New York: Negro Universities Press, 1969.

2495. Williams, Bruce E., and Orlando L. Taylor, eds. *International Conference on Black Communication: A Bellagio Conference, 1979.* New York: Rockefeller Foundation, 1980.

2496. Williams, John Alfred. *The Angry Black.* New York: Lancer Books, 1962.

2497. ————. *The Angry Ones.* New York: Ace Books, 1960. Reprint. New York: Pocket Book, 1970.

2498. ————. *The Berhama Account.* Far Hills, N.J.: New Horizon Press, 1985.

2499. ————. *Captain Blackman: A Novel.* Garden City, N.Y.: Doubleday and Co., 1972. Reprint. New York: Thunder's Mouth Press, 1988.

2500. ————. *!Click Song.* Boston: Houghton Mifflin Co., 1982. Reprint. New York: Thunder's Mouth Press, 1987.

2501. ————. *Flashbacks: A Twenty-Year Diary of Article Writing.* Garden City, N.Y.: Anchor Press, 1973.

2502. ———. *Jacob's Ladder: A Novel.* New York: Thunder's Mouth Press, 1987.

Set in the late 1960s, this novel is about the seamy underside of U.S. foreign policy in the Third World. It contains the twin tales of Chuma Fasseke, an independent soul and president of his independent African country, and Jake Henry, Afro-American and military man, a soul at war with his history.

2503. ———. *Journey out of Anger.* London: Eyre and Spottiswoode, 1965.

2504. ———. *The Junior Bachelor Society.* Garden City, N.Y.: Doubleday and Co., 1976.

2505. ———. *The Man Who Cried I Am.* Boston: Little, Brown and Co., 1967. Reprint. New York: Thunder's Mouth Press, 1985.

This novel is a panoramic account of Afro-American life between World War II and the 1960s. Among other things, it offers insights into the harsh segregation of the 1940s and the expatriation of black intellectuals to places such as Paris and Amsterdam.

2506. ———. *Minorities in the City.* New York: Harper and Row, 1975.

2507. ———. *Mothersill and the Foxes.* Garden City, N.Y.: Doubleday and Co., 1975.

2508. ———. *Night Song.* New York: Farrar, Straus and Cudahy, 1961. Reprint. Chatham, N.J.: Chatham Bookseller, 1975.

2509. ———. *One for New York.* Chatham, N.J.: Chatham Bookseller, 1975.

2510. ———. *Sissie.* Garden City, N.Y.: Doubleday and Co., 1963. Reprint. New York: Thunder's Mouth Press, 1988.

2511. ────. *Sons of Darkness, Sons of Light: A Novel of Some Probability*. Boston: Little, Brown and Co., 1969.

2512. ────. *Sweet Love Bitter*. New York: Farrar, Straus and Cudahy, 1961. Reprint. New York: Dell Publishing Co., 1966. Originall published as *Night Song*.

2513. ────, ed. *Beyond the Angry Black*. New York: Cooper Square Publishers, 1966. Reprint. New York: New American Library, 1971.

This is a reissue with new material of *The Angry Black*, published in 1962. Deals with Afro-Americans in literature.

2514. Williams, R. Ora. *An Alice Dunbar-Nelson Reader*. Washington, D.C.: University Press of America, 1978.

An anthology of essays, plays, poems, and short stories by a prominent black woman. Dunbar-Nelson was a suffragist, social worker, antilynching crusader, college professor, lecturer, and precursor of many contemporary Afro-American artists and writers.

2515. Williams, Robert L., ed. *Ebonics: The True Language of Black Folks*. St. Louis, Mo.: Institute of Black Studies, 1975.

This book takes a look at Afro-American language as viewed from a black perspective. It develops the meaning of the term *ebonics*, which was created by a caucus of black scholars from various disciplines at a national conference convened in 1973 to discuss language development in the black child. The text comprises both studies and viewpoints of the various essayists on black language and its relation to intelligence and intellectual development.

2516. Williams, Sherley Anne. *Dessa Rose*. New York: William Morrow and Co., 1986.

2517. ————. *Give Birth to Brightness: A Thematic Study in Neo-Black Literature.* New York: Dial Press, 1972.

2518. ————. *The Peacock Poems.* 1st ed. Middletown, Conn.: Wesleyan University Press, 1975.

2519. ————. *Semantic Behavior and Decision Making.* Ann Arbor, Mich.: Published for Center for Public Affairs, University of Southern California, by University Microfilms International, 1978.

2520. ————. *Some One Sweet Angel Chile.* 1st ed. New York: William Morrow and Co., 1982.

2521. Williamson, Juanita V. *A Phonological and Morphological Study of the Speech of the Negro of Memphis, Tennessee.* Publication of the American Dialect Society. Tuscaloosa: Published for the Society by University of Alabama Press, 1970.

2522. Williamson, Juanita V., and Virginia M. Burke,** eds. *A Various Language: Perspectives on American Dialects.* New York: Holt, Rinehart and Winston, 1971.

2523. Willis, Leydel Johnson. *Bits and Pieces.* Madison, Wis.: FAS Publishing Division, 1977.

2524. ————. *A Black Snowball: Poems.* Detroit: Harlo Press, 1977.

2525. ————. *The Rainbow Is Not Enough.* Little Rock, Ark.: Parkhurst, 1981; distributed by Clodele Enterprises.

2526. ————. *Yesterday, Today, and Tomorrow.* Book 1. Detroit: Harlo Press, 1976.

2527. ————. *Yesterday, Today, and Tomorrow.* Book 2. Detroit: Harlo Press, 1978.

2528. ————. *Yesterday, Today, and Tomorrow.* Book 3. Detroit: Harlo Press, 1980.

2529. Wilson, August. *Fences: A Play.* Introduction by Lloyd Richards. New York: New American Library, 1986.

2530. ————. *Joe Turner's Come and Gone: A Play in Two Acts.* New York: New American Library, 1988.

2531. Wilson, D. B. *Betrayed.* Los Angeles: Holloway House Publishing Co., 1984.

2532. Wilson, Julia. *Becky.* Illustrated by John Wilson. New York: Thomas Y. Crowell Co., 1967.

2533. Woodson, Carter Goodwin. *Negro Orators and Their Orations.* Washington, D.C.: Associated Publishers, 1925.

Woodson selects orations that represent the various stages in the history of the black man in America: defiant denunciations of slavery, speeches by blacks elected during Reconstruction, and optimistic and progressive–minded orations by blacks most illustrative of their time.

2534. Wright, Jerome Dyson. *Poor, Black, and in Real Trouble.* Los Angeles: Holloway House Publishing Co., 1976.

2535. ————. *Second Chance: A Novel.* Los Angeles: Holloway House Publishing Co., 1986.

2536. Wright, Nathan, Jr. *The Song of Mary: Poems.* Boston: Bruce Humphries, 1958.

2537. Wright, Richard. *American Hunger.* New York: Harper and Row, 1977.

The book *Black Boy* concludes with Wright's departure in 1934 for a new life in the North. It treats Wright's struggle to make his way in the North—in Chicago—as a store clerk, dishwasher, and eventually as a writer. This book, first published more than thirty years after the appearance of *Black Boy*, continues that story.

2538. ————. *Lawd Today.* New York: Walker and Co., 1963.

2539. ————. *The Long Dream: A Novel.* Garden City, N.Y.: Doubleday and Co., 1958. Reprint. Chatham, N.J.: Chatham Bookseller, 1969.

2540. ————. *Native Son.* New York: Harper and Brothers, 1940. Reprint. New York: Harper and Row, 1986.

2541. ————. *The Outsider.* New York: Harper and Brothers, 1953. Reprint. New York: Perennial Library, Harper and Row, 1965.

The Outsider, a violent story, tells of a man (Cross Damon) at odds with society and with himself, who hungers for peace but who brings terror and destruction wherever he goes. It is a gruesome presentation of a man who stands alone and apart from the rest of the world.

2542. ————. *Uncle Tom's Children.* New York: Harper and Row, 1938. Reprint. New York: New American Library, 1963.

This work contains five short stories and an autobiographical essay. The stories show southern blacks in the post–Civil War era living lives filled with hatred and violence as they struggle for survival.

2543. Wright, Sarah E. *This Child's Gonna Live.* With an appreciation by John Oliver Killens. New York: Feminist Press, 1986.

2544. Wynter, Sylvia. *The Hills of Hebron: A Jamaican Novel.* New York: Simon and Schuster, 1962.

2545. Yerby, Frank. *Griffin's Way: A Novel.* New York: Dial Press, 1962.

2546. Young, Al. *Ask Me Now*. New York: McGraw–Hill, 1980.

2547. ————. *The Blues Don't Change: New and Selected Poems*. Baton Rouge: Louisiana State University Press, 1982.

2548. ————. *Dancing: Poems*. 1st ed. New York: Corinth Books, 1969.

2549. ————. *Geography of the Near Past: Poems*. New York: Holt, Rinehart and Winston, 1976.

2550. ————. *Seduction by Light*. New York: Delta Books, 1988.

2551. ————. *Sitting Pretty: A Novel*. New York: Holt, Rinehart and Winston, 1976. Reprint. Berkeley: Creative Arts Book Co., 1986.

2552. ————. *Snakes: A Novel*. New York: Holt, Rinehart and Winston, 1970. Reprint. Berkeley: Creative Arts Book Co., 1981.

2553. ————. *The Song Turning Back into Itself: Poems*. 1st ed. New York: Holt, Rinehart and Winston, 1971.

2554. ————. *Who Is Angelina? A Novel*. 1st ed. New York: Holt, Rinehart and Winston, 1975. Reprint. London, Sidgwick and Jackson, 1978.

2555. Young, James O. *Black Writers of the Thirties*. Baton Rouge: Louisiana State University Press, 1973.

Young examines the works of Afro–Americans writing in a variety of political, economic, social, and cultural contexts during the Great Depression of the 1930s. Although he covers well-known writers such as W. E. B. DuBois, James Weldon Johnson, and Richard Wright, he places greater emphasis on less-celebrated individuals, such as Carter G. Woodson, Kelly Miller, George S. Schuyler, and Charles S. Johnson.

2556. Young, Joseph A. *Black Novelist as White Racist: The Myth of Black Inferiority in the Novels of Oscar Micheaux.* Westport, Conn.: Greenwood Press, 1989.

Young analyzes six novels by Oscar Micheaux (1884–1948?) who, according to Young, rejects "both his own blackness and that of his racial kinsmen." The novels are *The Conquest* (1913), *The Forged Note* (1915), *The Homesteader* (1917), *The Wind from Nowhere* (1941), *The Case of Mrs. Wingate* (1945), and *The Story of Dorothy Stanfield* (1946). Includes bibliography and index.

CHAPTER 8

PHILOSOPHY, PSYCHOLOGY, AND RELIGION

2557. Adams, Elizabeth Laura. *Dark Symphony*. New York: Sheed and Ward, 1942.

2558. Addo, Linda D., and James H. McCallum.* *To Be Faithful to Our Heritage: A History of Black United Methodism in North Carolina*. Raleigh: Western North Carolina Annual Conference, United Methodist Church, 1980.

2559. Akbar, Na'im. *The Community of Self*. Rev. ed. Tallahassee, Fla: Mind Productions and Associates, 1985.

2560. Baker, William H. *On Capital Punishment*. Chicago: Moody Press, 1985.

2561. ————. *Plain Pointed Practical Preaching: Old-Fashioned Bible Chautauqua Sermons*. New York: Greenwich Book Publishers, 1956.

2562. ————. *Sanctification: Why We Resist God, How to Overcome It*. Grand Rapids, Mich.: Lamplighter Books, 1986.

2563. Banner, William Augustus. *Ethics: An Introduction to Moral Philosophy*. New York: Charles Scribner's Sons, 1968.

467

2564.   ————. *Moral Norms and Moral Order: The Philosophy of Human Affairs.* Gainesville: University Presses of Florida, 1981.

In precise, elegant language that befits the classical views he supports, Banner presents a unified vision of matters that today are commonly regarded as distinct and are treated under the separate headings of ethics, politics, and law. Written in general agreement with Aristotle's view of the personal and public affairs of human beings, this book offers a careful and sustained argument for not separating questions of justice from questions of legality. The work concludes with a defense of the idea of punishment as restoration or restitution as opposed to retaliation, correction, or deterrence. Includes notes, bibliography, and indexes.

2565.   Bashir, Iman Abdul Alim. *A Serious Creation.* Jersey City, N.J.: New Mind Productions, 1987.

2566.   Bramble, Peter W. D. *The Overcome: A Black Passover.* Columbia, Md.: C. H. Fairfax Co., Publishers, 1989.

2567.   Brawley, James Phillip. *Climbing Jacob's Ladder.* Nashville: Board of Education; United Methodist Church, 1968.

2568.   ————. *Matthew Simpson Dauage: Elder Statesman and Revered Sage.* Nashville: Board of Education, United Methodist Church, 1973.

2569.   Breathett, George, ed. *The Catholic Church in Haiti, 1704–1785: Selected Letters, Memoirs, and Documents.* Salisbury, N.C.: Documentary Publications, 1983.

2570.   Brody, Emess Bright, and Nathan Brody.** *Intelligence: Nature, Determinants and Consequences.* New York: Academic Press, 1976.

Starting with the historical development of intelligence tests and their innovators, C. Spearman and L. Thurstone, the Brodys investigate "the results of seventy years of statistically oriented research on the structure of intelligence." Other areas, such as the quantitative properties of the numerical index and its stability and change over time; variable; biological and social determinants of intelligence and the uses of intelligence tests with a skeptical analysis of the utility of such tests, are also discussed.

2571. Brown, Carolyn T., ed. *Psycho–Sinology* = *Meng: The Universe of Dreams in Chinese Culture.* Washington, D.C.: Asia Program, Woodrow Wilson International Center for Scholars, 1988; distributed by University Press of America.

This work consist of papers from a conference held on May 27, 1986, in Washington, D.C., and sponsored by the Asia Program, Woodrow Wilson International Center for Scholars.

2572. Brown, Hubert L. *Black and Mennonite: A Search for Identity.* Scottdale, Pa.: Herald Press, 1976.

2573. Carriger, Sally A. *Stories About Jesus.* Illustrated by Terry McBride.* Washington, D.C.: Review and Herald Publishing Assoc., 1978.

2574. ————. *Stories from the Old Testament.* Illustrated by Terry Crews.* Washington, D.C.: Review and Herald Publishing Association. 1979.

2575. Cheek, Donald K. *Assertive Black . . . Puzzled White.* San Luis Obispo, Calif.: Impact, 1976.

Cheek presents a program specifically designed to aid blacks in the development of self–assertion and personal effectiveness skills. The black experience in America, which Cheeks refers to as the "Jim Crow Halo Effect," is integrated with this exclusive training program. (Also important in this presentation is an analysis of how black assertiveness is misinterpreted by whites.)

2576. Clark, Kenneth Bancroft. *Prejudice and Your Child.* 2d ed. Boston: Beacon Press, 1963.

In this psychological study based on *Brown v. Board of Education* (1954), Clark examines the effects of prejudice among children in both minority and dominant groups. He suggests that to overcome feelings of prejudice in children, specific courses of action must be implemented by parents, schools, churches, and social agencies.

2577.   Cleveland, Edward Earl. *Ask the Prophets.* Washington, D.C.: Review and Herald Publishing Assoc., 1970.

2578.   ————. *Come Unto Me.* Washington, D.C.: Review and Herald Publishing Assoc., 1968.

2579.   ————. *Free at Last.* Washington, D.C.: Review and Herald Publishing Assoc., 1970.

2580.   ————. *The Gates Shall Not.* Nashville: Southern Publishing Assoc., 1981.

2581.   ————. *Living Soul: "We Shall Overcome."* Nashville: Southern Publishing Assoc., 1974.

2582.   ————. *The Middle Wall.* Washington, D.C.: Review and Herald Publishing Assoc., 1969.

2583.   ————. *Mine Eyes Have Seen.* Washington, D.C.: Review and Herald Publishing Assoc., 1968.

2584.   ————. *Sparks from the Anvil.* Washington, D.C.: Review and Herald Publishing Assoc., 1971.

2585.   ————. *Without a Song.* Washington, D.C.: Review and Herald Publishing Assoc., 1972.

2586.   Clifford, Paul Rountree. *The Pastoral Calling.* Great Neck, N.Y.: Channel Press, 1961.

2587. Cone, James H. *Black Theology and Black Power.* New York: Seabury Press, 1969. Reprint. New York: Harper and Row, 1989.

> Developed within the sociopolitical context of the civil rights and black power movements of the 1960s, this book attempts to reconcile Christianity and black power. It includes a preface to the 1989 edition.

2588. Daniel, William Andrew. *The Education of Negro Ministers: Based upon a Survey of Theological Schools for Negroes in the United States.* New York: Doran, 1925. Reprint. New York: Negro Universities Press, 1969.

> Working from a list of Afro–American schools that advertised theological courses in 1923, the author visited these fifty–two schools in the late sixties to collect the material presented in this book. He discusses not only the administrative and educational organization and problems of these schools but also their origin and development. Particular emphasis here is placed on their historical background and the social forces influencing their development. The two appendixes include statistical data on each of the fifty–two departments and schools of theology.

2589. Davis, Allison. *Psychology of the Child in the Middle Class.* Pittsburgh: University of Pittsburgh Press, 1960.

> This is the topic of Davis's 1960 Horace Mann Lecture at the University of Pittsburgh. Here, he examines some of the processes involved in the emotional development of middle–class children, who often have to work their way up the ladder to positions in business or the professional world. Davis analyzes the relationship between these emotional processes and (1) success or failure in a career; and (2) the achievement of a sense of personal identity and autonomy.

2590. Dillard, John Milton. *Multicultural Counseling: Toward Ethnic and Cultural Relevance in Human Encounters.* Chicago: Nelson–Hall, 1983.

2591. Drake, John Gibbs St. Clair. *The Redemption of Africa and Black Religion.* Chicago: Third World Press, 1970.

Drake deals with the experience of black religion in North America and the Caribbean, indicating the crucial role of religion in our struggles toward freedom, identity, and self–determination. He also deals with the development of a mode of thinking that he calls "Ethiopianism" and with the concept of "providential design" as developed in the centuries of black exile and return.

2592. El–Amin, Mustafa. *Abraham's Legacy: Ancient Wisdom and Modern Reality.* Jersey City, N.J.: New Mind Productions, 1988.

El–Amin highlights two major concerns: faith and reasoning. He shows the progression of Prophet Abraham's faith in Allah and points to the fact that man should not give blind allegiance to any concepts. Man should consult his reasoning and ponder on those things that may not be clear to him. Al–Islam appeals to man's intellect.

2593. Ells,** Kenneth W., Allison Davis, et al.* *Intelligence and Cultural Differences: A Study of Cultural Learning and Problem Solving.* Chicago: University of Chicago Press, 1951.

This work is the product of an extended study of cultural learning as it relates to the solutions of problems in intelligence tests. The book is divided into three sections, with contributions by distinguished black scholars. The first section deals with the investigated problem and outlines its historical and sociological background. The second and third sections describe the procedures, findings, and conclusions of the study.

2594. Evans, Zelia Stephens, with J. T. Alexander,* eds. *The Dexter Avenue Baptist Church, 1877–1977.* 1st ed. Montgomery, Ala.: The Dexter Avenue Baptist Church, 1978.

2595. Fanon, Frantz. *Black Skin, White Masks.* New York: Grove Press, 1967.

Fanon makes a psychoanalytic study of the phenomenon of black men in a white–dominated society and examines the liberation of the man of color from the person of himself. He focuses on the duo–dimension of black and white, starting from the point of white superiority. His book is a study of the "massive existential complex" caused by the juxtaposition of the black and white races.

2596. Felder, Cain H. *Troubling Biblical Waters: Race, Class, and Family.* Maryknoll, N.Y.: Orbis Books, 1989.

The purpose of this book is "to provide some sorely needed correctives regarding the Bible in relation to ancient Africa and Black people today." Felder argues that the relation of blacks to the Bible is not a postbiblical experience. He shows the presence of blacks in the Bible and their association with biblical tradition. Includes notes, bibliography, general index, and a scripture index.

2597. Frazier, Edward Franklin. *The Negro Church in America.* New York: Schocken Books, 1964.

This text presents evidence that changes in the religious life of the Afro–American relates to evolution in the social organization or disorganization of Afro–American life. With documentary evidence taken from correspondence during the slavery era, Frazier analyzes the churches of the free Afro–American, the merger of the Free Negro Institutional Church with the "slave" congregational churches, black religion during and after the migration to the North, and the decline of the social influence of the church in the urban environment. This is a brief but informative analysis of the black church in America.

2598. Fuller, Thomas Oscar. *History of the Negro Baptists of Tennessee.* Memphis, Tenn.: Haskins, 1936.

This history documents the lives of several notable black Baptists of Tennessee and their churches. Fuller uses the available, rather incomplete data to present these personalities responsible for the continuation of the Baptist minority. Of special interest is chapter 9, devoted to white Baptists, which to some degree erases the stereotype that spotlights the Baptist faith as being overwhelmingly Afro-American.

2599. Garabedian,* John H., and Orde Coombs. *Eastern Religions in the Electric Age.* New York: Grosset and Dunlap, 1969.

2600. Goodwin, Bennie Eugene. *The Effective Leader: A Basic Guide to Christian Leadership.* Downers Grove, Ill.: Inter-Varsity Press, 1981.

2601. ————. *The Effective Teacher: A Christian's Guide to Teaching.* Downers Grove, Ill.: Inter-Varsity Press, 1985.

2602. ————. *How to Be a Growing Christian: A Basic Guide to Discipleship.* Downers Grove, Ill.: Inter-Varsity Press, 1987.

2603. ————. *Martin Luther King, Jr.: God's Messenger of Love, Justice, and Hope.* Jersey City, N.J.: Goodpatrick Publishers, 1976.

2604. ————. *Pray and Grow Rich.* Jersey City, N.J.: Goodpatrick Publishers, 1974.

2605. ————. *Pray Right! Live Right! Reflections on the Lord's Prayer.* 2d ed. Downers Grove, Ill.: Inter-Varsity Press, 1979.

2606. ————. *Reflections on Education: Meditations on King, Friere, and Jesus as Social and Religion Education.* East Orange, N.J.: Goodpatrick Publishers, 1978.

2607. Gregory, Dick. *Dick Gregory's Bible Tales, With Commentary.* Edited by James R. McGraw. 1974. Reprint. New York: Stein and Day, 1983.

2608. Grier, William H., and Price M. Cobbs. *Black Rage.* New York: Bantam Books, 1969.

Two psychiatrists discuss the causes of the black man's anger in America—white racism and the heritage of slavery. There are two sides to every issue, and this study brings out both sides of black rage. Thus, it is of interest to both Afro-Americans and whites who may be concerned about its causes.

2609. ————. *The Jesus Bag.* New York: McGraw-Hill, 1971.

2610. Hamilton, Charles V. *Black Preacher in America.* New York: William Morrow and Co., 1972.

A focus on the black preacher, his roles, and activities, with various selected topics. The chapters cover a wide spectrum, from the role of the preacher to his people, to the ministry during slavery, to the relationship between education and the ministry. Presented also are interviews with seven black preachers concerning the extent of their education.

2611. Hamilton, Virginia. *In the Beginning: Creation Stories from Around the World.* Illustrated by Barry Moser.* 1st ed. New York: Harcourt Brace Jovanovich, 1988.

An illustrated collection of twenty-five myths from various parts of the world explaining the creation of the world.

2612. Hansen,* James C., Richard W. Warner,* and Elsie J. Smith. *Group Counseling Theory and Process.* 2d ed. Chicago: Rand McNally College Publishing Co, 1980.

2613. Hargraves, J. Archie. *Stop Pussyfooting Through a Revolution: Some Churches That Did.* New York: Stewardship Council of the United Church of Christ and United Church Board for Homeland Ministeries, 1963.

This book highlights those churches involved in the present urban revolution. The objective is to take note of their efforts and successes so that other churches will follow suit. The author points out some new directions the churches can take for total involvement in their communities and calls for an acute sensitivity on the part of the church to the needs of the urban poor.

2614. Harris, Leonard, ed. *The Philosophy of Alain Locke: Harlem Renaissance and Beyond.* Philadelphia: Temple University Press, 1989.

2615. Harrison–Ross, Phyllis Anne. *Getting It Together: A Psychology Book for Today's Problems.* 2d ed. New York: Learning Trends, 1978.

2616. Haskins, James. *Religions.* New York: J. B. Lippincott Co., 1973.

This book discusses the history, practices, and beliefs of five major world religions: Hinduism, Buddhism, Judaism, Christianity, and Islam. No comparisons are offered; the essence of each is examined separately within its own context. The purpose is to provide insight into why many people are shedding old beliefs for an alternative in the seventies.

2617. ———. *Voodoo and Hoodoo: Their Tradition and Craft as Revealed by Actual Practitioners.* New York: Stein and Day, 1978.

2618. ———. *Witchcraft, Mysticism, and Magic in the Black World.* Garden City, N.Y.: Doubleday and Co., 1974.

Haskins seeks here to relate the supernatural beliefs and practices of Afro–Americans to African beliefs and practices. He contents that the importance of the supernatural in the lives of Afro–Americans today is a direct consequence of the important role the supernatural played, and is playing, in everyday African life. It is for this reason that chapter 2, "The Roots in Africa," deserves special attention as a link between African and Afro-American witchcraft. Another prevailing theme is the comparison between white and black witchcraft practices.

2619. Henderson, George. *A Religious Foundation of Human Relations: Beyond Games*. Norman: University of Oklahoma Press, 1977.

The author realizes the importance of being able to relate to one's fellow human beings, and this book is designed to help anyone interested in improving human relations. Christianity serves as support for most of the book, which covers such topics as divorce, civil rights, racism, and poverty. Divorce, discussed in chapter 4 under the main heading of "Marriage," is viewed from a secular as well as religious point of view. Included in this book are bibliographical references and an index.

2620. Holley, Joseph Winthrop. *Regnum Montis: Scriptural and Historical Evidence That the Destiny of the South Is Interwoven with the Second Coming of Christ*. New York: William-Frederick Press, 1954.

Holley sets forth his religious beliefs in this book and predicts that Christ's coming will bring an end to the present system. All signs indicate the end, according to Daniel's prophecy, now being realized. One of the most potent signs is the worldwide threat of communism. In chapter 12, Holley makes an urgent plea to bar communism from U.S. public schools and colleges.

2621. Hurston, Zora Neale. *The Sanctified Church*. Berkeley: Turtle Island, 1983.

2622. Jackson, Irene Viola, comp. *Lift Every Voice and Sing: A Collection of Afro-American Spirituals and Other Songs*. New York: Church Hymnal Corp., 1981.

2623. Johnson, Joseph Andrew, Jr. *Basic Christian Methodist Belief.* Shreveport, La.: The Fourth Episcopal District Press, 1978.

2624. ————. *Our Faith, Heritage, and Church.* Shreveport, La.: The Fourth Episcopal District Press, 1975.

2625. ————. *Proclamation Theology.* Shreveport, La.: The Fourth Episcopal District Press, 1977.

2626. ————. *The Soul of the Black Preacher.* Shreveport, La.: The Fourth Episcopal District Press, 1970.

2627. Jones, Reginald Lanier, ed. *Black Psychology.* New York: Harper and Row, 1972.

These readings cover psychology as applied to blacks, the psychological assessment of blacks, problems dealing with personality and motivation in blacks, reinterpretations and theoretical ideas about black behavior, counseling and education of blacks, and psychological perspectives on racism.

2628. Jules–Rosette, Bennetta. *African Apostles: Ritual and Conversion in the Church of John Maranke.* Ithaca, N.Y.: Cornell University Press, 1975.

2629. King, Martin Luther, Jr. *The Measure of Man.* Philadelphia: Christian Education Press, 1959. Reprint. Philadelphia: Fortress Press, 1988.

In this slim ecumenical book, King describes the religious, philosophical, and moral foundations upon which his commitment to the freedom movement was based. The book is part religious doctrine, part chastisement for an America that reneged on the promises made at its inception. "You started out right," King wrote. "You wrote the Declaration of Independence. . . . But, America, you strayed away from that sublime principle. You left the house of your great heritage and strayed away into a far country of segregation and discrimination." Pointing out that man is measured by more than wealth or occupation, King wrote: "No matter how small one thinks one's life work is . . . he must realize that it has cosmic significance if he is serving humanity and doing the will of God."

2630. ————. *Strength to Love.* New York: Harper and Row, 1963.

This book, a collection of sermons delivered between the mid-1950s and early 1960s, is one about which Dr. King had reservations. Sermons, he felt, were to be heard, not read. He states: "While I tried to rewrite these sermons for the eyes, I am convinced that this venture could never be entirely successful." The seventeen sermons tackle a variety of topics ranging from "Loving Your Enemies" to "How Should A Christian View Communism?" Besides Christianity, the connecting thread is the veiled message that blacks should steel themselves against the forces of oppression while marching toward equality.

2631. Lewis, Meharry H. *Seventy-fifth Anniversary Yearbook: The Church of the Living God, The Pillar and Ground of the Truth, Inc., 1903-1978.* Nashville: The New and the Living Way Publishing House, 1978.

2632. Lincoln, Charles Eric. *The Black Muslims in America.* Boston: Beacon Press, 1961. Reprint. Westport, Conn.: Greenwood Press, 1982.

2633. ————, ed. *The Black Experience in Religion: A Book of Readings.* Garden City, N.Y.: Doubleday and Co., 1974.

2634. Lincoln, Eugene A. *Right Face: A Handbook for Sabbathkeepers.* Nashville: Southern Publication Association, 1976.

2635. Lomax, Louis E. *When the Word is Given: A Report on Elijah Muhammad, Malcolm X, and the Black Muslim World.* New York: New American Library, 1963. Reprint. Westport, Conn.: Greenwood Press, 1979.

2636. Mays, Benjamin Elijah. *Disturbed About Man.* Richmond, Va.: John Knox Press, 1969.

A sermon to men of all races and faiths about deterring the inhumanities of mankind. Mays points out that man can be a noble creature if transformed by the light of Christianity. His eulogy for Dr. Martin Luther King, Jr., a close friend and student, is included in the first chapter of the book; the following chapters reflect a Christian's concern for his fellowman.

2637.   ————. *Seeking to be Christian in Race Relations.* 2d ed. New York: Friendship Press, 1964.

This book is concerned with the area of worsening human race relations. Assuming that man alone is incapable of solving race problems to any significant degree, the author attempts to provide a Christian basis for eliminating these problems, drawing upon a few essentials of the Christian faith. An interesting section consists of questions based on the subject of race relations; these questions are left to be answered by the reader.

2638.   Mays, Benjamin Elijah, and Joseph William Nicholson. *The Negro's Church.* New York: Negro Universities Press, 1969.

A description of the black church in contemporary U.S. society, based primarily on a study of 794 representative urban and rural churches in sixteen cities and counties. This comprehensive study provides a baseline for future studies of the black church. Outstanding chapters include "Origins of the Church," "Church in the Negro Life," and "Fellowship and Community Activities."

2639.   McDonald, Marjorie. *Not by the Color of Their Skin: The Impact of Racial Differences on the Child's Development.* New York: International University Press, 1971.

2640.   Middleton, Merlissie Ross. *The Black Church v. The System.* 1st ed. New York: Vantage Press, 1976.

The author examines the institution of the black church against the societal system, with particular reference to church status and membership, to ascertain the extent to which the black church has significantly contributed to the total life of America. In so doing, Middleton presents some of the inherent sociological challenges for church leadership to address.

The First Congregational Church in Atlanta was used as a sample, having been proven typical for the prescribed goal of the investigation. From the findings, a number of conclusions have been drawn: that the church is central to educational, fraternal, civic, and community advancements; that residential distribution and mobility of membership of high–status churches are trapped in low–status neighborhoods, and that the church is also an institution of political awakening.

2641. Miller, Kelly. *The Ministry: The Field for the Talented Tenth.* Washington, D.C.: Murray Bros. Press, 1911.

2642. Mitchell, Ella Pearson, ed. *Those Preaching Women.* 2 vols. Valley Forge, Pa.: Judson Press, 1985, 1988.

2643. Mitchell, Mozella Gordon. *Spiritual Dynamics of Howard Thurman's Theology.* Bristol, Ind.: Wyndham Hall Press, 1985.

2644. Moore, Bradley George. *Philosophy: Applied to Controversial Issues in a Democratic Society.* Washington, D.C.: University Press of America, 1979.

2645. Morrison–Reed, Mark D. *Black Pioneers in a White Denomination.* Boston: Beacon Press, 1980.

Through the stories of two pioneering black ministers—Egbert Ethelred Brown, founder of the first Unitarian Church in Harlem, and Lewis A. McGee, who started the Interracial Free Religious Fellowship in Chicago's black ghetto—Morrison–Reed provides insight into the disturbing and widespread problem of racism in religion. The introduction is by Andrew J. Young.

2646. Mosley, William. *What Color Was Jesus?* 1st ed. Chicago: African American Images, 1987.

2647.   Muhammad, Elijah. *Message to the Blackman in America.* Philadelphia: Hakim's Publications, 1965.

In addition to its message, this 350–plus–page book includes a guide to understanding the Bible, a guide to understanding the Holy Quran, and an index.

2648.   Nelson, William Stuart. *Bases of World Understanding: An Inquiry into the Means of Resolving Racial, Religious, Class, and National Misapprehensions & Conflicts.* Calcutta: Calcutta University, 1949.

2649.   ————, ed. *The Christian Way in Race Relations.* New York: Harper, 1948. Reprint. Freeport, N.Y.: Books for Libraries Press, 1971.

The result of a cooperative enterprise on the part of the members of the Institute of Religion at Howard University. Bibliographical references are included.

2650.   Pilgrim, David. *Human Oddities: An Exploratory Study.* Notre Dame, Ind.: The Foundations Press of Notre Dame, 1984.

This work deals with human and psychological aspects of abnormalities. Includes a bibliography.

2651.   ————, ed. *On Being Black: An In–Group Analysis.* Bristol, Ind.: Wyndham Hall Press, 1986.

This work comprises thirteen essays on the black experience. The essays are in honor of W. E. B. DuBois.

2652.   Pipes, William Harrison. *Say Amen Brother! Old–Time Negro Preaching: A Study in American Frustration.* New York: William–Frederick Press, 1951. Reprint. Westport, Conn.: Negro Universities Press, 1970.

This study focuses on old–fashioned preaching in the Afro–American tradition, as reflected in Macon County, Georgia, typical of that part of the "black belt" that has retained most of its traditional culture. This book includes seven sermons to exemplify the two basic types of old–fashioned black preaching identified with Macon County sermons and other traditional black preaching.

2653. Powell, Adam Clayton, Jr. *Keep the Faith, Baby!* New York: Trident Press, 1967.

2654. Raboteau, Albert J. *Slave Religion: The "Invisible Institution" in the Antebellum South.* New York: Oxford University Press, 1978.

In this 1979 winner of both the National Religious Book Award and the African Roots Award of the International African Institute, Raboteau provides a good synthesis of recent work on slave religion, and strengthens it with his own judgments and research into such materials as the slave narratives, spirituals, and church records.

2655. Reynolds, Louis B. *Bible Answers.* Nashville: Southern Publishing Association, 1980.

2656. ———. *The Dawn of a Brighter Day: Light Through the Darkness.* Nashville: Southern Publishing Association, 1945.

2657. ———. *Great Texts from Romans.* Nashville: Southern Publishing Association, 1972.

2658. ———. *Look to the Hills.* Nashville: Southern Publishing Association, 1960.

2659. Richardson, Harry Van Buren. *Dark Glory: A Study of the Rural Church Among Negroes.* New York: Friendship Press, 1947.

2660. ———. *Dark Salvation: The Story of the Methodist Movement As It Developed Among Black People in America.* New York: Doubleday and Co., 1976.

2661.   ————. *Walk Together, Children: The Birth and Growth of the Interdenominational Theological Center*. Atlanta, Ga.: I. T. C. Press, 1981.

2662.   Roberts, James Deotis. *Liberation and Reconciliation: A Black Theology*. Philadelphia: Westminster Press, 1971.

The author treats religion from a black perspective, with an emphasis on Christianity. For example, one of the many significant points in the chapter "The Black Man's God" is that the God of Moses, Abraham, and Issac is the black man's God. Even though blacks have suffered in America, they have kept their faith in God, who has revealed himself to them. Black theology takes into consideration that blacks who have achieved success and think they are free will not be free until their black brothers are free. There is also an emphasis on blacks and whites working together.

2663.   ————. *Roots of a Black Future: Family and Church*. 1st ed. Philadelphia: Westminster Press, 1980.

From its birth in America, the black church has, according to Roberts, provided a basis of social solidarity, a role that was extremely important to slaves in need of hope and faith that there would be a better tomorrow. He contends that the black church, no less now than in the days of slavery, shelters and protects blacks who endure and suffer the inequalities of a racist society. Although the success of the black church is often attributed to expediency, Roberts argues that the fundamental reason for its success is its role in helping to preserve and strengthen the black family. Includes bibliographical references.

2664.   Salley, Columbus, and Ronald Behm.** *Your God Is Too White*. Downers Grove, Ill.: Inter–Varsity, 1970.

Published in 1981 under the title *What Color Is Your God?* this book raises the issue of how Christianity can "be updated or redefined to deal with everyday problems of race." After stating that Christianity affirms a positive black self–concept and actively cooperates with blacks in their struggle, it then proceeds to examine how Christianity relates to both historical and present–day oppressive forces in America. The relations of Christianity to slavery, segregation, and "ghettorization" are discussed, together with attempts to analyze the types of new religion needed today.

2665. Samuda, Ronald J. *Psychological Testing of American Minorities: Issues and Consequences.* New York: Dodd, Mead and Co., 1975.

In this book the author discusses some of the arguments and problems surrounding the minority–testing controversy while presenting some alternatives to the standard forms of testing. Of special interest is the appendix, which contains a comprehensive listing of texts for minority adolescents and adults.

2666. Sewell, George Alexander. *A Motif for Living, and Other Sermons.* New York: Vantage Press, 1963.

2667. Tarry, Ellen. *Katharine Drexel, Friend of the Neglected.* New York: Farrar, Straus and Cudahy, 1958.

2668. Taylor, Gardner C. *Chariots Aflame.* Nashville: Broadman Press, 1988.

2669. ———. *How Shall They Preach.* Elgin, Ill.: Progressive Baptist Publishing House, 1977.

2670. ———. *The Scarlet Thread: Nineteen Sermons.* Elgin, Ill.: Progressive Baptist Publishing House, 1981.

2671. Teish, Luisah. *Jambalaya: The National Woman's Book of Personal Charms and Practical Rituals.* New York: Harper and Row, 1985.

This book concentrates on the voodoo of New Orleans. According to the author, New Orleans voodoo is like jambalaya—a spicy dish with many fine ingredients cooked together. Blending the practices of three continents into one tradition, it contains African ancestor reverence, native American earth worship, and European Christian occultism. The book includes an index and a bibliography.

2672. Thomas, Latta R. *Biblical Faith and the Black American.* Valley Forge, Pa.: Judson Press, 1976.

2673. Thurman, Howard. *Deep River.* Rev. and enl. New York: Harper and Brothers, 1955.

A treatise on the religious implications revealed in certain spirituals.

2674. Walker, Clarence E. *A Rock in a Weary Land: The African Methodist Episcopal Church During the Civil War and Reconstruction.* Baton Rouge: Louisiana State University Press, 1982.

2675. Warren, Mervyn Alonzo. *Black Preaching: Truth & Soul.* Washington, D.C.: University Press of America, 1977.

2676. Washington, Booker T. *Character Building: Being Addresses Delivered on Sunday Evenings to the Students at Tuskegee Institute.* New York: Doubleday, Page and Co., 1902. Reprint. New York: Haskell House Publishers, 1972.

2677. Washington, Joseph R., Jr. *Black Religion: The Negro and Christianity in the United States.* Boston: Beacon Press, 1964. Reprint. Lanham, Md.: University Press of America, 1984.

2678. ————. *Black Sects and Cults.* Garden City, N.Y.: Anchor Books, 1973. Reprint. Lanham, Md.: University Press of America, 1984.

This work examines the various sects and cults found within the black American religious experience, including Pentecostal, Sanctified Holiness, Baptists, and Methodists, as well as followers of Father Divine, Daddy Grace, and Reverend Albert B. Cleague, Jr. Black religious cults in America are interpreted as reactions to oppression.

2679. ————. *The Politics of God.* Boston: Beacon Press, 1967.

2680. White, Joseph L. *The Psychology of Blacks: An Afro-American Perspective.* Englewood Cliffs, N.J.: Prentice-Hall, 1984.

The author gives an overview of the psychological perspective of blacks shaped by certain dimensions, namely openness to self and others, tragedy and resilience, interdependence, the oral tradition, creative synthesis, the value of direct experience, and respect for the elderly. He cites black psychologists as well as novelists and celebrities (Ralph Ellison, James Baldwin, Aretha Franklin) who have shared in the black experience. The listing of E. Franklin Frazier and Aretha Franklin in the same reference group reflects the breadth of the book.

2681. Williams, William James. *Epistemics: Personalizing the Process of Change.* Los Angeles: University Publishers, 1974.

This book focuses on the general semantics process and on the newly developed discipline of epistemics. An attempt is made to combine the two to produce an abstract theoretical framework to be used as a vehicle for change on many levels. The individual is the central focus of this book, which is concerned with applying the precepts of epistemics for effective change.

2682. ————. *Uncommon Sense and Dimensional Awareness: Epistemics as a Process of Change and Personal Transformation.* 2d ed. Los Angeles: University Publishers, 1976.

2683. Willie, Charles Vert. *Church Action in the World: Studies in Sociology and Religion.* New York: Morehouse-Barlow, 1969.

This book is a personal discussion of the way in which the church acts or fails to act as a corporate body. Case studies of both its successful and unsuccessful actions are included. The issues are viewed from both a sociological and religious perspective. Specific goals and values of the church are also examined in their relationship to community structure and process.

2684. Wimberly, Edward P. *Pastoral Care in the Black Church.* Nashville: Abingdon Press, 1979.

2685. ———. *Pastoral Counseling and Spiritual Values: A Black Point of View.* Nashville: Abingdon Press, 1982.

2686. Wright, Nathan, Jr. *One Bread, One Body.* Greenwich, Conn.: Seabury Press, 1962.

This book, structured after the outline of the liturgy in the American Book of Common Prayer, focuses on early American church fathers and is derived from primary source material with the view that an appropriate forum may be invested by appointed authorities in church worship. This book is a commentary on the Lord's Supper, the focal point of church worship.

2687. ———. *The Riddle of Life, and Other Sermons.* Boston: Bruce Humphries, 1952.

This compilation of sermons and meditations implies faith in God's promises of the blessings of eternal life, which began in this world. This present life is fraught with many problems; however, the challenges can be overcome through God's love, as demonstrated by our creative abilities and actions in our daily lives. The author holds the view that the ultimate purpose of preaching is to render help and deliver blessings. This book was written "as the result of a community of effort in St. Cyprian's Church."

2688. Young, Henry James. *Major Black Religious Leaders, 1755–1940.* Nashville: Abingdon Press, 1977.

2689. ————. *Major Black Religious Leaders Since 1940.* Nashville: Abingdon Press, 1979.

2690. ————, ed. *God and Human Freedom: A Festschrift in Honor of Howard Thurman.* Richmond, Ind.: Friends United Press, 1983.

2691. ————, ed. *Preaching on Suffering and a God of Love.* Philadelphia: Fortress Press, 1978.

2692. ————, ed. *Preaching the Gospel.* Philadelphia: Fortress Press, 1976.

CHAPTER 9

SCIENCE AND TECHNOLOGY

2693. Alexis, Marcus, George H. Haines, Jr.,* and Leonard S. Simon.* *Black Consumer Profiles: Food Purchasing in the Inner City.* Ann Arbor: Division of Research, Graduate School of Business Administration, University of Michigan, 1980.

2694. Andrews, Malachi. *Psychoblackology, of Movement in Sports, Physical Education, Dance, Drama, Play, Gymnastics, Recreation, and the Soul Experience.* Oakland, Calif.: Achebe Enterprises, 1974.

2695. Ashley, Liza. *Thirty Years at the Mansion: Recipes and Recollections.* As told to Carolyn Huber.** Little Rock: August House, 1985.

Thirty Years at the Mansion, as told to Carolyn Huber, former mansion administrator, details the life of Liza Ashley as the cook at the Arkansas Governor's Mansion. Beginning as a maid in 1954 under Gov. Francis Cherry, Ashley became the cook a year later when Gov. Orval E. Faubus was elected to office (in 1955), and she cooked for seven governors and their families. It includes the favorite recipes of the various first families and her recollections of life with them.

2696. Bailey, Pearl. *Pearl's Kitchen: An Extraordinary Cookbook.* New York: Harcourt Brace Jovanovich, 1973.

Recipes in this book are combined with humorous anecdotes from the author's life as a celebrity.

2697. Berke,* Joseph, and Calvin C. Hernton. *The Cannabis Experience: An Interpretative Study of the Effects of Marijuana and Hashish.* London: P. Owen, 1974.

2698. Berkley, George. *On Being Black and Healthy: How Black Americans Can Lead Longer and Healthier Lives.* Englewood Cliffs, N.J.: Prentice–Hall, 1982.

2699. Berryman, Matilene S. *Science of Man's Environment: Principles of Science and Technology for Environmental, Marine, Engineering, and Ocean Science Technology.* Washington, D.C.: Market Place of Ideas, Inc., 1986.

This book describes interrelated science and technology principles. It provides an overview of the universe in terms of the energy sources and the resulting causes and effects to the atmosphere, the hydrosphere, and the lithosphere; concepts of pollution and radiation are included. The book also includes 170 figures, seventy tables, appendixes, and subject and name indexes, and is filled with illustrations, questions, answers, and examples.

2700. Blackwell, David Harold, and M. A. Girshick.* *Theory of Games and Statistical Decisions.* New York: John Wiley and Sons, 1954.

This book is intended primarily as a textbook in decision theory for first–year graduate students in statistics. The mathematical prerequisite for reading this book is an understanding of uniform convergence, limits of sequences, the Riemann integral, and the Heine–Borel theorem. Although a glossary of statistical concepts is given, the student without any previous knowledge of statistics may find some parts difficult.

2701. Boulware, Marcus Hanna. *The Riddle of Snoring.* Mokelumne Hill, Calif.: Health Research, 1969.

2702. Brown, Melanie. *Help with Finding a Job.* Boston: Houghton Mifflin Co., 1986.

2703. Brown, Roscoe Conkling, Jr., and Bryant J. Cratty,* eds. *New Perspectives of Man in Action.* Englewood Cliffs, N.J.: Prentice–Hall, 1969.

Written by younger members of physical education departments in America, this book focuses on the present status of the physical education profession and on different ways of enhancing its status as an academic discipline relating to the nature of man in action. Some of the articles deal with theories and techniques, others with subdisciplines and their interrelationships, and still others with teaching and working with young children.

2704. Brown, Roscoe Conkling, Jr., and Gerald S. Kenyon,* eds. *Classical Studies on Physical Activity.* Englewood Cliffs, N.J.: Prentice–Hall, 1968.

This compilation arose out of the spirit of scientific inquiry. The book includes significant contributions to our knowledge about physical activity. Each study, summarized and commented on by the editors, is comprehensive and includes charts, diagrams, reference tables, and graphs.

2705. Brumfiel,** Charles Francis, and Irvin E. Vance. *Algebra and Geometry for Teachers.* Reading, Mass.: Addison–Wesley Publishing Co., 1970.

A text aimed at providing a combined course in algebra and geometry for the training or retraining of elementary teachers. The material in the text gets progressively harder chapter by chapter, moving from basic concepts of algebra and geometry to their more complex forms. Chapter 5 can be used as an effective guide to a basic course in mathematics for junior high school teachers. The text includes numerous exercises, the answers to which are given at the back of the book.

2706. Bryce, Herrington J. *Financial and Strategic Management for Nonprofit Organizations.* Englewood Cliffs, N.J.: Prentice–Hall, 1987.

2707. Burke, Carolyn M. *The Pride and Beauty Handbook for Blackskinned Women.* Detroit: Heirloom Books, 1986.

2708. Burns, LaMont. *Down Home Southern Cooking.* 1st ed. Garden City, N.Y.: Doubleday and Co., 1987.

2709. Burton, Nathaniel, and Rudy Lombard, comps. *Creole Feast: 15 Master Chefs of New Orleans Reveal Their Secrets.* 1st ed. New York: Random House, Inc., 1978.

2710. Cameron, Randolph W. *The Minority Executives' Handbook: Your Essential Map and Guide to Success up the Corporate Ladder.* New York: Warner Books, 1989.

Among other topics, this work includes a chapter on "Outlook for the 1990s." The appendix includes average income by state as reported by the Commerce Department in 1986. A bibliography and an index are also included.

2711. Carter, Vertie L. *How to Get a Career Job.* 1st ed. Hicksville, N.Y.: Exposition Press, 1978.

2712. Chunn, Jay, II, Patricia Dunston, and Fariyal Ross–Sheriff.** *Mental Health and People of Color: Curriculum Development and Change.* Washington, D.C.: Howard University Press, 1983.

This book is a comprehensive presentation of curriculum development strategies and techniques relative to the disciplines of psychology, social work, psychiatry, and psychiatric nursing. Each chapter introduces the reader to the psychosocial development patterns of four racial and ethnic groups as well as to selected group idiosyncrasies, which influence the educational process. The authors discuss the importance of considering sociodemographic factors when designing and developing curricular elements for interracial or other ethnic groups. Includes diagrams and an index.

2713. Cobb, William Montague. *The First Negro Medical Society: A History of the Medico–Chirurgical Society of the District of Columbia, 1884–1939.* Washington, D.C.: Associated Publishers, 1939.

Cobb describes the founding of the oldest black medical society in the United States. Although there were only six black physicians at the time, he points out that the Chirurgical Society was formed to secure for black physicians "the advantage of regular meetings for medical improvement." General affairs, public relations, and the interrelationship of Freedmen's Hospital, Howard University Medical School, and the Medico–Chirurgical Society are discussed.

2714. ———. *Medical Care and the Plight of the Negro.* New York: NAACP, 1947.

Cobb addresses the status of Afro–American health, professional personnel, state board records, the AMA, internships, among other topics. He talks about the long, uphill struggle of blacks against discrimination in obtaining medical education and care. He stipulates that the quality of medical care is a function of the ability to pay, which results in the best medical care facilities being found in the regions with the most money. A comparison of black and white mortality rates shows gross disparities between the two groups. Includes illustrations and literature cited.

2715. ———. *Progress and Portents for the Negro in Medicine.* New York: NAACP, 1948.

With a foreword by Walter White, this study is a sequel to Cobb's *Medical Care and the Plight of the Negro*, published in 1947. It details some efforts to correct conditions acknowledged to be dangerous to the welfare and health of the general population. Sections on dentistry and pharmacy, which were not treated in the earlier work, are included.

2716. Conley, Houston, Chip Bowling, and Evans Harris. *A Handbook for Dynamic Supervision for the Public and Private Sector.* Washington, D.C.: College and University Press, 1975.

The book focuses on changing management practices. It challenges management to develop effect and responsible methods of policy formulation and decision making. Included are skills, techniques, methods, and exercises as aids to assist management and staff.

2717. Curtis, James L. *Blacks, Medical Schools, and Society.* Ann Arbor: University of Michigan Press, 1971.

This book describes the present situation of blacks in the nation's medical schools and the declining in the pattern of keeping blacks out of predominantly white medical schools. Curtis also discusses efforts to increase black enrollment in medical schools and to bolster blacks' premedical preparation by incorporating them in summer programs offered in some medical schools. Of particular interest are chapters 5 and 6, which examine the impact of such changes on both white and black medical schools.

2718. Davis, George, and Glegg Watson. *Black Life in Corporate America: Swimming in the Mainstream.* Garden City, N.Y.: Anchor Press, 1982.

Based on more than 160 interviews with black and white corporate managers and executives, the book provides an impressionistic view of the professional and personal lives of black men and women trying to make it in a "world created by and for white males." The authors conclude that swimming in the mainstream is a mixed blessing, and they describe some black managers as "waders," "floaters," "scuba divers," "splashers," and "backstrokers."

2719. Davis, Howard. *State Requirements in Physical Education for Teachers and Students.* Washington, D.C.: American Association for Health, Physical Education, and Recreation, 1973.

This physical education manual is designed to make certification requirements easy to find for the elementary and secondary physical education teacher. It sets forth the laws and regulations affecting physical education in each state. The information is aimed at both students aspiring to become professional physical educators and those who counsel prospective physical educators.

2720. DeKnight, Freda. *A Date with a Dish: A Cookbook of American Negro Recipes.* New York: Hermitage Press, 1948.

A nonregional cookbook that embraces recipes, cooking hints, and menus from all over the country.

2721. ————. *The Ebony Cookbook: A Date with a Dish.* Chicago: Johnson Publishing Co. 1962.

This selection contains a collection of thousands of soul food recipes—new ideas and old favorites. Its laminated jacket will protect it from spills in the kitchen.

2722. Dickens, Floyd, Jr., and Jacqueline B. Dickens. *The Black Managers: Making It in the Corporate World.* New York: AMACOM, 1982.

2723. Dillard, John Milton. *Lifelong Career Planning.* Columbus, Ohio: Charles E. Merrill Co., 1985.

This work covers all aspects of career planning. Also covered are decision–making strategies and sources for information on available careers. Such topics as networking and pyramiding are discussed. Practical advice is given on assertive behavior techniques, interviewing skills, and planning for advancement. Includes exercises and summaries in every chapter, as well as an index.

2724. Dunham, Melerson Guy. *The Centennial History of Alcorn Agricultural and Mechanical College.* Hattiesburg: University of Mississippi Press, 1971.

2725. Edmonds, Paul. *Microbiology: An Environmental Perspective.* New York: Macmillan Co., 1978.

2726. Godwin, Winfred L., ed. *Physicians for the South.* Atlanta, Ga.: Southern Educational Board, 1960.

2727. Granville, Evelyn B. *Theory and Application of Mathematics for Teachers.* 2d ed. Belmont, Calif.: Wadsworth Publishing Co., 1978.

2728. Gregory, Dick. *Dick Gregory's Natural Diet for Folks Who Eat: Cookin' with Mother Nature!* New York: Perennial Library, 1974.

2729. Harris, Thelma Bruner. *Good Foods for Good Health: A Cookbook Featuring Menu Tips and Easy-to-Prepare Recipes Calling for the Use of Vegetables, Fruit, Grain Foods, Nuts, and Dairy Products.* Nashville, Tenn.: Southern Publishing Association, 1972.

2730. Haskins, James. *The Consumer Movement.* New York: Franklin Watts, 1975.

2731. ————. *Exploring Careers: Jobs in Business and Office.* New York: Lothrop, Lee and Shepard Co., 1974.

One of a number of books in the *Exploring Careers* series which introduces the reader to careers in business and office management. The necessity for and benefits of a job in these fields are discussed. The well-illustrated text offers an informative examination of six particular jobs in the business and office field, as well as of various methods of seeking a career in one of these particular areas. This book is also excellent for juvenile readers and can be used as a vocational guide.

2732.   ———. *Jobs in Business and Office*. New York: Lothrop, Lee and Shepard Co., 1974.

2733.   ———. *Real Estate Careers*. New York: Franklin Watts, 1978.

2734.   Henderson, George, ed. *Human Relations in the Military: Problems and Programs*. Chicago: Nelson–Hall, 1975.

The focus in this book is on problems and solutions pertaining to seven topics: leadership, race relations, women's equality, military justice, drug and alcohol abuse, health care, and civil service. The book concerns not only students involved in military training programs, but all who are interested in acquiring techniques geared toward improving human relations. There are several case studies written by people actively involved in social change. Includes a bibliography.

2735.   Hine, Darlene Clark, ed. *Black Women in Nursing: An Anthology of Historical Sources*. New York: Garland Publishing, Inc., 1985.

Divided into three sections, this anthology examines the emergence and development of the early black hospital nursing schools, the career experiences of professionally trained black nurses, the limited financial and institutional resources of the black community, and the historical struggle of black nurses for professional opportunities, higher status, and integration. The twenty–seven articles, essays, surveys, and reports cover the period between 1898 to 1976.

2736.   ———, ed. *Black Women in the Nursing Profession: A Documentary History*. New York: Garland Publishing, Inc., 1985.

2737.   Jackson, Mary, and Lelia Wishart.** *The Integrated Cookbook: The Soul of Good Cooking.* Chicago: Johnson Publishing Co., 1972.

A black author joins with a white author to bring you over 150 soul food recipes, including one for whole opossum, and original George Washington Carver recipes in his own words! They also include favorite Jewish, Italian, Chinese, and Mexican dishes, plus a history of soul food, a nutrition chart, and a list of recommended soul food restaurants.

2738.   Jackson, William M., and Albert B. Harvey,** eds. *Lasers as Reactants and Probes in Chemistry.* Washington, D.C.: Howard University Press, 1985.

This book, the result of an international conference held at Howard University, reflects current thinking on the use of lasers in chemistry and scientific research.

2739.   Jay, James Monroe. *Modern Food Microbiology.* 3d ed. New York: Van Nostrand Co., 1986.

2740.   ———. *Negroes in Science: Natural Science Doctorates, 1876–1969.* Detroit: Balamp Publishing, 1971.

2741.   Just, Ernest Everett. *Basic Methods for Experiments on Eggs of Marine Mammals.* Philadelphia: P. Blakiston's Son and Co., 1939.

2742.   ———. *The Biology of the Cell Surface.* Philadelphia: P. Blakiston's Son and Co., 1939.

2743.   Kaufman, Cheryl Davidson. *Cooking the Caribbean Way.* Edited by Vicki Revsbech.* Photographs by Robert L. Wolfe* and Diane Wolfe.* Drawings by Jeanette Swofford.* Map by J. Michael Roy.* Minneapolis: Lerner Publications Co., 1988.

2744.   Kidd, Foster, ed. *Profile of the Negro in American Dentistry.* Washington, D.C.: Howard University Press, 1979.

Concisely written, the book traces the innovations in dentistry and relates the invaluable role blacks have played in this profession.

2745. Kittles, Emma Holmes. *Fashion Exhibition: A Guide for Planning Professional Fashion Shows.* Tallahassee: Florida Agricultural & Mechanical University 1975.

2746. Lawrence, Margaret Morgan. *Young Inner City Families: Development of Ego Strength Under Stress.* New York: Behavioral Publications, 1975.

2747. Lewis, Edna. *The Taste of Country Cooking.* New York: Alfred A. Knopf, 1976.

2748. Lewis, Edna, with Mary Goodbody.* *In Pursuit of Flavor.* Illustrated by Louisa Jones Waller.* New York: Alfred A. Knopf, 1988.

This cookbook contains about two hundred recipes, plus notes and special boxes on important ingredients (from black-eyed peas to Peking ducks). It contains techniques developed by the author to get the best flavor from the foods available today. Includes an index.

2749. Lewis, Edna, and Evangeline Peterson.* *The Edna Lewis Cookbook.* Indianapolis: Bobbs-Merrill, 1972. Reprint. New York: Ecco Press, 1983.

2750. Lloyd, Raymond Grann. *Tennessee Agricultural and Industrial State University, 1912-1962: Fifty Years of Leadership Through Excellence, 1912-1962.* Nashville: Tennessee A and I State University, 1962.

2751. McElroy, Samuel Ray Ford. *The Handbook on the Psychology of Hemoglobin-S: A Perspicacious View of Sickle Cell Disease.* Washington, D.C.: University Press of America, 1980.

2752. McLaughlin, Clara J. *The Black Parent's Handbook: A Guide to Healthy Pregnancy, Birth, and Child Care.* New York: Harcourt Brace Jovanovich, 1976.

A unique guide to young black parents, this four-part book investigates such areas as medical care during pregnancy, a child's formative years, and genetic and environmental factors affecting the black family. It presents an overall positive image of blackness to the reader.

2753. McQueen, Adele B., and Alan McQueen. *West African Cooking for Black American Families.* New York: Vantage Press, 1982.

2754. Nabwire, Constance R., and Bertha Vining Montgomery. *Cooking the African Way.* Photographs by Robert L Wolfe* and Diane Wolfe.* Minneapolis: Lerner Publications Co., 1988.

"An introduction to the cooking of East and West Africa, with information on the land and people of this area of the giant continent, and including recipes."

2755. Newell,* Virginia K., Joella Gipson, et al.,* eds. *Black Mathematicians and Their Works.* Ardmore, Pa.: Dorrance and Co., 1980.

2756. Nivens, Beatryce. *The Black Woman's Career Guide.* Rev. ed. Garden City, N.Y.: Doubleday and Co., 1987.

This book offers helpful hints to black women who want to improve their position in today's job market. It covers traditional and nontraditional job hunting procedures including career planning, resume writing, and interviewing techniques. Fashion and beauty tips are also discussed. This guide also contains profiles of about eighty black women representing a cross section of careers. The author states that she wrote this book to help black women "beat the odds." The book is designed, she says, "to help the displaced black woman move successfully to a new career in more marketable areas. It is for the recent college graduate seeking employment in this tight job market, the woman who is re-entering the job market, and the black woman who is looking for a job."

2757. ———. *Careers for Women Without College Degrees.* New York: McGraw-Hill Book Co., 1988.

2758. ———. *How to Change Careers.* New York: Perigee Books, 1990.

2759. Odarty, Bill. *A Safari of African Cooking.* Illustrated by Shirley Woodson.* 2d ed. Detroit: Broadside Press, 1971.

2760. Organ, Claude H., Jr., and Margaret M. Kosiba,* eds. *A Century of Black Surgeons: The U.S.A. Experience.* 2 vols. Norman, Okla.: Transcript Press, 1987.

This work discusses the experiences of black surgeons in seeking quality surgical training and in practicing surgery. A directory of black general and thoracic surgeons currently practicing in the United States is included.

2761. Paige, Howard. *Aspects of Afro-American Cookery.* Southfield, Mich.: Aspects Publishing Co., 1987.

The compilation of foods includes Creole, Cajun, Deep South, gourmet, contemporary, and soul. Includes an index.

2762. Pilgrim, David, ed. *Psychology and Psychotherapy: Current Trends and Issues.* Boston: Routledge and Kegan Paul, 1983.

2763. Ray,* Mary Frey, and Evelyn Jones Lewis. *Exploring Professional Cooking.* Peoria, Ill.: Charles A. Bennett Co., 1976.

Designed as a program text for vocational training in the field of food service, this book has five main parts: (1) the first two chapters introduce the world of food and food service; (2)

the next five chapters deal with food planning, cost control, sanitation, equipment, and cooking methods, which are the basic areas of food service and management; (3) chapter 8 discusses the efficient use of time, energy, and materials through the organization of good work centers; (4) the next six chapters discuss food preparation; and (5) a final chapter looks at work experience. Most chapters are prefaced by a short story about two people interested in food service as a career.

2764.   Sadler, William Anderson, and Winston A. Anderson,* eds. *Perspectives in Differentiation and Hypertrophy: Proceedings of the First Symposium Between Howard University and the University of the West Indies.* New York: Elseiver/North–Holland, 1982.

This work is based on the proceedings of the first symposium between Howard University and the University of the West Indies on Perspectives in Differentiation and Hypertrophy, held December 8–11, 1980, at Runaway Bay, Jamaica, West Indies.

2765.   Simpson, Bessie Chenauh. *Stuttering Therapy: A Guide for the Speech Clinician.* Danville, Ill.: Interstate Printers and Publishers, 1966.

Simpson draws upon the thinking and the personal experiences of experienced, competent speech therapists in developing this guide for the treatment of stuttering. Because stutters' problems are unique to them, no attempt is made toward prescribing a general treatment. Rather, directions a clinician may take toward trying to cope with a patient's problems are indicated. Therapies for primary, intermediate, and advanced groups are also considered. Particular attention should be paid to those sections that deal with various speech rules, methods or organization, and a testing program.

2766.   Sims, Naomi. *All About Health & Beauty for the Black Woman.* Rev. and expanded. Garden City, N.Y.: Doubleday and Co., 1986.

Sims, famed model and beauty expert, provides women of all ages with information on aging of the face and body, makeup, hairstyle, exercise and diet, coping with stress, dressing to succeed in business, dental care, ways of preventing weight gain after giving up smoking, and dealing with drug problems. Includes appendixes and an index.

2767. ————. *All About Success for the Black Woman.* 1st ed. Garden City, N.Y.: Doubleday and Co., 1982.

This book offers helpful hints to black women who want to improve their position in today's job market. Also this book covers traditional and nontraditional job hunting procedures, including career planning, resume writing, and interviewing techniques. Fashion and beauty tips are also included. In addition to these subjects, the book deals with the problems of negotiating raises and promotions, and explores the challenge of juggling "a career with marriage and motherhood—the double lives that black women in particular must often learn to cope with alone." Includes bibliographies and index.

2768. Stafford, Joseph. *The Black Gourmet: Favorite Afro-American and Creole Recipes from Coast to Coast.* Rev. and expanded. Detroit: Harlo, 1988.

2769. Taylor, Orlando L., ed. *Nature of Communication Disorders in Culturally & Linguistically Diverse Populations.* San Diego: College-Hill Press, 1986.

2770. ————, ed. *Treatment of Communication Disorders in Culturally & Linguistically Diverse Populations.* San Diego: College-Hill Press, 1986.

2771. Uggams, Leslie. *The Leslie Uggams Beauty Book.* Englewood Cliffs, N.J.: Prentice-Hall, 1966.

2772. Walker, Herschel, and Terry Todd.* *Herschel Walker's Basic Training.* 1st ed. Garden City, N.Y.: Doubleday and Co., 1985.

Walker, the famed former running–back for the Dallas Cowboys, and his coauthor provide an extensive exercise program for athletes and aspiring athletes.

2773. White, Augustus A., III., and Manohar M. Panjabi. *Clinical Biomechanics of the Spine.* Philadelphia: J. B. Lippincott Co., 1978.

2774. Willie, Charles Vert, Bernard M. Kramer,* and Bertram S. Brown,* eds. *Racism and Mental Health: Essays.* Pittsburgh: University of Pittsburgh Press, 1973.

These authors believe that healthy minds contribute to healthy nations and that a society that condones racism is not a just and healthy one. Arguing that mental health institutions and treatment practices have perpetuated racism in American society, they call for reforms in such institutions and for renewed mental self–examination.

2775. Young, Barbara H., and Herman A. Young. *Scientist in the Black Perspective.* Louisville, Ky.: The Lincoln Foundation, 1974.

This book traces the history of blacks in the area of science, focusing on their accomplishments and present progress. The material is divided into four parts: the black perspective and its psychosocial background; black pioneers in science and their inventions that contributed to the making of America; black inventors whose devises became practical everyday necessities; and black doctoral holders rated among the most outstanding black scientists in America today. Included in the text is an index of all the black scientists mentioned in the text.

CHAPTER 10

SOCIAL SCIENCE

2776. Abramowitz, Elizabeth A., ed. *Proceedings from the National Invitational Conference on Racial and Ethnic Data.* Washington, D.C.: Institute for the Study of Educational Policy, Howard University, 1976.

This book contains papers presented at the National Invitational Conference on Racial and Ethnic Data in Higher Education held in Washington, D.C., in February 1976 and sponsored by the Institute for the Study of Educational Policy. Problems in the collection and interpretation of racial and ethnic data are discussed. Specific measures are proposed to "resolve inconsistencies and conflicts in the data" and to "identify policy questions for which racial and ethnic data in higher education are needed." The question–and–answer session and summaries of the conference workshops are also included.

2777. Alexander,* Howard Wright, and Roland Frederick Smith. *Descriptive Statistics: A Self Instruction Program.* Boston: D. C. Heath and Co., 1965.

2778. Alexander, James I. *Blue Coats—Black Skin: The Black Experience in the New York City Police Department Since 1891.* 1st ed. Hicksville, N.Y.: Exposition Press, 1978.

2779.   Allen, Robert L., with Pamela P. Allen. *Reluctant Reformers: The Impact of Racism on American Social Reform Movements.* Washington, D.C.: Howard University Press, 1974.

Robert Allen, the author of *Black Awakening in Capitalist America*, discusses racism in seven major reform movements in the United States: the abolitionist, populist, progressive, woman's suffrage, labor, socialist, and communist movements. He views the internal dynamics of the different reform movements and characterizes their role in the larger flow of American and world history.

2780.   Amaker, Norman C., ed. *Civil Rights and the Reagan Administration.* Washington, D.C.: Urban Institute Press, 1988.

2781.   Avedon,* Richard, and James Baldwin. *Nothing Personal.* Photos by Richard Avedon* and text by James Baldwin. New York: Atheneum Publishers, 1964.

2782.   Baldwin, James. *The Fire Next Time.* New York: Dial Press, 1963. Reprint. New York: Dell Publishing Co., 1964.

This is a book of polemic essays, which became a major influence on the freedom movement of the 1960s. Its defiant ending, taken from an old spiritual, virtually became a rallying cry: "God gave Noah the rainbow sign, No more water, the fire next time!"

2783.   ————. *In the Evidence of Things Not Seen.* 1st ed. New York: Holt, Rinehart and Winston, 1985.

Baldwin uses the Wayne Williams/Atlanta child murder case as subject and springboard for analyzing of the state of the Union in the mid-1980s. Taking his title from St. Paul, Baldwin ranges over the whole landscape of American life and discusses black power, the black middle class, memory, guilt, terror, and redemption. He calls, in the end, for a fundamental reconstruction of social and political institutions.

2784. ————. *No Name in the Street.* New York: Dial Press, 1972.

2785. ————. *Nobody Knows My Name: More Notes of a Native Son.* New York: Dial Press, 1961.

These thirteen essays record the last months of this famed American writer's ten–year self–exile in Europe, his return to America and Harlem, and his first trip South at the time of the school integration battles. It contains Baldwin's controversial and intimate profiles of Norman Mailer, Richard Wright, and Ingmar Bergman. And it explores such varied themes as the relations between blacks and whites, the role of blacks in America and in Europe, and the question of sexual identity.

2786. ————. *Notes of a Native Son.* 1955. Reprint. Boston: Beacon Press, 1984.

2787. Baldwin, James, and Nikki Giovanni. *A Dialogue: James Baldwin and Nikki Giovanni.* Philadelphia: J. B. Lippincott Co., 1973.

This work is based on the transcript of a conversation taped for the television program "Soul," first shown in the United States on WNET–TV, December 1971.

2788. Bambara, Toni Cade. *The Black Woman: An Anthology.* New York: New American Library, 1970.

2789. Barbour, Floyd B., ed. *Black Power Revolt.* Boston: Porter Sargent, 1968.

Written by black authors, this collection of essays explores the concept of black power from the past (1700s) to the present. Includes a bibliography.

2790. Barclay,* William, Krishna Kuman,* and Ruth P. Simms, eds. *Racial Conflict, Discrimination, and Power: Historical and Contemporary Studies.* New York: AMS Press, 1976.

2791.   Barker, Lucius Jefferson, and Twiley W. Barker, Jr. *Civil Liberties and the Constitution: Cases and Commentaries.* 2d ed. Englewood Cliffs, N.J.: Prentice–Hall, 1978.

An aid to students and others who wish to interpret laws for themselves, this book examines several Supreme Court decisions. It is divided into six chapters, each supported by related court cases. Freedom of religion, freedom of expression, and other civil liberties are some of the areas covered in the book. It also describes how problems of civil liberty arise, what role organized interest groups play, what effect community attitudes and public opinion have, and what happens once court decisions are made.

2792.   ———. *Freedom, Courts, Politics: Studies in Civil Liberties.* Englewood Cliffs, N.J.: Prentice–Hall, 1965.

This book provides a framework within which civil liberty problems can be evaluated and better understood. It sets these problems, along with their moral aspects, in a pragmatic political context. Using a number of factual situations and court cases, the authors examine the dynamics of civil liberties in relationship to (1) how civil liberty problems arise, (2) what role organized interest groups play, (3) what impact community attitudes and public opinion have, and (4) what happens after a court decision is made, with respect to reactions to it and attempts to comply with, circumvent, or overcome it.

2793.   Barker, Lucius Jefferson, and Jessie J. McCory. *Black Americans and the Political System.* Cambridge, Mass.: Winthrop Publishers, 1976.

This book enables one to view the constitutional theory and structure of our political institutions in terms of everyday practices and operations. The book also shows that, to a large extent, the structures and operations of the political system impose a serious disadvantage on blacks and other minorities. The book includes an index, a glossary, a copy of the Constitution of the United States, tables, suggested readings, and topics for discussion. A separate teacher's manual is available, which includes lecture suggestions, behavioral objectives, and a variety of objective and essay questions.

2794. Barnes, Annie Shaw. *The Black Middle Class Family: A Study of Black Subsociety, Neighborhood, and Home in Interaction.* Bristol, Ind.: Wyndham Hall Press, 1985.

While lengthening the shadow of E. Franklin Frazier's historic study, this investigation of the black middle–class family is an effort at understanding the complexities of family life and social interaction.

2795. ————. *Black Women: Interpersonal Relationships in Profile: A Sociological Study of Work, Home, and the Community.* Bristol, Ind.: Wyndham Hall Press, 1986.

A sequel to her book, *The Black Middle Class Family*, this work is Barnes's investigation into the professional lifestyle of black women and how they relate to the pressures and challenges of career and family life.

2796. ————. *Single Parents in Black America: A Study in Culture and Legitimacy.* Bristol, Ind.: Wyndham Hall Press, 1987.

In this database study, Barnes describes and compares single motherhood and single fatherhood as seen through the eyes of the respondents, and she explores the fascinating but sometimes troubling complexes of kinship relations in the black community.

2797. ————, ed. *Social Science Research: A Skills Handbook.* Bristol, Ind.: Wyndham Hall Press, 1985.

2798. Bashful, Emmett W. *The Florida Supreme Court: A Study in Judicial Selection.* Tallahassee: Florida State University Bureau of Government Research, 1958.

This work is a revision of the author's thesis on the topic done at the University of Illinois.

2799. Bates,** Frederick L., and Clyde C. Harvey. *The Structure of Social Systems.* New York: Gardner Press, 1975.

2800. Bayton, James Arthur. *Tension in the Cities: Three Programs for Survival.* Philadelphia: Chilton Book Co., 1969.

A study of city government programs that primarily aim to alleviate urban tensions and crises. The programs of Washington, D.C., New York, and Atlanta were chosen because of their uniqueness in form of government, urban problems, and southern progressiveness, respectively. The book first discusses the crises of these urban areas and then describes the various programs each has initiated to combat them. Finally, Bayton evaluates the programs, discusses their implications, and offers recommendations for improved programs.

2801. Bayton, James Arthur, and Richard L. Chapman.** *Transformation of Scientists and Engineers into Managers.* Washington, D.C.: National Aeronautics and Space Administration Government Printeries Office, 1972.

This study is designed to help public officials in science and engineering cope with important problems of administration. More than one hundred interviews were held with officials in all levels of government to determine the critical factors in the transition from working as a specialist to working as a manager. Included are a summary of findings, panel recommendations, and an appendix describing survey techniques used.

2802. Beck, James D. *The Counselor and Black/White Relations.* Boston: Houghton Mifflin Co., 1973.

2803. Bell, Derrick Albert, Jr. *And We Are Not Saved: The Elusive Quest for Racial Justice.* New York: Basic Books, 1987.

The author takes a long probing look at the major battles fought on the legal front of the civil rights movement. Helping him analyze each decision is his fictitious heroine and alter ego, Geneva Crenshaw. Like Bell, Crenshaw is a civil rights attorney who, in Bell's allegorical tale, was a potent force in the courtroom clashes of the 1960s and 1970s. We encounter Crenshaw in the twilight of her career. In a whirlwind tour, she takes us through the history of civil rights litigation and legislation, recounting the joy and hope that followed the landmark decrees. In retrospect, however, she laments the folly of those who like herself, thought that judicial mandates and antidiscrimination laws would bring a sweeping end to racial oppression.

2804.   ———. *Race, Racism, and American Law.* 2d ed. Boston: Little, Brown and Co., 1980.

A discussion on American law and its relationship to race and racism in America. Bell considers the racial implications of laws associated with five basic rights: citizenship, education, housing, employment, and justice. As a pedagogical aid, some questions are given at the end of each section. The text is an excellent guide to understanding white America's attitudes toward nonwhites as these attitudes are reflected in the legal system.

2805.   ———, ed. *Civil Rights: Leading Cases.* Boston: Little, Brown and Co., 1980.

2806.   Bellegarde, Ida Rowland. *Understanding Cultural Values.* Pine Bluff, Ark.: Bell Enterprises, 1980.

2807.   Bellman,* Beryl Larry, and Bennetta Jules–Rosette. *A Paradigm for Looking: Cross–Cultural Research with Visual Media.* Norwood, N.J.: Ablex Publishing Corp., 1977.

2808.   Bennett, Lerone, Jr. *The Negro Mood, and Other Essays.* New York: Ballantine Books, 1965.

2809.   Bernstein, Daniel O., and John Conway.* *Wisconsin and Federal Civil Procedure.* Madison: University of Wisconsin Law School, 1986.

2810. Berry, Mary Frances. *Stability, Security, and Continuity: Mr. Justice Burton and Decision–Making in the Supreme Court, 1945–1958.* Westport, Conn.: Greenwood Press, Inc., 1978.

Drawing upon a variety of sources, including the private papers of Justices Harold Burton and Felix Frankfurter, Berry presents a critical analysis of Burton's career. Details of actual conferences and private discussions between the justices are included. She also analyzes major and minor cases with a view toward understanding how and why cases are decided in a certain way. Included are the school segregation cases, the Rosenberg case, and the Communist cases of the period.

2811. ———. *Why ERA Failed: Politics, Women's Rights, and the Amending Process of the Constitution.* Bloomington: Indiana University Press, 1986.

To show why the Equal Rights Amendment to the U.S. Constitution failed, Berry describes the history of the amending process. She focuses on the behavior of ERA proponents and opponents, and explains the inherent difficulties in the amending process. Includes appendixes, notes, and an index.

2812. Billingsley, Andrew. *Black Families and the Struggle for Survival: Teaching Our Children to Walk Tall.* New York: Friendship Press, 1974.

This book focuses on the strong fiber and resiliency of the Afro–American family, an institution that has contributed substantially to blacks' struggle for survival, meaning, and achievement in American society. Billingsley argues that the black family is the basis of Afro–American culture.

2813. ———. *Black Families in White America.* Englewood Cliffs, N.J.: Prentice Hall, 1968.

The family is highly interdependent with other social institutions and dependent on many of those institutions for its definition, survival, and achievement. The Afro–American family,

Billingsley argues, cannot be understood in isolation from these institutions, or by concentrating on its negative functions. Billingsley describes some of the problems and potentials associated with different patterns of Afro–American family life. He discusses the various approaches to these problems, which maybe taken by Afro–Americans themselves, by individuals and organizations interested in Afro–American affairs, and by the governmental agencies whose responsibility it is to provide leadership in the development of a viable democratic society that is at once interracial and pluralistic.

2814. Billingsley, Andrew, and Jeanne M. Giovannoni. *Children of the Storm: Black Children and American Child Welfare.* New York: Harcourt Brace Jovanovich, 1972.

This book describes the deleterious effects of racism on black children, and particularly the harmful effects of a child welfare system that harbors racist attitudes toward the children it purports to help. The book has three parts: part 1 traces the development of child welfare in America; part 2 covers the years 1937 to 1970; and part 3 covers patterns of organizational reform in child welfare.

2815. Blackwell, David Harold. *Basic Statistics.* New York: McGraw–Hill, 1969.

2816. Blackwell, James Edward. *The Black Community: Diversity and Unity.* 2d ed. New York: Harper and Row, 1985.

In this second edition, Blackwell brings together updated data to show the effect of racism and internal diversity within every aspect of the black community, including such areas as education, politics, economics, and the military.

2817. Blackwell, James Edward, and Phillip S. Hart. *Cities, Suburbs, and Blacks: A Study of Concerns, Distrust, and Alienation.* New York: General Hall, 1982.

This book is based upon an empirical investigation of urgent concerns, priorities, health needs, alienation, and distrust of the power structure, as identified by nearly one thousand black American residents of Atlanta, Boston, Cleveland, Houston, and Los Angeles. Substantial secondary data sources are also used to supplement the primary data. Priorities and concerns are tested against seven major hypotheses. Urban and suburban differences and similarities are examined with respect to micro- and macro-community issues. An analysis is made of the relationships that exist between degrees of alienation and/or social isolation and a number of important variables, such as position in the social structure, structural conditions, social class measures, age, sex, urban–suburban residence, and region of the country.

2818.   Blackwell, James Edward, and Morris Janowitz,** eds. *Black Sociologists: Historical and Contemporary Perspectives.* Chicago: University of Chicago Press, 1974.

A study of black sociologists and of sociology as it applies to black Americans. The first part of the book provides biographical data on the founders of black sociology, while the three remaining sections examine the black sociologist in various social settings. This book also provides discussion of theoretical issues and institutional adaptations in the light of this new approach to sociology.

2819.   Bond, Julian. *A Time to Speak, A Time to Act: The Movement in Politics.* New York: Simon and Schuster, 1972.

Bond urges black Americans to counter racism and militarism in American society by strengthening black communities where businesses, schools, and even the police can be controlled by blacks. Bond also discusses black self-awareness and forms of community socialism as ways of easing the problems of a racist society.

2820.   Bontemps, Arna Wendell, and Jack Conroy.* *Anyplace but Here.* New York: Hill and Wang, 1966.

Deals with the migration of blacks from the South. It is a revised and expanded version of *They Seek a City*, published in 1945.

2821. ―――――. *They Seek a City.* 1st ed. Garden City, N.Y.: Doubleday, Doran and Co., 1945.

2822. Boyer, James B. *Racial Integration and Learners from Limited Income Families: An Essay for American Educators.* Manhattan, Kans.: Mid-West Educational Associates, 1979.

2823. Bramwell, Jonathan Burton. *Courage in Crisis: The Black Professional Today.* Indianapolis: Bobbs-Merrill Co., 1972.

The author discusses―and dismisses―the theory that through "benign neglect" the racial, social, and economic gap between black and white professionals will diminish. He notes the resentment of whites charged―often quite rightly―with racism, and launches a bitter attack against the claim that blacks have been overcompensated to the extent that reverse discrimination is now apparent.

Jensen's highly controversial study of black intelligence and of the relationship between race and native intelligence is, for Bramwell, further evidence of the oppressive and unjust nature of white Americans, and Bramwell offers evidence against the theory. He suggests we use scientific technology to measure electronically the speed of neural responses to external stimuli as an essentially "culture-free" measurement of intelligence.

2824. Breneman,* William D., Louis E. Katz,* and Samuel Paschall. *Business Law Casebook.* Dubuque, Iowa: William C. Brown Co., 1981.

2825. Brown, Claude. *The Children of Ham.* New York: Stein and Day, 1976.

This book is about how abandoned children survive in a Harlem tenement. It depicts the lifestyle of these children and some of the people in one of America's famed black neighborhoods.

2826. Brown, H. Rap. *Die, Nigger, Die!* New York: Dial Press, 1969.

2827. Brown, Oliver. *Argument, Argument: The Oral Argument Before the Supreme Court in Brown v. Board of Education of Topeka, 1952-55.* Edited by Leon Friedman.** New York: Chelsea House Publishers, 1969.

2828. Bryant, Nathaniel H. *Urbanization and the Ecological Crisis: An Analysis of Environmental Pollution.* Washington, D.C.: University Press of America, 1976.

2829. Bryant, Spurgeon Quinton. *Black Leadership Fenced In by Racism.* Philadelphia: Dorrance and Co., 1974.

"A comparative study of the handicaps placed on black leadership, this book traces the effects of the white color caste system on blacks from the time of the Civil War to the present. The book covers impositions put on blacks and their successful attempts at leadership in the fields of education, politics, religion, and economics. Portraits of several black leaders, discussions of individual and personal experiences, as well as discussions on the Civil Rights movement and the black power surge reveal the author's thesis that the black man was visualized as a threat to the white man; thus, the white society chose segregation as a means of a psychological and physical barrier. The author is convinced that a fully integrated society would foster the best in black leadership to the benefit of all America and/or world society."

2830. Bryce-Laporte, Roy Simon, ed. *Sourcebook on the New Immigration: Implications for the United States and International Community.* New Brunswick, N.J.: Transaction Books, 1980.

2831. Bryce-Laporte, Roy Simon, and Claudewell S. Thomas,* eds. *Alienation & Contemporary Society: A Multidisciplinary Examination.* New York: Praeger Publishers, 1976.

Alienation, its manifestations in concept and in theory, is discussed in essays such as "A Culture of Discontent"; "Suicide: An End to Alienation"; and "Group Membership, Social Isolation, and Loneliness." These essays do more than analyze the disease of urbanized and industrialized man; in the section called "A Call for Action," they make recommendations for change. Brief biographies of the contributors to this collection are provided.

2832. Bryce, Herrington J. *Planning Smaller Cities.* Lexington, Mass.: Lexington Books, 1979.

2833. ———, ed. *Cities and Firms.* Lexington, Mass.: Lexington Books, 1980.

2834. ———, ed. *Urban Governance and Minorities.* New York: Praeger Publishers, 1976.

2835. Burgest, David R. *Social Casework Intervention with People of Color.* Lanham, Md.: University Press of America, 1985.

2836. ———, ed. *Social Work Practice with Minorities.* Metuchen, N.J.: Scarecrow Press, 1982.

2837. Butler, Johnella Elizabeth. *Black Studies—Pedagogy and Revolution: A Study of Afro-American Studies and the Liberal Arts Tradition Through the Discipline of Afro-American Literature.* Washington, D.C.: University Press of America, 1981.

Butler offers a conceptual framework for the criticism and teaching of Afro-American literature and proposes a liberating pedagogy for black studies. The literary criticism and pedagogy are developed within the context of two warring ideals, the African and the American, described by DuBois as central to the Afro-American experience and culture, and their counterparts found in Third World cultures, described by Paolo Freire. Proposing identity as the foundation of a pedagogy for black studies, Butler argues that the two warring ideals form the cultural context of Afro-American reality and thereby encourage an ambivalent aesthetic in Afro–American sensibility and literature. Arguing further that the recognition and explication of this ambivalence through an academic methodology and pedagogy that emphasizes the fusion of feeling (intuition) and intellect to effect learning is essential to the decolonization of the Afro–American mind.

2838.   Campbell, Bebe Moore. *Successful Women, Angry Men: Backlash in the Two–Career Marriage.* New York: Random House, 1986.

Having interviewed more than one hundred couples across the country (mostly white), Campbell relates personal stories (including her own) of what the respondents have experienced. These families describe how their ideal relationships have worked in actual practice. The first generation to start married life with a belief in equality between the sexes, they are finding that ideal difficult to live with, as well as threatening. According to Campbell, the phenomenon these couples are experiencing is backlash. (She notes that Audrey Chapman first advanced the theory of the first and subsequent stages of backlash.) Alvin F. Poussaint states in his introduction that "one element of backlash in these marriages focuses around the duties of raising children. Serious problems develop when the wife (or husband) does not want children at all or wishes to postpone childbearing beyond a time agreeable to the other partner." The solution to backlash, according to Campbell, isn't for women to be come less ambitious or successful, but for them to claim their own power and honestly communicate their needs to their husbands, believe those needs can be met, and prepare to take action if they are not met.

2839.   Carmichael, Stokely, and Charles V. Hamilton. *Black Power: The Politics of Liberation in America.* New York: Random House, 1967.

The authors express the view that "American Negroes can no longer afford to believe that their 'liberation' will come through traditional political processes," and they offer an alternative solution. Since racism in American society negates the existent political attitudes and institutions, blacks should organize their own political systems as a means of obtaining social change. The authors suggest that the political ideology of black power can lead to racial progress.

2840. Carson, Clayborne. *In Struggle: SNCC and the Black Awakening of the 1960s.* Cambridge: Harvard University Press, 1981.

2841. Chapman, Audrey B. *Man Sharing: Dilemma or Choice? A Radical New Way of Relating to the Men in Your Life.* New York: William Morrow and Co., 1986.

Chapman takes a look at the pros and cons of sharing a man in an era when exclusive relationships are rare, and she demonstrates how women can actually benefit from this harsh predicament.

2842. Clark, Kenneth Bancroft. *King, Malcolm, Baldwin: Three Interviews.* Middletown, Conn.: Wesleyan University Press, 1985.

2843. ————. *Pathos of Power.* 1st ed. New York: Harper and Row, 1974.

This two–part book is adapted from papers written by Clark over the past three decades. It represents his thinking on the complexities of power and social interaction in a nuclear era. Chapter 4, "Toward a Unifying Theory of Power," is of particular interest to social psychologists.

2844. Clark, Kenneth Bancroft, and Jeanette Hopkins.* *A Relevant War Against Poverty: A Study of Community Action Programs and Observable Change.* New York: Harper and Row, 1969.

This study assesses the nature, effectiveness, and consequences of community action programs. The authors begin with a definition of community action programs and then proceed to report in–depth studies of community action programs in New

York, Cleveland, Chicago, Los Angeles, and eight other cities, as well as fifty–one project proposals from other areas and regions. Clark and Hopkins maintain that the failure of many of these programs is due to a lack of any "rational understanding of the phenomena of power and of social change."

2845.   Clarke, John Henrik, with Amy Jacques Garvey, eds. *Marcus Garvey and the Vision of Africa.* New York: Vintage Books, 1974.

With the assistance of Amy Jacques Garvey, Clarke presents a collection of articles by and about Marcus Garvey, the early twentieth–century black leader. The collection provides an illuminating portrait of his life and work, his aspirations and accomplishments. Includes notes and an index.

2846.   Cogdell, Roy Thomas, and Sybil Wilson.* *Black Communication in White Society.* Saratoga, Calif.: Century Twenty One Publishers, 1980.

2847.   Comer, James Pierpoint, and Alvin F. Poussaint. *Black Child Care: How to Bring Up a Healthy Black Child in America: A Guide to Emotional and Psychological Development.* New York: Simon and Schuster, 1975.

Focusing on the mental health of black children in the formative years from infancy to adolescence, the authors, two black psychiatrists, examine what effects living in a white–dominated society can have on the development of black minds. They describe ways black children can acquire healthy mental attitudes and values. This book also includes a helpful, thorough bibliography on mental health development.

2848.   Coney, John C. *Exploring the Known and Unknown Factors in the Rates of Alcoholism Among Black and White Females.* San Francisco: R and E Research Associates, 1978.

2849.   ———. *The Precipitating Factors in the Use of Alcoholic Treatment Services: A Comparative Study of Black and*

White Alcoholics. San Francisco: R and E Research Associates, 1977.

2850. Conyers, James E., and Walter L. Wallace. *Black Elected Officials: A Study of Black Americans Holding Governmental Office.* New York: Russell Sage Foundation, 1976.

This book, based on questionnaire surveys of black elected officials compared with surveys of white officials in the same biographical region, presents a nationwide, in–depth profile of black elected officials. Areas surveyed by the study include ideological attitudes, perceptions of electoral constituencies, and perspectives on the future. Interesting discussions center around those officials who supported black independence, those who supported socioeconomic liberalism, and those who supported equality for women. Included also are sample questionnaires used and statistical data showing results to specific questions.

2851. Conyers, James E., William Farmar,** with Martin Levin.** *Black Youth in a Southern Metropolis: Socioeconomic Characteristics, Attitudes, and Values of Negro High School Students in Atlanta.* Atlanta, Ga.: Southern Regional Council, 1968.

2852. Coombs, Orde. *Do You See My Love for You Growing?* New York: Dodd, Mead and Co., 1972.

2853. Cosby, Bill. *Fatherhood.* Introduction and Afterword by Alvin F. Poussaint, M.D. Garden City, N.Y.: Doubleday and Co., 1986.

In this book, "Bill Cosby makes fatherhood come alive. He takes us on a Comedic yet insightful journey through the awesome shifting sands of parenthood. Along the way, he selects for emphasis those stages of fatherhood through which most men, who elect to participate actively in the great spiritual and psychological adventure of parenting, must pass." With amusing tales of his own experiences at fathering, Cosby challenges the reader to reflect on the phenomenon of fatherhood.

2854.   Cruse, Harold. *Plural but Equal: Blacks and Minorities in America's Plural Society.* New York: William Morrow and Co., 1987.

Cruse begins with a lengthy attack on the U.S. Supreme Court's 1954 *Brown v. Board of Education* decision. He argues that "separate but equal" might not have been an entirely bad idea if the "equal" part had been strictly enforced. He posits that those such as the NAACP who emphasize government action rather than self-help as the main avenue of progress for blacks have followed the wrong course. The black movement should focus on developing black organizations. Cruse favors establishing a black political party as "the first initial step toward a total reorganization of black life over the remainder of the twentieth century" into "first a political bloc, then cultural blocs, and then into whatever internal economic organizations are possible within a capitalistic, free–market system." Includes notes, bibliography, and an index.

2855.   Darden, Joe Turner, ed. *The Ghetto: Readings and Interpretations.* Port Washington, N.Y.: Kennikat Press, 1981.

This work provides an in–depth, comprehensive understanding of the ghetto, its problems, and solutions to those problems as viewed by eminently qualified and distinguished scholars. The authors represent a variety of disciplines including geography, political science, and economics. The result is an interdisciplinary perspective on a little–understood section of cities.

2856.   Darden, Joe Turner, Richard Child Hill, June Thomas, et al. *Detroit: Race and Uneven Development.* Philadelphia: Temple University Press, 1987.

Using sociology, geography, history, and planning, the authors view Detroit not only as the hub of the American auto industry and the site of the celebrated Riverfront Renaissance, but also as a city of poverty, unemployment, and racial segregation. They examine the genesis of this city, its recent redevelopment policies, and the ensuing political conflicts. Joe Darden, Richard Hill, June Thomas, and Richard Thomas argue that the current situation of metropolitan Detroit is a logical result of trends that have gradually escalated through the post–World War II era.

2857. David, Wilfred L. *Political Economy of Economic Policy: The Quest for Human Betterment.* New York: Praeger Publishers, 1988.

In this book, concerned with development policy, David advocates a balanced political economy, with emphasis on basic human rights and the realization of unfulfilled needs.

2858. Davidson, Chandler, ed. *Minority Vote Dilution.* Washington, D.C.: Howard University Press, 1984.

With an introduction by Davidson, this collection of essays documents and analyzes the historical basis for vote dilution and delineates the various techniques—at–large elections, white bloc voting, run–off primaries—used in the process that continue to preclude minorities from winning political office or gaining equal access to political power.

2859. Davis, Abraham Lincoln. *Blacks in the Federal Judiciary: Neutral Arbiters or Judicial Activists?* Bristol, Ind.: Wyndham Hall Press, 1989.

2860. ———, ed. *The United States Supreme Court and the Uses of Social Science Data.* New York: Irvington, 1975.

2861. Davis, Allison, and Robert J. Havighurst.** *Father of the Man: How Your Child Gets His Personality.* Boston: Houghton–Mifflin Co., 1947.

In this book, the authors trace the stages of individual development, as the child becomes a unique human being with his own personality and characteristics, different even from those of his siblings even though they have the same parents, family life, and perhaps even the same social environment beyond the family. Two fictitious American families are used to demonstrate the contrasts in the growing–up process. The authors offer suggestions that parents will find helpful in understanding and facilitating their child's development.

2862.   Davis, Allison, Burleigh B. Gardner,** Mary R. Gardner,** et al. *Deep South: A Social Anthropological Study of Caste and Class.* Chicago: University of Chicago Press, 1941.

This book, based on anthropological research conducted in the Deep South by a team of two blacks and two whites, presents their findings on the culture of the community and the social life of its people, particularly the prevalent caste and class systems.

2863.   Davis, Angela Yvonne. *Women, Culture, & Politics.* New York: Random House, 1984.

This book, which has as its central concern the struggle for racial, sexual, and economic equality, is the result of old speeches and articles that reflects the author's involvement in various movements: national committee member of the Ccommunist party, co–chairperson of the National Alliance Against Racial and Political Repression, and member of the executive boards of the National Black Women's Health Project and the National Political Congress of Black Women.

2864.   ————. *Women, Race, and Class.* New York: Vintage Books, 1983.

This documented study of the women's movement in the United States from abolitionist days to the present demonstrates how it has always been hampered by the racist and classist biases of its leaders. Although its focus is primarily historical, contemporary women's legal issues—rape, reproductive rights, and the socialization of housework—are discussed. Includes bibliographical references.

2865. Davis, Angela Yvonne, Ruchell Magee, et al.* *If They Come in the Morning: Voices of Resistance.* New York: New American Library, 1971.

This is a critical examination of the American penal system by such notables as Julian Bond, James Baldwin, George Jackson, Huey Newton, and Ericka Huggins. The authors attempt to rally popular support for prison reform by presenting historical and current examples of political repression in America and by emphasizing that many of those incarcerated in America are political prisoners. The book includes a letter to Angela Davis from James Baldwin and the case descriptions of "Trials of Political Prisoners Today" by Angela Davis.

2866. Davis, Frank Green. *The Black Community's Social Security.* Washington, D.C.: University Press of America, 1977.

2867. Davis, George. *Love, Black Love.* 1st ed. Garden City, N.Y.: Anchor Press, 1978.

Presents twenty-five personal narratives that capture the essence of how black Americans feel about their lives and loves.

2868. Dawkins, Marvin Phillip. *Alcohol and the Black Community: Exploratory Studies of Selected Issues.* Saratoga, Calif.: Century Twenty One Publishers, 1980.

2869. Day, Mary W. *The Socio-Cultural Dimensions of Mental Health: A Curriculum Practice Mode.* New York: Vantage Press, 1985.

2870. Dennis, Rutledge M., and Charles Jarmon, comps. *Afro-Americans: A Social Science Perspective.* Washington, D.C.: University Press of America, 1980.

2871. Devore, Wynetta, and Elfriede G. Schlesinger.** *Ethnic–Sensitive Social Work Practice.* 2d ed. Columbus, Ohio: Merrill Publishing Co., 1987.

   Concentrating on building sound social work skills and using them to enhance ethnic sensitivity, the text focuses on a unique ethnic–sensitive practice model easily adapted to existing social work practice models. Includes numerous case studies, many new invention strategies, an appendix ("Community Profile"), and an index.

2872. Dressler,** David, with William M. Willis. *Sociology: The Study of Human Interaction.* 3d ed. New York: Alfred A. Knopf, 1976.

2873. DuBois, W. E. B. *W. E. B. DuBois: A Reader.* Edited, and with an introduction by Meyer Weinberg.** New York: Harper Torchbooks, 1970.

2874. DuBois, W. E. B., and Augustus Granville Dill, eds. *The Negro American Artisan: Report of a Social Study Made by Atlanta University Under the Patronage of the Trustees of the John F. Slater Foundation.* Atlanta, Ga.: Atlanta University Press, 1912. Reprint. New York: Arno Press, 1968.

2875. Duster, Troy S. *The Legislation of Morality: Law, Drugs, and Moral Judgement.* New York: Free Press, 1970.

   Duster takes Svend Ranulf's thesis that the middle classes have a near monopoly on moral indignation to show how morality and social class are closely related. With irony and sometimes even sarcasm, he uses the case of drug addiction to illustrate how moralistic indignation is conditioned according to whether the finger of indignation is pointed by or at the middle, class and he argues that middle America's attitudes toward drugs are often absurd. Duster elaborates his thesis in discussions of the legislation morality, deviance, analytic and empirical approaches to the study of morality, and mental illness and criminal intent.

2876.   Edelman, Marian Wright. *Families in Peril: An Agenda for Social Change.* Cambridge: Harvard University Press, 1987.

With abundant documentation, Edelman, president of the Children's Defense Fund, paints a somber portrait of a deepening crisis: the rising curve of teen-age pregnancy, the massive joblessness of young blacks, the national trend toward single-parent households, and the increase in hungry and neglected children. She dispels common assumptions about these developments. For example, she shows that the birth rate for black women is stabilizing while that for unmarried white women continues to rise.

2877.   ————. *Portrait of Inequality: Black and White Children in America.* Washington, D.C.: Children's Defense Fund, 1980.

In this book, Edelman presents a discussion, supported by statistics, that documents the disparity between societal benefits to black and white families. She encourages enlightened advocacy and provides many suggestions for action.

2878.   El-Amin, Mustafa. *Freemasonry, Ancient Egypt, and the Islamic Destiny.* Jersey City, N.J.: New Mind Productions, 1988.

The author accentuates the connection between freemasonry, America, and ancient Egypt. He explores the contributions that the ancient Africans of Egypt made to the West and to the entire world. Includes a bibliography.

2879.   El-Khawas,** Elaine, Deborah J. Carter, and Cecilia A. Ottinger, eds. *The Community College Fact Book.* New York: American Council on Education: Macmillan Co., 1989.

Using charts, graphs, and tables, this book summarizes current statistics about enrollment trends, student characteristics, student outcomes, staffing, and financial data on two-year colleges. It also includes data on minorities in two-year colleges, as well as social and demographic data for the country. In short, it answers a wide range of questions.

2880. Emecheta, Buchi. *In the Ditch.* London: Barrie and Jenkins, 1972.

2881. Esedebe, P. Olisanwuche. *Pan-Africanism: The Idea and Movement, 1776-1963.* Enugu, Nigeria: Fourth Dimension Press, 1980. Reprint. Washington, D.C.: Howard University Press, 1982.

The author explores the Pan-African movement through the documents of the Pan-Africanists themselves: from the Chicago Congress of 1893, to the London Congress of 1921 and the emergence of the West African Students' Union, to the birth of the Organization of African Unity in 1963. Includes appendix, bibliography, and index.

2882. Evans,** Frank B., and Harold T. Pinkett, eds. *Research in the Administration of Public Policy.* Washington, D.C.: Howard University Press, 1975.

This book explores the wide range of valuable documents pertaining to the administration of public policy and examines the major federal agencies, especially their administrative policies and their relations with the public.

2883. Everett, Faye Philip. *The Colored Situation: A Book of Vocational and Civic Guidance for the Negro Youth.* Boston: Meador Publishing Co., 1938.

2884. Fanon, Frantz. *The Wretched of the Earth.* 1963. Reprint. New York: Grove Press, 1968.

2885. Farley,** Reynolds, and Walter R. Allen. *The Color Line and the Quality of Life in America.* New York: Russell Sage Foundation, 1987.

This is the third in a series of volumes (*The Population of the United States in the 1980s*) aimed at converting the vast statistical yield of the 1980 census into authoritative analyses of major changes and trends in American life. This analysis of the comparative status of blacks and whites encompasses such dimensions as fertility, mortality, and migration; family structure and educational attainment; employment and earnings. The authors also refine their description of black/white differences to reflect the internal diversity of the black population, comparing native–born and foreign blacks. Above all, Farley and Allen are sensitive to the powerful nexus between economic status and racial identity in the United States.

2886. Farmer, George L. *Afro–American Problems in Sociology and Psychology.* Los Angeles: Artgo Publications, 1970. Reprint. San Bernardino, Calif.: Borgo Press, 1983.

2887. Farmer, James. *Freedom—When? New York: Random House, 1965.*

A founder and former director of CORE, Farmer asks the crucial questions facing the civil rights revolution.

2888. Ferguson, Samuel Allan. *Chasing Rainbows.* Nashville: Southern Publishing Association, 1974.

2889. Fortune, Timothy Thomas. *Black and White: Land, Labor, and Politics in the South.* New York: Fords, Howard and Hulbert, 1884. Reprint. New York: Arno Press, 1969.

The author, born a slave in 1856 (Florida), states that "My purpose is to show that poverty and misfortune make no invidious distinctions of 'race, color, or previous condition,' but that wealth unduly centralized oppresses all alike." He contends that social problems in the South are universal and that the conflict in that area is between capital and labor. A new preface by James M. McPherson is included.

2890. Franklin, Jimmie Lewis. *Born Sober: Prohibition in Oklahoma, 1907–1959.* Norman: University of Oklahoma Press, 1971.

2891. Franklin, John Hope, and Isidore Starr,* comps. *The Negro in Twentieth Century America: A Reader on the Struggle for Civil Rights.* New York: Vintage Books, 1967.

2892. Frazier, Edward Franklin. *Black Bourgeoisie: The Rise of a New Middle Class in the United States.* New York: The Free Press, 1957. Reprint. New York: Collier Books, 1962.

In this work, Frazier sets forth his views on the frustrations and insecurities of middle–class American blacks. Analyzing the behavior, values, and attitudes of a group that, in his judgment, has become isolated as a result of its rejection by the "white world" and its break with its own cultural traditions, he posits the theory of a collective inferiority complex, which creates a world of make–believe centered around the myths of "Negro business" and "Negro society." Includes notes and an index.

2893. ————. *The Negro Family in the United States.* Chicago: University of Chicago Press, 1939.

2894. ————. *The Negro in the United States.* New York: Macmillan Co., 1957.

2895. ————. *Negro Youth at the Crossroads: Their Personality Development in the United States.* Washington, D.C.: American Council on Education, 1940.

This book is a clinical study of the results of enforced segregation and isolation of black youth from the American mainstream.

2896. Fuller, Thomas Oscar. *Banks and Banking.* Memphis, Tenn.: Pilcher Co., 1920.

This book, addressed to high school students, is arranged in lessons with helpful questions after each lesson. It begins with an investigation into banking from ancient times. Next it goes into the language of banking and looks into signature, kinds of accounts, loans, notes, checks, drafts, and the clearinghouse. The

final lesson, contributed by George W. Henderson, president of
Henderson Business College in Memphis, Tennessee, focuses on
the value of business education.

2897. Gary, Lawrence E. *The Afro-American Experience and the
Social Work Curriculum: Some Specific Suggestions.*
Washington, D.C.: Institute for Urban Affairs and Research,
Howard University, 1974.

2898. ————, ed. *Black Men.* Beverly Hills, Calif.: Sage Publications,
1981.

To dispel the unflattering light in which the American black
man has often been portrayed, Gary has assembled this collection
of eighteen articles, which he contends more genuinely reflect the
black man's experience. These essays examine the black man's
demographics, his relationships with women and family, his
psychological and social coping strategies, and his role in major
institutions—school, church, social welfare, and the legal system.
Includes bibliographies.

2899. ————, ed. *Mental Health: A Challenge to the Black
Community.* Philadelphia: Dorrance and Co., 1978.

2900. Gary, Lawrence E., and Lee P. Brown, eds. *Crime and Its Impact
on the Black Community.* Washington, D.C.: Institute for
Urban Affairs and Research, Howard University, 1975.

This work consist of a selection of papers presented at the
third annual research conference sponsored by the Institute for
Urban Affairs and Research, Howard University, held in
Washington, D.C., June 4–6, 1975.

2901. Gavins, Raymond. *The Perils and Prospects of Southern Black
Leadership: Gordon Blaine Hancock, 1884–1970.* Durham,
N.C.: Duke University Press, 1977.

2902.   Gibbs, Jewelle Taylor, ed. *Young, Black, and Male in America: An Endangered Species.* Dover, Mass.: Auburn House Publishing Co., 1988.

This book provides detailed analyses of the economic, social, cultural, and political factors that have contributed to the weakening status of black youth, particularly black males. The volume recommends a comprehensive family policy and a network of services that address the causes of the multiple problems facing black youth.

2903.   Giddings, Paula. *When and Where I Enter: The Impact of Black Women on Race and Sex in America.* New York: William Morrow and Co., 1984.

Using interviews as well as primary sources—speeches, diaries, letters, among others—Giddings set out to write a narrative history of black women from the seventeenth century to the contemporary period, tracing their concerns and what they did about them—that is, how they transcended double discrimination. Her book provides the material for vivid portraits that show how black women have been involved in two great social reform movements in this country—the struggles for racial and sexual equality.

2904.   Gifford, Bernard R., ed. *Test Policy and the Politics of Allocation: The Workplace and the Law.* Norwell, Mass.: Kluwer Academic Publishers, 1989.

Proceedings prepared under the aegis of the National Commission on Testing and Public Policy, this volume reviews testing use and policy. With contributors providing the background to a set a issues central to standardized test use policy, it presents the view that standardized test use and the interpretation of its results are affected by political factors.

2905.   Gill, Gerald R. *Meanness Mania: The Changed Mood.* Washington, D.C.: Howard University Press, 1981.

This book follows and complements *The Changing Mood in America: Eroding Commitment?* by Faustine C. Jones (Howard University Press, 1977). Gill's analysis shows that the national mood, too gently dubbed "conservative," has been long and viciously building. It also shows that the sources of this mood are marked by narrowness of interest and meanness of spirit. He cites a "new negativism" marked by "cultural narcissism," "social solipsism," and "hedonism." He supports Benjamin Hooks's assertion "that inflation makes people mean, vicious and selfish."

2906. Glasgow, Douglas G.. *The Black Underclass: Poverty, Unemployment, and Entrapment of Ghetto Youth.* San Francisco: Jossey–Bass Publishers, 1980. Reprint. New York: Vintage Books, 1981.

Provides an analysis of why, despite costly antipoverty programs, there continues to exist in this country a black under-class of hundreds of thousands of men and women who have neither the education nor the skills to emerge from abject poverty. Based on his study of hard–core "problem" youth in Watts, which he made from 1965 to 1968 with a follow–up in 1975, Glasgow outlines the dimensions of the problem and offers a new understanding of the aspirations and motivations of ghetto youth.

2907. Gloster, Jesse Edward. *Economics of Minority Groups.* 1st ed. Houston, Tex.: Premier Printing Company, 1973.

2908. ———. *Economics–in–Action.* Dubuque, Iowa: William C. Brown Co., 1968.

2909. ———. *Minority Economic, Political, and Social Development.* Washington, D.C.: University Press of America, 1978.

2910. ———. *North Carolina Mutual Life Insurance Company: Its Historical Development and Current Operations.* New York: Arno Press, 1975.

2911.   Goss, Linda, and Marian E. Barnes,* eds. *Talk That Talk: An Anthology of African–American Storytelling.* New York: Simon and Schuster, 1989.

2912.   Green, Charles. *Elitism vs. Democracy in Community Organizations: The Agonies of a South Bronx Group.* Bristol, Ind.: Wyndham Hall Press, 1985.

Green analyzes the iron law of oligarchy in a South Bronx community and provides insight into the organizational patterns and tendencies of emerging community groups.

2913.   Green, Ely. *Ely: Too Black, Too White.* Edited by Elizabeth N. Chitty* and Arthur Ben Chitty.* Amherst: University of Massachusetts Press, 1970.

2914.   Green, Robert L., et al.* *Discrimination and the Welfare of Urban Minorities.* Springfield, Ill.: Charles C. Thomas, 1981.

2915.   Greene, Lorenzo Johnston, and Myra Colson Callis. *The Employment of Negroes in the District of Columbia.* Washington, D.C.: Association for the Study of Negro Life and History, 1932.

This book is the result of a survey of Negro life and employment opportunities in the District of Columbia to determine the extent of unemployment among blacks, to ascertain whether a relatively greater proportion of blacks than whites were unemployed, to inquire into the causes for the same, and to suggest methods and means of combating that condition. It includes details of survey questionnaires, survey findings, and areas of interest covered by the survey. An analysis of the findings, as well as the interpretations and implications, are discussed. A summary and conclusion chapter is also included.

2916.   Greene, Lorenzo Johnston, and Carter G. Woodson. *The Negro Wage Earner.* Washington, D.C.: Association for the Study of Negro Life and History, 1931. Reprint. New York: AMS Press, 1970.

2917. Gregory, Dick. *Dick Gregory's Political Primer*. Edited by James R. McGraw.* 1st ed. New York: Harper and Row, 1972.

2918. ————. *The Shadow That Scares Me*. 1st ed. Garden City, N.Y.: Doubleday and Co., 1968.

2919. Gregory, Dick, and Mark Lane.* *Code Name "Zorro": The Murder of Martin Luther King, Jr*. Englewood Cliffs, N.J.: Prentice-Hall, 1977.

2920. Hall, Raymond Londell. *Black Separatism in the United States*. Hanover, N.H.: University Press of New England, 1978.

2921. ————. *Ethnic Autonomy: Comparative Dynamics—The Americas, Europe, and the Developing World*. Elmsford, N.Y.: Pergamon Press, 1979.

2922. ————, ed. *Black Separatism and Social Reality: Rhetoric and Reason*. Elmsford, N.Y.: Pergamon Press, 1977.

2923. Hamilton, Charles V. *The Bench and the Ballot: Southern Federal Judges and Black Voters*. New York: Oxford University Press, 1973.

This book is a study of the struggle to register black voters in the South. Hamilton analyzes the different judicial styles and temperaments of the various southern judges in some fifteen cases brought up in federal courts in the states of Alabama, Mississippi, Louisiana, and Tennessee. He also provides historical background for each case. Hamilton argues that the work of the judiciary is affected by the other two branches of government, and he shows how recent judicial and political history is affecting present trends.

2924. Harding, Vincent. *There Is a River: The Black Struggle for Freedom in America.* New York: Harcourt Brace Jovanovich, 1981. Reprint. New York: Vintage Books, 1983.

In this book, Harding discusses black leaders in history and the meaning of the black historical experience in America in an attempt to understand the true nature of black struggles for freedom. He implies that the dream of freedom—like the river—flows on.

2925. Hare, Nathan, and Julia Hare. *Bringing the Black Boy to Manhood: The Passage.* San Francisco: Black Think Tank, 1985.

2926. ―――. *The Endangered Black Family.* San Francisco: Black Think Tank, 1984.

2927. Harper, Frederick Douglas, ed. *Alcohol Abuse and Black America.* Alexandria, Va.: Douglas Publishers, 1976.

Using both a historical and a sociological approach, Harper discusses what he considers to be the primary health and social problem among Afro-Americans—alcohol abuse. He analyzes alcohol–related problems within the black community and examines the causes, impact, and implications of alcohol abuse. Of particular interest are the chapters on alcohol abuse and black women, black adolescents, and the black family in general. A glossary of alcohol–related terms as used by blacks is included together with a list of organizations and programs for treating alcoholism.

2928. Harris, Charles Wesley. *Perspectives of Political Power in the District of Columbia: The Views and Opinions of 110 Members of the Local Political Elite.* Washington, D.C.: National Institute of Public Management, 1981.

2929. ―――. *Regional COG's and the Central City.* Detroit: Metropolitan Fund, 1970.

A research brief on councils of government and the central city. A research project of Metropolitan Fund, Inc. Includes a bibliography.

2930. ————. *Resolving the Legislative Veto Issue: A Review of Proposals and Opinions.* Washington, D.C.: National Institute of Public Management, 1979.

2931. Harris,** Fred R., and Roger W. Wilkins, eds. *Quiet Riots: Race and Poverty in the United States.* New York: Pantheon Books, 1988.

This book confirms the inability of this country's political, economic, and social institutions to respond to the urgent messages sent out of the ghettos in the uprisings of the 1960s. The purpose of the editors and their contributors is to force our attention away from those black Americans who have done so well onto those millions of others who still live in deprivation and despair in the rural and urban poor.

2932. Harris, Joseph Earl. *Africans and Their History.* New York: New American Library, 1972.

2933. Harris, William Hamilton. *Keeping the Faith: A. Philip Randolph, Milton P. Webster, and the Brotherhood of Sleeping Car Porters, 1925–37.* Urbana: University of Illinois Press, 1977.

This book focuses upon the charismatic leadership of A. Philip Randolph, on his articulation of the sleeping car porters' grievances, and on his close working relationship with his lieutenant, who organized the porters while he appealed for support among the public. Includes an appendix, a note on sources, and an index.

2934. Harrison–Ross, Phyllis Anne, and Barbara Wyden.** *The Black Child—A Parents' Guide.* New York: Peter H. Wyden, Inc., 1973.

Two women—one black, one white, both deeply concerned about racial prejudice—have collaborated on this book, urging people to deal constructively with the issue of race, even—and especially—in interacting with their own children. The book is written for white and black parents alike in the hope that they will see the need for removing racial prejudice from themselves and their young, and so act upon this need.

2935.   Haskins, James. *The Guardian Angels.* Hillside, N.Y.: Enslow Publishers, 1983.

2936.   ————. *The Long Struggle: The Story of American Labor.* Philadelphia: Westminster Press, 1976.

This history of American labor from colonial days to present times discusses trade unions and associations, and mechanization and its influence on labor, as well as specific historical periods, such as the Great Depression and the labor boom that followed. Haskins provides a glossary of labor terminology and a comprehensive bibliography.

2937.   ————. *The New Americans: Vietnamese Boat People.* Hillside, N.J.: Enslow Publishers, 1980.

2938.   ————. *A New Kind of Joy: The Story of the Special Olympics.* Garden City, N.Y.: Doubleday and Co., 1976.

This illustrated book about the mentally retarded and their successes as Special Olympians is a tribute to their stamina and drive to become acceptable citizens to society. Haskins describes their struggles and victories that occur even before they reach the finish line, and emphasizes the vast support to the Special Olympics program given by the communities themselves.

2939.   ————. *A Piece of the Power: Four Black Mayors.* New York: Dial Press, 1972.

The four black mayors discussed in this book—Richard Hatcher, Kenneth Gibson, Carl Stokes, and Charles Evers—are evidence of some black political power, despite the overall powerlessness of black Americans. These four men demonstrate the positive ways that political power can be used to benefit themselves and their people. The book includes photographs of these four men in various activities.

2940. ————. *Profiles in Black Power.* Garden City, N.Y.: Doubleday and Co., 1972.

2941. ————. *Resistance: Profiles in Non-Violence.* Garden City, N.Y.: Doubleday and Co., 1970.

Haskins defines nonviolence and compares the views on nonviolence of Bertrand Russell, Mahatma Gandhi, Martin Luther King, Jr., Jesus of Nazareth, and other well-known proponents of it.

2942. ————. *Revolutionaries: Agents of Change.* 1st ed. Philadelphia: J. B. Lippincott Co., 1971.

In this book Haskins describes the lives of eleven revolutionaries—including Malcolm X, Mao Tse Tung, and Fidel Castro—representing a wide cross-section of revolutionary mentalities. He uses their lives to illustrate the meanings of *revolution* and *revolutionary*, two key terms in today's society.

2943. ————. *Street Gangs: Yesterday and Today.* New York: Hastings House, 1974.

This history of street gangs in urban New York City demonstrates the similarities between all gangs regardless of their nationality. Haskins stresses the fact that gangs are not just common to the lower classes but are to be found among the higher strata of society as well. The text includes many interesting illustrations and photographs.

2944. ————. *Teen-Age Alcoholism.* New York: Hawthorn Books, 1976.

Haskins argues that addiction to alcohol is very much like addiction to heroin and that young alcoholics are more emotionally disturbed than their adult counterparts. Using a self–help approach, he examines facts and misconceptions about alcohol, including its effects on the body and mind, use and abuse of alcohol, and youth and alcoholism. Appendixes contain a nationwide listing of the National Council on Alcoholism, Inc. directories.

2945.   ————. *Werewolves.* New York: Franklin Watts, 1981.

2946.   ————. *Who Are the Handicapped?* New York: Doubleday and Co., 1978.

2947.   ————. *Your Rights, Past and Present: A Guide for Young People.* New York: Hawthorn Books, 1975.

This book discusses specific rights of young people and laws affecting them. The rights include the right to work, education, justice, and home life. Chapter 5, which deals with the rights of young people at home, is especially interesting because it discusses the necessary evolution of the child from being a total parent possession to being a protectee under the law.

2948.   Haskins, Jim, with Pat Connolly.* *The Child Abuse Help Book.* Reading, Mass.: Addison–Wesley Publishing Co., 1982.

2949.   Haskins, Jim, with J. M. Stifle.* *The Quiet Revolution: The Struggle for the Rights of Disabled Americans.* New York: Thomas Y. Crowell Co., 1979.

2950.   Hayes, Leola G. *Occupational and Vocational Interest for the Exceptional Individual.* Washington, D.C.: University Press of America, 1977.

2951.   Haynes, Leonard L., III, Henry E. Cobbs,* and Robert A. Holmes III,* eds. *An Analysis of the Arkansas–Georgia Statewide Desegregation Plans.* Washington, D.C.: Institute for Services to Education, 1979.

This book analyzes the state plans for desegregation of higher education, submitted by Arkansas and Georgia and approved by the Department of Health, Education, and Welfare as a result of the *Adams v. Richardson* (1973) case, in which ten states were accused of operating dual systems of education. Not only are the state plans evaluated in terms of meeting HEW criteria, but questions are also raised as to the relevancy and adequacy of the HEW criteria themselves.

2952. Henderson, George. *To Live in Freedom: Human Relations Today and Tomorrow.* 1st ed. Norman: University of Oklahoma Press, 1972.

The author ingeniously combines aspects of social psychology, social science, urban studies, Afro-American studies, and current issues into a skillful essay on human relations. The book is designed for the first-year college course in related social sciences. A list of sources for further reading is included at the end of each chapter.

2953. ———, ed. *Human Relations: From Theory to Practice.* Norman: University of Oklahoma Press, 1974.

In this text, the editor introduces each essay with an extended discussion of the area and follows it with an article that further illustrates the thesis. "The Process of the Encounter Group," by Carl R. Rodgers, and "Fifth Avenue, Uptown: A Letter from Harlem," by James Baldwin, illustrate encounter groups, and a prelude to violence and nonviolence, respectively. A list of suggested readings is included in each chapter. The result is a comprehensive examination of human relations and techniques for positive improvement in this area. The appendixes include individual, group, and community change questionnaires, along with guidelines for community problem analysis.

2954. Henderson, Lenneal J., Jr. *Administrative Advocacy: Black Administrators in Urban Bureaucracy.* Palo Alto, Calif.: R and E Research Associates, 1979.

2955. Hernton, Calvin C. *Coming Together: Black Power, White Hatred, and Sexual Hang-ups.* New York: Random House, 1971.

2956. ———. *Sex and Racism in America.* 1st ed. Garden City, N.Y.: Doubleday, 1965.

2957. ———. *White Papers for White Americans.* 1st ed. Garden City, N.Y.: Doubleday and Co., 1966. Reprint. Westport, Conn.: Greenwood Press, 1982.

2958. Higginbotham, A. Leon, Jr. *In the Matter of Color: Race and the American Legal Process: The Colonial Period.* New York: Oxford University Press, 1978.

This four-part book—"Race and the American Legal Process," "The Black Experience in Colonial America," "The English Experience with Slavery," and "The Revolution"—clearly establishes that law has played a vast role in the degradation of black Americans. An epilogue, an appendix (a note on the indentured servant system), a bibliography, notes, an index, and a table of cases are included.

2959. Hill, Robert A. *The Strength of Black Families.* New York: Emerson Hall, 1973.

Using social science methodology, Robert Hill analyzes a previous research study conducted by the National Urban League about the myths surrounding the black family—matriarchy, dependency, illegitimacy, and related issues. Hill uncovers substantial evidence that the black family is the nourishing foundation for blacks. He discusses family structure, attitudes toward work, goals, and religious orientations.

2960. Hill, Robert Bernard. *Informal Adoption Among Black Families.* Washington, D.C.: Research Department, National Urban League, 1977.

2961. ———. *Youth Employment in American Society.* Washington, D.C.: Bureau of Social Science Research, 1984.

The thrust of this volume is on private industry's attitudes and practices toward youth employment, with special attention to minority youth. It addresses questions such as the following: Where are youth hires located in the private sector? What positions do they typically occupy? What are private employers' guidelines for hiring youth? What are private employers' attitudes toward wage subsidies for young people? The work concludes with a careful set of recommendations based on growth projections by region; changes in technological sophistication in the work force; and an evaluation of industries with high and low growth potential.

2962. Himes, Joseph Sandy. *Conflict and Conflict Management.* Athens: University of Georgia Press, 1980.

This book, an integration and summation of both recent and earlier works in the field, is subdivided into analysis and treatment sections. Himes cites and uses a wide range of materials including his own research as he first deals with the nature of social conflict and draws upon the works of sociologists such as Parsons, Merton, Simmel, Coser, and Dahrendorf. He also deals with the management of conflict, with its prevention and treatment, which he suggests is more developed in advanced societies. Includes a bibliography and an index.

2963. ———. *Social Planning in America: A Dynamic Interpretation.* Garden City, N.Y.: Doubleday and Co., 1954.

An analysis of the nature, methods, and problems of democratic social planning in industry, agriculture, science, government, and community, addressed to both college students and lay readers. The incorporation of sound sociological principles is especially evident in the discussion of community-level social planning.

2964.   ————. *The Study of Sociology: An Introduction.* Glenview,
        Ill.: Scott, Foresman and Co., 1968.

In this six-part book with glossary, Himes takes topics that
are fairly standard in introductory sociology texts, and brings
them into sharp focus by organizing them around three basic
issues: social organization, personality, and social change.

2965.   Hine, Darlene Clark. *Black Victory: The Rise and Fall of the
        White Primary in Texas.* Millwood, N.Y.: Kraus-Thomson
        Organization, 1979.

This book reflects the struggle by blacks to gain the right to
vote. A voting rights conflict began in Texas when a middle-
class black man decided that he wanted to vote and was denied
that right. Nixon (the prospective voter), local blacks, and the
NAACP challenged this decision. Their challenges brought about
four major U.S. Supreme Court cases: *Nixon v. Herndon*, 1927;
Nixon v. Condon, 1932; *Grovey v. Townsend*, 1935; and *Smith v.
Allwright*, 1944. Hine describes the white primary as being the
most effective scheme in southern states to deny blacks the right
to vote. The Texas Democratic white primary was declared
unconstitutional in the 1944 case above. The book also includes
a bibliography and an index.

2966.   Hogan, Lloyd L. *Principles of Black Political Economy.* Boston:
        Routledge and Kegan Paul, 1984.

Hogan questions the "standard" wisdom in the field of
political economy regarding race and racial questions, particularly
about the black experience in America. His thesis is that black
oppression is based on the virtually total exploitation of black
labor. According to Hogan, to comprehend this exploitation we
must understand the social reproduction of the black population
over the past five centuries. He then outlines the mechanisms that
determine the social reproduction of any population in any
political economy, including blacks in the United States. Includes
an index and a bibliography.

2967. Holden, Matthew. *The Politics of the Black "Nation."* New York: Chandler Publishing Co., 1973.

2968. Holley, Joseph Winthrop. *What if the Shoe Were on the Other Foot?—Slavery in Reverse.* New York: William–Frederick Press, 1953.

2969. Holt, Thomas C., Cassandra Smith–Parker, and Rosalyn Terborg–Penn. *A Special Mission: The Story of Freedmen's Hospital, 1862–1962.* Washington, D.C.: Office of Academic Affairs Division, Howard University, 1975.

2970. Hooks, Bell. *Ain't I a Woman: Black Women and Feminism.* Boston: South End Press, 1981.

The author examines the impact of sexism on black women during slavery, the historic devaluation of black womanhood, black male sexism, racism within the recent women's movement, and black women's involvement with feminism.

2971. ————. *Talking Back: Thinking Feminist, Thinking Black.* Boston: South End Press, 1989.

This work, by a black feminist and social critic, is a collection of essays on the issues of race, class, gender and the rise of the black feminist movement.

2972. Hoskins, Linus A. *Carrot and Bigstick: Perspectives on U.S.– Caribbean–Jamaican Relations.* Inglewood, Calif.: Tele-Artists Co., 1985.

2973. ————. *The New International Economic Order: A Bibliographic Handbook.* Washington, D.C.: University Press of America, 1982.

2974. ————. *The Political Economy of Pan-African Nationalism: Historical Origins and Contemporary Forms.* Baltimore, Md.: Pyramid Publications, 1987.

In this essay Hoskins challenges Pan–Africanist views on the movement's development and offers alternative ideas.

2975. Hughes, Langston. *Fight for Freedom: The Story of the NAACP.* New York: W. W. Norton and Co., 1962.

2976. Hull, Gloria T., Patricia Bell Scott, and Barbara Smith, eds. *All the Women Are White, All the Blacks Are Men, But Some of Us Are Brave: Black Women's Studies.* Old Westbury, N.Y.: Feminist Press, 1982.

2977. Hunt,* Chester L., and Lewis Walker. *Ethnic Dynamics: Patterns of Intergroup Relations in Various Societies.* 2d ed. Holmes Beach, Fla.: Learning Publications, 1979.

2978. Ince, Basil Andre. *Decolonization and Conflict in the United Nations: Guyana's Struggle for Independence.* Cambridge, Mass.: Schenkman Publishing Co., 1974.

The story of a nation's struggle for political independence through the United Nations. It looks at the views on decolonization and self–determination offered by the United Nations and at their subsequent role in securing independence for Guyana. The text includes a UN Charter and some General Assembly resolutions on the topic.

2979. Jackson, Jacquelyne Johnson. *Minorities and Aging.* Belmont, Calif.: Wadsworth Publishing Co., 1980.

2980. ———, ed. *Research Conference on Minority Group Aged in the South.* Durham, N.C.: Center for the Study of Aging and Human Development, Duke University Medical Center, 1972.

2981. Jackson, Jacquelyne Johnson, with Faith Hampton Childs* and Robin Ficker,* eds. *Aging Black Women: Selected Readings for NCBA.* Washington, D.C.: College and University Press, 1975.

This work is a compilation to provide related background material for participants in the third annual conference of the National Caucus on the Black Aged, held in Washington, D.C., April 13–15, 1975. Includes a bibliography.

2982. Jarmon, Charles. *Nigeria: Reorganization and Development Since the Mid-Twentieth Century.* New York: E. J. Brill Press, 1988.

The book focuses on urbanization and national development in the postcolonial era of Nigeria.

2983. Johnson, Charles Spurgeon. *Bitter Canaan.* New Brunswick, N.J.: Transaction Books, 1987.

This book is a historical–sociological account of Liberian society. Written in 1930 and revised in 1948 by the influential, pioneering sociologist Charles S. Johnson, it traces the historical development of American race relations that led to the emigration of thousands of black to Liberia. Their struggle in leaving America and settling the African wilderness is detailed. Johnson shows how a Liberian nationality evolved and how social, economic, and political foundations of the nascent state affected its history. He critically evaluates American corporate intervention in Liberian society in the twentieth century.

2984. ———. *Growing Up in the Black Belt: Negro Youth in the Rural South.* Washington, D.C.: American Council on Education, 1941. Reprint. New York: Schocken Books, 1967.

After a study of over two thousand southern rural blacks, Johnson chose for this book ten rural youths whose experiences in the familiar institutions of community life and in the setting of the rural South are described. Through the use of life history documents, family case studies, individual interviews, and aptitude and psychological tests, the author has woven the results of many methods of research into a unified statement. He includes sample personal attitude tests used for the study and a detailed index.

2985.   ————. *A Preface to Racial Understanding.* New York: Friendship Press, 1936.

2986.   Johnson, Charles Spurgeon, Edwin R. Embree, and W. W. Alexander.* *The Collapse of Cotton Tenancy: Summary of Field Studies & Statistical Surveys, 1933–35.* Freeport, N.Y.: Libraries Press, 1972.

2987.   Johnson, Edward Augustus. *Adam vs. Ape–Man and Ethiopia.* New York: J. J. Little and Ives Co., 1931.

Johnson compares two theories of creation and the original man, the agamic theory and the scientific theory, and argues that while both are equally reasonable, the former has more human value and should be considered the real foundation of human life.

2988.   Johnson, George Marion. *Education Law.* East Lansing: Michigan State University Press, 1969.

2989.   ————. *Handbook on Michigan Education Law.* East Lansing: Michigan State University Press, 1970.

2990.   Jones, Dionne J., and Stanley F. Battle, eds. *Teenage Pregnancy: Developing Strategies for Change in the Twenty–First Century.* New Brunswick, N.J.: Transaction Publishers, 1990.

2991.   Jones, Faustine Childress, with Cynthia Smith, John McClendon, et al. *The Changing Mood in America: Eroding Commitment?* Washington, D.C.: Howard University Press, 1977.

Using Gunnar Myrdal's *An American Dilemma* as a framework, Jones (with the assistance of Cynthia Smith, John McClendon, and Reginald Hildebrand) examines the changing mood in America in the 1970s and concludes that this mood is working to the detriment of blacks and other minorities. Supported by the Institute for the Study of Educational Policy at Howard University, Jones bases her conclusion on various published documents of groups and institutions. These are listed in a comprehensive bibliography.

2992. Jones, LeRoi. *Home: Social Essays.* New York: William Morrow and Co., 1966.

In this work, LeRoi Jones (now known as Imamu Amiri Baraka) conveys very personal feelings about being black in a world dominated by white practicalities.

2993. Jones, Marcus Earl. *Black Migration in the United States with Emphasis on Selected Central Cities.* Saratoga, Calif.: Century Twenty One Publishers, 1980.

2994. Jones, Reginald Lanier, and George Trentin.* *Budgeting: Key to Planning and Control, Practical Guidelines for Managers.* Rev. ed. New York: American Management Association, 1971.

Describes the various roles a business administrator must assume when budgeting. Numerous diagrams supplement the discussion of how a business can best profit from a well–organized budget.

2995. Jules–Rosette, Bennetta. *The Mushecho: A Girl's Purity Rite.* San Diego: University of California, 1976.

This work looks at puberty rites, celibacy, and marriage customs and rites in Zimbabwe. It is a companion to the videotape, "The Muschecho," first presented at the seventh annual conference on visual anthropology, Temple University, March 1976. Includes a bibliography.

2996. ————. *The New Religions of Africa.* Norwood, N.J.: Ablex Publishing Corp., 1979.

2997.   ————. *Symbols of Change: Urban Transition in a Zambian Community.* Norwood, N.J.: Ablex Publishing Corp., 1981.

2998.   Karenga, Maulana. *The African American Holiday of Kwanzaa: A Celebration of Family, Community, & Culture.* Los Angeles: University of Sankore Press, 1988.

Discusses the origins, values, symbols, and activities of Kwanzaa. Created by Karenga in 1966, Kwanzaa is an Afro-American holiday based on African agricultural celebrations and collective principles that contribute to the unity and development of the African community.

2999.   Karnig,** Albert K., and Paula D. McClain, eds. *Urban Minority Administrators: Politics, Policy, and Style.* Westport, Conn.: Greenwood Press, 1988.

With a foreword by Julian Bond, this volume presents the views of minority administrators, together with analyses by three prominent scholars in the field. The group, which includes two women, consists of two city managers, two police chiefs, a deputy mayor, and the director of a quasi-governmental health organization. The editors conclude the volume with an examination of the differences and similarities in the experiences of the contributing authors and attempt to place common issues in a broader context.

3000.   Kennedy, Theodore R. *You Gotta Deal with It: Black Family Relations in a Southern Community.* New York: Oxford University Press, 1980.

This book explodes the myth that the lives of southern rural blacks have changed dramatically as a result of the civil rights revolution. It offers proof that the stereotypical southern town—replete with poverty, prejudice, and hopelessness—still exists. Presenting an overview of the community and an in-depth analysis of four extended families, this study illuminates the nature of family structure among different classes of blacks. The book lets the families speak for themselves as the dialogues, blended with Kennedy's narrative, demonstrate that the southern black family is not "breaking down" or "matrilocal," but has a well-defined, coherent, viable structure.

3001. Killens, John Oliver. *Black Man's Burden.* New York: Trident Press, 1965. Reprint. New York: Simon and Schuster, 1970.

3002. King, Charles Edward. *The Sociology of Small Groups: A Handbook of Theory and Experiment.* New York: Pageant Press, 1962.

This hundred-page college text examines several aspects of the small group, such as structure, group cohesiveness, goal achievement, and the process of leadership. Theory is supported through experiments reported at the end of each chapter. Of great interest to the sociology major.

3003. King, Martin Luther, Jr. *Stride Toward Freedom: The Montgomery Story.* New York: Harper and Row, 1958.

This book gives a fascinating account of the year-long boycott of Montgomery's segregated bus system—a protest that sparked the freedom movement. The book outlines the events that galvanized Montgomery's diverse black community and spurred it to take action against the policy relegating blacks to the back of buses. The citywide bus system was a daily reminder of the indignities of segregation. Dr. King generously praised the men and women who carried out the protest—not just the leaders, but the people he described as followers, many of them beyond middle age, who walked to work and home again as much as twelve miles a day for over a year rather than submit to the discourtesies and humiliation of the segregated buses.

3004. ———. *The Trumpet of Conscience.* New York: Harper and Row, 1968.

This book is a transcript of a series of radio broadcasts presented by Dr. King for the Canadian Broadcasting Corporation in 1967. During this five-part-series, he turned his magnifying glass on the world and examined its shortcomings. The result is a compelling collection of essays espousing love and peace.

3005.   ————. *Where Do We Go from Here: Chaos or Community?* 1st ed. New York: Harper and Row, 1967.

Written to counter arguments that the birth of the black power movement was a sign that the nonviolent faction of the movement was in a "state of ideological disarray," this book acknowledges that the dreams of the movement have only partially been realized. Dr. King, understanding the frustration felt by many blacks in the face of white indifference, nevertheless urges them to stay the course of nonviolence while at the same time urging government to act, to be concerned that the potential of the individual is not wasted.

3006.   ————. *Why We Can't Wait.* New York: Signet Books, 1964.

This book provides an answer to the question of why the civil rights movement of the 1950s and 1960s occurred. Dr. King traces the black man's path of oppression from slavery to the present day and evaluates the future of the struggle in the areas of education, legislation, and employment.

3007.   ————. *The Words of Martin Luther King, Jr.* 1st ed. Selected by Coretta Scott King. 1983. Reprint. New York: Newmarket Press, 1987.

Selected quotations and maxims of Dr. Martin Luther King, Jr., noted civil rights leader. Includes bibliographical references.

3008.   King, Mary Elizabeth. *Freedom Song: A Personal Story of the 1960's Civil Rights Movement.* 1st ed. New York: William Morrow and Co., 1987.

3009.   King, Woodie, Jr., and Earl Anthony, eds. *Black Poets and Prophets: The Theory, Practice, and Esthetics of the Pan-Africanist Revolution.* New York: New American Library, 1972.

3010. Kunjufu, Jawanza. *Motivating and Preparing Black Youth to Work.* 1st ed. Chicago: African American Images, 1986.

3011. Lacy, Leslie Alexander. *The Soil Soldiers: The Civilian Conservation Corps in the Great Depression.* Radnor, Pa.: Chilton Book Co., 1976.

3012. Ladner, Joyce A. *Mixed Families: Adopting Across Racial Boundaries.* Garden City, N.Y.: Anchor Press/Doubleday and Co., 1977.

This very interesting study about white American parents who adopt black children was conducted in Georgia, Missouri, Washington, D.C., Maryland, Virginia, Connecticut, and Minnesota. Ladner records her in-depth interview with each set of parents and the reactions of relatives, friends, and neighbors, as well as the relationship between adopted and biological children. she attempts to clarify the motives for interracial adoption.

3013. Lamont, Barbara. *City People.* New York: Macmillan Co., 1975.

3014. Landry, Bart. *The New Black Middle Class.* Berkeley: University of California Press, 1987.

Landry argues that the Civil Rights Act of 1964 and a prosperous economy together gave rise to the new black middle class consisting of all white-collar workers and small business men plus a number of service occupations such as firemen, policemen, and dental assistants. As a result, this new black middle class differs from its predecessor—the old black middle class—in the variety of occupations comprising it. The author shows that the new class generally falls behind its white counterpart in economic well-being and differs from it in lifestyle.

3015. Lester, Julius. *Look Out, Whitey! Black Power's Gon' Get Your Mama!* New York: Dial Press, 1968.

3016.   Lewis, David Levering. *King: A Critical Biography.* 1st ed. New York: Praeger Publishers, 1970.

3017.   Lewis, Evelyn Jones. *Backways of Kent.* Chapel Hill: University of North Carolina Press, 1955.

Lewis's intimate study of the lives of blacks in a small southern town examines family life, economics, education, and government primarily from a sociological point of view. The material is divided into three parts. Part 1 introduces the black subculture, part 2 examines what goes into the making of the subculture; and part 3 discusses the integration of the subculture into the dominant white society. The text includes numerous figures and tables.

3018.   Lewis, Mary C. *Herstory: Black Female Rites of Passage.* Chicago: African American Images, 1988.

Where do parents and daughters disagree? When does a girl become a woman? How can we reduce teenage pregnancy? What's the real deal between black males and black females? Do black females trust each other? These are a few questions addressed in this 138–page work. Includes footnotes and a selected bibliography.

3019.   Lewis, Raphael O. *People, Politics, and the Political Life: An Introduction to Political Science.* Washington, D.C.: University Press of America, 1979.

3020.   Lincoln, Charles Eric. *My Face Is Black.* Boston: Beacon Press, 1964.

Five essays written during the civil rights movement, including one on Malcolm X.

3021.   ————. *Race, Religion, and the Continuing American Dilemma.* New York: Hill and Wang, 1984.

In 1944, Gunnar Myrdal evaluated the American character and concluded that it was flawed by what he called "the American Dilemma"—a deeply rooted contradiction between the high ideals Americans espouse and the low realities they live by. Forty years later C. Eric Lincoln reassessed that evaluation and decided that the American dilemma is "essentially intact" and that the cost in money, self-respect, and human potential is astronomical. The roots of the dilemma, Lincoln argues in this book, are in the "easy rapprochements" between religion and politics. He further argues that Protestantism, Catholicism, and Judaism have accommodated themselves to American political mores and have thus created a "religion of culture" that protects the American conscience from racial indictments.

3022.   ————. *Sounds of the Struggle: Persons and Perspectives in Civil Rights.* New York: William Morrow and Co., 1967.

3023.   ————, ed. *Is Anyone Listening to Black America?* New York: Seabury Press, 1968.

3024.   Littlejohn, Walter L., and Clara Murphy Jennings,* eds. *Good Programs for Young Children: A Guide for Caregivers.* Little Rock, Ark.: Heritage Press, 1978.

3025.   Lloyd, Raymond Grann. *White Supremacy in the United States: An Analysis of Its Background, with Especial Reference to the Poll Tax.* Washington, D.C.: Public Affairs Press, 1952.

3026.   Locke, Alain LeRoy, ed. *The New Negro: An Interpretation.* Decorations and portraits by Winold Reiss.* Albert and Charles Boni, Inc., 1925. Reprint. New York: Atheneum Publishers, 1968.

This volume aims to document the "New Negro" culturally and socially and to present the artistic and social goals of the "New Negro" movement, also known as the Harlem Renaissance. Includes a list of early books by blacks, a select list of plays about black life, and a bibliography of black music.

3027. Locke, Hubert G. *The Care and Feeding of White Liberals: The American Tragedy and the Liberal Dilemma*. New York: Newman Press, 1970.

3028. Logan, Rayford Whittingham. *The Betrayal of the Negro, From Rutherford B. Hayes to Woodrow Wilson*. 1965. Reprint. New York: Collier Books, 1972.

Originally published as *The Negro in American Life and Thought: The Nadir, 1877–1901*, this work shows how various presidential administrations thwarted the aspirations of black Americans.

3029. ————. *The Diplomatic Relations of the United States with Haiti, 1776–1891*. Chapel Hill: University of North Carolina Press, 1941. Reprint. New York: Kraus Reprint Co., 1969.

3030. ————. *Two Bronze Titans: Frederick Douglass and William Edward Burghardt DuBois*. Washinghton, D.C.: Department of History, Howard University, 1972.

3031. ————, ed. *The Attitude of the Southern White Press Toward Negro Suffrage, 1932–1940*. Washington, D.C.: Foundation Publishers, 1940.

3032. ————, ed. *What the Negro Wants*. Chapel Hill: University of North Carolina Press, 1944. Reprint. New York: Agathon Press, 1966.

3033. Lynch, Hollis Ralph, comp. *The Black Urban Condition: A Documentary History, 1866–1971*. New York: Thomas Y. Crowell and Co., 1973.

3034. Madhubuti, Haki R. *Enemies: The Clash of Races*. Chicago: Third World Press, 1978.

3035. Madhubuti, Haki R., and Jawanza Kunjufu. *Black People and the Coming Depression*. Chicago: Institute of Positive Education, 1975.

3036. Manley, Michael. *The Politics of Change: A Jamaican Testament.* Washington, D.C.: Howard University Press, 1975.

This book is a declaration that the needs of the new Jamaica are radically different from those of colonial Jamaica. Manley, a former prime minister, uses a steep knowledge and understanding of the past to offer convincing solutions for removing his country from the economic, political, psychological, and social strangulation resulting from centuries of colonial and human bondage.

3037. ————. *Up the Down Escalator: Development and the International Economy—A Jamaican Case Study.* Washington, D.C.: Howard University Press, 1987.

Manley's book examines the ideals, objectives, and proposals that have come to be described as the "new international economic order." In analyzing the problems of economic development in a Third World country, Manley focuses on Jamaica and its experiences with the problems of economic development in the eight and one-half years he was prime minister.

3038. Mann, Coramae Richey. *Female Crime and Delinquency.* University, Ala.: University of Alabama Press, 1984.

3039. Manuel, Ron C., ed. *Minority Aging: Sociological and Social Psychological Issues.* Westport, Conn.: Greenwood Press, 1982.

3040. Marr, Warren, II, and Maybelle Ward,** eds. *Minorities and the American Dream: A Bicentennial Perspective.* New York: Arno Press, 1976.

This interesting collection of articles was written for the American Issues Forum sponsored by the National Endowment for the Humanities. The articles examine fundamental issues relating to the development and future of American society, including such topics as "Who Represents America?—Who

Governs?" "The Black Worker in America," and "How to Combat Racism and Bigotry." Contributors include Andrew Young and Eli Ginzberg.

3041. Martin, Eddie J., and James F. Blumstein,** eds. *The Urban Scene in the Seventies: Proceedings.* Nashville: Vanderbilt University Press, 1974.

These papers, originally delivered in slightly different form at a 1972 conference, address three issues: definitions of the problems of public policy, evaluation of existing programs, and policy strategies and alternatives. Bibliographies are included for each paper.

3042. McAdoo, Harriette Pipes, ed. *Black Families.* 2d ed. Beverly Hills, Calif.: Sage Publications, 1988.

The 1981 first edition of this publication addressed some unresolved issues regarding black families. Since that publication, the status of the black family in America has changed dramatically. New questions have arisen: What is the current economic status of the black family in America today? What educational opportunities exist today for blacks? What role do black families play in the socialization of their children? How does teenage pregnancy affect the black family? The revised second edition provides a current and comprehensive overview on the state of the black family.

3043. McAdoo, Harriette Pipes, with Jim T. Parham,** eds. *Services to Young Families: Program Review and Policy Recommendations.* Washington, D.C.: American Public Welfare Association and Ford Foundation, 1985.

3044. McClure, Jesse F. *Managing Human Services.* Davis, Calif.: International Dialogue Press, 1979.

3045. McDaniel, Reuben Roosevelt, Jr., and Kenneth E. Knight.** *Organizations: An Information Systems Perspective.* Belmont, Calif.: Wadsworth Publishing Co., 1979.

3046. McGuire, Phillip. *He, Too, Spoke for Democracy: Judge Hastie, World War II, and the Black Soldier.* Westport, Conn.: Greenwood Press, 1988.

3047. McKissick, Floyd. *Three-Fifths of a Man.* London: Macmillan and Co., 1969.

The former director of CORE presents a bold and scathing denunciation of racist attitudes and practices in America.

3048. McMillon, Doris, with Michele Sherman. *Mixed Blessing.* New York: St Martin's Press, 1985.

This book tells the story of McMillon's successful search for her biological mother, who is white.

3049. Mead,** Margaret, and James Baldwin. *A Rap on Race.* Philadelphia: J. B. Lippincott Co., 1971.

Mead and Baldwin candidly speak to each other about race, violence, responsibility, and the past and future of America. They compare blacks in America with whites in South Africa. Both groups have suffered and died for their respective lands; both are in an absolutely hostile environment, and both are outnumbered and surrounded by a different ethnic group. Mead and Baldwin speak of possible solutions to racial problems.

3050. Medley,** Morris L., and James E. Conyers, eds. *Sociology for the Seventies: A Contemporary Perspective.* New York: John Wiley and Sons, 1972.

3051. Miles, Johnnie Harris, and James P. Clouse.* *Career Advising for Adults.* Blacksburg, Va.: Virginia Department of Vocational Education and College of Education at Virginia Polytechnical Institute and State University, 1981.

3052. Milgram, Morris. *Good Neighborhood: The Challenge of Open Housing.* New York: W. W. Norton and Co., 1979.

3053. Miller, Carroll L. *Role Model Blacks: Known but Little Known Role Models of Successful Blacks.* Muncie, Ind.: Accelerated Development Inc., 1982.

Presents sixty biographical profiles of contributing recognized blacks in often–considered nontraditional careers for blacks. Contains thought questions for each profile. The role models were selected by eminent and distinguished Afro–Americans. Includes bibliographical references and indexes.

3054. Miller, Kelly. *Radicals and Conservatives, and Other Essays on the Negro in America.* 1908 Reprint. New York: Schocken Books, 1968. Originally published as *Race Adjustment.*

Topics Miller discusses include: "An Appeal to Reason on the Race Problem," "The City Negro," "The Land of Goshen," "Surplus Negro Women," "What Walt Whitman Means to the Negro," "Jefferson and the Negro," "The Artistic Gifts of the Negro," "The Early Struggle for Education," "A Brief for the Higher Education of the Negro," and "Roosevelt and the Negro."

3055. Moore,** Kristin A., Margaret C. Simms, and Charles L. Betsey. *Choice and Circumstance: Race Differences in Adolescent Sexuality and Fertility.* New Brunswick, N.J.: Transaction Publishers, 1986.

The authors explore three factors underlying the racial differences in the incidence of early childbearing: information about sex, pregnancy, and contraception; need for family planning and abortion services; and motivation for postponing parenthood, including aspirations for schooling, employment plans, and desire for children within marriage. They consider which teens postpone sex and pregnancy and why, and whether the kinds of motivation necessary to prevent early pregnancy vary by race.

3056. Moses, Wilson Jeremiah. *Black Messiahs and Uncle Toms: Special and Literary Manipulation of a Religious Myth.* University Park: Pennsylvania State University Press, 1982.

3057. Moss, Larry Edward. *Black Political Ascendancy in Urban Centers, and Black Control of the Local Police Functions: An Exploratory Analysis.* San Francisco: R and E Research Associates, 1977.

      Moss confirms the view that there is institutionalized conflict between the police and the black community, and he attempts to determine the extent to which selected black communities in the United States—Atlanta, Newark, and Washington, D.C.—have been able to translate enhanced political potential into control of the policing function in their communities and the means by which such control has been attempted. His examination of the aforementioned urban centers is followed by a series of tentative hypotheses, some methodological observations, and some conclusions as to the optimum strategy for blacks seeking to use local political offices to control the local police.

3058. Murray, Albert. *The Omni–Americans: Some Alternatives to the Folklore of White Supremacy.* New York: Outerbridge and Dienstfrey, 1970, Distributed by E. P. Dutton. Reprint. New York: Vintage Books, 1983.

      This work, a series of essays on various cultural topics, includes attacks on white supremacy movements and on a variety of nationally known figures who hold disparaging views of Afro–Americans.

3059. Murray, Pauli, and Verge Lake,* eds. *States' Laws on Race and Color.* Cincinnati, Ohio: Women's Division of Christian Services, 1955.

3060. Mutharika, Arthur Peter. *The Alien Under American Law: Text, Materials, Cases.* Dobbs Ferry, N.Y.: Oceana Publications, 1980.

3061. ———. *The Regulation of Statelessness Under International and National Law.* Dobbs Ferry, N.Y.: Oceana Publications, 1977.

3062. ————, ed. *The International Law of Development.* Dobbs Ferry, N.Y.: Oceana Publications, 1978.

3063. Nelson, William E., Jr., and Phillip J. Meranto.* *Electing Black Mayors: Political Action in the Black Community.* Columbus: Ohio State University Press, 1977.

3064. Newton, Huey P., with Herman Blake.* *Revolutionary Suicide.* New York: Harcourt Brace Jovanovich, 1973.

3065. Offiong, Daniel A. *Imperialism and Dependency: Obstacles to African Development.* Washington, D.C.: Howard University Press, 1982.

This book contributes to the debate on problems of Third World development. It includes chapters on "A Critique of Modernization," "Imperialism and Dependency," "Development of Underdevelopment: Slavery," "Development of Underdevelopment: Colonial Imperialism," "Development of Underdevelopment: Neocolonialism," "The CIA and U.S. Capitalism," "Impact of Underdevelopment on Third World Societies," and "Toward a New International Economic Order." The author states that a change in the status quo will come about only when the underdeveloped countries come together to take a common stand against their exploiters. Includes an index.

3066. Ottley, Roi. `New World A–Coming': Inside Black America.* Boston: Houghton Mifflin Co., 1943. Reprint. New York: Arno Press, 1968.

Writing an intimately detailed story of Afro–American life, the author focuses on Harlem, viewing it as the barometer of black America. Using knowledge gathered mainly from black newspapers and the records of black organizations, as well as from personal observations and interviews, Ottley provides a picture of Harlem during the late 1930s and early 1940s. A new preface by Benjamin Quarles is included.

3067. Owens, Jesse, with Paul G. Neimark.* *Blackthink: My Life as Black Man and White Man.* New York: William Morrow and Co., 1970.

3068. ————. *I Have Changed.* New York: William Morrow and Co., 1972.

3069. Owens, Leslie Howard. *This Species of Property: Slave Life and Culture in the Old South.* New York: Oxford University Press, 1977.

3070. Painter, Nell Irvin. *The Narrative of Hosea Hudson: His Life as a Negro Communist in the South.* Cambridge: Harvard University Press, 1979.

3071. Palley,* Marian Lief, and Michael B. Preston, eds. *Race, Sex, and Policy Problems.* Lexington, Mass.: Lexington Books, 1979.

3072. Parks, Arnold G. *Black Elderly in Rural America: A Comprehensive Study.* Bristol, Ind.: Wyndham Hall Press, 1988.

3073. Parsons,** Talcott, and Kenneth Bancroft Clark, eds. *The Negro American.* Boston: Beacon Press, 1967.

This comprehensive survey examines the racial crisis in America. Using demographic data, economic factors, and social-psychological perspectives, thirty academic figures and civil rights leaders present essays on the problems and status of blacks in the sixties. Some of these essays originally appeared in 1965 and 1966 issues of *Daedalus*, the journal of the American Academy for Arts and Sciences. Foreword is by Lyndon B. Johnson.

3074. Peirson, Gwynne W. *Police Operations.* Chicago: Nelson–Hall, 1976.

3075. Penn, Nolan E., and Charles W. Thomas. *Urban and Rural Studies.* Lexington, Mass.: Ginn Custom Publishing Co., 1979.

3076. Pentecoste, Joseph. *Systems of Poverty.* Washington, D.C.: University Press of America, 1977.

3077. Perry, Huey L. *Democracy and Public Policy: Minority Input in the National Energy Policy of the Carter Administration.* Bristol, Ind.: Wyndham Hall Press, 1985.

3078. Pinkney, Alphonso. *The American Way of Violence.* New York: Vintage Books, 1972.

In this documented study, Alphonso Pinkney traces the roots of America's propensity for violence to its culture and the demands of its economic system. He identifies domestic occurrences of violence—for example, exploitation, labor violence, racism, and police violence, as well as violence in international relations, such as America's involvement in Vietnam.

3079. ————. *Black Americans.* Englewood Cliffs, N.J.: Prentice–Hall, 1969.

The author describes and analyzes the history, social characteristics, and socioeconomic status of blacks in America for the purpose of understanding the roots of their continuing oppression. The chapter entitled "Assimilation into American Society" may be of special interest to the sociologist, student, and layman alike. Bibliographies have been included at the end of each chapter.

3080. ————. *The Myth of Black Progress.* New York: Cambridge University Press, 1984.

Disturbed by the suggestion that race is no longer a salient variable in relations between blacks and whites, Pinkney analyzes the status of black Americans since the Civil Rights Act of 1964 and reminds us that race remains a lamentably powerful force in

American political life. He discusses affirmative action, busing, open admissions, and other educational issues. Measured in his analysis, he depicts a bleak outlook, particularly for ghetto youth. Includes notes and an index.

3081. Pipes, William Harrison. *Death of an "Uncle Tom."* New York: Carlton Press, 1967.

3082. Powell,** Norman, and Robert A. Holmes III. *Black Politics and Public Policy.* New York: Emerson–Hall, 1975.

3083. Prestage, Jewel Limar, and Marianne Githens,** eds. *A Portrait of Marginality: The Political Behavior of the American Woman.* New York: David McKay Co., 1979.

3084. Preston, Michael B. *Black Machine Politics in the Post–Daley Era.* Evanston, Ill.: Center for Urban Affairs, Northwestern University, 1979.

3085. ————. *The Politics of Bureaucratic Reform: The Case of the California State Employment Service.* Urbana: University of Illinois Press, 1984.

3086. Preston, Michael B., Lenneal J. Henderson, Jr., and Paul Puryear, eds. *The New Black Politics: The Search for Political Power.* 2d ed. New York: Longman, 1987.

3087. Quarles, Benjamin. *Black Abolitionists.* New York: Oxford University Press, 1970.

3088. Rampersad, Arnold. *The Art and Imagination of W. E. B. DuBois.* Cambridge: Harvard University Press, 1976.

3089. Redding, J. Saunders. *The Lonesome Road: The Story of the Negro in America.* Garden City, N.Y.: Doubleday and Co., 1958.

3090.   ————. *No Day of Triumph.* With an introduction by Richard Wright. New York: Harper and Brothers, 1942. Reprint. New York: J. and J. Harper, 1968.

3091.   ————. *On Being Negro in America.* 1st ed. Indianapolis: Bobbs–Merrill, 1951. Reprint. New York: Harper and Row, 1969.

3092.   ————. *They Came in Chains: Americans from Africa.* Rev. ed. Philadelphia: J. B. Lippincott Co., 1973.

3093.   Reed, Adolph L., Jr. *The Jesse Jackson Phenomenon: The Crisis of Purpose in Afro–American Politics.* New Haven: Yale University Press, 1986.

   The central thesis of this book is that the 1984 Jesse Jackson phenomenon reflects the inadequacy of conventional patterns of discourse, concerning black political activity, for generating either critical interpretations or appropriate strategic responses. According to Reed, the Jackson phenomenon must be understood in relation to (1) the development of competing criteria for legitimation of claims to black political leadership; (2) the sharpening of lines of socioeconomic stratification within the Afro–American population; and (3) the growth of centrifugal pressures within and external attacks on the national policy consensus represented in the Democratic coalition.

3094.   Robinson, Luther D. *Sound Minds in a Soundless World.* Washington, D.C.: U.S. Department of Health, Education, and Welfare, 1978.

3095.   Rodgers–Rose, La Frances, ed. *The Black Woman.* Beverly Hills, Calif.: Sage Publications, 1980.

   The contributors to this volume—all of them black women—analyze the black woman and examine her relationship to the black man, the family, the community, the political and educational systems, and the economy. The wide array of topics and methodological approaches shows the richness of this area for future study and provides much of interest for all concerned with race relations and sex roles. Includes bibliographies.

3096. Rodney, Walter. *The Groundings with my Brothers.* 1969. Reprint. London: Bogle–L'Ouverture Publications, 1975.

3097. ———. *How Europe Underdeveloped Africa.* 1974. Reprint. Washington, D.C.: Howard University Press, 1982.

Rodney explores and analyses the complex interrelationship of Europe and Africa from the fifteenth century to the mid–twentieth century. Rodney traces the history of Europe's development as it relates to Africa's underdevelopment and examines the correlation between the two.

3098. Rose,** Peter Issac, Stanley Rotham,** and William Julius Wilson, eds. *Through Different Eyes: Black and White Perspectives on American Race Relations.* New York: Oxford University Press, 1973.

A thought–provoking collection of essays covering various aspects of race relations in America today, including black/white perspectives, schools, and other social institutions that continue to be plagued by racial problems. Contributors include Joyce Ladner, Edgar Epps, Lewis Killian, Andrew Greeley Chuck Stone, Lawrence Rosen, Jan Dizard, and Sethard Fisher. Includes notes.

3099. Rose, Harold M. *The Black Ghetto: A Spatial Behavioral Perspective.* New York: McGraw–Hill, 1971.

3100. ———. *Black Suburbanization: Access to Improved Quality of Life or Maintenance of the Status Quo.* Cambridge, Mass.: Ballinger Publishing Co., 1976.

3101. Ross, Edyth L., ed. *Black Heritage in Social Welfare: 1860–1930.* Metuchen, N.J.: Sacrecrow Press, 1978.

Legacies of the slave institutions, segregation, and public policy decisions are addressed by various writers to illustrate the meaning of social welfare to the black community. Documentary evidence, including landmark events and court cases, underscores the reasons and demonstrates the need for social work among blacks. The work constitutes an excellent source for the student of social work.

3102. Rowan, Carl Thomas. *Just Between Us Blacks.* New York: Random House, 1974.

This collection of Rowan's brilliantly written commentaries, originally presented on the "Black Perspectives" radio broadcasts, comments on the Nixon administration and national security with refreshing frankness. Rowan addresses the issue of the black family and the failures and confusions of blacks in an equally forthright manner. Provocative, enlightening, and extraordinary insight into issues that affect all black Americans directly and all white Americans indirectly.

3103. Rubin,* Leslie, and Pauli Murray. *The Constitution and Government of Ghana.* London: Sweet and Maxwell, 1961.

3104. Russell,** John Caro, Jr., and Walter D. Broadnax. *Minorities in Kansas: In Quest for Equal Opportunity.* Topeka, Kans.: Economic Opportunity Office, 1968.

3105. Sabir, Waliyyuddin Abdul. *Reconstruction of the African–American Male.* Jersey City, N.J.: New Mind Productions, 1989.

This book re–addresses the impact of slavery as a peculiar institution. It explains how slavery reduced the African–American male to three–fifths of a man, thus fulfilling the description ascribed to slaves. The thesis of the book concludes that the "Three–Fifths concept" has been carefully orchestrated and intentionally perpetuated. It also speaks to the responsibility of the oppressed in removing the burden of oppression.

3106. Salaam, Kalamu Ya. *Tearing the Roof off the Sucker: The Fall of South Afrika.* New Orleans: Ahidiana, 1977.

3107. Scott, Emmett Jay. *Negro Migration During the Civil War.* New York: Oxford University Press, 1920. Reprint. New York: Arno Press, 1969.

Supported by a grant from the Carnegie Endowment for International Peace, Scott details the black migration to northern cities during World War I. He shows why it took place, where it took place, what efforts were made to check the movement, the effects of the movement on the South when entire communities were depopulated, and what remedies for relief were offered by national organizations. Includes a bibliography and index, as well as a new preface by Thomas R. Cripps.*

3108. Scott, Joseph W. *The Black Revolts: Racial Stratification in the U.S.A.: The Politics of Estate, Caste, and Class in the American Society.* Cambridge, Mass.: Schenkman Publishing Co., 1976.

"This book is a socio–historical study of racial stratification in America. It argues and supports the thesis that the black population was turned into a statutorily ascribed estate and hence a political class. Political racism superseded economic racism and led to the enslavement and subsequent containment of the blacks."

3109. Sikes, Melvin P. *The Administration of Injustice.* New York: Harper and Row, 1975.

Seeking to improve the relationship between police and the community, Sikes describes the beleaguered system of American justice and the many dedicated law enforcement persons involved in the criminal justice system who represent the professional ideal. By making us aware of the weaknesses of the law enforcement system, Sikes attempts to increase American minorities' understanding and tolerance for law enforcement persons.

3110. Simms, Margaret C., and Julianne M. Malveaux,* eds. *Slipping Through the Cracks: The Status of Black Women*. New Brunswick, N.J.: Transaction Publishers, 1986.

This volume focuses on black women as a special group, and includes articles on employment, educational attainment, and job training, as well as on the role of women in developing country economies.

3111. Sinclair, William Albert. *The Aftermath of Slavery:A Study of the Condition and Environment of the American Negro*. Boston: Small, Maynard and Company, 1905. Reprint. New York: Arno Press, 1969.

Born a South Carolina slave in 1858, Sinclair, who later became a founder of the NAACP, addresses various manifestations of white racism—legal persecution, economic exploitation, imprisonment and peonage, brutality, and lynching. Includes a new preface by Otto H. Olsen.*

3112. Smith, Barbara, ed. *Home Girls: A Black Feminist Anthology*. New York: Kitchen Table—Women of Color Press, 1983.

3113. Smith, Ed Calvin, and J. B. Cannon,** *Resources for Affirmative Action: An Annotated Directory of Books, Periodicals, Films, Training Kits, and Consultants on Equal Opportunity*. Garrett Park, Md.: Garrett Park Press, 1982.

3114. Smith, James Wesley. *The Strange Way of Truth*. New York: Vantage Press, 1968.

3115. Smith, Shelby Lewis, ed. *Black Political Scientists and Black Survival: Essays in Honor of a Black Scholar*. Detroit: Balamp Publishing, 1977.

A collection of essays and lectures by American political scientists honoring Jewel Limar Prestage (1931–). Includes bibliographical references.

3116.   Smith, William Gardner. *Return to Black America.* Englewood
Cliffs, N.J.: Prentice–Hall, 1970.

3117.   Sowell, Thomas. *Civil Rights: Rhetoric or Reality?* New York:
William Morrow and Co., 1984.

After more than three decades since the landmark *Brown v.
Board of Education* decision, Sowell examines what has actually
happened over these decades—as distinguished from the promise
with which they began or the rhetoric with which they continue.
How much of the promise of the *Brown v. Board of Education*
and the Civil Rights Act of 1964 has been fulfilled. How much
has it been perverted? How well has the social vision behind the
civil rights movement been understood—or even questioned?
These questions, and the assumptions behind the civil rights
revolution, are the focus of Sowell's analysis. Includes notes and
an index.

3118.   ————. *Classical Economics Reconsidered.* Princeton, N.J.:
Princeton University Press, 1974.

The text is divided into four chapters: social philosophy,
macroeconomics, microeconomic, and methodology. The chapter
on macroeconomics includes a thorough discussion of Say's Law
and Monetary Theory.

3119.   ————. *Compassion Versus Guilt and Other Essays.* New
York, N.Y.: William Morrow and Co. 1987.

This book contains a collection of eighty essays on subjects
ranging from child abuse to Tom Brokaw's patriotism, from
South America to comparable worth. It discredits commonly held
myths in order to point out the obvious contradictions in some
viewpoints. It also questions the premises of Left and Right alike.

3120.   ————. *A Conflict of Visions: Ideological Origins of Political
Struggles.* New York: William Morrow and Co., 1987.

Conflicts that endure for generations or centuries show a remarkably consistent pattern. The analysis of this pattern is the purpose of this book. Its theme is that the enduring political controversies of the past two centuries reflect radically different assumptions about the nature of man. The meaning of such words as *freedom, equality, rights,* and *power* is drastically different in the context of different visions of man. According to Sowell, "The analysis here is not intended to reconcile visions or determine their validity, but to understand what they are about, and what role they play in political, economic, and social struggles."

3121.   ————. *Economics: Analysis and Issues.* Glenview, Ill.: Scott, Foresman and Co., 1971.

The text studies the underlying principles involved in economic behavior. Sowell begins with a discussion of the process of price setting and the role price plays in an economy. He continues by analyzing price determinants operating in noncompetitive markets, as well as other economic elements and policy problems on the national level.

3122.   ————. *The Economics and Politics of Race: An International Perspective.* New York: William Morrow and Co., 1983. Reprint. New York: Quill, 1985.

Sowell uses hard facts to demonstrate that, internationally as well as domestically, discrimination, however heinous, is not a cause of poverty.

3123.   ————. *Knowledge and Decisions.* New York: Basic Books, 1980.

Building on the pioneering work of F.A. Hayek, Sowell explains how decentralized knowledge is used in society and how markets transmit the knowledge and coordinate the decisions of millions of individuals.

3124. ———. *Markets and Minorities.* New York: Basic Books, 1985.

Sowell not only dismantles widespread myths about the nature of discrimination in economic life but shows how minorities can use the market to improve their economic condition.

3125. ———. *Marxism: Philosophy and Economics.* 1st ed. New York: William Morrow and Co., 1985.

3126. ———. *Pink and Brown People and Other Controversial Essays.* Stanford, Calif.: Hoover Institution Press, 1981.

This book contains some sixty of Sowell's short essays, which were previously published in some of America's largest newspapers between 1977 and 1981. The essays are divided into sections: race and ethnicity, politics, economic policy, the social scene (focusing on social problems as well as education), courts and the law, and foreign policy.

3127. ———. *Say's Law: An Historical Analysis.* Princeton, N.J.: Princeton University Press, 1972.

A discussion and analysis of the controversy surrounding the notion that supply creates its own demand—Say's Law. Sowell discusses the views of such notable opponents to this law as Karl Marx and John Maynard Keynes. The period of controversy considered in this study is between the early nineteenth century and close to the mid–twentieth century.

3128. Spencer, Margaret Beale, Geraldine Kearse Brookins, and Walter R. Allen, eds. *Beginnings: The Social and Affective Development of Black Children.* Hillsdale, N.J.: Lawrence Erlbaum Associates, 1985.

In this volume, noted psychologists, sociologists, anthropologists, historians, and psychiatrists offer empirical assessments of the ecological contexts, interpersonal relationships, and psychological states that influence black children's growth. To fill the conceptual and empirical void in the interpretation of black children's development, this book goes a long way toward abetting the sensitive interpretation of the development of children of all minorities.

3129.   Spiva, Ulysses Van. *How to Get a Grant for Your Own Special Project.* Bloomington, Ind.: T. I. S. Publications, 1980.

The grant–seeking approach suggested in this publication is an integrated and systematic one that is the culmination of training received by the author through numerous grantsmanship workshops and conferences attended over the past several years and through job–related experiences as a research project administrator, a consultant to national research and development projects for the United States Office of Education, a Washington Policy Fellow, and a university director of sponsored research and training programs.

3130.   Spruill, Albert W. *Great Recollections from Aggieland: A Human Interest Account of the Development of the A & T College of N. Carolina from 1893–1960.* Wilmington, N.C.: Whitehead Printing Co., (Private) 1964.

3131.   Staples, Robert E. *Black Masculinity: The Black Male's Role in American Society.* San Francisco: Black Scholar Press, 1982.

3132.   ————. *Introduction to Black Sociology.* New York: McGraw-Hill, 1976.

As a study of sociology from the black perspective, this book provides interesting insights into the nature of the discipline and examines such areas as personality, religion, crime, and social class as they relate to the black culture.

3133.   ————. *The Lower Income Family in Saint Paul.* St. Paul, Minn.: St. Paul Urban League, 1967.

3134. ————. *The World of Black Singles: Changing Patterns of Male/Female Relations.* Westport, Conn.: Greenwood Press, 1981.

3135. ————, comp. *The Black Family: Essays and Studies.* 3d ed. Belmont, Calif.: Wadsworth Publishing Co., 1986.

3136. Stevens, Joseph H., Jr. and Marilyn Mathews,** eds. *Mother/Child Father/Child Relationships.* Washington, D.C.: National Association for the Education of Young Children, 1978.

An anthology of selected research that appears to have the greatest bearing on the work of practitioners who counsel parents, in the hope that it will inspire further research for a more comprehensive view of parent–child relationships. Reports on significant research studies and position papers outlining critical issues in relation to research and practice are outlined. In addition, two chapters outline issues surrounding a study of the parent and child, and applications of this knowledge are included.

3137. Stone, Chuck. *Black Political Power in America.* Rev. ed. Indianapolis: Bobbs–Merrill Co., 1968.

Not only examines the history of the Afro–American in American politics from the Civil War through the 1960s, but also analyses the very nature of our political process. Showing how other ethnic groups—through pressure tactics, bloc voting, and patronage—have achieved power, Stone points out why this has not been true for the blacks and tells how the political process can be made to work.

3138. ————. *Tell It Like It Is.* New York: Trident Press, 1970.

3139. Strickland, Arvarh E. *History of the Chicago Urban League.* Urbana: University of Illinois Press, 1966.

3140. Sullivan, Leon Howard. *Build, Brother, Build.* Philadelphia: Macrae Smith, 1969.

3141.   Swan, Llewelyn Alex. *Families of Black Prisoners: Survival and Progress.* Boston: G. K. Hall and Co., 1981.

3142.   ————. *The Politics of Riot Behavior.* Washington, D.C.: College and University Press, 1975. Reprint. Washington, D.C.: University Press of America, 1980.

3143.   ————. *Survival and Progress: The Afro-American Experience.* Westport, Conn.: Greenwood Press, 1981.

3144.   Swan, Llewelyn Alex, with Betty B. Cox.* *Issues in Marriage, Family, and Therapy.* 2d ed. Lexington, Mass.: Ginn Custom Publishing Co., 1983.

3145.   Taylor, Alrutheus Ambush. *The Negro in Tennessee, 1865–1880.* Washington, D.C.: Associated Publishers, 1941. Reprint. Spartanburg, S.C.: Reprint Co., 1974.

3146.   Taylor, Arnold H. *American Diplomacy and the Narcotics Traffic, 1900–1939: A Study in International Humanitarian Reform.* Durham, N.C.: Duke University Press, 1969.

3147.   Taylor, Howard F. *Balance in Small Groups.* New York: Van Nostrand Reinhold Co., 1970.

3148.   ————. *The I.Q. Game: A Methodological Inquiry into the Heredity–Environment Controversy.* New Brunswick, N.J.: Rutgers University Press, 1980.

This text presents various analyses of the IQ games. In chapter 1, it notes that the genetic heritability of human IQ scores within a given population cannot be reliably estimated. Chapter 2 states that IQ heritability has no implications for educational policy. Chapter 3 reveals that there are certain errors in Jensen's statement on the study of separated identical twins kinship correlation, and that there is no reason to postulate the existence of any genes for intelligence. Chapters 4 and 5 indicate that some hypothetical gene or set of genes might affect the scores of an IQ test. In chapter 6, Taylor suggests that the ill-defined methodologically inadequate Jensen–like pair–wise equation for calculating the heritability coefficient should be abandoned. Includes notes, and an index.

3149. Teague, Bob. *Letters to a Black Boy.* New York: Walker and Co., 1968.

3150. Terborg–Penn, Rosalyn, Sharon Harley, and Andrea Benton Rushing, eds. *Women in Africa and the African Diaspora.* Washington, D.C.: Howard University Press, 1987.

This book examines the role and place of women in the African diaspora. The collection of essays included is a result of the conference "Women in the African Diaspora: An Interdisciplinary Perspective," sponsored by the Association of Black Women Historians and held June 12–14, 1983, at Howard University. Contributors clarify the concepts, methodology, and projected guidelines for studies of women throughout the African diaspora. An index is included.

3151. Thibodeax, Mary Roger. *A Black Nun Looks at Black Power.* New York: Sheed and Ward, 1972.

In these personal reflections on black power, a black nun writes about "God and Black Power," "Black Power in America," "Black Womanhood," "Nuns and Black Power," and "Faith and Black Power." Included in the book are thirty–six black–and–white photographs of life in the black community.

3152. Thompson, Alton. *Quality of Life Among Rural Residents in North Carolina: Community and Life Satisfaction.* Bristol, Ind.: Wyndham Hall Press, 1985.

Conducted under sponsorship of the U.S. Department of Agriculture, this study focuses on rural residents of North Carolina, with special attention to black Americans. Includes charts and diagrams.

3153.   Thompson, Daniel Calbert. *A Black Elite: A Profile of Graduates of UNCF Colleges.* Westport, Conn.: Greenwood Press, 1986.

Focusing on graduates of the forty–two United Negro College Fund member institutions and using questionnaires, interview data, and personal documents, as well as published information from a variety of secondary sources, Thompson presents a comprehensive profile. Beginning with an overview of the group as a whole and of the political, economic, and social changes that have affected them, Thompson addresses the general question of racial equality. There follows a systematic description and interpretation of the social and economic characteristics of black college graduates, including social origins and the educational, occupational, and income levels of their parents. Education is studied in terms of the racial composition of high schools attended, black students' honors and achievements, areas of study, advanced degrees, and the perceptions of the group concerning their education. An analysis of employment includes types of careers, work history, racial mix in the workplace, qualifications compared with those of white employees, rate and degree of advancement, and individual and family income. Tables, bibliography, and an index are included.

3154.   ————. *Sociology of the Black Experience.* Westport, Conn.: Greenwood Press, 1974.

Thompson analyzes the experience of blacks in American society, using such variables as time, age, sex, geographic location, level of achievement, and social class status. Special attention is given to those experiences directly related to the black subculture, such as life in the ghetto, poverty, and family life. Sociological interpretations pervade the text with a view to reflecting a black perspective.

3155.   Thurman, Howard. *The Luminous Darkness: A Personal Interpretation of the Anatomy of Segregation and the Ground of Hope.* New York: Harper and Row, 1965. Reprint. Richmond, Ind.: Friends United Press, 1989.

3156. Tryman, Mfanya Donald. *Afro-American Mass Political Integration: A Causal and Deductive Model*. Washington, D.C.: University Press of America, 1982.

3157. Tucker, James F. *Anatomy of High-Earning Minority Bank, 1972-1975*. Washington, D.C.: American Bankers Association, 1978.

3158. ————. *Buying Treasury Securities at Federal Reserve Bank*. 6th ed. Richmond, Va.: Federal Reserve Bank of Richmond, 1982.

3159. ————. *Current Economic Issues and Problems for the Consumer, Worker and Taxpayer*. Chicago: Rand McNally and Co., 1976.

3160. ————. *Essentials of Economics*. Englewood Cliffs, N.J.: Prentice-Hall, 1975.

3161. ————. *Personal Money Management: A Guide to the Family's Financial Affairs*. Washington, D.C.: Howard University Press, 1984.

Written for the average wage earner who wants to increase household income. Tucker, a vice president at the Federal Reserve Bank of Richmond, Virginia, explains the basics of money management, realistic budgeting, and simple investing for the person with little financial expertise. He outlines how these proven techniques can generate additional income no matter how modest the resources.

3162. Turner, John B., ed. *Neighborhood Organization for Community Action*. New York: National Association of Social Workers, 1968.

This book is the record of a conference on "Citizen Self-Help Organizations: Relevance and Problems" held in Cleveland, Ohio, in March of 1967. The conference was a report on various neighborhood action programs initiated by both private and government organizations to find ways of motivating people to self–help group action. The programs included regional workshops that served as information–gathering–and–compiling stations. The book includes discussions of areas investigated by the conferences, listings of the workshop staff and conference participants, and case records produced at the workshops.

3163.   Tweedle, John. *A Lasting Impression: A Collection of Photographs of Martin Luther King, Jr.* Columbia: University of South Carolina Press, 1983.

After Dr. Martin Luther King, Jr., went north to Chicago and focused the civil rights movement on that city, Tweedle became the unofficial photographer of Dr. King and the movement in Chicago. He captured an astonishing variety of King's moods as the civil rights leader moved along Chicago streets, through slums, into speakers' platforms, and into churches. This book presents Tweedle's work. The foreword is by the Reverend Jesse L. Jackson.

3164.   Upton, James Nathaniel. *A Social History of 20th Century Urban Riots.* Bristol, Ind.: Wyndham Hall Press, 1984.

3165.   Vincent, Charles. *Black Legislators in Louisiana During Reconstruction.* Baton Rouge: Louisiana State University Press, 1976.

3166.   Walker, Harry J. *The Negro in American Life.* New York: Oxford Book Co., 1954.

3167.   Wallace, Michele. *Black Macho and the Myth of the Superwoman.* New York: Dial Press, 1979.

Wallace treats the relationship of the black man to the black woman, with an emphasis on the role of the black woman in America. She examines the concept that the black woman has been and continues to be a matriarch in terms of its relevance to the belief that the dominating role of the black woman has caused the black man to lose his position as head of the household.

Social Science 583

Wallace uses several personal situations from her life, the Moynihan report, and aspects of slavery and the civil rights movement, as well as references to Afro-American literature and poets to support her work. In addition, she cites Richard Wright's Bigger Thomas in *Native Son* as the starting point of "the black writer's love affair with Black Macho."

3168. Wallace, Walter L. *The Logic of Science in Sociology.* Chicago: Aldine-Atherton Publishing Co., 1971.

This helpful guide explores five aspects of the scientific method commonly found in sociological observation, empirical generalization, theories, hypotheses, and decisions to accept or reject hypotheses. The author also looks into thirteen scientific methods and initiates a detailed discussion of theories and their structures, as well as of the explanatory and research strategies they imply.

3169. ————. *Principles of Scientific Sociology.* Hawthorne, N.Y.: Aldine Publishing Co., 1983.

This book emphasizes the relationship between pure and applied sociological analysis and specifies the indispensable contributions of each to the other. Relationships between the substantive concepts of the sociology of humans on the one hand, and the sociology of nonhumans on the other, are systematized.

3170. ————, ed. *Sociological Theory.* Hawthorne, N.Y.: Aldine Publishing Co., 1969.

3171. Walters, Ronald W. *Black Presidential Politics in America: A Strategic Approach.* Albany, N.Y.: State University of New York Press, 1988.

Walters outlines an aggressive political posture for blacks. He argues that aggressive political strategies cannot always be left up to black politicians because they have become institutionalized. Using political opportunities such as presidential elections effectively is what Walters believes to be one of the routes to political power for minority groups that find themselves in a socioeconomic status similar to that of blacks in this country.

3172. ————. *South Africa and the Bomb: Responsibility and Deterrence.* Lexington, Mass.: Lexington Books, 1987.

In these eight chapters, Walters gives details of South Africa's initial incentives to possess nuclear weapons and of the role of the United States in developing nuclear relations with Africa.

3173. Walton, Hanes, Jr. *Black Political Parties: An Historical and Political Analysis.* New York: Free Press, 1972.

3174. ————. *Black Politics: A Theoretical and Structural Analysis.* Philadelphia: J. B. Lippincott Co., 1972.

3175. ————. *Black Republicans: The Politics of the Black and Tans.* Metuchen, N.J.: Scarecrow Press, 1975.

3176. ————. *Black Women at the United Nations: The Politics, a Theoretical Model, and the Documents.* San Bernardino, Calif.: Borgo Press, 1989.

3177. ————. *Invisible Politics: Black Political Behavior.* Albany, N.Y.: State University of New York Press, 1985.

3178. ————. *The Negro in Third Party Politics.* Philadelphia: Dorrance and Co., 1969.

3179. ————. *The Political Philosophy of Martin Luther King, Jr.* Westport, Conn.: Greenwood Press, 1971.

This work is a revision of the author's thesis, Howard University, 1967. Includes an introduction by Samuel DuBois, as well as a bibliography.

3180. ————. *When the Marching Stopped: The Politics of Civil Regulatory Agencies.* Albany, N.Y.: State University of New York Press, 1988.

3181. Washington, Booker T. *The Future of the American Negro.* Boston: Small, Maynard and Co., 1899. Reprint. New York: Haskell House Publishers, 1968.

3182. Washington, Booker T., et al. *The Negro Problem: A Series of Articles by Representative Negroes of Today.* New York: James Potts and Co., 1903. Reprint. Miami, Fla.: Mnemosyne Publishers, 1969.

Contains the following essays: "Industrial Education for the Negro," by Booker T. Washington; "The Talented Tenth," by W. E. B. DuBois; "The Disfranchisement of the Negro," by Charles W. Chesnutt; "The Negro and the Law," by Wilford H. Smith; "The Characteristics of the Negro People," by H. T. Kealing; "Representative American Negroes," by Paul Laurence Dunbar; and "The Negro's Place in American Life at the Present Day," by T. Thomas Fortune.

3183. Watkins,** Kathleen Pullan, and Lucius Durant, Jr. *Day Care: A Source Book.* New York: Garland Publishing, Inc., 1987.

Divided into eight chapters, this work explores the topics and issues of greatest concern to parents and professionals in the child care community. Each chapter contains an essay followed by a comprehensive, annotated bibliography that cites books, articles, and dissertations published in English from 1980 to 1986, and classic works on specific topics. Includes an introduction and index.

3184. Watson, Bernard C. *Stupidity, Sloth, and Public Policy: Social Darwinism Rides Again.* Washington, D.C.: National Urban Coalition, 1973.

Some people clamor that what could be done to help the less fortunate has been done, so federal aid to them should either cease or be cut drastically. In this study Watson attempts to identify and analyze such arguments against social welfare. Three particular bases for these arguments are discussed: some races are inferior genetically; the poor are poor because of their own laziness; and educational institutions have not proven effective in changing individual circumstances. The theories of Darwin, Moynihan, Shockley, and Jensen, just to mention a few, provide the material for analysis.

3185.   Weaver, Robert Clifton. *The Negro Ghetto.* New York: Harcourt, Brace and Co., 1948. Reprint. New York: Russell and Russell, 1967.

This book takes a look at the economic factors that created residential segregation in the North.

3186.   ————. *The Urban Complex: Human Values in Urban Life.* New York: Anchor Books, 1966.

The administrator of the Housing and Home Finance Agency under the Johnson administration discusses at length the Urban Renewal Program and the types of activities it facilitates. An in-depth analysis of the federal and fiscal policies is recounted in the chapter on economic considerations. Weaver also probes the role and reactions of ethnic minorities. The text may be of special interest to educators and students of economics, political science, and sociology.

3187.   Wells, Elmer Eugene. *The Mythical Negative Black Self Concept.* San Francisco: R and E Research Associates, 1978.

The media, as well as some educators, have developed the belief that blacks have a low self–concept. This study treats that belief. The subjects for this study were twelve black high school dropouts between the ages of sixteen and eighteen, and they included nine males and three females. The black self–concepts were found to be somewhat positive, and the subjects became even more positive as more time was spent on the project.

3188. Wells–Barnett, Ida B. *On Lynching: Southern Horrors, A Red Record, Mob Rule in New Orleans.* New York: Arno Press, 1969. Reprint. Salem, N.H.: Ayer Co., 1987.

As editor of a Memphis black newspaper, the author denounced the lynching in 1892 of three black businessmen from her city and was forced to flee the city. Through lectures and pamphlets, she continued her crusade against lynching. This work consist of three of her pamphlets: *Southern Horrors* (1892), *A Red Record* (1895), and *Mob Rule in New Orleans* (1900). Includes a new preface by August Meier.**

3189. Wesley, Charles Harris. *Negro History in the United States, 1850–1925: A Study in American Economic History.* New York: Vanguard Press, 1927. Reprint. New York: Russell and Russell, 1967.

3190. Wharton, Clifton R., Jr. *The U.S. Graduate Training of Asian Agricultural Economics.* New York: Council on Economic Cultural Affairs, 1959.

This study of the problems encountered by Asians studying agricultural economics in the United States is based on some two hundred interviews with U.S. faculty and their Asian graduate students enrolled in training programs in agricultural economy at U.S. universities. Wharton records the problem areas and trouble spots he discovered in these interviews, and makes recommendations for dealing with these problems.

3191. ————, ed. *Subsistence Agriculture and Economic Development.* Chicago: Aldine Publishing Co., 1969.

These essays examine the subsistence farmer in agrarian cultures and peasant societies. The format of the book consists of introductory remarks by the editor and comments by experts and authorities, followed by case studies. The chapter on change and growth may be of special interest to students of economics.

3192. White, Walter Francis. *Rope & Faggot: A Biography of Judge Lynch*. New York: Alfred A. Knopf, 1929. Reprint. New York: Arno Press, 1969.

This book includes the following chapters: "The Mind of the Lyncher," "The Extent of the Industry," "Religion and Judge Lynch," "Sex and Lynching," "The Economic Foundations of Lynch–Law," "Science, Nordicism, Lynching," "The Changing Scene," "Lynching and Laws: Is There a Way Out?" It also includes an appendix, an index, and a new preface by Roy Wilkins.

3193. Wilkinson, Doris Yvonne. *Workbook for Introductory Sociology*. Minneapolis: Burgess Publication Co., 1968.

3194. ————, ed. *Black Male/White Female: Perspectives on Interracial Marriage and Courtship*. Cambridge, Mass.: Schenkman Publishing Co., 1975.

This book examines the various social forces at work in interracial marriages and courtships, and provides a general overview of the sociology of interracial liaisons. Contributions include sociological research, historical materials, psychological research, and legal articles and essays.

3195. ————, ed. *Social Structure and Assassination Behavior: The Sociology of Political Murder*. Cambridge, Mass.: Schenkman Publishing Co., 1976.

3196. Wilkinson, Doris Yvonne, and Ronald L. Taylor, eds. *The Black Male in America: Perspectives on His Status in Contemporary Society*. Chicago: Nelson–Hall Publishers, 1977.

This anthology includes essays by sociologists, psychologists, anthropologists, and psychiatrists on a variety of topics: the role and status of the Afro–American father; past and present myths about the psychological and biological nature of the Afro-American male; and the projected future of the Afro-American male in postindustrial society.

3197. Williams, John Alfred. *The King God Didn't Save: Reflections on the Life and Death of Martin Luther King, Jr.* New York: Coward-McCann, 1970.

3198. ————. *This Is My Country Too.* New York: New American Library, 1965.

This work is about a distinguished black novelist who travels across the nation trying to discover his own identity.

3199. Williams, John Alfred, and Charles F. Harris,* eds. *Amistad: Writings on Black History and Culture.* New York: Vintage Books, 1970. Reprint. New York: Random House, 1971.

3200. Williams, Juan. *Eyes on the Prize: America's Civil Rights Years, 1954-1965.* New York: Viking Penguin, 1987.

This book is the companion volume to the six-part PBS television series "Eyes on the Prize: America's Civil Rights Years." It recaptures the dramatic and poignant events in the years between the U.S. Supreme Court's 1954 ruling that segregated schools were unconstitutional and Congress's approval of the 1965 Voting Rights Act. It is a history of the civil rights movement as seen by the participants, black and white, then and now. Here are the stories of the Montgomery bus boycott, the freedom rides, the Selma to Montgomery march, and the individuals who found themselves at the center of the maelstrom. Includes illustrations, a selected bibliography, an index, and an introduction by Julian Bond.

3201. Williams, Loretta J. *Black Freemasonry and Middle-Class Realities.* Columbia: University of Missouri Press, 1980.

3202. Williams, Melvin D. *Community in a Black Pentecostal Church: An Anthropological Study.* Pittsburgh: University of Pittsburgh Press, 1974.

This work seeks to study the social relations and behavior of a Zionist religious group—in particular, the members of the Zion Holiness Church and of its larger affiliation to the international Church of Christ. Chapter 8 provides Williams's analysis of this group as a community as well as a church. Their apparent cohesiveness is due to a strong communal ideology; the congregation has direct and indirect influence on the lifestyle of its individual members in the context of both the church and the community. Williams has examined very carefully the native content and character of these groups on which he bases his conclusions.

3203. ———, ed. *Selected Readings in Afro–American Anthropology.* Lexington, Mass.: Xerox Publishing Co., 1975.

3204. Williams, Robert Franklin. *Negroes with Guns.* New York: Marzani and Munsell, 1962. Reprint. Chicago: Third World Press, 1973.

3205. Williams, Vernon J., Jr. *From a Caste to a Minority: Changing Attitudes of American Sociologists Toward Afro–Americans, 1896–1945.* Westport, Conn.: Greenwood Press, 1989.

This book examines the changing attitudes held toward blacks by the nation's leading sociologists. It explores how and why sociology transformed itself from a discipline that rationalized castelike arrangements in the United States to one that actively supported the full assimilation of Afro–Americans into the American mainstream.

3206. Williams, William James. *General Semantics and the Social Sciences: Reflections and New Directions.* New York: Philosophical Library, 1972.

Williams provides a theoretical framework for examining special problems in public administration, such as racial and social problems, which he discusses in an informative and stimulating manner. Advocating a "modern" scientific methodology for dealing with these problems, he calls for new leadership that will be more aware of social conflict.

3207. Willie, Charles Vert. *Black and White Families: What They Can Teach Each Other.* Bayside, N.Y.: General Hall, 1985.

Willie's book centers on family research and focuses on an comparative examination of minority and majority families which encompassed both race and social class. His students at Harvard University prepared descriptive reports on the similarities and differences between the families and related these findings to the literature in the field. The reports, coupled with the author's own research, became the basis for this book.

3208. ————. *Five Black Scholars.* Cambridge, Mass.: Abt Books, 1983.

Through reputational analysis, this text examines five black scholars in the social sciences and humanities in the United States. It goes on to determine how they achieved their eminence by focusing on the unfolding of their careers, identifying the decisive moments in their lives, and analyzing the structural supports that sustained their scholarly careers, such as their families and their educational background. It is in essence a study of social institutions and their interrelationship, as manifested in the lives of professional scholars.

3209. ————. *A New Look at Black Families.* 2d edition. Bayside, N.Y.: General Hall, 1981.

This second edition has been completely revised, with six new case studies and two new chapters added. These review theoretical issues in race relations and make a strong case for rejecting the Marxist and colonialist theories, using the situational sociologist perspective in analyzing race–related issues. Eighteen case studies provide a window through which readers see patterns of variations in the life–style of affluent or middle–class and poor black families. A comparative analysis of black and of white families is introduced.

The findings of this book appear to contradict the Moynihan thesis that a weak family structure among blacks *perpetuates the cycle of poverty.* Willie's analysis finds that more than 90 percent of affluent black and affluent white families are two–parent households. *The problem is that too few blacks are affluent.*

3210.   ———. *Oreo: A Perspective on Race and Marginal Men and Women.* Wakefield, Mass.: Parameter Press, 1975.

This ninety–five–page book (including references) deals in a refreshing, innovative way with the agony and the ecstasy of being a marginal man. Of particular interest is the chapter entitled "Marginality and Social Change."

3211.   ———. *Race, Ethnicity, and Socioeconomic Status: A Theoretical Analysis of Their Interrelationship.* Bayside, N.Y.: General Hall, 1983.

The goal of this book is to provide an adequate conceptual apparatus with which to explain and interpret behavior associated with race, ethnicity, and socioeconomic status. Adaptations associated with these factors are analyzed from the perspective of sociology as a science of humanity. Historical trends as well as contemporary situations are considered; social psychological, and geographical factors are researched as contextual variables in intergroup relations.
Based on the empirical findings resulting from examination of racial and ethnic group relations during a quarter of a century, Willie presents twelve theoretical propositions concerning self and society, social structure, social process, and the social context. These principles are designed to enhance our conceptual knowledge about social organization and intergroup relations.

3212.   ———, ed. *Black/Brown/White Relations: Race Relations in the 1970s.* New Brunswick, N.J.: Transaction Books, 1977.

3213.   ———, ed. *Caste and Class Controversy.* Bayside, N.Y.: General Hall, 1979.

This book is a response to William Julius Wilson's book, *The Declining Significance of Race*. Willie states that it is important to challenge Wilson's book because "it is part of a series of publications dating back to *Inequality* by Christopher Jencks and *The Negro Family: A Case for National Action* by Daniel Moynihan that cast doubt on the focus of the freedom movement among minorities." Willie's book includes commentaries from both black and white scholars: Hollie West, Dorothy Newman, Thomas F. Pettigrew, Bernard M. Kramer, Harry Edwards, Charles Payne, James Hefner, Robert Hill, and Richard Margolis. The book ends with the statement of the Association of Black Sociologists calling the Wilson book a "misrepresentation of the black experience."

3214.   ———, ed. *The Family Life of Black People*. Columbus, Ohio: Charles E. Merrill Co., 1970.

Questioning common myths about the black family, essays in this collection address such issues as family stability, the family as an economic unit, external social factors affecting the family, and other functional aspects of the family. The information contained in the book is of value in analyzing and understanding the black family in relation to social problems.

3215.   Willie, Charles Vert, and Susan L. Greenblatt,** eds. *Community Politics and Educational Change: Ten School Systems Under Court Order*. New York: Longman, 1981.

The editors seek to provide a clearer understanding of the social process of effective public policies. Desegregation is highlighted as an endorsement of social change, critical to the achievement of an equitable society. The publication is a particularly useful source for policymakers, as it analyzes the effects of policy and court decisions using ten case studies. Many of these are examined by various authors within the context of the dynamics of power, community resistance, business intervention, and ethnic experience.

3216.   Wilson, George D. *Progressive Units for Student Teaching in High School.* 4th ed. Minneapolis: Burgess, 1954.

3217.   Wilson, William Julius. *The Declining Significance of Race: Blacks and Changing American Institutions.* 2d ed. Chicago: University of Chicago Press, 1980.

In the first edition of this book, Wilson contends that, for the first time in our history, class has become more important than race in determining black access to privilege and power. In this new paperback edition, Wilson includes a major new essay in which he not only reflects on the debate surrounding his 1978 book but also presents a provocative discussion of race, class, and social policy. Includes bibliography and index.

3218.   ————. *Power, Racism, and Privilege: Race Relations in Theoretical and Sociohistorical Perspectives.* New York: Macmillan Co., 1973.

In this theoretical study, Wilson examines the social and historical factors contributing to race relations in the United States and the Republic of South Africa.

3219.   ————. *The Truly Disadvantaged: The Inner City, the Underclass, and Public Policy.* Chicago: University of Chicago Press, 1987.

Wilson challenges liberal and conservative orthodoxies in confronting the inner–city problems of poor urban blacks in the United States. Extending his exposition of the black underclass begun in *The Declining Significance of Race*, Wilson here candidly discusses the social pathologies of the ghetto and provides a comprehensive explanation of the rise of this "ghetto underclass"; he then offers a far–reaching social–democratic policy agenda that moves beyond race–specific issues to confront fundamental problems of industrial society. Inner–city decay cannot be explained by racism alone, Wilson argues, but instead is related to a complex web of factors involved in the urban economy, the most important of which is the changing class structure of ghetto neighborhoods. The movement of middle-class black professionals from the innercity, followed by the exodus of increasing numbers of working–class blacks, has left behind a concentration of the most disadvantaged segments of the black urban population. At the same time, urban minorities have been particularly vulnerable to broader changes in the economy that have caused major reductions in the workforce, which in turn has exacerbated other social problems.

In critically examining publicpolicy approaches to the ghetto underclass, Wilson argues that civil rights organizations should broaden their agendas by recognizing that poor minorities are affected by problems that go beyond racial considerations.

3220. Wintersmith, Robert F. *The Police and the Black Community*. Lexington, Mass.: Lexington Books, 1974.

A study of the relationship between the police and blacks, this book contains "a brief history of police–black community relations; a discussion of the social psychology of the police occupation; and a brief discussion of the nature of diverse black attitudes towards police practices." It also includes tabular data, which basically treat the frequency of various situations as they relate to blacks, whites, and policemen. For example, one table is entitled the "Frequency with Which Black Citizens Are Believed to be Harassed and Intimidated by the Police Without Reason."

3221. Woodard, Maurice Compton. *Directory of Black Americans in Political Science*. 2d ed. Washington, D.C.: American Political Science Assoc., 1988.

This directory contains the names, addresses, telephone numbers, degrees, and fields of specialty of over four hundred black American political scientists. Also included are an index by fields of academic specialization and research interest, and the names and addresses of predominantly black colleges and universities, including the name and telephone number of department chairpersons.

3222.   ———, ed. *Blacks and Political Science.* Washington, D.C.: American Political Science Assoc., 1977.

    Commissioned by the APSA Committee on the Status of Blacks in the Profession, this 133–page monograph includes "Report of the Conference on Political Science Curriculum at Predominately Black Institutions," "The Comparative Status of Black and White Political Scientists," and "Political Science in Black Colleges: 1969 and 1976."

3223.   Wright, Bruce. *Black Robes, White Justice.* Secaucus, N.J.: Lyle Stuart Inc., 1987.

    Wright tells of the influence of his early years, of the kinds of confusions that harassed his childhood—the adverse effect of racism. Having spent more than sixteen years as a judge in the City of New York, Wright, nicknamed "Turn 'em loose Bruce" when he released an accused police slasher on his own recognizance, states: "It is the pageant of the poor that concerns me, and the simultaneous but different ordeals of the judged and their judges, as each continues to confront the other." Wright reveals the inequities of our judicial system. He examines their origins and proposes remedies that must be taken if the courts are to be a place of hope for all Americans.

3224.   Wright, Charles H. *Robeson: Labor's Forgotten Champion.* Detroit: Balamp Publishing, 1977.

3225.   Wright, Nathan, Jr. *Black Power and Urban Unrest: Creative Possibilities.* New York: Hawthorn Books, 1967.

    Wright holds that despite its frightening aspects, "the power issue and the creative possibilities inherent in the concept of Black Power may provide a key to new approaches to a number of increasingly critical problems related to the nation's urban life." The book attempts to examine these "creative possibilities." Chapters include "Power and Conscience," "A National Necessity," "The Creative Use of Black Power," "Race Economics," "Self–Development and Self–Respect," "The Public

Education Battleground," "Race-Related Problems," "Black Leadership and American Goals," "A Religious Opportunity," "The Difficulties of Self-Awareness," and "Is Brotherhood Enough?" The appendix contains a statement issued by the National Committee of Negro Churchmen, July 1966, on black power. Includes an index.

3226. ———. *Ready to Riot.* 1st ed. New York: Holt, Rinehart and Winston, 1968.

An in-depth look at the social dynamics of riots in the 1960s. Using available statistical data, Nathan Wright, Jr., presents a personal interpretation of these dynamics to clarify the behavior of blacks under riot conditions and to determine exactly what social phenomena incite them to riot. Wright's own experience is with Newark, New Jersey, but he refers to other metropolitan areas as well.

3227. ———, ed. *What Black Politicians Are Saying.* New York: Hawthorn Books, 1972.

This anthology presents various perspectives on the black political experience. The underlying suggestion throughout the text is that blacks will become an integral part of American political life to the extent that they are allowed to assume influential roles in public affairs.

3228. Wright, Richard. *White Man, Listen!* 1st ed. Garden City, N.Y.: Doubleday and Co., 1957. Reprint. Westport, Conn.: Greenwood Press, 1978.

3229. X, Malcolm. *Malcolm X Speaks.* Edited with prefatory notes by George Breitman.** New York: Merit Publishers, 1965.

This work is a selection of speeches made during the last year of his life after he withdrew from the Black Muslin movement. Includes index.

3230. Yette, Samuel F. *The Choice: The Issue of Black Survival in America.* New York: G. P. Putnam's Sons, 1971. Reprint. Silver Spring, Md.: Cottage Books, 1982.

Yette's book discusses America of the late 1960s and early 1970s, and reviews the Johnson and Nixon administrative programs for blacks and poor people. Provocative issues such as birth control as a subtle form of black genocide, Nixon's and Moynihan's "benign neglect" of blacks, and the comparison of the war on poverty with the Vietnam conflict are elucidated. The well-documented facts of this book suggest a crisis in the survival of blacks in America.

3231. Young, Carlene, ed. *Black Experience: Analysis and Synthesis.* San Rafael, Calif.: Leswing Press, 1972.

The black experience is explored in these ways from many different points of view by those who have lived and are still living it, and by those who have studied and reflected on it. Among some of the different aspects presented are "Original Narratives," "Historical Genesis," and "African Heritage," and the sociological, psychological, economic, and political dimensions of black community life.

3232. Young, Henry James, ed. *The Black Church and the Harold Washington Story: The Man, the Message, the Movement.* Bristol, Ind.: Wyndham Hall Press, 1988.

3233. Young, Whitney M., Jr. *To Be Equal.* New York: McGraw-Hill, 1964.

Young, who became executive director of the National Urban League on October 1, 1961, treats the need for blacks to have equality. He cites four points that the reader should be aware of if the book is to be of value: the conditions and problems of blacks are real, the problems are no longer regional, civil rights is dedicated, and blacks will no longer be ignored. Topics he treats include education, housing, and employment.

3234. Zigler,* Edward F., and Edmund Wyatt Gordon, eds. *Day Care: Scientific and Social Policy Issues.* Boston: Auburn House Publishing Co., 1982.

NOTES

1. The Library of Congress classification system was used in determining which books should be included in this field.

2. *Black Authors and Education: An Annotated Bibliography of Books* (Washington, D.C.: University Press of America, 1980); "Black Authors: An Annotated Bibliography of Autobiographies and Biographies," *Black Books Bulletin* 6 (1980): 90–96; "Black Authors in Philosophy, Psychology, and Religion: An Annotated Bibliography of Selected Books," *The Journal of Religious Thought* 36 (Spring–Summer 1979): 61–65; "Language, Literature, and Communication: An Annotated Bibliography of Books by Black Authors," *Journal of Black Studies* 15 (December 1984): 155–176.

3. Verification of an author's ethnic identity included appearance of author's photograph in publication(s); my personal knowledge of the author; indication of ethnicity in the card catalog of the Moorland–Spingarn Research Center, Howard University; author's identification in a biographical directory on blacks; or the knowledge of two or more individuals.

4. The Library of Congress classification system includes a range of topics within each main class. Thus some works are in a chapter where you would least expect to find them—cookbooks in science and technology and sports in fine arts.

SELECTED BIBLIOGRAPHY

Baker, Augusta. *The Black Experience in Children's Books*. New York: New York Public Library, 1971.

————, ed. *The Young Years: Anthology of Children's Literature*. New York: Parents Magazine Press, 1950.

Brignano,** Russell Carl. *Black Americans in Autobiography: An Annotated Bibliography of Autobiographies and Autobiographical Books Written Since the Civil War*. Rev. and expanded ed. Durham, N.C.: Duke University Press, 1984.

Corrigan,** Robert A. "Afro-American Fiction: A Checklist, 1853–1970." *Mid-Continent American Studies Journal* 11 (Fall 1970): 114–135

Davis, Arthur Paul. *From the Dark Tower: Afro-American Writers from 1900 to 1960*. Washington, D.C.: Howard University Press, 1974.

Fischer,* Russell G. "James Baldwin: A Bibliography, 1947–1962." *Bulletin of Bibliography* 24 (January–April 1965): 127–130.

Matney, William C., ed. *Who's Who Among Black Americans*. 1st ed. 1975–1976 Vol 1. Northbrook, Ill.: Who's Who Among Black Americans, Inc., Publishing Co., 1976.

Page, James Allen, and Jae Min Roh,** comps. *Selected Black American, African, and Caribbean Authors: A Bio-Bibliography.* rev. and expanded. Littleton, Colo.: Libraries Unlimited, Inc., 1985.

Porter, Dorothy Burnett, comp. *A Working Bibliography on the Negro in the United States.* Ann Arbor, Mich.: Xerox, University Microfilms, 1969.

Robinson, Wilhelmena S. *International Library of Negro Life and History: Historical Negro Biographies.* New York: Publishers Co., Inc., 1967.

Rollock, Barbara. *Black Authors and Illustrators of Children's Books: A Biographical Dictionary.* New York: Garland Publishing, Inc., 1988.

Rudman, Masha Kabakow. *Children's Literature: An Issues Approach.* 2d ed. New York: Longman, 1984.

Rush, Theressa Gunnels, et al. *Black American Writers Past and Present.* Metuchen, New Jersey: Scarecrow Press, Inc., 1975.

Shockley, Ann Allen, and Sue P. Chandler. *Living Black American Authors: A Biographical Directory.* New York: R. R. Bowker Co., 1973.

Trent, Toni. "Stratification Among Blacks by Black Authors." *Negro History Bulletin* 34 (December 1971): 179–181.

Turner, Darwin T. *Afro-American Writers.* New York: Appleton-Century-Crofts, 1970.

AUTHOR INDEX

Note: Includes illustrators and translators where indicated.

Aaron, Henry 187
Abdul, Raoul 187, 277, 425
Abdul-Jabbar, Kareem 3
Abdullah, Omanii 60
Abernathy, Ralph David 4
Abrahams, Peter 355
Abramowitz, Elizabeth A. 71, 507
Abramowitz,* Jack 355
Achebe, Chinua 278
Adair, Alvis V. 72
Adams, Effie Kaye 72
Adams, Elizabeth Laura 467
Adams, Russell L. 278
Adams, William 355–356
Addo, Linda D. 55, 467
Addo, Peter Eric Adotey 356
Akbar, Na'im 467
Akpan, Moses E. 205
Alexander, Alpha Vernell 193
Alexander,* David M. 73
Alexander,* Howard Wright 507
Alexander,* J. T. 473

Alexander, James I. 507
Alexander, Rae Pace 278
Alexander,* W. W. 550
Alexis, Marcus 491
Ali, Muhammad 4
Allen,** Anne 448
Allen, Elizabeth L. 241
Allen, Pamela P. 508
Allen, Robert L. 205, 508
Allen, Samuel 278
Allen, Walter R. 55, 530, 575
Amaker, Norman C. 508
Amos, W. J. 356
Andersen,** Charles J. 73
Anderson,** Archibald W. 94
Anderson, James Douglas 73, 109
Anderson,* Peggy Perry (illus.) 333
Anderson,* Winston A. 504
Andrews, Malachi 357, 491
Angelou, Maya 4–5, 357
Ansa, Tina McElroy 357

Anselment,** Carol 399
Anthony, Earl 73, 554
Appleberry,** Mary Hilton 185
Archer, Leonard Courtney 187
Archer,* Peter (illus.) 299
Arkhurst, Joyce 278
Armstrong, Louis 5
Armstrong,* Margaret (illus.) 389, 391
Arnez, Nancy Levi 74, 358, 433
Arrington,* Bennie (illus.) 391
Asante, Molefi Kete 358–359, 378. *See also* Smith, Arthur Lee, Jr.
Asbury, Charles Alexander 91
Ashe, Arthur R., Jr. 6, 187, 279
Ashely, Liza 491
Aubert, Alvin 360
Austin,* Lettie J. 205
Avedon,* Richard 508
Avery, Burniece 205
Awkward, Michael 360

Bacote, Clarence A. 74
Bailey,** Judith 96
Bailey, Minnie Thomas 206
Bailey, Pearl 6, 55, 360, 491
Bailey–Jones,* Suzanne (illus.) 303
Bair,* Barbara 29
Baker, Augusta 55, 279
Baker,* David N. 188
Baker, Gwendolyn C. 98
Baker, Houston A., Jr. 360–361
Baker, William H. 467
Bala,* Virginia (illus.) 333

Baldwin, James 279, 361–362, 508–509, 561
Ballard, Allen B. 75, 206
Bambara, Toni Cade 279–280, 509
Banks, Cherry A. McGee 77, 280
Banks, James A. 75–78, 134, 280
Banner, William Augustus 467–468
Baptiste, H. Prentice, Jr. 78
Baraka, Amina 363
Baraka, Imamu Amiri 6, 188, 206, 363. *See also* Jones, LeRoi
Barbour, Floyd B. 206, 509
Barclay,* William 509
Barker, Lucius Jefferson 510
Barker, Twiley W., Jr. 510
Barkley,* James (illus.) 325
Barksdale, Richard 363
Barnes, Annie Shaw 511
Barnes,* Cornell (illus.) 324
Barnes,* Marian E. 536
Barnett, Moneta (illus.) 295, 305, 306, 307, 336, 347
Barrett, Joyce Durham 280
Barrett, Lindsay 364
Barrow, Joe Louis, Jr. 188
Bartholomew* (illus.) 329–330, 333
Bartlett,* Joy Ellis 106
Bartley, Lua Stewart 188
Bashful, Emmett W. 511
Bashir, Iman Abdul Alim 468
Basie, William (Count) 6

Bass de Martinez, Bernice 158
Bates, Daisy 6
Bates,** Frederick L. 512
Battle, Stanley F. 550
Battle, Thomas C. 67
Baugh, Delores M. 281
Baxter, Milton 438
Baylor, Don 189
Bayton, James Arthur 512
Beady, Charles H., Jr. 85
Bearden, Romare H. 278, 281
Beck, James D. 512
Beck, Robert 364
Beck, Sherman (illus.) 380
Becket, Sidney 7
Beckham, Barry 78–79, 364
Behm,** Ronald 484
Beker,* Jerome 179
Bell, Derrick Albert, Jr. 79,
512–513
Bell,* Willis E. 344
Bellegarde, Ida Rowland 7,
365–366, 513
Bellman,* Beryl Larry 513
Bellman,** Richard Earnest 56
Belt,* Lida M. 188
Bennett, Lerone, Jr. 207, 281–
283, 513
Bennett,* Rainey (illus.) 379
Benson,** Kathleen 28, 29, 194,
235, 316
Benston,** Kimberley W. 411
Bentley,** Robert H. 383
Berger,* David G. 195
Berger,* Maxine 197
Berke,* Joseph 492
Berkley, George 492
Bernstein, Daniel O. 513
Berrian, Albert 386
Berry, Chuck 7

Berry, Faith 366
Berry, Leonidas H. 207
Berry, Mary Frances 207, 514
Berryman, Matilene S. 492
Bertrand, Yolande 366
Betsey, Charles L. 562
Bibens,** Robert F. 124
Bible, Charles 283
Biller,** Edward L. 166
Billingsley, Andrew 514–515
Binch,* Caroline (illus.) 309
Black, Luther H. 79, 366
Blackwell, David Harold 56,
492, 515
Blackwell, James Edward 79–80,
515–516
Blaine, Laurence 366
Blake, Cecil A. 359
Blake, Clarence Napoleon 207
Blake,* Herman 564
Blakely, Allison 208
Blassingame, John W. 56, 207,
208–209
Blockson, Charles 8, 209
Bloom,** Benjamin S. 80
Blubaugh,** Jon A. 438
Blumstein,** James F. 560
Boddy,* Joe (illus.) 328, 331
Bogle, Donald 189–190
Bogus, S. Diane 366–367
Boles, Robert 367
Bond, Horace Mann 80–81, 241
Bond, Jean Carey 283
Bond, Julian 212, 516
Bondurant,* Bill 139
Bonner, Mary Winstead 81–82
Bontemps, Arna Wendell 8, 82,
210, 283–285, 367–368, 414,
516–517
Boone, Mark Allen 368

Border-Patterson, Anne 140
Boulware, Marcus Hanna 368, 492
Bowles,** Frank 82
Bowling, Chip 496
Boyar,** Burt 191
Boyar,** Jane 191
Boyd, Candy Dawson 285
Boyd, Sue Abbott 369
Boyd, William M. 82
Boyer,** Ernest L. 159
Boyer, James B. 83, 517
Boyer, Joe L. 83
Bradley, David 369
Bramble, Peter W. D. 468
Bramwell, Jonathan Burton 517
Branch,* Kip 187
Brawley, Benjamin Griffith 8, 83, 210, 369-370
Brawley, James Phillip 84, 468
Bray,* Barbara (trans.) 444
Brazziel, William F. 84
Breathett, George 468
Brehan, Delle 370
Breinburg, Petronella 285-286
Breneman,* William D. 517
Bricktop, 8
Bright, Jean M. 453
Britts, Maurice W. 85
Broadnax, Walter D. 570
Brody, Erness Bright 468
Brody,** Nathan 468
Brooke, Amos 370
Brookins, Geraldine Kearse 575
Brookover,** Wilbur P. 85
Brooks, Charlotte Kendrick 85, 371
Brooks, George Washington 86
Brooks, Glenwood C., Jr. 157

Brooks, Gwendolyn 9, 286-287, 371-373
Brooks,* Kevin (illus.) 291
Brooks, Lyman Beecher 86
Broudy,* Eric 210
Brown,* Bertram S. 506
Brown, Carolyn T. 469
Brown, Charles Allen 86
Brown, Claude 9, 517
Brown,* David Scott (illus.) 334, 340
Brown, Donna B. 86
Brown, Frank 165
Brown, Frank London 373
Brown, H. Rap 518
Brown, Hubert L. 469
Brown, Hugh Victor 86-87
Brown, James, Jr. (illus.) 303
Brown, Kay 287-288, 302
Brown, Lee P. 533
Brown, Lillian B. 213
Brown, Lloyd Wellesley 373
Brown, Martha H. 261
Brown, Melanie 493
Brown, Oliver 518
Brown,* Ray 127
Brown, Roscoe Conkling, Jr. 210, 255, 493
Brown,* Sandford 319
Brown, Sterling Allen 374
Brown, Thomas J. 87
Brown, Virginia Suggs 288, 289
Brown, William Wells 374
Browne, Robert S. 211
Browne, Rose Butler 9
Brown-Guillory, Elizabeth 375
Browning,* Colleen (illus.) 328
Brucklacher,** Linda L. 161
Brumfiel,** Charles Francis 493

Bryan, Ashley (illus.) 289, 300, 390
Bryant, Henry A., Jr. 211
Bryant, Nathaniel H. 518
Bryant, Spurgeon Quinton 87, 518
Bryce, Herrington J. 494, 519
Bryce-Laporte, Roy Simon 518
Buckler,** John 250
Buckley, Gail Lumet 9
Bullock, Clifton 375
Bullock, Henry Allen 88, 97
Burford,* Kay (illus.) 323
Burger,* Mary W. 245
Burgest, David R. 519
Burke, Carolyn M. 375, 494
Burke,** Virginia M. 461
Burns, LaMont 494
Burns,* Robert (illus.) 299
Burr, Dane (illus.) 277
Burrell, Leon F. 88, 89, 293
Burrell, Natelkka E. 9, 89
Burroughs, Margaret Taylor G. 290
Burton, Nathaniel 494
Burton,* Virginia Lee (illus.) 285
Bush,* Terri 324
Butcher, Margaret Just 375
Butcher, Philip 376-377
Butler, Addie Louise Joyner 89
Butler, Frieda R. 56
Butler, Johnella E. 519
Butts, Hugh F. 406
Byard, Carole (illus.) 304, 305, 327, 334, 341, 349, 353

Cain, George 377
Caines, Jeannette Franklin 290-291

Calbert,* Roosevelt 183
Caldwell, Dista H. 89
Caliver, Ambrose 56, 89-91
Callender, Red 10
Callis, Myra Colson 536
Callum, Agnes Kane 10
Cameron, Howard K. 91
Cameron, Randolph W. 494
Cameron, Winifred F. 91
Campanella, Roy 10
Campbell, Barbara 291
Campbell, Bebe Moore 211, 520
Campbell,* E. Simms (illus.) 285
Campbell, Thomas Monroe 92
Cannon,** J. B. 572
Carew, Jan Rynveld 211, 291-292
Carew, Rod 190
Carlton,* Bennett (illus.) 198
Carmichael, Stokely 520
Carn, John Benjamin 377
Carriger, Sally A. 469
Carroll, Diahann 10
Carruthers, Jacob H. 211, 243
Carson, Clayborne 521
Carter, Deborah J. 73, 529
Carter, Lamore J. 93
Carter, Mary Kennedy 292
Carter, Vertie L. 92, 494
Cartey, Wilfred G. 292, 377
Cartier, Xam W. 377
Carty, Leo (illus.) 328, 337
Cary, Willie Mae 92
Casilla,* Robert (illus.) 318
Casmier, Adam A. 377
Cassata,** Mary B. 378
Castaneda,** Alfredo 92
Cat,* Christopher 378-379
Cayton, Horace R. 218

Cazac,** Yavan (illus.) 279
Cazort, Jean E. 11
Chalk, Ocania 187
Chamberlain, Wilt 11
Chambers, Lucille Arcola 212
Chandler, Sue P. 45
Chapman, Audrey B. 521
Chapman, Dorothy Hilton 56
Chapman,** Richard L. 512
Charles, Bernard 139
Charles, Ray 11
Chase-Riboud, Barbara 292, 379
Chatfield,* Hale 389
Cheek, Donald K. 469
Cheek, James Edward 93
Cheers, Arlynne Lake 93
Chesley, Donald 379
Chestnutt, Charles Waddell 292
Childress, Alice 292–293, 379
Childs,* Faith Hampton 548
Ching* (illus.) 331
Chisholm, Shirley 12
Chitty,* Arthur Ben 536
Chitty,* Elizabeth N. 536
Chrisman, Robert 212
Christian, Barbara 380
Christian, Mary 101
Chunn, Eva Wells 161
Chunn, Jay, II 494
Church, Annette Elaine 12
Church, Roberta 12
Church, Vivian 380
Clapp, Ouida H. 293
Clark, Al C. *See* Goines, Donald
Clark, Barbara Randall 56
Clark, Felton Grandison 93
Clark, Kenneth Bancroft 94, 158,
    212, 469, 521, 565
Clark, Reginald M. 94

Clark, Septima Poinsette 12
Clarke, John Henrik 213, 380,
    522
Clarke, Nina L. 213
Clarke, Robert Lewis 214
Clay, Stanley Bennett 380
Cleaver, Eldridge 214
Cleaves, Mary W. 61
Clegg,** Ambrose A., Jr. 77
Clements,** Zacharie J. 88, 293
Cleveland, Edward Earl 214, 470
Clifford, Paul Rountree 470
Clift, Virgil A. 65, 94
Clifton, Fred J. 95
Clifton, Lucille 293, 380–381
Clouse,* James P. 561
Coan, Josephus Roosevelt 13
Coates, W. Paul 67
Cobb, Martha Kendrick 381
Cobb, William Montague 495
Cobbs,* Henry E. 542
Cobbs, Price M. 475
Cogdell, Roy Thomas 381, 522
Coger, Rick 95, 125
Cohen,* Elaine 10
Cohen,** Joel 187
Coleman, Floyd W. 200
Coleridge-Taylor, Samuel 190
Collier, Eugenia W. 425, 446
Collins, Marva 95
Collins,* Pat (illus.) 291
Colson, Edna Meade 95
Colter, Cyrus 382
Comer, James Pierpoint 13, 96,
    522
Cone, James H. 471
Coney, John C. 522
Conley, Houston 73, 96, 496
Conn, Peter 355–356

Connelly,* Gwen (illus.) 331
Connolly,* Pat 542
Conrad,* Earl 191
Conroy,* Jack 285, 516
Conway,* John 513
Conyers, James E. 523, 561
Cook, Mercer 382, 414
Cook,* Scott (illus.) 329
Coombs, Orde 194, 214, 382, 523
Cooper,* Floyd (illus.) 305, 317
Cooper, T. G. 190
Cordasco,** Francesco 97
Cornelius, James 190
Cornish, Sam 296
Cortez, Jayne 383
Cosby, Bill 383, 523
Costello, Bagz 383
Cox,* Betty B. 578
Cox, George O. 97
Cozart, Leland Stanford 97
Crain,** Robert L. 121
Cratty,* Bryant J. 493
Crawford, George Williamson 98
Crawford, Samuel D. 383
Crew, Donald 296–297
Crews,* Terry (illus.) 469
Crichlow, Ernest (illus.) 307, 344
Crockett, Harry J. 214
Crogman, William Henry 215, 244
Cromwell, Adelaide M. 13, 215
Cromwell,* Otelia 283
Cross, Dolores E. 98
Crowe, Larry (illus.) 342
Cruse, Harold 215, 524
Cruz,* Ray (illus.) 323
Cullen, Countee 378–379, 384

Culp, Daniel Wallace 98
Cummings, Pat Marie (illus.) 191, 280, 291, 297, 305, 350
Cummings, Robert J. 211
Curry, George 191
Curry, Gladys J. 384
Curtis, James L. 496
Cyphert,* Frederick Ralph 99

Dabney, Lillian Gertrude 99
Daise, Ronald 216
Dance,* Stanley 192
Dandridge, Dorothy 191
Daniel, Sadie Iola 13
Daniel, Walter C. 56
Daniel, Walter Green 99
Daniel, William Andrew 471
Daniels, Douglas Henry 216
Dansby, B. Baldwin 99
Darden, Joseph Turner 56, 216, 524
Davey,** Beth 166
David, Wilfred L. 525
Davidson, Chandler 525
Davidson, Edmonia White 100
Davis, Abraham Lincoln 525
Davis, Allison 13, 80, 100, 217, 471, 472, 525–556
Davis, Angela Yvonne 14, 526–527
Davis, Arthur, Jr. 101
Davis, Arthur Paul 14, 374, 385
Davis, Charles Twitchell 385
Davis, Frank Green 527
Davis, George 386, 496, 527
Davis, Howard 191, 497
Davis, John Preston 217
Davis,* Lambert (illus.) 310
Davis, Lenwood G. 57–59, 217

Davis,* Lillie S. 143
Davis, Marianna White 14, 217, 386
Davis, Miles 14
Davis, Nathaniel 59
Davis, Nolan 386
Davis, Ossie 297
Davis, Sammy, Jr. 191
Davis, Thulani 387
Dawkins, Marvin Phillip 527
Dawson, Martha Easton 101
Day, Mary W. 527
DeCarava, Roy 389
DeCosta, Frank 82
DeCosta-Willis, Miriam 387
DeCoy, Robert H. 387
Dee, Ruby 297, 387
Deeter,** Catherine (illus.) 348
DeKnight, Freda 497
Delaney, William H. 101
Delany, Martin Robison 218
Delany, Samuel R. 387
Delessert,* Etienne 415
Delk, Fannie Mitchell 387
Della-Dora,** Delmo 101
Dennis, Rutledge M. 527
Derbigny, Irving Antony 102
Derry,* Art (illus.) 286
Devall, William Sigure, Jr. 191
DeVeaux, Alexis 298
De Velasco,* Joe E. (illus.) 290
Devore, Wynetta 528
Dewart, Janet 218
Dexter,* Charles 200
Dickens, Floyd, Jr. 497
Dickens, Jacqueline B. 497
Dickerson, Dolores Pawley 166
DiGrazia,* Thomas (illus.) 294, 295, 347

Dill, Augustus G. 103, 528
Dillard, Joey Lee 387
Dillard, John Milton 388, 472, 497
Dillon,** Diane (illus.) 292, 305, 312, 327, 349
Dillon, Leo (illus.) 292, 305, 312, 327, 349
Dilworth, Mary Elizabeth 102
Dinsdale,* Mary (illus.) 286
Diop, Birago 298
Dobler,* Lavinia 268
Dodson, Owen 298
Dollard,** John 217
Dorsey, James W. 218
D'Orso,* Michael 42
Douglas,* Aaron (illus.) 322
Douglas, Stephanie (illus.) 295
Douglass, Frederick 14
Dove, Rita 388
Drake, John Gibbs St. Clair 218, 472
Dressler,** David 528
Drisko,* Carol 268
DuBois, Shirley Lola Graham 16, 219, 299
DuBois, W. E. B. 16, 103, 219–220, 388–389, 528
Dufty,* William F. 195
Duke, Romare 389. *See also* Riley, Cole
Dumas, Glenda 389
Dumas, Henry 389
Dunbar, Paul Laurence 299, 389–391
Dunbar-Nelson, Alice Moore 16
Duncan, Lionel Sebastian 103
Dunham, Katherine 16, 191, 221, 391

Dunham, Melerson Guy 498
Dunn,* Jessica M. 56
Dunnigan, Alice Allison 17, 221
Dunnington,* Tom (illus.) 330–331, 333
Dunston, Patricia 494
Durant, Lucius, Jr. 585
Durham, John Stephens 221
Durham, Richard 4
Durr,* William Kirtley 391
Duster, Alfreda M. 528
Duster, Troy S. 528
DuVall,* Taiwo (illus.) 342
Dykes,* Eva B. 383
Dyson, Walter 222

Earley, Charity Adams 222
Earnhardt,* Kay S. 391
Edelman, Marian Wright 529
Edmonds, Paul 498
Edmonds, Ronald R. 179
Edwards, Audrey 299
Edwards, Harry 103
Edwards, Junius 392
Edwards, Norma S. 103
Edwards, Thomas Bentley 104–105
Edwards, Vetress Bon 222
Egypt, Ophelia Settle 299
El-Amin, Mustafa 472, 529
El-Khawas,** Elaine 529
Elam, Julia C. 105
Elder, Lonne, III 392
Ellington, Duke (Edward Kennedy) 192
Ellington, Mercer 192
Elliott,** Peggy G. 106
Ellis, Dock 23
Ellis, Mary Jackson 106
Ellison, Ralph 392

Ells,** Kenneth W. 472
Embleton,* Gerry A. (illus.) 287, 288
Embree, Edwin R. 550
Emecheta, Buchi 17, 299–300, 393, 530
English, Richard Allyn 55
English,* James W. 9
Engs, Robert Francis 222
Epps, Edgar G. 106, 118, 222
Esedebe, P. Olisanwuche 530
Esko,* Pearl K. 106
Espinosa,** Paul 397
Ets,* Marie Hall 450
Eugene, Georgia 96
Evans,** Frank B. 530
Evans, Mari 300, 393–394
Evans, Zelia Stephens 107, 473
Everett, Faye Philip 107, 530
Evers, Charles James 17
Evers, Myrlie 17

Faggett, Harry Lee 223, 394
Fairbairn, Ann 395
Falkner,** David 49
Fanon, Frantz 473, 530
Farbstein,* Marvin 161
Farley,** Reynolds 530
Farmar,** William 523
Farmer, George L. 531
Farmer, James 223, 531
Farmer, Marjorie 107, 395
Farnsworth,* Robert M. 441
Farris, Christine King 18
Farrow, W. M. (illus.) 430
Favors, Aaron 111
Favors, Kathryne 223
Favors,* John S. 223
Fax, Elton C. 192, 223, 300
Feelings, Muriel 301

Feelings, Tom (illus.) 301, 307, 325, 326, 348
Felder, Cain H. 473
Fenderson, Lewis H. 205
Ferguson, Amos 302
Ferguson, Ira Lunan 18, 395
Ferguson, Samuel Allan 531
Ficker,* Robin 548
Fields, Alonzo 223
Fields, Barbara Jeanne 223
Fields, Julia 302
Fields, Karen 18
Fields, Mamie Garvin 18
Finney, Nikky 395
Firestone,* Rose 10
Fishel, Leslie H., Jr. 223
Fisher,* Margaret Barrow 107
Fisher, Miles Mark, Sr. 192
Fisher,* Richard I. 107
Fisher, Rudolph 395
Fitzgerald,* Ed 21
Fleming,* Daniel 224
Fleming, Jacqueline 107
Fleming, John E. 108
Fleming, Mickey C. 395
Fleming, Robert. *See* Duke, Romare; Riley, Cole
Flemns,* Delois M. 395
Fletcher, Tom 192
Flipper, Henry Ossian 18
Flournoy, Valerie R. 302
Foner,** Philip Sheldon 15
Ford, George, Jr. (illus.) 302, 306, 327, 352
Ford, Nick Aaron 224, 394
Forman, James 224
Fortune, Timothy Thomas 531
Foster,* Craig C. 257
Foster, Frances Smith 395

Foster, Marcus A. 109
Fowler, Carolyn 18
Fowler,* David H. 224
Franklin,* Harold (illus.) 320, 351
Franklin, J. E. 395
Franklin, Jimmie Lewis 224, 531
Franklin, John Hope 19, 224–225, 532
Franklin, Vincent P. 109, 226
Fraser,** Al 193
Frazier, Edward Franklin 473, 532
Frazier, Walt 19
Freedle,* Roy O. 404
Freese,* Mathias 210
Froe, Otis D. 110
Froe,* Otyce B. 110
Fry,* Ron 8
Frye,** Jerry K. 359
Fufuka, Karama 302
Fufuka,* Mahiri (illus.) 302
Fuller, Charles 396
Fuller, Chet 226
Fuller, Thomas Oscar 226, 474, 532

Gaines, Earnst J. 20, 396
Gallot, Mildred B. G. 110
Galloway, Phyllis Hyacinth 396
Gandy, Oscar H., Jr. 59, 397
Garabedian,* John H. 474
Gardner,** Burleigh B. 526
Gardner,** Mary R. 526
Gardner, William E. 111
Garibaldi, Antoine M. 111
Garland,* Michael (illus.) 296
Garnet, Henry Highland 269
Garvey, Amy Jacques 522

Gary, Lawrence E. 111, 226, 533
Gates, Henry Lewis, Jr. 385, 397
Gatewood,** Willard B., Jr. 29
Gavins, Raymond 533
Gayle, Addison, Jr. 20, 192, 227, 398
Gayles, Anne Richardson 111-112
Gentry, Atron A. 112
George, Nelson 192-193
Gewecke,* Clifford G., Jr. 6
Gibbons, Ashton F. E. 60
Gibbs, Jewelle Taylor 534
Gibbs,* Michele 414
Gibson, Althea 21
Gibson, Bob 193
Gibson, Donald B. 398-399
Gibson,** Gail S. 60
Giddings, Paula 534
Gifford, Bernard R. 112, 227, 534
Gilchrist, Jan Spivey 425
Giles, Raymond H., Jr. 112, 227
Gill, Gerald R. 108, 534
Gillespie, Dizzy 193
Gilliam, Dorothy Butler 21
Gilmer, J. Lance 399
Gilpin,* Sandra 302
Ginsburg,** Max (illus.) 345
Giovanni, Nikki 21, 302-303, 399-400, 509
Giovannoni, Jeanne M. 515
Gipson, Joella 502
Girshick,* M. A. 492
Githens,** Marianne 567
Glasgow, Ann Duncan 113
Glasgow, Douglas G. 535
Gloster, Jesse Edward 535

Gober, Dom 401. *See also* Nazel, Joseph; Lezan, Joyce
Godwin, Winfred L. 113, 498
Goines, Donald 401
Golden, Marita 21, 402
Goodbody,* Mary 501
Goodwin, Bennie Eugene 114, 402, 474
Gordon, Asa Hines 227-228
Gordon, Edmund Wyatt 114, 599
Gordon, Ethel 402
Gordy, Berry, Sr. 21
Goss, Clay 303, 402
Goss,* Erwin 119
Goss, Linda 303, 536
Grady,** Michael K. 114
Graham, Lorenz 303-304
Graham, Maryemma 402
Graham, Shirley Lola 304
Grambs,** Jean D. 78
Grant, Carl A. 114-115, 159
Grant, J. Jason 402
Grant, Janie Aiken 22
Grant, Moses Alexander 22
Grant, Nancy L. 228
Granville, Evelyn B. 498
Gray, Alma Long 61
Green, Charles 536
Green, Ely 22, 536
Green, Ethel G. 56
Green, Joseph E. 403
Green, Mildred Denby 193
Green, Robert Lee 116-117, 536
Green, Robert W. 403
Green, Tina Sloan 193
Greenblatt,* Susan L. 593
Greene, Ellin 279
Greene, Harry Washington 117

Greene, Lorenzo Johnston 22, 228–229, 536
Greene, Robert Ewell 229
Greene,* Ethel J. 155
Greenfield, Eloise 301–302, 304, 327
Gregory, Dick 22, 403, 475, 498, 537
Gregory, James M. 22
Gregory, Montgomery 425
Grier, William H. 475
Griese,** Bob 193
Grifalconi,* Ann (illus.) 294, 295, 317
Griffin, Judith Berry 307
Griffith, Helen 23
Grimes, Nikki 307
Guirma, Frederic 308
Gumble,* Gray (illus.) 333
Gurin,** Patricia 118
Guthrie,** James W. 118
Guthrie, Robert V. 229
Guy, Rosa 298, 308–309
Guzman, Jessie Parkhurst 60, 229–230
Gwaltney, John Langston 230

Hackney,* Richard (illus.) 332
Haines,* George H., Jr. 491
Hale-Benson, Janice E. 118
Haley, Alex 53, 403
Hall, Carol 309
Hall,* Donald 23
Hall,* James 35
Hall, Jo Anne 55
Hall, Raymond Londell 537
Hall, William S. 404
Halliburton, Warren Jennings 119, 210, 230, 243, 309, 355, 404

Hamilton, Charles V. 230, 475, 520, 537
Hamilton,* Fred J. 200
Hamilton, Virginia 23, 309–314, 475
Hampton, Lionel 23
Handy, William Christopher 23, 193
Hankerson, Henry Edward 119
Hankins, Lela Ruth 119
Hanna,* Cheryl (illus.) 298
Hansberry, Lorraine 231, 404
Hansen,* James C. 475
Hansen, Joyce W. 314–315
Harding, Vincent 538
Hare, Julia 538
Hare, Nathan 212, 231, 538
Hargraves, J. Archie 475
Harley, Sharon 579
Harper, Frederick Douglas 119, 404, 538
Harper, Michael S. 404–405
Harris,* Charles F. 589
Harris, Charles Wesley 538–539
Harris, Charlie Avery 405
Harris, Evans 496
Harris,** Fred R. 539
Harris,* Jacqueline 317
Harris, Janie Miller 59
Harris,* Jeff 198
Harris, Joseph Earl 24, 231–233, 539
Harris, Leonard 233, 476
Harris, Marquis Lafayette 120
Harris,* Norene 120
Harris, Randolph 405
Harris, Thelma Bruner 498
Harris, William Hamilton 233, 539
Harris, William Henry 234

Harris, William McKinley, Sr 120, 234
Harrison, Daphne 193
Harrison-Ross, Phyllis Anne 476, 539
Hart, Phillip S. 515
Harvey,** Albert B. 500
Harvey, Clyde C. 512
Haskins, James 8, 23, 24–29, 120–121, 194, 234–235, 315–316, 405–406, 476, 498–499, 540–542. *See also* Haskins, Jim
Haskins, Jim 33, 194, 202, 542. *See also* Haskins, James
Hatch, James Vernon 60, 406
Hatch, Rodger D. 235
Hatcher, Richard G. 212
Havighurst,** Robert J. 525
Hawkins, Odie 406–407
Hawley,** Willis D. 121
Hayden, Robert Carter 316–317
Hayes, Leola G. 407, 542
Haynes, Carrie Ayers 121
Haynes, Leonard L., III 122, 542
Hays,* Michael (illus.) 345
Haywood, Jacquelyn Slaughter 224
Hazard,** William R. 165
Heilman,** Arthur W. 122
Henderson, Edwin Bancroft 194
Henderson, George 123–124, 153, 477, 499, 543
Henderson, Henry 281
Henderson, Lenneal J., Jr. 235, 543, 567
Henderson, Mae G. 56, 210
Henderson, Stephen Evangelist 382, 407

Henderson, Thomas (Hollywood) 29
Hendrick,** Irving G. 124
Herling,* Eleanor B. 61
Hernandez,** Deluvina 448
Hernton, Calvin C. 407–408, 492, 544
Hesburgh,** Theodore Martin 124
Hess,** Robert E. 80
Higginbotham, A. Leon, Jr. 544
Higgins, Chester, Jr. 194, 236
Hill, Bennett D. 250
Hill,** Beverly 125
Hill, Clifton Thompson (illus.) 433
Hill, George H. 59, 60, 217
Hill, Johnny R. 125
Hill, Richard Child 524
Hill, Robert A. 29, 236, 544–545
Hill, Robert Bernard 544
Hill, Roy L. 408
Hillson,* Maurie 97
Himes, Chester B. 29, 408–410
Himes, Joseph Sandy 237, 545–546
Himler,* Ronald (illus.) 291
Hine, Darlene Clark 237, 499, 546
Hinton, Milt 195
Hobson, Constance Tibbs 11
Hockerman,* Dennis (illus.) 331
Hodges, Willis Augustus 29
Hoefer,* George 200
Hogan, Lloyd L. 546
Hogrogian,* Nonny (illus.) 313
Hogue, W. Lawrence 410
Hohenshil,** Thomas H. 125

Holden, Matthew 547
Holiday, Billie 195
Holland, Antony F. 229
Holland, Jerome H. 237
Holley, Joseph Winthrop 30, 125, 477, 547
Holmes, Butch 410
Holmes, Dwight Oliver W. 125
Holmes, Elizabeth Ann 122
Holmes, Robert A., III 542, 567
Holt, Thomas C. 238, 547
Holtzclaw, William Henry 125
Hooks, Bell 547
Hopkins, Lee Bennett 317
Hopkins,* Jeanette 521
Horne, Lena 195
Hornsby, Alton, Jr. 238
Hoskins, Linus A. 547
Hoskins, Thurman 410
House, James E. 101
Howard, Elizabeth Fitzgerald 60, 317–318
Howard, Moses Leon 318
Howard, Vanessa 318
Huber,** Carolyn 491
Hudson, Cheryl Willis 318
Hudson, Herman C. 126, 188, 410
Hudson, Theodore R. 60, 411
Hudson, Valerie Willis 318
Hudson, Wade 318
Huggins, Nathan Irvin 238
Hughes, Langston 30, 195, 239, 285, 319–320, 387, 411–414, 548
Hughes,* William Hardin 30
Hull, Gloria T. 16, 30, 414, 548
Hullfish,** Gordon H. 94
Hunt,* Chester L. 548

Hunte, Christopher Norman 126
Hunter, Kristin 320
Hunter, William Andrew 126
Hurst, Charles G. 126
Hurston, Zora Neale 30, 239, 415–416, 477
Hutchins, Fred Lew 239
Hylton, Patrick C. 239

Imhoot,** Maurice L. 410
Ince, Basil Andre 548
Ingle, Edward 239
Inkelis,* Ellen 29
Iroaganachi,* John 278
Isadora,* Rachel (illus.) 329

Jackman, Oliver 416
Jackson, Andrew Stonewall 31
Jackson, Blyden 416–417
Jackson, Edward Merica 417
Jackson, Irene Viola 60, 196, 477. *See also* Jackson–Brown, Irene Viola
Jackson, Jacquelyne Johnson 240, 548
Jackson, Jesse J. 320–322
Jackson, John Henry 127
Jackson, Mahalia 31
Jackson, Mary 500
Jackson, Michael 196
Jackson, Miles Merrill, Jr. 60–61
Jackson, Nathaniel 120
Jackson, Reggie 31
Jackson, William M. 500
Jackson,* Sidney L. 61
Jackson–Brown, Irene Viola. *See* Jackson, Irene Viola
Jackson–Coppin, Fanny 127
Jacques–Garvey, Amy 240

Jahannes, Ja Arthur 127, 417
James, Felix 240
James,* Harold Laymount (illus.) 321
James, Richard L. 92, 127
Janowitz,** Morris 516
Jarmon, Charles 527, 549
Jay, James Monroe 500
Jeffers, Lance 417, 418
Jefferson, Roland S. 418
Jemie, Onwuchekwa 418
Jenkins, Betty Lanier 62
Jenkins, Lee Clinton 418
Jenkins, Martin D. 128
Jenkins, William Sumner 240
Jennings,* Clara Murphy 557
Jeschke,* Susan (illus.) 296
Johns,* Jeanne (illus.) 296
Johnson, Angela 322
Johnson,* Bonnie Helene (illus.) 350
Johnson, Charles Richard 418
Johnson, Charles Spurgeon 128, 240–241, 248, 270, 418, 549–550
Johnson, Deborah Jean 159
Johnson, Earvin (Magic) 31
Johnson, Edward Augustus 242, 550
Johnson, George Marion 550
Johnson, Harper 284
Johnson, Harry Alleyn 62, 128
Johnson, James Weldon 31, 196, 243, 322–323, 418
Johnson, John Rosamond 196
Johnson, Joseph Andrew, Jr. 478
Johnson, Kenneth R. 129
Johnson, Robert E. 32
Johnson, Roosevelt 129

Johnson, Simon Otis 129–130
Johnson, Sylvia T. 131
Johnson, Timothy V. 32
Johnston,* A. P. 73
Johnston, Gladys Styles 131
Jones, Adrienne Lash 243
Jones, Dionne J. 550
Jones, Edward Allen 132, 418
Jones, Faustine Childress 132, 550
Jones, Gayl 418–419
Jones, Gilbert Haven 132
Jones, Jesse B., III 419
Jones,* Ken (illus.) 332
Jones, Lawrence Clifton 32
Jones, Leon 133
Jones, LeRoi 419, 551. *See also* Baraka, Imamu Amiri
Jones, Lewis Wade 133
Jones, Marcus Earl 551
Jones,* Michael R. (illus.) 303
Jones, Reginald Lanier 124, 133–134, 478, 551
Jones,* Sherman 183
Jones,* Timothy (illus.) 287
Jones–Jackson, Patricia 419
Jordan, June Meyer 243, 323–324, 420
Joseph,* Stephen M. 21
Joseph,* Thomas (illus.) 300
Josey, Elonnie Junius 61, 62–63
Joyce, Donald Franklin 63
Joyce,** William W. 77, 134
Juilliard,* Ahrgus 52
Jules–Rosette, Bennetta 197, 478, 513, 551–552
Just, Ernest Everett 500

Kaiser, Ernest 230

Kane,* Robert 106
Kaplan,** Jerome 175–176
Karenga, Maulana 243, 552
Karnig,** Albert K. 552
Katz,* Louis E. 517
Katz,** William Loren 230, 243
Kauffer,* E. McKnight (illus.) 412
Kaufman, Cherly Davidson 500
Keats,** Ezra Jack (illus.) 55
Keith,* Eros (illus.) 310
Kelley, William Melvin 420–421
Kellogg,** Steven (illus.) 290
Kemble,* E. W. (illus.) 390
Kendrick, Dolores 421
Kennedy, Theodore R. 552
Kent,* Lorna 62
Kenyon,* Gerald S. 493
Khalil, Amma 381
Kidd, Foster 500
Killens, John Oliver 421, 553
Kilson, Martin 244
Kim, Jody (illus.) 335
Kimmons, Willie James 134
Kincaid, Jamaica 244, 422
King, Charles Edward 140, 553
King, Coretta Scott 244
King,* Edith W. 166
King, Martin Luther, Jr. 478–479, 553–554
King, Martin Luther, Sr. 32
King, Mary Elizabeth 554
King, Woodie, Jr. 197, 422–423, 554
Kinnamon, Kenneth 363
Kirpatrick, Oliver Austin 324
Kittles, Emma Holmes 501
Kletzing,* Henry F. 244
Knight,** Kenneth E. 560

Knobler,** Peter 3, 29
Knowles, Timothy S. 89
Knox, Ellis O. 135
Knuckles, Jeffery 423
Koering, Ursula (illus.) 319
Kopper,* Lisa (illus.) 326
Kosiba,* Margaret M. 503
Kramer,* Bernard M. 506
Kremer,** Gary R. 229
Kremer,* Marjean G. 34
Kuman,* Krishna 509
Kunjufu, Jawanza 135–136, 324, 555, 558
Kushner,* Bill 202
Kwak,** Tony 125

Lacey, Henry Clark 423
Lacy, Leslie Alexander 32, 33, 324–325, 427, 555
Ladner, Joyce A. 244–245, 555
Lake,* Verge 563
Lakin, Mattie Temple T. 423
Lamming, George 423
Lamont, Barbara 555
Landau,* Elaine 322
Landry, Bart 555
Lane,* Mark 537
Lane, Pinkie Gordon 424
Lapchick,* Richard 159
LaPoint, Velma D. 69
Latta, Morgan London 33
Lawrence, Jacob 325, 411
Lawrence, Margaret Morgan 136, 501
Lee, Andrea 245, 424
Lee, Don Luther. *See* Madhubuti, Haki R.
Lee** Maurice A. 110
Lee, Ulysses 374

LeFlore, Ron 33
Lemelle, Tilden J. 136
Lemelle, Wilbert J. 136
Lester, Julius 33, 197, 245, 278,
  325–326, 424, 555
Levin,** Martin 523
Levin,** Richard 31
Levine,** Daniel U. 149
Levy,** Eugene D. 261
Lewin, Hugh 326
Lewin, Ted (illus.) 290
Lewis, David Levering 34, 197,
  556
Lewis, Edna 501
Lewis, Evelyn Jones 503, 556
Lewis, James, Jr. 136–137
Lewis, Mary C. 556
Lewis, Meharry H. 479
Lewis, Raphael O. 556
Lewis,** Ronald L. 253
Lewis, Selma S. 34
Lezan, Joyce 424–425. *See also*
  Nazel, Joseph; Gober, Dom
Lightfoot, Sara Lawrence 34,
  137
Lilly, Charles (illus.) 307, 338
Lincoln, Charles Eric 320, 479,
  556–557
Lincoln, Eugene A. 479
Lipscomb,* George Dewey 16
Lipsyte,* Robert 22
Little, Lessie Jones 307, 327,
  425
Littlejohn, Walter L. 557
Littleton, Arthur C. 245
Lloyd, Errol (illus.) 327, 285, 286
Lloyd, Raymond Grann 501, 557
Locke, Alain LeRoy 197, 246,
  425, 557

Locke, Hubert G. 558
Logan, Rayford Whittingham 34,
  47, 138, 246–247, 558
Lomax,** Allan 425
Lomax, Louis E. 247, 425, 479
Lombard, Ruby 494
Lomotey, Kofi 138
Long, Herman Hodge 133, 248
Long, Richard A. 197, 425
Lopez,* Peter E. 366
Lorde, Audre 381, 425–426
Louis, Joe 35
Lovinggood, Penman 197
Low, Joseph (illus.) 378
Low, W. Augustus 64
Lufkin, Raymond (illus.) 284
Lupica,** Mike 31
Lyda, Wesley J. 38
Lyles, Carl C., Sr. 248
Lynch, Hollis Ralph 248, 558
Lynch,** James 78
Lynch, John Roy 35, 248
Lynch, Lorenzo 327, 335
Lynk, Miles Vandahurst 35, 138,
  249

MacCann, Donnarae 426
Macmillan,** Donald L. 134
Madhubuti, Haki R. 426, 558
Magee, Ruchell 527
Magubane, Peter 327
Major, Clarence 426
Major, Geraldyn Hodges 249
Makeba, Miriam 35
Makward,* Edris 427
Malizio,** Andrew G. 73
Malveaux,* Julianne M. 572
Manley, Michael 559
Mann, Coramae Richey 559

Mann,* Peter B. 113
Manning, Kenneth R. 36
Manuel, Ron C. 559
Mapplethorpe, Robert 197
Marfo, Kofi 139
Marlow, Eric (illus.) 306
Marr, Warren II 559
Marrett, Cora Bagley 174
Marshall, Paule 427
Marshall,* Rita 415
Martin,* Clovis (illus.) 330
Martin, Donald F. 207
Martin, Eddie J. 560
Martin,** Sonia 458
Martinez, Maurice M., Jr. 139
Martins,* George 303
Mataka, Laini 427
Mathews,** Marilyn 577
Mathews,* Tom 51
Mathis, Sharon Bell 327–328
Matney, William C., Jr. 36
Maupin, Madeline Taylor 139
May, Lola June 139–140
Mayberry, Claude, Jr. 140
Mayer,** Robert R. 140
Mays, Benjamin Elijah 36, 479–480
Mays, Robert E. 106, 140
Mays,* Victor (illus.) 339
Mays, Willie 197–198
McAdoo, Harriette Pipes 249, 560
McAdoo, John Lewis 249
McAllister, Jane Ellen 141
McBride,* Terry (illus.) 469
McCallum,* James H. 467
McCannon, Dindga 328, 351
McCarthy,* Agnes 328
McCarthy,** Mignon 3
McClain, Paula D. 552

McClendon, John 550
McClure, Jesse F. 560
McCord,* Arline Sakuma 179
McCory, Jessie J. 510
McCourt,* Anne A. 391
McCully,* Emily A. (illus.) 347
McDaniel, Reuben Roosevelt, Jr. 560
McDonald, Marjorie 480
McDowell, Deborah E. 428
McElroy, Colleen J. 428
McElroy, Samuel Ray Ford 501
McFadden,** Elizabeth S. 9
McFerrin, Bobby 198
McGovern,* Penny 163
McGraw,* James R. 403, 537
McGuire, Phillip 250, 561
McKay, Claude 428
McKay,** John P. 250
McKay, Nellie Y. 37, 429
McKinney, Richard Ishmael 141
McKinney, Theophilus Elisha 141
McKissack, Fredrick 328, 329–333
McKissack, Patricia C. 328–333
McKissick, Floyd 561
McLaughlin, Clara J. 502
McLean,** Sammis (illus.) 309, 346
McLemore, William Prince 142
McMillan, Terry 429
McMillon, Doris 561
McNeil, Genna Rae 37, 250
McPherson, James M. 64
McQueen, Adele B. 502
McQueen, Alan 502
McSweeny,* William 44
Mead,** Margaret 561
Meddaugh,* Susan (illus.) 297

Medley,** Morris L. 561
Meier,** August 19
Meisel,* Paul (illus.) 329
Melham, D. H. 429
Meltzer,* Milton 195, 320
Mendez, Phil 334
Meranto,* Phillip J. 564
Mercer, Walter Alexander 142
Meredith, James Howard 142
Meriwether, Louise M. 334
Merrill,* Reed (illus.) 332
Micheaux, Oscar 250, 430
Middleton, Merlissie Ross 480
Mikesell,* Janice H. 442
Miles, Johnnie Harris 125, 561
Milgram, Morris 561
Millender, Dharathula Hood 334-335
Miller, Abie 250
Miller, Carroll L. 562
Miller, Don (illus.) 294, 347, 348
Miller, E. Ethelbert 430
Miller,** Inabeth 180
Miller, Kelly 250-251, 481, 562
Miller, Lamar P. 142-143
Miller, Loren 251
Miller, May 430-431, 442
Miller, Melba 335
Miller,* Paul A. 124
Miller,** Susan 59
Millican, Arthenia Bates 431
Milner, Ron 423
Miner,* Leigh Richmond (illus.) 389
Mitchell, Ella Pearson 481
Mitchell, Lofton 198
Mitchell, Mozella Gordon 481
Mitgang,** N. R. 28
Mitter,* Kathy (illus.) 333

Mohr, Paul B. 143
Molette, Barbara J. 198
Molette, Carlton W. 198
Montgomery, Bertha Vining 502
Moody, Anne 37
Moore, Bradley George 143, 481
Moore, Carmen Leroy 335
Moore, Emily R. 335
Moore,** Kristin A. 562
Moore, Marsha L. 58, 59
Moore, William, Jr. 144-145, 251
Morgan, Gordon Daniel 37, 251-252
Morgan, Kathryn L. 252
Morninghouse, Sundaira 335
Morris, Aldon D. 252
Morris, Lorenzo 252
Morrison, Toni 431-432
Morrison-Reed, Mark D. 481
Morrow,* Barbara (illus.) 318
Morse, L. C. 432
Morton,* Lee Jack (illus.) 334
Moseley, Clifton L. 145
Moser,* Barry 475
Moses, Wilson Jeremiah 562
Mosley, Charles C. 252
Mosley, William 481
Moss, Alfred A., Jr. 225, 252
Moss, Geoffrey (illus.) 346
Moss, Larry Edward 563
Motley, Willard 432-433
Moton, Robert Russa 37, 252
Moustakas,** Clark E. 150
Moutoussamy-Ashe, Jeanne 198, 252
Muhammad, Elijah 482
Muhammad, Farid I. 146
Muhammad, Fonda K. 335
Muller,* Gilbert H. 433

Mulvoy,* Mark 48
Munder,** Barbara 188
Murphy, Beatrice M. 335, 433
Murray, Albert 6, 198, 253, 433
Murray,* Ossie (illus.) 286
Murray, Pauli 38, 434, 563, 570
Musgrove, Margaret 335
Mutharika, Arthur Peter 563–564
Myers, Walter Dean 336–338

Nabrit, Samuel M. 146
Nabwire, Constance R. 502
Nagenda, John 338
Nagenda, Musa 338
Napper, George 146
Nast,* Bernhard (illus.) 411
Naylor, Gloria 434
Nazel, Joseph 39, 434–436. *See also* Gober, Dom; Lezan, Joyce
Neal, Annie W. 338
Neal, Larry 415, 419, 436
Neimark,* Paul G. 39, 565
Nelson, Sophia P. 205
Nelson, William E., Jr. 564
Nelson, William Stuart 482
Ness,* Evaline (illus.) 294, 296
Nettles, Michael Terrael 147
Newby, James Edward 65, 147
Newell,* Virginia K. 502
Newman,* David 196
Newmark,** Eileen 359
Newton, Eunice Sheed 147
Newton, Huey P. 564
Newton, James E. 148, 253 148, 253
Neyland, Leedell Wallace 148, 253

Nicholas,* Frank (illus.) 321
Nicholson, Joseph William 480
Nivens, Beatryce 502–503
Noble, Jeanne L. 107, 148
Norris, Cornell (illus.) 446
Norton, Kimberly 436
Nwagbaraocha,* Joel O. 184

O'Daniel, Therman B. 437
Odarty, Bill 503
O'Meally, Robert G. 437
Offen,** Neil 19
Offiong, Daniel A. 564
Ogbu, John U. 149
Ogilvie,* Donald H. 257
Oglesby,** Carole A. 193
Oliver, Elizabeth Murphy 338
Olu,* Yaounde (illus.) 324
Ongiri, David O. 149
Orden,* Bob 403
Ordover,** Janusz A. 397
Organ, Claude H., Jr. 503
Ornstein,** Allen C. 149
Ottinger, Cecilia A. 529
Ottley, Roi 564
Owens, Jesse 39, 565
Owens, Leslie Howard 565
Owens,* Paul T. 357
Oyemade, Ura Jean 171

Page, James Allen 65, 199
Paige, Howard 503
Painter, Nell Irvin 253, 565
Paisner,* Daniel 203
Palfi,* Marian (illus.) 284
Palley,* Marian Lief 565
Palmer, Cyril Everard 338–339
Panjabi, Manohar M. 506
Paquet, Sandra Pouchet 437

Parham,** Jim T. 560
Parker, Marjorie H. 254
Parker, Robert 254
Parker,** Tom 52
Parks, Arnold G. 65, 565
Parks, David 254
Parks, Gordon 39, 199
Parsons,** Talcott 565
Paschall, Samuel 517
Pasteur, Alfred B. 437
Pate,* Rodney (illus.) 336
Patterson, Frederick D. 30
Patterson, Lillie G. 339
Patterson, Lindsay 199, 438
Patterson, Orlando 438
Payne, Charles Ray 149–150
Payne, Daniel Alexander 39
Payne,** James S. 150
Payson, Dale (illus.) 295
Payton, Vanessa 339
Paznik–Bondarin,* Jane 438
Pearson, Preston 199
Peeples, Kenneth Eugene, Jr. 63
Peirson, Gwynne W. 565
Penn, Nolan E. 566
Pennington, Dorothy L. 438
Pentecoste, Joseph 566
Pepe,* Phil 193
Peplow,* Michael W. 385
Perinbam, B. Marie 40
Perkins, Hattie Logan 254
Perry, Cereta 150
Perry, Huey L. 566
Perry,* Jeanne 62
Perry, Margaret 439
Perry, Thelma Davis 151
Perry,* V. Y–Tessa 102
Peters,* William 17
Peterson, Carla L. 439
Peterson,* Evangeline 501

Petry, Ann Lane 339–340, 439–440
Pfaff, Françoise 199
Pickens, William Garfield 440
Picott, John Rupert 151
Pilgrim, David 152, 482, 503
Pinkett, Harold T. 530
Pinkney, Alphonso 254, 566
Pinkney, Jerry (illus.) 278, 302, 306, 326, 329, 340–341, 345–346
Pinto,* Ralph (illus.) 325
Pipes, William Harrison 482, 567
Ploski,* Harry A. 255
Plotkin,** Lawrence 94
Plummer, Brenda Gayle 255
Poindexter, Hildrus A. 40
Poitier, Sidney 40
Polite, Carlene Hatcher 440
Polloway,** Edward A. 150
Ponderhughes,* J. (illus.) 318
Porter, Dorothy Burnett 65, 255
Porter, James Amos 200
Poussaint, Alvin F. 255, 522
Powell, A. Clayton 40
Powell, Adam Clayton, Jr. 41, 483
Powell,** Norman 567
Prather, Ray (illus.) 313, 340
Prator, Ralph 152
Pratt,* John (illus.) 391
Prestage, Jewel Limar 567
Preston, Michael B. 565, 567
Price,* Christine (illus.) 341
Price, Linda Whitson 152
Priestley, Eric 440
Prince,* Leonora E. (illus.) 350
Proctor, Samuel Dewitt 256
Pruitt, Anne S. 152–153

Pryse,* Marjorie 440
Pugh, Charles 440
Pulsifer,* Marjorie P. 281
Puryear, Paul 567

Quarles, Benjamin 41, 47, 223, 256, 567

Raboteau, Albert J. 483
Rackley, Larney G. 112
Ragan,* William Burke 153
Rampersad, Arnold 41, 42, 428, 440, 567
Ramsey,** Patricia G. 153
Ransome,* James (illus.) 322
Rashke,* Richard 254
Ratteray, Joan D. 66
Ray, David 441
Ray,* Mary Frey 503
Readus, James–Howard 441
Redbury,** Dennis 150
Reddick, Lawrence Dunbar 42, 328
Redding, J. Saunders 257, 385, 441, 567–568
Redford, Dorothy Spruill 42
Redmond,* Eugene B. 389
Redmond,** Patricia 361
Reed, Adolph L., Jr. 568
Reed, Ishmael 200, 441–442
Reed, Rodney J. 118, 154
Reich,** Jerome R. 166, 263
Reilly,** Robert R. 388
Reiss,* Winold (illus.) 557
Rembert, Emma White 154
Render, Sylvia Lyons 442
Revis,* Alesia 307
Revsbech, Vicki 500
Reynolds, Barbara A. 42–43

Reynolds, Louis B. 483
Rhodes, Odis Odean 185
Richard, Henry J. 257
Richardson, Craig 442
Richardson, Harry Van Buren 483–484
Richardson, Joe Martin 154
Richardson,** John Adkins 200
Richardson, Marilyn 257, 442
Richardson,* Willis 442
Richmond, Mossie J., Jr. 154
Riley,* Clayton 32
Riley, Cole 443. *See also* Duke, Romare; Fleming, Robert
Riley,* John W. 148
Ritz,** David 11, 44
Rive, Richard 443
Rivers,** William 59
Rivlin,** Harry N. 165
Robbins,** Webster 92
Robbs,** Stephen 448
Roberts, James Deotis 484
Robeson, Paul 43
Robinet, Harriette Gillem 340
Robinson, Adjai 340–341
Robinson, Armstead L. 257
Robinson, Frank 200
Robinson, Ian Paul 288
Robinson, Jackie 341. *See also* Robinson, John Roosevelt
Robinson, John Roosevelt 43–44, 200. *See also* Robinson, Jackie
Robinson, Kitty Kidd 155
Robinson, Louie, Jr. 279, 341
Robinson, Luther D. 568
Robinson, Robert 257
Robinson, Smokey 44
Rockwell,* Anne (illus.) 339

Rodgers, Carolyn M. 443
Rodgers, Frederick A. 155
Rodgers-Rose, La Frances 568
Rodney, Walter 569
Rogers, Joel A. 258
Rogers,* Kathy (illus.) 330
Roh,** Jae Min 66
Rollins, Charlemae Hill 66, 341
Rollock, Barbara 66
Romano,* Clare (illus.) 292
Romanowski,* Patricia 52
Romero,* Patricia W. 270
Rose, Harold M. 569
Rose,** Peter Issac 569
Rose,* Richard (illus.) 286
Ross, Edyth L. 569
Ross,* John (illus.) 292
Ross-Sheriff,** Fariyal 494
Rossell,** Christine H. 121
Rotham,** Stanley 569
Rout, Leslie B., Jr. 258
Rowan, Carl Thomas 44, 570
Roy, J. Michael (illus.) 500
Rubin,* Leslie 570
Rubin,* Louis D., Jr. 417
Ruffin, Reynold 341
Rushing, Andrea Benton 579
Russell, Bill 44
Russell, Charlie London 443
Russell,* Jim (illus.) 286
Russell,** John Caro, Jr. 570
Rust, Art, Jr. 35
Rust, Edna 35
Rustin, Bayard 258
Rydingsword,* Carl E. 120

Sabir, Waliyyuddin Abdul 570
Sadler, William Anderson 504
Salaam, Kalamu Ya 443, 571
Salbert, Ronni (illus.) 286

Salkey, Andrew 341
Salley, Columbus 259, 484
Sample, Johnny 200
Samuda, Ronald J. 155, 485
Samuels, Charles 51
Sanchez, Sonia 342, 443-444
Sanders, Doris E. 444
Sandle, Floyd L. 444
Sarden, Claudia 444
Saunders, Doris E. 249, 259
Sayers, Gale 193, 200
Saylor,** John Galen 155
Schickel,* Richard 195
Schlesinger,** Elfriede G. 528
Schulman,* Jerome L. 214
Schulte,* Rainer 451
Schwartz,* Sonny 200
Schwarz-Bart, Simone 444
Scott, EdRoyal 44
Scott, Emmett Jay 259, 571
Scott, Hugh Jerome 156
Scott, John Irving Elias 156-157
Scott, Joseph W. 571
Scott, Julius Samuel, Jr. 146
Scott, Patricia Bell 548
Scott,* Trudy (illus.) 340
Seale, Bobby 44, 259
Sedlacek,** William E. 157
Seeger,* Peter 197
Sekora,* John 444
Sellers, Cleveland 45
Seuling,* Barbara (illus.) 318
Sewell, George Alexander 45, 157, 485
Sewell,* Helen (illus.) 319
Shabazz, Abdul-Alin 157
Shade, Barbara J. Robinson 158
Shakur, Assata 45
Shange, Ntozake 444-446
Sharp, Saundra 446

Shaw, Charles (illus.) 338
Shaw,** Dave 11
Shea,* Thomas M. 169
Shearer, John 342
Shearer, Ted (illus.) 342
Sheffey, Ruthe T. 446
Shepard,* Ray Anthony 292
Sherlock, Hilary 342
Sherlock, Philip 342
Sherman, Michele 561
Sherriffs, Alex C. 158
Shimin, Symeon (illus.) 314
Shockley, Ann Allen 45, 66
Shockley, Grant Sneed 250
Shoemaker,* Kathryn E. (illus.) 329
Sikes, Melvin P. 571
Sikorski,* Anne (illus.) 331
Silverman,** Al 200
Simms, Margaret C. 562, 572
Simms, Ruth P. 260, 509
Simon,* Leonard S. 491
Simons, Rita Dandridge 395
Simpson, Bessie Chenauh 504
Sims, Janet L. 58. *See also* Sims-Wood, Janet L.
Sims, Naomi 504–505
Sims, William E. 107, 158, 260
Sims-Wood, Janet L. 59, 67, 69. *See also* Sims, Janet L.
Sinclair, William Albert 572
Singleton, Carole 190
Sinnette, Elinor Des Verney 46, 67
Sitaram,** K. 381
Sizemore, Barbara A. 159
Slaton, Nellie 342
Slaton, William 342
Slaughter, Diana T. 159

Slaughter, John 159
Slaughter,** Reid 203
Slayton,* Paul, Jr. 224
Sleeter,** Christine E. 159
Slepian, Barry 355–356
Slevin,* Jonathan 257
Slim, Iceberg. *See* Beck, Robert
Smalley,* Webster 411
Smith, Arthur Lee, Jr. 446–448. *See also* Asante, Molefi Kete
Smith, Barbara 548, 572
Smith, Benjamin Julian 46
Smith,* Claire 189
Smith, Cynthia J. 160, 550
Smith, Ed Calvin 160, 260, 572
Smith, Elsie J. 160, 475
Smith, Ida Ragins 161
Smith, James E., Jr. 150
Smith, James Wesley 161, 261, 572
Smith, Joshua L. 155
Smith,** Michael J. 200
Smith, Roland Frederick 507
Smith, Roland McFatridge 261
Smith, Shelby Lewis 572
Smith, William Gardner 573
Smith, Willie ("the Lion") 200
Smith, Willy DeMarcell 161
Smitherman, Geneva 161
Smith-Parker, Cassandra 547
Snowden, Frank M., Jr. 201, 261
Soman,* David (illus.) 322
Sommerville, Joseph C. 161–162
Souder,* Sally 377
Southall, Geneva H. 201
Southern, Eileen Jackson 201–202
Sowell,* Floyd (illus.) 334, 338, 346

Sowell, Thomas 162–163, 261–262, 573–575
Spaights, Ernest 99, 163
Spellman, Cecil Lloyd 46, 262
Spencer, Margaret Beale 575
Spiegel,* Doris (illus.) 320
Spillers, Hortense Jeanette 440
Spiva, Ulysses Van 163–164, 576
Spivey, Donald 164
Spradling, Mary (Louis) Mace 46
Springs, John B., III 448
Spruill, Albert W. 165, 576
St. Clair, Ronald 446
Stadley, Quandra Prettyman 448
Stafford, Joseph 505
Staples, Robert E. 263, 576–577
Starks, John Jacob 47
Starling, Marion Wilson 263
Starr,* Isidore 532
Stent, Madelon Delany 165
Stepto, Robert Burns. 405, 449
Steptoe, John 343–344, 293, 298, 306
Sterling, Dorothy 47, 263, 344
Sterling,* Philip 47
Stern,* Bernhard J. 246
Stetson, Erlene LaQuetta 449
Stevens, Joseph H., Jr. 166, 577
Stewart, Rae Shawn 449
Stewart, Rex 202
Stewart, Ruth Ann 47
Stifle,* J. M. 29, 542
Stiles**, Lindley J. 98
Stingley, Darryl 48
Stock,* Catherine 349
Stockett, Thomas A. (illus.) 338
Stone, Chuck 449, 577
Stone, Donald P. 48

Story, Rosalyn M. 202
Stowe,** Lyman Beecher 259
Strain, Lucille B. 166
Strickland, Arvarh E. 22, 166, 263, 577
Strickland, Dorothy S. 449
Suba,* Susanne (illus.) 339
Sullivan,** Dorothy D. 166
Sullivan, Leon Howard 577
Sutherland, Efua 344
Swan, Llewelyn Alex 578
Swinburne,* Laurence 210
Swinton, David H. 108
Swisher,* Elizabeth (illus.) 332
Swofford,* Jeanette (illus.) 500

T, Mr. 48
Tamarkin,* Civia 95
Tarry, Ellen 48, 344, 449–450, 485
Tate, Claudia 450
Tate, Eleanora E. 344
Tate, Elfleda Jackson 167
Tatum, Jack 202
Taulbert, Clifton L. 49
Taylor, Alrutheus Ambush 264, 578
Taylor, Arnold H. 269, 578
Taylor, Clyde R. 264
Taylor, Gardner C. 485
Taylor, Howard F. 578
Taylor, Lawrence 49
Taylor, Mildred D. 345–346
Taylor, Orlando L. 458, 505
Taylor,* Prentiss (illus.) 411, 412
Taylor, Ronald L. 588
Taylor, Ruth Sloan 167
Teague, Bob 68, 579
Teish, Luisah 485

Terborg–Penn, Rosalyn 547, 579
Terrell, Mary Church 49
Terrell, Robert L. 45
Terry, Wallace 264
Theony,** A. Robert 147
Thibodeax, Mary Roger 579
Thiede,** Robert 162
Thomas, Charles Cyrus 450
Thomas, Charles W. 265, 566
Thomas,* Claudewell S. 518
Thomas, Dawn C. 347
Thomas, Duane 202
Thomas,* Frances S. 116
Thomas, Gail Elaine 167
Thomas, Ianthe 347
Thomas, Joyce Carol 348, 450
Thomas, June 524
Thomas, Latta R. 486
Thomas, Will 49
Thompson, Alton 579
Thompson, Cleopatra Davenport 168
Thompson, Daniel Calbert 168, 265, 580
Thompson, Era Bell 49, 265
Thompson, Mozelle (illus.) 323
Thompson,* Quentin (illus.) 332
Thornton, J. Mills 266
Thorpe, Earl E. 50, 68, 266–267
Thurman, Howard 50, 486, 580
Thurman, Wallace 450
Timmons, Eleanor Lewis 168
Tinker, Barbara Wilson 451
Todd,* Terry 505
Toldson, Ivory L. 437
Tollett, Kenneth S. 168
Tolson, Arthur L. 267
Tomes,* Margot (illus.) 307
Toppin, Edgar Allan 224, 268

Toulmin–Rothe,* Ann (illus.) 347
Travis, Dempsey J. 50, 268
Trentin,* George 551
Troup, Cornelius V. 50, 157
Troupe, Quincy 14, 451
Tryman, Mfanya Donald 581
Tucker, James F. 581
Turkle,* Brinton (illus.) 294
Turner, Bridges Alfred 169
Turner, Darwin T. 68, 444, 451–453
Turner, Ethel Marie 268
Turner, Glennette Tilley 269, 453
Turner, John B. 581
Turner, Lorenzo Dow 383, 453
Turner, Patricia 69
Tweedle, John 582

Uggams, Leslie 505
Upton, James Nathaniel 582

Van Sertima, Ivan 269
Vance, Irvin E. 493
Vandi, Abdulai S. 359, 454
Vernon, William Tecumseh 454
Vincent, Charles 169, 582
Vinson, James 411
Vivian, Octavia 50
Vold, Edwina Battle 153
Vontress, Clemmont E. 169

Wade–Gayles, Gloria Jean 454
Wagstaff, Lonnie H. 145
Walker, A. (illus.) 415
Walker, Alice 454–455
Walker, Clarence E. 486
Walker, David 269

Walker, David Anthony 202
Walker, Harry J. 582
Walker, Herschel 505
Walker, James E. 169
Walker, Juliet E. K. 269
Walker, Lewis 548
Walker, Mae 170
Walker, Margaret 400, 455–456
Walker, Sylvia 139
Wall, Cheryl A. 456
Wallace, Michele 582
Wallace, Susan J. 456
Wallace, Walter L. 170, 523, 583
Waller,* Louisa Jones (illus.) 501
Walter, Mildred Pitts 349–350
Walter, Ronald Anderson 12
Walters, Ronald W. 583
Walton, Darwin McBeth 351
Walton, Hanes, Jr. 69, 584–585
Walton, Sidney F., Jr. 170
Warbash, Denver 456
Ward,** Maybelle 559
Warner, Malcolm–Jamal 203
Warner,* Richard W. 475
Warren, Mervyn Alonzo 486
Washington, Booker T. 51, 171, 270, 486, 585
Washington, Joseph R., Jr. 486–487
Washington, Mary Helen 456–457
Washington, Valora 69, 171
Waterland,* Jean C. 163
Waters, Elroy 457
Waters, Ethel 51, 203
Watkins, Frank E. 235
Watkins,** Kathleen Pullan 585
Watson, Bernard C. 172, 585

Watson, Glegg 496
Wattenbarger,* James Lorenzo 113
Weatherford,** Willis Duke 270
Weaver, Robert Clifton 586
Webb, Frank J. 457
Webb, Spud 203
Webster, Staten Wentford 172–173, 270
Wells, Elmer Eugene 586
Wells–Barnett, Ida B. 587
Wesley, Charles Harris 173, 270, 274, 587
Weston,* Josepha M. 139
Weston, Rubin Francis 271
Wharton, Clifton R. 124, 587
Wharton, Dolores Duncan 203
Wheatley, Phillis 457
Whitaker, Ginger 457
White, Augustus A., III. 506
White, Charles (illus.) 282
White, Edgar B. 351, 458
White, Joseph L. 487
White, Oscar 458
White, Walter Francis 51, 458, 588
Whiting, Helen Adele 173
Wilcox, Preston 173–174
Wilkerson, Doxey A. 114, 149, 174
Wilkins, Roger W. 51, 539
Wilkins, Roy 51
Wilkinson, Brenda Scott 351
Wilkinson, Doris Yvonne 271, 588
Wilkinson,* Louise Cherry 174
William,* Napoleon 138
Williams, Audrey 291
Williams, Bruce E. 458
Williams, Chancellor 271

Williams, Eric Eustace 174, 271
Williams, George Washington 272
Williams, John Alfred 52, 272, 433, 458–460, 589
Williams, John B., III 175
Williams,* Joshua 143
Williams, Juan 589
Williams,** Leslie R. 153
Williams, Loretta J. 589
Williams, Lorraine Anderson 272
Williams, Lucius L. 175–176
Williams, Melvin D. 272, 589–590
Williams, R. Ora 69, 460
Williams, Robert Franklin 590
Williams, Robert L. 176, 460
Williams, Sherley Anne 460–461
Williams, Vernon J., Jr. 590
Williams, William James 487, 590
Williams, William Taylor B. 176–177
Williams–Garcia, Rita 352
Williamson, Juanita V. 461
Williamson, Mel 352
Willie, Charles V. 114, 177–180, 487, 506, 591–593
Willis, Leydel Johnson 461–462
Willis, William M. 528
Willis–Thomas, Deborah 204
Wilson,* Alan B. 104
Wilson, August 462
Wilson, Beth 352
Wilson, Charles H., Sr. 180
Wilson, D. B. 462
Wilson, George D. 180, 594
Wilson, John (illus.) 462

Wilson, Johnniece Marshall 352
Wilson, Julia 462
Wilson, Mary 52
Wilson,* Sybil 522
Wilson, Thomasyne Lightfoot 180
Wilson, William Julius 569, 594
Wimberly, Edward P. 488
Windley, Vivian O. 391
Winfield, Dave 52
Winston, Michael R. 34, 247, 250, 273
Wintersmith, Robert F. 595
Wirt,* Frederick 105
Wishart,** Lelia 500
Wohl,* Gary 299
Wolfe,* Diane (illus.) 500, 502
Wolfe,* Robert L. (illus.) 500, 502
Woll, Allen 204
Wood, Forrest G. 273
Woodard, Gloria 426
Woodard, Maurice Compton 595–596
Woodard, Samuel L. 181
Woods,* Sandra L. 155
Woodson, Carter G. 181–182, 273–274, 352, 462, 536
Woodson, Jacqueline 353
Woodson, Shirley 503
Woolfolk, E. Oscar 182–184
Woolfolk, George R. 184, 274
Work, Monroe Nathan 69
Wright, Bruce 596
Wright, Charles H. 596
Wright, Jerome Dyson 462
Wright, Nathan, Jr. 184, 274, 462, 488, 596–597

Wright, Richard   52, 275, 462, 463, 597
Wright, Richard Robert   184
Wright, Sarah E.   463
Wyden,** Barbara   539
Wylie,* Evan McLeod   31
Wynn, Cordell   185
Wynter, Sylvia   291, 463

X, Malcolm   53, 597

Yarbrough, Camille   353
Yeakey, Carol Camp   131
Yerby, Frank   463
Yette, Frederick Walton   275
Yette, Samuel F.   275, 598
Young, Al   200, 204, 464
Young, Andrew Sturgeon N.   353
Young, Barbara H.   506

Young, Bernice Elizabeth   353
Young,** Beverly Sue   185
Young, Carlene   598
Young,** Ethel   185
Young, Glenell S.   69
Young, Henry James   488–489, 598
Young, Herman A.   506
Young, James O.   464
Young, Joseph A.   465
Young, Margaret Buckner   353, 354
Young, Richard P.   275
Young, Tommie Morton   53
Young, Whitney M., Jr.   598
Yulsman, Jerry   403

Zigler,* Edward F.   599
Zimmerman,* Paul   202

TITLE INDEX

Abby 290
About Courage 395
About Michael Jackson 24
Abraham's Legacy: Ancient Wisdom and Modern Reality 472
Abram, Abram, Where Are We Going? 328
Absence of Ruins, An 438
Academic Common Market, The 113
Accent African Fashions 259
Access of Black Students to Graduate and Professional Schools 79
Accountability in Reading Instruction 166
Achievement Among Minority Americans: A Conference Report 214
Adah's Story: A Novel 393
Adam By Adam: The Autobiography of Adam Clayton Powell, Jr. 41
Adam Clayton Powell: Portrait of a Marching Black 24
Adam in Blunderland 346
Adam vs. Ape-Man and Ethiopia 550
Administering Early Childhood Education Programs 166
Administering the Individualized Instruction Program 136
Administration of Injustice, The 571
Administrative Advocacy 543
Advancing Equality of Opportunity: A Matter of Justice 160
Advantage Ashe 6
Adventures in Educational Progress 107

Adventures of Aku, The 289
Adventures of Fathead, Smallhead, and Squarehead, The 342
Adventures of Spider: West African Folk Tales, The 278
Affirmative Action Reconsidered. Was It Necessary in Academia? 162
Afraid of the Dark 375
Africa and the Afro–American Experience 272
Africa Dream 304
Africa, Land of My Fathers 265
Africa: Her History, Lands, and People, Told with Pictures 272
African–American Genealogy 53
African American Holiday of Kwanzaa The 552
African–American Principals 138
African Americans and the Sacred 266
African and African American Communication Continuities 358
African Apostles 478
African Experience in Spanish America, 1502 to the Present, The 258
African Goals and Diplomatic Strategies in the United Nations 205
African Heroes and Heroines 352
African Mandates in World Politics, The 246
African Myths 352
African Presence in Asia, The 231
African Rhythms: Selected Stories and Poems 371
African Treasury, An 413
African Vignettes 251
Africanisms in the Gullah Dialect 453
Africans and Their History 539
Afro–American Authors 355
Afro–American Experience and the Social Work Curriculum, The 533
Afro–American History: Sources for Research 214
Afro–American Literary Style in the 1990s 361
Afro–American Literature: Fiction 356
Afro–American Literature: Nonfiction 355
Afro–American Mass Political Integration 581
Afro–American Poetics 360
Afro–American Problems in Sociology and Psychology 531
Afro–American Reference 59
Afro–American Religious Music 60

Afro-American School Speaker and Gems of Literature for School Commencements, Literary Circles, Debating Clubs, and Rhetoricals Generally, The 138
Afro-American Singers 69
Afro-American Writers 68
Afro-American Writing: An Anthology of Prose and Poetry 425
Afro-Americans in Pittsburgh 216
Afro-Americans: A Social Science Perspective 527
Afro-Bets 123 Book 318
Afro-Bets ABC Book 318
Afro-Bets Book of Black Heroes from A to Z 318
Afro-Victorian Feminist, An 13
Afrocentric Idea, The 358
Afrocentricity: The Theory of Social Change 358
After the School Bell Rings 115
Aftermath of Slavery, The 572
Aftermaze 369
Against the Blues: Poems 360
Against the Odds 144
Against the Tide: An Autobiography 40
Agent K-13, the Super-Spy 346
Aging Black Women: Selected Readings for NCBA 548
Ain't Got Time to Die 386
Ain't I A Woman: Black Women and Feminism 547
Airtight Willie & Me 364
Alcohol Abuse and Black America 538
Alcohol and the Black Community 527
Alesia 307
Algebra and Geometry for Teachers 493
Alice Dunbar-Nelson Reader, An 460
Alien Under American Law: Text, Materials, Cases, The 563
Alienation & Contemporary Society 518
All About Health & Beauty for the Black Woman 504
All About Success for the Black Woman 505
All-American Girl 339
All God's Children Need Traveling Shoes 4
All is Well: An Autobiography 33
All Paths Lead to Bethlehem 329
All Shot Up 408

All the Women Are White, All the Blacks Are Men, but Some of Us Are Brave 548
All Us Come Cross the Water 293
Aloneness 371
Along This Way: The Autobiography of James Weldon Johnson 31
Alpha Kappa Alpha: In the Eye of the Beholder 254
Alternative Strategies: Reading in the Elementary School 154
Always Movin' On: A Biography of Langston Hughes 24
Amen Corner: A Play 361
America as Story: Historical Fiction for Secondary Schools 61
America's Color Caravan 119
America's Other Children: Public Schools Out–Side Suburbia 123
America's Tenth Man 212
American Addition: History of a Black Community, The 240
American Black Women in the Arts and Social Sciences 69
American Daughter 49
American Diplomacy and the Narcotics Traffic, 1900–1939 578
American Ethnic Groups 262
American Hunger 462
American in India, An 257
American Majorities and Minorities 230
American Negro Academy: Voices of the Talented Youth, The 252
American Negro Poetry 284
American Negro Reference Book, The 217
American Negro Short Stories 380
American Slavery and the American Novel, 1852–1977 417
American Way of Violence, The 566
Amifika 294
Amistad: Writings on Black History and Culture 589
Amoralists & Other Tales: Collected Stories, The 382
Analysis and Projection of Research in Teacher Education, An 99
Analysis of the Arkansas–Georgia Statewide Desegregation Plans, An 542
Analysis of the Specific References to Negroes in Selected Curricula for the Education of Teachers, An 95
Anansi, the Spider Man 342
Anatomy of High–Earning Minority Bank 1972–1975 581
Anchor Man 320
And I Heard a Bird Sing 308

And So I Sing: African–American Divas of Opera and Concert   202
And Still I Rise   357
And Still We Rise: Interviews with 50 Black Achievers   42
And the Walls Came Tumbling Down: An Autobiography   4
And Then We Heard the Thunder   421
And We Are Not Saved: The Elusive Quest for Racial Justice   512
Andrew Young: Man with a Mission   315
Angel of Beale Street: A Biography of Julia Ann Hooks, The   34
Angela Davis—An Autobiography   14
Angry Black, The   458
Angry Ones, The   458
Annie Allen   372
Annie John   422
Another Country   361
Anthology of the Afro–American in the Theatre   199
Anthony and Sabrina   340
Anthony Burns: The Defeat and Triumph of a Fugitive Slave   309
Anti–Slavery Sentiment in American Literature Prior to 1865   453
Antislavery Newspapers and Periodicals   56
Anyplace But Here   516
Appeal to Conscience, An   250
Appraising Teacher Performance   137
Argument; Argument: The Oral Argument Before the Supreme Court   518
Arilla Sun Down   310
Arkansas Baptist College: A Historical Perspective, 1884–1982   92
Art and Imagination of W. E. B. DuBois, The   567
Art of Slave Narrative, The   444
Arthur Alfonso Schomburg, Black Bibliophile & Collector   46
Arthur Ashe, Tennis Champion   341
Ashanti to Zulu: African Traditions   335
Ask Me Now   464
Ask the Prophets   470
Ask Your Mama: 12 Moods for Jazz   411
Aspects of Afro–American Cookery   503
Assata: An Autobiography   45
Assertive Black   469
At the Bottom of the River   422

Attitude of the Southern White Press Toward Negro Suffrage, 1932–1940, The 558

Attitudes of High School Students as Related to Success in Sch 104

Autobiography of an Ex–Colored Man, The 31

Autobiography of Black Chicago, An 268

Autobiography of LeRoi Jones/Amiri Baraka, The 6

Autobiography of Lieut. Henry Ossian Flipper 18

Autobiography of Malcolm X, The 53

Autobiography of Miss Jane Pittman, The 20

Autobiography of W. E. B. DuBois, The 16

Baba and Mr. Big 338

Babe Ruth and Hank Aaron: The Home Run Kings 24

Babel–17 387

Baby Chocolate and Other Short Stories 375

Baby Leopard: "How and Why" Story, The 303

Baby of the Family 357

Baby Say 343

Background Study of Negro College Students, A 89

Backways of Kent 556

Bacteria and Viruses: Friends or Foes? 342

Bahamian Scene 456

Balance in Small Groups 578

Ballad of Beta–2, The 387

Balm in Gilead: Journey of a Healer 34

Banjo: A Story Without a Plot 428

Banks and Banking 532

Barbara Jordan: Speaking Out 315

Baseball Has Done It 200

Bases of World Understanding 482

Basic Christian Methodist Belief 478

Basic Design: Systems, Elements, Applications 200

Basic Methods for Experiments on Eggs of Marine Mammals 500

Basic Statistics 515

Bass Line: The Stories and Photographs of Milt Hinton 195

Be–Bop, Re–Bop 377

Beach Umbrella, The 382

Beat the Story Drum, Pum–Pum 289

Beauty and the Beast 287

Because We Are 349
Beckonings: Poems 372
Becky 462
Before Color Prejudice: The Ancient Views of Blacks 261
Before the Mayflower: A History of Black America 281
Beginnings 575
Behavior Management: A Practical Approach for Educators 169
Being Black: Psychological–Sociological Dilemmas 229
Bells of Christmas, The 310
Beloved 431
Bench and the Ballot, The 537
Berhama Account, The 458
Beside Still Waters 402
Besieged School Superintendent, The 74
Best of Simple, The 411
Best Short Stories by Afro–American Writers, 1925–1950 394
Best Short Stories by Black Writers, The 413
Best Short Stories by Negro Writers, The 413
Best Time of Day, The 302
Betrayal of the Negro, The 558
Betrayed 462
Betsey Brown 444
Better Discipline: A Practical Approach 129
Between Two Worlds: A Novel 444
Between Two Worlds: A Profile of Negro Higher Education 82
Between You and Me: Loving Reminiscences 6
Beyond Agenda Setting: Information Subsidies and Public Policy 396
Beyond Black and White 13
Beyond the Angry Black 460
Beyond the Basics: A Rhetoric Reader 386
Bible Answers 483
Biblical Faith and the Black American 486
Bibliographical Guide to Black Studies Programs in the United States 59
Bibliography of Materials by and About Negro Americans for You 61
Bibliography of Negro History and Culture for Young Readers, A 61
Bibliography of the Negro in Africa and America, A 69
Bicycle from Bridgetown, A 347
Bicycle Race 296

Big Bug Book of Counting, The 329
Big Bug Book of Opposites, The 330
Big Bug Book of Places to Go, The 330
Big Bug Book of the Alphabet, The 330
Big Bug Book of Things to Do, The 330
Big Doc Bitteroot 338
Big Gold Dream, The 408
Big Hit, The 441
Big Sea: An Autobiography, The 30
Bikes 281
Bill Cosby: America's Most Famous Father 25
Bill Cosby: In Words and Pictures 32
Billion Dollar Death 436
Billy Jo Jive and the Midnight Voices 342
Bio–Bibliography of Countee P. Cullen, 1903–1946, A 439
Biographical History of Blacks in America Since 1528, A 268
Biography of G. Wash Carter, White, The 395
Biology of the Cell Surface, The 500
Biology: A Problem Solving Approach 119
Bird at My Window 405
Birthday 343
Birthday Present for Katheryn Kenyatta, A 443
Bitch 402
Bits of Ivory 373
Bitter Canaan 549
Bittersweet: Poems 450
Black Abolitionists 567
Black Administrators in Public Community Colleges 134
Black Adult Development and Aging 133
Black Aesthetic, The 192
Black Africa 248
Black Africa on the Move 324
Black Aged in the United States, The 57
Black Agenda for Career Education 129
Black Almanac, The 238
Black American Experience, The 263
Black American Families, 1965–1984 55
Black American in Books for Children, The 426
Black American in United States History, The 268

Black American Literature: Essays, Poetry, Fiction, Drama 451
Black American Literature: Fiction 451
Black American Literature: Poetry 452
Black American Scholars: A Study of Their Beginnings 80
Black American Spirituals. Vol. 2, *I'm Going to Sing* 289
Black American Spirituals. Vol. 1, *Walk Together Children* 289
Black Americans 566
Black Americans and the Political System 510
Black and Deadly 405
Black and Mennonite: A Search for Identity 469
Black and White Families: What They Can Teach Each Other 591
Black and White: Land, Labor and Politics in the South 531
Black and White: Stories of American Life 399
Black Anglo-Saxons, The 231
Black Apollo of Science: The Life of Ernest Everett Just 36
Black Artists in the United States 58
Black Artists of the New Generation 192
Black Arts Annual 189
Black Athlete: Emergence and Arrival, The 194
Black Authors and Education 65
Black Authors and Illustrators of Children's Books 66
Black Awakening in Capitalist America 205
Black BC's, The 294
Black Bibliophiles and Collectors: Preservers of Black History 67
Black Boogaloo: Notes on Black Liberation 436
Black Book 197
Black Bourgeoisie 532
Black Boy: A Record of Childhood and Youth 52
Black/Brown/White Relations: Race Relations in the 1970s 592
Black Business and Economics: A Bibliography 60
Black Businesses, Employment, Economics, and Finance in Urban 57
Black Champions of the Gridiron: Leroy Keys and O. J. Simpson 353
Black Child 328
Black Child 349
Black Child—A Parents' Guide, The 539
Black Child Care 522
Black Children and American Institutions: An Ecological Review 69
Black Children: Social, Educational, and Parental Environments 249
Black Children: Their Roots, Culture, and Learning Styles 118

Black Christ & Other Poems, The 384
Black Church and the Harold Washington Story, The 598
Black Church v. The System, The 480
Black College: Strategy for Achieving Relevancy, The 136
Black Colleges and Universities: Challenges for the Future 111
Black Colleges as Instruments of Affirmative Action 168
Black Colleges in America 179
Black Communication in White Society 522
Black Community Development 234
Black Community: Diversity and Unity, The 515
Black Community's Social Security, The 527
Black Composer Speaks, The 188
Black Consciousness, Identity, and Achievement 118
Black Consumer Profiles: Food Purchasing in the Inner City 491
Black Cop 401
*Black Curriculum: Developing a Program in Afro–American Studies,
    The* 170
Black Defenders of America, 1775–1973 229
Black Diamond in the Queen's Tiara, A 14
Black Drama Anthology 423
Black Drama in America: An Anthology 452
Black Drama: The Story of the American Negro in the Theatre 198
Black Education in Contemporary America: A Crisis in Ambiguity 127
Black Education: A Quest for Equity and Experience 161
Black Education: Myths and Tragedies 162
Black Educators in White Colleges: Progress and Prospects 145
Black Elderly in Rural America: A Comprehensive Study 565
Black Elected Officials 523
Black Elite: A Profile of Graduates of UNCF Colleges, A 580
Black English: Its History and Usage in the United States 387
Black Exorcist, The 434
Black Experience, The 210
Black Experience in American Politics, The 230
Black Experience in Children's Books, The 55
Black Experience in Religion: A Book of Readings, The 479
Black Experience: Analysis and Synthesis 598
Black Expression 398
Black–Eyed Susans: Classic Stories by and about Black Women 456
Black Families 560

Black Families and the Struggle for Survival 514
Black Families in White America 514
Black Family in the United States: A Revised, Updated, Selectively Annotated Bibliography, The 57
Black Family in the United States: A Selected Bibliography of Annotated Books, Articles, and Dissertations on Black Families in America, The 58
Black Family in Urban Areas in the United States: A Bibliography of Published Works on the Black Family in Urban Areas in the United States, The 57
Black Family: Essays and Studies, The 577
Black Feeling, Black Talk 399
Black Feeling, Black Talk, Black Judgement 399
Black Feminist Criticism: Perspectives on Black Women Writers 380
Black Films and Film-Makers 199
Black Fire: An Anthology of Afro-American Writing 419
Black Folktales 325
Black Foremothers: Three Lives 47
Black Freemasonry and Middle-Class Realities 589
Black Fury 434
Black Gangster 401
Black Genealogy 8
Black Gestapo, The 434
Black Ghetto: A Spatial Behavioral Perspective, The 569
Black Girl Lost 401
Black Girl: From Genesis to Revelations 395
Black Gourmet, The 505
Black Heritage in Social Welfare: 1860-1930 569
Black Heroes and Heroines: Book 1 7
Black Heroes and Heroines: Book 2 7
Black Heroes and Heroines: Book 3 7
Black High School and Its Community, The 155
Black Historians: A Critique 266
Black History and the Organic Perspective 68
Black Images 377
Black Images in the American Theatre 187
Black in a White Paradise 370
Black in America: A Fight for Freedom 321
Black Is Beautiful Beauty Book, The 335

Black is the Color of the Cosmos 385
Black Is Back 434
Black-Jewish Relations in the United States, 1752–1984 217
Black Journals of the United States 56
Black Judgement 399
Black Language 357
Black Language Reader 383
Black Lark Caroling, A 450
Black Leaders of the Twentieth Century 19
Black Leadership Fenced In by Racism 518
Black Leadership in Urban Schools 113
Black Legislators in Louisiana During Reconstruction 582
Black Librarian in America, The 63
Black Life in Corporate America: Swimming in the Mainstream 496
Black Literature in America 360
Black Literature: Essays 452
Black Machine Politics in the Post–Daley Era 567
Black Macho and the Myth of the Superwoman 582
Black Magic 195
Black Male in America, The 588
Black Male/White Female: Perspectives on Interracial Marriage 588
Black Man and the Promise of America, The 205
Black Man in American Politics: Three Views, The 212
Black Man's Burden, The 125
Black Man's Burden 553
Black Managers: Making It in the Corporate World, The 497
Black Manhattan 243
Black Manifesto for Education 121
Black Masculinity 576
Black Mathematicians and Their Works 502
Black Men 533
Black Messiahs and Uncle Toms 562
Black Metropolis: A Study of Negro Life in a Northern City 218
Black Midas 291
Black Middle Class Family, The 511
*Black Migration in the United States with Emphasis on Selected Central
    Cities* 551
Black Misery 319
Black Mosaic 256

Black Mother Goose Book 338
Black Music 188
Black Music in America: A History Through Its People 315
Black Musical Theatre: From Coontown to Dreamgirls 204
Black Muslims in America, The 479
Black New Orleans, 1860–1880 208
Black Novelist as White Racist: The Myth of Black Inferiority 465
Black Nun Looks at Black Power, A 579
Black Odyssey: The Afro-American Ordeal in Slavery 238
Black Oklahomans: A History, 1541–1972, The 267
Black Olympian Medalists 199
Black on Black: Baby Sister and Selected Writings 408
Black on Red 257
Black Opportunity 237
Black over White 238
Black Parent's Handbook, The 502
Black Pearl and the Ghost, The 336
Black Pearls: Blues Queens of the 1920s 193
Black People and the Coming Depression 558
Black Photographers, 1840–1940 204
Black Pilgrimage 301
Black Pioneers in a White Denomination 481
Black Playwrights, 1823–1977 60
Black Poetry in America 417
Black Poets and Prophets 554
Black Political Ascendancy in Urban Centers, and Black Control of the Local Police Functions 563
Black Political Life in the United States 235
Black Political Parties: An Historical and Political Analysis 584
Black Political Power in America 577
Black Political Scientists and Black Survival 572
Black Politics and Public Policy 567
Black Politics and Race 211
Black Politics: A Theoretical and Structural Analysis 584
Black Power and Urban Unrest: Creative Possibilities 596
Black Power Revolt 509
Black Power U.S.A. 282
Black Power: The Politics of Liberation in America 520
Black Preacher in America 475

Black Preaching: Truth & Soul 486
Black Presidential Politics in America 583
Black Prophet 435
Black Psychology 478
Black Rage 410
Black Rage 475
Black Reconstruction in America 219
Black Religion 486
Black Renegades 441
Black Republicans 584
Black Revolt: Strategies of Protest 271
Black Revolts, The 571
Black Robes, White Justice 596
Black Scare 273
Black Scenes 379
Black Scholars on Higher Education in the 70's 129
Black School Superintendent: Messiah or Scapegoat?, The 156
Black Sects and Cults 486
Black Self-Concept 78
Black Self-Determination 226
Black Separatism and Social Reality: Rhetoric and Reason 537
Black Separatism in the United States 537
Black Seventies, The 206
Black Short Story Anthology 422
Black Sister: Poetry by Black American Women 1746-1980 449
Black Situation, The 227
Black Skin, White Masks 473
Black Slang: A Dictionary of Afro-American Talk 426
Black Snowman, The 334
Black Society 249
Black Sociologists: Historical and Contemporary Perspectives 516
Black Spirits: A Festival of New Black Poets in America 422
Black Spokesman 248
Black Student's Guide to Colleges, The 78
Black Students 103
Black Students at White Colleges 179
Black Students in Higher Education 167
Black Students in Interracial Schools 160
Black Students in White Schools 106

Black Students: White Campus 119
Black Studies in Public Schools 112
Black Studies in the University: A Symposium 257
Black Studies—Pedagogy and Revolution 519
Black Studies: Pitfalls and Potential 260
Black Studies: Threat-or-Challenge 224
Black Suburbanization 569
Black Theater in America 405
Black Theater, U.S.A. 406
Black Theater 438
Black Theatre, Present Condition 197
Black Theatre: Premise and Presentation 198
Black Theology and Black Power 470
Black Thunder 367
Black Tradition in American Dance, The 197
Black Troopers, The 249
Black Troubador: Langston Hughes 341
Black Underclass, The 535
Black Urban Condition: A Documentary History, 1866–1971, The 558
Black Vendetta 379
Black Victory 546
Black Viewpoints 245
Black Woman, The 568
Black Woman in White America, The 263
Black Woman: An Anthology, The 509
Black Woman's Career Guide, The 502
Black Woman's Experience, A 17
Black Women at the United Nations 584
Black Women Composers: A Genesis 193
Black Women in Nursing 499
Black Women in Sport 193
Black Women in the Nursing Profession 499
Black Women Novelists 380
Black Women Writers (1950–1980) 394
Black Women Writers at Work 450
Black Women Writers: Arguments and Interviews 394
Black Women: Interpersonal Relationships in Profile 511
Black Women: Their Problems and Power 240
Black Writer in Africa and the Americas, The 373

Black Writers of America: A Comprehensive Anthology 363
Black Writers of the Thirties 464
Black Youth in a Southern Metropolis 523
Blacker Than Thou: The Struggle for Campus Unity 146
Blacks 372
Blacks and Other Minorities in Shakespeare's England 223
Blacks and Political Science 692
Blacks in America: Bibliographical Essays 64
Blacks in America: Then and Now 268
Blacks in American Film and Television 189
Blacks in Antiquity 261
Blacks in Classical Music: A Personal History 187
Blacks in Oklahoma, The 224
Blacks in the American Armed Forces, 1776–1983 217
Blacks in the Federal Judiciary 525
Blacks in the Humanities, 1750–1984 63
Blacks in College 107
Blacks, Medical Schools, and Society 496
Blacks on White Campuses 105
Blacks on White College Campuses 85
Blackthink: My Life as Black Man and White Man 565
Blessing: Poems 348
Blind Man on a Freeway 144
Blind Man with a Pistol 408
Blind Tom 201
Bloods: An Oral History of the Vietnam War by Black Veterans 264
Blue Coats 507
Blue Tights 352
Blues Book for Blue Black Magical Women, A 443
Blues Don't Change: New and Selected Poems, The 464
Blues for Mister Charlie: A Play 361
Blues, Ideology, and Afro–American Literature 360
Blues Merchant: Songs (Poems) for Blackfolk, The 443
Blues People: Negro Music in White America 188
Blues 193
Blueschild Baby 377
Bluest Eye, The 431
Bob McAdoo: Superstar 25
Bodies and Soul: Musical Memoirs 204

Bondage, Freedom and Beyond 398
Bone Flames: Poems 428
Book of American Negro Poetry, The 418
Book of American Negro Spirituals, The 196
Book of Negro Folklore, The 414
Book of Negro Humor, The 413
Booker T. Washington, Builder of Civilization 259
Booker T. Washington: Educator of Hand, Head, and Heart 304
Borderline: The Case of Too Many Graves, A Novel 356
Born Sober: Prohibition in Oklahoma, 1907–1959 531
Born to Play: The Life and Career of Hazel Harrison 11
Born to Rebel 36
Borrowed Moments 366
Boss Cat 320
Boy at the Window: A Novel 298
Boy Who Didn't Believe in Spring, The 294
Boys No More 265
Breadsticks and Blessing Places 285
Break of Dawn, The 446
Break Dancing 194
Breakout: From Prison to the Big Leagues 33
Bricktop 8
Bride Price: A Novel, The 393
Brief Historical Sketch on Negro Education in Georgia, A 184
Brief History of Jackson College, A 99
Brief History of the Division of Health, Physical Education, and Recreation at Florida A & M University, A 188
Bright Shadow 348
Bringing Teaching to Life 114
Bringing the Black Boy to Manhood: The Passage 538
Broad Players 405
Broadside Treasury, A 373
Bronzeville Boys and Girls 286
Brother Ray: Ray Charles Own Story 11
Brother to the Wind 349
Brown Girl, Brownstones 427
Brown Is a Beautiful Color 283
Brown Sugar 190
Bubbles 304

Buckingham Palace,' District Six 443
Budgeting 551
Bugs! 330
Build, Brother, Build 577
Building the United States 166
Business Law Casebook 517
Busting Out of an Ordinary Man, The 406
Buying Treasury Securities at Federal Reserve Bank 581

C.L.O.U.D.S 297
Cactus in Bloom 375
Call Me Charley 320
Cavalcade 385
Candle in the Dark: A History of Morehouse College, A 132
Candle–Lightin' Time 389
Cane: An Authoritative Text, Backgrounds, Criticisms 452
Cannabis Experience, The 492
Cannibals 410
Cannon Shot and Glass Beads: Modern Black Writing 423
Capitol Hill in Black and White 254
Captain Blackman: A Novel 458
Captain of the Planter: The Story of Robert Smalls 47
Care and Feeding of White Liberals, The 558
Career Advising for Adults 561
Career Education and the Teaching of English 107
Careers for Women Without College Degrees 503
Caroling Dusk: An Anthology of Verse by Negro Poets 384
Carousel 296
Carrot and Bigstick 547
Case for Affirmative Action for Blacks in Higher Education, The 108
Case for Improved College Teaching, The 147
Case of Mrs. Wingate, The 430
Case of Rape, A 408
Cast the First Stone: Novel 408
Caste and Class Controversy 592
Cat's Purr, The 289
Catholic Church in Haiti, 1704–1785, The 468
Centennial History of Alcorn Agricultural and Mechanical College, The
    498

Centennial History of Southern University and A&M College, A   169
Central Theme of Black History, The   266
Century of Black Surgeons: The U.S.A. Experience, A   503
Century of Negro Education in Louisville, Kentucky, A   180
Century of Service, A   61
Ceremonies in Dark Old Men   392
Challenge of Blackness, The   282
Chaneysville Incident, The   369
Changing Mood in America: Eroding Commitment?, The   550
Chant of Saints   405
Chaperone, The   402
Character Building   486
Characteristics of Teachers   154
Chariot in the Sky: A Story of the Jubilee Singers   283
Chariots Aflame   485
Charles W. Chesnutt   442
Charley Starts from Scratch   321
Charlie Pippin   285
Chasing Rainbows   531
Cheer the Lonesome traveler   325
Chicago Hustle   406
Child Abuse Help Book, The   542
Childhood Disability in Developing Countries   139
Children Are the Reward of Life   135
Children of Bondage   217
Children of Ham, The   517
Children of Long Ago   425
Children of Longing   309
Children of Night   351
Children of Sisyphus, The   438
Children of Strangers: The Stories of a Black Family   252
Children of the Storm   515
Children of the Sun   291
Children's ABC Christmas, The   330
Childtimes: A Three Generation Memoir   307
Chili: Memoirs of a Black Casannova   407
Chilly Stomach   291
Chita's Christmas Tree   317
Chocolate Soldier: A Novel, A   382

Choice and Circumstance 562
Choice of Weapons, A 39
Choice: The Issue of Black Survival in America, The 598
Chosen Place, The Timeless People, The 427
Christian Way in Race Relations, The 482
Christmas Gif' 341
Chuck Berry: The Autobiography 7
Church Action in the World 487
Cinderella 330
Cinema of Ousmane Sembene, A Pioneer African Film, The 199
Circle of Gold 285
Cities and Firms 519
Cities, Suburbs and Blacks 515
City of a Thousand Suns 387
City People 555
Civil Liberties and the Constitution 510
Civil Rights and the Reagan Administration 508
Civil Rights: Leading Cases 513
Civil Rights Movement in America from 1865 to the Present, The 330
Civil Rights: Rhetoric or Reality? 573
Civil Wars 243
Clark College Legacy, The 84
Classical Economics Reconsidered 573
Classical Studies on Physical Activity 493
Claude McKay: The Black Poet at War 398
Clearing and Beyond, The 430
!Click Song 458
Climate of Candor: A Novel of the 1970s, The 450
Climbing Jacob's Ladder 468
Clinical Biomechanics of the Spine 506
Clotel, or, The President's Daughter 374
Cloud with the Silver Lining, The 339
Clover 444
Coagulations: New and Selected Poems 383
Coal 402
Code Name "Zorro" 537
Cold Black Preach 387
Collapse of Cotton Tenancy, The 550
Collected Poems 374

Collected Poems of Sterling A. Brown, The   405
College Education as Personal Development   107
College President, The   152
College Selection Workbook, The   79
Color   384
Color Line and the Quality of Life in America, The   530
Color Purple, The   454
Color, Sex and Poetry   30
Colored Girls and Boys   234
Colored Situation, The   530
Colored Woman in a White World, A   49
Colors Around Me   380
Come and Get It   407
Come September   366
Come Unto Me   470
Coming Home   386
Coming of Age in Mississippi   37
Coming of Chronos to the House of Nightsong, The   407
Coming Together   544
Coming Together: Modern Stories by Black and White Americans   377
Common School and the Negro American, The   103
Communications: A Key to Economic and Political Change   397
Community College Fact Book, The   529
Community College in the South: Progress and Prospects, The   113
Community College Response to the High–Risk Student   144
Community in a Black Pentecostal Church   589
Community of Self, The   467
Community Politics and Educational Change   593
Comparative and International Librarianship   60
Compassion Versus Guilt and Other Essays   573
Compensatory Education for Cultural Deprivation   80
Compensatory Education for the Disadvantaged   114
Competency–Based Teacher Education   143
Complete Poems of Frances E. W. Harper   402
Complete Poems of Paul Laurence Dunbar, The   389
Con Man   405
*Condition, Elevation, Emigration, and Destiny of the Colored People of
   the United States, The*   218
Confessions of a Dirty Ballplayer   200

Confirmation: An Anthology of African American Women 363
Conflict and Conflict Management 545
Conflict of Visions, A 573
Confrontation: Black and White 207
Conjure Tales 292
Conjure Woman, The 292
Conjuring: Black Women, Fiction, and Literary Tradition 440
Conquest, The 250
Consensus and Dissent 395
Constance Stumbles 331
Constitution and Government of Ghana, The 570
Consumer Movement, The 498
Contemporary Administrative and Supervisory Challenges 162
Contemporary African Literature 427
Contemporary Artists of Malaysia 203
Contemporary Black Leaders 300
Contemporary Black Thought 359
Contemporary Black Thought: The Best From Black Scholars 212
Contemporary Poets 411
Contemporary Public Communication Applications 359
Contingency Planning for a Unitary School System 96
*Continuing "Enslavement" of Blind Tom, the Black Pianist–Composer
    (1865–1887), The* 201
Contributions of Black Women to America 217
Contributions of Blacks to the Physical Education Profession 191
*Control of State–Supported Teacher–Training Programs for Negroes,
    The* 93
Cooking the African Way 502
Cooking the Caribbean Way 500
Copper Sun 384
Corazon Aquino: Leader of the Philippines 25
Coretta Scott King 339
Coretta: The Story of Mrs. Martin Luther King, Jr. 50
Cornrows 353
Corregidora 418
Cotillion, or, One Good Bull is Half the Herd, The 421
Cotton Candy on a Rainy Day: Poems 399
Cotton Club, The 234
Cotton Comes to Harlem 408

Cotton Regency, The 274
Counseling Negroes 169
Counseling the Culturally Different Black Youth 160
Counselor and Black/White Relations, The 512
Count on Me 292
Count Your Way Through the Arab World/China/Japan/Russia 315
Countering the Conspiracy to Destroy Black Boys 135
Country Mouse and City Mouse 331
Country Place 439
Courage in Crisis: The Black Professional Today 517
Cow Called Boy, A 339
Craft of Ralph Ellison, The 437
Crazy Kill, The 409
Creole Feast 494
Creoles of Color of New Orleans, The 234
Crime and Its Impact on the Black Community 533
Crime Partners 401
Crisis of the Negro Intellectual, The 215
Crispus Attucks, Boy of Valor 334
Critical Essays on Toni Morrison 429
Critical Examination of the Adams Case: A Source Book, A 122
Cross–Cultural Education 176
*Cross–Cultural Program for Attitude Modification of White Students on
    Predominantly Black University Campus, A* 143
Crossing Difference—Interracial Communication 438
Crusade for Civic Democracy 229
Crusader Without Violence, A Biography of Martin Luther King, Jr. 42
Cry Baby! 404
Cry Revenge 401
Crystal 336
Crystal Breezes: Poems 450
Cultural Pluralism 106
Cultural Pluralism in Education: A Mandate for Change 165
Culture and Language: The Black American Experience 404
Culture, Style, and the Educative Process 158
Curling: A Novel 367
Current Economic Issues and Problems for the Consumer 581
Curriculum and Instruction after Desegregation 83
Curriculum and Instruction in the Elementary School 155

Curriculum Change in Black Colleges 182
Curriculum Change in Black Colleges III 184
Curriculum Change in Black Colleges IV 183
Curriculum Desegregation in Public School 83
Curriculum Evaluation of Black Studies in Relation to Student Knowledge of Afro-American History and Culture, A 148

Daddy 291
Daddy Cool 401
Daddy Is a Monster . . . Sometimes 343
Daddy King: An Autobiography 32
Daddy was a Number Runner 334
Dancers on the Shore 420
Dances of Haiti 191
Dancing Granny, The 289
Dancing: Poems 464
Danger in Centerfield 198
Daniel Alexander Payne, Christian Educator 13
Daniel Defoe: Moll Flanders 358
Daring Black Leaders 228
Dark Ghetto: Dilemmas of Social Power 212
Dark Glory 483
Dark Road Home 366
Dark Salvation 483
Dark Symphony 467
Dark Testament and Other Poems 434
Darl 95
Darlene 304
Darryl Stingley: Happy to Be Alive 48
Date with a Dish: A Cookbook of American Negro Recipes, A 497
Daufuskie Island: A Photographic Essay 252
Daughter's Geography, A 445
Dauntless in Mississippi 23
David, the Story of a King 339
Dawn of a Brighter Day, The 483
Day Care: A Source Book 585
Day Care: Scientific and Social Policy Issues 599
Daydreamers 301
Dead Lecturer: Poems, The 363

Dear John, Dear Coltrane: Poems 404
Death and Duplicity 377
Death for Hire 435
Death List 401
Death Merchants, The 441
Death of an "Uncle Tom." 567
Death of Rhythm and Blues, The 192
Death of White Sociology, The 245
Deception by Stratagem 152
Declining Significance of Race, The 594
Decolonization and Conflict in the United Nations 548
Dedicated . . . Committed 46
Deep River 486
Deep South 526
Deep Woods 442
Deity Nodded, The 431
Delta Crossing 435
Dem 420
Democracy and Public Policy 566
Democracy and the District of Columbia Public Schools 135
Descriptive Statistics: A Self Instruction Program 507
Desegregating America's College 82
Desegregating America's Colleges and Universities 175
Desegregation: The Illusion of Black Progress 72
Desertion of Man, The 267
Design for Desegregation Evaluation, A 120
Dessa Rose 460
Destination Biafra: A Novel 393
Destruction of Black Civilization, The 271
Determined Reader, The 439
Detroit: Race and Uneven Development 524
Developing Effective Instructional Systems 95
Developing Positive Self-Images and Discipline in Black Children 136
Development of Higher Education in the West Indies, The 126
Dexter Avenue Baptist Church, 1877-1977, The 473
Diahann: An Autobiography 10
Dialogue: James Baldwin and Nikki Giovanni, A 509
Diana Ross: Star Supreme 25
Diaries of Willard Motley, The 433

Diary of a Harlem School Teacher 120
Dick Gregory's Bible Tales, With Commentary 475
Dick Gregory's Natural Diet for Folks Who Eat 498
Dick Gregory's Political Primer 537
Dictionary of American Negro Biography 34
Did You Feed My Cow? Street Games, Chants, and Rhymes 290
Die, Nigger, Die! 518
Die the Long Day 438
Different Drummer, A 420
Different Kind of Christmas, A 403
Diplomatic Relations of the United States with Haiti, The 558
Directory of Black Americans in Political Science 595
Disadvantaged Learner: Knowing, Understanding, Educating, The 173
Disappearance, The 308
Disappearing Acts 429
Discipline in the Classroom 172
Discourse and the Other 410
Discrimination and the Welfare of Urban Minorities 536
Distinctive Black College, The 89
Distinguished Negro Georgians 50
Disturbed About Man 479
Diva 380
Do Like Kyla 322
Do Lord Remember Me 424
Do You See My Love for You Growing? 523
Dock Ellis in the Country of Baseball 23
Doctor Dillard of the Jeanes Fund 83
Doctor Shawn 285
Dogs of Fear: A Story of Modern Africa 338
Doing Time 370
Don Baylor: Nothing but the Truth, A Baseball Life 189
Don't Explain: A Song of Billie Holiday 298
Don't Ride the Bus on Monday: The Rosa Parks Story 334
Don't Worry, be Happy 198
Don't You Remember? 294
Don't You Turn Back: Poems 317
Donna Summer: An Unauthorized Biography 29
Dopefiend 401
Double Dog Dare 340

Double Dutch 202
Double Yoke 393
Down Home Southern Cooking 494
Down the Line 258
Dowry: A Novel, The 457
Dr. George Washington Carver, Scientist 16
Dr. J: A Biography of Julius Erving 25
Dr. Martin Luther King, Jr.: Man of Peace 339
Drama in Bahamas 190
Dream Keeper and Other Poems, The 319
Dreamgirl: My Life as a Supreme 52
Drop of Patience, A 421
Drugstore Cat, The 339
Drums of Life 194
Dry Victories 323
Drylongso: A Self-Portrait of Black America 230
Duane Thomas and the Fall of America's Team 202
DuBois: A Pictorial Biography 16
Duey's Tale 360
Duke Ellington in Person: An Intimate Memoir 192
Dunfords Travels Everywheres 421
Duplication of Schools for Negro Youth 176
Dusk of Dawn 219
Dust of Uncertain Journey 430
Dust Tracks on a Road: An Autobiography 30
Dustland 310
Dutchman and the Slave: Two Plays 363
Dying Is So Easy 449
Dynamics of the African Afro-American Connection 215

Early Field Experiences in Teacher Education 106
Early Negro American Writers 370
Ears and Tails and Common Sense 342
Earthquake 341
Earthquakes and Sunrise Missions 426
Eastern Religions in the Electric Age 474
Easy Steps to a Large Vocabulary 365
Easy Steps to Correct Speech 365
Easy Steps to Good Grammar 365

Easy Way to Better Grades, The 110
Ebonics: The True Language of Black Folks 460
Ebony and Topaz, a Collectanea 418
Ebony Cookbook: A Date with a Dish, The 497
Ebony Handbook, The 259
Ebony Rhythm 433
Ebony Tree and the Spirit of Christmas, The 403
Echo in My Soul 12
Echo of Lions: A Novel 379
Economic Status of Negroes, The 240
Economic Value of Negro Education, The 103
Economics and Politics of Race, The 574
Economics-in-Action 535
Economics of Minority Groups 535
Economics: Analysis and Issues 574
Edith Jackson 308
Edna Lewis Cookbook, The 501
Education and the Cultural Crisis 128
Education and the Segregation Issue 125
Education for an Open Society 101
Education for Black Humanism: A Study of Approaching It 173
Education for Negroes in Mississippi Since 1910 180
Education for Peace: Focus on Mankind 123
Education for the Black Race 97
Education in the 80's: Multiethnic Education 76
Education in the British West Indies 174
Education in Theory and Practice 132
Education Law 550
Education of Black Americans, The 172
Education of Black Folk, The 75
Education of Black People in Florida, The 156
Education of Black Philadelphia, The 109
Education of Blacks in the South, 1860–1935, The 73
Education of Negro Ministers, The 471
Education of Negro Teachers 90
Education of Negroes: A 5-Year Bibliography, 1931–1935 56
Education of the Afro-American in America 170
Education of the Negro Child, The 89
Education of the Negro in the American Social Order 80

Education of the Negro Prior to 1861, The 181
Education: Assumptions Versus History: Collected Essays 163
Educational Administration and Policy 118
Educational Alternatives for Colonized People 176
Educational Needs of Minority Groups, The 92
Educational Psychology and Teaching 161
Educational Psychology for the Secondary School Teacher 107
*Educational Status of Children During the First School Year Following
    Four Years of Little or no Schooling, The* 116
Educational Status of Children in a District Without Public Schools, The
    117
*Educators' Diagnostic Guidebook and Reference Manual for Problems
    in Reading* 81
Edward Wilmot Blyden: Pan-Negro Patriot, 1832-1912 248
Effective Education: A Minority Policy Perspective 177
Effective Leader, The 474
Effective Teacher, The 474
Ego-Tripping and Other Poems for Young People 302
Egypt Revisited 269
Eight Black American Inventors 316
Eldorado Red 401
Electing Black Mayors 564
Elitism vs. Democracy in Community Organizations 536
Eliza's Daddy 347
Elm City, A Negro Community in Action 262
Elusive Equality 145
Ely: An Autobiography 22
Ely: Too Black, Too White 536
Emancipation Proclamation, The 224
Emergence of Black Colleges, The 114
Emerging Concepts for Collaboration: Selected Papers 127
Emigrants, The 423
Empire Star 387
Employment of Negroes in the District of Columbia, The 536
Enchanted Hair Tale, An 298
Encyclopedia of Black America, The 64
Endangered Black Family, The 538
Enemies: The Clash of Races 558
Energies: Americanfolk Poetry 375

Epistemics: Personalizing the Process of Change 487
Equal Educational Opportunity for Blacks in U.S. Higher Education 71
Equal Educational Opportunity: More Promise Than Progress 71
E-Qual-ity Education in North Carolina Among Negroes 86
Equality of Educational Opportunity: A Hand-book for Research 142
Era of Reconstruction 1863-1877, The 273
Eros and Freedom in Southern Life and Thought 267
Escape to Freedom: A Play About Young Frederick Douglass 297
Essays in Ancient Egyptian Studies 211
Essays on Criticism, Theory, and Writing by Black Women 456
Essentials of Economics 581
Ethics in College Sports 159
Ethics: An Introduction to Moral Philosophy 467
Ethnic America: A History 261
Ethnic American Minorities 62
Ethnic Autonomy—Comparative Dynamics, the Americas, Europe, 537
Ethnic Dynamics 548
Ethnic Image in Modern American Literature-1900-1950, The 376
Ethnic-Sensitive Social Work Practice 528
Eva's Man 418
Everett Anderson's 1 2 3 294
Everett Anderson's Christmas Coming 294
Everett Anderson's Friend 294
Everett Anderson's Goodbye 295
Everett Anderson's Nine Month Lag 295
Everett Anderson's Year 295
Evers 17
Every Goodbye Ain't Gone 435
Everything and Nothing: The Dorothy Dandridge Tragedy 191
Evolution of the Negro College, The 125
Execution by Choice 456
Exodusters 253
Experiences of a Fulbright Teacher 72
Exploring Careers: Jobs in Business and Office 498
Exploring Professional Cooking 503
*Exploring the Known and Unknown Factors in the Rates of Alcoholism
    Among Black and White Females* 522
Eyes on the Prize 589

Faces of America: A History of the U.S. 261
Facts of Reconstruction, The 248
Fallen Angels 336
Fallen Prince 48
Families in Peril: An Agenda for Social Change 529
Families of Black Prisoners: Survival and Progress 578
Family and Personal Development in Adult Basic Education 100
Family Life and School Achievement 94
Family Life of Black People, The 593
Family Pictures 372
Famous American Negro Poets 341
Famous American Negroes 319
Famous Black Entertainers of Today 277
Famous Modern Negro Musicians 197
Famous Negro Athletes 284
Famous Negro Entertainers of Stage, Screen and TV 341
Famous Negro Heroes of America 30
Famous Negro Music Makers 319
Fannie Lou Hamer 323
Fascinating Story of Black Kentuckians, A 221
Fashion Exhibition 501
Fast Sam, Cool Clyde, and Stuff 336
Fast Sounder Hound, The 285
Fast Track 405
Father of the Blues: An Autobiography 23
Father of the Man: How Your Child Gets His Personality 525
Fatherhood 523
Faulkner and Black–White Relations 418
Feeling Through: New Poems 360
Female Crime and Delinquency 559
Femi and Old Grandaddie 340
Fences: A Play 462
Fiction of Stephen Crane, The 398
Fifteen Methods of Teaching Secondary School Subjects 143
Fifth Sunday: Stories 388
Fight for Freedom: The Story of the NAACP 548
Fighting Shirley Chisholm 25
Figures in Black 397
Filipino Nation, The 235

Financial and Strategic Management for Nonprofit Organizations 494
Finders Keepers, Losers Weepers: A Novel 435
Finding A Way Out: An Autobiography 37
Finding My Way 156
Fire in the Flint, The 458
Fire Next Time, The 508
Firespitter 383
First Book of Africa, The 319
First Book of American Negroes, The 353
First Book of Jazz, The 195
First Book of Negroes, The 319
First Book of Rhythms, The 195
First Book of the West Indies, The 239
First Grade Log 106
First Negro Medical Society, The 495
First Pink Light 305
Five Black Lives 8
Five Black Scholars 591
Five Black Writers 399
Five French Negro Authors 382
Five on the Black Hand Side: A Play in Three Acts 443
Five Plays 411
Flagellants, The 440
Flashbacks: A Twenty-Year Diary of Article Writing 458
Flight 458
Florida Supreme Court, The 511
Flossie and the Fox 329
Fly Jimmy Fly! 336
Flying 296
Flying High 203
Focus on Curriculum Change in Black Colleges II 182
*For Colored Girls Who Have Considered Suicide/When the Rainbow Is
    Enuf* 445
For Love of Imabelle 409
For My People 455
For Us, the Living 17
Forerunners: Black Poets in America, The 423
Forever Free 344
Forever Friends 285

Forward March 185
Foundations of American Education 153
Foundations of Intercultural Communication 381
Foundations of Urban Education 142
Four Took Freedom 47
Fourteenth Cadillac, The 321
Foxtrap: A Novel 435
Frederick Douglass 41
Frederick Douglass: The Black Lion 331
Frederick Douglass: Freedom Fighter 339
Frederick Douglass: The Orator 22
Free at Last 470
Free at Last: The Life of Frederick Douglass 210
Free Frank: A Black Pioneer on the Antebellum Frontier 269
Free Man of Color 29
Free Negro in North Carolina, 1790–1860, The 225
Free Negro in Texas, 1800–1860 274
Freedom, Courts, Politics: Studies in Civil Liberties 510
Freedom Ship of Robert Smalls, The 334
Freedom Song 554
Freedom Train: The Story of Harriet Tubman 344
Freedom – When? New York: Random House, 1965 531
Freedom's First Generation 222
Freedom's Plow 411
Freemasonry, Ancient Egypt and the Islamic Destiny 529
Freight Train 296
Friends, The 308
Friendship, The 345
From a Caste to a Minority 590
From a Land Where Other People Live 425
From a Plow to a Doctorate—So What? 169
From Behind the Veil 449
From Brown to Boston 133
From Columbus to Castro 271
From Ghetto to Glory: The Story of Bob Gibson 193
From LeRoi Jones to Amiri Baraka: The Literary Works 411
From Lew Alcindor to Kareem Abdul Jabbar 25
From Okra to Greens: A Different Kinda Love Story 445
From Okra to Greens: Poems 445

From Paragraph to Theme: Understanding and Practice 410
From Slavery to Freedom: A History of Negro Americans 225
From the Back of the Bus 403
From the Dark Tower: Afro–American Writers 1900 to 1960 385
From the Windows of My Mind: Poems 446
Fulcrums of Change 211
Fundamentals of Islamic Education 157
Future of the American Negro, The 585

Gambling: Who Really Wins? 194
Games as Learning Tools 166
Garies and their Friends, The 457
Garvey: Story of a Pioneer Black Nationalist 300
Gatekeepers of Black Culture 63
Gates Shall Not, The 470
Gather Together in My Name 5
Gathering, The 310
Gathering of Old Men, A 396
Gemini 21
Gender Influences in Classroom Interaction 174
General Education in the Negro College 102
General Semantics and the Social Sciences 590
Generations: A Memoir 295
Generations: Poetry, 1969–1985 443
Gentleman Pimp: An Autobiography 31
Geography of the Near Past: Poems 464
George McGinnis: Basketball Superstar 26
George Washington Carver 60
George Washington Williams: A Biography 19
Georgia Negro: A History, The 227
Getting It Together 476
Getting Started in Tennis 279
Getting the Most out of High School 156
Ghana Folk Tales: Ananse Stories from Africa 356
Ghetto: A Bibliography, The 56
Ghetto: Readings and Interpretations, The 524
GI Diary 254
Giant Steps: The Autobiography 3
Giant Talk: An Anthology of Third World Writers 451

Giants for Justice 352
Gift-Giver, The 314
Gift of Black Folk, The 220
Gilded Six-Bits: Love is Fragile, The 415
Giovanni's Room: A Novel 362
Girl Called Bob, A Horse Named Yoki, A 291
Girl on the Outside, The 349
Give Birth to Brightness 461
Give Us Each Day: The Diary of Alice Dunbar-Nelson 16
Global Dimensions of the African Diaspora 232
Go South with Christ: A Study in Race Relations 222
Go Tell it on the Mountain 362
Go Up for Glory 44
God and Human Freedom 489
God Bless the Child 415
God Made Alaska for the Indians: Selected Essays 441
God Made Something Wonderful 331
God Wash the World and Start Again 303
God's Beloved Rebel: An Autobiography 9
God's Trombones 322
Going to Meet the Man 362
Going to the Territory 392
Going to School: The African-American Experience 138
Gold Cadillac, The 345
Golden Lynx, The 279
Golden Pasture, The 348
Golden Shaft, The 435
Golden Slippers 284
Goldwater and the Republic That Was 261
Good Foods for Good Health 498
Good High School: Portraits of Character and Culture, The 137
Good Morning Blues: The Autobiography of Count Basie 6
Good Morning Mrs. "B" 130
Good Neighborhood: The Challenge of Open Housing 561
Good News 305
Good News About Earth: New Poems 380
Good News on Grape Street 121
Good Night Willie Lee, I'll See You in the Morning 454
Good Programs for Young Children 557

Good, Says Jerome 295
Good Times: Poems 295
Good Woman: Poems and a Memoir, 1969–1980 295
Gorilla, My Love 279
Gotta Pay to Live 449
Grace Notes: Poems 388
Grandmama's Joy 305
Grandmother's Pictures 296
Grandpa's Face 305
Grandsire: Poems 419
Great American Crazies, The 29
Great Gittin' Up Morning 421
Great Minu 352
Great Negroes Past and Present 278
Great Recollections From Aggieland 576
Great Teachers 143
Great Texts from Romans 483
Greatest: My Own Story, The 4
Green Lion of Zion Street, The 302
Griffin's Way: A Novel 463
Griot: A Novel, The 440
Groundings with my Brothers, The 569
Groundwork 37
Group Counseling Theory and Process 475
Growin' 307
Growing up in the Black Belt 549
Guardian Angels, The 540
Guests in the Promised Land 320
Gwendolyn Brooks: Poetry and the Heroic Voice 429

Haiku Reflections 365
Haiti and the Dominican Republic 246
Haiti and the Great Powers, 1902–1915 255
Halfway to the Sun 430
Hamdaani: A Traditional Tale from Zanzibar 283
Hamp: An Autobiography 23
Handbook for Dynamic Supervision for the Public and Private Sector,
    A 496
Handbook of Intercultural Communication 359

Handbook on Michigan Education Law 550
Handbook on the Psychology of Hemoglobin – S, The 501
Hansel and Gretel 287
Harbor 297
Hard Road to Glory, A 187
Harder We Run: Black Workers Since the Civil War, The 233
Harlem, Haiti, and Havana 381
Harlem Renaissance Remembered: Essays, The 368
Harlem, U.S.A. 213
Harlem: A Community in Transition 213
Harlem: A History of Broken Dreams 230
Harlem: The Story of a Changing Community 353
"Harold," The People's Mayor 50
Harriet and the Promised Land 325
Harriet Tubman 339
Have a Happy 349
He, Too, Spoke for Democracy 561
Head Above Water 17
Healing Heat: Poems, 1973–1988 414
Hearing the Noise: My Life in the NFL 199
Heart As Evergreen, The 443
Heart of a Woman, The 5
Heart of Man: Dr. Daniel Hale Williams, The 334
Heartbeat 424
Heat's On, The 409
Heirloom Poetry Sample 375
Heist, The 404
Hell Has No Exit 399
Hell Is Forever 399
Help With Finding a Job 493
Her Poems: An Anniversaric Chronology 366
Here I Stand 43
Hermit–Woman: Poems, The 418
Hero Ain't Nothin' but a Sandwich, A 292
Hero and the Blues, The 433
Herschel Walker's Basic Training 505
Herstory: Black Female Rites of Passage 556
Hezekiah Horton 449
Hi, Mrs. Mallory! 347

Hidden Lookout 288
Higher Education Among Negroes 141
Higher Education: Myths, Realities, and Possibilities 113
Higher Education's Responsibility for Advancing Equality of Opportunity and Justice 93
Hills of Hebron, A Jamaican Novel, The 463
Hippodrome: A Novel, The 382
His Day Is Marching On: A Memoir of W.E.B. DuBois 16
His Eye Is On the Sparrow: An Autobiography 51
His Own Where. 323
Historic Tour of N.C. A and T State University, The 165
Historical Judgements Reconsidered 250
History in the School: What Shall We Teach? 227
History of Alpha Phi Alpha, The 173
History of Black Americans, A 243
History of Blacks in Higher Education, 1875–1975, A 58
History of Education from the Greeks to the Present Time 127
History of Fisk University, 1865–1946, A 154
History of Florida Agricultural and Mechanical University, The 148
History of Grambling State University, A 110
History of Morehouse College 83
History of My Life and Work, The 33
History of Negro Education in the South, A 88
History of Negro Soldiers in the Spanish–American War and Other Items of Interest 242
History of Public Library Service to Negroes in the South, A 66
History of Schools for Negroes in the District of Columbia, The 99
History of the American Teachers Association 151
History of the Association of Colleges and Secondary Schools, A 97
History of the Chicago Urban League 577
History of the Education of Negroes in North Carolina, A 87
History of the Mississippi Teachers Association, The 168
History of the Negro Baptists of Tennessee 474
History of the Negro Race in America From 1619 to 1880 272
History of the Tennessee Education Congress, 1923–1967 86
History of the Virginia Teachers Association 151
History of World Societies, A 250
History of the Black Public Schools of Montgomery County, Maryland 1872–1961 213

Hitting the Aaron Way 187
Hold Fast to Dreams: Poems Old and New 284
Holders of Doctorates Among American Negroes 117
Holt English 293
Holy Violence 40
Home Boy 314
Home Coming: Poems 443
Home Girls: A Black Feminist Anthology 572
Home to Harlem 428
Home: Social Essays 551
Homecookin': Five Plays 402
Homegirls and Handgrenades 443
Homespun Images 387
Homesteader: A Novel, The 430
Honey, I Love and Other Love Poems 305
Hoo-doo 5, Special Women's Issue 381
Hoodoo Hollerin' Bebop Ghosts 436
Hoops 336
Hooray! Hooray! David Is the One 331
Hornes: An American Family, The 9
Horses Make a Landscape Look More Beautiful: Poems 455
Hot Day, Hot Night 409
Hot Dog Man, The 327
Hot Snake Nights 389
House of Dies Drear, The 310
How Europe Underdeveloped Africa 569
How I Got Ovah 443
How It Is 369
How Relevant Is Education in America Today? 158
How Shall They Preach 485
How the Leopard Got His Claws 278
How to Be a Growing Christian 474
How to Become a Successful Student 110
How to Change Careers 503
How to Get a Career Job 494
How to Get a Grant for Your Own Special Project 576
How to Make Animal Models 302
How to Make It in College 126

How to Talk "With" People of Other Races, Ethnic Groups, and Cultures 448
Howard University Department of History, 1913–1973, The 273
Howard University The Capstone of Negro Education 222
Howard University 138
Howdy, Honey, Howdy 389
Human Mandolin, The 318
Human Oddities: An Exploratory Study 482
Human Relations in the Military 499
Human Relations: From Theory to Practice 543
Humanities: Lecture–Discussion Syllabus 254
Humanizing the Desegregated School 142
Hundred Penny Box, The 327
Hungry Catch the Foolish Boy 303
Hurricane 341
Hurry Up, America, & Spit 55
Hypertension Among Blacks 60

I Always Wanted to Be Somebody 21
I Am a Black Woman 393
I Am Third 200
I Can Do It by Myself 327
I Dug Graves at Night to Attend College by Day 18
I Greet the Dawn: Poems 389
I Have Changed 565
I Hear Them Calling My Name 226
I Know Why the Caged Bird Sings 5
I Look at Me 300
I Love Myself When I am Laughing 415
I Need a Lunch Box 291
I Never Had It Made: The Autobiography of Jackie Robinson 43
I Never Scream: New and Selected Poems 424
I Swore I'd Never Lose It Again 357
I Wish I Had an Afro 342
I Wonder as I Wander: An Autobiographical Journey 30
I Wouldn't Take Nothin' for My Journey 207
I'm Gonna Make You Love Me: The Story of Diana Ross 26
I'm Off to See the Goddam Wizard, Alright! 366
I've Been a Woman: New and Selected Poems 444

Iceman: Canadian Kill, The 435
Iceman: Spinning Target, The 435
Idylls of the Season 365
If Beale Street Could Talk 362
If He Hollers, Let Him Go 409
If They Come in the Morning: Voices of Resistance 527
If We Must Die 392
Iguana's Tail 342
Illustrated Bio–Bibliography of Black Photographers, An 204
Image of the Black in Western Art, The 201
Images of Kin: New and Selected Poems 404
Images of the Negro in America 453
Imamu Amiri Baraka (Leroi Jones) 411
Impact of School Desegregation in A Southern City, The 140
Impact on Reading 371
Imperialism and Dependency 564
Implications of Existential Psychology for the Black Experience with Application to Education, The 152
Impressions 391
Impressions in Asphalt 446
In a Minor Chord 451
In Black and White: Afro–Americans in Print 46
In Love and Trouble: Stories of Black Women 455
In Pursuit of Equality in Higher Education 153
In Pursuit of Flavor 501
In Search of America 224
In Search of Our Mothers' Gardens 455
In Spite of the System 172
In Struggle: SNCC and the Black Awakening of the 1960s 521
In the Beginning: Creation Stories from Around the World 475
In the Cage: Eyewitness Accounts of the Freed Negro 238
In the Castle of My Skin 423
In the Ditch 530
In the Evidence of Things Not Seen 508
In the Midst of Change: Poems 446
In The Matter of Color 544
Index to Poetry by Black American Women 56
Infants in the Spring 450
Informal Adoption Among Black Families 544

Inner City Hoodlum 401
Inspiriting Influences 360
Instructional Development 125
Instructional Planning in the Secondary School 111
Integrated Cookbook: The Soul of Good Cooking, The 500
Integration of American Schools, The 120
Integration or Separation in Education: K–12 174
Intelligence and Cultural Differences 472
Intelligence: Nature, Determinants and Consequences 468
International Conference on Black Communication 458
International   Handbook   of   Contemporary   Developments   in
Librarianship 61
International Law of Development, The 564
Into the Clearing 430
Into the Mainstream 241
Introduction to American Education 123
Introduction to Black Literature in America, An 438
Introduction to Black Sociology 576
Invented Lives: Narratives of Black Women 1860–1960 457
Inventory of Academic Leadership 146
Invisible Man, The 393
Invisible Politics: Black Political Behavior 584
I.Q. Game, The 578
Irritated Genie: An Essay on the Haitian Revolution, The 211
Is Anyone Listening to Black America? 557
Is for Africa, A 283
Is Massa Day Dead? Black Moods in the Caribbean 214
Isaac Watts: His Life and Works 14
Islamic Social and Educational Issues 146
Island Possessed 221
Issues in Marriage, Family and Therapy 578
Issues in Year–Round Education 154
It Ain't All for Nothin' 336
It's a New Day: Poems for Young Brothers and Sistuhs 342
It's Good to Be Alive 10
Ivory and Ebony Towers, The 177

J. D. 300
Jack and the Beanstalk 287

Jackie Robinson, My Own Story 44
Jackie Robinson's Little League Baseball Book 341
Jacob's Ladder: A Novel 459
Jafta 326
Jahdu 311
Jake Gaither, America's Most Famous Black Coach 191
Jambalaya 485
Jambo Means Hello: Swahili Alphabet Book 301
James Baldwin: A Critical Evaluation 437
James Van DerZee: The Picture–Takin' Man 315
James Weldon Johnson 299
Jane Edna Hunter 243
Janie Belle 449
Jasper the Drummin' Boy 290
Jay and the Marigold 340
Jazz Masters of the Thirties 202
Jazz. 319
Jean Toomer, Artist 37
Jean Toomer: A Critical Evaluation 437
Jeffrey Bear Cleans Up His Act 343
Jennifer's New Chair 283
Jesse Jackson Phenomenon, The 568
Jesse Jackson: America's David 43
Jesse: A Spiritual Autobiography 39
Jesus and Fat Tuesday and Other Short Stories 428
Jesus Bag, The 475
Jim Flying High 300
Jimmy Lee Did It 297
Jive and Slang of Students in Negro Colleges 368
Jobs in Business and Office 499
Joe Louis: 50 Years an American Hero 188
Joe Louis 58
Joe Louis: My Life 35
Joe Turner's Come and Gone: A Play in Two Acts 462
John Brown 220
John Brown: A Cry for Freedom 303
Jojo 298
Jokes from Black Folks 406
Jonah Simpson 341

Jonah's Gourd Vine 415
Journey 450
Journey Back: Issues in Black Literature and Criticism, The 360
Journey out of Anger 459
Journey Toward Hope: A History of Blacks in Oklahoma 224
Joys of Motherhood: A Novel, The 393
Jubilee 456
Julius K. Nyerere: Teacher of Africa 304
Jump Bad: A New Chicago Anthology 373
Junior Bachelor Society, The 459
Junior High School Art Curriculum 191
Junius Over Far 311
Just Above My Head 362
Just an Overnight Guest 344
Just Between Us Blacks 570
Just Give Me a Cool Drink of Water 'fore I Diiie 357
Just My Luck 335
Just Us Women 291
Justice and Her Brothers 311
Justin and the Best Biscuit in the World 349

Kane–Butler Genealogy: History of a Black Family 10
Kansas: A Novel 448
Kareem 3
Kasamance: A Fantasy 391
Kasho and the Twin Flutes 341
Katharine Drexel, Friend of the Neglected 485
Katharsis 451
Katherine Dunham 26
Katherine Dunham's Journey to Accompong 221
Katrina Stands Alone 89
Keep the Faith, Baby! 483
Keeping the Faith 539
Kemet and the African Worldview 243
Kennedy Years and the Negro, The 259
Kenneth B. Clark, A Bibliography 62
Kenyatta's Escape 401
Kenyatta's Last Hit 401
Kicks is Kicks 370

Killer Cop 435
Killing Memory, Seeking Ancestors 426
Kimako's Story 323
Kind of Marriage, A 394
Kindergarten Log, The 106
Kinds of Blues: Musical Memoirs 204
King God Didn't Save, The 589
King, Malcolm, Baldwin: Three Interviews 521
King Strut 449
King: A Biography of Martin Luther King, Jr. 34
King: A Critical Biography 556
King's New Clothes, The 331
Knee-High Man and Other Tales, The 325
Knock Ten: A Novel of Mining Life 287
Knot in the Thread, A 18
*Knowing and Understanding the Socially Disadvantaged Ethnic
    Minority Groups* 270
Knowledge and Decisions 574
Ku Klux Klan: A Bibliography, The 59

Lady Cavaliers, The 424
Lady Sings the Blues 195
Lagos Plan of Action Versus the Berg Report, The 211
Lakestown Rebellion, The 415
Langston Hughes, American Poet 348
Langston Hughes, Black Genius 437
Langston Hughes Reader, The 411
Langston Hughes: An Introduction to the Poetry 418
Langston Hughes: Before and Beyond Harlem 366
Langston: A Play 297
Language, Communication, and Rhetoric in Black America 447
Lasers as Reactants and Probes in Chemistry 500
Last Summer with Maizon 353
Last Toke, The 370
Lasting Impression, A 582
Laughing to Keep from Crying 411
Lawd Today 463
Lay Bare the Heart 223
Leaders of the Middle East 235

Leadership, Love, and Aggression   13
Leadership Plus Administration in School Management   163
Learn By Doing   101
Learning Disabilities for the Classroom Teacher   86
*Learning English as a Second Language for Secondary Schools and
    Continuing Education*   458
Learning To Be Free   150
Legal Outlook   164
Legal Rights of Teachers and Students   73
Legend of Tarik, The   336
Legend of the Saints   339
Legends of Suriname   286
Legislation of Morality, The   528
Lemon Swamp and Other Places: A Carolina Memoir   18
Lena   195
Lena Horne   26
Lena: A Personal and Professional Biography of Lena Horne   28
Lengthening Shadow of Slavery, The   108
LeRoi Jones (Amiri Baraka) Bibliography, A   60
Leslie Uggams Beauty Book, The   505
Lessons From History: A Celebration in Blackness   324
Let No Man Write My Epitaph   432
Let Noon Be Fair: A Novel   432
Let the Circle Be Unbroken   345
Let's Face Racism   274
Let's Go!   281
Let's Hear It for the Queen   293
Let's See the Animals   281
Let's Take a Trip   281
Let's Work Together   274
Letters to a Black Boy   579
Liberation and Reconciliation: A Black Theology   484
Lie and Say You Love Me: Poems   428
Life and Death of Martin Luther King, Jr., The   26
Life and Times of Frederick Douglass, The   14
Life and Works of Paul Laurence Dunbar, The   390
Life and Writings of Frederick Douglass, The   15
Life of Langston Hughes, Vol. 1: 1902–1941, The   41
Life of Langston Hughes, Vol. 2: 1941–1967, The   42

Lifelong Career Planning   497
Lift Every Voice and Sing   323
Lift Every Voice and Sing: A Collection of Afro–American Spirituals and Other Songs   477
Lift Every Voice   47
Light   297
Light Ahead for the Negro   242
Lillie of Watts Takes a Giant Step   350
Lillie of Watts: A Birthday Discovery   350
Lincoln and the Negro   41
Linden Hills   434
Lines to A Little Lady   394
Lion and the Ostrich Chicks and Other African Tales   290
Lisping Leaves   365
Listen Children: An Anthology of Black Literature   449
Listen for the Fig Tree   327
Little   305
Little Brown Baby   299
Little Love, A   311
Little Man in the Family   342
Little Man, Little Man: A Story of Childhood   279
Little Red Hen, The   331
Little Stepping Stones to Correct English   365
Little Stepping Stones to Correct Speech   365
Little Tree Growing in the Shade, A   353
Live and Off–Color: News Biz   68
Living Black American Authors   45
Living Room: New Poems   420
Living Soul: "We Shall Overcome   470
Living with Others   157
Lo These Many Years: An Autobiographical Sketch   47
Logic of Science in Sociology, The   583
Lonely Crusade   409
Lonely Rage, A   44
Lonesome Boy   284
Lonesome Road, The   567
Long Black Song   360
Long Dream: A Novel, The   463
Long Hard Journey, A   332

Long Journey Home: Stories from Black History 325
Long Memory: The Black Experience in America 207
Long Shadow of Little Rock, a Memoir, The 6
Long Struggle: The Story of American Labor, The 540
Long Way from Home, A 428
Long White Con 364
Look Out, Whitey! Black Power's Gon' Get Your Mama! 555
Look to the Hills 483
Looking Back 22
Looking for a Country Under Its Original Name 428
Lordy, Aunt Hattie 347
Lost Zoo, The 378
Lou in the Limelight 320
Louis Armstrong, Young Music Maker 334
Love, Black Love 527
Love Is a Terrible Thing 433
Love My Children: An Autobiography 9
Love of Landry, The 390
Love Poems 444
Love's Silken Web 436
Lover's Holiday 425
Lovesong: Becoming A Jew 33
Lower Income Family in Saint Paul, The 576
LT: Living on the Edge 49
Lucky Stone, The 295
Ludell 351
Ludell and Willie 351
Ludell's New York Time 351
Luminous Darkness, The 580
Lyles Station: Yesterday and Today 248
Lyrics of Love and Laughter 390
Lyrics of Lowly Life 390
Lyrics of the Hearthside 390

M. C. Higgins, the Great 311
M. I. A.: Saigon 356
Mabel Mercer: A Life 26
Macking Gangster 405
Maggie's American Dream 13

Magic 31
Magic Mirrors, The 307
Magic of Black Poetry, The 277
Magic: A Biography of Earvin Johnson 26
Magical Adventures of Pretty Pearl, The 312
Mainstreaming Outsiders 79
Major Black Religious Leaders, 1755–1940 488
Major Black Religious Leaders Since 1940 489
Make a Joyful Noise Unto the Lord! 321
Makeba: My Story 35
Making Choices for Multicultural Education 159
Making of an Afro-American, The 47
Making of Black Revolutionaries, The 224
Making Schools Work 109
Malcolm X Speaks 597
Malcolm X 32
Mama 429
Mama Black Widow 364
Mama Day 434
Man Ain't Nothin' but a Man, A 421
Man Called White, A 51
Man Sharing: Dilemma or Choice? 521
Man Who Cried I Am, The 459
Man's Life: An Autobiography, A 51
Managing Human Services 560
Manchild in the Promised Land 9
Mansart Builds a School 388
March Toward Freedom 280
Marcia 343
Marcus Garvey: An Annotated Bibliography 58
Marcus Garvey and the Vision of Africa 522
Marcus Garvey and Universal Negro Improvement Association 236
Marcus Garvey and Universal Negro Improvement Association 236
Marcus Garvey: Life and Lessons 29
Maria W. Stewart, America's First Black Woman Political Writer 257
Mariah Loves Rock 350
Marian Anderson 67
Marianna 252
Mark Well Made, A 268

Marked by Fire 348
Markets and Minorities 575
Marrow of Tradition, The 379
Martin Luther King, Jr. 352
Martin Luther King, Jr., Boy with a Dream 335
Martin Luther King, Jr.: God's Messenger of Love, Justice, and Hope
    474
Martin Luther King, Jr.: His Life and Dream 18
Marva Collins' Way 95
Marxism: Philosophy and Economics 575
Mary Jane 344
Mary McLeod Bethune 306
Masquerade, an Historical Novel, The 430
Mass Communication: Principles and Practices 377
Master Plan: A Novel, The 375
Masters of the Dew 414
Matthew Simpson Dauage 468
Maude Martha 372
Maya Angelou: Poems 357
McGraw–Hill Introduction to Literature, The 433
Me and Neesie 306
Me, Mop, and the Moondance Kid 336
Meanness Mania: The Changed Mood 534
Measure of Man, The 478
Measure of Time, A 309
"Measurement Mystique," The 131
Mechanics and Conventions in Formal Writing 396
Medea and Some Poems, The 384
Media and Government: An Annotated Bibliography 59
Medical Care and the Plight of the Negro 495
Medicine Man: Collected Poems 409
Medley 391
Melville's Israel Potter: A Pilgrimage and Progress 440
Memoirs of Dolly: A High School Graduate, The 444
Mental Health and People of Color 494
Mental Health Team in the Schools, The 136
Mental Health: A Challenge to the Black Community 533
Meridan 455
Message of Tourist Art, The 197

Message to the Blackman in America   482
Messy Bessey   332
Messy Bessey's Closet   332
Metropolitan Desegregation   116
Metropolitan School Desegregation   114
Mets from Mobil: Tommie Agee, Cleon Jones, The   353
Microbiology: An Environmental Perspective   498
Middle Wall, The   470
Midnight Birds   457
Midnight's Daughter   419
Migrations of the Heart   21
Miles: The Autobiography   14
Militant Black Writer in Africa and the United States, The   382
Mind of the Negro, The   267
Mine Eyes Have Seen   470
Ministry: The Field for the Talented Tenth, The   481
Mink: A Novel   448
Minorities and Aging   548
Minorities and the American Dream   559
Minorities in Kansas: In Quest for Equal Opportunity   570
Minorities in the City   462
Minorities in U.S. Institutions of Higher Education   165
Minority Access and Achievement in Higher Education   166
Minority Aging   559
Minority Economic, Political and Social Development   535
Minority Education and Caste   149
Minority Executives' Handbook, The   494
Minority Presence in American Literature, 1600–1900, The   376
Minority Vote Dilution   525
Mirandy and Brother Wind   329
Mirror of Her Own   309
Mis–Education of the Negro, The   182
Mississippi Black History Makers   45
Missouri's Black Heritage   229
Mixed Blessing   561
Mixed Families: Adopting Across Racial Boundaries   555
Model of Mass Communications and National Development, A   454
Modern Black Poets: A Collection of Critical Essays   399
Modern Food Microbiology   500

Modern Negro Art 200
Modernism and the Harlem Renaissance 361
Moderns: An Anthology of New Writing in America, The 363
Moja Means One: The Swahili Counting Book 301
Monkey–Monkey's Trick 329
Montage of a Dream Deferred 411
Moonlight Bride, The 299
Moonwalk 196
Moonwalker: The Storybook 196
Moral Norms and Moral Order 468
More Adventures of Spider 278
More Tales of Uncle Remus 326
More Than Dancing 196
More Than Drumming 196
Morgan State College Program, The 128
Morris Brown College 157
Moses, Man of the Mountain 415
Most Native of Sons, The 52
Mother/Child Father/Child Relationships 577
Mother Crocodile = Maiman–Caiman 298
Mothersill and the Foxes 459
Motif for Living and Other Sermons, A 485
Motivating and Preparing Black Youth to Work 555
Motown and Didi: A Love Story 337
Mouth on Paper 383
Movable School Goes to the Negro Farmer, The 92
Movement: Documentary of a Struggle for Equality, The 231
Movin' On Up 31
Movin' Up 21
Mr. Bojangles: The Biography of Bill Robinson 28
Mr. Kelso's Lion 284
Mr. Monkey and the Gotcha Bird 337
Mr. T: The Man with the Gold: An Autobiography 48
Mrs. Flowers: A Moment of Friendship 357
Mufaro's Beautiful Daughters 343
Muhammad Ali 352
Muhammad Ali, the People's Champ 299
Mukasa 338
Mules and Men 416

Mules Done Long Since Gone, The 428
Multi-Cul 149
Multi-Cultural Education Clinic Papers 150
Multicultural Counseling 471
Multicultural Education in Western Societies 78
Multicultural Education Through Competency-Based Teacher Education 126
Multicultural Education Through Competency-Based Teacher Education 185
Multicultural Education: A Source Book 153
Multicultural Education: A Synopsis 78
Multicultural Education: Issues and Perspectives 77
Multicultural Elementary Classrooms 130
Multiethnic Education: Theory and Practice 75
Multimedia Materials for Afro-American Studies 128
Museum: Poems 388
Mushecho: A Girl's Purity Rite, The 551
Music from Home: Selected Poems 428
Music is My Mistress 192
Music of Black Americans: A History, The 201
Music on My Mind: The Memoirs of an American Pianist 200
My 21 Years in the White House 223
My Bible ABC Book 332
My Bondage and My Freedom 15
My Brother Fine With Me 295
My Brother Never Feeds the Cat 341
My Brother Sean 286
My Daddy is a Cool Dude and Other Poems 302
My Dog Rinty 450
My Face is Black 556
My Friend Jacob 295
My House: Poems 399
My Larger Education 171
My Life is Baseball 200
My Life of Absurdity 29
My Life with Martin Luther King, Jr. 244
My Lives and How I Lost Them 379
My Love, My Love, or, The Peasant Girl 309
My Main Mother 364

My Mama Needs Me 350
My Menfriends 407
My One Good Nerve: Rhythm, Rhymes, Reasons 387
My Special Best Words 343
My Street's a Morning Cool Street 347
My World of Reality: An Autobiography 40
Mystery of Drear House, The 312
Mystic Female: Poems, The 424
Myth Maker: A Novel, The 373
Myth of Black Progress, The 566
Mythical Negative Black Self Concept, The 586

Naja the Snake and Mangus the Mongoose 324
Naked Soul of Iceberg Slim, The 364
Na–Ni 298
Nappy Edges 445
Narrative of Hosea Hudson, The 565
Narrative of the Life of Frederick Douglass 15
Narrows, The 439
Nat King Cole 28
Nat Turner 307
National Survey of the Higher Education of Negroes 90
Native Daughter 32
Native Son 463
*Nature of Communication Disorders in Culturally & Linguistically
    Diverse Populations* 505
Near–Johannesburg Boy, and Other Poems, The 372
Neglected History 270
Negotiation of Desegregation in Ten Southern Cities, The 133
Negro Almanac, The 255
Negro American, The 565
Negro American Artisann, The 528
Negro American: A Documentary History, The 223
Negro Americans in the Civil War 270
Negro and His Music, The 197
Negro and the Great Society, The 250
Negro and the Post–War World: A Primer, The 246
Negro Builders and Heroes 8
Negro Caravan: Writings by American Negroes, The 374

Negro Church in America, The 473
Negro College Graduate, The 128
Negro Education in Alabama 81
Negro Education in American 94
Negro Family in the United States, The 532
Negro Geniuss, The 369
Negro Ghetto, The 586
Negro History Compendium, A 268
Negro History in the United States, 1850–1925 587
Negro History in Thirteen Plays 442
Negro in American Civilization, The 240
Negro in American Culture, The 375
Negro in American Fiction, The 374
Negro in American History, The 55
Negro in American Life, The 582
Negro in American Life and Thought, The 246
Negro in Colonial New England, 1620–1776, The 228
Negro in Literature and Art in the United States, The 370
Negro in Mississippi History, The 252
Negro in Music and Art, The 199
Negro in our History, The 274
Negro in Revolutionary Georgia, The 238
Negro in Sports, The 194
Negro in Tennessee, 1865–1880, The 578
Negro in the American Educational Theater, The 444
Negro in the American Revolution, The 256
Negro in the Civil War, The 256
Negro in the District of Columbia, The 239
Negro in the Making of America, The 256
Negro in the Reconstruction of Virginia, The 264
Negro in the United States, The 532
Negro in the United States Vol. 1, The 247
Negro in the United States Vol. 2, The 247
Negro in the United States: A Brief History, The 246
Negro in the United States: A Selected Bibliography, The 65
Negro in Third Party Politics, The 584
Negro in Twentieth Century America, The 531
Negro Leadership Class, The 265
Negro Makers of History 273

Negro Migration During the Civil War 571
Negro Mood, and Other Essays, The 513
Negro Mother, and Other Dramatic Recitations, The 411
Negro Orators and Their Orations 462
Negro Pictorial Review of the Great World War, The 249
Negro Problem, The 585
Negro Protest Pamphlets 255
Negro Protest, The 212
Negro Revolt, The 247
Negro Slave Songs in the United States 192
Negro Student at Integrated Colleges, The 94
Negro Students and Their Colleges 157
Negro Voices 433
Negro Wage Earner, The 536
Negro Woman's College Education, The 148
Negro Youth at the Crossroads 532
Negro's Church, The 480
Negroes in Science 500
Negroes with Guns 590
Neighborhood Organization for Community Action 581
Nettie Joe's Friends 329
Never as Strangers 427
Never Die Along 401
New Americans: Cuban Boat People, The 316
New Americans: Vietnamese Boat People, The 540
New and Collected Poems 441
New Black Middle Class, The 555
New Black Politics, The 567
New Days: Poems of Exile and Return 420
New Dimensions for Academic Library Service 62
New Directions in Special Education 133
New Essays on Invisible Man 437
New Guys Around the Block 309
New International Economic Order, The 547
New Kind of Joy: The Story of the Special Olympics, A 540
New Life: New Room 323
New Look at Black Families, A 591
New Negro Poets, U.S.A. 413
New Negro Renaissance: An Anthology, The 385

New Negro: An Interpretation, The 557
New Neighbors 340
New Perspectives of Man in Action 493
New Perspectives on Black Educational History 109
New Perspectives on Black Studies. 209
New Religions of Africa, The 551
New Students and Coordinated Counseling 152
`New World A-Coming': Inside Black America 564
New York Head Shop and Museum 425
Next: New Poems 380
Nigeria 549
Nigger: An Autobiography 22
Night Comes Softly 399
Night Song 459
Night Studies 382
Nightfeathers 335
Nine Black American Doctors 317
1989-1990 Fact Book on Higher Education 73
Nineteenth Century Memphis Families of Color, 1850-1900 12
Nini at Carnival 327
No Crystal Stair 454
No Day of Triumph 567
No Name in the Street 509
No Stranger Now 214
No Trespassing 340
Nobody Knows My Name 509
North American Poets 65
North Carolina Mutual Life Insurance Company 535
North Town 303
Northern J. Calloway Presents: I Been There 309
Not by the Color of Their Skin 480
Not Separate, Not Equal 351
Not That Far 430
Not Without Laughter 320
Notes of a Native Son 509
Nothing Personal 508
Novels of George Lamming, The 437
Now Is the Thing to Praise: Poems 421
Now Sheba Sing the Song 357

Nowhere to Play 299
Nuts and Bolts of Elementary Education, The 101

Oak and Ivy: A Biography of Paul Laurence Dunbar 20
Occupational and Vocational Interest for the Exceptional Individual
    542
Of Love and Dust 396
Offensive Football 193
Oh, Brother 352
Oh, Happy, Happy Day! 332
Oh Pray My Wings Are Going to Fit Me Well 357
Old South: A Psychohistory, The 50
Old South, The 368
Omar at Christmas 351
Omni—Americans, The 563
On Being Black and Healthy 492
On Being Black: An In—Group Analysis 482
On Being Negro in America 568
On Call: Political Essays 243
On Capital Punishment 467
On Games Involving Bluffing 56
On Lynching 587
On Stage in America 190
On the Street Where I Lived 272
On These I Stand 384
On to Freedom 292
On Wings Made of Gauze 395
Once Upon a Time When We Were Colored 49
One Bread, One Body 488
One Day, Another Day 286
One for New York 459
One Hundred Years of Negro Freedom 284
One Hundred Years of the Negro in Show Business 192
One More Day's Journey 206
One More Day's Journey: The Story of a Family and a People 206
One—Way Ticket 411
One Way to Heaven 384
One Woman's Army 222
Opening the Public School Curriculum 140

Operation Burning Candle: A Novel 416
Operation COPE 100
Opportunities for Minorities in Librarianship 63
Oratory of Negro Leaders, 1900–1968, The 368
Ordeal of Mansart, The 389
Ordinary Woman, An 381
Oreo 592
Organizations: An Information Systems Perspective 560
*Origin and Development of Secondary Education for Negroes in
   Metropolitan Area of Birmingham, Alabama, The* 86
Origins of the Civil Rights Movement, The 252
Ostrich Chase, The 318
Ostrich Girl, The 340
Other Slaves, Mechanics, Artisans, and Craftsmen, The 253
Our Dead Behind Us: Poems 426
Our Faith, Heritage, and Church 478
Out from This Place 314
Out Jumped Abraham 288
Out of Control: Confessions of An NFL Casualty 29
Out of Our Lives 448
Outnumbered, The 371
Outside Shot, The 337
Outsider, The 463
Overcome: A Black Passover, The 468
Ox of the Wonderful Horns, and Other African Folktales, The 290

Pan–Africanism: The Idea and Movement, 1776–1963 530
Panther and the Lash: Poems of Our Times, The 412
Parade 297
Paradigm for Looking, A 513
Paris, Pee Wee, and Big Dog 309
Participation of Blacks in Graduate and Professional Schools, The 80
Pasaderitas Hacia El Ingles Correcto: Un Mini–libro par El Mej 366
Passion: New Poems, 1977–1980 420
Passion's Surrender 436
Passport to Freedom, Education, Humanism, and Malcolm X 126
Pastoral Calling, The 470
Pastoral Care in the Black Church 490
Pastoral Counseling and Spiritual Values 488

Patchwork Quilt, The 302
Pathos of Power 521
Pathways to the World of English 355
Patterns for Lifelong Learning 124
Patterns of Negro Segregation 240
Paul Laurence Dunbar Reader, The 390
Paul Laurence Dunbar: Poet of His People 370
Paul Robeson 306
Paul Robeson, All-American 21
Paul Robeson: Citizen of the World 304
Paul Robeson: The Life and Times of a Free Black Man 312
Peaches 328
Pearl's Kitchen: An Extraordinary Cookbook 491
Peer Group Counseling Policies and Human-Relations Workshops
    Procedures 139
Peer Tutoring Programs for the Academically Deficient Student 154
Pele: A Biography 26
Pennsylvania Black History 209
People Could Fly: American Black Folktale, The 312
People One Knows: A Novel, The 367
People, Politics, and the Political Life 556
People v Property 248
Perception of Administrators and Minority Students of Minority Student
    Experience on Predominantly White Campuses 89
Perils and Prospects of Southern Black Leadership, The 533
Personal Money Management 581
Personnel Study of Negro College Students, A 90
Perspectives in Differentiation and Hypertrophy 504
Perspectives in Immigrant and Minority Education 155
Perspectives in Multicultural Education 158
Perspectives of Political Power in the District of Columbia 538
Petitioners, The 251
Philadelphia Negro: A Social Study, The 220
Philosophy and Opinions of Marcus Garvey 241
Philosophy Born of Struggle 233
Philosophy of Alain Locke, The 476
Philosophy 481
Phoebe and the General 307
Photograph: Lovers in Motion, A 445

Physicians for the South 498
Pictorial History of Black Americans, A 320
Pictorial History of the American Negro 226
Picture life of Stevie Wonder, The 299
Picture Life of Bobby Orr, The 299
Picture Life of Jesse Jackson, The 309
Picture Life of Martin Luther King, Jr., The 354
Picture Life of Muhammad Ali, The 299
Picture Life of Malcolm X, The 316
Picture Story of Frank Robinson, The 353
Picture Story of Hank Aaron, The 353
Piece of the Power: Four Black Mayors, A 540
Pied Piper of Hamelin, The 287
Pimp: The Story of My Life 364
Pinckney Benton Stewart Pinchback 27
Piney Woods and Its Story 32
Pink and Brown People and Other Controversial Essays 581
Pinktoes 409
Pinocchio 288
Pioneer Urbanites 216
Pioneers and Patriots 268
Pioneers in Protest 282
Plain Pointed Practical Preaching 467
Planet of Junior Brown, The 313
Planning Smaller Cities 519
Planning the Academic Program 183
Plato to IBM 103
Play Ebony: Play Ivory 389
Play for Love, A 366
Playing the Changes 387
Plays of Negro Life 425
Playtime in Africa 344
Plural but Equal 524
Pocket: A Novel, The 448
Poems 430
Poems by Blacks 369
Poems by Blacks 424
Poems from Africa 278
Poems from Black Africa 414

Poems of Cabin and Fields 390
Poems of Phillis Wheatley, The 457
Poems on Love and Life 404
Poet's Song, The 417
Poetic Equation, A 400
Poetry for My People 389
Poetry of the Negro, 1746–1970, The 414
Police and the Black Community, The 595
Police Operations 565
Political Change in a West African State 244
Political Economy of Economic Policy 525
Political Economy of Pan–African Nationalism, The 547
Political Education in Black and White 158
Political Philosophy of Martin Luther King, Jr., The 584
Politics and Power in a Slave Society 266
Politics of Bureaucratic Reform, The 567
Politics of Change: A Jamaican Testament, The 559
Politics of God, The 487
Politics of Literary Expression, The 399
Politics of Miseducation, The 164
Politics of Riot Behavior, The 578
Politics of the Black "Nation," The 547
Poor, Black and in Real Trouble 462
Popo and Fifina: Children of Haiti 285
Portia: The Biography of Portia Washington Pittman 47
Portico of the Temple 423
Portrait of Inequality 529
Portrait of Marginality, A 567
Postdoctoral Study in the U.S. 1977–78 127
Poverty Without Bitterness 37
Power, Racism and Privilege 594
Prairie View: A Study in Public Conscience, 1878–1946 184
Praisesong for the Widow 427
Pray and Grow Rich 474
Pray Right! Live Right! Reflections on the Lord's Prayer 474
Preaching on Suffering and a God of Love 489
Preaching the Gospel 489
Precipitating Factors in the Use of Alcoholic Treatment Services, The
    522

Predator, The 419
Preface to Racial Understanding, A 550
Prejudice and Your Child 469
Preparing for Reflective Teaching 115
Prescriptions for Adult Education and Secondary Education 79
Price of the Ticket, The 362
Pride and Beauty Handbook for Blackskinned Women, The 494
Pride and Power: From Watts to Mexico City 227
Primary Education 173
Primative, The 409
Princess of the Full Moon 308
Principles of Black Political Economy 546
Principles of Scientific Sociology 583
Private Black Colleges at the Crossroads 168
Private Conversations: A Novel 423
Pro-Slavery Thought in the Old South 240
Problems and Issues in Education of Exceptional Children 134
*Proceedings from the National Invitational Conference on Racial and
    Ethnic Data* 507
*Proceedings from the Tenth Annual Telecommunications Policy
    Research Conference* 397
Proclamation Theology 478
Professional Roles of Urban School Psychology 91
Profile of the Negro in American Dentistry 500
Profiles in Black Power 541
Profiles of Black Achievers, 1930-1950 44
Profiles: A Collection of Short Biographies 293
Progress and Portents for the Negro in Medicine 495
*Progress of a Race, or, The Remarkable Advancement of the Afro-
    American* 244
Progress of Afro-American Women, The 67
Progressive Units for Student Teaching in High School 594
Project Head Start 171
Promoting Pre-School Curriculum and Teaching 119
Prophets of a New Day 456
Proud Shoes: The Story of an American Family 38
Proven and Promising Educational Innovations in Secondary Schools
    112
Pseudo Cool 403

Psychoblackology, of Movement in Sports, Physical Education, Dance, Drama, Play, Gymnastics, Recreation, and the Soul Experience 491

Psychoeducational Assessment of Minority Group Children 134

Psychological Testing of American Minorities 485

Psychology and Mental Health of Afro-American Women, The 69

Psychology and Psychotherapy 503

Psychology of Black Language, The 406

Psychology of Blacks, The 487

Psychology of the Child in the Middle Class 471

Psycho-Sinology = Meng 469

Putting It All Together 155

Quality Education for All Americans 84

Quality of Hurt: The Autobiography of Chester Himes, The 29

Quality of Life Among Rural Residents in North Carolina 579

Quarter Century of the Black Experience in Elementary and Secondary Education, 1950–1975, A 151

Queen of Gospel Singers 321

Queen of the Blues: The Story of Dinah Washington 29

Queen of the Ebony Isles 428

Quiet Revolution, The 542

Quiet Riots: Race and Poverty in the United States 539

Quiz Book on Black America 207

Race Adjustment and the Everlasting Stain 251

Race and Economics 262

Race, Ethnicity, and Socioeconomic Status 592

Race Mixing in the Public Schools 179

Race, Racism and American Law 513

Race Relations 270

Race Relations: Current Perspectives 222

Race, Religion, and the Continuing American Dilemma 556

Race, Sex, and Policy Problems 565

"Race," Writing, and Difference 379

Racial and Ethnic Relations 237

Racial Conflict, Discrimination and Power 509

Racial Conflict in American Society 237

Racial Crisis in American Education 116

Racial Crisis in Public Education 101
Racial Integration and Learners from Limited Income Families 517
Racism and Mental Health 506
Racism in American Education 157
Racism in U.S. Imperialism 271
Radical and Conservatives, and Other Essays on the Negro in America
  562
Rainbow Is Not Enough, The 461
Rainbow Jordan 293
Raise, Race, Rays, Raze: Essays Since 1965 206
Raisin in the Sun: A Drama in Three Acts, A 404
Ralph Bunche: A Most Reluctant Hero 27
Ramadan: Through the Eyes of a Child 335
Ransomed Wait: Poems, The 431
Rap on Race, A 561
Rap Stories 300
Rape of Shavi 393
Raw Dog 440
Raw Pearl, The 6
Ray Charles 327
Recreation 400
Reading How and Why 185
Reading Interests and Needs of Negro College Freshmen Regarding
  Social Science Materials, The 99
Readings from Negro Authors, for Schools and Colleges, with a
  Bibliography of Negro Literature 383
Readings in Black American Music 202
Ready to Riot 597
Real Cool Killers, The 410
Real Estate Careers 499
Real Winner, A 332
Really Reading 122
Reckless Eyeballing 574
Recollections of James Juma Mbotela 24
Recollections of Seventy Years 39
Reconstruction in Indian Territory 206
Reconstruction of the African–American Male 570
Red Badge of Courage, The 399
Red, Black and Green 254

Red Riding Hood 288
Redemption of Africa and Black Religion, The 472
Reducing Aspiration Conflict Among Minority Youth 111
Reducing Stress on Black Administrators 181
Reena and Other Stories 427
Reflections 56
Reflections on Education 474
Reforming Metropolitan Schools 149
Reggie: The Autobiography 31
Regional COG's and the Central City 538
Regional Project in Secondary Education, The 104
Regnum Montis 477
Regulation of Statelessness Under International and National Law, The
    563
Relevant Expository Techniques and Programmed Grammar 395
Relevant War Against Poverty, A 521
Religion in Higher Education Among Negroes 141
Religions 476
Religious Foundation of Human Relations: Beyond Games, A 477
Reluctant Reformers 508
Reminiscences of School Life and Hints on Teaching 127
Reminiscences of an Active Life 35
Reminiscences of Sea Island Heritage 216
Removing Barriers to Humaneness in the High School 155
Repatriates and Refugees in a Colonial Society 231
Report from Part One: An Autobiography 9
Report on Negro Universities in the South 177
Research and Thought in Administrative Theory 131
Research Conference on Minority Group Aged in the South 548
Research in the Administration of Public Policy 530
Resistance: Profiles in Non-Violence 544
Resolving the Legislative Veto Issue 539
Resource Guide on Black Aging, A 56
Resources for Affirmative Action 572
Restructuring the Educational Process 111
Return to Black America 573
Return to South Town 303
Reunion 368
Revolutionaries: Agents of Change 541

Revolutionary Love: Poems & Essays 443
Revolutionary Notes 245
Revolutionary Petunias and Other Poems 455
Revolutionary Suicide 564
Rhetoric of Black Revolution 446
Rhetoric of Racial Revolt 408
Richard Pryor: A Man and His Madness 27
Richard Pryor: The Man Behind the Laughter 39
Richard Wright 456
Richard Wright: Impressions and Perspectives 440
Richard Wright: Ordeal of a Native Son 20
Riddle of Life, and Other Sermons, The 488
Riddle of Snoring, The 492
Ride the Red Circle 340
Ridin' the Moon in Texas: Word Paintings 445
Right Face: A Handbook for Sabbathkeepers 479
Rip & Run 410
Rise and Fall of a Proper Negro, The 33
River of No Return, The 45
Rivers of Eros, The 382
Robert R. Churches of Memphis, The 12
Robert Russa Moton of Hampton and Tuskegee 30
Robeson: Labor's Forgotten Champion 546
Rock Against the Wind, A 438
Rock in a Weary Land, A 486
Rocks Cry Out, The 433
Rod Carew's Art and Science of Hitting 190
Role Model Blacks 562
Roll of Thunder, Hear My Cry 345
Room for Randy 321
Roots of a Black Future 484
Roots of Rebellion 275
Roots of Soul, The 437
Rootworker: A Novel, The 389
Rope & Faggot 588
Rope the Sun 292
Rosa Parks 306
Rough Steps on my Stairway 46
Rough Trade 443

Ruby 309
Run Man, Run 410
Runner Mack 364
Ruptured Diamond, The 159
Rural Negro, The 273
Russia and the Negro 208
Russian Journal 245

Sacred Cows and Other Edibles 400
Safari of African Cooking, A 503
Sally–Ann in the Snow 286
Sally Hemings: A Novel 292
Salt Eaters, The 279
Sanctification 467
Sanctified Church, The 477
Sapphire's Sampler 367
Sarah Phillips 424
Sassafrass 445
Sassafrass, Cypress, and Indigo 446
Satan's Master 435
Satchmo: My Life in New Orleans 5
Sati the Rastafarian 351
Saw the House in Half: A Novel 416
Say Amen Brother! Old–Time Negro Preaching 482
Say's Law: An Historical Analysis 575
Scarecrow 407
Scarifications 383
Scarlet Thread: Nineteen Sermons, The 485
Scars and Memories 407
School and Community Issues and Alternatives 139
School and Home Communications 149
School Bus 297
School Desegregation in the North 105
School Desegregation Plans That Work 176
School Guidance Services 125
School History of the Negro Race in America from 1619 to 1890, A
     242
School in the Social Order, The 97
School Power 96

School Social Systems and Student Achievement 85
Schooling for the New Slavery 164
Science of Man's Environment 492
Scientist in the Black Perspective 506
Scorpions 337
Scott Joplin: The Man Who Made Ragtime 28
Scottsboro Limited: Four Poems and a Play in Verse 412
Screaming Whisper, A 318
Seabirds Are Still Alive, The 280
Sean's Red Bike 286
Search for Talent, The 81
Search for the New Land 245
Second Chance: A Novel 462
Second-Class Citizen 393
Secondary Education for Negroes 90
Secret Below 103rd Street, The 418
Secret Music: A Book 407
Secret of Gumbo Grove, The 345
Seduction by Light 464
See No Evil 446
Seeds Beneath the Snow 431
Seeking, The 49
Seeking to be Christian in Race Relations 480
Seize the Time 259
Selected Black American, African, and Caribbean Authors 65
Selected Black American Authors 65
Selected Group Analysis of Administrative Field Experience Problems 161
Selected Letters of Edward Wilmot Blyden 248
Selected Poems 372
Selected Poems 429
Selected Poems of Langston Hughes 412
Selected Readings in Afro-American Anthropology 590
Sequoyah: The Cherokee Who Captured Words 339
Seraph on the Suwanee: A Novel 416
Serious Creation, A 468
Services to Young Families 560
Seven Black American Scientists 317
Seventeen Black Artists 300

Seventh Son, The 245

Seventy–fifth Anniversary Yearbook 479

Sex and Racism in America 544

Sexual Mountain and Black Women Writers, The 408

Shades of Brown 79

Shadow and Act 392

Shadow of the Plantation 241

Shadow That Scares Me, The 537

Shakedown, The 436

Shaker, Why Don't You Sing? 357

Shakespeare in Harlem 412

Shaping of Black America, The 282

Shawn Goes to School 286

She Come Bringing Me That Little Baby Girl 306

Shirley Temple Black: Actress to Ambassador 28

Short Fiction of Charles W. Chesnutt, The 442

Short History of the American Negro, A 210

Short Walk, A 293

Sickest Don't Always Die the Quickest, The 321

Sidewalk Story 328

Sifting and Winnowing 115

Sign in Sidney Brustein's Window, The 404

Signifying Monkey, The 397

Silence to the Drums 439

Simple Omnibus, The 412

Simple Speaks His Mind 412

Simple Stakes a Claim 412

Simple Takes a Wife 412

Simple's Uncle Sam 412

Singers of Daybreak 361

Singin' and Swingin' and Gettin' Merry Like Christmas 5

Singing Tales of Africa 341

Single Parents in Black America 511

'Sippi 422

Sissie 459

Sister 307

Sister Outsider: Essays and Speeches 426

Sister X and the Victims of Foul Play 440

Sitting Pretty: A Novel 464

Six Black Masters of American Art 281
Sixties Reader, The 235
Sixty Years of Medicine 35
Sketches of Negro Life and History in South Carolina 228
Slave Community, The 208
Slave Girl: A Novel, The 393
Slave Narrative, The 263
Slave Religion 483
Slave Testimony 209
Slavery and Freedom on the Middle Ground 223
Slavery and the Literary Imagination 428
Slaves 422
Sleeping Beauty 288
Slick Revenge 436
Slipping Through the Cracks 572
Small Place, A 244
Smokey: Inside My Life 44
Smuggling Language into the Teaching of Reading 122
Snakes: A Novel 464
Snow Sculpture and Ice Carving 194
Snow White and the Seven Dwarfs 288
Snowfire 436
Social Casework Intervention with People of Color 519
Social Class Influences upon Learning 100
Social Goals and Educational Reform 180
Social History of 20th Century Urban Riots, A 582
Social History of the American Negro, A 210
Social Planning in America 545
Social Research and the Black Community 226
Social Science Research: A Skills Handbook 511
Social Structure and Assassination Behavior 588
Social Studies Strategies for Today's Learners 142
Social Uses of Mass Communication, The 378
Social Work Practice with Minorities 519
Socio-Cultural Dimensions of Mental Health, The 527
Sociological Theory 583
Sociology for the Seventies 561
Sociology of Small Groups, The 553
Sociology of the Black Experience 580

Sociology of Urban Education, The 178
Sociology: The Study of Human Interaction 528
Soil Soldiers, The 555
Soldier's Play: A Play, A 396
Some Achievements of the Negro Through Education 230
Some Changes 420
Some of the Days of Everett Anderson 296
Some Things That Glitter 404
Some Time Ago 236
Somebody's Angel Child 335
Somerset Homecoming 42
Something in Common, and Other Stories 412
Something on My Mind 307
Something to Count On 335
Song for Anninho 418
Song for Mumu 364
Song in a Weary Throat 38
Song of Mary: Poems, The 462
Song of Solomon 431
Song of the Boat 304
Song of the Trees 346
Song Turning Back into Itself, The 464
Sonora Beautiful 296
Sons of Darkness, Sons of Light 460
Sorcerer's Apprentice, The 418
Soul Brothers and Sister Lou, The 320
Soul Clap Hands and Sing 427
Soul of the Black Preacher, The 478
Soul on Ice 214
Souls of Black Folk, The 220
Soulscript: Afro–American Poetry 420
Sound Investment, A 342
Sound Minds in a Soundless World 568
Sounds of the Struggle 557
Sourcebook on the New Immigration 518
South Africa and the Bomb 584
South Carolina's Blacks and Native Americans 14
South of Freedom 44
South Street 369*

South to a Very Old Place 253
Southern Odyssey, A 225
Southern Road, Poems by Sterling A. Brown 374
Space Challenger: The Story of Guion Bluford 316
Sparks from the Anvil 470
Speak Out in Thunder Tones 263
Special Delivery, A 103
Special Education in Transition 134
Special Mission, A 547
Special Problems of Negro Education 174
Spell #7: A Theater Piece in Two Acts 446
Spin a Soft Black Song: Poems for Children 303
Spirits in the Street 298
Spiritual Dynamics of Howard Thurman's Theology 481
Spring Embrace 425
Stability, Security, and Continuity 514
Stack A Dollar 457
Stained Glass 375
Standing Fast: The Autobiography of Roy Wilkins 51
State of Afro-American History, The 237
State of Black America 1988, The 218
State Requirements in Physical Education for Teachers and Students
     497
States' Laws on Race and Color 563
Statistical Atlas of Southern Counties 241
Statue of Liberty: America's Proud Lady, The 235
Stevie 343
Stevie Wonder 352
Stevie Wonder Scrapbook, The 194
Stomping the Blues 198
Stop Pussyfooting Through a Revolution 475
Stories About Jesus 469
Stories from the Old Testament 469
Story of Alanta University, The 74
Story of Dorothy Stanfield, Based on a Great Insurance Swindle, and
     a Woman, The 430
Story of George Washington Carver, The 284
Story of Jumping Mouse, The 343
Story of My Life and My Work, The 171

Story of Phillis Wheatley, The 299
Story of Stevie Wonder, The 316
Story of the Negro 284
Story of the Negro Retold, The 274
Story of the Negro: The Rise of the Race from Slavery, The 270
Storytelling, Art and Technique 279
Straight from the Heart 235
Strange Way of Truth, The 572
Stranger and Alone: A Novel 441
Strategies for Effective Desegregation 121
Strategies for Language Acquisition 386
Strategies for Teaching the Mentally Retarded 150
Street, The 440
Street Gangs: Yesterday and Today 541
Street in Bronzeville, A 372
Street Players. 402
Street Wars: A Novel 436
Strength of Black Families, The 544
Strength of Gideon and Other Stories, The 390
Strength to Love 479
Stressed Out: A Novel 377
Stride Toward Freedom: The Montgomery Story 558
Structure of Social Systems, The 512
Struggle of the Caribbean People (1492–1984), The 239
Student Culture 170
Student Dissent in the Schools 124
Student's Self–Directing Computational Guide I 175
Student's Self–Directing Computational Guide II 176
Study and Analysis of Black Politics, The 69
Study Guide and Resource Manual for Introduction to Exceptional Children 82
Study of Sociology: An Introduction, The 546
Study of Some Social and Psychological Factors Influencing Educational Achievement, A 104
Study of the Public–Assisted Black College Presidency, A 125
Stupidity, Sloth and Public Policy 585
Stuttering Therapy 504
Subsistence Agriculture and Economic Development 587
Successful Women, Angry Men 520

Such Things from the Valley 431
Such Was the Season: A Novel 426
Sugar Ray Leonard 28
Sula 432
Summer Blues 425
Sun Salutes You, The 339
Sunday Fix 436
Sunday Hell 410
Sundial 432
Super−Spy K−13 in Outer Space 346
Supermarket 281
Supervising Student Teachers 140
Suppression of the African Slave−Trade to the United States of American, 1638−1870, The 220
Sure Hands, Strong Heart 339
Surfaces and Masks: A Poem 426
Surprise for Mrs 453
Survival and Progress 578
Survival Kit for Brothers & Sisters Going to Grey Colleges, A 88
Swallow the Lake 426
Swamp Man 402
Sweet Flypaper of Life, The 387
Sweet Love Bitter 460
Sweet Peter Deeder 407
Sweet Street Blues 366
Sweet Summer 213
Sweet Whispers, Brother Rush 313
Swings 281
Symbols of Change 552
Symptoms & Madness: Poems 426
Syncopated Cakewalk, The 426
Systematic Interviewing 388
System of Dante's Hell 363
Systems of Poverty 566

Taking a Stand Against Racism and Racial Discrimination 332
Tales 419
Tales and Stories for Black Folks 280
Tales of a Dead King 337

Tales of Mogho 308
Tales of the Congaree 437
Tales of Uncle Remus, The 326
Talk About a Family 307
Talk That Talk 536
Talk with Jawanza, A 136
Talkin' & Testifyin' 161
Talking Back: Thinking Feminist, Thinking Black 547
Talking to Myself 6
Talking Tree, The 279
Talks for the Times 215
Tall Black Texans 72
Tall Phil and Small Bill 333
Talladega Manual of Vocational Guidance, The 98
Tambourines to Glory: A Novel 413
Taps for a Jim Crow Army 250
Tar Baby 432
Taste of Country Cooking, The 501
Teacher's Guide for Medley 391
Teacher's Totter 102
Teachers Should Care: Social Perspectives of Teaching 124
Teaching and Learning in the Model Classroom 93
Teaching English 168
Teaching Ethnic Studies: Concepts and Strategies 76
Teaching Faculty in Black Colleges and Universities 147
Teaching in a Multi-Cultural Society 98
Teaching in the Desegregated Classroom 167
Teaching in the Desegregated School 142
Teaching Mathematics in the Elementary School 139
Teaching Minorities More Effectively 87
Teaching Resources for the Kindergarten 106
Teaching Social Studies to Culturally Different Children 77
Teaching Strategies for Ethnic Studies 75
Teaching Strategies for the Social Studies 76
Teaching Strategies for the Social Studies 77
Teaching the Black Experience: Methods and Materials 76
Teaching the Culturally Disadvantaged 129
Teaching the Disadvantaged: A Teacher's Manual 167
Teaching the Economically Poor (the Disadvantaged) 83

Teaching the Inner-City Child 74
Teaching the Language Arts to Culturally Different Children 134
Teacup Full of Roses 328
Tearing the Roof off the Sucker 577
Techniques for Teaching Disadvantaged Youth 163
Teen-Age Alcoholism 541
Teenage Pregnancy 550
Tell It Like It Is 577
Tell Me a Story, Mama 322
Tell Me How Long the Train's Been Gone 363
Tell My Horse 239
Temple of My Familiar, The 455
Tennessee Agricultural and Industrial State University 501
Tension in the Cities 512
Tessie 321
Test Policy and Test Performance 112
Test Policy and the Politics of Allocation 534
Testing of Black Students: A Symposium, The 143
Testing of Cultural Groups, The 66
That Man Cartwright: A Novel 395
Their Eyes Were Watching God: A Novel 416
Their Place on the Stage 375
Theo and Me: Growing Up Okay 203
Theory and Application of Mathematics for Teachers 498
Theory of Games and Statistical Decisions 492
There is a River 537
There Was Once a Slave 219
They Call Me Assassin 202
They Came Before Columbus 269
They Came in Chains: Americans from Africa 568
They Can Learn English 85
They Had a Dream 210
They Seek a City 517
They Showed the Way: Forty American Negro Leaders 341
Things Ain't What They Used To Be: Musical Memoirs 204
Things That I Do in the Dark 420
Third Door, The 48
Third Generation, The 410
Third Gift, The 292

Third Life of Grange Copeland, The 455
Thirty Years at the Mansion 491
This Child's Gonna Live 463
This is My Country Too 589
This Life 366
This Life 40
This Species of Property 565
This Strange New Feeling 326
Thomas and Beulah: Poems 389
Those Preaching Women 481
Those Who Ride the Night Winds 400
Three African Tales 341
Three Bears, The 333
Three Billy Goats Gruff 333
Three–Dimensional Approach to Teaching in the Urban Schools 149
Three–Fifths of a Man 561
Three Pieces 446
Three Thousand Years of Black Poetry 425
Three Years in Mississippi 142
Through Black Eyes 223
Through Different Eyes 569
Through the Ceiling 421
Tiger, Paleface and Me 286
Tiger, Tinker and Me 286
Tiger Who Wore White Gloves, The 287
Time–Ago Lost: More Tales of Jahdu 313
Time–Ago Tales of Jahdu, The 313
Time Flies 383
Time of the Furnaces, The 73
Time to Speak, A Time to Act, A 516
Times They Used to Be, The 296
Titch the Cat 300
Tituba of Salem Village 340
To Be a Slave 326
To Be Equal 598
To Be Faithful to Our Heritage 467
To Be or Not—To Bop: Memoirs 193
To Be Popular or Smart: The Black Peer Group 324
To Disembark 372

To Hell with Dying   348
To Kill a Black Man   425
To Live in Freedom   543
To Make a Poet Black   441
To Me It's Wonderful   203
To Raise, Destroy, and Create   423
To Smile in Autumn: A Memoir   199
To Stem This Tide   241
To Teach the Negro History   221
Today's Negro Voices   335
Tomorrow's Tomorrow: The Black Woman   244
Toms, Coons, Mulattoes, Mammies, and Bucks   190
Topics in Afro-American Studies   257
Torch Glows, The   145
Touch of Innocence, A   16
Toward Black Undergraduate Student Equality in American Higher Education   147
Toward Equitable Education for Multicultural Consciousness for Early Childhood   180
Toward Viable Directions in Postsecondary Education   180
Towards Transracial Communication   447
Traditional Model of Educational Excellence, A   132
Tragedies in American Education, The   137
Train Ride   343
Train to Lulu's, The   318
Train Whistle Guitar   433
Training of Negro Teachers in Louisiana   141
Transformation of Scientists and Engineers into Managers   512
Transformational Grammar and Written Sentences   386
Transracial Communication   447
Travail and Triumph   264
Treat it Gentle: An Autobiography   7
Treat Them Like Animals   449
Treatment of Communication Disorders in Culturally & Linguistically Diverse Populations   505
Trends in Southern Sociolinguistics   440
Trick Baby   364
Tricks of the Trade for Teachers of Language Arts   107
Trickshot: The Story of a Black Pimp   405

Troll in a Hole, A   333
Trouble They Have Seen, The   263
Trouble's Child   350
Troubling Biblical Waters   473
Trucks   297
Trucks and Cars to Ride   281
Truly Disadvantaged, The   594
Trumpet of Conscience, The   553
Turmbull Park: A Novel   373
Turning on Learning   115
Tuskegee and Its People   171
TVA and Black Americans   228
Twelve Black Floridians   253
Twelve Million Black Voices   275
Twelve–String Guitar as Played by Leadbelly, The   197
Twentieth Century Negro Literature   98
Twenty–Five Black African Filmmakers   199
Twenty–Four Negro Melodies   190
Twins of Ilora, The   292
Twins Strike Back, The   302
Two Bronze Titans   558
Two Centuries of Methodist Concern   84
Two–Headed Woman   381
Two Love Stories   424
Two Ways to Count to Ten   297

U.S. Graduate Training of Asian Agricultural Economics, The   587
Ugly Little Duck, The   333
Unbought and Unbossed   12
Uncle Tom's Children   463
Uncommon Sense and Dimensional Awareness   487
Under a Soprano Sky   444
Under the Sunday Tree   302
Underground Railroad in DuPage County, Illinois, The   269
Underground: Four Plays   458
Understanding Cultural Values   513
Understanding the New Black Poetry   407
Understanding the New Generation in Africa   260
Unfinished Dream: The Musical World of Red Callender   10

Unfinished March, The 268
United States Supreme Court and the Uses of Social Science Data, The
  525
Up from Nigger 405
Up from Slavery: An Autobiography 51
Up South: Blacks in Chicago's Suburbs, 1719–1983 218
Up the Down Escalator 559
Upbuilding of a Race, The 454
Uprising 436
Uptown 344
Upward: A History of Norfolk State University 86
Urban and Rural Studies 566
Urban Challenge: Poverty and Race, The 116
Urban Complex: Human Values in Urban Life, The 586
Urban Education: An Annotated Bibliography 66
Urban Education: The City as a Living Curriculum 140
Urban Education: The Hope Factor 112
Urban Governance and Minorities 519
Urban Minority Administrators 552
Urban Scene in the Seventies, The 560
Urbanization and the Ecological Crisis 518
Urbanization in West Africa 257
Us Boys of Westcroft 286

Vacation Time: Poems for Children 400
Venture of Faith, A 97
Vertical Ghetto, The 251
Vietnam and Black America 264
Vietnam Blues 377
Viewfinders: Black Women Photographers 198
Viewpoints from Black America 384
Virginia History and Government 224
Visible Now: Blacks in Private Schools 159
Vocational Education and Guidance of Negroes 91
Voice in the Wilderness, The 120
Voice of Black Rhetoric: Selections, The 448
Voice of the Children, The 324
Voices from the Black Experience: African and Afro–American
  Literature 453

Voices of Negritude 418
Voodoo and Hoodoo 476
Voodoo Gods 239

W. E. B. DuBois: A Biography 23
W. E. B. DuBois: A Profile 34
W. E. B. DuBois: A Reader 528
W. E. B. DuBois: Writings 238
Wade in the Water 283
Wait Till Next Year 44
Waiting Years, The 416
Walk Home Tired, Billy Jenkins 347
Walk On 352
Walk Quietly Through the Night and Cry Softly 205
Walk Together, Children 484
Walker's Appeal in Four Articles (David Walker) 269
Walls of Jericho, The 395
Walt Frazier 19
War and the Protest: Vietnam, The 235
Washington and Two Marches 1963 and 1983 275
Watch Out for C 289
Water Girl 348
Watercolor 375
Way of the New World, The 398
Ways of White Folks, The 413
Wayward and the Seeking, The 452
Wayward Child: A Personal Odyssey 21
We Are Not Afraid, Elijah's God Is Great! 328
We Are Your Sisters 263
We Be Word Sorcerers 444
We Build Together 66
We Fished All Night 432
We Have Tomorrow 284
We Read: A to Z 297
We Speak as Liberators 382
We Walk the Way of the New World 426
Weary Blues, The 413
Werewolves 542
West African Cooking for Black American Families 502

West African Vignettes 300
West Indian Experience in British Schools, The 113
West Indies Folk Tales 342
West Indies: Islands in the Sun, The 292
What Black Educators Are Saying 184
What Black Librarians Are Saying 63
What Black Politicians Are Saying 597
What Color Are You? 351
What Color Was Jesus? 481
What Happened at Rita's Party 286
What Happened in Memphis 239
What if the Shoe Were on the Other Foot? 547
What Manner of Man 283
What the Negro Thinks 252
What the Negro Wants 558
What We Must See 382
What's Happening? 403
When and Where I Enter 534
When Do You Talk to God? 333
When Harlem Was in Vogue 197
When I Am Old with You 322
When Malindy Sings 391
When People Meet 246
When Roots Die 419
When the Fire Reaches Us 451
When the Marching Stopped 584
When the Rattle Snake Sounds 293
When the Truth Is Told 237
When the Word Is Given 479
Where Are the Love Poems for Dictators? 430
Where Did Our Love Go? 193
Where Do We Go From Here: Chaos or Community? 554
Where Does the Day Go? 337
Where Have All the Little Girls Gone? 383
Where to, Black Man 260
Where's Geraldine? 338
Which Way Freedom? 315
White Americans Who Cared 223
White Man, Listen! 597

White Man's Justice: Black Man's Grief 400
White Papers for White Americans 544
White Rat: Short Stories 418
White Romance, A 314
White Supremacy in the United States 557
Who Are The Handicapped? 542
Who Cares? 289
Who I Am 424
Who Is Angelina? A Novel 464
Who Look at Me 323
Who's Who Among Black Americans 36
Who's Who Among Negro Principals 138
Who's Who Among Virginia State Graduates 161
Whore–Daughter 405
Whoreson: The Story of a Ghetto Pimp 402
Whose Town? 304
Why Blacks Kill Blacks 255
Why ERA Failed 514
Why I Don't Like Bussing 87
Why Me? The Sammy Davis, Jr., Story 191
Why We Can't Wait 554
William Leo Hansberry African History Notebook, The. Vol. 1 233
William Leo Hansberry African History Notebook, The. Vol. 2 232
William Stanley Braithwaite Reader, The 377
Willie Bea and the Time the Martians Landed 314
Willie Blows a Mean Horn 347
Willie Mays: "Play Ball!" 197
Willie Mays 197
Willie's Not the Hugging Kind 280
Willy's Summer Dream 288
Wilt 11
Wind from Nowhere, The 430
Wind Thought: Poems 424
Window Wishing 291
Wines in the Wilderness 375
Winfield: A Player's Life 52
Winnie Mandela: Life of Struggle 28
Wisconsin and Federal Civil Procedure 513
Witchcraft, Mysticism, and Magic in the Black World. 476

With Head and Heart 50
Without a Song 470
Witnessing Slavery 395
Wolves of Summer 436
Woman in the Moon 367
Woman's Place, A 402
Women and the Men, The 400
Women Builders 13
Women, Culture, & Politics 526
Women Houses & Homes 442
Women in Africa and the African Diaspora 579
Women of Brewster Place, The 434
Women, Race and Class 526
Won't Know Till I Get There 338
Words of Martin Luther King, Jr., The 554
Workbook for Introductory Sociology 588
Working With Carter G. Woodson 22
Working With the Hands 171
Works of Alice Dunbar–Nelson, The 414
World of Black Singles, The 577
World of Gwendolyn Brooks, The 373
World's Great Men of Color Vol. 1 258
World's Great Men of Color Vol. 2 258
Worlds Apart 137
Worlds of Color 389
Worse Than Silence: The Black Child's Dilemma 92
Worth Fighting For 328
Wreath for Udomo, A 355
Wrestling Match, The 300
Wretched of the Earth, The 530
Write and Write Again 438
Writings of W. E. B. DuBois, The 314

Xarque and Other Poems 419

Yardbird Lives! 200
Yellow Bird and Me 315
Yellow House on the Corner: Poems, The 388
Yes I Can 191

Yesterday, Today, and Tomorrow. Book 1 461
Yesterday, Today, and Tomorrow. Book 2 461
Yesterday, Today, and Tomorrow. Book 3 462
You Can't Build a Chimney from the Top 30
You Can't Keep a Good Woman Down 455
You Gotta Deal With It 552
Young and Black in America 278
Young, Black, and Male in America 533
Young Booker: Booker T. Washington's Early Days 82
Young Inner City Families 501
Young Jim 344
Young Landlords, The 338
Young Negro in America, 1960–1980, The 256
Young Years, The 279
Youngblood 422
Your God Is Too White 484
Your Hand in Mind 296
Your Rights, Past and Present 542
Youth Employment in American Society 542

Zamani Goes to Market 301
Zeely 314